This false-colour composite image was recorded in June. Glasgow and Edinburgh and other settlements in the Forth–Clyde Valley are clearly visible in blue. The bright red areas are fields of healthy crops. Imagery such as this is used to police EU agricultural subsidies. *(EROS)*

PHILIP'S

MODERN SCHOOL ATLAS

96TH EDITION

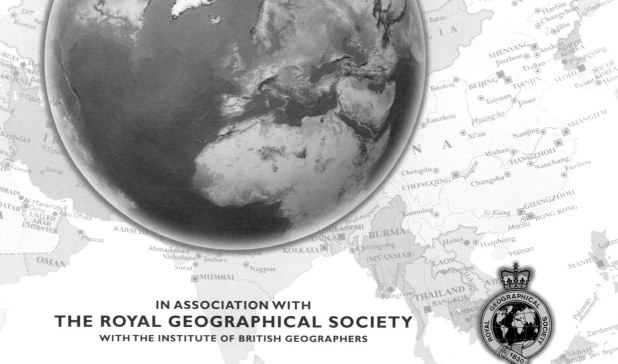

IN ASSOCIATION WITH
THE ROYAL GEOGRAPHICAL SOCIETY
WITH THE INSTITUTE OF BRITISH GEOGRAPHERS

MAP SYMBOLS

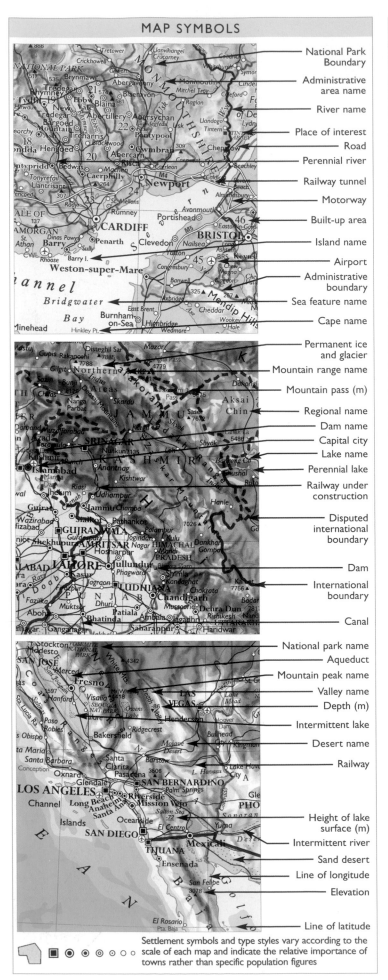

- National Park Boundary
- Administrative area name
- River name
- Place of interest
- Road
- Perennial river
- Railway tunnel
- Motorway
- Built-up area
- Island name
- Airport
- Administrative boundary
- Sea feature name
- Cape name
- Permanent ice and glacier
- Mountain range name
- Mountain pass (m)
- Regional name
- Dam name
- Capital city
- Lake name
- Perennial lake
- Railway under construction
- Disputed international boundary
- Dam
- International boundary
- Canal
- National park name
- Aqueduct
- Mountain peak name
- Valley name
- Depth (m)
- Intermittent lake
- Desert name
- Railway
- Height of lake surface (m)
- Intermittent river
- Sand desert
- Line of longitude
- Elevation
- Line of latitude

Settlement symbols and type styles vary according to the scale of each map and indicate the relative importance of towns rather than specific population figures

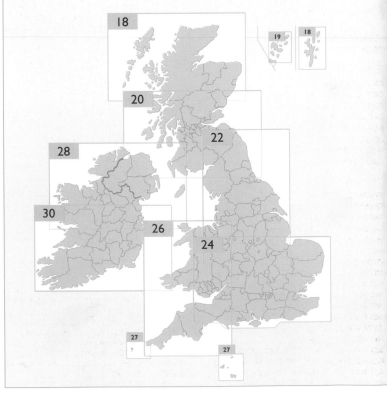

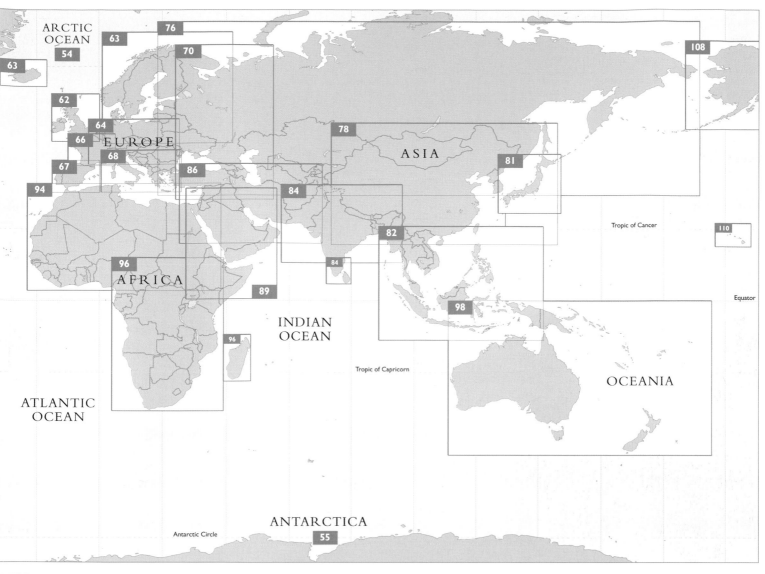

CONTENTS

CALE, LATITUDE AND LONGITUDE 4
AP PROJECTIONS...5

REMOTE SENSING   **6–16**

TRODUCTION 6–7
OLOUR COMPOSITES 8
GETATION AND LANDFORMS...9
OBAL MONITORING..10–11
IVIRONMENTAL MONITORING 12–13
EOLOGICAL INTERPRETATION 14
NTHETIC APERTURE RADAR 15
HE URBAN ENVIRONMENT 16

UNITED KINGDOM AND IRELAND   **17–48**

ORTHERN SCOTLAND 18–19
UTHERN SCOTLAND 20–21
ORTHERN ENGLAND 22–23
UTH AND SOUTH-EAST ENGLAND 24–25
ALES AND SOUTH-WEST ENGLAND 26–27
ELAND – NORTH 28–29
ELAND – SOUTH 30–31
C AND IRELAND: GEOLOGY 32
C AND IRELAND: RELIEF OF LAND.....................................33
C AND IRELAND: CLIMATE 34–35
C AND IRELAND: ENVIRONMENT 36–37
C AND IRELAND: AGRICULTURE, INDUSTRY
AND TRADE 38–39
C AND IRELAND: ENERGY 40–41
C AND IRELAND: TRANSPORT AND TOURISM 42–43
C AND IRELAND: COUNTIES AND REGIONS 44–45
C AND IRELAND: POPULATION TRENDS.......................46–47
C AND IRELAND: STANDARDS OF LIVING 48

THE WORLD   **49–122**

THE WORLD: RELIEF OF LAND...................................50–51
THE WORLD: COUNTRIES..52–53
ARCTIC OCEAN AND ANTARCTICA.............................54–55
EUROPE: RELIEF OF LAND..56
EUROPE: COUNTRIES...57
EUROPE: CLIMATE AND BIOMES......................................58
EUROPE: POPULATION...59
EUROPEAN UNION..60–61
UK AND IRELAND...62
SCANDINAVIA AND THE BALTIC LANDS...........................63
CENTRAL EUROPE..64–65
FRANCE..66
SPAIN AND PORTUGAL...67
ITALY AND THE BALKAN STATES...............................68–69
EASTERN EUROPE AND TURKEY................................70–71
ASIA: RELIEF OF LAND..72
ASIA: COUNTRIES...73
ASIA: CLIMATE AND BIOMES..74
ASIA: POPULATION AND WEALTH.....................................75
RUSSIA AND NORTHERN ASIA...................................76–77
CHINA AND THE FAR EAST..78–79
CHINA: INDUSTRY AND HYDROELECTRICITY.....................80
JAPAN..81
SOUTH-EAST ASIA..82–83
SOUTH ASIA...84–85
THE MIDDLE EAST...86–87
THE MIDDLE EAST: OIL AND WATER.................................88
ARABIA AND THE HORN OF AFRICA.................................89
AFRICA: RELIEF OF LAND..90
AFRICA: COUNTRIES...91
AFRICA: CLIMATE AND BIOMES.......................................92
AFRICA: POPULATION AND WEALTH.................................93
NORTHERN AFRICA...94–95
CENTRAL AND SOUTHERN AFRICA.............................96–97
OCEANIA..98–99
OCEANIA: CLIMATE AND POPULATION.....................100–101

PACIFIC OCEAN...102–103
NORTH AMERICA: RELIEF OF LAND 104
NORTH AMERICA: COUNTRIES 105
NORTH AMERICA: CLIMATE AND BIOMES......................106
NORTH AMERICA: POPULATION AND WEALTH...............107
CANADA..108–109
UNITED STATES 110–111
NORTH-EAST UNITED STATES AND THE ST LAWRENCE....112–113
MEXICO, CENTRAL AMERICA AND THE CARIBBEAN 114–115
CARIBBEAN: HURRICANES 116
SOUTH AMERICA: RELIEF OF LAND 117
SOUTH AMERICA: CLIMATE AND BIOMES 118
SOUTH AMERICA: POPULATION AND WEALTH 119
SOUTH AMERICA...120–121
SOUTH-EAST BRAZIL 122

WORLD THEMES   **123–160**

THE WORLD: VOLCANOES AND EARTHQUAKES.............124–125
THE WORLD: TEMPERATURE AND OCEAN CURRENTS.........126
THE WORLD: PRESSURE, WINDS AND PRECIPITATION 127
THE WORLD: CLIMATE..128–129
THE WORLD: CLIMATE CHANGE.................................130–131
THE WORLD CLIMATE STATISTICS 132–133
THE WORLD: BIOMES..134–135
THE WORLD: AGRICULTURE.......................................136–137
THE WORLD: ENERGY AND MINERALS 138–139
THE WORLD: INDUSTRY AND TRADE...........................140–141
THE WORLD: TRAVEL AND TOURISM 142–143
THE WORLD: STANDARDS OF LIVING 144–145
THE WORLD: POPULATION DISTRIBUTION...................146–147
THE WORLD: POPULATION TRENDS.............................148–149
THE WORLD: LANGUAGES AND RELIGION 150
THE WORLD: INTERNATIONAL ORGANIZATIONS 151
THE WORLD: HUMAN CONCERNS 152–153
THE WORLD: SOCIAL AND ECONOMIC STATISTICS......154–159
THE WORLD: PHYSICAL DIMENSIONS 160

INDEX   **161–184**

SCALE

The scale of a map is the relationship of the distance between two points shown on the map and the distance between the same two points on the Earth's surface. For instance, 1 inch on the map represents 1 mile on the ground, or 10 kilometres on the ground is represented by 1 centimetre on the map.

Instead of saying 1 centimetre represents 10 kilometres, we could say that 1 centimetre represents 1 000 000 centimetres on the map. If the scale is stated so that the same unit of measurement is used on both the map and the ground, then the proportion will hold for any unit of measurement. Therefore, the scale is usually written 1:1 000 000. This is called a 'representative fraction' and usually appears at the top of the map page, above the scale bar.

Calculations can easily be made in centimetres and kilometres by dividing the second figure in the representative fraction by 100 000 (i.e. by deleting the last five zeros). Thus at a scale of 1:5 000 000, 1 cm on the map represents 50 km on the ground. This is called a 'scale statement'. The calculation for inches and miles is more laborious, but 1 000 000 divided by 63 360 (the number of inches in a mile) shows that 1:1 000 000 can be stated as 1 inch on the map represents approximately 16 miles on the ground.

Many of the maps in this atlas feature a scale bar. This is a bar divided into the units of the map – miles and kilometres – so that a map distance can be measured with a ruler,

dividers or a piece of paper, then placed along the scale bar, and the distance read off. To the left of the zero on the scale bar there are usually more divisions. By placing the ruler or dividers on the nearest rounded figure to the right of the zero, the smaller units can be counted off to the left.

The map extracts below show Los Angeles and its surrounding area at six different scales. The representative fraction, scale statement and scale bar are positioned above each map. Map 1 is at 1:27 000 and is the largest scale extract shown. Many of the individual buildings are identified and most of the streets are named, but at this scale only part of central Los Angeles can be shown within the given area. Map 2 is much smaller in scale at 1:250 000. Only a few important buildings and streets can be named, but the whole of central Los Angeles is shown. Maps 3, 4 and 5 show how greater areas can be depicted as the map scale decreases, down to Map 6 at 1:35 000 000. At this small scale, the entire Los Angeles conurbation is depicted by a single town symbol and a large part of the south-western USA and part of Mexico is shown.

The scales of maps must be used with care since large distances on small-scale maps can be represented by one or two centimetres. On certain projections scale is only correct along certain lines, parallels or meridians. As a general rule, the larger the map scale, the more accurate and reliable will be the distance measured.

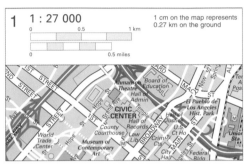

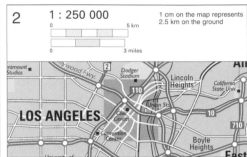

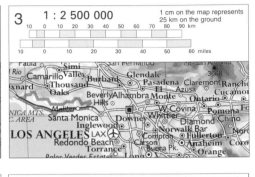

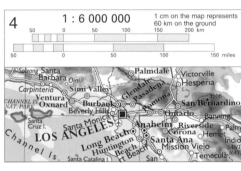

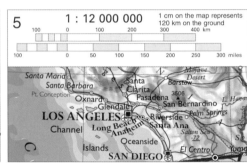

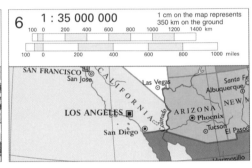

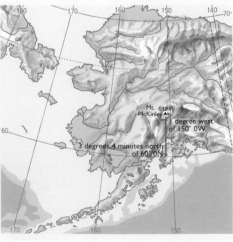

LATITUDE AND LONGITUDE

Accurate positioning of individual points on the Earth's surface is made possible by reference to the geometric system of latitude and longitude.

Latitude is the distance of a point north or south of the Equator measured at an angle with the centre of the Earth, whereby the Equator is latitude 0 degrees, the North Pole is 90 degrees north and the South Pole 90 degrees south. Latitude parallels are drawn west–east around the Earth, parallel to the Equator, decreasing in diameter from the Equator until they become a point at the poles. On the maps in this atlas the lines of latitude are represented by blue lines running across the map in smooth curves, with the degree figures in blue at the sides of the maps. The degree interval depends on the scale of the map.

Lines of longitude are meridians drawn north–south, cutting the lines of latitude at right angles on the Earth's surface and intersecting with one another at the poles. Longitude is measured by an angle at the centre of the Earth from the prime meridian (0 degrees), which passes through Greenwich in London. It is given as a measurement east or west of the Greenwich Meridian from 0 to 180 degrees. The meridians are

normally drawn north–south vertically down the map, with the degree figures in blue in the top and bottom margins of the map.

In the index each place name is followed by its map page number, its letter-figure grid reference, and then its latitude and longitude. The unit of measurement is the degree, which is subdivided into 60 minutes. An index entry states the position of a place in degrees and minutes. The latitude is followed by N(orth) or S(outh) and the longitude E(ast) or W(est).

For example:
Helston, U.K.   27 G3   50 7N   5 17W
Helston is on map page 27, in grid square G3, and is 50 degrees 7 minutes north of the Equator and 5 degrees 17 minutes west of Greenwich.

McKinley, Mt., U.S.A.   108 B4   63 4N   151 0W
Mount McKinley is on map page 108, in grid square B4, and is 63 degrees 4 minutes north of the Equator and 151 degrees west of Greenwich.

HOW TO LOCATE A PLACE OR FEATURE

The two diagrams (left) show how to estimate the required distance from the nearest line of latitude or longitude on the map page, in order to locate a place or feature listed in the index (such as Helston in the UK and Mount McKinley in the USA, as detailed in the above example).

In the left-hand diagram there are 30 minutes between the lines and so to find the position of Helston an estimate has to be made: 7 parts of the 30 minutes north of the 50 0N latitude line, and 17 parts of the 30 minutes west of the 5 0W longitude line.

In the right-hand diagram it is more difficult to estimate because there is an interval of 10 degrees between the lines. In the example of Mount McKinley, the reader has to estimate 3 degrees 4 minutes north of 60 0N and 1 degree west of 150 0W.

MAP PROJECTIONS

A map projection is the systematic depiction of the imaginary grid of lines of latitude and longitude from a globe on to a flat surface. The grid of lines is called the 'graticule' and it can be constructed either by graphical means or by mathematical formulae to form the basis of a map. As a globe is three dimensional, it is not possible to depict its surface on a flat map without some form of distortion. Preservation of one of the basic properties listed below can only be secured at the expense of the others and thus the choice of projection is often a compromise solution.

Correct area

In these projections the areas from the globe are to scale on the map. This is particularly useful in the mapping of densities and distributions. Projections with this property are termed 'equal area', 'equivalent' or 'homolographic'.

Correct distance

In these projections the scale is correct along the meridians, or, in the case of the 'azimuthal equidistant', scale is true along any line drawn from the centre of the projection. They are called 'equidistant'.

Correct shape

This property can only be true within small areas as it is achieved only by having a uniform scale distortion along both the 'x' and 'y' axes of the projection. The projections are called 'conformal' or 'orthomorphic'.

Map projections can be divided into three broad categories – **'azimuthal'**, **'conic'** and **'cylindrical'**. Cartographers use different projections from these categories depending on the map scale, the size of the area to be mapped, and what they want the map to show.

AZIMUTHAL OR ZENITHAL PROJECTIONS

These are constructed by the projection of part of the graticule from the globe on to a plane tangential to any single point on it. This plane may be tangential to the equator (equatorial case), the poles (polar case) or any other point (oblique case). Any straight line drawn from the point at which the plane touches the globe is the shortest distance from that point and is known as a 'great circle'. In its 'gnomonic' construction any straight line on the map is a great circle, but there is great exaggeration towards the edges and this reduces its general uses. There are five different ways of transferring the graticule on to the plane and these are shown below. The diagrams below also show how the graticules vary, using the polar case as the example.

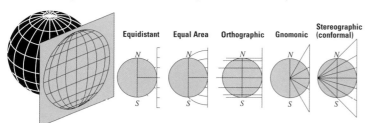

Equidistant   Equal Area   Orthographic   Gnomonic   Stereographic (conformal)

Polar case

The polar case is the simplest to construct and the diagram on the right shows the differing effects of all five methods of construction, comparing their coverage, distortion, etc, using North America as the example.

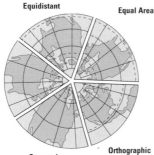

Equidistant   Equal Area   Stereographic   Gnomonic   Orthographic

Oblique case

The plane touches the globe at any point between the Equator and poles. The oblique orthographic uses the distortion in azimuthal projections away from the centre to give a graphic depiction of the Earth as seen from any desired point in space.

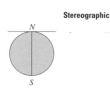

Equatorial case

The example shown here is Lambert's Equivalent Azimuthal. It is the only projection which is both equal area and where bearing is true from the centre.

CONICAL PROJECTIONS

These use the projection of the graticule from the globe on to a cone which is tangential to a line of latitude (termed the 'standard parallel'). This line is always an arc and scale is always true along it. Because of its method of construction, it is used mainly for depicting the temperate latitudes around the standard parallel, i.e. where there is least distortion. To reduce the distortion and include a larger range of latitudes, the projection may be constructed with the cone bisecting the surface of the globe so that there are two standard parallels, each of which is true to scale. The distortion is thus spread more evenly between the two chosen parallels.

Simple Conical with one standard parallel

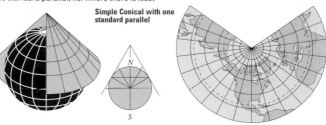

Bonne

This is a modification of the simple conic, whereby the true scale along the meridians is sacrificed to enable the accurate representation of areas. However, scale is true along each parallel but shapes are distorted at the edges.

Albers Conical Equal Area

This projection uses two standard parallels. The selection of these relative to the land area to be mapped is very important. It is equal area and is especially useful for large land masses oriented east–west, such as the USA.

CYLINDRICAL AND OTHER WORLD PROJECTIONS

This group of projections are those which permit the whole of the Earth's surface to be depicted on one map. They are a very large group of projections and the following are only a few of them. Cylindrical projections are constructed by the projection of the graticule from the globe on to a cylinder tangential to the globe. Although cylindrical projections can depict all the main land masses, there is considerable distortion of shape and area towards the poles. One cylindrical projection, Mercator, overcomes this shortcoming by possessing the unique navigational property that any straight line drawn on it is a line of constant bearing ('loxodrome'). It is used for maps and charts between 15° either side of the Equator. Beyond this, enlargement of area is a serious drawback, although it is used for navigational charts at all latitudes.

Mercator

Simple Cylindrical

Cylindrical with two standard parallels

Eckert IV (pseudo-cylindrical equal area)

Hammer (polyconic equal area)

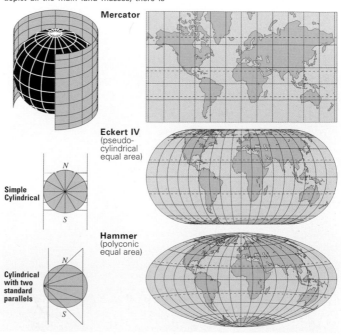

The first satellite to monitor our environment systematically was launched as long ago as April 1961. It was called TIROS-1 and was designed specifically to record atmospheric change. The first of the generation of Earth resources satellites was Landsat-1, launched in July 1972.

The succeeding decades have seen a revolution in our ability to survey and map our global environment. Digital sensors mounted on satellites now scan vast areas of the Earth's surface day and night. They collect and relay back to Earth huge volumes of geographical data which is processed and stored by computers.

Satellite imagery and remote sensing

Continuous development and refinement, and freedom from national access restrictions, have meant that sensors on these satellite platforms are increasingly replacing surface and airborne data-gathering techniques. Twenty-four hours a day, satellites are scanning and measuring the Earth's surface and atmosphere, adding to an ever-expanding range of geographic and geophysical data available to help us identify and manage the problems of our human and physical environments. Remote sensing is the science of extracting information from such images.

Satellite orbits

Most Earth-observation satellites (such as the Landsat, SPOT and IRS series) are in a near-polar, Sun-synchronous orbit (*see diagram opposite*). At altitudes of around 700–900 km the satellites revolve around the Earth approximately every 100 minutes and on each orbit cross a particular line of latitude at the same local (solar) time. This ensures that the satellite can obtain coverage of most of the globe, replicating the coverage typically within 2–3 weeks. In more recent satellites, sensors can be pointed sideways from the orbital path, and 'revisit' times with high-resolution frames can thus be reduced to a few days.

Exceptions to these Sun-synchronous orbits include the geostationary meteorological satellites, such as Meteosat. These have a 36,000 km high orbit and rotate around the Earth every 24 hours, thus remaining above the same point on the Equator.

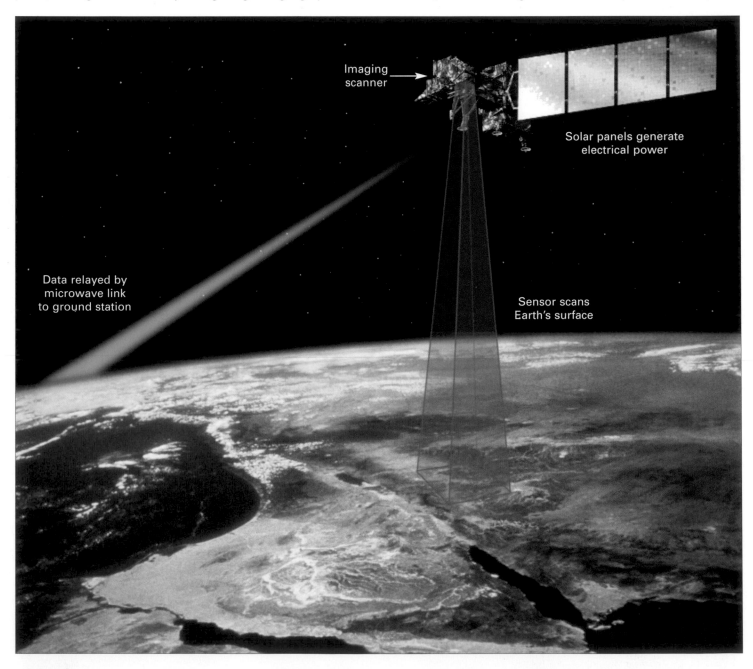

Imaging scanner

Solar panels generate electrical power

Data relayed by microwave link to ground station

Sensor scans Earth's surface

Landsat-7
This is the latest addition to the Landsat Earth-observation satellite programme, *orbiting at 705 km above the Earth. With onboard recorders, the satellite can store data until it passes within range of a* *ground station. Basic geometric and radiometric corrections are then applied before distribution of the imagery to users.*

These satellites acquire frequent images showing cloud and atmospheric moisture movements for almost a full hemisphere.

In addition, there is the Global Positioning System (GPS) satellite 'constellation', which orbits at a height of 20,200 km, consisting of 24 satellites. These circle the Earth in six different orbital planes, enabling us to fix our position on the Earth's surface to an accuracy of a few centimetres. Although developed for military use, this system is now available to individuals through hand-held receivers and in-car navigation systems. The other principal commercial uses are for surveying and air and sea navigation.

Digital sensors

Early satellite designs involved images being exposed to photographic film and returned to Earth by capsule for processing, a technique still sometimes used today. However, even the first commercial satellite imagery, from Landsat-1, used digital imaging sensors and transmitted the data back to ground stations (*see diagram opposite*).

Passive, or optical, sensors record the radiation reflected from the Earth for specific wavebands. Active sensors transmit their own microwave radiation, which is reflected from the Earth's surface back to the satellite and recorded. The SAR (Synthetic Aperture Radar) Radarsat images on page 15 are examples of the latter.

Whichever scanning method is used, each satellite records image data of constant width but potentially several thousand kilometres in length. Once the data has been received on Earth, it is usually split into approximately square sections or 'scenes' for distribution.

Spectral resolution, wavebands and false-colour composites

Satellites can record data from many sections of the electromagnetic spectrum (wavebands) simultaneously. Since we can only see images made from the three primary colours (red, green and blue), a selection of any three wavebands needs to be made in order to form a picture that will enable visual interpretation of the scene to be made. When any combination other than the visible bands are used, such as near or middle infrared, the resulting image is termed a 'false-colour composite'. An example of this is shown on page 8.

The selection of these wavebands depends on the purpose of the final image – geology, hydrology, agronomy and environmental requirements each have their own optimum waveband combinations.

GEOGRAPHIC INFORMATION SYSTEMS

A Geographic Information System (GIS) enables any available geospatial data to be compiled, presented and analysed using specialized computer software.

Many aspects of our lives now benefit from the use of GIS – from the management and maintenance of the networks of pipelines and cables that supply our homes, to the exploitation or protection of the natural resources that we use. Much of this is at a regional or national scale and the data collected from satellites form an important part of our interpretation and understanding of the world around us.

GIS systems are used for many aspects of central planning and modern life, such as defence, land use, reclamation, telecommunications and the deployment of emergency services. Commercial companies can use demographic and infrastructure data within a GIS to plan marketing strategies, identifying where their services would be most needed, and thus decide where best to locate their businesses. Insurance companies use GIS to determine premiums based on population distribution, crime figures and the likelihood of natural disasters, such as flooding or subsidence.

Whatever the application, all the relevant data can be prepared in a GIS so that a user can extract and display the information of particular interest on a map, or compare it with other material in order to help analyse and resolve a specific problem. From analysis of the data that has been acquired it is often possible to use a GIS to create a computer 'model' of possible future situations and see what impact various actions may have. A GIS can also monitor change over time, aiding the interpretation of long term trends.

A GIS may also use satellite data to extract useful information and map large areas, which would otherwise take many man-years using other methods. For applications such as hydrocarbon and mineral exploration, forestry, agriculture, environmental monitoring and urban development, these developments have made it possible to undertake projects on a global scale unheard of before.

To find out more about how GIS works and how it affects our lives, why not go the Ordnance Survey's Mapzone website at: http://mapzone.ordnancesurvey.co.uk/mapzone/giszone.html

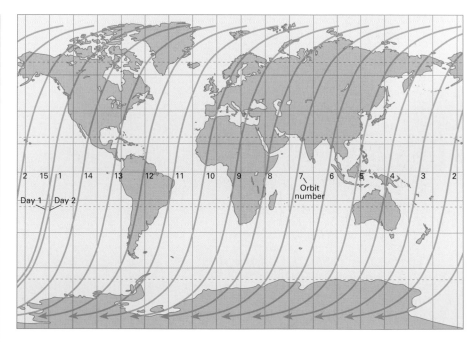

SELECTED REMOTE SENSING SATELLITES			
Year Launched	Satellite	Country	Pixel Size (Resolution)
Passive Sensors (Optical)			
1972	Landsat-1 MSS	USA	80 m
1978	NOAA AVHRR	USA	1.1 km
1981	Cosmos TK-350	Russia	10 m
1982	Landsat-4 TM	USA	30 m
1986	SPOT-1	France	10 / 20 m
1988	IRS-1A	India	36 / 72 m
1989	Cosmos KVR-1000	Russia	2 m
1991	IRS-1B	India	36 / 72 m
1995	IRS-1C	India	5.8 / 23.5 m
1997	IRS-1D	India	5.8 / 23.5 m
1999	Landsat-7 ETM	USA	15 / 30 m
1999	UoSAT-12	UK	10 / 32 m
1999	IKONOS-2	USA	1.0 / 4 m
1999	ASTER	USA	15 m
2000	Hyperion	USA	30 m
2000	EROS-A1	International	1.8 m
2001	Quickbird	USA	0.61 / 2.4 m
2002	SPOT-5	France	2.5 / 5 / 10 m
2002	DMC AlSat-1	Algeria (UK)	32 m
2003	DMC UK	UK	32 m
2003	DMC NigeriaSat-1	Nigeria (UK)	32 m
2003	DMC BilSat	Turkey (UK)	32 m
2003	OrbView-3	USA	1.0 / 4 m
2004	Formosat-2	Taiwan	2.0 / 8 m
2004	KOMPSAT-2	South Korea	1.0 / 4 m
2006	ALOS PRISM & AVNIR	Japan	2.5 m
2007	Worldview-1	USA	0.5 m
2008	GeoEye	USA	0.4 m
Active Sensors (Synthetic Aperture Radar)			
1991	ERS-1	Europe	25 m
1992	JERS-1	Japan	18 m
1995	ERS-2	Europe	25 m
1995	Radarsat	Canada	8–100 m
2002	ENVISAT	Europe	25 m
2006	ALOS PALSAR	Japan	10 m
2007	Radarsat-2	Canada	3 m
2007	TERRASAR-X	Germany	1 m
2007	COSMO-SkyMed	Italy	1 m

Satellite orbits
Landsat-7 makes over 14 orbits per day in its Sun-synchronous orbit. During the full 16 days of a repeat cycle, coverage of the areas between those shown is achieved.

Natural-colour and false-colour composites
These images show the salt ponds at the southern end of San Francisco Bay, which now form the San Francisco Bay National Wildlife Refuge. They demonstrate the difference between 'natural colour' (*top*) and 'false colour' (*bottom*) composites.

The top image is made from visible red, green and blue wavelengths. The colours correspond closely to those one would observe from an aircraft. The salt ponds appear green or orange-red due to the

colour of the sediments they contain. The urban areas appear grey and vegetation is either dark green (trees) or light brown (dry grass).

The bottom image is made up of near-infrared, visible red and visible green wavelengths. These wavebands are represented here in red, green and blue, respectively. Since chlorophyll in healthy vegetation strongly reflects near-infrared light, this is clearly visible as red in the image.

False-colour composite imagery is therefore very sensitive to the presence of healthy vegetation. The bottom image thus shows better discrimination between the 'leafy' residential urban areas, such as Palo Alto (south-west of the Bay) from other urban areas by the 'redness' of the trees. The high chlorophyll content of watered urban grass areas shows as bright red, contrasting with the dark red of trees and the brown of natural, dry grass. *(EROS)*

Western Grand Canyon, Arizona, USA
This false-colour image shows in bright red the sparse vegetation on the limestone plateau, including sage, mesquite and grasses. Imagery such as this is used to monitor this and similar fragile environments. The sediment-laden river, shown as blue-green, can be seen dispersing into Lake Mead to the north-west. Side canyons cross the main canyon in straight lines, showing where erosion along weakened fault lines has occurred. *(EROS)*

Ayers Rock and Mt Olga, Northern Territory, Australia
These two huge outliers are the remnants of Precambrian mountain ranges created some 500 million years ago and then eroded away. Ayers Rock (*seen at right*) rises 345 m above the surrounding land and has been a part of Aboriginal life for over 10,000 years. Their dramatic coloration, caused by oxidized iron in the sandstone, attracts visitors from around the world. *(EROS)*

Mount St Helens, Washington, USA
A massive volcanic eruption on 18 May 1980 killed 60 people and devastated around 400 sq km of forest within minutes. The blast reduced the mountain peak by 400 m to its current height of 2,550 m, and volcanic ash rose some 25 km into the atmosphere. The image shows Mount St Helens eight years after the eruption in 1988. The characteristic volcanic cone has collapsed in the north, resulting in the devastating 'liquid' flow of mud and rock. *(EROS)*

Niger Delta, West Africa
The River Niger is the third longest river in Africa after the Nile and Congo. Deltas are by nature constantly evolving sedimentary features and often contain many ecosystems within them. In the case of the Niger Delta, there are also vast hydrocarbon reserves beneath it with associated wells and pipelines. Satellite imagery helps to plan activity and monitor this fragile and changing environment. *(EROS)*

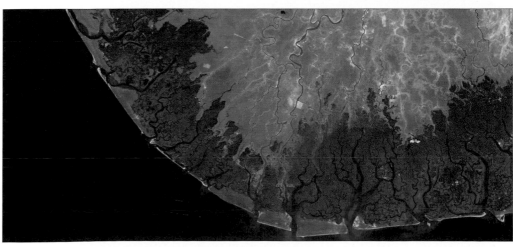

Europe at night

This image was derived as part of the Defense Meteorological Satellite Program. The sensor recorded all the emissions of near-infrared radiation at night, mainly the lights from cities, towns and villages. Note also the 'lights' in the North Sea from the flares of the oil production platforms. This project was the first systematic attempt to record human settlement on a global scale using remote sensing. *(© Fugro-NPA)*

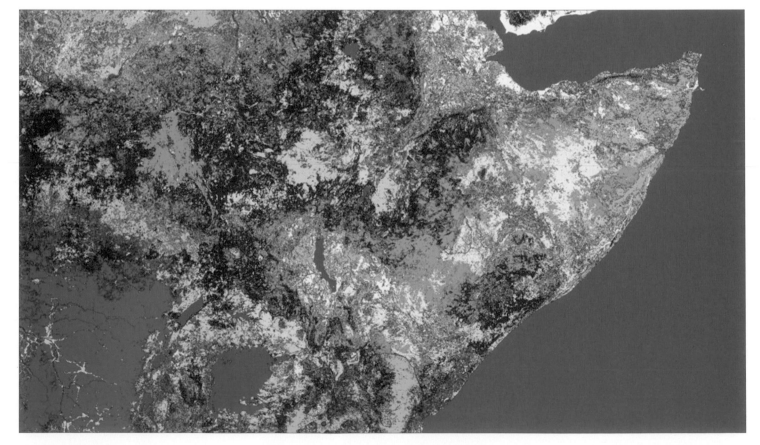

World Land Cover

The European Space Agency's (ESA) GlobCover project between 2004 and 2006 has produced the first complete global land cover data down to a resolution of 300 metres. It is an ongoing process and differentiates between 22 different land cover types, including croplands, wetlands, forests, artificial surfaces, water and snow. This will allow scientists to perform much more accurate research and prediction on sustainable environmental management, humanitarian issues and climate change modelling. *(© ESA/ESA GlobCover Project, led by MEDIAS-France)*

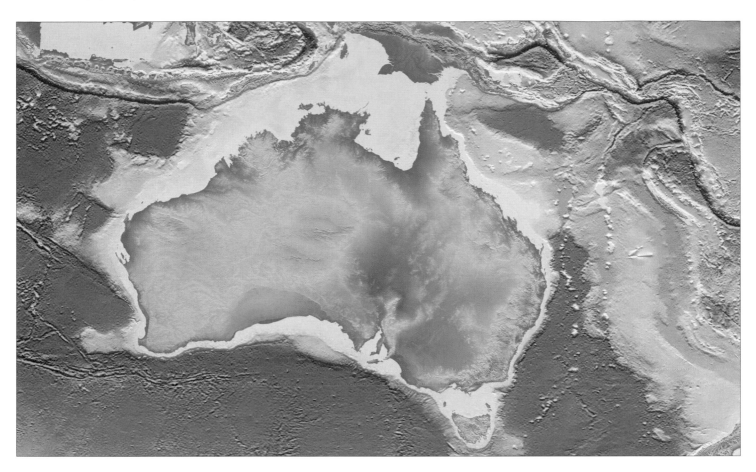

Mapping the Ocean Floors

The accurate global mapping of whole ocean floors has only been possible since the advent of satellite radar altimetry. From a precisely known orbit microwave pulses measure the ocean surface. The effects of tides, waves and currents can mathematically be removed from these measurements and the resultant ocean surface shape reflects that of the ocean floor beneath due the gravitational effects of the water over the sea floor topography. However for large scale navigational charts shipboard echo soundings are still used. *(© Fugro-NPA)*

Weather monitoring

Geostationary and polar orbiting satellites monitor the Earth's atmospheric movements, giving us an insight into the global workings of the atmosphere and permitting us to predict weather change. *(NASA image courtesy GOES Project Science Office)*

Tropical Cyclone 'Billy'

On Christmas Day 2008 the storm approaches Western Australia from the Indian Ocean. Such images aid in monitoring the development and track of weather systems. *(Jeff Schmaltz, MODIS Rapid Response Team at NASA Goddard Space Flight Center)*

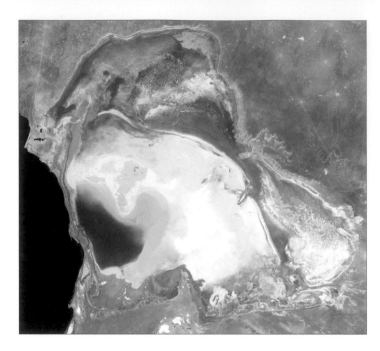

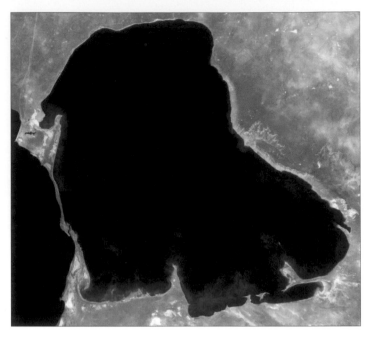

Kara-Bogaz-Gol, Turkmenistan
The Kara-Bogaz-Gol (*above, left and right*) is a large, shallow lagoon joined by a narrow, steep-sided strait to the Caspian Sea. Evaporation makes it one of the most saline bodies of water in the world. Believing the Caspian sea level was falling, the strait was dammed by the Soviet Union in 1980 with the intention of conserving the water to sustain the salt industry. However, by 1983 it had dried up completely (*above left*), leading to widespread wind-blown salt, soil poisoning and health problems downwind to the east. In 1992 the Turkmenistan government began to demolish the dam to re-establish the flow of water from the Caspian Sea (*above right*). Satellite imagery has helped to monitor and map the Kara-Bogaz-Gol as it has fluctuated in size. *(EROS)*

Antarctic warming
Antarctica was generally considered to be less affected by global warming than the Arctic, but gathering data was difficult because of its isolation. This false-colour image however displays the results of scientific analysis of 50 years of temperature recordings between 1957–2007. Temperature records for the early years, before satellite data was available, are extrapolated from ground weather station records. The darker orange tones indicate the highest temperature rise, showing that western Antarctica, including the peninsula, has warmed most during this period. *(Image courtesy Trent Schindler, NASA Goddard Space Flight Center Scientific Visualization)*

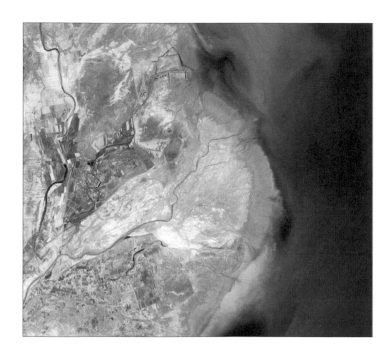

Yellow River Delta

The image on the left was captured in 1979, whilst the one on the right was obtained in 2000. They both cover exactly the same area of the Yellow River (Huang He) Delta in China, as can be seen from the course of the river in the top left hand corner. Much further upstream, the river erodes large amounts of sediment as it cuts through soft plateaux in its upper course. It carries this load until it deposits it at its mouth, as it slows to meet the sea. Notice as well how much other change has taken place on the land over the same period. *(NASA image created by Jesse Allen, using Landsat data provided by the United States Geological Survey)*

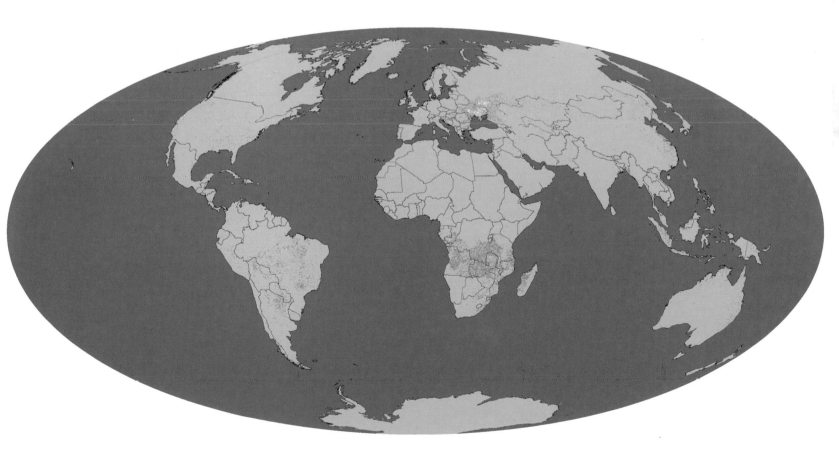

World Fires

This image shows all the fires worldwide which were burning during August 2008, whether they were man-made, to clear ground for crops, for example, or occurs naturally from, say, lightning strikes. The orange tint indicates where fires are at their fiercest. Over any given year the areas affected by the fires move with the seasons, February being the month with most fires in the tropics. Acquiring this data from satellites allows efficient management of scarce resources in remote and environmentally threatened areas. *(NASA image by Reto Stockli and Jesse Allen using data courtesy the MODIS Land Science Team at NASA Goddard Space Flight Center)*

Sichuan Basin, China

The north-east/south-west trending ridges in this image are anticlinal folds developed in the Earth's crust as a result of plate collision and compression. Geologists map these folds and the lowlands between them formed by synclinal folds, as they are often the areas where oil or gas are found in commercial quantities. The river shown in this image is the Yangtze, near Chongqing. *(China RSGS)*

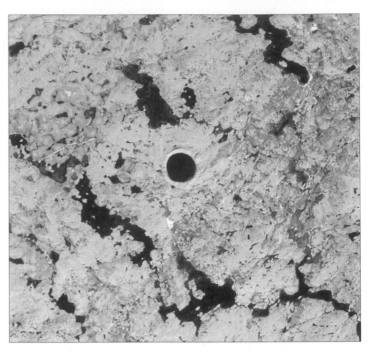

Pingualuit Crater

The circular feature is a meteorite crater in the Ungava Peninsula, Québec, formed by an impact over 1.4 million years ago. It is 3.4 km wide and the lake within is 264 m deep. The lake has no link to any water sources and has been formed only by rain and snow. Thus the water is very pure and among the world's clearest and least saline. Sediments at the bottom have been unaffected by ice sheets and are important for scientific research. *(© Fugro-NPA)*

Wadi Hadhramaut, Yemen

Yemen is extremely arid – however, in the past it was more humid and wet, enabling large river systems to carve out the deep and spectacular gorges and dried-out river beds (*wadis*) seen in this image. The erosion has revealed many contrasting rock types. The image has been processed to exaggerate this effect, producing many shades of red, pink and purple, which make geological mapping easier and more cost-effective. *(EROS)*

Zagros Mountains, Iran

These mountains were formed as Arabia collided with Southern Eurasia. The upper half of this colour-enhanced image shows an anticline that runs east–west. The dark grey features are called *diapirs*, which are bodies of viscous rock salt that are very buoyant and sometimes rise to the surface, spilling and spreading out like a glacier. The presence of salt in the region is important as it stops oil escaping to the surface. *(EROS)*

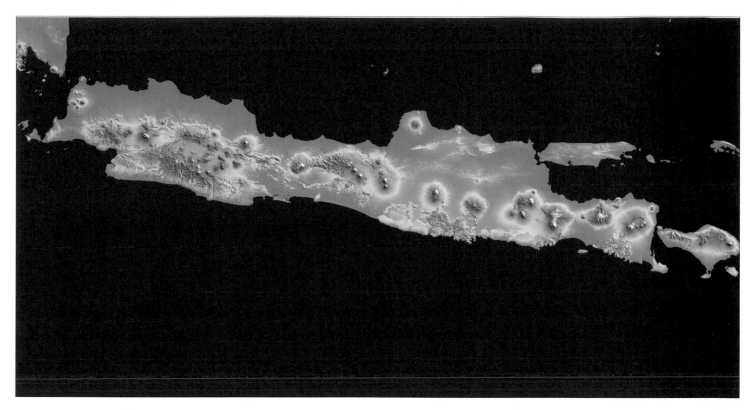

Topographic Survey

In February 2000 the Shuttle Radar Topography Mission (SRTM) was launched. Over 11 days, using specially developed radar equipment, it captured the topography of 80% of the earth's land area at high resolution. This was the first time that this had been done on a consistent basis globally and for many inaccessible areas was the first survey. The volcanic cones of the Indonesian islands of Java and Bali are clearly visible. (© Fugro-NPA)

Environmental Monitoring

Synthetic Aperture Radar (SAR) uses microwaves to penetrate cloud and needs no solar illumination, so is ideal for monitoring remote and difficult areas. In the middle of this image the David Glacier in Antarctica is seen flowing to the sea. Here it floats onwards and is known as the Drygalski Ice Tongue. At its end, a tabular iceberg is breaking off, or calving, whilst to the right is part of a 120km long iceberg which almost collided with it. (© ESA)

Lidar Surveying.

Lasers based on aircraft or satellites can be used to scan surface elevations to an accuracy of a few centimetres. This extract from a survey of the whole of London shows the City of London (from St Paul's Cathedral in the north-west to the Tower of London and Tower Bridge in the south-east. The very narrow and deep urban canyons and atriums in this area clearly demonstrate the advantages of airborne laser scanning (Lidar), which only requires a single line-of-sight to obtain precise measurements. A basic variant of this technology has been used for several years from satellites to acquire elevation profiles of the surface of Mars. Sensors capable of more detailed scanning are currently under development for Earth-orbiting satellites. *(Precision Terrain Surveys Ltd – www.precisionterrain.com)*

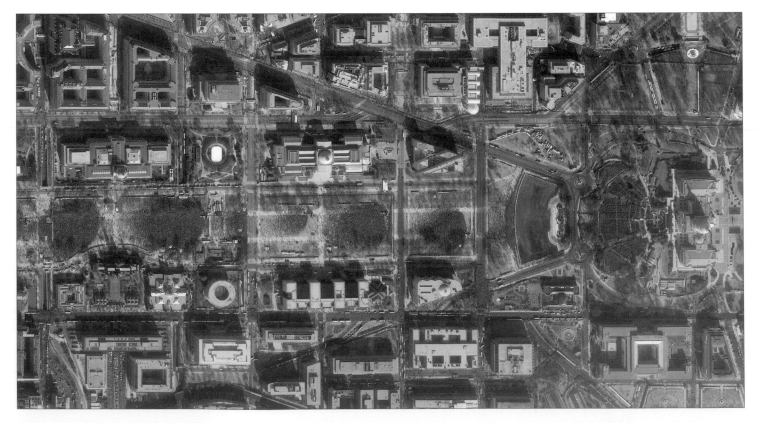

Washington DC, January 20th, 2009

Modern satellite and sensor technology now mean that imagery goes down to resolutions of less than 0.5m. Thus human beings become visible for the first time on commercially available imagery. On this image, crowds can clearly be seen gathering on the Mall in the early morning sunshine leading up to Barrack Obama's inauguration. The large building on the right with blue roofs is the U.S. Capitol. *(Image courtesy GeoEye)*

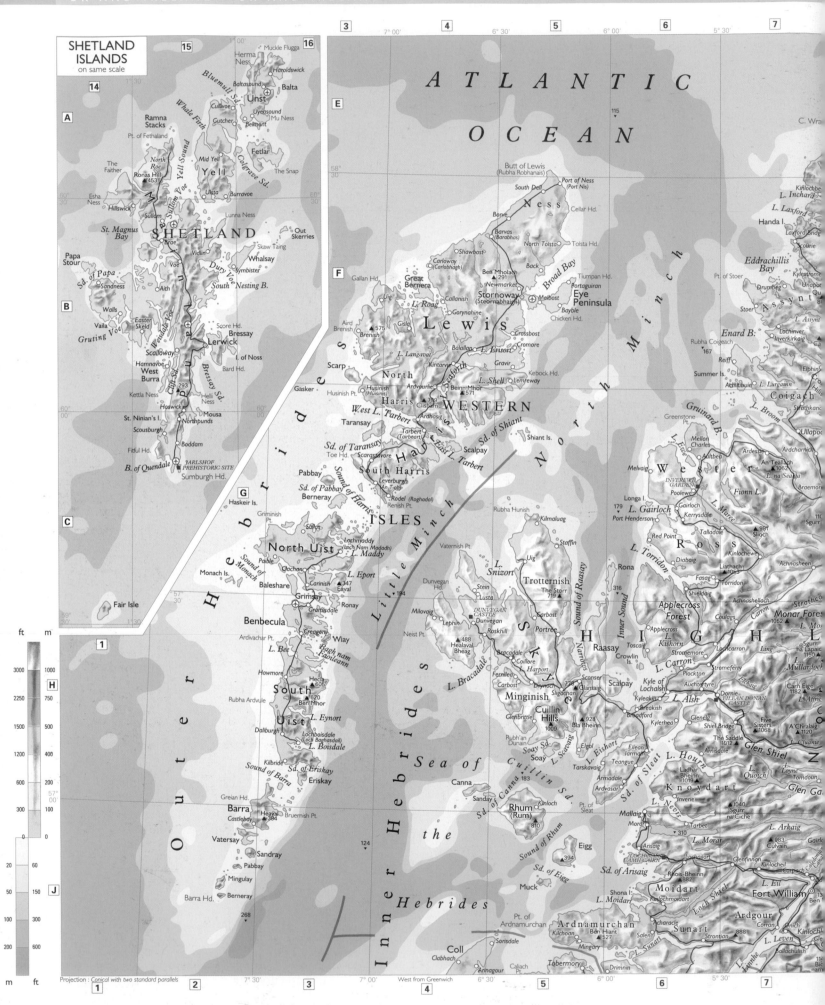

SHETLAND
ISLANDS
on same scale

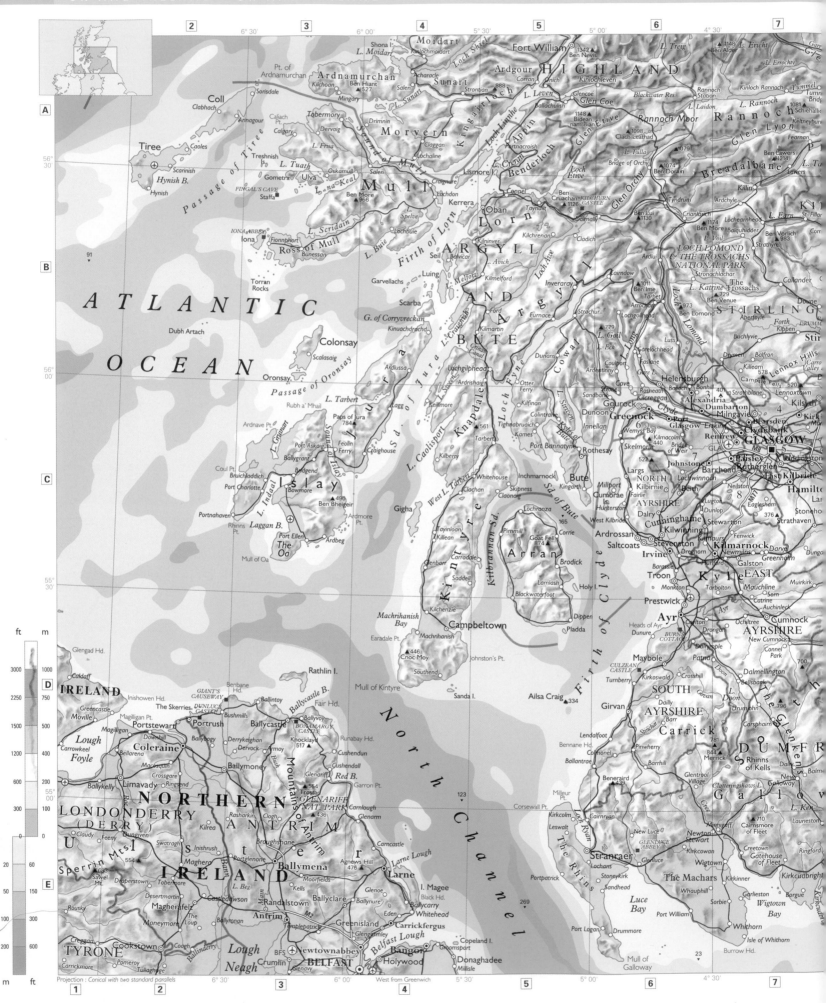

Key to Scottish unitary
authorities on map
2 DUNDEE CITY
3 WEST DUNBARTONSHIRE
4 EAST DUNBARTONSHIRE
5 CITY OF GLASGOW
6 INVERCLYDE
7 RENFREWSHIRE
8 EAST RENFREWSHIRE
9 NORTH LANARKSHIRE
10 FALKIRK
11 CLACKMANNANSHIRE
12 WEST LOTHIAN
13 CITY OF EDINBURGH
14 MIDLOTHIAN

NORTH

SEA

SCOTTISH
BORDERS

NORTHUMBERLAND

NORTHUMBERLAND
NATIONAL PARK

CHEVIOT HILLS

TYNE
& WEAR

CUMBRIA

DURHAM

COPYRIGHT PHILIP'S

1:1 000 000

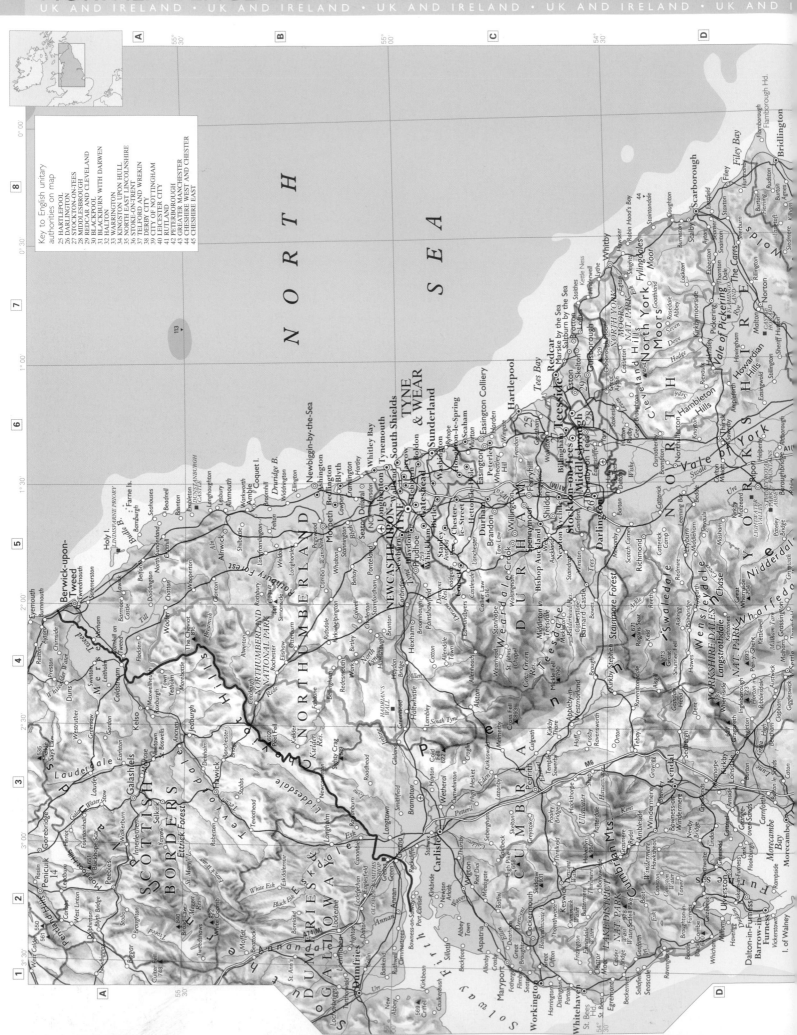

Key to English unitary authorities on map

25 HARTLEPOOL
26 DARLINGTON
27 STOCKTON-ON-TEES
28 MIDDLESBROUGH
29 REDCAR AND CLEVELAND
30 BLACKPOOL
31 BLACKBURN WITH DARWEN
32 HALTON
33 WARRINGTON
34 KINGSTON UPON HULL
35 NORTH EAST LINCOLNSHIRE
36 STOKE-ON-TRENT
37 TELFORD AND WREKIN
38 DERBY CITY
39 CITY OF NOTTINGHAM
40 LEICESTER CITY
41 RUTLAND
42 PETERBOROUGH
43 GREATER MANCHESTER
44 CHESHIRE WEST AND CHESTER
45 CHESHIRE EAST

1:1 000 000

Projection: Conical with two standard parallels

STAFFORDSHIRE
SHROPSHIRE
HEREFORDSHIRE
WORCESTERSHIRE
WARWICKSHIRE
WEST MIDLANDS
GLOUCESTERSHIRE
OXFORDSHIRE
POWYS
CARMARTHEN-SHIRE
MONMOUTHSHIRE
WILTSHIRE
HAMPSHIRE
WEST BERKSHIRE
SOMERSET
DEVON
DORSET
NORTHAMPTONSHIRE

BIRMINGHAM
WOLVERHAMPTON
COVENTRY
LEICESTER
NOTTINGHAM
DERBY
Shrewsbury
Telford
Hereford
Gloucester
Cheltenham
Worcester
Oxford
Swindon
Newport
CARDIFF
BRISTOL
Bath
Swansea
Port Talbot
Bridgend
Weston-super-Mare
Taunton
Exeter
Yeovil
Salisbury
Winchester
SOUTHAMPTON
BOURNEMOUTH
Poole
Dorchester
Weymouth
ISLE OF WIGHT

Bristol Channel
Bridgwater Bay
Swansea Bay
Lyme Bay
The Solent

BRECON BEACONS NATIONAL PARK
EXMOOR NATIONAL PARK
Exmoor
NEW FOREST NATIONAL PARK
Cotswold Hills
Mendip Hills
Quantock Hills
Blackdown Hills
Salisbury Plain
Vale of Pewsey
Marlborough Downs
Berkshire Downs
Vale of White Horse
Cranborne Chase
South Dorset Downs
North Dorset Downs
Blackmoor Vale
Black Mountains
Mynydd Eppynt
Clun Forest
Radnor Forest
Wyre Forest
Forest of Dean
Chesil Beach

Projection : Conical with two standard parallels
West from Greenwich

ft m
2250 750
1500 500
1200 400
900 300
600 200
300 100
0 0

Grid references: 7, 8, 9, 10, 11, 12 (top); A, B, C, D, E (right); 7, 8, 9, 10, 11, 12 (bottom)

0° 30′ 0° 00′ 0° 30′ 1° 00′ 1° 00′

The Wash

LINCOLNSHIRE **NORFOLK** **CAMBRIDGESHIRE** **SUFFOLK** **ESSEX**
HERTFORDSHIRE **BUCKINGHAMSHIRE** **GREATER LONDON** **KENT**
SURREY **WEST SUSSEX** **EAST SUSSEX**

Major places: Grantham, Boston, Hunstanton, Wells-next-the-Sea, Cromer, Sheringham, King's Lynn, Norwich, Great Yarmouth, Lowestoft, Peterborough, Ely, Cambridge, Bury St. Edmunds, Thetford, Diss, Ipswich, Felixstowe, Newmarket, Harwich, Colchester, Clacton-on-Sea, Frinton-on-Sea, Walton-on-the-Naze, Chelmsford, Southend-on-Sea, Harlow, Luton, Stevenage, Welwyn Garden City, Hertford, St. Albans, Watford, Aylesbury, Hemel Hempstead, High Wycombe, Milton Keynes, Bedford, Northampton, Kettering, Wellingborough, Rushden, LONDON, Maidenhead, Slough, Bracknell, Woking, Guildford, Dorking, Reigate, Crawley, Horsham, Maidstone, Rochester, Chatham, Gillingham, Canterbury, Margate, Broadstairs, Ramsgate, Sandwich, Deal, Dover, Folkestone, Ashford, Tunbridge Wells, Tonbridge, Sevenoaks, Gravesend, Dartford, Bromley, Croydon, Epsom, Sutton, Kingston-upon-Thames, Farnborough, Aldershot, Godalming, Haslemere, Midhurst, Chichester, Bognor Regis, Littlehampton, Worthing, Brighton, Hove, Newhaven, Seaford, Eastbourne, Bexhill, Hastings, Rye, Lewes, Burgess Hill, Haywards Heath, East Grinstead, Uckfield, Crowborough, Heathfield, Battle, Romney Marsh, New Romney, Hythe, Dymchurch

Thames Estuary

Strait of Dover

FRANCE — Calais, Boulogne-sur-Mer, Le Portel, Outreau, Wimereux, Wimille, Marquise, C. Gris-Nez, Guînes, Sangatte

Isle of Sheppey, I. of Thanet, North Foreland, South Foreland, Beachy Hd., Dungeness, Orford Ness, The Naze, Foulness I., Mersea I.

North Downs, The Weald, Ashdown Forest, South Downs, Romney Marsh, Breckland, The Fens, Rutland Water, Grafham Water

Key to English unitary authorities on map
37 TELFORD AND WREKIN
38 DERBY CITY
39 CITY OF NOTTINGHAM
40 LEICESTER CITY
41 RUTLAND
42 PETERBOROUGH
43 MILTON KEYNES
44 LUTON
45 NORTH SOMERSET
46 CITY OF BRISTOL
47 BATH AND NORTH EAST SOMERSET
48 SWINDON
49 READING
50 WOKINGHAM
51 WINDSOR AND MAIDENHEAD
52 SLOUGH
53 BRACKNELL FOREST
54 THURROCK
55 SOUTHEND-ON-SEA
56 MEDWAY
59 POOLE
60 BOURNEMOUTH
61 SOUTHAMPTON
62 PORTSMOUTH
63 BRIGHTON AND HOVE
64 BEDFORD
65 CENTRAL BEDFORDSHIRE

Key to Welsh unitary authorities on map
16 NEATH PORT TALBOT
17 BRIDGEND
18 RHONDDA CYNON TAFF
19 MERTHYR TYDFIL
20 CAERPHILLY
21 BLAENAU GWENT
22 TORFAEN
23 CARDIFF
24 NEWPORT

East from Greenwich

1:1 000 000

5 0 10 20 30 40 50 km
5 0 5 10 15 20 25 30 35 miles

COPYRIGHT PHILIP'S

1:1 000 000

FRANCE

CHANNEL ISLANDS
on same scale

Jersey

CHANNEL ISLANDS

Passage de la Déroute

COPYRIGHT PHILIP'S

Key to Welsh unitary
authorities on map
15 SWANSEA
16 NEATH PORT TALBOT
17 BRIDGEND
18 RHONDDA CYNON TAFF
19 MERTHYR TYDFIL
20 CAERPHILLY
21 BLAENAU GWENT
22 TORFAEN
23 CARDIFF
24 NEWPORT

Isles of Scilly
on same scale

Key to English unitary
authorities on map
32 HALTON
33 WARRINGTON
37 TELFORD AND WREKIN
45 NORTH SOMERSET
46 CITY OF BRISTOL
47 BATH AND NORTH EAST SOMERSET
57 PLYMOUTH
58 TORBAY
59 WEST CHESHIRE AND CHESTER
60 EAST CHESHIRE

Projection : Conical with two standard parallels

1:1 000 000

COPYRIGHT PHILIP'S

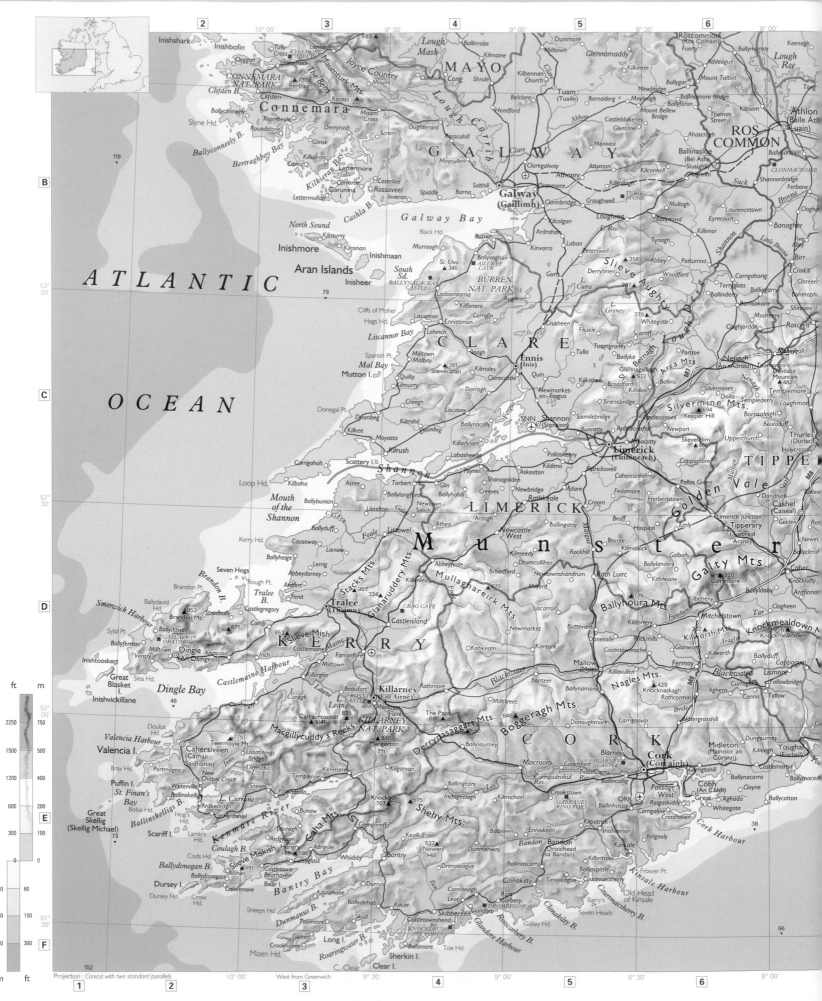

IRISH SEA

CELTIC SEA

St. George's Channel

WALES

WESTMEATH

MEATH

OFFALY

KILDARE

LEINSTER

LAOIS

WICKLOW

CARLOW

KILKENNY

WEXFORD

WATERFORD

Wicklow Mountains

Blackstairs Mts.

Comeragh Mts.

DUBLIN
(Baile Atha Cliath)

PEMBROKESHIRE
COAST NATIONAL PARK

1:1 000 000

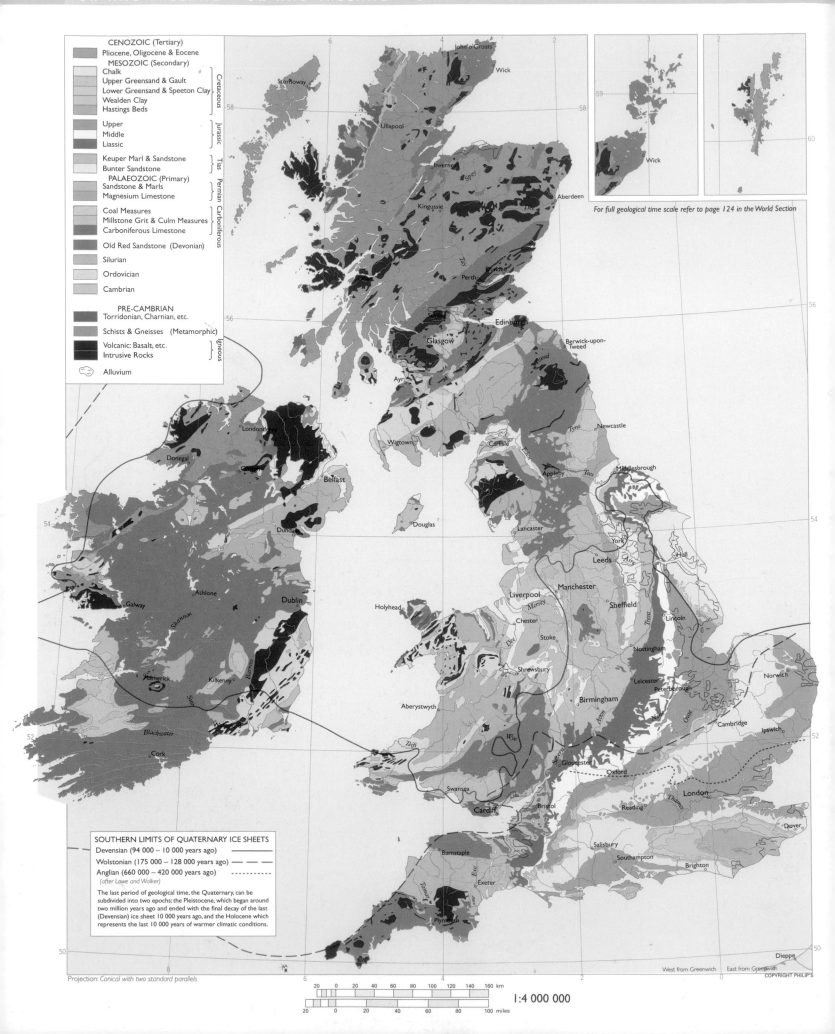

CENOZOIC (Tertiary)
Pliocene, Oligocene & Eocene

MESOZOIC (Secondary)
Chalk — *Cretaceous*
Upper Greensand & Gault
Lower Greensand & Speeton Clay
Wealden Clay
Hastings Beds

Upper — *Jurassic*
Middle
Liassic

Keuper Marl & Sandstone — *Trias*
Bunter Sandstone

PALAEOZOIC (Primary)
Sandstone & Marls — *Permian*
Magnesium Limestone

Coal Measures — *Carboniferous*
Millstone Grit & Culm Measures
Carboniferous Limestone

Old Red Sandstone (Devonian)

Silurian

Ordovician

Cambrian

PRE-CAMBRIAN
Torridonian, Charnian, etc.

Schists & Gneisses (Metamorphic)

Volcanic: Basalt, etc. — *Igneous*
Intrusive Rocks

Alluvium

For full geological time scale refer to page 124 in the World Section

SOUTHERN LIMITS OF QUATERNARY ICE SHEETS

Devensian (94 000 – 10 000 years ago) ⎯⎯⎯
Wolstonian (175 000 – 128 000 years ago) ⎯ ⎯ ⎯
Anglian (660 000 – 420 000 years ago) ⋯⋯⋯⋯
(after Lowe and Walker)

The last period of geological time, the Quaternary, can be subdivided into two epochs; the Pleistocene, which began around two million years ago and ended with the final decay of the last (Devensian) ice sheet 10 000 years ago, and the Holocene which represents the last 10 000 years of warmer climatic conditions.

Projection: Conical with two standard parallels

West from Greenwich   East from Greenwich
COPYRIGHT PHILIP'S

1:4 000 000

20 0 20 40 60 80 100 120 140 160 km
20 0 20 40 60 80 100 miles

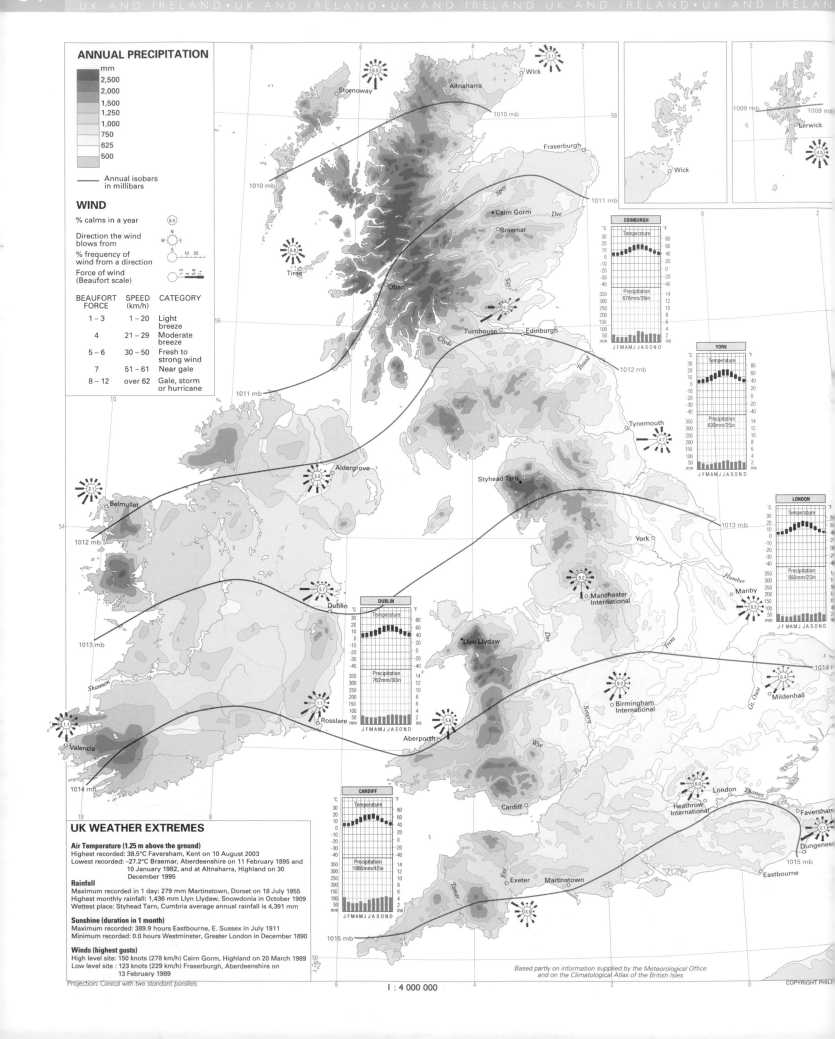

ANNUAL PRECIPITATION

mm
2,500
2,000
1,500
1,250
1,000
750
625
500

—— Annual isobars
in millibars

WIND

% calms in a year   6.5

Direction the wind
blows from
                    N
                W ✧ E
                    S   10 20
% frequency of
wind from a direction

Force of wind
(Beaufort scale)   1-3
                           4
                           5-6
                           7+

BEAUFORT FORCE	SPEED (km/h)	CATEGORY
1 – 3	1 – 20	Light breeze
4	21 – 29	Moderate breeze
5 – 6	30 – 50	Fresh to strong wind
7	51 – 61	Near gale
8 – 12	over 62	Gale, storm or hurricane

UK WEATHER EXTREMES

Air Temperature (1.25 m above the ground)
Highest recorded: 38.5°C Faversham, Kent on 10 August 2003
Lowest recorded: –27.2°C Braemar, Aberdeenshire on 11 February 1895 and
10 January 1982, and at Altnaharra, Highland on 30
December 1995

Rainfall
Maximum recorded in 1 day: 279 mm Martinstown, Dorset on 18 July 1955
Highest monthly rainfall: 1,436 mm Llyn Llydaw, Snowdonia in October 1909
Wettest place: Styhead Tarn, Cumbria average annual rainfall is 4,391 mm

Sunshine (duration in 1 month)
Maximum recorded: 389.9 hours Eastbourne, E. Sussex in July 1911
Minimum recorded: 0.0 hours Westminster, Greater London in December 1890

Winds (highest gusts)
High level site: 150 knots (278 km/h) Cairn Gorm, Highland on 20 March 1989
Low level site : 123 knots (229 km/h) Fraserburgh, Aberdeenshire on
13 February 1989

Projection: Conical with two standard parallels

1 : 4 000 000

*Based partly on information supplied by the Meteorological Office
and on the Climatological Atlas of the British Isles*

COPYRIGHT PHILI

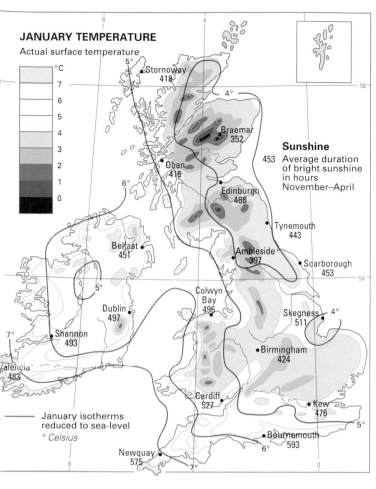

JANUARY TEMPERATURE

Actual surface temperature

°C
7
6
5
4
3
2
1
0

Sunshine

453 Average duration of bright sunshine in hours November–April

— January isotherms reduced to sea-level
° Celsius

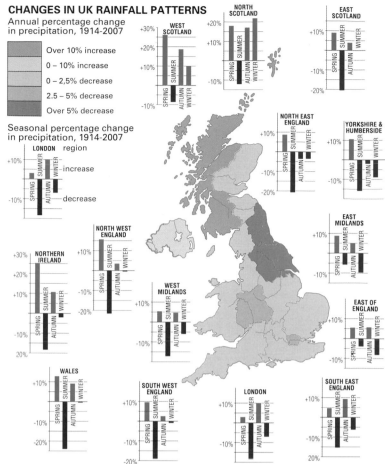

CHANGES IN UK RAINFALL PATTERNS

Annual percentage change in precipitation, 1914-2007

Over 10% increase
0 – 10% increase
0 – 2,5% decrease
2.5 – 5% decrease
Over 5% decrease

Seasonal percentage change in precipitation, 1914-2007 region

WEST SCOTLAND
NORTH SCOTLAND
EAST SCOTLAND
LONDON
NORTH EAST ENGLAND
YORKSHIRE & HUMBERSIDE
NORTHERN IRELAND
NORTH WEST ENGLAND
WEST MIDLANDS
EAST MIDLANDS
EAST OF ENGLAND
WALES
SOUTH WEST ENGLAND
LONDON
SOUTH EAST ENGLAND

increase
decrease

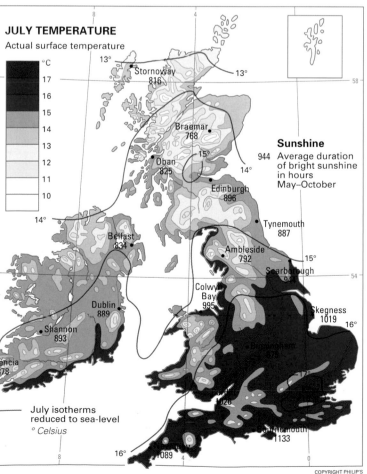

JULY TEMPERATURE

Actual surface temperature

°C
17
16
15
14
13
12
11
10

Sunshine

944 Average duration of bright sunshine in hours May–October

— July isotherms reduced to sea-level
° Celsius

COPYRIGHT PHILIP'S

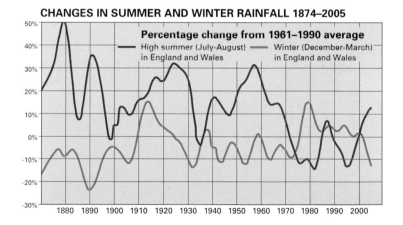

CHANGES IN SUMMER AND WINTER RAINFALL 1874–2005

Percentage change from 1961–1990 average

— High summer (July-August) in England and Wales
— Winter (December-March) in England and Wales

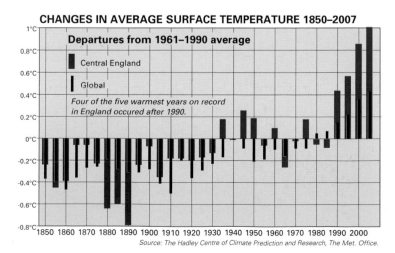

CHANGES IN AVERAGE SURFACE TEMPERATURE 1850–2007

Departures from 1961–1990 average

■ Central England
■ Global

Four of the five warmest years on record in England occured after 1990.

Source: The Hadley Centre of Climate Prediction and Research, The Met. Office.

WATER SUPPLY

Regions of reliably high rainfall (more than 1,250 mm in at least 70% of the years)

③ Major reservoirs (capacity over 20 million cubic metres, see list opposite for details)

→ Existing inter-regional transfers of water (by pipeline and river)

→ Proposed inter-regional transfers of water (by pipeline and river)

☐ Proposed estuary storage site

▽ Proposed groundwater storage site

Principal sources of groundwater (porous and jointed aquifers)

There are no water authorities in Ireland, each county and urban borough is responsible for its own water supply

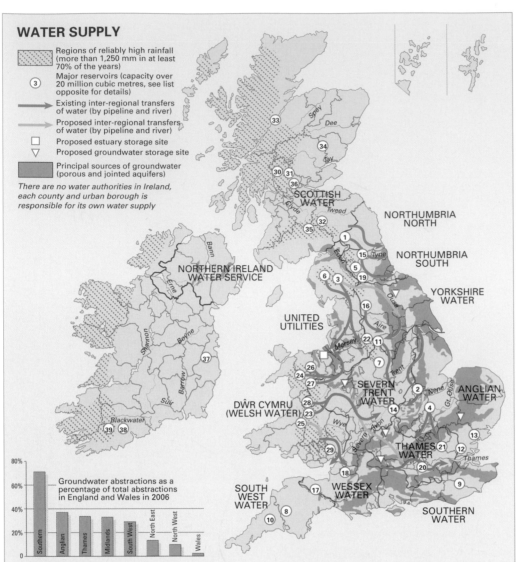

Groundwater abstractions as a percentage of total abstractions in England and Wales in 2006

MAJOR RESERVOIRS (with capacity in million m

England
1	Kielder Reservoir	198
2	Rutland Water	123
3	Haweswater	85
4	Grafham Water	59
5	Cow GreenReservoir	41
6	Thirlmere	41
7	Carsington Reservoir	36
8	Roadford Reservoir	35
9	Bewl Water Reservoir	31
10	Colliford Lake	29
11	Ladybower Reservoir	28
12	Hanningfield Reservoir	27
13	Abberton Reservoir	25
14	Draycote Water	23
15	Derwent Reservoir	22
16	Grimwith Reservoir	22
17	Wimbleball Lake	21
18	Chew Valley Lake	20
19	Balderhead Reservoir	20
20	Thames Valley (linked reservoirs)	
21	Lea Valley (linked reservoirs)	
22	Longendale (linked reservoirs)	

Wales
23	Elan Valley
24	Llyn Celyn
25	Llyn Brianne
26	Llyn Brenig
27	Llyn Vyrnwy
28	Llyn Clywedog
29	Llandegfedd Reservoir

Scotland
30	Loch Lomond
31	Loch Katrine
32	Megget Reservoir
33	Loch Ness
34	Blackwater Reservoir
35	Daer Reservoir
36	Carron Valley Reservoir

Ireland
37	Poulaphouca Reservoir
38	Inishcarra Reservoir
39	Carrigadrohid Reservoir

WATER SUPPLY IN THE UK

Total water abstraction in England and Wales in 200 was approximately 58,000 million litres a day. The pie graph represents the almost 19,000 million litres a day that were supplied by the water service and supply companies in the U.K. in 2006.

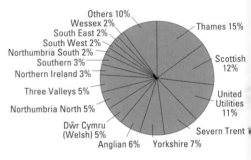

Others 10%
Wessex 2%
South East 2%
South West 2%
Northumbria South 2%
Southern 3%
Northern Ireland 3%
Three Valleys 5%
Northumbria North 5%
Dŵr Cymru (Welsh) 5%
Anglian 6%
Yorkshire 7%
Severn Trent
Thames 15%
Scottish 12%
United Utilities 11%

WASTE RECYCLING

The percentage of household waste recycled in 2007

■	Over 35%
	30 – 35%
	25 – 30%
	Under 25%

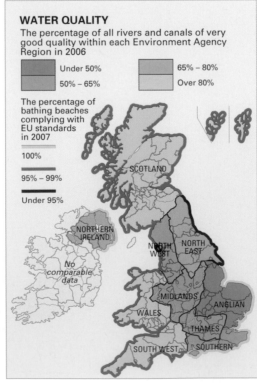

WATER QUALITY

The percentage of all rivers and canals of very good quality within each Environment Agency Region in 2006

■	Under 50%
	50% – 65%
	65% – 80%
	Over 80%

The percentage of bathing beaches complying with EU standards in 2007

━━ 100%

━━ 95% – 99%

━━ Under 95%

FLOOD RISK IN ENGLAND AND WALES

■ Areas at greatest risk from flooding (as designated by the Environment Agency

⬩ Counties worst affected by flooding in summer 2007

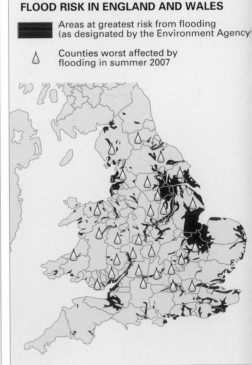

COPYRIGHT PH

EU AIR QUALITY

Greenhouse gas emissions in thousand tonnes

	Sulphur dioxide			Nitrogen oxides		
	1975	1990	2005	1975	1990	2005
Austria	–	90	26	–	221	237
Belgium/Lux.	–	105	146	–	172	285
Denmark	418	183	22	182	270	184
Finland	–	260	69	–	290	177
France	3,329	1,200	465	1,608	1,487	1,412
Germany	3,325	5,633	560	2,532	3,033	1,447
Greece	–	–	529	–	338	332
Ireland	186	187	70	60	128	124
Italy	3,250	1,682	496	1,499	2,041	1,112
Netherlands	386	204	62	447	575	325
Portugal	178	286	214	104	216	289
Spain	–	2,205	1,359	–	1,247	1,529
Sweden	–	169	40	–	411	181
United Kingdom	5,310	3,754	706	2,365	2,731	1,619

SOILS

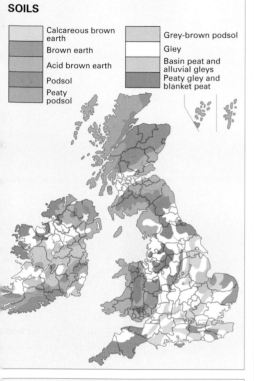

- Calcareous brown earth
- Brown earth
- Acid brown earth
- Podsol
- Peaty podsol
- Grey-brown podsol
- Gley
- Basin peat and alluvial gleys
- Peaty gley and blanket peat

NATURAL VEGETATION

The plant cover associated with a particular environment if it was unaffected by human activity

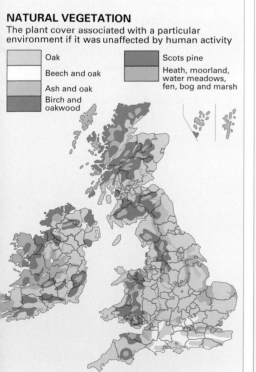

- Oak
- Beech and oak
- Ash and oak
- Birch and oakwood
- Scots pine
- Heath, moorland, water meadows, fen, bog and marsh

ACID RAIN

Average acidity of precipitation in the UK (pH scale)

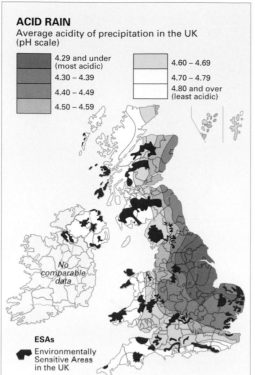

- 4.29 and under (most acidic)
- 4.30 – 4.39
- 4.40 – 4.49
- 4.50 – 4.59
- 4.60 – 4.69
- 4.70 – 4.79
- 4.80 and over (least acidic)

ESAs
Environmentally Sensitive Areas in the UK

GREENHOUSE GAS EMISSIONS*

CO_2 emissions in tonnes per capita 2006

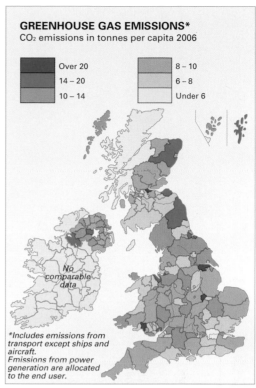

- Over 20
- 14 – 20
- 10 – 14
- 8 – 10
- 6 – 8
- Under 6

*Includes emissions from transport except ships and aircraft. Emissions from power generation are allocated to the end user.

CONSERVATION

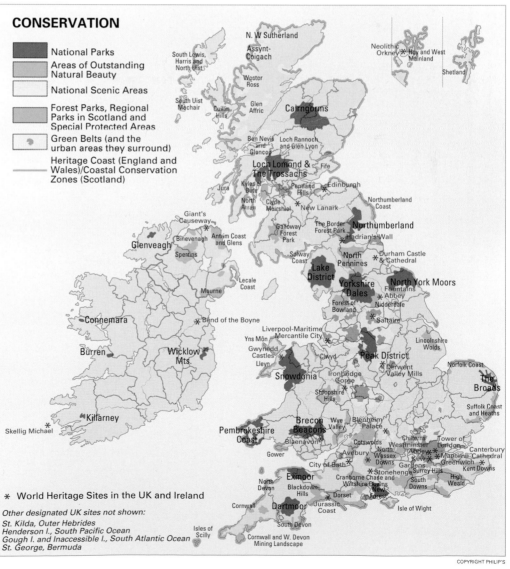

- National Parks
- Areas of Outstanding Natural Beauty
- National Scenic Areas
- Forest Parks, Regional Parks in Scotland and Special Protected Areas
- Green Belts (and the urban areas they surround)
- Heritage Coast (England and Wales)/Coastal Conservation Zones (Scotland)

* World Heritage Sites in the UK and Ireland

Other designated UK sites not shown:
St. Kilda, Outer Hebrides
Henderson I., South Pacific Ocean
Gough I. and Inaccessible I., South Atlantic Ocean
St. George, Bermuda

N. W Sutherland
Assynt-Coigach
South Lewis, Harris and North Uist
Wester Ross
South Uist Machair
Cuillin Hills
Glen Affric
Cairngorms
Ben Nevis and Glencoe
Loch Rannoch and Glen Lyon
Loch Lomond & The Trossachs
Fife
Kyles of Bute
Pentland Hills
Edinburgh
Jura
North Arran
Clyde Muirshiel
New Lanark
Northumberland Coast
Giant's Causeway
Galloway Forest Park
The Border Forest Park
Northumberland
Binevenagh
Antrim Coast and Glens
Hadrian's Wall
Glenveagh
Sperrins
Solway Coast
North Pennines
Durham Castle & Cathedral
Lecale Coast
Lake District
Mourne
Yorkshire Dales
North York Moors
Connemara
Bend of the Boyne
Forest of Bowland
Fountains Abbey
Nidderdale
Saltaire
Burren
Yns Môn
Gwynedd Castles: Llŷn
Liverpool-Maritime Mercantile City
Clwyd
Lincolnshire Wolds
Wicklow Mts.
Peak District
Derwent Valley Mills
Norfolk Coast
Snowdonia
Ironbridge Gorge
Shropshire Hills
The Broads
Killarney
Suffolk Coast and Heaths
Pembrokeshire Coast
Brecon Beacons
Wye Valley
Blenheim Palace
Blaenavon
Gower
Cotswolds
North Wessex Downs
Chilterns
Westminster Abbey
Kew Gardens
Tower of London
Canterbury Cathedral
Maritime Greenwich
Avebury
City of Bath
Stonehenge
Cranborne Chase and Wiltshire Downs
Surrey Hills
High Weald
Kent Downs
South Downs
Exmoor
North Devon
Blackdown Hills
New Forest
Dorset
Cornwall
Dartmoor
South Devon
Jurassic Coast
Isle of Wight
Skellig Michael
Neolithic Orkney
Hoy and West Mainland
Shetland
Isles of Scilly
Cornwall and W. Devon Mining Landscape
St. George

COPYRIGHT PHILIP'S

TYPES OF FARM

- Dairy cattle
- Beef cattle
- Sheep
- ● Pigs and/or poultry
- Mixed farming
- Market gardening (fruit and vegetables)
- Cereals
- Other crops (mainly potatoes, sugar beet)
- — Northern limit of 9 month growing season
- Forests
- Built-up areas
- Areas with over 1,000 mm rainfall per year

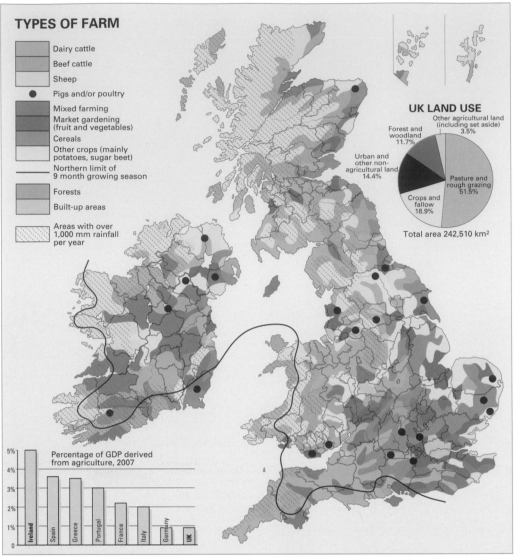

UK LAND USE

- Other agricultural land (including set aside) 3.5%
- Forest and woodland 11.7%
- Urban and other non-agricultural land 14.4%
- Pasture and rough grazing 51.5%
- Crops and fallow 18.9%

Total area 242,510 km²

Percentage of GDP derived from agriculture, 2007

(bar chart: Ireland 5%, Spain ~3.6%, Greece ~3.5%, Portugal ~3%, France ~2.2%, Italy ~2%, Germany ~1%, UK ~1%)

CEREAL FARMING

The percentage of the total farmland used for growing cereals in 2007

- Over 40%
- 30 – 40%
- 20 – 30%
- 10 – 20%
- 0 – 10%
- No data

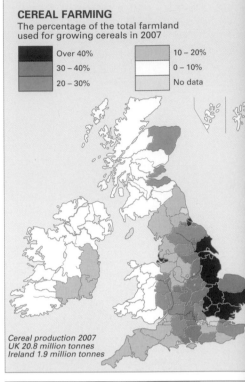

Cereal production 2007
UK 20.8 million tonnes
Ireland 1.9 million tonnes

DAIRY FARMING

The number of dairy cows per 100 hectares of farmland in 2007

- Over 40
- 30 – 40
- 20 – 30
- 10 – 20
- 0 – 10
- No data

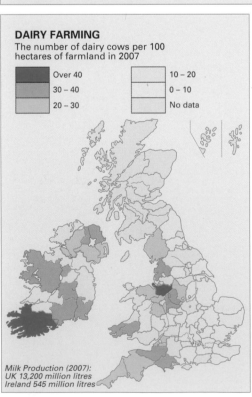

Milk Production (2007):
UK 13,200 million litres
Ireland 545 million litres

LIVESTOCK FARMING

The number of beef cattle, sheep and pigs per 100 hectares of farmland in 2007

- Over 400
- 300 – 400
- 200 – 300
- 100 – 200
- Under 100
- No data

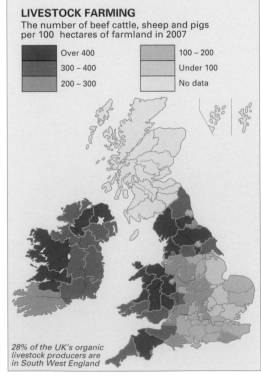

28% of the UK's organic livestock producers are in South West England

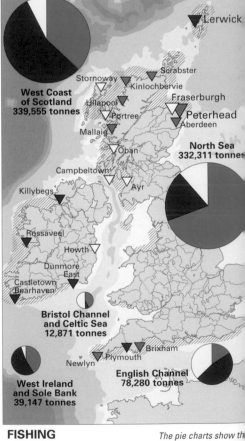

West Coast of Scotland 339,555 tonnes

Lerwick
Stornoway
Scrabster
Kinlochbervie
Ullapool
Fraserburgh
Portree
Peterhead
Mallaig
Aberdeen
Oban
North Sea 332,311 tonnes
Campbeltown
Killybegs
Ayr
Rossaveel
Howth
Dunmore East
Castletown Bearhaven
Bristol Channel and Celtic Sea 12,871 tonnes
Brixham
Plymouth
Newlyn
West Ireland and Sole Bank 39,147 tonnes
English Channel 78,280 tonnes

FISHING
Major fishing ports

- ▼ Demersal e.g. cod (Deep sea fish)
- ▼ Pelagic e.g. mackeral (Shallow sea fish)
- ▽ Shellfish e.g. lobster

The most important inshore fishing grounds

The pie charts show the total amount in tonnes and the colours show the type of fish caught in each fishing region

- Deep-sea fish
- Shellfish
- Shallow sea fish

Depth of sea in metres
1000 500 200 100 50 m

EMPLOYMENT IN SERVICES

The percentage of the workforce employed in the service industry in 2007

Over 85%
80 – 85%
75 – 80%
70 – 75%
Under 70%

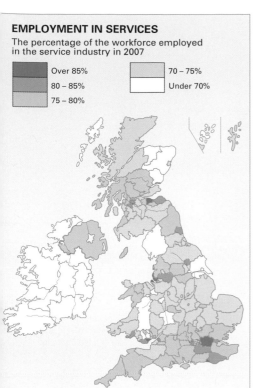

EMPLOYMENT IN MANUFACTURING

The percentage of the workforce employed in manufacturing in 2007

Over 20%
16 – 20%
14 – 16%
12 – 14%
10 – 12%
Under 10%

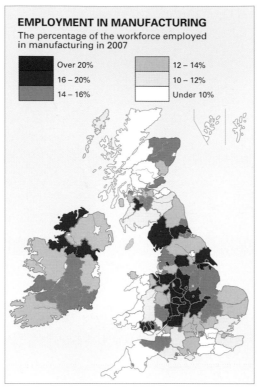

MOTOR MANUFACTURING IN ENGLAND AND WALES

■ Car manufacturing sites
▣ Commercial vehicle manufacturing sites
□ Selected engine manufacturing sites

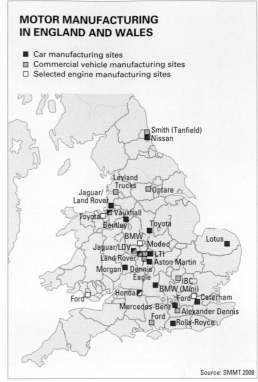

Source: SMMT 2008

CHANGES IN EMPLOYMENT IN THE UK

Employment by industry

Services
Transport
Manufacturing
Mining & energy supply
Agriculture, forestry & fishing

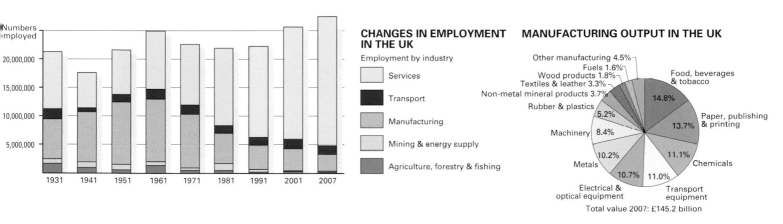

MANUFACTURING OUTPUT IN THE UK

Other manufacturing 4.5%
Fuels 1.6%
Wood products 1.8%
Textiles & leather 3.3%
Non-metal mineral products 3.7%
Rubber & plastics 5.2%
Machinery 8.4%
Metals 10.2%
Electrical & optical equipment 10.7%
Transport equipment 11.0%
Chemicals 11.1%
Paper, publishing & printing 13.7%
Food, beverages & tobacco 14.8%

Total value 2007: £145.2 billion

UK FOREIGN TRADE

TOP TEN TRADING PARTNERS One container represents 1% of the total value of imports or 1% of the total value of exports in 2007

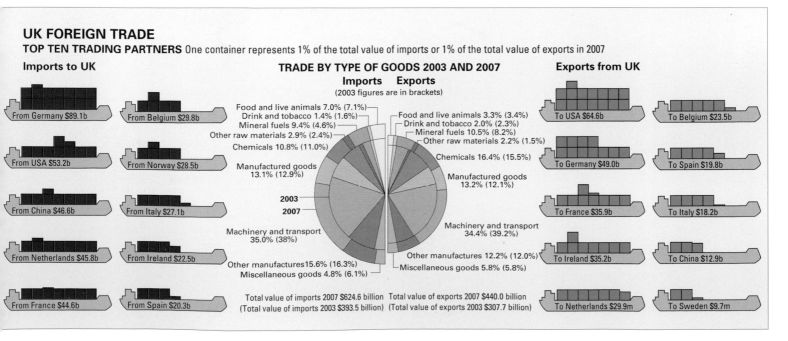

Imports to UK

From Germany $89.1b
From Belgium $29.8b
From USA $53.2b
From Norway $28.5b
From China $46.6b
From Italy $27.1b
From Netherlands $45.8b
From Ireland $22.5b
From France $44.6b
From Spain $20.3b

TRADE BY TYPE OF GOODS 2003 AND 2007

Imports   Exports
(2003 figures are in brackets)

Food and live animals 7.0% (7.1%)
Drink and tobacco 1.4% (1.6%)
Mineral fuels 9.4% (4.6%)
Other raw materials 2.9% (2.4%)
Chemicals 10.8% (11.0%)
Manufactured goods 13.1% (12.9%)

2003
2007

Machinery and transport 35.0% (38%)
Other manufactures 15.6% (16.3%)
Miscellaneous goods 4.8% (6.1%)

Food and live animals 3.3% (3.4%)
Drink and tobacco 2.0% (2.3%)
Mineral fuels 10.5% (8.2%)
Other raw materials 2.2% (1.5%)
Chemicals 16.4% (15.5%)
Manufactured goods 13.2% (12.1%)
Machinery and transport 34.4% (39.2%)
Other manufactures 12.2% (12.0%)
Miscellaneous goods 5.8% (5.8%)

Total value of imports 2007 $624.6 billion
(Total value of imports 2003 $393.5 billion)

Total value of exports 2007 $440.0 billion
(Total value of exports 2003 $307.7 billion)

Exports from UK

To USA $64.6b
To Belgium $23.5b
To Germany $49.0b
To Spain $19.8b
To France $35.9b
To Italy $18.2b
To Ireland $35.2b
To China $12.9b
To Netherlands $29.9m
To Sweden $9.7m

NORTH SEA OIL AND GAS

- Oilfield
- Gasfield
- Gas condensate field
- Oil pipeline
- under construction
- Gas pipeline
- under construction
- Oil terminal
- Gas terminal
- Tanker terminal
- Oil refinery
- International dividing line

UK OIL AND GAS RESERVES

- Oil and gas reserves (estimated)
- Value of oil and gas reserves

Reserves in billion tonnes
Value in £ billion at December 2007 prices

1998 1999 2000 2001 2002 2003 2004 2005 2006 2007

Projection : Conical with two standard parallels

West from Greenwich   East from Greenwich

1 : 7 640 000

COPYRIGHT PHILIP'S

CHANGES IN UK GAS SUPPLY

- UK produced gas
- Gas imports
- Gas exports

1998 **2007**

from Norway 226,000 GWh
from EU (and Russia) 83,000 GWh

Total 1998   Total 2007
1,090,600 GWh   1,299,300 GWh

as imports are on a contractual basis and may not correspond to physical gas flows

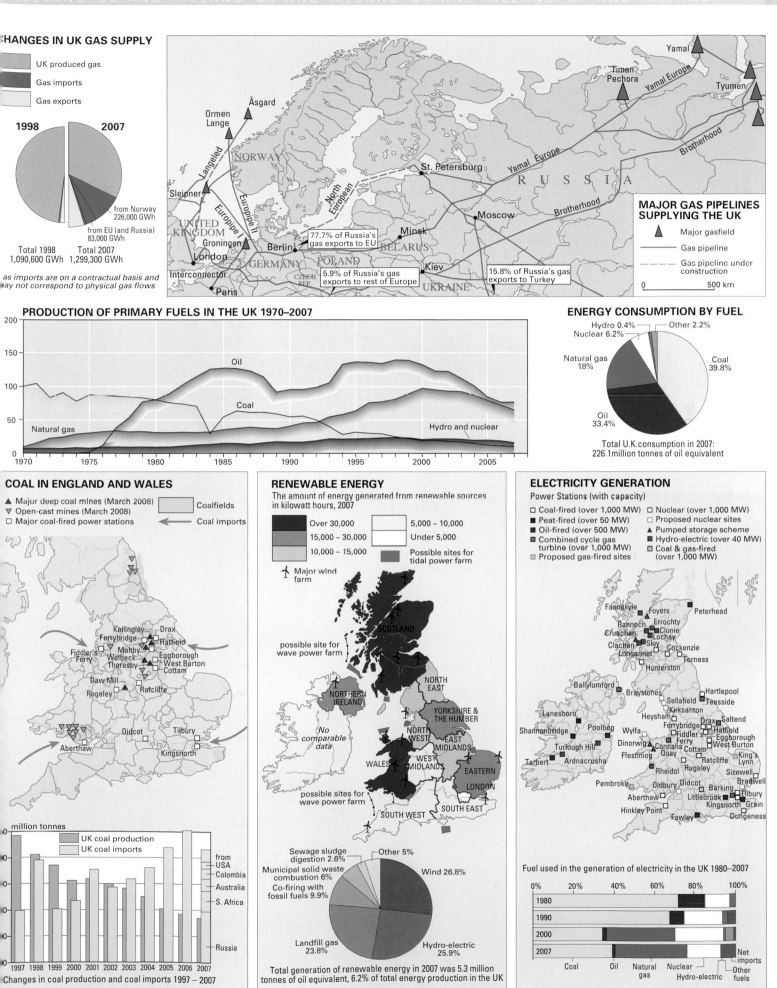

MAJOR GAS PIPELINES SUPPLYING THE UK

▲ Major gasfield
— Gas pipeline
- - - Gas pipeline under construction

0   500 km

77.7% of Russia's gas exports to EU

5.9% of Russia's gas exports to rest of Europe

15.8% of Russia's gas exports to Turkey

PRODUCTION OF PRIMARY FUELS IN THE UK 1970–2007

Oil
Coal
Natural gas
Hydro and nuclear

ENERGY CONSUMPTION BY FUEL

Hydro 0.4% — Other 2.2%
Nuclear 6.2%
Natural gas 18%
Coal 39.8%
Oil 33.4%

Total U.K.consumption in 2007:
226.1 million tonnes of oil equivalent

COAL IN ENGLAND AND WALES

▲ Major deep coal mines (March 2008)
▽ Open-cast mines (March 2008)
□ Major coal-fired power stations
☐ Coalfields
← Coal imports

Kellingley — Drax
Ferrybridge — Hatfield
Fiddler's Ferry
Maltby
Welbeck
Thoresby
Eggborough
West Burton
Cottam
Daw Mill
Rugeley
Ratcliffe
Didcot
Tilbury
Aberthaw
Kingsnorth

million tonnes

- UK coal production
- UK coal imports

from
USA
Colombia
Australia
S. Africa
Russia

1997 1998 1999 2000 2001 2002 2003 2004 2005 2006 2007
Changes in coal production and coal imports 1997 – 2007

RENEWABLE ENERGY

The amount of energy generated from renewable sources in kilowatt hours, 2007

- Over 30,000
- 15,000 – 30,000
- 10,000 – 15,000
- 5,000 – 10,000
- Under 5,000
- Possible sites for tidal power farm

🛧 Major wind farm

SCOTLAND

possible site for wave power farm

NORTHERN IRELAND

No comparable data

NORTH EAST
YORKSHIRE & THE HUMBER
NORTH WEST
EAST MIDLANDS
WALES
WEST MIDLANDS
EASTERN
LONDON
SOUTH WEST
SOUTH EAST

possible sites for wave power farm

Sewage sludge digestion 2.6%
Municipal solid waste combustion 6%
Co-firing with fossil fuels 9.9%
Other 5%
Wind 26.8%
Landfill gas 23.8%
Hydro-electric 25.9%

Total generation of renewable energy in 2007 was 5.3 million tonnes of oil equivalent, 6.2% of total energy production in the UK

ELECTRICITY GENERATION

Power Stations (with capacity)

- □ Coal-fired (over 1,000 MW)
- ■ Peat-fired (over 50 MW)
- ■ Oil-fired (over 500 MW)
- ■ Combined cycle gas turbine (over 1,000 MW)
- ▨ Proposed gas-fired sites
- □ Nuclear (over 1,000 MW)
- □ Proposed nuclear sites
- ▲ Pumped storage scheme
- ■ Hydro-electric (over 40 MW)
- □ Coal & gas-fired (over 1,000 MW)

Fasnakyle
Foyers
Peterhead
Rannoch
Errochty
Cruachan
Clunie
Lochay
Clachan
Sloy
Cockenzie
Longannet
Torness
Hunterston
Ballylumford
Braystones
Hartlepool
Lanesboro
Sellafield
Teesside
Kirksanton
Heysham
Shannonbridge
Poolbeg
Wylfa
Ferrybridge
Saltend
Dinorwig
Connahs Quay
Fiddler's
Ferry
Hatfield
Eggborough
West Burton
Turlough Hill
Ffestiniog
Cottam
Tarbert
Ardnacrusha
King's Lynn
Rheidol
Ratcliffe
Sizewell
Pembroke
Oldbury
Didcot
Barking
Bradwell
Aberthaw
Littlebrook
Tilbury
Hinkley Point
Kingsnorth
Grain
Fawley
Dungeness

Fuel used in the generation of electricity in the UK 1980–2007

	0%	20%	40%	60%	80%	100%
1980						
1990						
2000						
2007						

Coal   Oil   Natural gas   Nuclear   Hydro-electric   Net imports   Other fuels

COPYRIGHT PHILIP'S

ROADS AND FERRIES

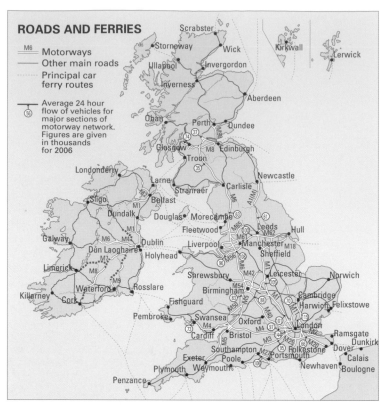

- M6   Motorways
- ——   Other main roads
- ······   Principal car ferry routes
- 50   Average 24 hour flow of vehicles for major sections of motorway network. Figures are given in thousands for 2006

RAILWAYS

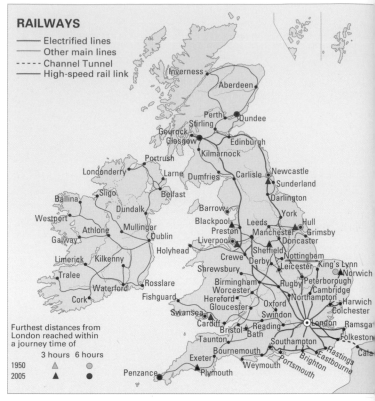

- ——   Electrified lines
- ——   Other main lines
- -----   Channel Tunnel
- ——   High-speed rail link

Furthest distances from London reached within a journey time of

	3 hours	6 hours
1950	▲	●
2005	▲	●

CHANNEL TUNNEL AND HIGH-SPEED RAIL LINKS IN EUROPE
Estimated journey times between London and other European cities

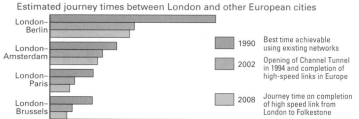

- 1990   Best time achievable using existing networks
- 2002   Opening of Channel Tunnel in 1994 and completion of high-speed links in Europe
- 2008   Journey time on completion of high speed link from London to Folkestone

MEANS OF TRANSPORTATION WITHIN THE UK

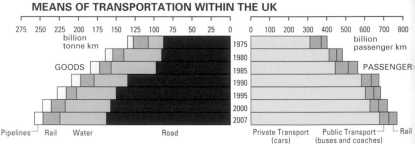

GOODS — billion tonne km — Pipelines, Rail, Water, Road

PASSENGER — billion passenger km — Private Transport (cars), Public Transport (buses and coaches), Rail

SEAPORTS

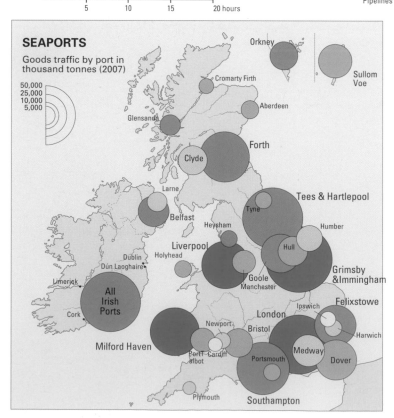

Goods traffic by port in thousand tonnes (2007)

50,000
25,000
10,000
5,000

AIRPORTS

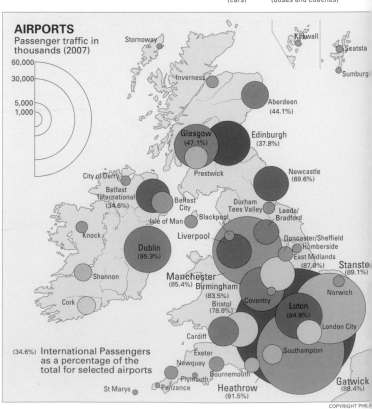

Passenger traffic in thousands (2007)

60,000
30,000
5,000
1,000

(34.6%) International Passengers as a percentage of the total for selected airports

COPYRIGHT PHIL

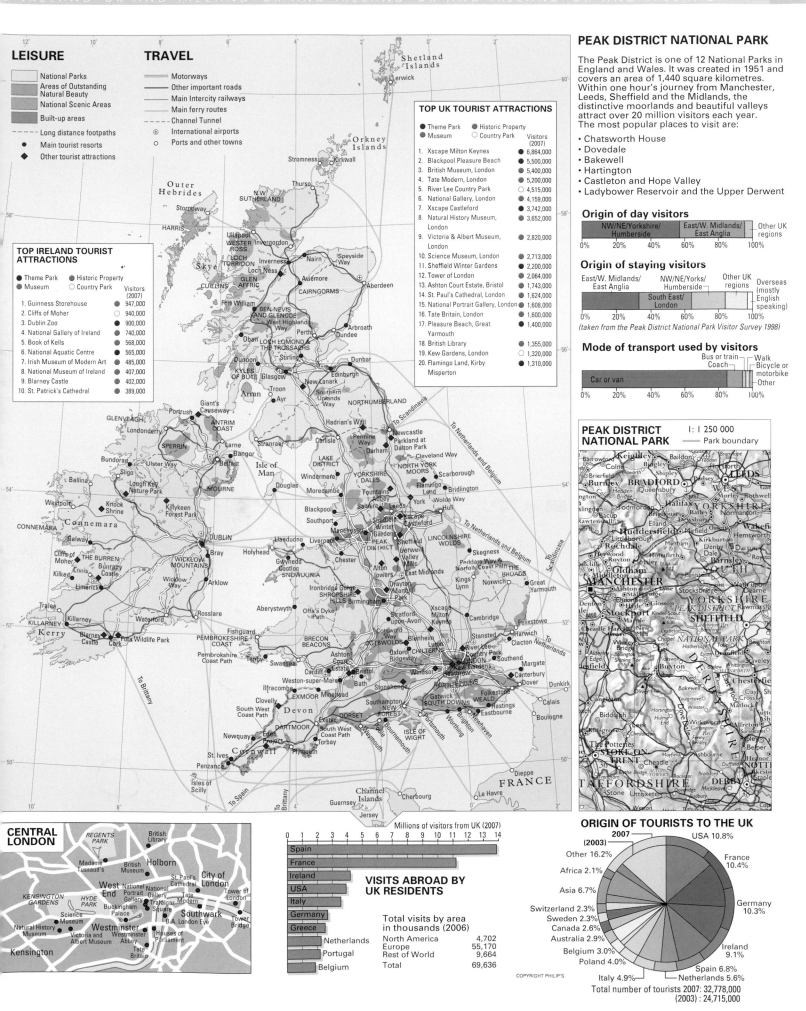

LEISURE

- National Parks
- Areas of Outstanding Natural Beauty
- National Scenic Areas
- Built-up areas
- Long distance footpaths
- ● Main tourist resorts
- ◆ Other tourist attractions

TRAVEL

- Motorways
- Other important roads
- Main Intercity railways
- Main ferry routes
- Channel Tunnel
- ⊕ International airports
- ○ Ports and other towns

TOP IRELAND TOURIST ATTRACTIONS

- ● Theme Park
- ○ Museum
- ■ Historic Property
- ○ Country Park

	Visitors (2007)	
1. Guinness Storehouse	●	947,000
2. Cliffs of Moher	○	940,000
3. Dublin Zoo	●	900,000
4. National Gallery of Ireland	●	740,000
5. Book of Kells	●	568,000
6. National Aquatic Centre	●	565,000
7. Irish Museum of Modern Art	●	485,000
8. National Museum of Ireland	●	407,000
9. Blarney Castle	●	402,000
10. St. Patrick's Cathedral	●	389,000

TOP UK TOURIST ATTRACTIONS

- ● Theme Park
- ● Museum
- ● Historic Property
- ○ Country Park

		Visitors (2007)
1. Xscape Milton Keynes	●	6,864,000
2. Blackpool Pleasure Beach	●	5,500,000
3. British Museum, London	●	5,400,000
4. Tate Modern, London	●	5,200,000
5. River Lee Country Park	○	4,515,000
6. National Gallery, London	●	4,159,000
7. Xscape Castleford	●	3,742,000
8. Natural History Museum, London	●	3,652,000
9. Victoria & Albert Museum, London	●	2,820,000
10. Science Museum, London	●	2,713,000
11. Sheffield Winter Gardens	●	2,200,000
12. Tower of London	●	2,064,000
13. Ashton Court Estate, Bristol	●	1,743,000
14. St. Paul's Cathedral, London	●	1,624,000
15. National Portrait Gallery, London	●	1,608,000
16. Tate Britain, London	●	1,600,000
17. Pleasure Beach, Great Yarmouth	●	1,400,000
18. British Library	●	1,355,000
19. Kew Gardens, London	○	1,320,000
20. Flamingo Land, Kirby Misperton	●	1,310,000

PEAK DISTRICT NATIONAL PARK

The Peak District is one of 12 National Parks in England and Wales. It was created in 1951 and covers an area of 1,440 square kilometres. Within one hour's journey from Manchester, Leeds, Sheffield and the Midlands, the distinctive moorlands and beautiful valleys attract over 20 million visitors each year. The most popular places to visit are:

- Chatsworth House
- Dovedale
- Bakewell
- Hartington
- Castleton and Hope Valley
- Ladybower Reservoir and the Upper Derwent

Origin of day visitors

NW/NE/Yorkshire/ Humberside	East/W. Midlands/ East Anglia	Other UK regions

0% 20% 40% 60% 80% 100%

Origin of staying visitors

East/W. Midlands/ East Anglia	NW/NE/Yorks/ Humberside	Other UK regions	Overseas (mostly English speaking)

South East/ London

0% 20% 40% 60% 80% 100%

(taken from the Peak District National Park Visitor Survey 1998)

Mode of transport used by visitors

Bus or train — Walk
Coach — Bicycle or motorbike — Other

Car or van

0% 20% 40% 60% 80% 100%

PEAK DISTRICT NATIONAL PARK

1: 1 250 000
— Park boundary

CENTRAL LONDON

Millions of visitors from UK (2007)

0 1 2 3 4 5 6 7 8 9 10 11 12 13 14

- Spain
- France
- Ireland
- USA
- Italy
- Germany
- Greece
- Netherlands
- Portugal
- Belgium

VISITS ABROAD BY UK RESIDENTS

Total visits by area in thousands (2006)	
North America	4,702
Europe	55,170
Rest of World	9,664
Total	**69,636**

COPYRIGHT PHILIP'S

ORIGIN OF TOURISTS TO THE UK

2007
(2003)

- USA 10.8%
- France 10.4%
- Germany 10.3%
- Ireland 9.1%
- Spain 6.8%
- Netherlands 5.6%
- Italy 4.9%
- Poland 4.0%
- Belgium 3.0%
- Australia 2.9%
- Canada 2.6%
- Sweden 2.3%
- Switzerland 2.3%
- Asia 6.7%
- Africa 2.1%
- Other 16.2%

Total number of tourists 2007: 32,778,000
(2003): 24,715,000

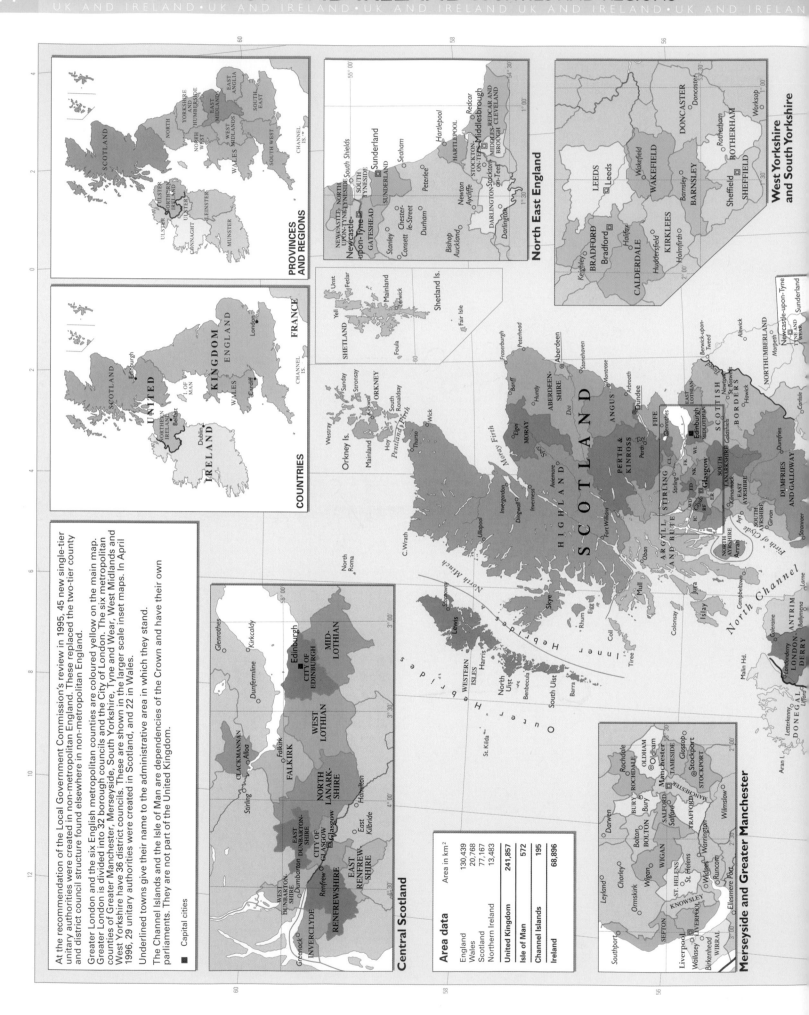

At the recommendation of the Local Government Commission's review in 1995, 45 new single-tier unitary authorities were created in non-metropolitan England. These replaced the two-tier county and district council structure found elsewhere in non-metropolitan England.

Greater London and the six English metropolitan counties are coloured yellow on the main map. Greater London is divided into 32 borough councils and the City of London. The six metropolitan counties of Greater Manchester, Merseyside, South Yorkshire, Tyne and Wear, West Midlands and West Yorkshire have 36 district councils. These are shown in the larger scale inset maps. In April 1996, 29 unitary authorities were created in Scotland, and 22 in Wales.

Underlined towns give their name to the administrative area in which they stand.

The Channel Islands and the Isle of Man are dependencies of the Crown and have their own parliaments. They are not part of the United Kingdom.

■ Capital cities

PROVINCES AND REGIONS

COUNTRIES

North East England

West Yorkshire and South Yorkshire

Central Scotland

Area data

	Area in km²
England	130,439
Wales	20,768
Scotland	77,167
Northern Ireland	13,483
United Kingdom	**241,857**
Isle of Man	572
Channel Islands	195
Ireland	68,896

Merseyside and Greater Manchester

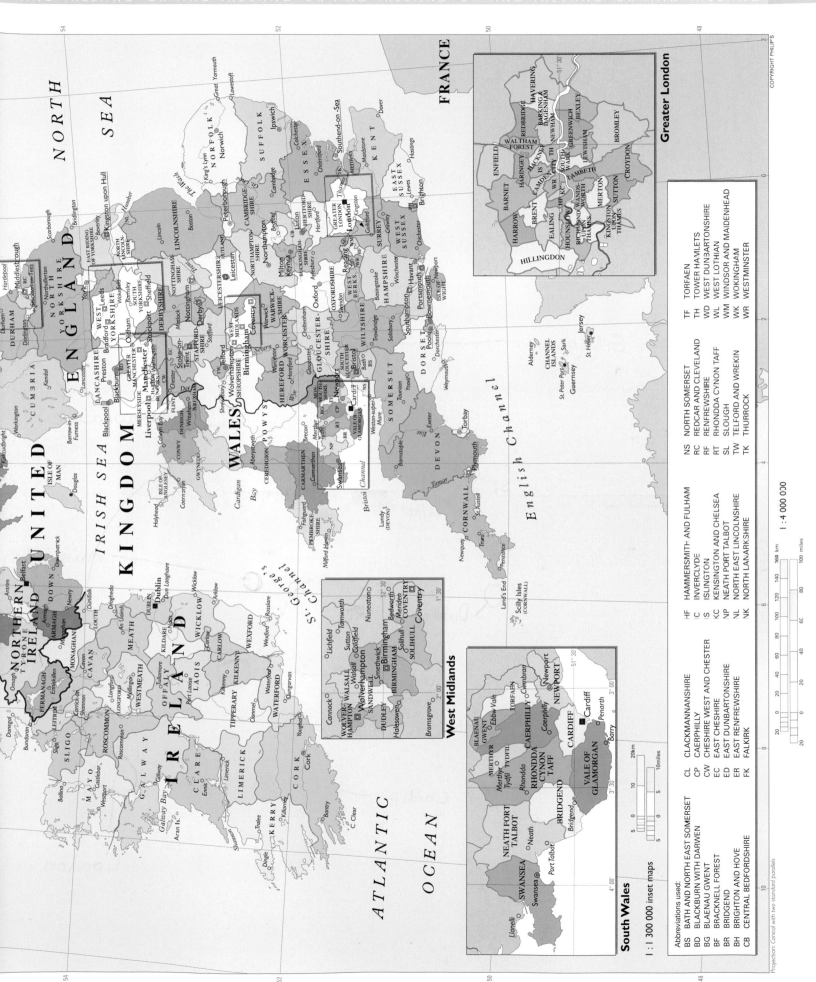

Greater London

NORTH

SEA

FRANCE

UNITED

KINGDOM

NORTHERN IRELAND

IRELAND

ENGLAND

WALES

ATLANTIC

OCEAN

IRISH SEA

St. George's Channel

English Channel

Bristol Channel

West Midlands
1 : 300 000 inset maps

South Wales
1 : 1 300 000 inset maps

Abbreviations used:
BS	BATH AND NORTH EAST SOMERSET	HF	HAMMERSMITH AND FULHAM
BD	BLACKBURN WITH DARWEN	IC	INVERCLYDE
BG	BLAENAU GWENT	IS	ISLINGTON
BF	BRACKNELL FOREST	KC	KENSINGTON AND CHELSEA
BR	BRIDGEND	NP	NEATH PORT TALBOT
BH	BRIGHTON AND HOVE	NL	NORTH EAST LINCOLNSHIRE
CB	CENTRAL BEDFORDSHIRE	NK	NORTH LANARKSHIRE
CL	CLACKMANNANSHIRE	NS	NORTH SOMERSET
CP	CAERPHILLY	RC	REDCAR AND CLEVELAND
CW	CHESHIRE WEST AND CHESTER	RF	RENFREWSHIRE
EC	EAST CHESHIRE	RT	RHONDDA CYNON TAFF
ED	EAST DUNBARTONSHIRE	SL	SLOUGH
ER	EAST RENFREWSHIRE	TW	TELFORD AND WREKIN
FK	FALKIRK	TK	THURROCK
		TF	TORFAEN
		TH	TOWER HAMLETS
		WD	WEST DUNBARTONSHIRE
		WL	WEST LOTHIAN
		WM	WINDSOR AND MAIDENHEAD
		WK	WOKINGHAM
		WR	WESTMINSTER

1 : 4 000 000

COPYRIGHT PHILIP'S

Projection: Conical with two standard parallels

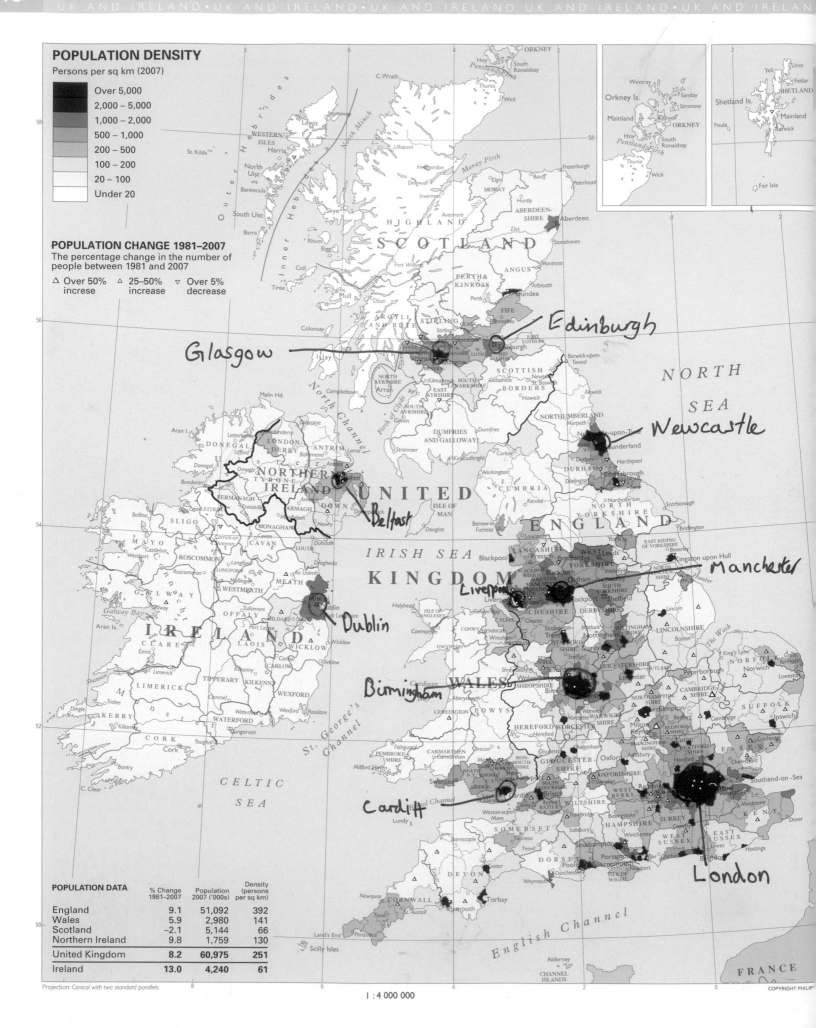

POPULATION DENSITY
Persons per sq km (2007)

■	Over 5,000
■	2,000 – 5,000
■	1,000 – 2,000
■	500 – 1,000
	200 – 500
	100 – 200
	20 – 100
	Under 20

POPULATION CHANGE 1981–2007
The percentage change in the number of people between 1981 and 2007

△ Over 50% increse △ 25–50% increase ▽ Over 5% decrease

POPULATION DATA

	% Change 1981–2007	Population 2007 ('000s)	Density (persons per sq km)
England	9.1	51,092	392
Wales	5.9	2,980	141
Scotland	–2.1	5,144	66
Northern Ireland	9.8	1,759	130
United Kingdom	8.2	60,975	251
Ireland	13.0	4,240	61

Projection: Conical with two standard parallels

1 : 4 000 000

COPYRIGHT PHILIP'

POPULATION DENSITY IN 1891

Persons per sq km

- Over 1,000
- 500 – 1,000
- 200 – 500
- 100 – 200
- 50 – 100
- 25 – 50
- Under 25

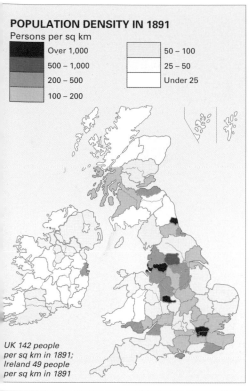

UK 142 people
per sq km in 1891;
Ireland 49 people
per sq km in 1891

ETHNIC GROUPS

Ethnic minorities as a percentage of total
population in 2003

- Over 30%
- 10 – 30%
- 5 – 10%
- 0 – 5%

Ethnic minority groups

- Indian/ Pakistani/ Bangladeshi
- W. Indian/ African
- Other

77 000 Total number of
ethnic minority
people in each
region

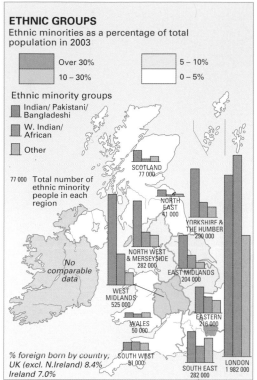

SCOTLAND
77 000

NORTH
EAST
41 000

YORKSHIRE &
THE HUMBER
290 000

NORTH WEST
& MERSEYSIDE
282 000

EAST MIDLANDS
204 000

WEST
MIDLANDS
525 000

EASTERN
216 000

(No
comparable
data

WALES
50 000

SOUTH WEST
91 000

SOUTH EAST
282 000

LONDON
1 982 000

% foreign born by country;
UK (excl. N.Ireland) 8.4%
Ireland 7.0%

MIGRATION

The difference between the number moving in and
the number moving away per 1,000 inhabitants 2007*

- Over 10 moved in
- 5 – 10 moved in
- 0 – 5 moved in
- 0 – 5 moved away
- 5 – 10 moved away
- Over 10 moved away

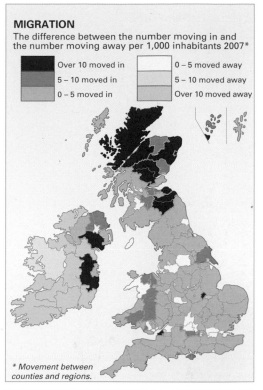

* Movement between
counties and regions.

NATURAL POPULATION CHANGE

The difference between the number of births and the
number of deaths per thousand inhabitants in 2007

- Over 7.5 more births
- 5 – 7.5 more births
- 2.5 – 5 more births
- 0 – 2.5 more births
- 0 – 2.5 more deaths
- Over 2.5 more deaths

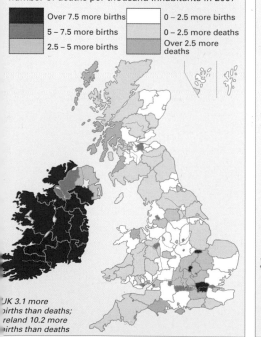

UK 3.1 more
births than deaths;
Ireland 10.2 more
births than deaths

YOUNG PEOPLE

The percentage of the population
under 15 years old in 2007

- Over 21%
- 20 – 21%
- 19 – 20%
- 18 – 19%
- 17 – 18%
- Under – 17%

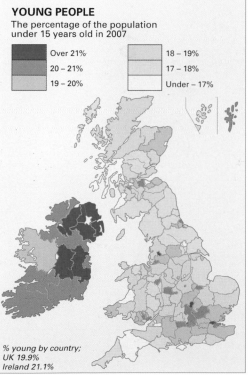

% young by country;
UK 19.9%
Ireland 21.1%

OLD PEOPLE

The percentage of the population
over pensionable age* in 2007

- Over 26%
- 24 – 26%
- 22 – 24%
- 20 – 22%
- 18 – 20%
- Under 18%

*Pensionable age is
65 for males, 60 for
females

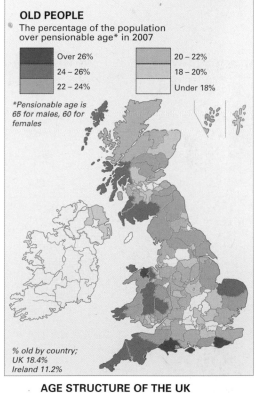

% old by country;
UK 18.4%
Ireland 11.2%

UK VITAL STATISTICS (1900–2007)

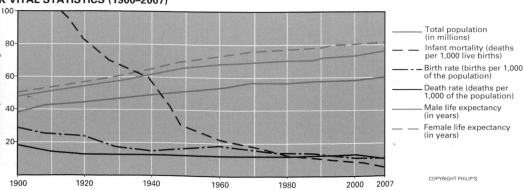

- Total population (in millions)
- Infant mortality (deaths per 1,000 live births)
- Birth rate (births per 1,000 of the population)
- Death rate (deaths per 1,000 of the population)
- Male life expectancy (in years)
- Female life expectancy (in years)

COPYRIGHT PHILIP'S

AGE STRUCTURE OF THE UK

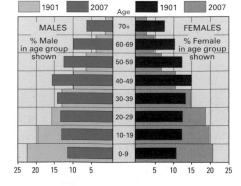

| 1901 | 2007 | Age | 1901 | 2007 |

MALES   FEMALES
% Male   70+   % Female
in age group   60-69   in age group
shown   50-59   shown
                40-49
                30-39
                20-29
                10-19
                0-9

25 20 15 10 5   5 10 15 20 25

HOUSE PRICES
Annual percentage increase
in house prices, 1996–2007

- Over 25%
- 20 – 25%
- 15 – 20%
- Under 15%

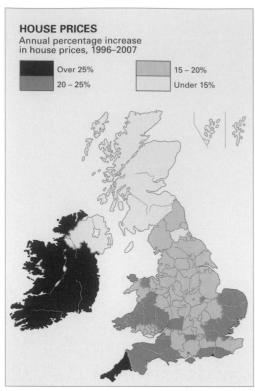

UNEMPLOYMENT
The percentage of the workforce
unemployed in 2007

- Over 8%
- 7 – 8%
- 6 – 7%
- 5 – 6%
- 4 – 5%
- Under 4%

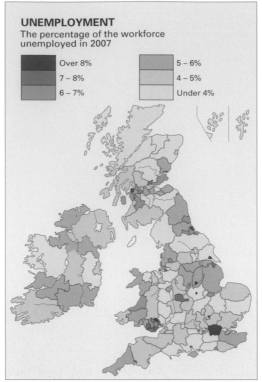

INCOME
The average gross weekly earnings of males
and females in full employment in 2007

- Over £550
- £500 – £550
- £450 – £500
- £400 – £450
- Under £400
- No data

No comparable data

Average weekly;
earnings (2007)
UK £422
Ireland €705

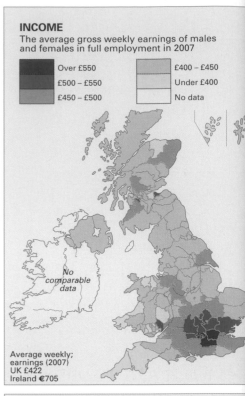

HEALTH
The number of doctors per 100,000 people
by Strategic Health Authority in 2007

- Over 160
- 150 – 160
- 140 – 150
- 130 – 140
- Under 130

SCOTLAND

NORTHERN
IRELAND

No comparable data

NORTH
EAST

YORKSHIRE &
THE HUMBER

NORTH
WEST

EAST
MIDLANDS

WEST
MIDLANDS

EAST OF
ENGLAND

WALES

SOUTH
CENTRAL

LONDON

SOUTH EAST
COAST

SOUTH WEST

NHS Strategic
Health Authority
boundaries

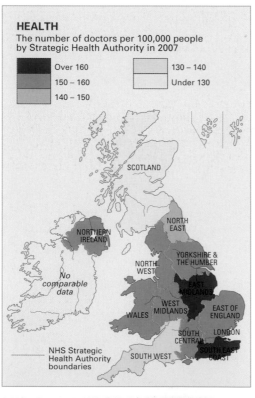

EDUCATION
The percentage of pupils achieving
5 grade A* – C at GCSE in 2007

- Over 70%
- 65 – 70%
- 60 – 65%
- 55 – 60%
- Under 60%

No comparable data

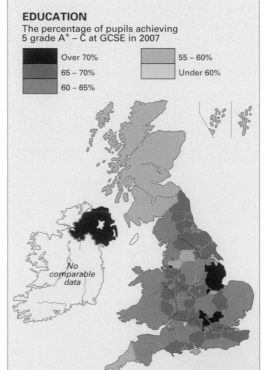

CRIME RATE
The number of recorded crimes per
thousand people in 2007

- Over 100
- 90 – 100
- 80 – 90
- 70 – 80
- 60 – 70
- Under 60

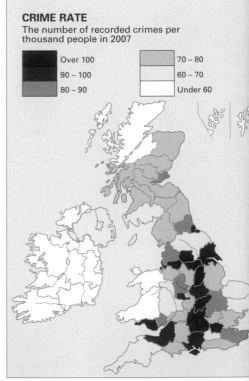

COMPARISON OF HOUSEHOLD EXPENDITURE IN THE UK, 2007

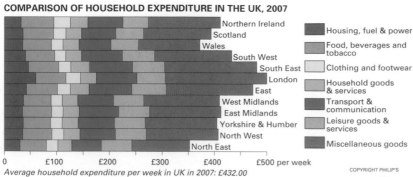

Northern Ireland
Scotland
Wales
South West
South East
London
East
West Midlands
East Midlands
Yorkshire & Humber
North West
North East

- Housing, fuel & power
- Food, beverages and tobacco
- Clothing and footwear
- Household goods & services
- Transport & communication
- Leisure goods & services
- Miscellaneous goods

0   £100   £200   £300   £400   £500 per week

Average household expenditure per week in UK in 2007: £432.00

COPYRIGHT PHILIP'S

HOUSEHOLDS WITH INTERNET ACCESS, 2006

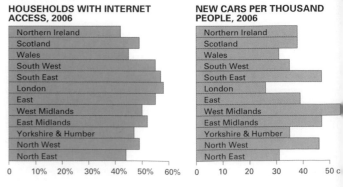

Northern Ireland
Scotland
Wales
South West
South East
London
East
West Midlands
East Midlands
Yorkshire & Humber
North West
North East

0   10%   20%   30%   40%   50%   60%

NEW CARS PER THOUSAND PEOPLE, 2006

Northern Ireland
Scotland
Wales
South West
South East
London
East
West Midlands
East Midlands
Yorkshire & Humber
North West
North East

0   10   20   30   40   50 c

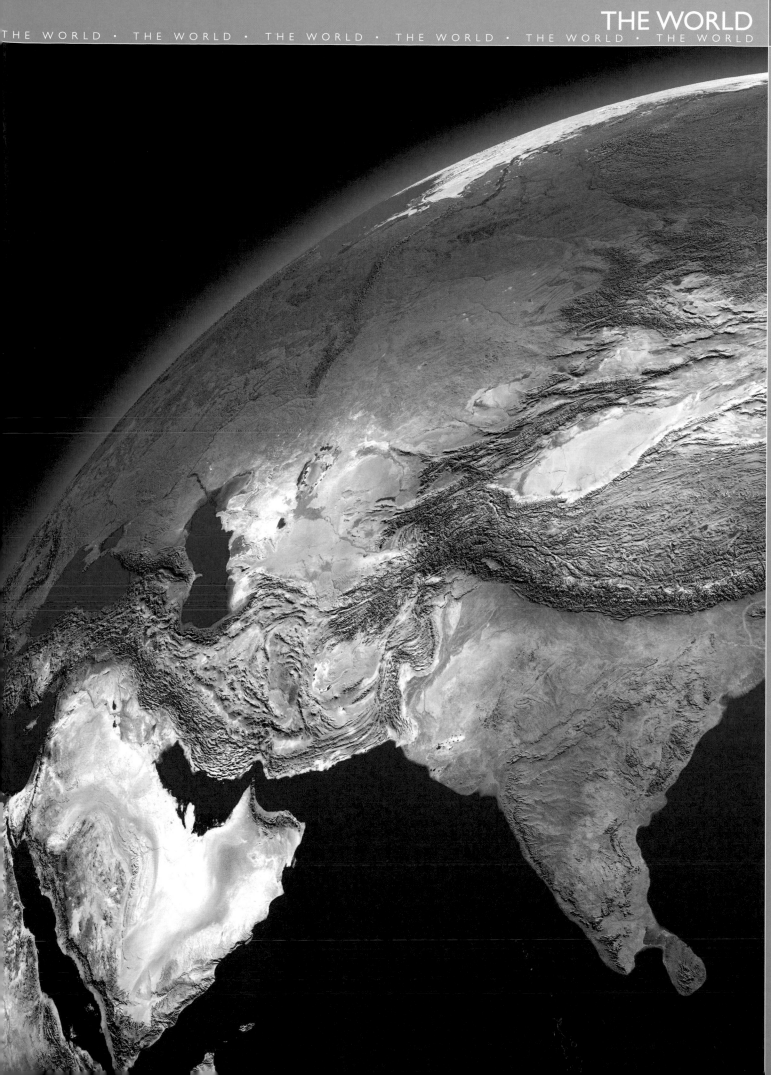

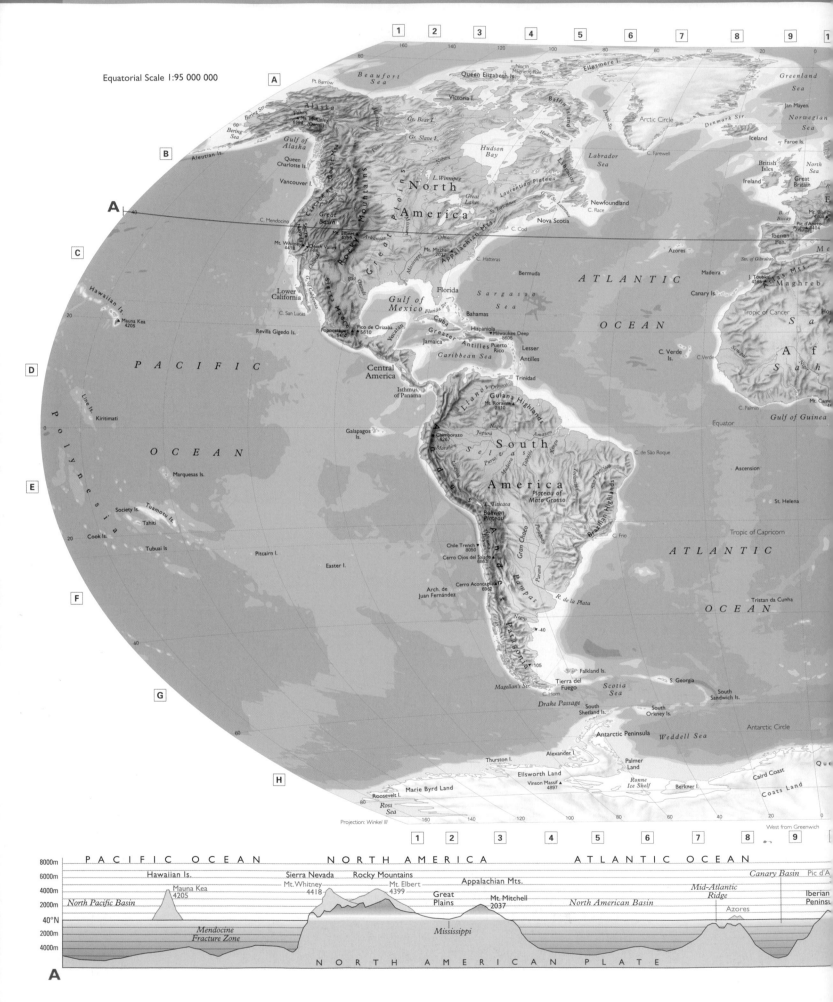

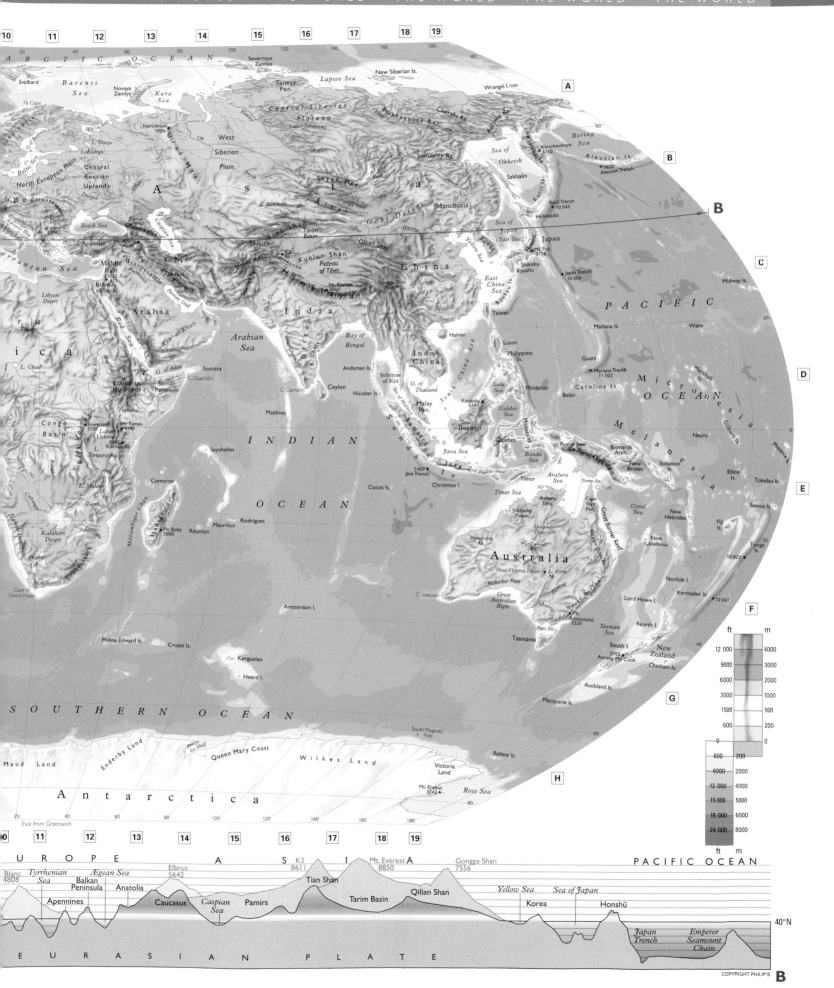

COPYRIGHT PHILIP'S

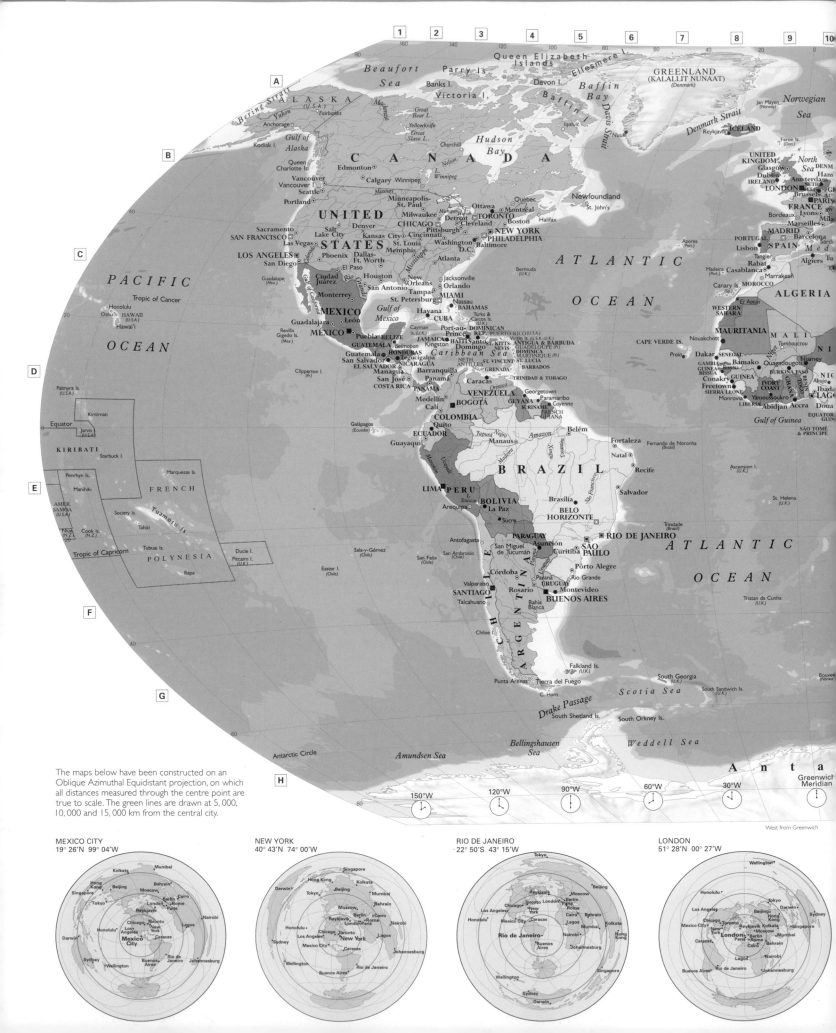

The maps below have been constructed on an Oblique Azimuthal Equidistant projection, on which all distances measured through the centre point are true to scale. The green lines are drawn at 5,000, 10,000 and 15,000 km from the central city.

West from Greenwich

MEXICO CITY
19° 26'N 99° 04'W

NEW YORK
40° 43'N 74° 00'W

RIO DE JANEIRO
22° 50'S 43° 15'W

LONDON
51° 28'N 00° 27'W

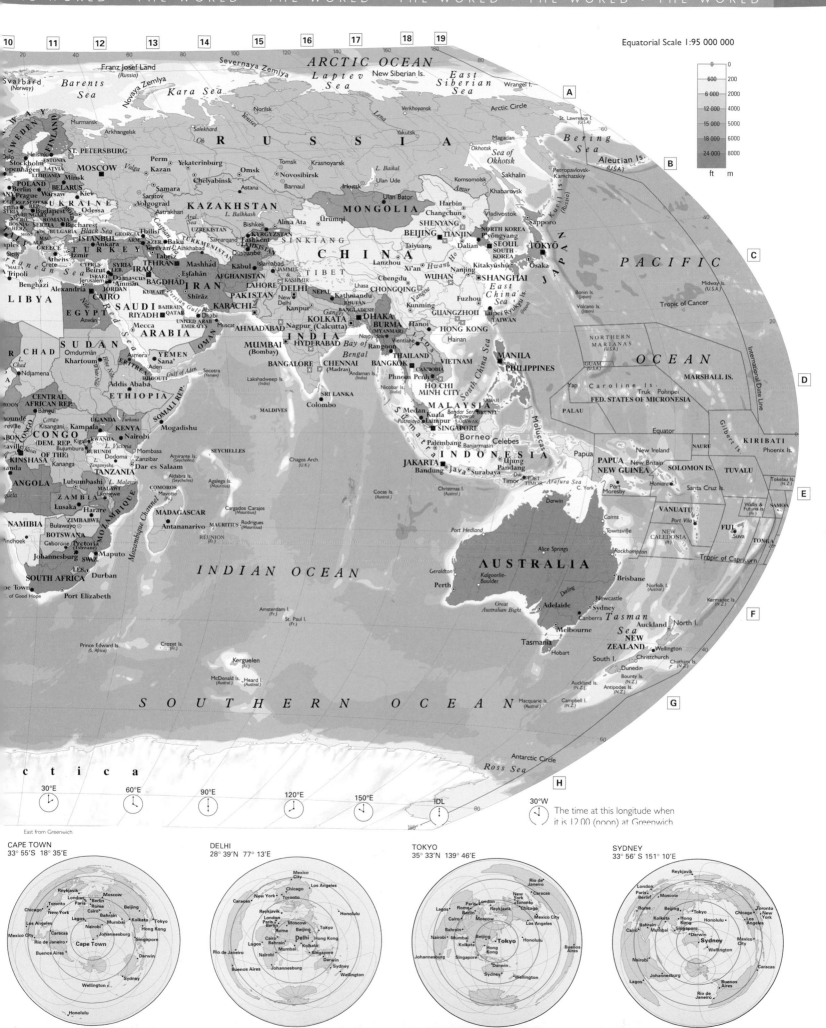

Equatorial Scale 1:95 000 000

| 10 | 11 | 12 | 13 | 14 | 15 | 16 | 17 | 18 | 19 |

ft   m
0   0
600   200
6 000 2000
12 000 4000
15 000 5000
18 000 6000
24 000 8000

CAPE TOWN
33° 55'S 18° 35'E

DELHI
28° 39'N 77° 13'E

TOKYO
35° 33'N 139° 46'E

SYDNEY
33° 56'S 151° 10'E

East from Greenwich

30°W
The time at this longitude when
it is 12.00 (noon) at Greenwich

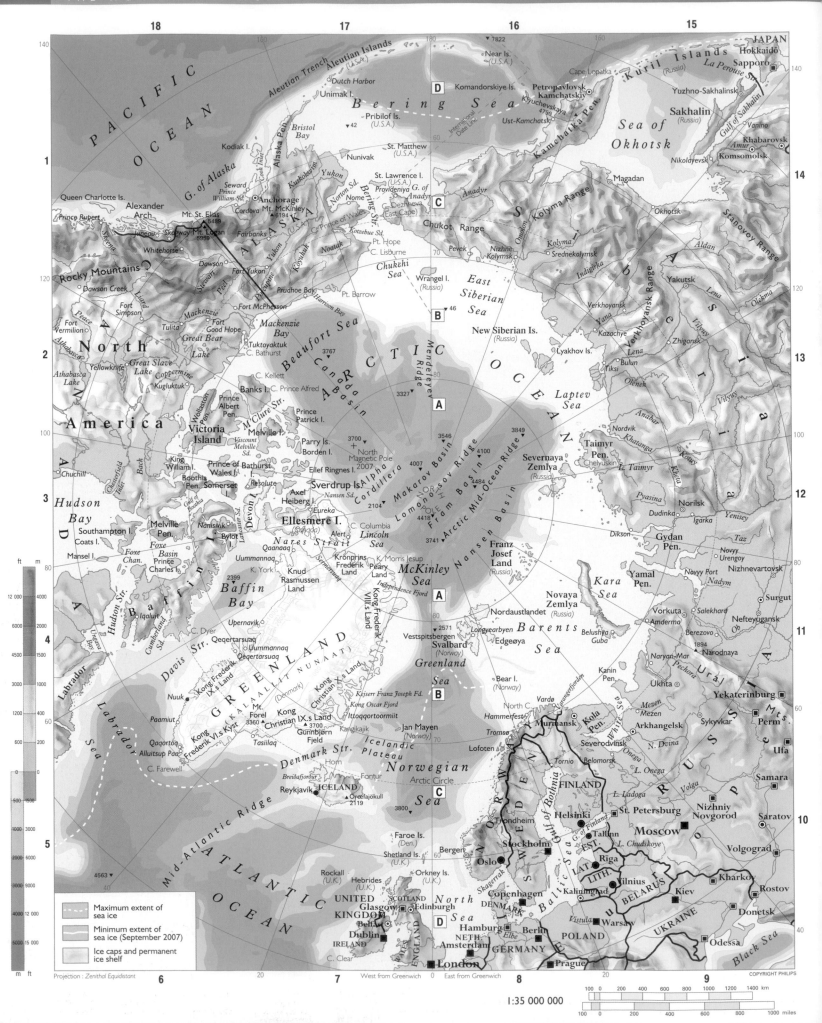

Projection : Zenithal Equidistant

West from Greenwich   East from Greenwich

COPYRIGHT PHILIPS

1:35 000 000

Maximum extent of sea ice
Minimum extent of sea ice (September 2007)
Ice caps and permanent ice shelf

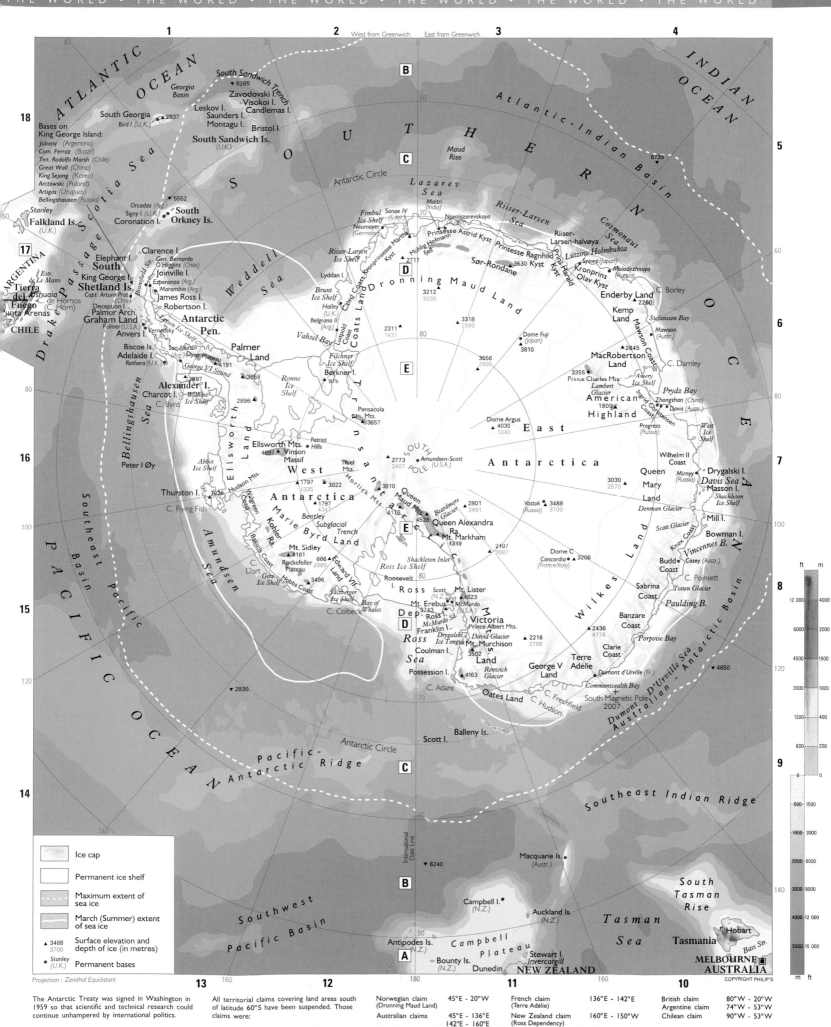

Legend

- Ice cap
- Permanent ice shelf
- Maximum extent of sea ice
- March (Summer) extent of sea ice
- ▲ 3488 / 3700 Surface elevation and depth of ice (in metres)
- • Stanley Permanent bases

Projection: Zenithal Equidistant

The Antarctic Treaty was signed in Washington in 1959 so that scientific and technical research could continue unhampered by international politics.

All territorial claims covering land areas south of latitude 60°S have been suspended. Those claims were:

Norwegian claim (Dronning Maud Land)	45°E – 20°W
Australian claims	45°E – 136°E / 142°E – 160°E
French claim (Terre Adélie)	136°E – 142°E
New Zealand claim (Ross Dependency)	160°E – 150°W
British claim	80°W – 20°W
Argentine claim	74°W – 53°W
Chilean claim	90°W – 53°W

COPYRIGHT PHILIP'S

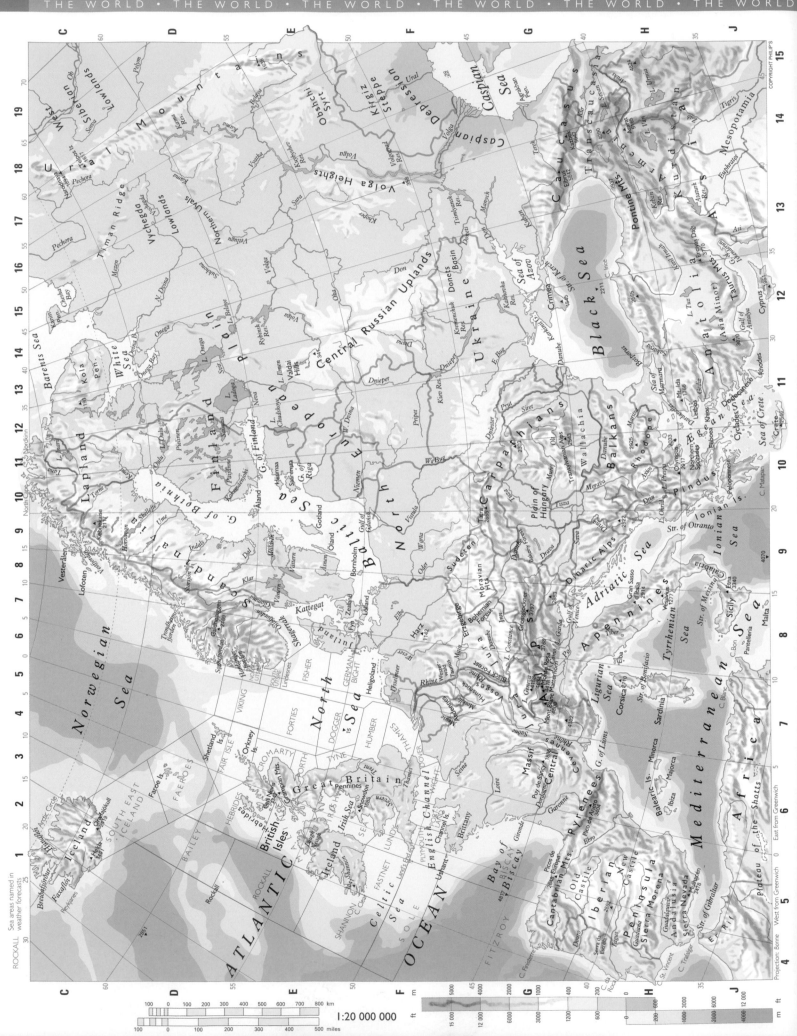

1:20 000 000

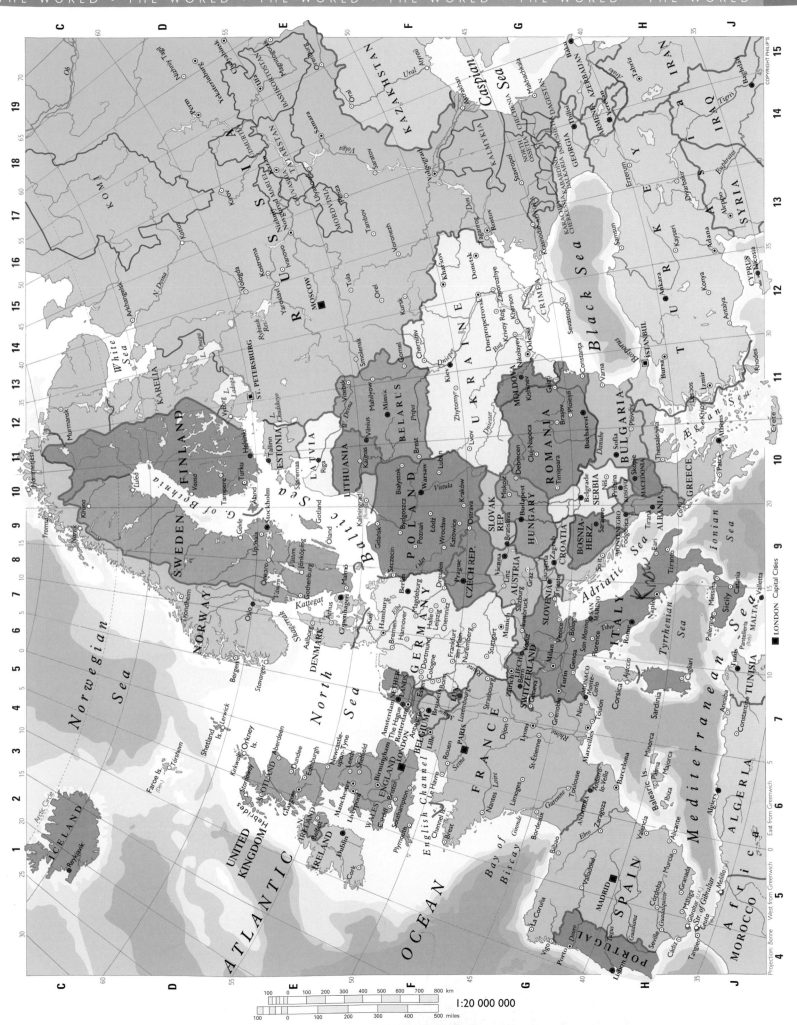

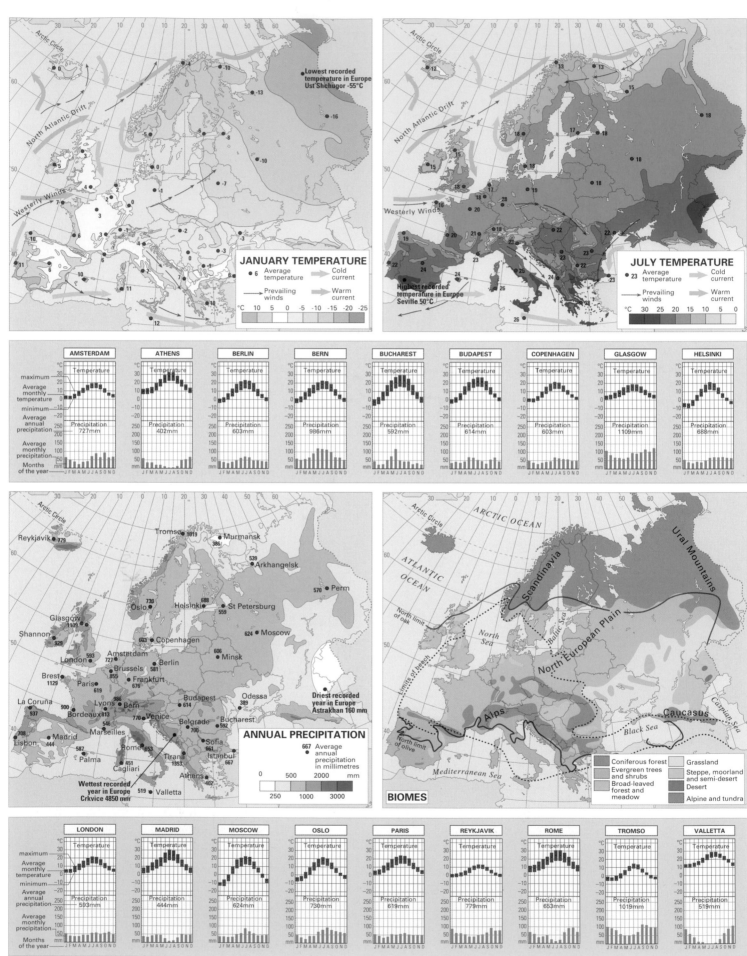

JANUARY TEMPERATURE

Lowest recorded temperature in Europe Ust'Shchugor -55°C

- 6 Average temperature
- Prevailing winds
- Cold current
- Warm current

°C 10 5 0 -5 -10 -15 -20 -25

JULY TEMPERATURE

Highest recorded temperature in Europe Seville 50°C

- 23 Average temperature
- Prevailing winds
- Cold current
- Warm current

°C 30 25 20 15 10 5 0

Climate graphs: AMSTERDAM 727mm, ATHENS 402mm, BERLIN 603mm, BERN 986mm, BUCHAREST 592mm, BUDAPEST 614mm, COPENHAGEN 603mm, GLASGOW 1109mm, HELSINKI 688mm

maximum / Average monthly temperature / minimum / Average annual precipitation / Average monthly precipitation / Months of the year

ANNUAL PRECIPITATION

Driest recorded year in Europe Astrakhan 160 mm

Wettest recorded year in Europe Crkvice 4850 mm

- 667 Average annual precipitation in millimetres

0 250 500 1000 2000 3000 mm

Reykjavik 179, Tromsø 1019, Murmansk 386, Arkhangelsk 539, Perm 570, Oslo 730, Helsinki 688, St Petersburg 559, Glasgow 1109, Shannon 929, Copenhagen 603, Moscow 624, Amsterdam 727, Berlin 581, Minsk 606, London 593, Brussels 855, Frankfurt 676, Brest 1129, Paris 619, Lyons 813, Bern 986, La Coruña 937, Bordeaux 546, Venice 770, Budapest 614, Odessa 389, Bucharest 592, Belgrade 700, Madrid 444, Marseilles 1333, Sofia 661, Istanbul 667, Lisbon 708, Palma 587, Rome 653, Tirana, Athens 402, Cagliari 451, Valletta 519

BIOMES

- Coniferous forest
- Evergreen trees and shrubs
- Broad-leaved forest and meadow
- Grassland
- Steppe, moorland and semi-desert
- Desert
- Alpine and tundra

Arctic Circle, ARCTIC OCEAN, ATLANTIC OCEAN, Scandinavia, Ural Mountains, North Sea, Baltic Sea, North European Plain, North limit of oak, limits of beech, Alps, North limit of olive, Caucasus, Black Sea, Caspian Sea, Mediterranean Sea

Climate graphs: LONDON 593mm, MADRID 444mm, MOSCOW 624mm, OSLO 730mm, PARIS 619mm, REYKJAVIK 779mm, ROME 653mm, TROMSO 1019mm, VALLETTA 519mm

maximum / Average monthly temperature / minimum / Average annual precipitation / Average monthly precipitation / Months of the year

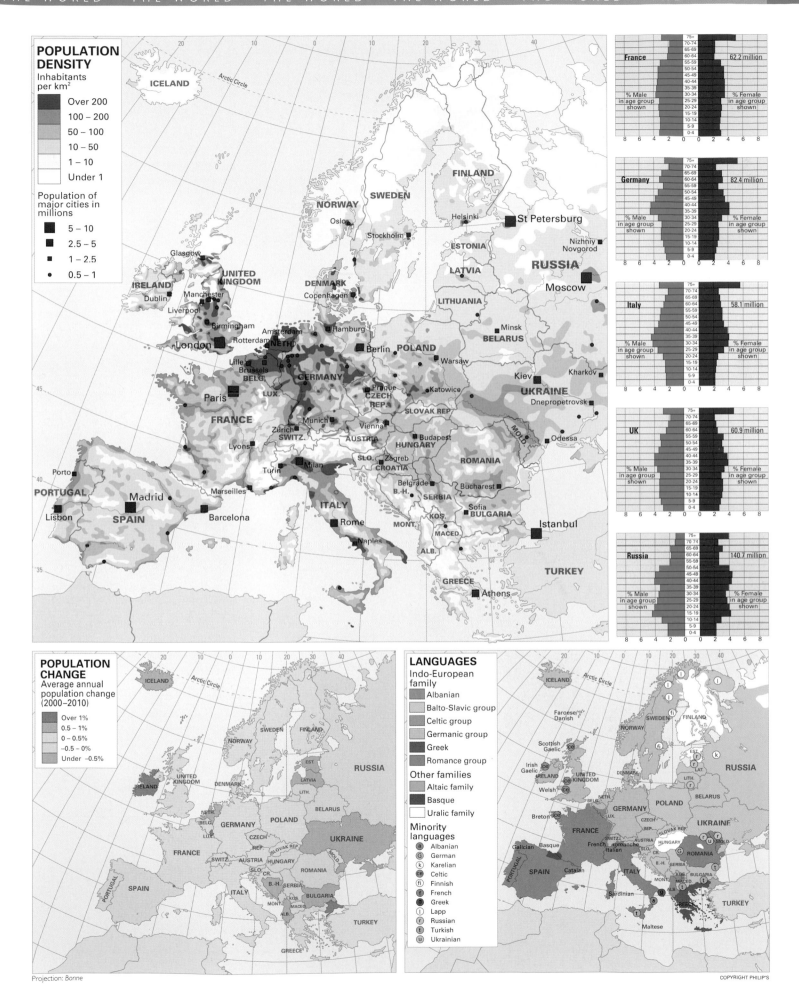

POPULATION DENSITY
Inhabitants per km²
- Over 200
- 100 – 200
- 50 – 100
- 10 – 50
- 1 – 10
- Under 1

Population of major cities in millions
- 5 – 10
- 2.5 – 5
- 1 – 2.5
- 0.5 – 1

France — 62.2 million
Germany — 82.4 million
Italy — 58.1 million
UK — 60.9 million
Russia — 140.7 million

% Male in age group shown / % Female in age group shown

POPULATION CHANGE
Average annual population change (2000–2010)
- Over 1%
- 0.5 – 1%
- 0 – 0.5%
- –0.5 – 0%
- Under –0.5%

LANGUAGES
Indo-European family
- Albanian
- Balto-Slavic group
- Celtic group
- Germanic group
- Greek
- Romance group

Other families
- Altaic family
- Basque
- Uralic family

Minority languages
- (a) Albanian
- (G) German
- (k) Karelian
- (ce) Celtic
- (fi) Finnish
- (f) French
- (g) Greek
- (l) Lapp
- (r) Russian
- (t) Turkish
- (u) Ukrainian

Projection: Bonne

COPYRIGHT PHILIP'S

COUNTRIES OF THE EU

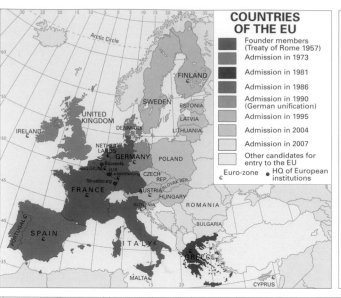

Legend:
- Founder members (Treaty of Rome 1957)
- Admission in 1973
- Admission in 1981
- Admission in 1986
- Admission in 1990 (German unification)
- Admission in 1995
- Admission in 2004
- Admission in 2007
- Other candidates for entry to the EU

Euro-zone   • HQ of European institutions

EU COUNTRY COMPARISONS	Population (thousands)	Annual Income (US$ per capita)
Germany	82,370	34,400
France	62,200	33,800
United Kingdom	60,944	35,300
Italy	58,145	31,000
Spain	40,491	33,700
Poland	38,501	16,200
Romania	22,247	11,100
Netherlands	16,645	38,600
Greece	10,723	30,500
Portugal	10,677	21,800
Belgium	10,404	36,500
Czech Republic	10,221	24,400
Hungary	9,931	19,500
Sweden	9,045	36,900
Austria	8,206	39,000
Bulgaria	7,263	11,800
Denmark	5,485	37,400
Slovakia	5,455	19,800
Finland	5,245	35,500
Ireland	4,156	55,600
Lithuania	3,565	16,700
Latvia	2,245	17,700
Slovenia	2,008	27,300
Estonia	1,308	21,800
Cyprus	793	24,600
Luxembourg	486	80,800
Malta	404	23,200
Total EU 2008 (27 countries)	**491,021**	**30,181**

REGIONS OF THE EU

Austria (States) — A
1 Niederösterreich	4 Kärnten	7 Tirol
2 Oberösterreich	5 Salzburg	8 Wien
3 Burgenland	6 Steiermark	9 Vorarlberg

Belgium (Regions) — B
1 Bruxelles	2 Vlaanderen	3 Wallonie

Bulgaria (Regions) — BU
1 Severen tsentralen	3 Severozapaden	5 Yugozapaden
2 Severoiztochen	4 Yugoiztochrn	6 Yuzhen tsentralen

Cyprus (member state with no corresponding division) — CY

Czech Republic (Kraj) — CZ
1 Jihovychod	4 Praha	7 Stredni Cechy
2 Jihozapad	5 Severovychod	8 Stredni Morava
3 Moravskoslezsko	6 Severozapad	

Denmark (member state with no corresponding division) — DK

Estonia (member state with no corresponding division) — EE

Finland (Provinces) — FIN
1 Åland	3 Väli-Suomi	5 Uusimaa (Suuralue)
2 Itä-Suomi	4 Pohjois-Suomi	6 Etelä-Suomi

France (Regions) — F
1 Alsace	9 Franche-Comté	17 Normandie (Basse-)
2 Aquitaine	10 Île-de-France	18 Normandie (Haute-)
3 Auvergne	11 Languedoc-Roussillon	19 Picardie
4 Bourgogne	12 Limousin	20 Poitou-Charentes
5 Bretagne	13 Loire (Pays de la)	21 Provence-Alpes-Côte d'Azur
6 Centre	14 Lorraine	22 Rhône-Alpes
7 Champagne-Ardenne	15 Midi-Pyrénées	
8 Corse	16 Nord-Pas-de-Calais	

Germany (Länder) — D
1 Baden-Württemberg	7 Hamburg	11 Rheinland-Pfalz
2 Niedersachsen	8 Hessen	12 Saarland
3 Bayern	9 Mecklenburg-Vorpommern	13 Sachsen
4 Berlin		14 Sachsen-Anhalt
5 Brandenburg	10 Nordrhein-Westfalen	15 Schleswig-Holstein
6 Bremen		16 Thüringen

Greece (Regions) — EL
1 Anatoliki Makedonia kai Thraki	5 Epiros	10 Dytiki Makedonia
2 Kriti	6 Attiki	11 Kentriki Makedonia
3 Voreio Aigaio	7 Sterea Ellas	12 Peloponnese
4 Notio Aigaio	8 Dytiki Ellas	13 Thessaly
	9 Ionioi Nisoi	

Hungary (Megyék) — HU
1 Del-Alfold	4 Eszak-Magyarorszag	7 Nyugat-Dunantul
2 Del-Dunantul	5 Kozep-Dunantul	
3 Eszak-Alfold	6 Kozep-Magyarorszag	
		3 Eszak-Alfold

Ireland (Provinces) — IRL
1 Border, Midlands & Western	
2 Southern & Eastern	

Italy (Regions) — I
1 Abruzzo	8 Liguria	15 Sardegna
2 Basilicata	9 Lombardia	16 Sicilia
3 Calábria	10 Marche	17 Toscana
4 Campánia	11 Molise	18 Trentino-Alto Adige
5 Emília-Romagna	12 Umbria	19 Valle d'Aosta
6 Friuli-Venézia Giulia	13 Piemonte	20 Venéto
7 Lazio	14 Puglia	

Latvia (member state with no corresponding division) — L

Lithuania (member state with no corresponding division) — L

Luxembourg (member state with no corresponding division) — L

Malta (member state with no corresponding division) — MT

Netherlands (Regions) — NL
1 Noord-Nederland	3 West-Nederland	
2 Oost-Nederland	4 Zuid-Nederland	

Poland (Voivodships) — PL
1 Dolnośląskie	7 Mazowieckie	13 Swietokrzyskie
2 Kujawsko-Pomorskie	8 Opolskie	14 Warmińsko-Mazurskie
3 Łódzkie	9 Podkarpackie	15 Wielkopolskie
4 Lubelskie	10 Podlaskie	16 Zachodniopomorskie
5 Lubuskie	11 Pomorskie	
6 Małopolskie	12 Śląskie	

Portugal (Autonomous regions) — P
1 Alentejo	3 Centro	5 Norte
2 Algarve	4 Lisboa-Vale do Tejo	

Romania (Regions) — RO
1 Bucureşti	4 Nord-Vest	7 Sud-Vest
2 Centru	5 Sud	8 Vest
3 Nord-Est	6 Sud-Eest	
		2 Centru

Slovak Republic (Kraj) — SK
1 Bratislavsky Kraj	3 Vychodne Slovensko	
2 Stredne Slovensko	4 Zapadne Slovensko	

Slovenia (member state with no corresponding division) — SI

Spain (Autonomous communities) — E
1 Andalucía	7 Cantabria	13 Madrid
2 Aragon	8 Castilla y Léon	14 Murcia
3 Asturias	9 Castilla-La Mancha	15 Navarra
4 Islas Baleares	10 Cataluña	16 Rioja (La)
5 País Vasco	11 Extremadura	17 Valencia
6 Islas Canarias	12 Galicia	

Sweden (Regions) — S
1 Stockholm	4 Västsverige	7 Övre Norrland
2 Östra Mellansverige	5 Norra Mellansverige	8 Småland med öarna
3 Sydsverige	6 Mellersta Norrland	

United Kingdom (Government Office Regions) — UK
1 North East	5 West Midlands	9 South West
2 North West	6 Eastern	10 Wales
3 Yorkshire & The Humber	7 London	11 Scotland
4 East Midlands	8 South East	12 Northern Ireland

Projection: Bonne

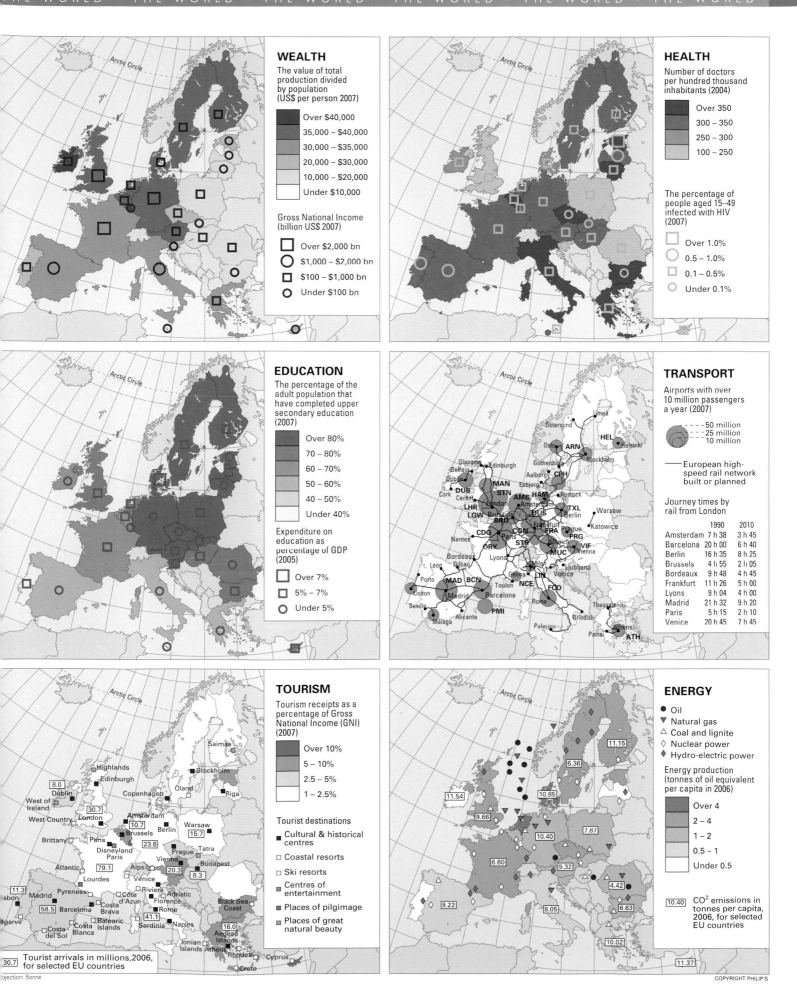

WEALTH

The value of total production divided by population (US$ per person 2007)

- Over $40,000
- 35,000 – $40,000
- 30,000 – $35,000
- 20,000 – $30,000
- 10,000 – $20,000
- Under $10,000

Gross National Income (billion US$ 2007)

- ☐ Over $2,000 bn
- ◯ $1,000 – $2,000 bn
- ☐ $100 – $1,000 bn
- ◯ Under $100 bn

HEALTH

Number of doctors per hundred thousand inhabitants (2004)

- Over 350
- 300 – 350
- 250 – 300
- 100 – 250

The percentage of people aged 15–49 infected with HIV (2007)

- ☐ Over 1.0%
- ◯ 0.5 – 1.0%
- ☐ 0.1 – 0.5%
- ◯ Under 0.1%

EDUCATION

The percentage of the adult population that have completed upper secondary education (2007)

- Over 80%
- 70 – 80%
- 60 – 70%
- 50 – 60%
- 40 – 50%
- Under 40%

Expenditure on education as percentage of GDP (2005)

- ☐ Over 7%
- ☐ 5% – 7%
- ◯ Under 5%

TRANSPORT

Airports with over 10 million passengers a year (2007)

- 50 million
- 25 million
- 10 million

— European high-speed rail network built or planned

Journey times by rail from London

	1990	2010
Amsterdam	7 h 38	3 h 45
Barcelona	20 h 00	6 h 40
Berlin	16 h 35	8 h 25
Brussels	4 h 55	2 h 05
Bordeaux	9 h 48	4 h 45
Frankfurt	11 h 26	5 h 00
Lyons	9 h 04	4 h 00
Madrid	21 h 32	9 h 20
Paris	5 h 15	2 h 10
Venice	20 h 45	7 h 45

TOURISM

Tourism receipts as a percentage of Gross National Income (GNI) (2007)

- Over 10%
- 5 – 10%
- 2.5 – 5%
- 1 – 2.5%

Tourist destinations

- ■ Cultural & historical centres
- ☐ Coastal resorts
- ☐ Ski resorts
- ■ Centres of entertainment
- ■ Places of pilgimage
- ■ Places of great natural beauty

30.7 Tourist arrivals in millions, 2006, for selected EU countries

ENERGY

- ● Oil
- ▼ Natural gas
- △ Coal and lignite
- ◇ Nuclear power
- ◆ Hydro-electric power

Energy production (tonnes of oil equivalent per capita in 2006)

- Over 4
- 2 – 4
- 1 – 2
- 0.5 – 1
- Under 0.5

10.40 CO_2 emissions in tonnes per capita, 2006, for selected EU countries

Projection: Bonne

COPYRIGHT PHILIP'S

Projection: Conical with two standard parallels

1:5 000 000

East from Greenwich COPYRIGHT PHILIP'S

Projection: Conical with two standard parallels

1:5 000 000

COPYRIGHT PHILIP'S

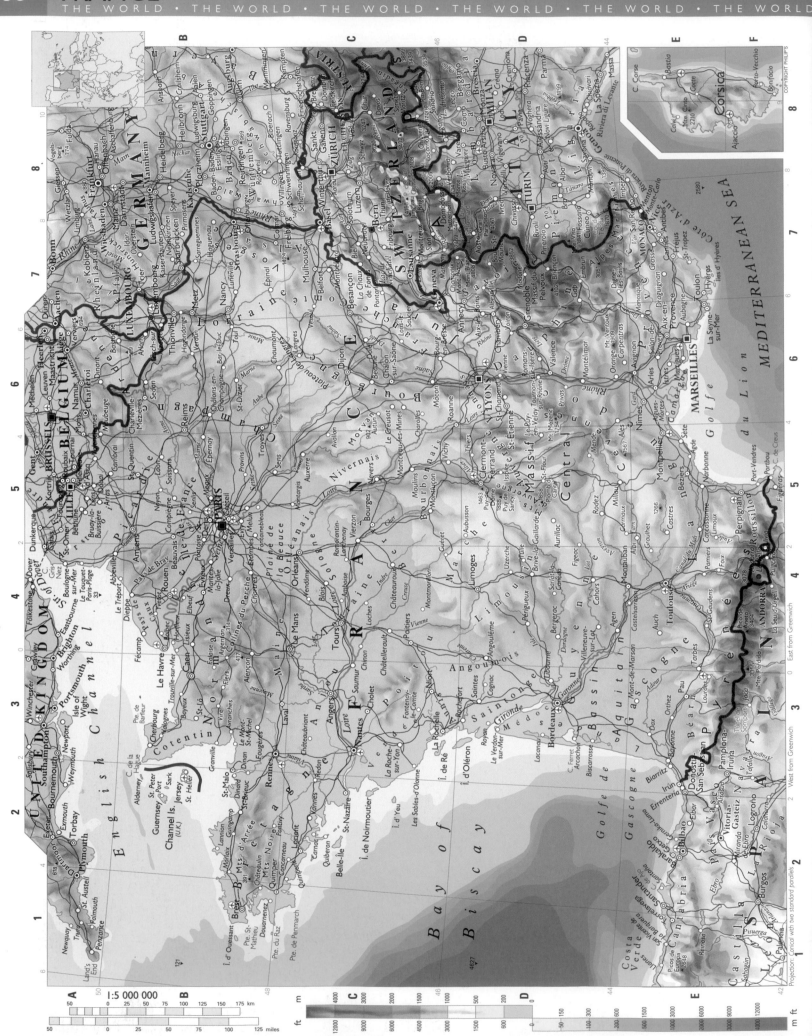

1:5 000 000

Projection: Conical with two standard parallels

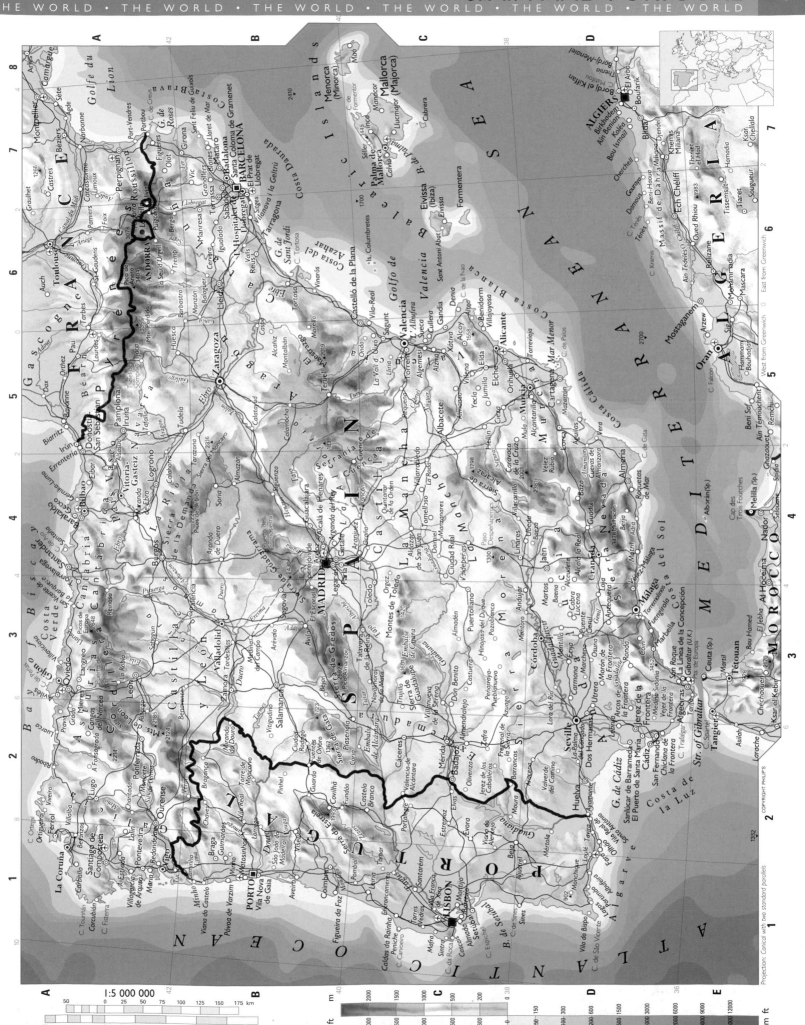

1:5 000 000

Projection: Conical with two standard parallels

COPYRIGHT PHILIP'S

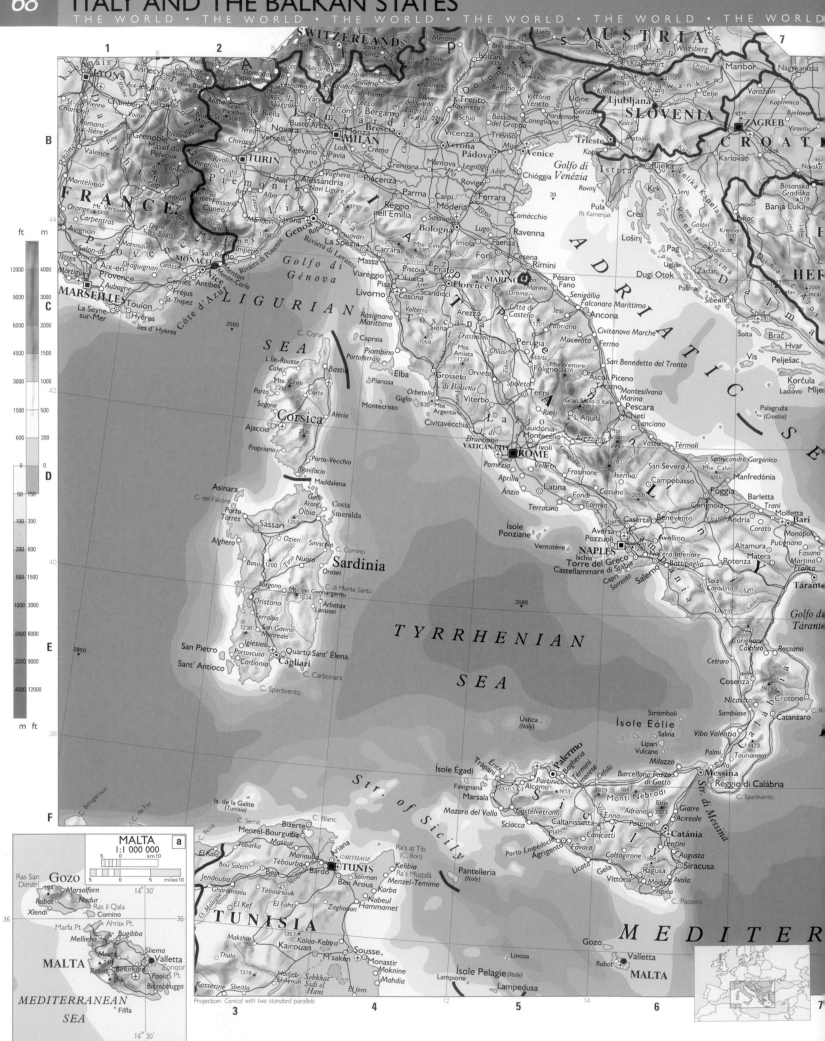

Projection: Conical with two standard parallels

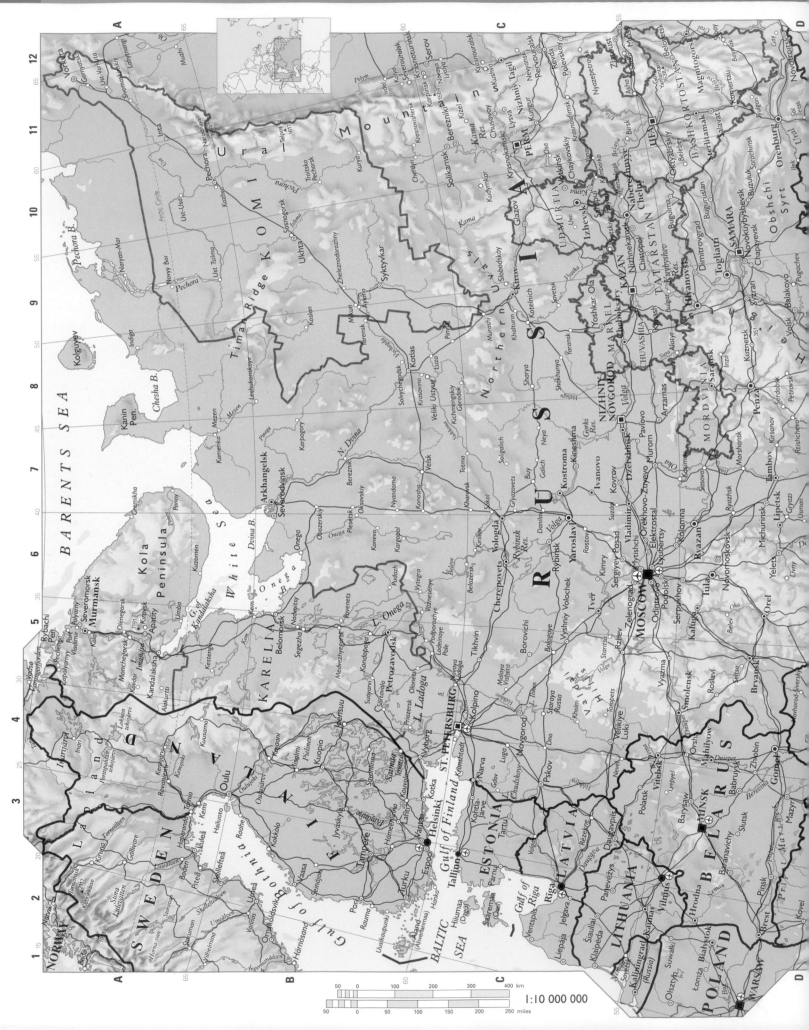

BARENTS SEA

Kola Peninsula

White Sea

Ural Mountains

KOMI

Timan Ridge

KARELIA

FINLAND

SWEDEN

NORWAY

Lapland

Gulf of Bothnia

BALTIC SEA

Gulf of Finland

Gulf of Riga

ESTONIA

LATVIA

LITHUANIA

BELARUS

POLAND

MOSCOW

ST. PETERSBURG

RUSSIA

Helsinki

Tallinn

Riga

Vilnius

Minsk

Warsaw

Murmansk

Arkhangelsk

Syktyvkar

Vologda

Kazan

PERM

SAMARA

UFA

NIZHNIY NOVGOROD MARI EL

UDMURTIA

TATARSTAN

CHUVASHIA

MORDVIA

BASHKORTOSTAN

Volga

1:10 000 000

50   0   100   200   300   400 km

50   0   50   100   150   200   250 miles

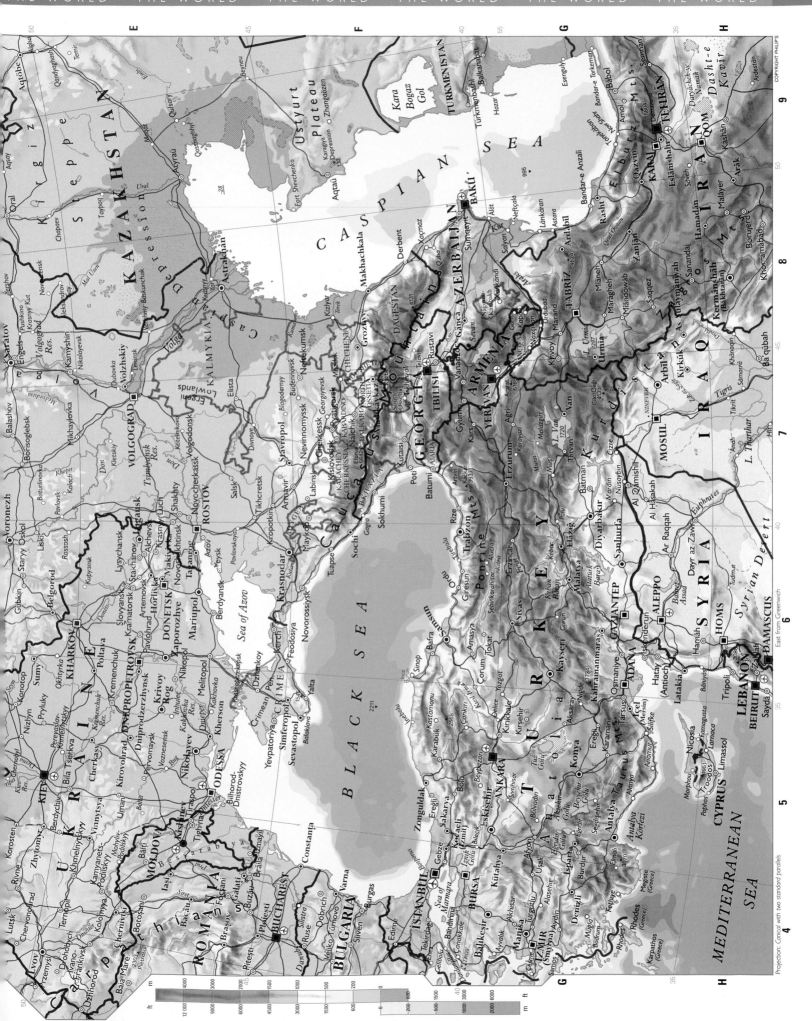

East from Greenwich

Projection: Conical with two standard parallels

1:50 000 000

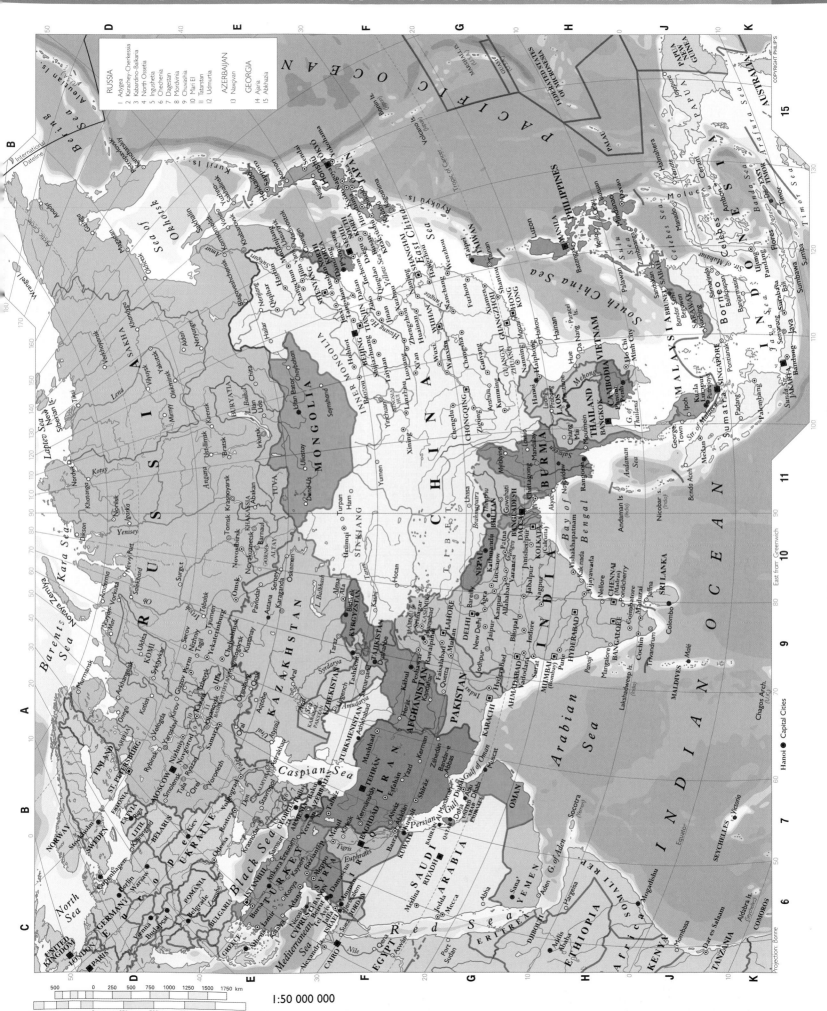

RUSSIA
1 Adygea
2 Karachey-Cherkessia
3 Kabardino-Balkaria
4 North Ossetia
5 Ingushetia
6 Chechenia
7 Dagestan
8 Mordvinia
9 Chuvashia
10 Mari El
11 Tatarstan
12 Udmurtia

AZERBAIJAN
13 Naxçıvan

GEORGIA
14 Ajaria
15 Abkhazia

1:50 000 000

Hanoi ● Capital Cities

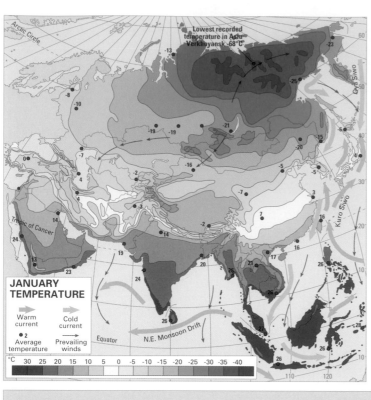

JANUARY TEMPERATURE

→ Warm current
⇒ Cold current
● 2 Average temperature
→ Prevailing winds

°C 30 25 20 15 10 5 0 -5 -10 -15 -20 -25 -30 -35 -40

Lowest recorded temperature in Asia Verkhoyansk -68°C

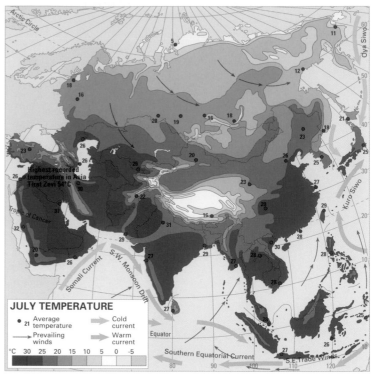

JULY TEMPERATURE

● 21 Average temperature
→ Prevailing winds
⇒ Cold current
⇒ Warm current

°C 30 25 20 15 10 5 0 -5

Highest recorded temperature in Asia Tirat Zevi 54°C

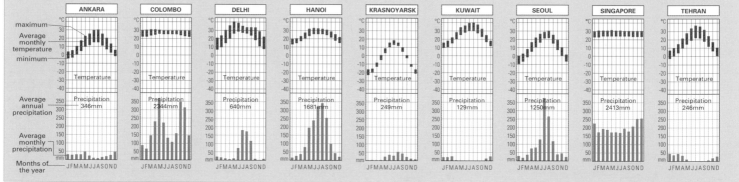

	ANKARA	COLOMBO	DELHI	HANOI	KRASNOYARSK	KUWAIT	SEOUL	SINGAPORE	TEHRAN
Precipitation	346mm	2344mm	640mm	1681mm	249mm	129mm	1250mm	2413mm	246mm

maximum
Average monthly temperature
minimum

Temperature

Average annual precipitation

Average monthly precipitation

Months of the year: JFMAMJJASOND

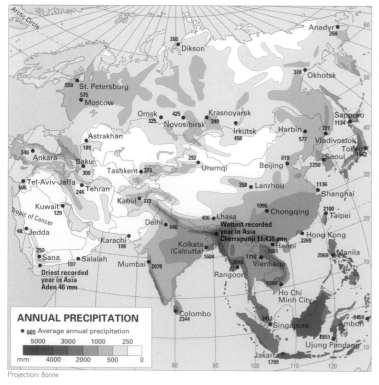

ANNUAL PRECIPITATION

● 665 Average annual precipitation

mm 5000 4000 3000 2000 1000 500 250 0

Anadyr 260
Dikson 266
Okhotsk 378
St. Petersburg 559
Moscow 575
Omsk 425
Krasnoyarsk 249
Novosibirsk 325
Sapporo 1134
Irkutsk 458
Harbin 577
Vladivostok 721
Astrakhan 189
Tokyo 1562
Ankara 346
Baku 300
Urumqi 292
Seoul 1250
Tashkent 373
Beijing 619
Tel-Aviv-Jaffa 506
Tehran 246
Lanzhou 358
Shanghai 1136
Kabul 372
Chongqing 1090
Lhasa 406
Taipei 2100
Delhi 640
Hong Kong 2265
Kuwait 129
Jedda 48
Karachi 198
Manila 2069
Kolkata (Calcutta) 1604
Hanoi 1681
Sana 252
Mumbai 2078
Vientiane 1716
Salalah 107
Rangoon 2616
Ho Chi Minh City 1984
Colombo 2344
Singapore 2413
Ambon 2851
Ujung Pandang
Jakarta 1799

Wettest recorded year in Asia Cherrapunji 11,430 mm

Driest recorded year in Asia Aden 46 mm

Projection: Bonne

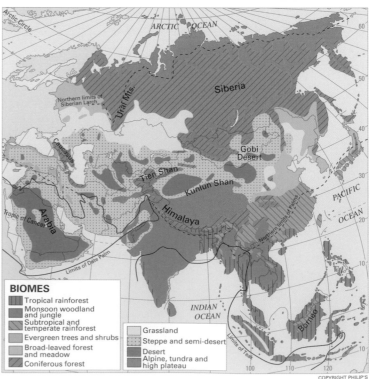

BIOMES

■ Tropical rainforest
■ Monsoon woodland and jungle
■ Subtropical and temperate rainforest
■ Evergreen trees and shrubs
■ Broad-leaved forest and meadow
■ Coniferous forest
□ Grassland
▦ Steppe and semi-desert
■ Desert
■ Alpine, tundra and high plateau

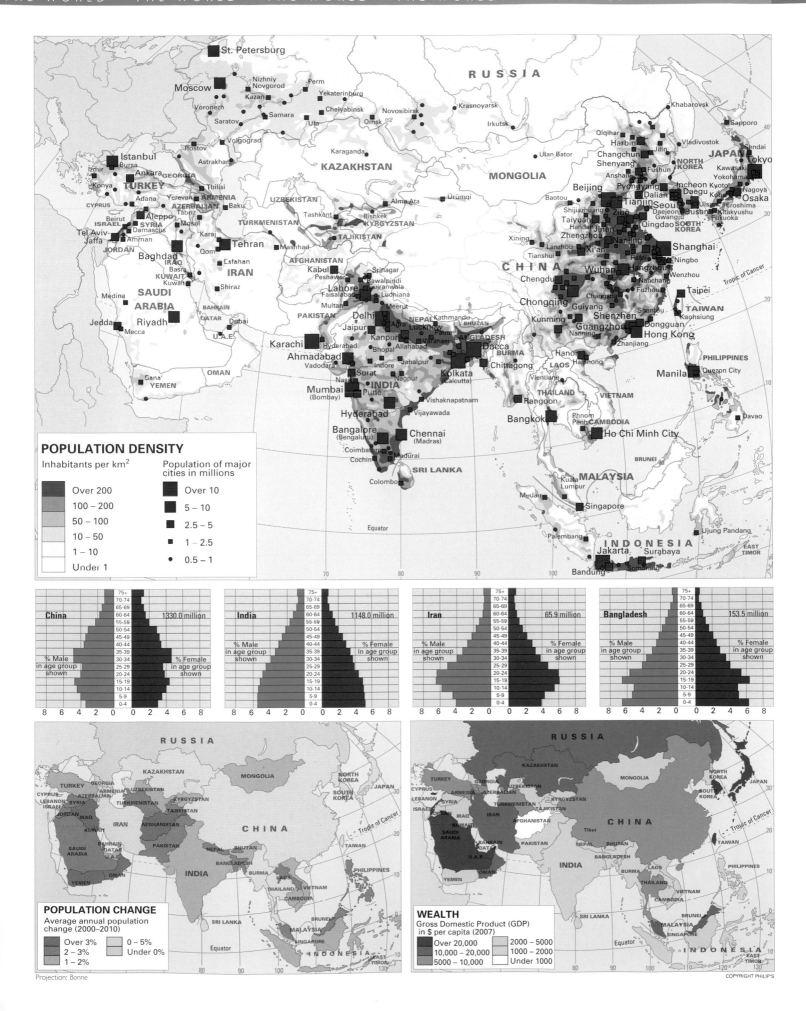

POPULATION DENSITY

Inhabitants per km²

	Over 200
	100 – 200
	50 – 100
	10 – 50
	1 – 10
	Under 1

Population of major cities in millions

■	Over 10
■	5 – 10
■	2.5 – 5
■	1 – 2.5
•	0.5 – 1

China 1330.0 million
% Male in age group shown
% Female in age group shown

India 1148.0 million
% Male in age group shown
% Female in age group shown

Iran 65.9 million
% Male in age group shown
% Female in age group shown

Bangladesh 153.5 million
% Male in age group shown
% Female in age group shown

POPULATION CHANGE
Average annual population change (2000–2010)

	Over 3%		0 – 5%
	2 – 3%		Under 0%
	1 – 2%		

WEALTH
Gross Domestic Product (GDP) in $ per capita (2007)

	Over 20,000		2000 – 5000
	10,000 – 20,000		1000 – 2000
	5000 – 10,000		Under 1000

Projection: Bonne

COPYRIGHT PHILIP'S

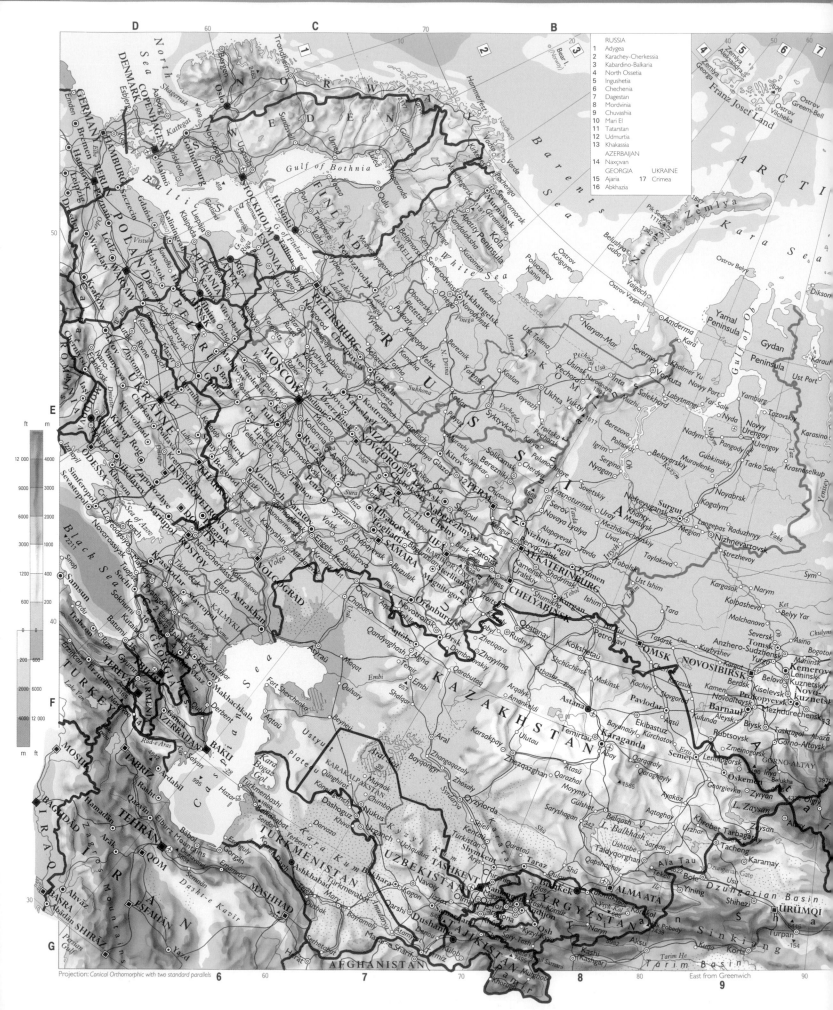

A · B · C

8 · 9 · 10 · 15 · 16 · 17 · 18 · 19

OCEAN

Laptev Sea · New Siberian Islands · East Siberian Sea · Wrangel I. · Chukot Range · Chukchi Sea · C. Dezhneva (East C.) · St. Lawrence I. (U.S.A.) · Bering Sea

Severnaya Zemlya · Ostrov Komsomolets · Ostrov Oktyabrskoy Revolyutsii · Ostrov Bolshevik · Ostrova Delonga · Ostrov Faddeyevsky · Ostrov Novaya Sibir · Ostrov Kotelnyf · Lyakhov Islands · Dmitri Laptev Str.

Vilkitski Strait · Chelyuskin · Byrranga Ra. · Taimyr Peninsula · Nordvik · L. Taimyr

Pevek · Ust Chaun · Ambarchik · Cherski · Bilibino · Anadyr · Gulf of Anadyr · Provideniya · Beringovskiy

Nizhne Kolymsk · Srednekolymsk · Omolon · Koryak Range · Sredinnyy Range

Kamchatka Peninsula · Ust-Kamchatsk · Klyuchi · Petropavlovsk-Kamchatskiy · Viluchinsk

Dudinka · Talnakh · Norilsk · Gory Putorana · Yessey · Kheta · Khatanga · Novorybnoye

Turukhansk · Noginsk · Lower Tunguska · Tura · Yukta

Verkhoyansk · Batagay · Cherski Range · Khandyga · Okhotskiy Perevoz · Arka · Magadan · Ola

Sea of Okhotsk · Sakhalin · Nikolayevsk-na-Amur · Aleksandrovsk-Sakhalinskiy · Yuzhno-Sakhalinsk · Korsakov

R U S S I A

Yartsevo · Severo-Yeniseyskiy · Stony Tunguska · Kuyumba · Mutoray · Vanavara · Yerbogachen · Yenyuka · Olekma · Stanovoy Range · Tynda · Skovorodino · Magdagachi

Yeniseysk · Lesosibirsk · Angara · Kodinsk · Boguchany · Chuna · Kondratyevo · Ust-Ilimsk · Makarovo · Ust-Kut · Kirensk · Korshunovo · Mama · Bodaybo · Chara · Ust-Nyukzha · Zeya

Achinsk · Zelenogorsk · Kansk · Ilanskiy · Krasnoyarsk · Krasnoyarsk Res. · Artemovsk · Salyan Mountains · Chernogorsk · Abakan · Minusinsk · Sayanogorsk

Nizhneudinsk · Tulun · Zima · Zalari · Usolye Sibirskoye · Cheremkhovo · Angarsk · Irkutsk · L. Baikal · Slyudyanka · Ulan Ude

Turan · Kyzyl · TUVA · Samagaltay · Toora-Khem · Munku-Sardyk · Hovsgol Nuur · Hatgal · Mörön

Hangayn Nuruu · Hentiyn Nuruu · Ulan Bator · Öndörhaan · Baruun-Urt · Tamsagbulag

M O N G O L I A

Uliastay · Tsetserleg · Altay · Bayanhongor · Arvayheer · Mandalgovi · Buyant-Uhaa · Choyr · Choybalsan

(Aerhtai Shan) · Dalandzadgad · G o b i · Erenhot

Hami · Gaxun Nur · BAOTOU · HOHHOT · ZHANGJIAKOU · Chengde · BEIJING · TANGSHAN

C H I N A · Xilinhot · Linxi · CHIFENG · SHENYANG · JINXI · ANSHAN · Yingkou · DALIAN

Manchouli · Hulun Nur · Hailar · Great Khingan Mts · Zalantun · Baicheng · Taonan · Siping · CHANGCHUN · FUSHUN · Tonghua

QIQIHAR · DAQING · Suihua · HARBIN · JILIN · Hegang · JIAMUSI · JIXI · MUDANJIANG · FUYU · FUYU · Manchuria

Bei'an · Nenjiang · Yichun · Songhua · Vladivostok

Khabarovsk · Sikhote-Alin Ra. · Komsomolsk-na-Amur · Birobidzhan · Blagoveshchensk · Heihe · Amur

Hokkaido · SAPPORO · Hakodate · Kuril Islands

NORTH KOREA · Ch'ongjin · Kimch'aek · Hamhung · Wonsan · PYONGYANG · NAMP'O · Dandong

SOUTH KOREA · SEOUL · INCHEON · DAEJON · DAEGU · BUSAN · GWANGJU

JAPAN · Akita · Niigata · Honshu · KOBE · OSAKA · KYOTO · Kanazawa · Toyama

Sea of Japan (East Sea)

Aomori · Hachinohe

10 · 11 · 12 · 13 · 14

100 0 100 200 300 400 500 600 700 800 km
100 0 100 200 300 400 500 miles
1:20 000 000

COPYRIGHT PHILIP'S

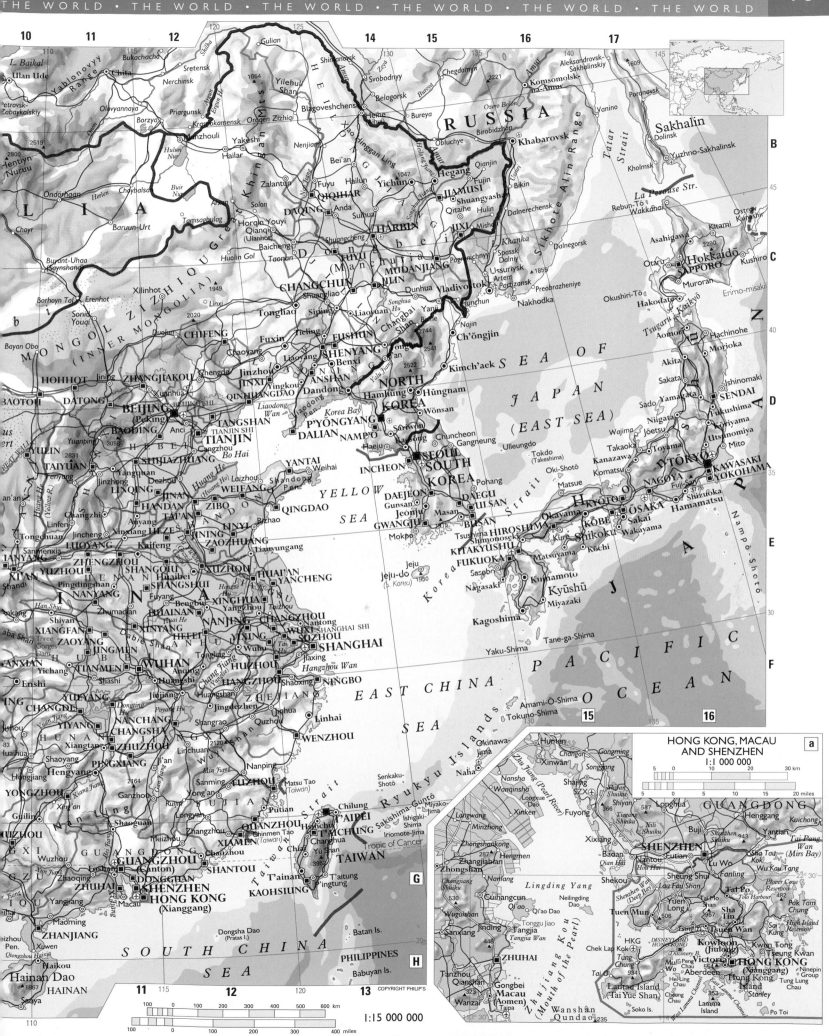

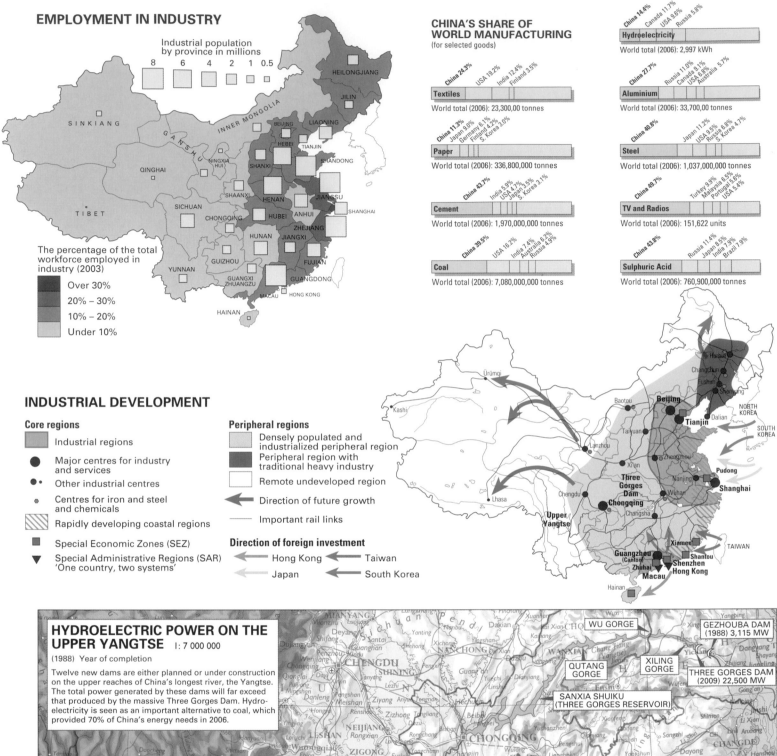

EMPLOYMENT IN INDUSTRY

Industrial population
by province in millions

8   6   4   2   1   0.5

The percentage of the total
workforce employed in
industry (2003)

- Over 30%
- 20% – 30%
- 10% – 20%
- Under 10%

CHINA'S SHARE OF WORLD MANUFACTURING
(for selected goods)

Textiles — China 24.3% | USA 19.2% | India 12.4% | Finland 3.5%
World total (2006): 23,300,00 tonnes

Paper — China 11.3% | Japan 9.0% | Germany 6.1% | Finland 4.2% | S. Korea 3.0%
World total (2006): 336,800,000 tonnes

Cement — China 43.7% | India 5.9% | USA 4.7% | Japan 3.5% | S. Korea 3.1%
World total (2006): 1,970,000,000 tonnes

Coal — China 39.5% | USA 16.2% | India 7.4% | Australia 6.2% | Russia 4.9%
World total (2006): 7,080,000,000 tonnes

Hydroelectricity — China 14.4% | Canada 11.7% | USA 9.6% | Russia 5.8%
World total (2006): 2,997 kWh

Aluminium — China 27.7% | Russia 11.0% | Canada 9.1% | USA 6.8% | Australia 5.7%
World total (2006): 33,700,00 tonnes

Steel — China 40.8% | Japan 11.2% | USA 9.5% | Russia 6.8% | S. Korea 4.7%
World total (2006): 1,037,000,000 tonnes

TV and Radios — China 49.7% | Turkey 9.9% | Malaysia 6.5% | Portugal 5.6% | USA 5.4%
World total (2006): 151,622 units

Sulphuric Acid — China 43.8% | Russia 11.4% | Japan 8.5% | India 7.9% | Brazil 7.9%
World total (2006): 760,900,000 tonnes

INDUSTRIAL DEVELOPMENT

Core regions

- Industrial regions
- ● Major centres for industry and services
- ●·· Other industrial centres
- ● Centres for iron and steel and chemicals
- Rapidly developing coastal regions
- ■ Special Economic Zones (SEZ)
- ▼ Special Administrative Regions (SAR) 'One country, two systems'

Peripheral regions

- Densely populated and industrialized peripheral region
- Peripheral region with traditional heavy industry
- Remote undeveloped region
- ← Direction of future growth
- — Important rail links

Direction of foreign investment
- ← Hong Kong   ← Taiwan
- ← Japan   ← South Korea

HYDROELECTRIC POWER ON THE UPPER YANGTSE   1: 7 000 000

(1988) Year of completion

Twelve new dams are either planned or under construction
on the upper reaches of China's longest river, the Yangtse.
The total power generated by these dams will far exceed
that produced by the massive Three Gorges Dam. Hydroelectricity is seen as an important alternative to coal, which
provided 70% of China's energy needs in 2006.

WU GORGE

GEZHOUBA DAM (1988) 3,115 MW

QUTANG GORGE

XILING GORGE

THREE GORGES DAM (2009) 22,500 MW

SANXIA SHUIKU (THREE GORGES RESERVOIR)

UPPER JINSHA DAMS (2020) 8,900 MW

XIANGJJIABA DAM (2015) 6,000 MW

LIYUAN DAM

MIDDLE JINSHA DAMS (2018) 21,150 MW

XILUODU DAM (2015) 12,600 MW

LIANGJIAREN DAM

AHAI DAM

HUTIAOXIA DAM

JINANQIAO DAM

BAIHETAN DAM (2015) 14,000 MW

GUANYINGYAN DAM

LONGKAIKOU DAM

LUDILA DAM

WUDONGDE DAM (2015) 7,400 MW

WORLD'S TEN LARGEST HYDROELECTRIC POWER STATIONS

(1986) Year of completion
1. Three Gorges Dam, China (2009) 22,500 MW
2. Itaipu, Brazil/Paraguay (2003) 14,000 MW
3. Guri, Venezuela (1986) 10,200 MW
4. Tucuruí, Brazil (1984) 8,370 MW
5. Sayano Shushenskaya, Russia (1989) 6,400 MW
6. Grand Coulee, USA (1942) 6,809 MW
7. Krasnoyarskaya, Russia (972) 6,000 MW
8. Robert-Bourassa, Canada (1981) 5,616 MW
9. Churchill Falls, Canada (1971) 5,429 MW
10. Longtan Dam, China (2009) 6,300 MW

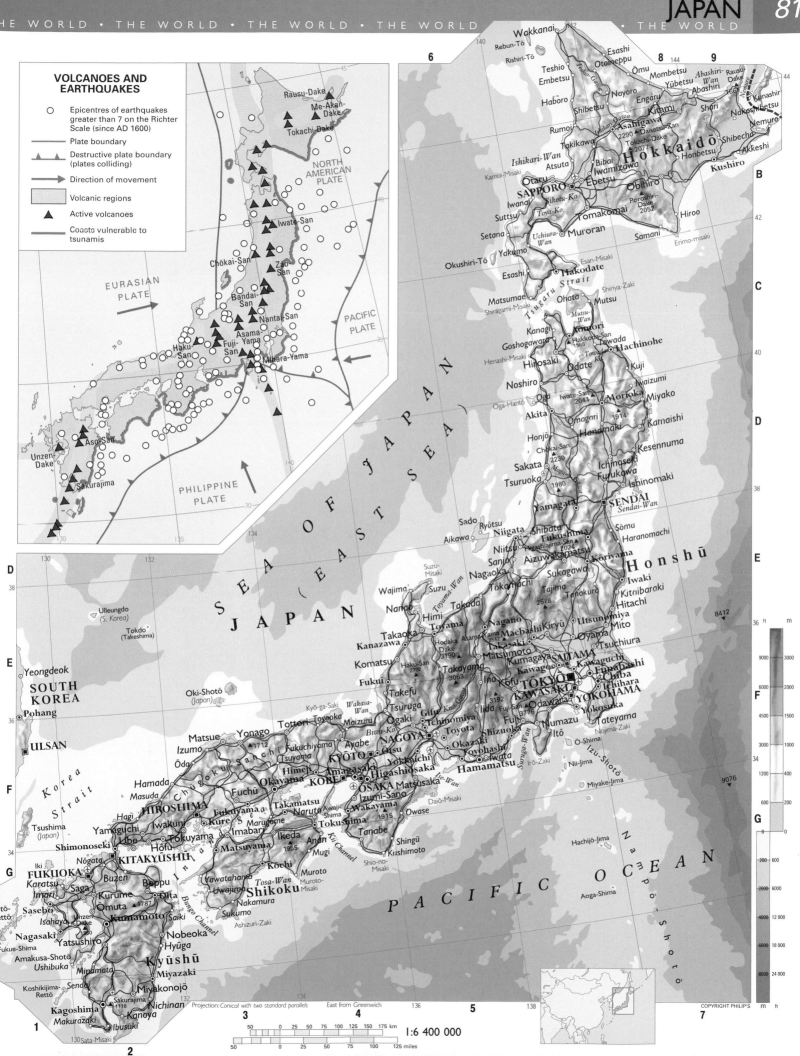

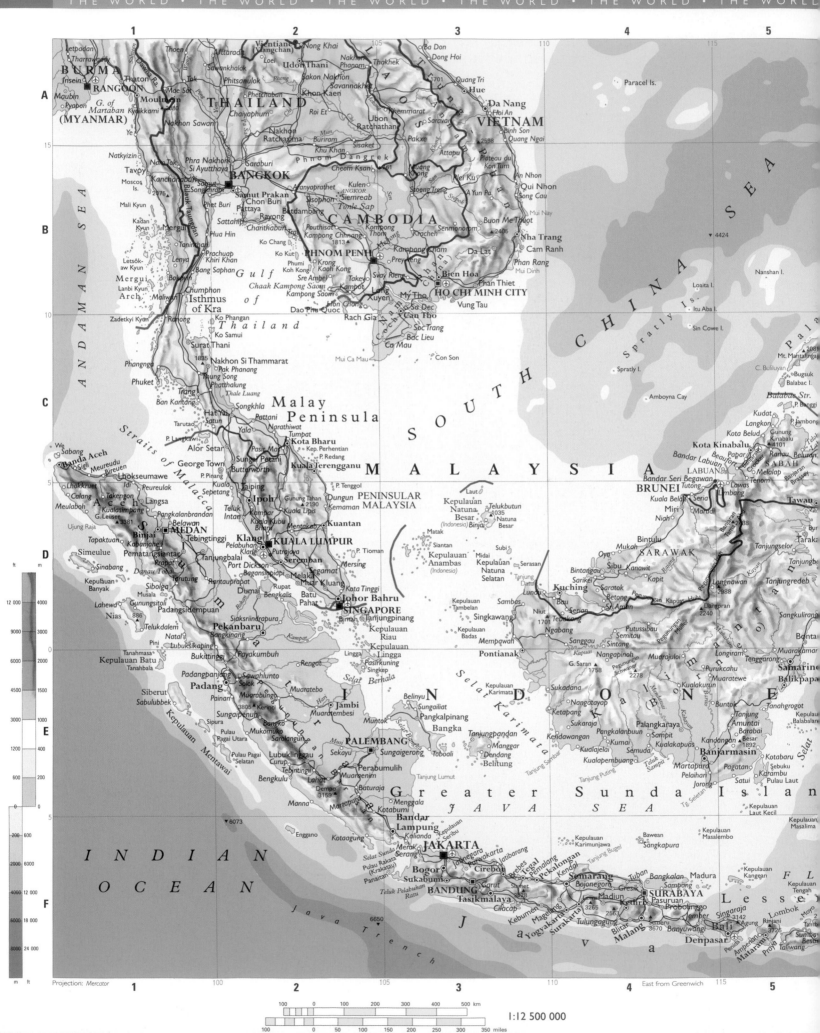

Projection: Mercator

1:12 500 000

East from Greenwich

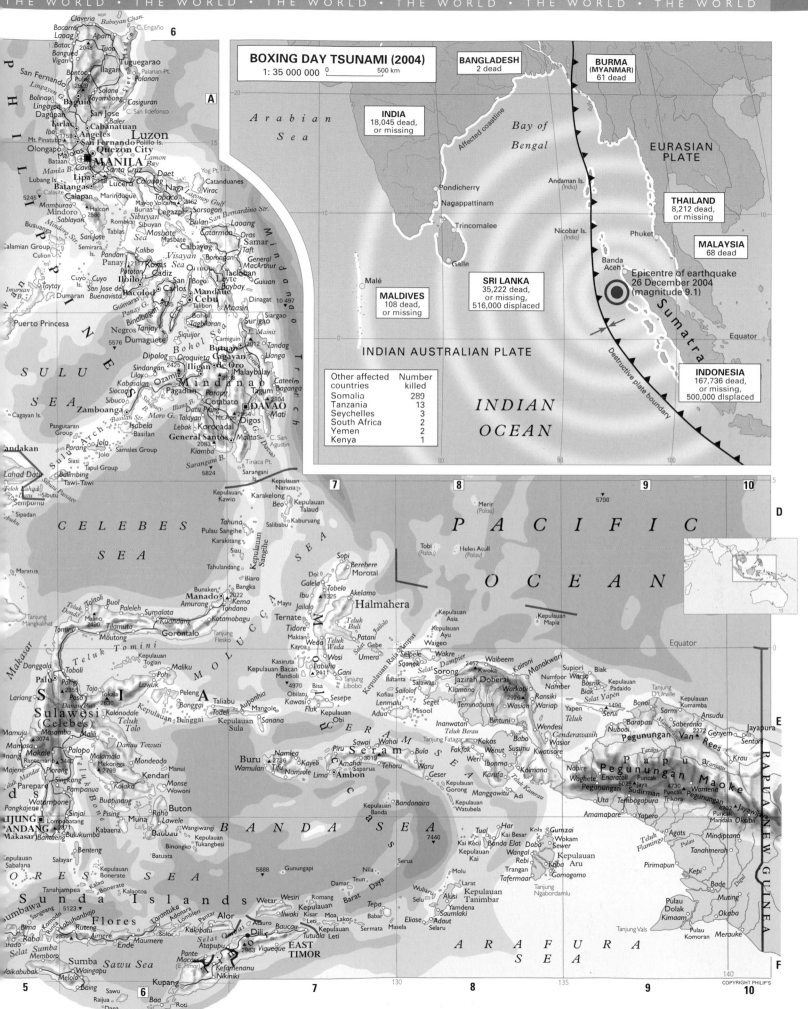

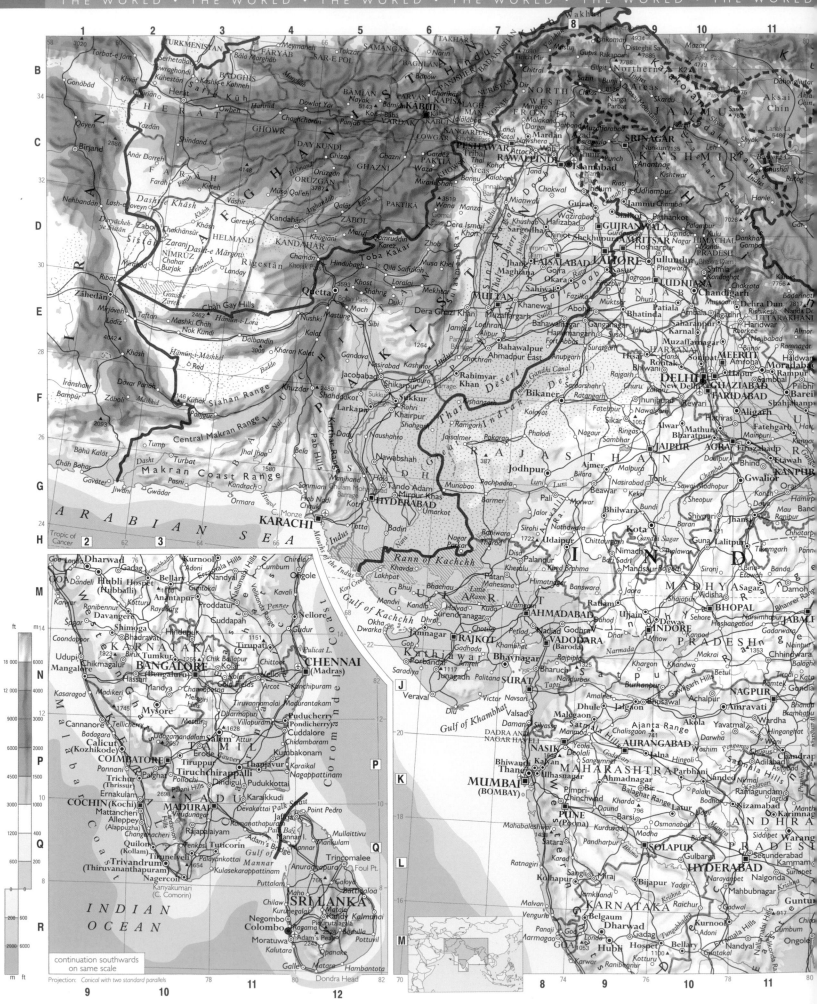

continuation southwards on same scale

Projection: Conical with two standard parallels

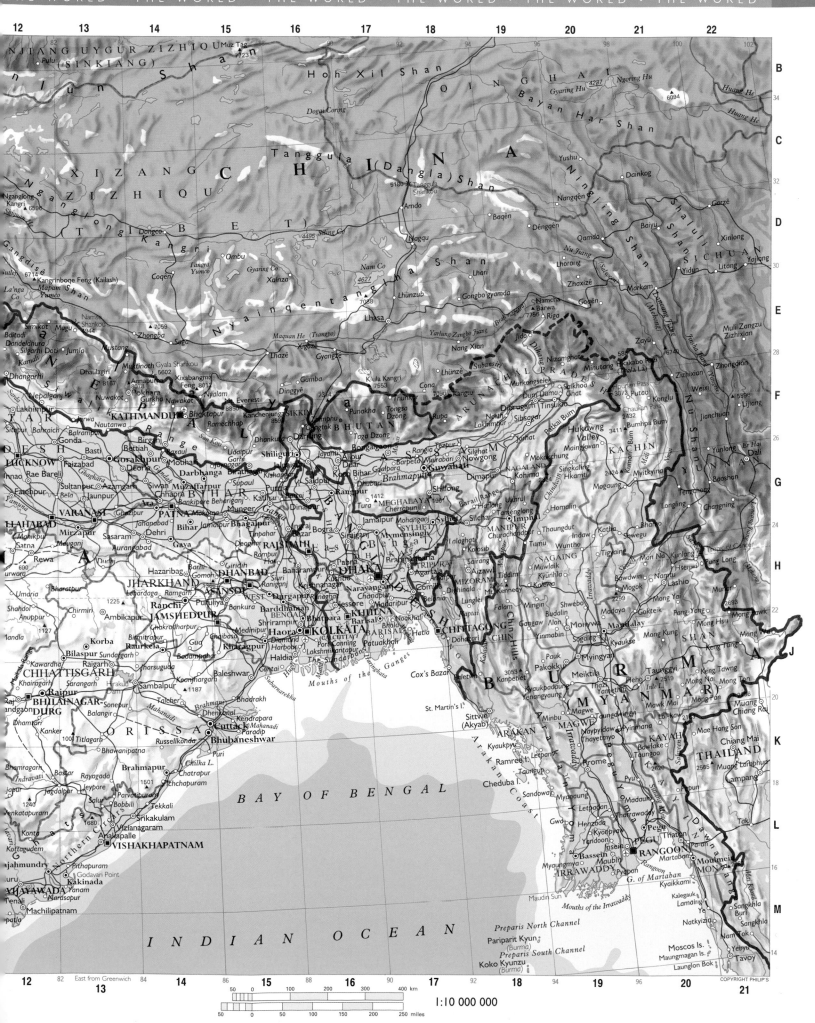

1:10 000 000

COPYRIGHT PHILIP'S

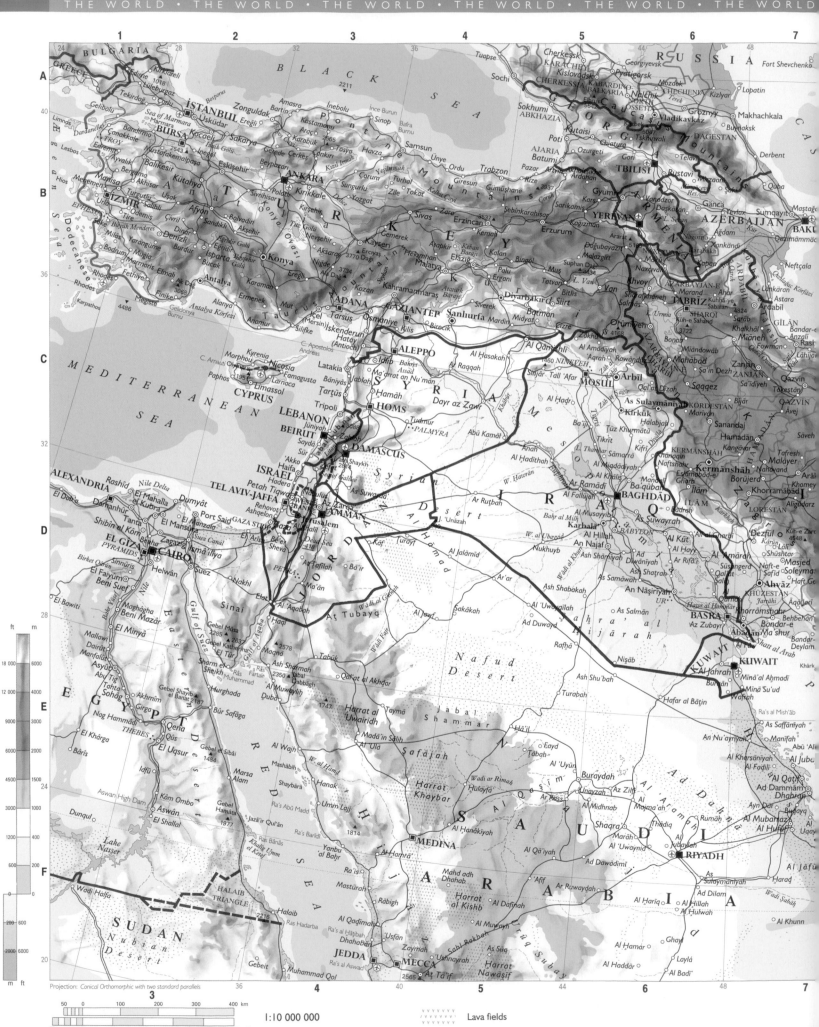

Projection: Conical Orthomorphic with two standard parallels

1:10 000 000

v v v v v
v v v v v v   Lava fields
v v v v v

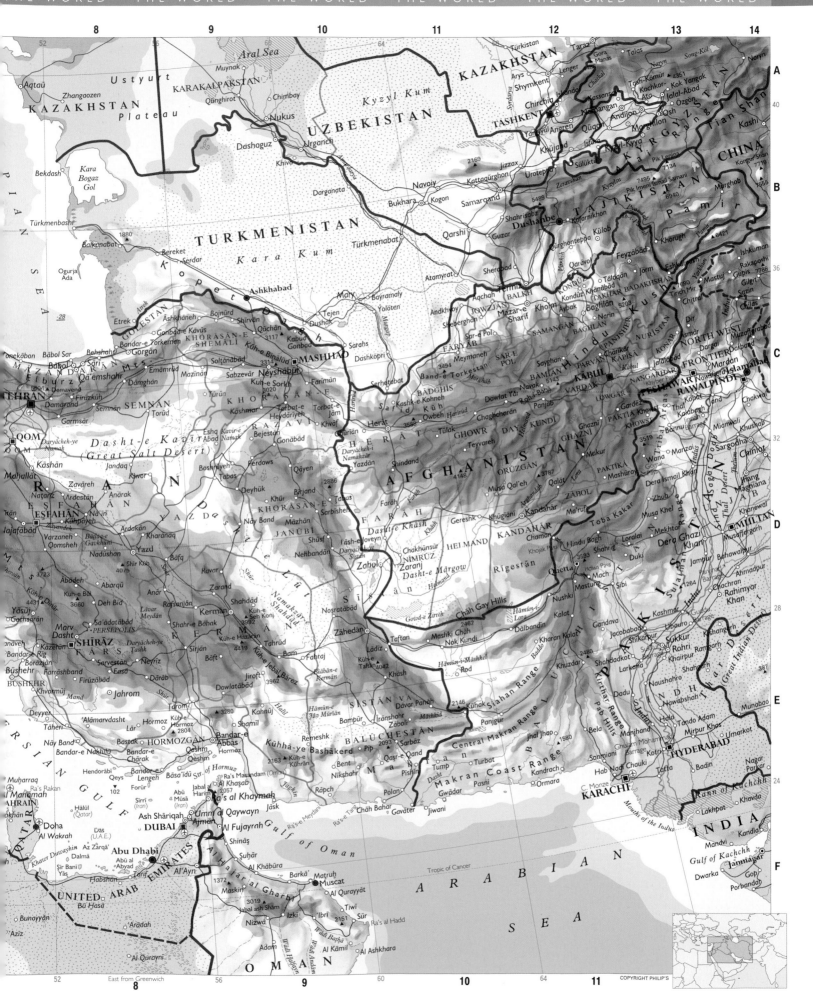

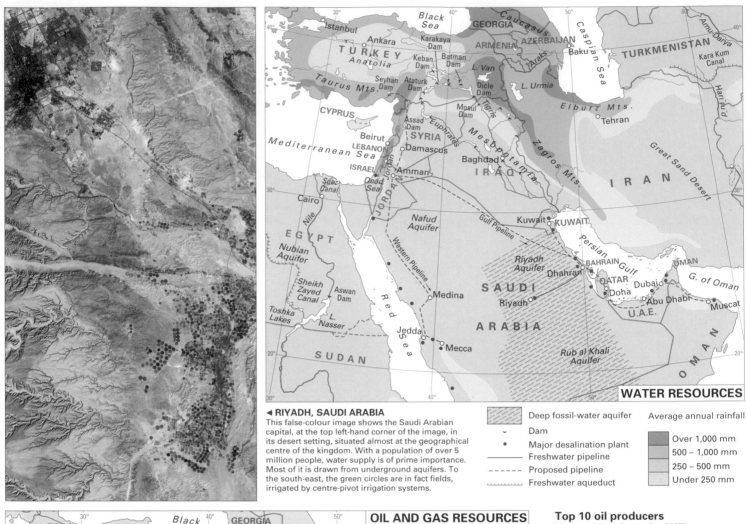

◄ RIYADH, SAUDI ARABIA
This false-colour image shows the Saudi Arabian capital, at the top left-hand corner of the image, in its desert setting, situated almost at the geographical centre of the kingdom. With a population of over 5 million people, water supply is of prime importance. Most of it is drawn from underground aquifers. To the south-east, the green circles are in fact fields, irrigated by centre-pivot irrigation systems.

WATER RESOURCES

- Deep fossil-water aquifer
- Dam
- Major desalination plant
- Freshwater pipeline
- Proposed pipeline
- Freshwater aqueduct

Average annual rainfall
- Over 1,000 mm
- 500 – 1,000 mm
- 250 – 500 mm
- Under 250 mm

OIL AND GAS RESOURCES

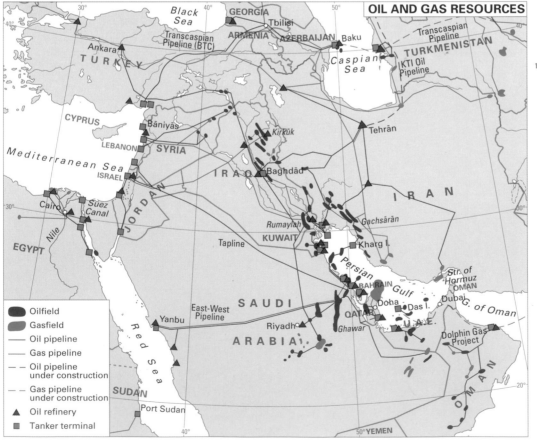

- Oilfield
- Gasfield
- Oil pipeline
- Gas pipeline
- Oil pipeline under construction
- Gas pipeline under construction
- ▲ Oil refinery
- ■ Tanker terminal

Top 10 oil producers
(thousand barrels per day 2007)

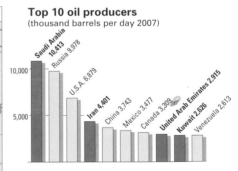

Saudi Arabia 10,413; Russia 9,978; U.S.A. 6,879; Iran 4,401; China 3,743; Mexico 3,477; Canada 3,309; United Arab Emirates 2,915; Kuwait 2,626; Venezuela 2,613

Oil production by region

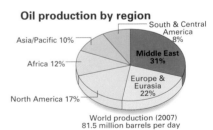

Middle East 31%; Europe & Eurasia 22%; North America 17%; Africa 12%; Asia/Pacific 10%; South & Central America 8%

World production (2007) 81.5 million barrels per day

Oil reserves by region

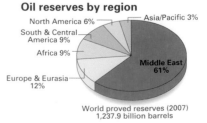

Middle East 61%; Europe & Eurasia 12%; Africa 9%; South & Central America 9%; North America 6%; Asia/Pacific 3%

World proved reserves (2007) 1,237.9 billion barrels

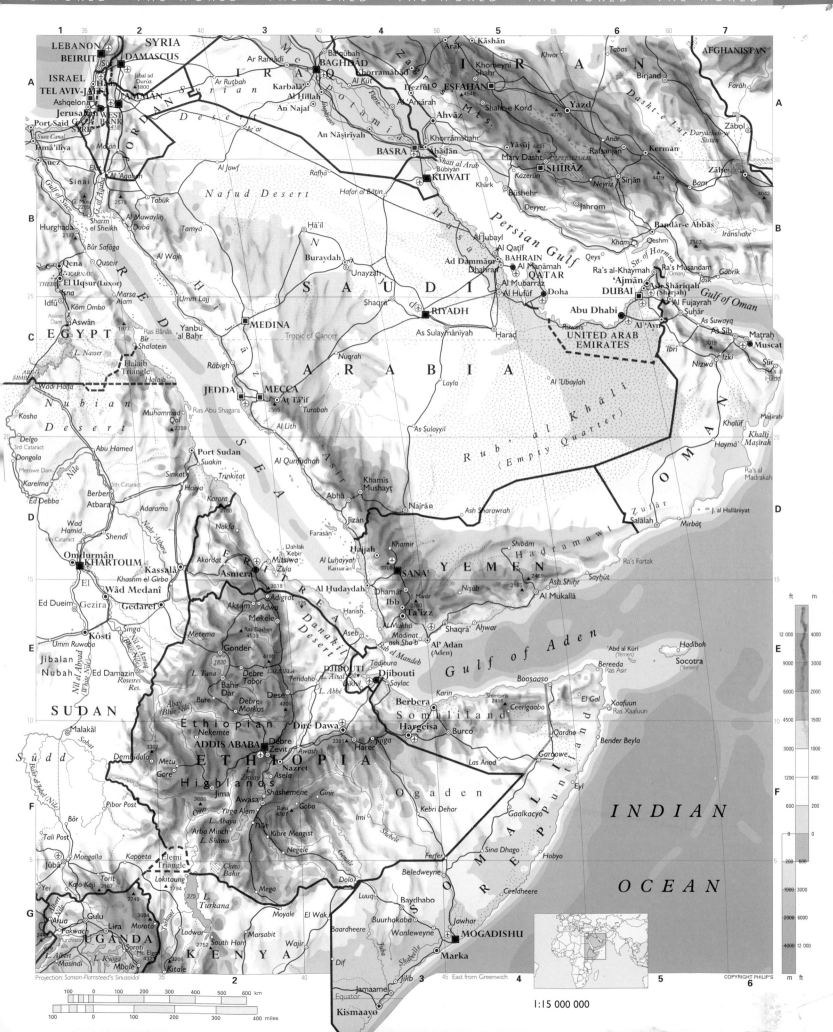

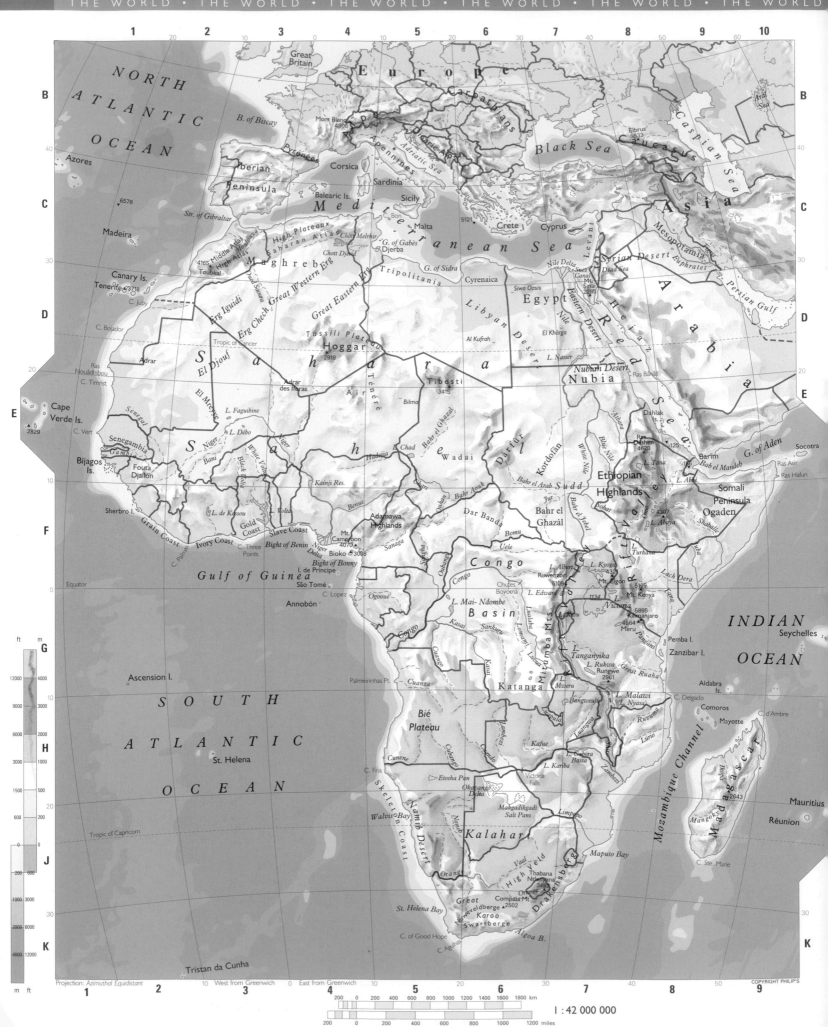

Projection: Azimuthal Equidistant

West from Greenwich | East from Greenwich

COPYRIGHT PHILIP'S

1 : 42 000 000

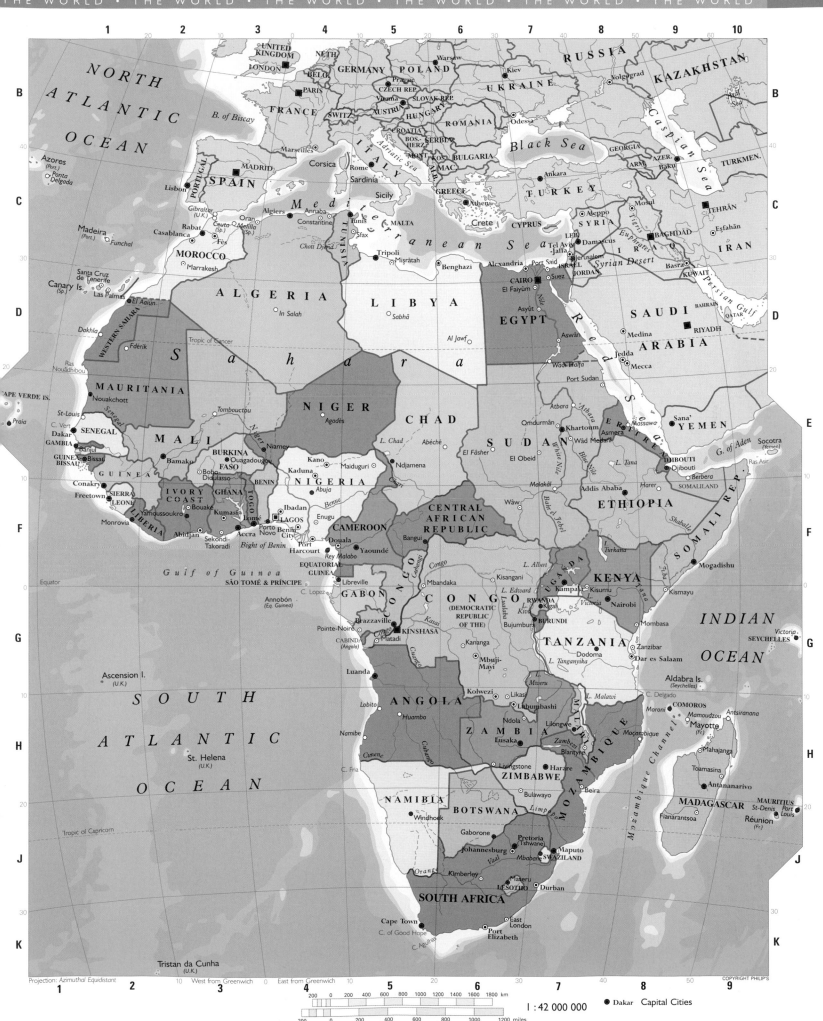

Projection: Azimuthal Equidistant

West from Greenwich / East from Greenwich

1 : 42 000 000

• Dakar Capital Cities

COPYRIGHT PHILIP'S

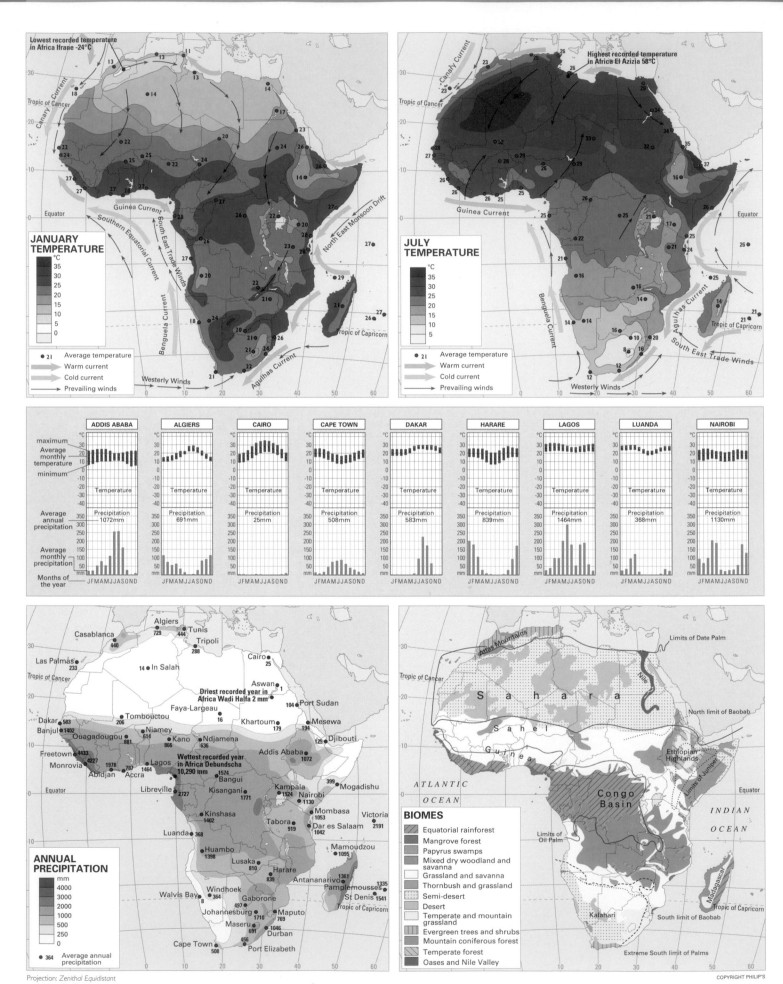

Lowest recorded temperature in Africa Ifrane -24°C

JANUARY TEMPERATURE

°C
35
30
25
20
15
10
5
0

• 21 Average temperature
→ Warm current
→ Cold current
→ Prevailing winds

Canary Current
Tropic of Cancer
Equator
Guinea Current
Southern Equatorial Current
South East Trade Winds
Benguela Current
North East Monsoon Drift
Agulhas Current
Westerly Winds
Tropic of Capricorn

Highest recorded temperature in Africa El Azizia 58°C

JULY TEMPERATURE

°C
35
30
25
20
15
10
5

• 21 Average temperature
→ Warm current
→ Cold current
→ Prevailing winds

Canary Current
Tropic of Cancer
Guinea Current
Benguela Current
Agulhas Current
South East Trade Winds
Westerly Winds
Equator
Tropic of Capricorn

ADDIS ABABA — maximum / Average monthly temperature / minimum — Temperature — Precipitation 1072mm — Average annual precipitation — Average monthly precipitation — Months of the year JFMAMJJASOND

ALGIERS — Temperature — Precipitation 691mm — JFMAMJJASOND

CAIRO — Temperature — Precipitation 25mm — JFMAMJJASOND

CAPE TOWN — Temperature — Precipitation 508mm — JFMAMJJASOND

DAKAR — Temperature — Precipitation 583mm — JFMAMJJASOND

HARARE — Temperature — Precipitation 839mm — JFMAMJJASOND

LAGOS — Temperature — Precipitation 1464mm — JFMAMJJASOND

LUANDA — Temperature — Precipitation 368mm — JFMAMJJASOND

NAIROBI — Temperature — Precipitation 1130mm — JFMAMJJASOND

Algiers 729
Tunis 444
Casablanca 440
Tripoli 288
Las Palmas 233
Cairo 25
14 • In Salah
Tropic of Cancer
Aswan 1
Driest recorded year in Africa Wadi Halfa 2 mm
Faya-Largeau
Port Sudan 104
Tombouctou 16
Khartoum 179
Mesewa 194
Dakar 583
Niamey
Kano 614
Ndjamena 636
Djibouti 129
Banjul 1402
Ouagadougou 881
866
Addis Ababa 1072
Freetown 4433
4227
Lagos 1464
Wettest recorded year in Africa Debundscha 10,290 mm
Bangui 1574
399 • Mogadishu
Monrovia 1978
787
Accra
Abidjan
Libreville 2727
Kisangani 1402
Kampala 1524
Nairobi 1771
1130
Kinshasa
Tabora 919
Mombasa 1053
Victoria 2191
Luanda 368
Dar es Salaam 1042
Huambo 1398
Mamoudzou 1095
Lusaka 810
Harare 839
Antananarivo 1361
Pamplemousses 1335
St Denis 1541
Windhoek 364
Walvis Bay 8
Gaborone 497
Johannesburg 1710
Maputo 769
Maseru 1046
Durban 456
Cape Town 508
Port Elizabeth

ANNUAL PRECIPITATION

mm
4000
3000
2000
1000
500
250
0

• 364 Average annual precipitation

Atlas Mountains
Limits of Date Palm
Tropic of Cancer
Sahara
Nile
North limit of Baobab
Sahel
Guinea
Ethiopian Highlands
Limits of Juniper
ATLANTIC OCEAN
Congo Basin
Equator
INDIAN OCEAN
Limits of Oil Palm
Kalahari
South limit of Baobab
Madagascar
Tropic of Capricorn
Extreme South limit of Palms

BIOMES

- Equatorial rainforest
- Mangrove forest
- Papyrus swamps
- Mixed dry woodland and savanna
- Grassland and savanna
- Thornbush and grassland
- Semi-desert
- Desert
- Temperate and mountain grassland
- Evergreen trees and shrubs
- Mountain coniferous forest
- Temperate forest
- Oases and Nile Valley

Projection: Zenithal Equidistant

COPYRIGHT PHILIP'S

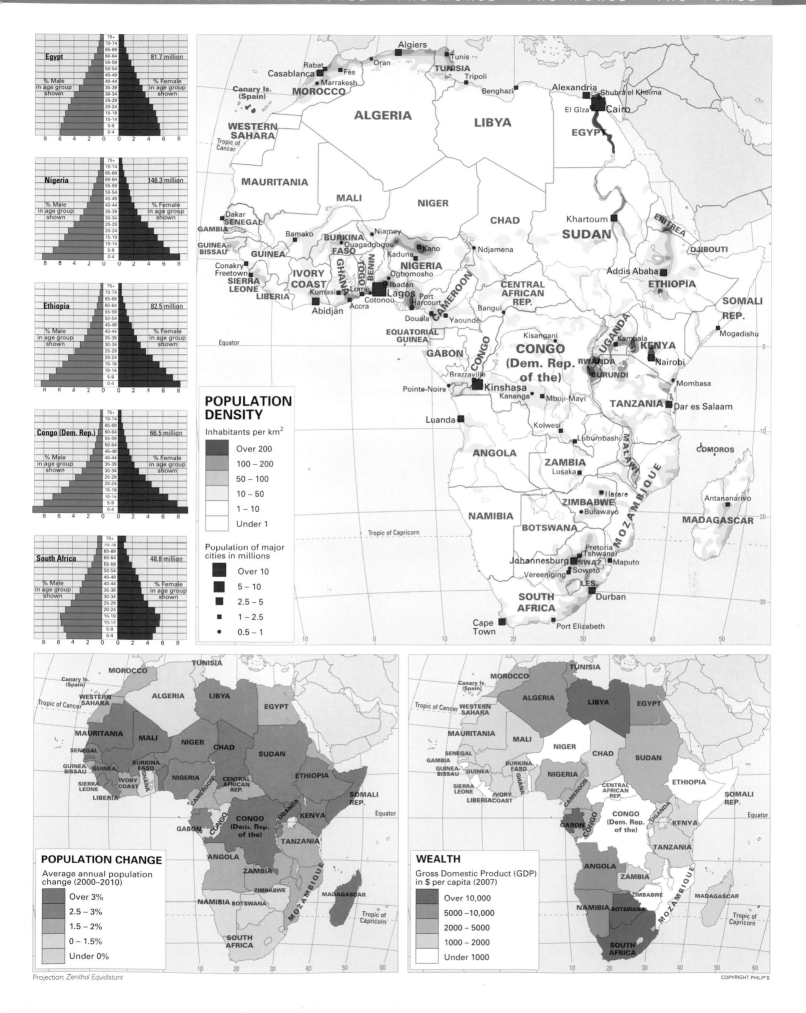

Egypt   81.7 million
% Male in age group shown   % Female in age group shown

Nigeria   146.3 million
% Male in age group shown   % Female in age group shown

Ethiopia   82.5 million
% Male in age group shown   % Female in age group shown

Congo (Dem. Rep.)   66.5 million
% Male in age group shown   % Female in age group shown

South Africa   48.8 million
% Male in age group shown   % Female in age group shown

POPULATION DENSITY

Inhabitants per km²

- Over 200
- 100 – 200
- 50 – 100
- 10 – 50
- 1 – 10
- Under 1

Population of major cities in millions

- Over 10
- 5 – 10
- 2.5 – 5
- 1 – 2.5
- 0.5 – 1

POPULATION CHANGE

Average annual population change (2000–2010)

- Over 3%
- 2.5 – 3%
- 1.5 – 2%
- 0 – 1.5%
- Under 0%

WEALTH

Gross Domestic Product (GDP) in $ per capita (2007)

- Over 10,000
- 5000 – 10,000
- 2000 – 5000
- 1000 – 2000
- Under 1000

Projection: Zenithal Equidistant

COPYRIGHT PHILIP'S

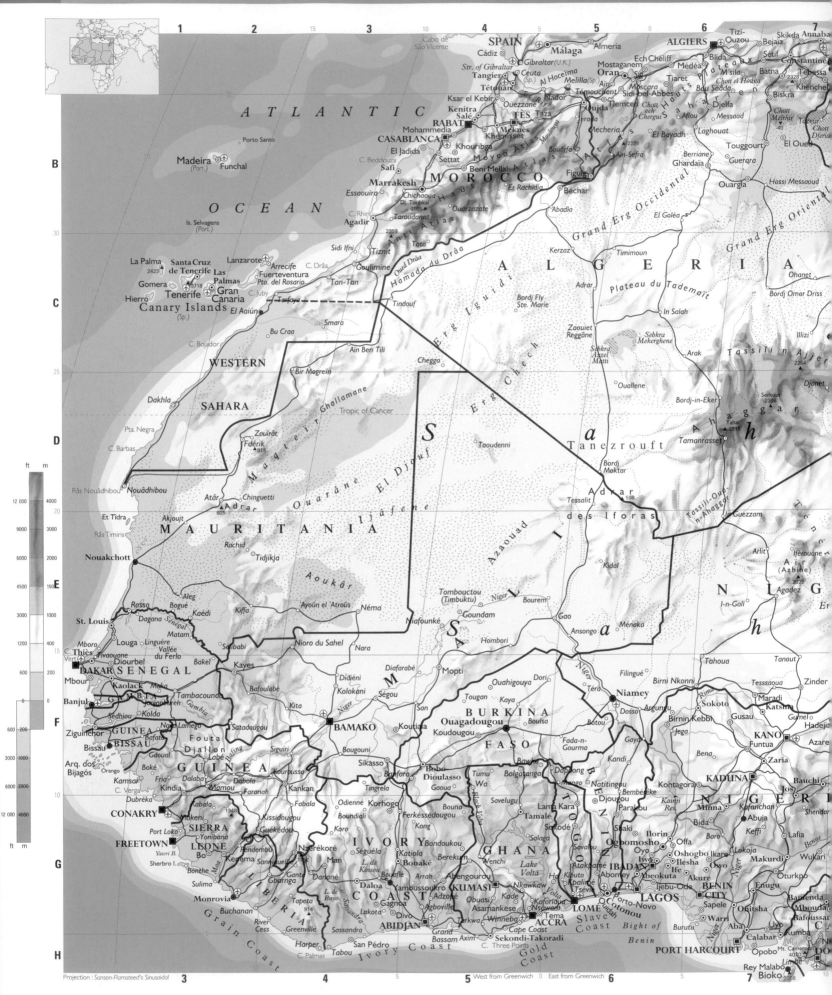

1:15 000 000

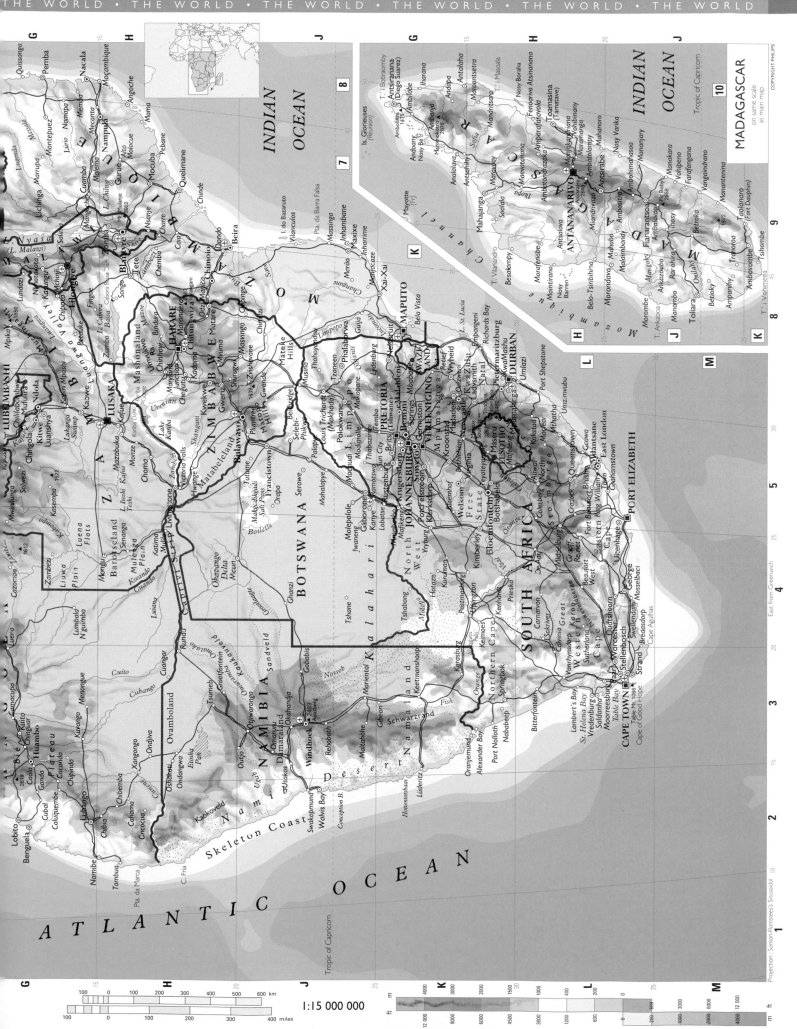

MADAGASCAR
on same scale
as main map

10

COPYRIGHT PHILIPS

INDIAN
OCEAN

INDIAN
OCEAN

ATLANTIC OCEAN

Projection : Sanson-Flamsteen's Sinusoidal

1:15 000 000

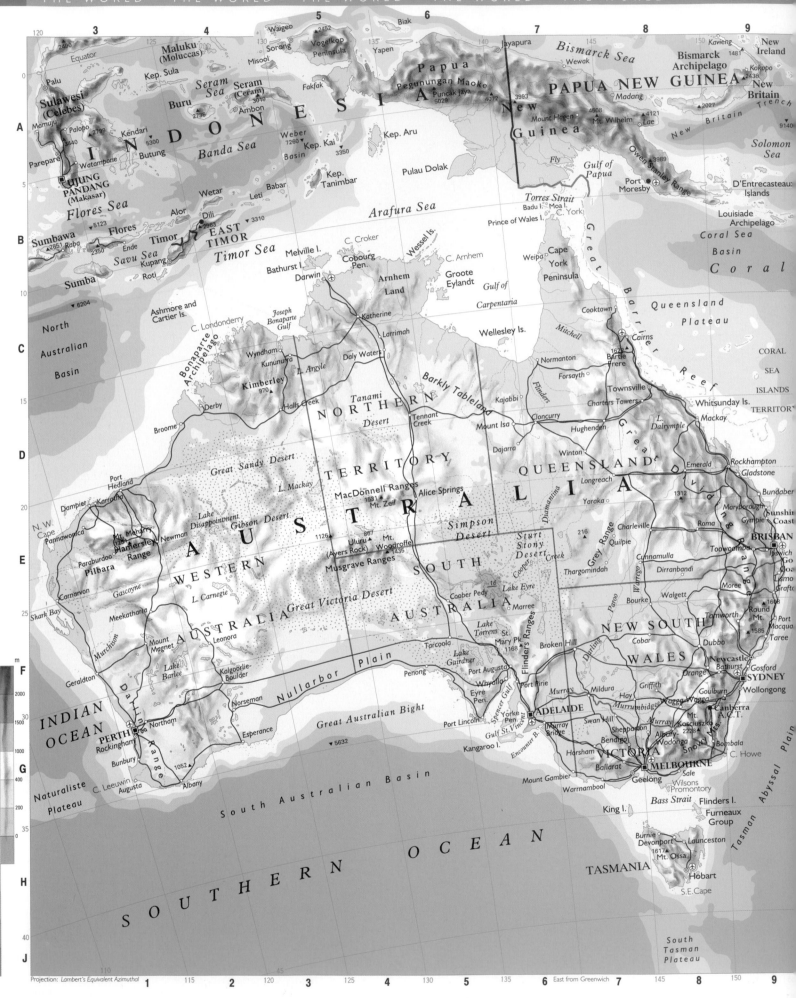

Projection: Lambert's Equivalent Azimuthal

11   12   13   14   15   16

M e l a n e s i a

Ontong Java
Plateau

Solomon Rise

2743 Bougainville
Mt. Balbi
Shortland Is.
1067
Yella Lavella
Choiseul
Santa Isabel
SOLOMON
1219
New
Georgia Is.
Vangunu
Russell Is.
Florida
1432
Is.
Malaita
2439
Honiara
ISLANDS
Guadalcanal
Makira
(San Cristóbal)
1250
Bellona
Pocklington
Reef
Rennell
South Solomon Trench
7223
Reef Is.
Duff Is.
Nendo
Santa Cruz
Is.
9165
Vanikoro
Fataka
Tikopia

Sea

Is. Torres
Vanua Lava
Is. Banks
Gaua
Espíritu Santo
1879
VANUATU
Malakula
863
(New Hebrides)
Epi
Île D'Entrecasteaux
Shepherd Is.
Port Vila
Efate
Île
Bélep
Erromango
Îles Chesterfield
1084
Tanna
4628
Î. Lifou
Aneityum
New
Caledonia
La Foa
(Fr.)
Nouméa
Yate
Î. Maré
Î. des Pins
Î. Matthew

Vitiaz Trench

W e s t
F i j i
B a s i n

Ceve-i-Ra

Rotuma

Mata-Utu
Uvea
Wallis & Futuna
Horn
(Fr.)
Alofi

Vanua Levu
1031
Taveuni
Viti Levu
FIJI
1323
Suva
Kadavu
Lau Group
Lau Ridge
Lau Basin

Niuafo'ou
Niua
Group
Niuatoputapu

Vava'u Group
Late
Ha'apai Group
TONGA
Nuku'alofa
Eua
Tongatapu
Group
Ata

Tabiteuea
Beru
Nikunau
Onotoa
Tamana
Gilbert
Arorae
Is.
6195
K I R I B A T I

Namumea
Niutao
Nanumanga
Nui
Vaitupu
TUVALU
(Ellice Is.)
Funafuti
Fongafale
Nukulaelae
Niulakita

Baker I.
(U.S.A.)
Equator

Winslow
Reef
McKean
Abariringa
Birnie
Enderbury
Nikumaroro
Phoenix Is.
Orona
Rawaki
Carondelet
Reef
Manra

Atafu
Nukunonu
Tokelau Is.
(N.Z.)
Fakaofo

International Date Line

SAMOA
Savai'i
1858
Apia
Upolu
Pago
Tutuila
Pago
American
Samoa
(U.S.A.)

Alofi
Niue
(N.Z.)

10 882
Tonga Trench

P A C I F I C

Lord Howe Seamount Chain

Caledonia Trough

Norfolk Ridge

South New Hebrides Trench

5303

New

O C E A N

Tropic of Capricorn

Norfolk I.
(Austral.)
Norfolk
Basin

Lord Howe I.
(Austral.)
734

Lord Howe Rise

S o u t h
F i j i
B a s i n

Raoul I.
Kermadec Is.
(N.Z.)
Macauley I.
Curtis I.
10 047

Kermadec Trench

Colville Ridge

S o u t h w e s t
P a c i f i c
B a s i n

T a s m a n   S e a

5267

North C.
Kaitaia
Whangarei
AUCKLAND
Hamilton
Challenger
New Plymouth
Plateau
North Island
Bay of
Plenty
Tauranga
Rotorua
Gisborne
Ruapehu
1797
Napier
NEW
Wanganui
Palmerston
North
ZEALAND
Masterton
Nelson
Wellington
Greymouth
Blenheim
Cook Strait
South Island
Aoraki Mt. Cook
3753
Christchurch
Southern Alps
Chatham
Queenstown
Timaru
Rise
Chatham I.
Invercargill
Dunedin
Pitt I.
Chatham Is.
Stewart I.
(N.Z.)

International Date Line

COPYRIGHT PHILIP'S

1:20 000 000

100 0 100 200 300 400 500 600 700 800 km
100 0 100 200 300 400 500 miles

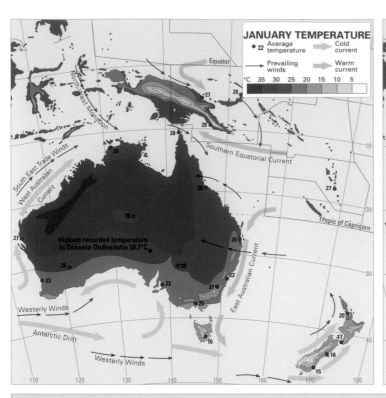

JANUARY TEMPERATURE

• 22 Average temperature
→ Prevailing winds
⇒ Cold current
⇒ Warm current

°C 35 30 25 20 15 10 5

Highest recorded temperature in Oceania Oodnadatta 50.7°C

North West Monsoon
South East Trade Winds
West Australian Current
Southern Equatorial Current
Equator
Tropic of Capricorn
East Australian Current
Westerly Winds
Antarctic Drift
Westerly Winds

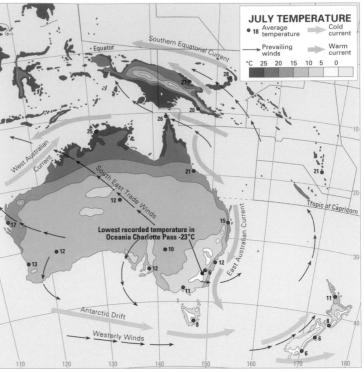

JULY TEMPERATURE

• 18 Average temperature
→ Prevailing winds
⇒ Cold current
⇒ Warm current

°C 25 20 15 10 5 0

Lowest recorded temperature in Oceania Charlotte Pass -23°C

Southern Equatorial Current
Equator
West Australian Current
South East Trade Winds
East Australian Current
Tropic of Capricorn
Antarctic Drift
Westerly Winds

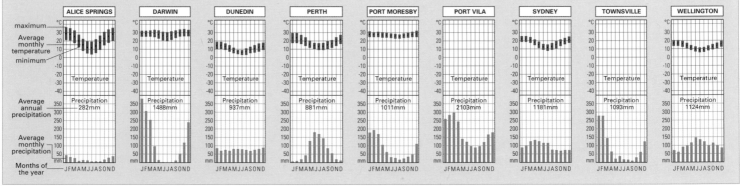

	ALICE SPRINGS	DARWIN	DUNEDIN	PERTH	PORT MORESBY	PORT VILA	SYDNEY	TOWNSVILLE	WELLINGTON
maximum	Temperature	Temperature	Temperature	Temperature	Temperature	Temperature	Temperature	Temperature	Temperature
Average monthly temperature									
minimum									
Average annual precipitation	Precipitation 282mm	Precipitation 1488mm	Precipitation 937mm	Precipitation 881mm	Precipitation 1011mm	Precipitation 2103mm	Precipitation 1181mm	Precipitation 1093mm	Precipitation 1124mm
Average monthly precipitation									
Months of the year	JFMAMJJASOND	JFMAMJJASOND	JFMAMJJASOND	JFMAMJJASOND	JFMAMJJASOND	JFMAMJJASOND	JFMAMJJASOND	JFMAMJJASOND	JFMAMJJASOND

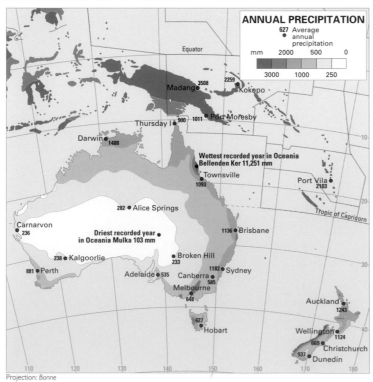

ANNUAL PRECIPITATION

• 627 Average annual precipitation

mm 2000 500 0
3000 1000 250

Equator
Madang 3508
2259 Kokopo
Thursday I 900 1011 Port Moresby
Darwin 1488
Wettest recorded year in Oceania Bellenden Ker 11,251 mm
Townsville 1093
Port Vila 2103
Tropic of Capricorn
282 Alice Springs
Carnarvon 236
Driest recorded year in Oceania Mulka 103 mm
1136 Brisbane
238 Kalgoorlie
Broken Hill 233
881 Perth
1182 Sydney
Adelaide 535
Canberra 585
Melbourne 648
Auckland 1243
627 Hobart
Wellington 1124
669 Christchurch
937 Dunedin

Projection: Bonne

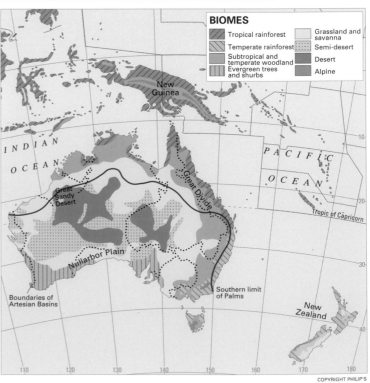

BIOMES

- Tropical rainforest
- Temperate rainforest
- Subtropical and temperate woodland
- Evergreen trees and shrubs
- Grassland and savanna
- Semi-desert
- Desert
- Alpine

New Guinea
INDIAN OCEAN
PACIFIC OCEAN
Great Sandy Desert
Great Divide
Nullarbor Plain
Tropic of Capricorn
Southern limit of Palms
Boundaries of Artesian Basins
New Zealand

COPYRIGHT PHILIP'S

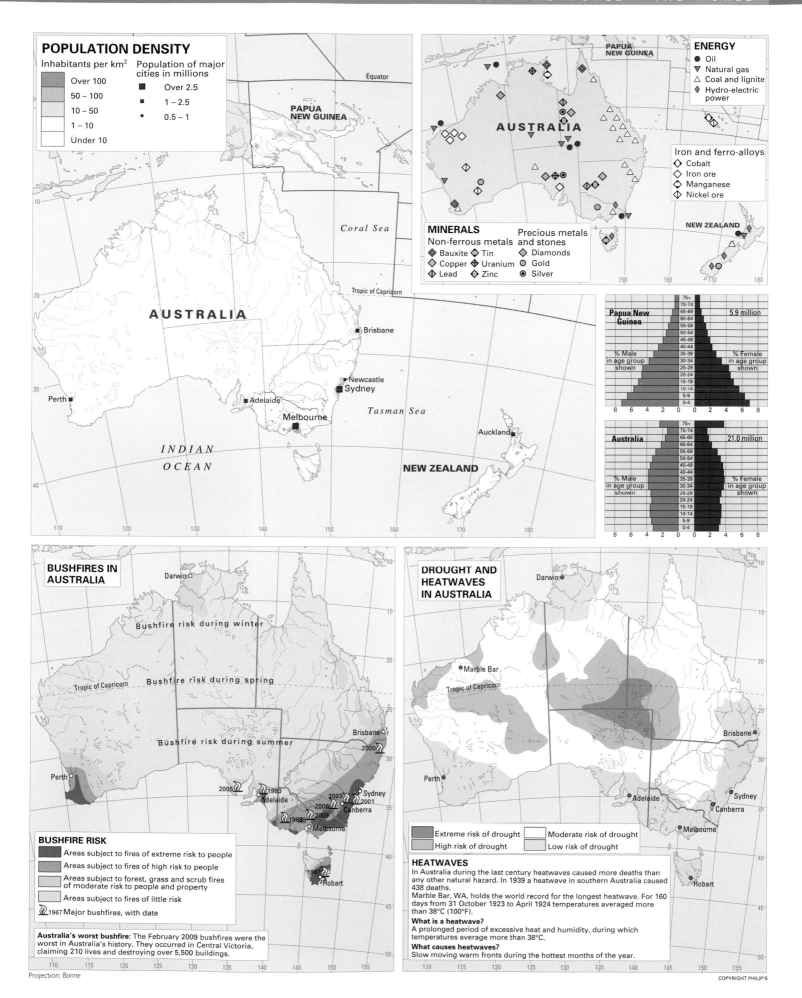

POPULATION DENSITY

Inhabitants per km²

	Over 100
	50 – 100
	10 – 50
	1 – 10
	Under 10

Population of major cities in millions

- ■ Over 2.5
- ▪ 1 – 2.5
- • 0.5 – 1

ENERGY

- ● Oil
- ▼ Natural gas
- △ Coal and lignite
- ◆ Hydro-electric power

Iron and ferro-alloys

- ◇ Cobalt
- ◇ Iron ore
- ◇ Manganese
- ◈ Nickel ore

MINERALS

Non-ferrous metals

- ◈ Bauxite
- ◇ Copper
- ◈ Lead

- ◇ Tin
- ◆ Uranium
- ◇ Zinc

Precious metals and stones

- ◇ Diamonds
- ● Gold
- ◉ Silver

Papua New Guinea — 5.9 million

Australia — 21.0 million

% Male in age group shown — % Female in age group shown

BUSHFIRES IN AUSTRALIA

Bushfire risk during winter

Bushfire risk during spring

Bushfire risk during summer

2000
2005
1983
2003
2006 2001
2009 Canberra
1983
Hobart 1967

BUSHFIRE RISK

- Areas subject to fires of extreme risk to people
- Areas subject to fires of high risk to people
- Areas subject to forest, grass and scrub fires of moderate risk to people and property
- Areas subject to fires of little risk
- 〰1967 Major bushfires, with date

Australia's worst bushfire: The February 2009 bushfires were the worst in Australia's history. They occurred in Central Victoria, claiming 210 lives and destroying over 5,500 buildings.

Projection: Bonne

DROUGHT AND HEATWAVES IN AUSTRALIA

- Extreme risk of drought
- High risk of drought
- Moderate risk of drought
- Low risk of drought

HEATWAVES

In Australia during the last century heatwaves caused more deaths than any other natural hazard. In 1939 a heatwave in southern Australia caused 438 deaths.

Marble Bar, WA, holds the world record for the longest heatwave. For 160 days from 31 October 1923 to April 1924 temperatures averaged more than 38°C (100°F).

What is a heatwave?
A prolonged period of excessive heat and humidity, during which temperatures average more than 38°C.

What causes heatwaves?
Slow moving warm fronts during the hottest months of the year.

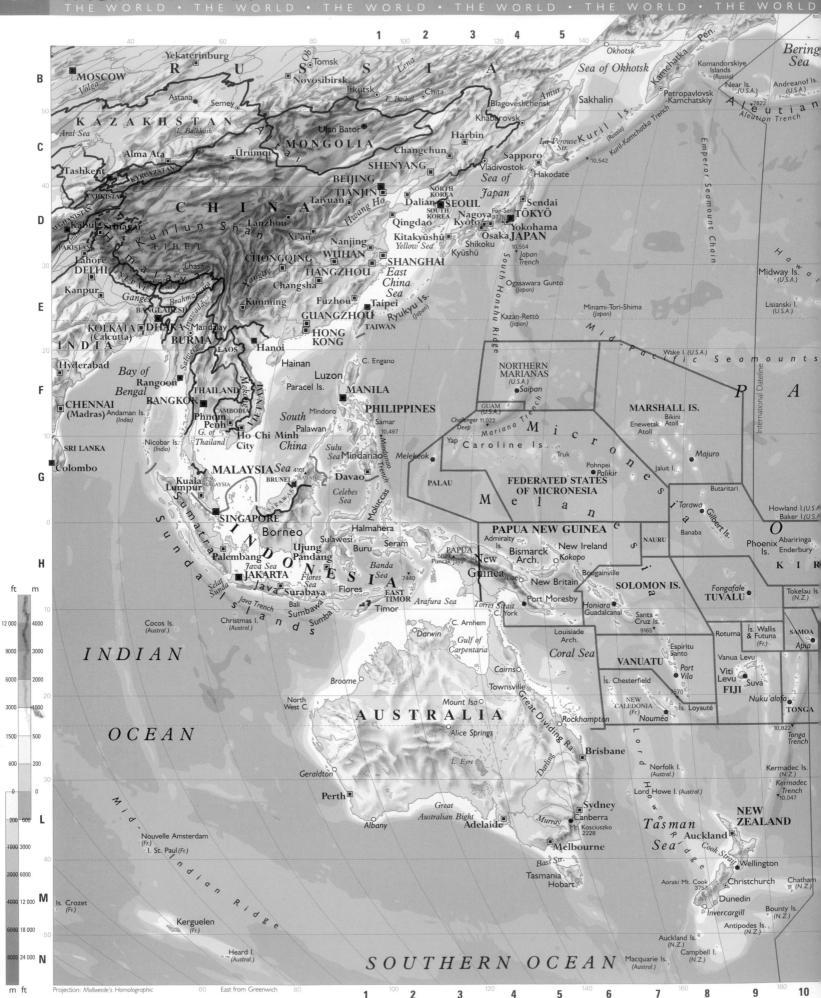

16 17 18 19 20

ALASKA
(U.S.A.)
Anchorage
Bristol Bay
Gulf of Alaska
Juneau
Prince of Wales I.
(U.S.A.) Prince Rupert
Queen Charlotte Is.
(Canada)
Is. (U.S.A.)

CANADA

Edmonton
L. Winnipeg
Newfoundland

Vancouver
Vancouver I.
Calgary
Regina
Winnipeg
L. Superior
Québec
St. Lawrence

NORTH

Victoria
Seattle
Portland
Boise
Minneapolis
Missouri
L. Michigan
Toronto
Detroit
L. Huron
Montréal
Ottawa
L. Ontario
Buffalo
Boston
St. John's

St. Louis
Salt Lake City
Denver
Kansas City
CHICAGO
Pittsburgh
Cincinnati
L. Erie
NEW YORK
PHILADELPHIA
Baltimore
Washington D.C.

ATLANTIC

Sacramento
SAN FRANCISCO
UNITED STATES
Oklahoma City
Memphis
Atlanta
Appalachian Mts.
C. Hatteras
Bermuda
(U.K.)

LOS ANGELES
San Diego
Phoenix
Dallas
Houston
Jacksonville

OCEAN

Ciudad Juárez
Mississippi
New Orleans
New Antonio
San Antonio
Gulf of Mexico
Miami
BAHAMAS
Sargasso Sea

Guadalupe
(Mex.)
Golfo de California
Baja California
Monterrey
Havana
Florida Str.
West Indies

Tropic of Cancer

Honolulu
O'ahu
HAWAI'I
(U.S.A.)
Hawai'i
C. San Lucas
Guadalajara
Yucatan Channel
CUBA
OCEAN

Johnston I.
(U.S.A.)
Is. de Revillagigedo
(Mex.)
MEXICO
Puebla
Mérida
JAMAICA
HAITI
DOMINICAN REP.
Leeward Is.

C I F I C
Acapulco
BELIZE
Kingston
PUERTO RICO
(U.S.A.)

North West Christmas I. Ridge
Palmyra Is.
(U.S.A.)
Teraina
Tabuaeran
Kiritimati
GUATEMALA
Guatemala
San Salvador
EL SALVADOR
HONDURAS
NICARAGUA
Managua
Caribbean Sea
BARBADOS
Windward Is.

O C E A N
Jarvis I.
(U.S.A.)
Malden I.
Equator
Barranquilla
San José
COSTA RICA
Colón
PANAMÁ
Maracaibo
Caracas
VENEZUELA

I B A T I
Starbuck I.
Galápagos
(Ecuador)
I. del Coco
(Costa Rica)
Medellín
Bogotá
COLOMBIA
Orinoco

Tongareva
Vostok I.
Caroline I.
(Millennium I.)
I. de Malpelo
(Colombia)
Quito
ECUADOR
Amazonas

Pukapuka
Manihiki
Flint I.
Guayaquil
C. Paliñas
Iquitos
BRAZIL

MER. AMOA (U.S.A.)
Suwarrow Is.
Société
Trujillo

Niue
(N.Z.)
Cook Is.
(N.Z.)
Papeete
Tahiti
uamotu
6369
PERU
Cuzco
L. Titicaca
Nevada Ancohuma
6550

Rarotonga
FRENCH POLYNESIA
Mururoa
Arequipa
6866
La Paz
BOLIVIA
Peru-
Arica

Tropic of Capricorn
Iquique
East Pacific Rise

Henderson I.
Antofagasta
PARAGUAY

Pitcairn I.
(U.K.)
8050
Trench
San Miguel de Tucumán
Asunción

Rapa
Sala-y-Gómez
(Chile)
(Chile)
San Ambrosio
(Chile)
PORTO ALEGRE

I. de Pascua
(Chile)
San Felix
(Chile)
Córdoba
Aconcagua
6962
Rosario
URUGUAY

Arch. de Juan Fernández
(Chile)
Valparaíso
SANTIAGO
BUENOS AIRES
Rio de la Plata
Montevideo

Concepción
ARGENTINA

SOUTH

Chile Rise
ATLANTIC

Pacific-Antarctic Ridge
Patagonia
6212
OCEAN

Punta Arenas
Magellan's Str.
Falkland Is.
(U.K.)
South Georgia
(U.K.)

Tierra del Fuego
C. Horn

11 12 13 14 15 16 17 18 19 20

West from Greenwich

Equatorial Scale 1:54 000 000

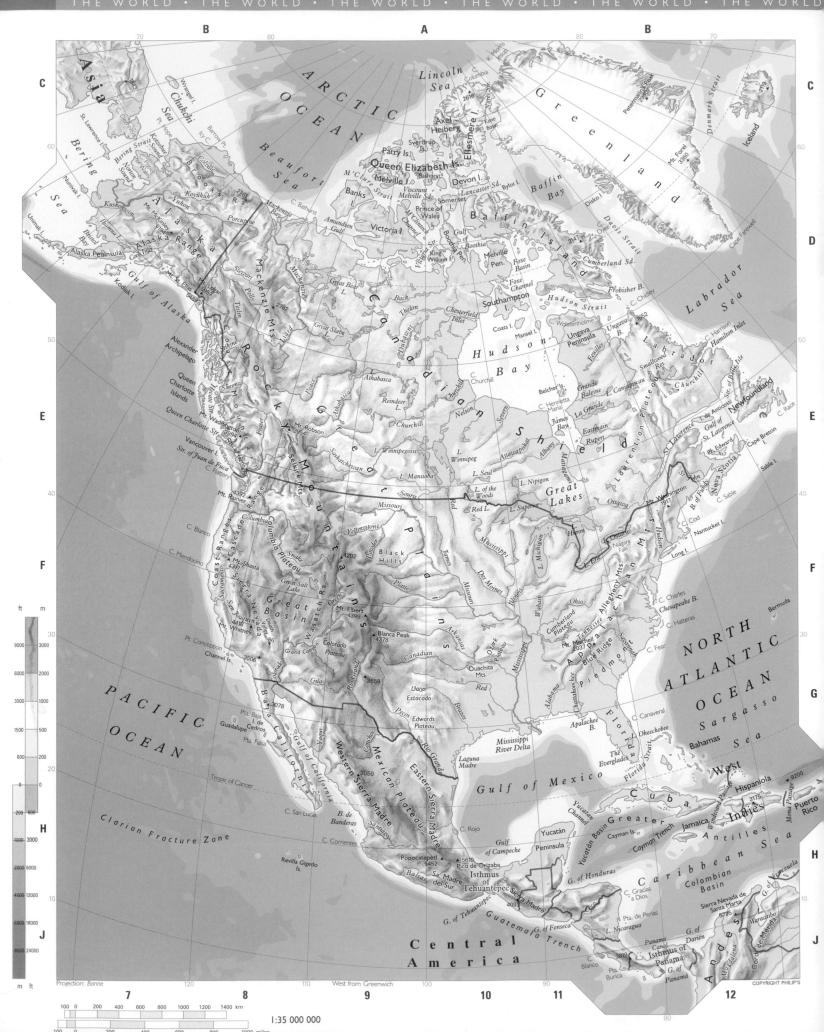

Projection: Bonne

West from Greenwich

1:35 000 000

COPYRIGHT PHILIP'S

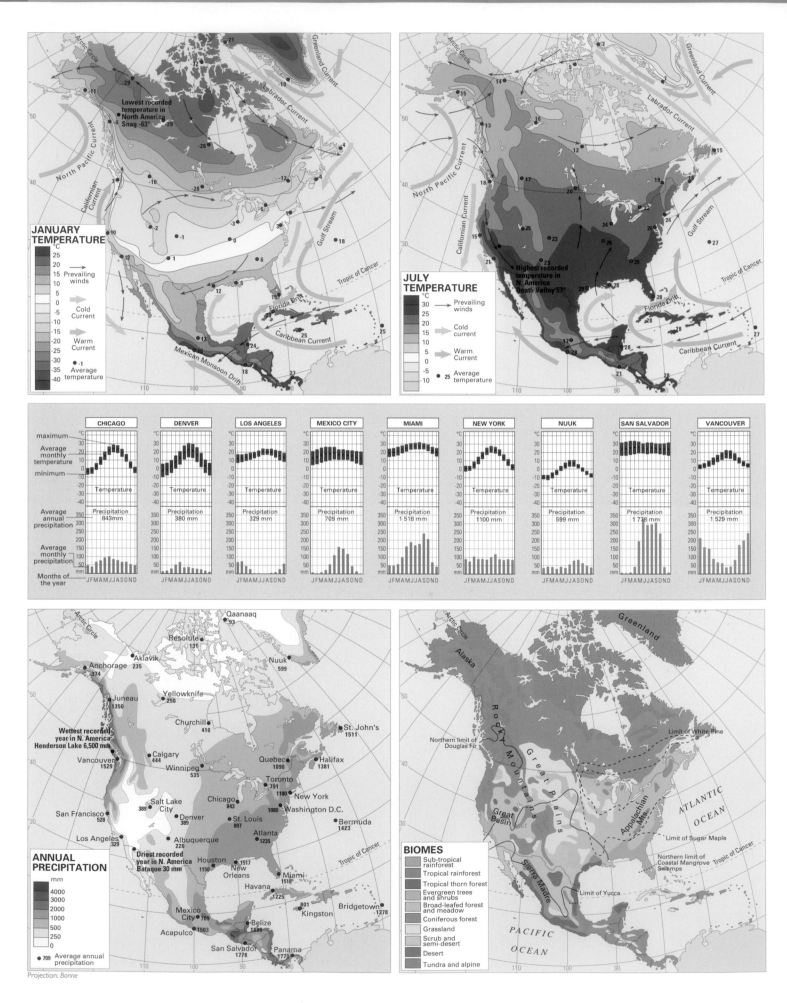

JANUARY TEMPERATURE
°C
25
20
15 Prevailing winds
10
5
0
-5 Cold Current
-10
-15
-20 Warm Current
-25
-30
-35 • -1 Average temperature
-40

Lowest recorded temperature in North America Snag -63°

Arctic Circle
North Pacific Current
Californian Current
Labrador Current
Greenland Current
Gulf Stream
Florida Drift
Caribbean Current
Mexican Monsoon Drift
Tropic of Cancer

JULY TEMPERATURE
°C
30
25
20 Prevailing winds
15
10 Cold current
5
0 Warm Current
-5
-10 • 25 Average temperature

Highest recorded temperature in N. America Death Valley 57°

Arctic Circle
North Pacific Current
Californian Current
Labrador Current
Greenland Current
Gulf Stream
Florida Drift
Caribbean Current
Tropic of Cancer

CHICAGO — Temperature — Precipitation 843mm
DENVER — Temperature — Precipitation 380 mm
LOS ANGELES — Temperature — Precipitation 329 mm
MEXICO CITY — Temperature — Precipitation 709 mm
MIAMI — Temperature — Precipitation 1 518 mm
NEW YORK — Temperature — Precipitation 1100 mm
NUUK — Temperature — Precipitation 599 mm
SAN SALVADOR — Temperature — Precipitation 1 778 mm
VANCOUVER — Temperature — Precipitation 1 529 mm

maximum
Average monthly temperature
minimum
Average annual precipitation
Average monthly precipitation
Months of the year
JFMAMJJASOND

ANNUAL PRECIPITATION
mm
4000
3000
2000
1000
500
250
0
• 709 Average annual precipitation

Qaanaaq 93
Resolute 131
Aklavik 235
Anchorage 374
Nuuk 599
Juneau 1350
Yellowknife 250
Churchill 410
St. John's 1511
Wettest recorded year in N. America Henderson Lake 6,500 mm
Calgary 444
Quebec 1090
Halifax 1381
Vancouver 1529
Winnipeg 535
Toronto 791
Salt Lake City 389
Chicago 843
New York 1100
San Francisco 528
Denver 389
St. Louis 897
Washington D.C. 1080
Bermuda 1423
Los Angeles 329
Albuquerque 226
Atlanta 1235
Driest recorded year in N. America Bataque 30 mm
Houston 1517
New Orleans 1150
Miami 1518
Havana 1225
Mexico City 709
Belize 1590
Kingston 801
Bridgetown 1278
Acapulco 1503
San Salvador 1778
Panama 1770
Arctic Circle
Tropic of Cancer

Projection: Bonne

BIOMES
Sub-tropical rainforest
Tropical rainforest
Tropical thorn forest
Evergreen trees and shrubs
Broad-leafed forest and meadow
Coniferous forest
Grassland
Scrub and semi-desert
Desert
Tundra and alpine

Greenland
Alaska
Rocky Mountains
Great Plains
Great Basin
Appalachian Mts.
Sierra Madre
ATLANTIC OCEAN
PACIFIC OCEAN
Northern limit of Douglas Fir
Limit of White Pine
Limit of Sugar Maple
Northern limit of Coastal Mangrove Swamps
Limit of Yucca
Arctic Circle
Tropic of Cancer

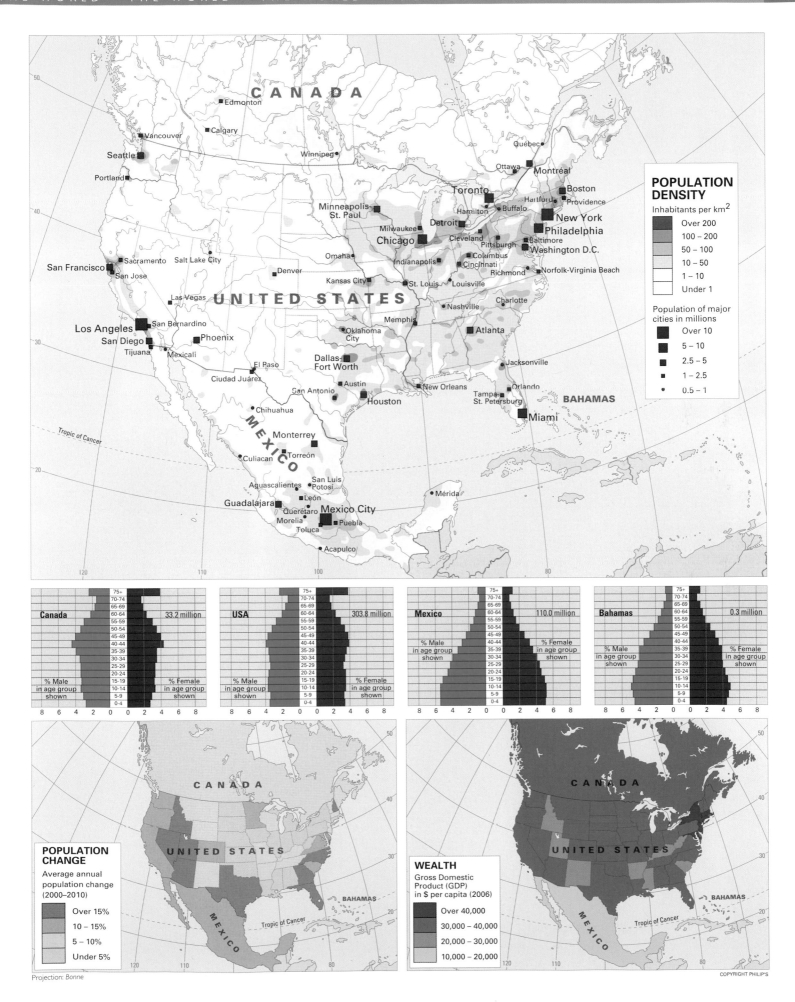

POPULATION DENSITY

Inhabitants per km²

Over 200
100 – 200
50 – 100
10 – 50
1 – 10
Under 1

Population of major cities in millions

Over 10
5 – 10
2.5 – 5
1 – 2.5
0.5 – 1

Canada 33.2 million
% Male in age group shown
% Female in age group shown

USA 303.8 million
% Male in age group shown
% Female in age group shown

Mexico 110.0 million
% Male in age group shown
% Female in age group shown

Bahamas 0.3 million
% Male in age group shown
% Female in age group shown

75+
70-74
65-69
60-64
55-59
50-54
45-49
40-44
35-39
30-34
25-29
20-24
15-19
10-14
5-9
0-4

8 6 4 2 0 0 2 4 6 8

POPULATION CHANGE

Average annual population change (2000–2010)

Over 15%
10 – 15%
5 – 10%
Under 5%

WEALTH

Gross Domestic Product (GDP) in $ per capita (2006)

Over 40,000
30,000 – 40,000
20,000 – 30,000
10,000 – 20,000

Projection: Bonne

COPYRIGHT PHILIP'S

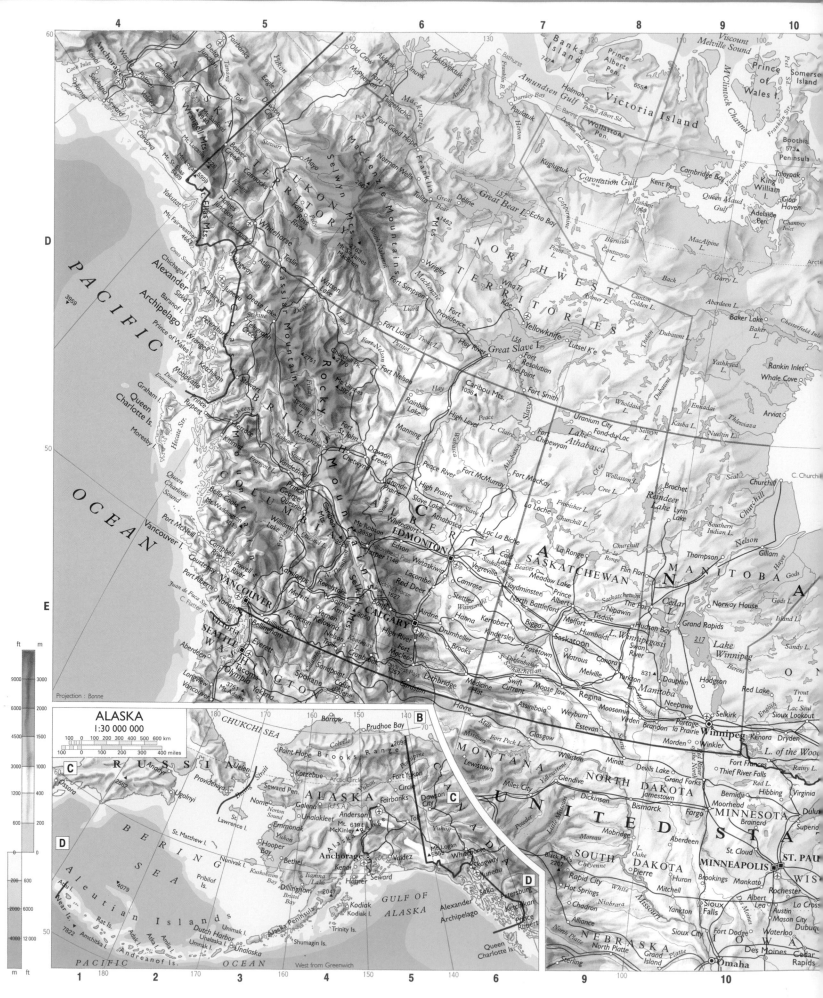

Projection : Bonne

ALASKA
1:30 000 000

West from Greenwich

NORTHERN CANADA
Continuation northwards on same
scale as main map

West from Greenwich

COPYRIGHT PHILIP'S

1:15 000 000

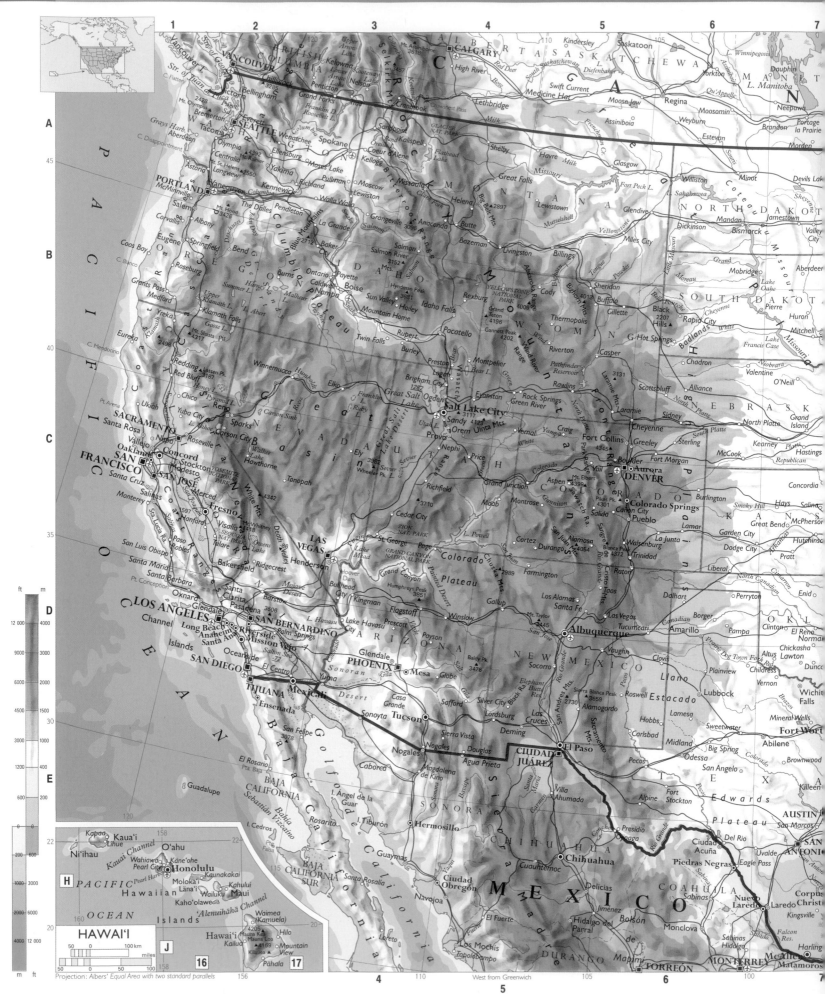

HAWAI'I

Projection: Albers' Equal Area with two standard parallels

West from Greenwich

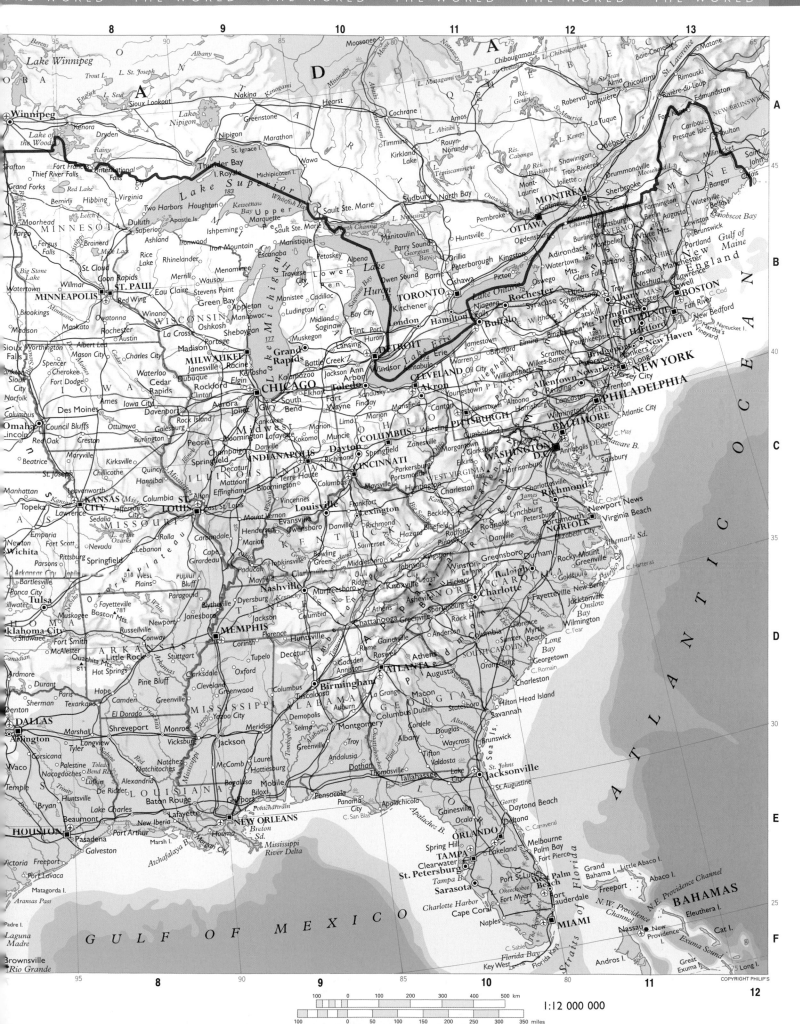

1:12 000 000

COPYRIGHT PHILIP'S

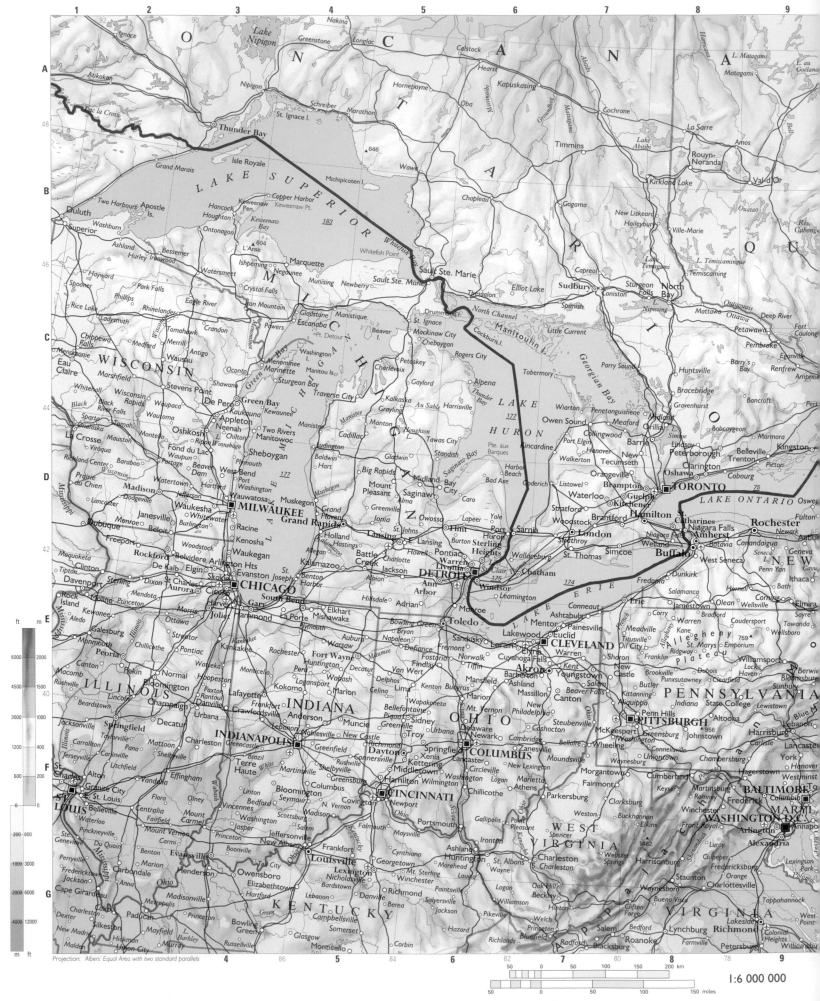

Projection: Albers' Equal Area with two standard parallels

1:6 000 000

TOURISM IN THE USA

Major tourist centres
Major concentration of hotels
Major National Parks

COPYRIGHT PHILIP'S

UNITED STATE

GULF OF MEXICO

Tropic of Cancer

PACIFIC OCEAN

Major labels and places:

San Diego, Tijuana, Mexicali, Ensenada, Phoenix, Tucson, Ciudad Juárez, El Paso, Roswell, Lubbock, Wichita Falls, Little Rock, Huntsville, Fort Worth, Dallas, Birmingham, Tuscaloosa, Abilene, Shreveport, Monroe, Jackson, Meridian, Montgomery, Austin, Houston, San Antonio, New Orleans, Pensacola, Mobile, Baton Rouge, Lafayette, Beaumont, Galveston, Corpus Christi, Brownsville, Matamoros, Reynosa, McAllen, Laredo, Nuevo Laredo

Hermosillo, Ciudad Obregón, Navojoa, Los Mochis, Culiacán, Durango, Torreón, Monterrey, Saltillo, Ciudad Victoria, Mazatlán, Zacatecas, Aguascalientes, San Luis Potosí, Tampico, Ciudad Madero, Guadalajara, León, Irapuato, Celaya, Querétaro, Morelia, MÉXICO, TOLUCA, PUEBLA, Cuernavaca, Veracruz, Xalapa, Córdoba, Orizaba, Acapulco, Chilpancingo, Oaxaca, Coatzacoalcos, Villahermosa, Tuxtla Gutiérrez

Sierra Madre Occidental, Sierra Madre Oriental, Baja California, Golfo de California, Istmo de Tehuantepec, G. de Tehuantepec

MÉRIDA, Cancún, Cozumel, Campeche, Yucatán, Chetumal, BELIZE, Belize City, GUATEMALA, HONDURAS, TEGUCIGALPA, San Pedro Sula, La Ceiba, SAN SALVADOR, EL SALVADOR, NICARAGUA, MANAGUA, León, Golfo de Honduras, Gulf of Honduras

Inset maps:

JAMAICA
1:3 000 000

CARIBBEAN SEA

Montego Bay, Lucea, Negril, Savanna-la-Mar, Black River, Mandeville, May Pen, Spanish Town, Portmore, Kingston, Port Antonio, Port Maria, Ocho Rios, St. Ann's Bay, Falmouth, Runaway Bay, Blue Mountains, Blue Mt. Pk. 2256, Mount Denham 985, Morant Point, Portland Point

GUADELOUPE (Fr.)
Port-Louis, Grande-Terre, Petit-Canal, Le Moule, Ste-Rose, Pointe-à-Pitre, Ste-Anne, Le Gosier, Basse-Terre, Bouillante, Soufrière 1467, Capesterre-Belle-Eau, Trois-Rivières, Basse-Terre, Marie-Galante, Grand-Bourg, Capesterre-de-Marie-Galante 204, Îles des Saintes

MARTINIQUE (Fr.)
Cap St-Martin, Basse-Pointe, Ste-Marie, La Trinité, Presqu'île de la Caravelle, Le Prêcheur, Montagne Pelée 1397, St-Pierre, Le Robert, Le François, Schœlcher, Fort-de-France, Le Lamentin, Rivière-Salée, St-Esprit, Le Marin, Rivière-Pilote, Pte. d'Enfer

GUADELOUPE AND MARTINIQUE
1:2 000 000

Projection: Bonne

Elevation legend (ft / m):
12 000 / 4000, 9000 / 3000, 6000 / 2000, 4500 / 1500, 3000 / 1000, 1200 / 400, 600 / 200, 0 / 0, 200 / 600, 2000 / 6000, 4000 / 12000, 6000 / 18000

PUERTO RICO d
1:3 000 000

ATLANTIC OCEAN

PUERTO RICO
(U.S.A.)

Pta. Agujereada
Isabela
Aguadilla
Arecibo   Barceloneta   Vega   Manati   Rio Grande   SAN JUAN
San   Baja   Bayamón   Carolina   Dewey
Mayagüez   Sebastián   Utuado   Caguas   Sierra de   Fajardo   Culebra
Adjuntas   Cordillera Central   Luquillo   Pta.   Vieques
Uroyan Mts.   C. de Punta   Cayey   Humacao   Puerca
San German   Yauco   1338   Coamo   Yabucoa   Esperanza
Pta. Aguila   Guanica   Ponce   Guayama   18
I. Caja de Muertos
67   66

VIRGIN IS. e
1:2 000 000

Ruffling Pt.   The Settlement
Anegada   East
Pt.

Virgin Islands
(U.K.)

Great
Camanoe
Virgin Is.   Jost Van   Guana I.   Beef   Virgin Gorda
(U.S.A.)   Hans   Dyke I.   521   Tortola   I.   Spanish Town
Lollik I.   Cruz   Guana I.   Road Town   Peter I.
Charlotte   Bay   St. John I.
Amalie   St.
Thomas I.
65   64° 30'

ST. LUCIA f
1:1 000 000

Cap Point   Pte. Hardy
Gros Islet   Anse Lavoutte
Castries   Marquis
Girard
L'Anse la Raye   Dennery
Canaries   Millet
Soufrière   Mt. Gimie   Trou Gras Pt.
Soufrière   750   950
Bay   Petit Piton   Micoud
Gros Piton Pt.   795   Vierge Pt.
Choiseul   Gros Piton
Laborie   Vieux Fort
C. Moule à Chique   ST. LUCIA
61

BARBADOS g
1:1 000 000

ATLANTIC
OCEAN

Crab Hill   North Point
Spring Hall
Fustic   Boscobelle
245   Belleplaine
Speightstown   Bathsheba   BARBADOS
Westmoreland   840   Martin's Bay
Alleynes Bay   Mt. Hillaby   Hillcrest
Holetown   Jackson   Massiah
Bridgefield   Street   Six Cross Roads
Black Rock   Ellerton   The Crane
Bridgetown   Oistins   St. Martins
Carlisle Bay   Worthing   Chancery Lane
Oistins   South Point
Bay
59° 30'

—— Main map ——

ATLANTA
Columbia   Wilmington
Augusta   C. Fear   Long Bay
Macon   Savannah   Charleston
Columbus
Albany   Altamaha
Tallahassee   Jacksonville
Daytona Beach
ORLANDO   C. Canaveal
TAMPA   Melbourne
St. Petersburg   West
Sarasota   L. Okeechobee   Palm   Grand
Beach   Bahama
MIAMI   Fort   I.   Freeport   Abaco I.
Lauderdale
Bimini Is.
Key West   New   Eleuthera I.
Providence I.   Nassau
Straits of Florida   Andros I.   Cat I.
BAHAMAS   San Salvador I.
LA HABANA   Matanzas   Great Exuma I.   Long I.
(Havana)   Cárdenas   Crooked I.
Pinar   Santa Clara   Placetas   Mayaguana I.
del Rio   Güines   Morón   Acklins
Guane   G. de   Cienfuegos   Camagüey   Great Inagua
Batabanó   Trinidad   Sancti Spíritus   Nuevitas   Turks & Caicos Is.   (U.K.)
I. de   CUBA   Ciego de Ávila   Banes   Cockburn
la Juventud   Las Tunas   Holguín   Town
Manzanillo   Baracoa   Port-de-Paix
Bayamo   Santiago   Cap-Haïtien   Puerto Plata   Monte Cristi
Cayman Is.   1972   de Cuba   GUANTANAMO   Gonaïves   Pico   San Francisco
Grand   George Town   BAY (U.S.A.)   St-Marc   Duarte   de Macorís
Cayman   Cayman   Guantánamo   Windward   HAITI   3175   La Vega   La Romana
(U.K.)   7680   Trench   Passage   Jérémie   DOMINICAN   San Pedro de Macorís
Montego Bay   2256   Les Cayes   Jacmel   San Juan   REP.   Barahona
Mandeville   Spanish   Kingston   PORT-AU-PRINCE   SANTO
JAMAICA   Town   Hispaniola   DOMINGO
Is. Santanilla   A   n   t   i   l   l   e   s
(Honduras)
L. de Caratasca   C. Gracias a Dios
Puerto Cabezas
I. de Providencia   CARIBBEAN   SEA
(Colombia)
I. de San Andrés   Antilles
(Colombia)
Bluefields   Pta. Gallinas   Aruba (Neth.)   Curaçao   Bonaire
COSTA RICA   Pen. de la   Willemstad
Ican Irazú   Guajira   Puerto   NETH.
3432   Limón   Santa Marta   Fijo   ANTILLES
Cartago   BARRANQUILLA   Sierra Nevada   San   Puerto Cabello   MARACAY
JOSE   Volcán Barú   CARTAGENA   de Santa Marta   Felipe   MARACAIBO   Coro   CARACAS
3475   Panama   Soledad   5775   BARQUISIMETO   VALENCIA   Barcelona
PANAMÁ   Canal   Sincelejo   Calamar   Cabimas   VALERA   Acarigua   Maturín
Puerto   G. del   Monteria   Valledupar   L. de   El Tigre   Ciudad
Armuelles   Santiago   Darién   Mompos   Maracaibo   Merida   Barinas   San Fernando   Guayana
I. de   Chitré   La Palma   5007   de Apure   Ciudad Bolívar
Coiba   Pen. de   El Real   Puerto Wilches   Cúcuta   Pico Bolívar   Embalse de Guri
Azuero   Jaque   Barrancabermeja   San Cristóbal   Tumeremo
Isthmus of   G. de   Riosucio   Yarumal   Pamplona   Caicara   Mt. Roraima
Panama   Panamá   4960   BUCARAMANGA   VENEZUELA   2772
G. de Cupica   Antioquia   Puerto Carreño   GUYANA
C. Corrientes   Bello   MEDELLÍN   Sogamoso   Puerto Ayacucho   Georgetown
I. de Malpelo   Quibdó   COLOMBIA   Tunja   Meta   Bartica   New Amsterdam
(Colombia)   Manizales   Villavicencio   Puerto Inírida   Linden
Pereira   Tolima   Vichada   Sierra Pacaraima
Buenaventura   Armenia   Ibagué   BOGOTÁ   Boa Vista
CALI   Huila   Girardot   Guaviare   BRAZIL
Neiva   Orinoco
Popayán   Guaviare
Volcán Puracé

CAYMAN TRENCH   7680
Cayman Trench

Puerto Rico Trench   8605
PUERTO RICO TRENCH

MONA PASSAGE

Virgin Is.   Anguilla (U.K.)
(U.K. - U.S.A.)   St-Martin (Fr. - Neth.)
SAN JUAN   St. KITTS & NEVIS
Arecibo   1338   Basseterre   ANTIGUA &
Caguas   Mayagüez   St. John's   BARBUDA
Ponce   St. Croix   1156   Montserrat (U.K.)   914
(U.S.A.)   Leeward   GUADELOUPE (Fr.)
PUERTO RICO   Islands   1467   Pointe-à-Pitre
(U.S.A.)   Basse-Terre   Roseau
1447   DOMINICA
L   e   s   s   e   r   1397   MARTINIQUE (Fr.)
Fort-de-France
A   n   t   i   l   l   e   s   Castries   ST. LUCIA
ST. VINCENT &   1234   Kingstown
THE GRENADINES   Kingstown   BARBADOS
Bridgetown
Windward
Islands   GRENADA
St. George's   Tobago
I. Blanquilla (Ven.)   TRINIDAD & TOBAGO
I. de Margarita   Güiria   Port of Spain
Polamar   Cumaná   San Fernando
Carúpano   G. de
La Tortuga   Puerto La   Cruz   Paria
Maiquetía   Cruz   2640

West from Greenwich   80   75   70   65   60   Equator   0°
8   9   10   11   12   13
100   0   100   200   300   400   500   600 km
1:15 000 000
100   0   100   200   300   400 miles
COPYRIGHT PHILIP'S

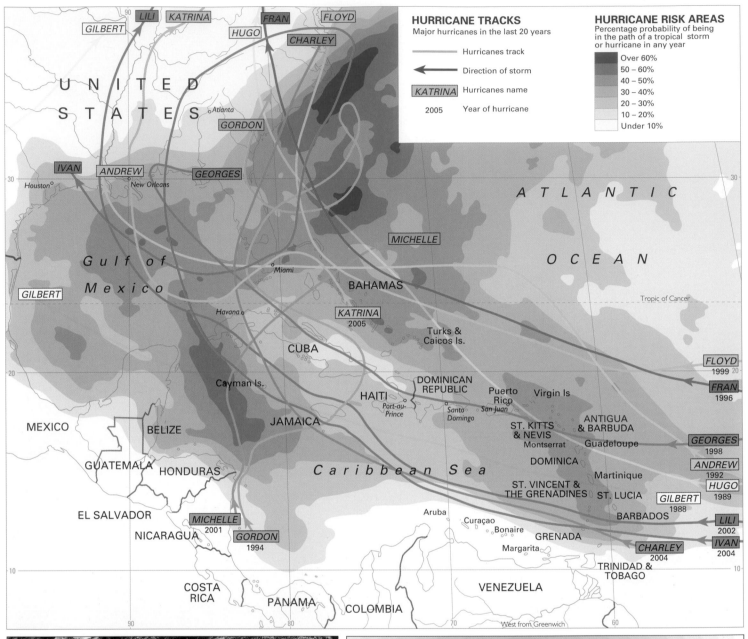

HURRICANE TRACKS
Major hurricanes in the last 20 years

— Hurricanes track

← Direction of storm

KATRINA Hurricanes name

2005 Year of hurricane

HURRICANE RISK AREAS
Percentage probability of being in the path of a tropical storm or hurricane in any year

- Over 60%
- 50 – 60%
- 40 – 50%
- 30 – 40%
- 20 – 30%
- 10 – 20%
- Under 10%

UNITED STATES

GILBERT   LILI   KATRINA   FRAN   FLOYD
HUGO   CHARLEY

Atlanta

GORDON

ATLANTIC

IVAN   ANDREW   GEORGES
Houston   New Orleans

OCEAN

GILBERT

Gulf of Mexico

Miami

MICHELLE

BAHAMAS

Tropic of Cancer

Havana

KATRINA
2005

CUBA

Turks & Caicos Is.

FLOYD
1999

Cayman Is.

HAITI   DOMINICAN REPUBLIC
Port-au-Prince   Santo Domingo

Puerto Rico   Virgin Is
San Juan

FRAN
1996

JAMAICA

MEXICO   BELIZE

ANTIGUA & BARBUDA

GEORGES
1998

GUATEMALA   HONDURAS

Caribbean Sea

ST. KITTS & NEVIS
Montserrat   Guadeloupe

DOMINICA

ANDREW
1992

Martinique

HUGO
1989

ST. VINCENT & THE GRENADINES   ST. LUCIA

GILBERT
1988

EL SALVADOR

Aruba   Curaçao

BARBADOS

MICHELLE
2001

NICARAGUA

GORDON
1994

Bonaire

GRENADA

LILI
2002

Margarita

CHARLEY
2004

IVAN
2004

COSTA RICA   PANAMA   COLOMBIA

VENEZUELA

TRINIDAD & TOBAGO

West from Greenwich

▲ Hurricane Katrina hit the USA's Gulf Coast on 29th August 2005. It was the costliest and one of the five deadliest hurricanes ever to strike the United States. This satellite image shows the storm approaching the US coastline.

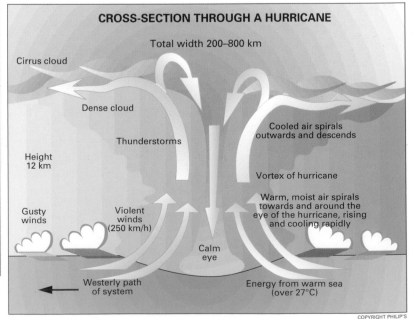

CROSS-SECTION THROUGH A HURRICANE

Total width 200–800 km

Cirrus cloud

Dense cloud

Cooled air spirals outwards and descends

Thunderstorms

Vortex of hurricane

Height 12 km

Warm, moist air spirals towards and around the eye of the hurricane, rising and cooling rapidly

Gusty winds

Violent winds (250 km/h)

Calm eye

Westerly path of system

Energy from warm sea (over 27°C)

COPYRIGHT PHILIP'S

Projection: Lambert's Azimuthal Equal Area

1:35 000 000

100 0 200 400 600 800 1000 1200 1400 km
100 0 200 400 600 800 1000 miles

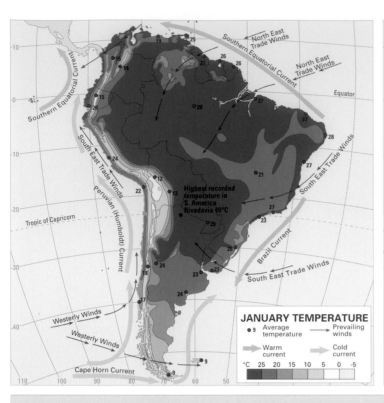

JANUARY TEMPERATURE

- 9 Average temperature
- → Prevailing winds
- ⇒ Warm current
- ⇒ Cold current

°C 25 20 15 10 5 0 -5

Highest recorded temperature in S. America Rivadavia 49°C

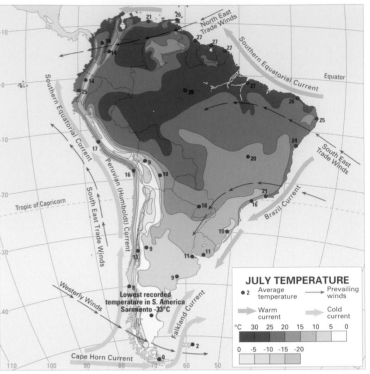

JULY TEMPERATURE

- 2 Average temperature
- → Prevailing winds
- ⇒ Warm current
- ⇒ Cold current

°C 30 25 20 15 10 5 0
0 -5 -10 -15 -20

Lowest recorded temperature in S. America Sarmiento -33°C

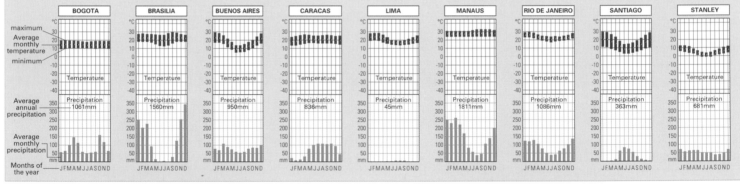

Climate graphs for: BOGOTA, BRASILIA, BUENOS AIRES, CARACAS, LIMA, MANAUS, RIO DE JANEIRO, SANTIAGO, STANLEY

- maximum
- Average monthly temperature
- minimum
- Average annual precipitation
- Average monthly precipitation
- Months of the year

Annual precipitation values:
- BOGOTA: 1061mm
- BRASILIA: 1560mm
- BUENOS AIRES: 950mm
- CARACAS: 836mm
- LIMA: 45mm
- MANAUS: 1811mm
- RIO DE JANEIRO: 1086mm
- SANTIAGO: 363mm
- STANLEY: 681mm

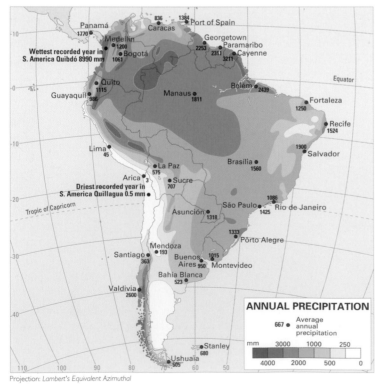

ANNUAL PRECIPITATION

- 667 Average annual precipitation

mm 3000 1000 250
4000 2000 500 0

Wettest recorded year in S. America Quibdó 8990 mm
Driest recorded year in S. America Quillagua 0.5 mm

Station values: Panamá 1770, Medellín 1200, Bogotá 1061, Caracas 836, Port of Spain 1384, Georgetown 2253, Paramaribo 2311, Cayenne 3211, Quito 1115, Guayaquil 986, Manaus 1811, Belém 2439, Fortaleza 1250, Recife 1524, Lima 45, La Paz 575, Sucre 707, Arica 3, Brasília 1560, Salvador 1900, São Paulo 1086, Rio de Janeiro 1425, Asunción 1318, Pôrto Alegre 1333, Mendoza 193, Santiago 363, Buenos Aires 950, Montevideo 1015, Bahía Blanca 523, Valdivia 2600, Stanley 680, Ushuaia 505

Projection: Lambert's Equivalent Azimuthal

BIOMES

- Tropical rainforest
- Tropical thorn forest
- Temperate rainforest
- Evergreen trees and shrubs
- Grassland and savanna
- Semi-desert
- Desert
- Alpine and high plateau

Labels: Guiana Highlands, Amazon Basin, South limit of wild rubber, Atacama Desert, Andes, Brazilian Highlands, South limit of Quebracho, PACIFIC OCEAN, Pampas, Patagonia, ATLANTIC OCEAN, Equator, Tropic of Capricorn

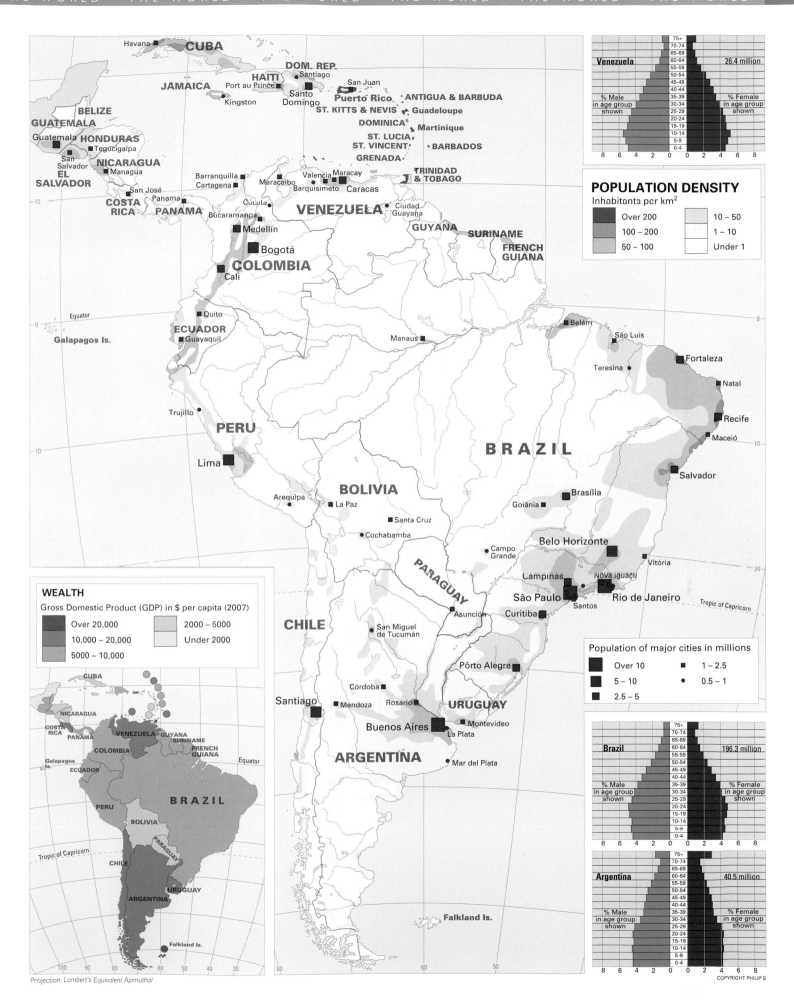

Venezuela 26.4 million

% Male in age group shown | % Female in age group shown

POPULATION DENSITY
Inhabitants per km²

Over 200	10 – 50
100 – 200	1 – 10
50 – 100	Under 1

WEALTH
Gross Domestic Product (GDP) in $ per capita (2007)

Over 20,000	2000 – 5000
10,000 – 20,000	Under 2000
5000 – 10,000	

Population of major cities in millions

Over 10	1 – 2.5
5 – 10	0.5 – 1
2.5 – 5	

Brazil 196.3 million

% Male in age group shown | % Female in age group shown

Argentina 40.5 million

% Male in age group shown | % Female in age group shown

Projection: Lambert's Equivalent Azimuthal

COPYRIGHT PHILIP'S

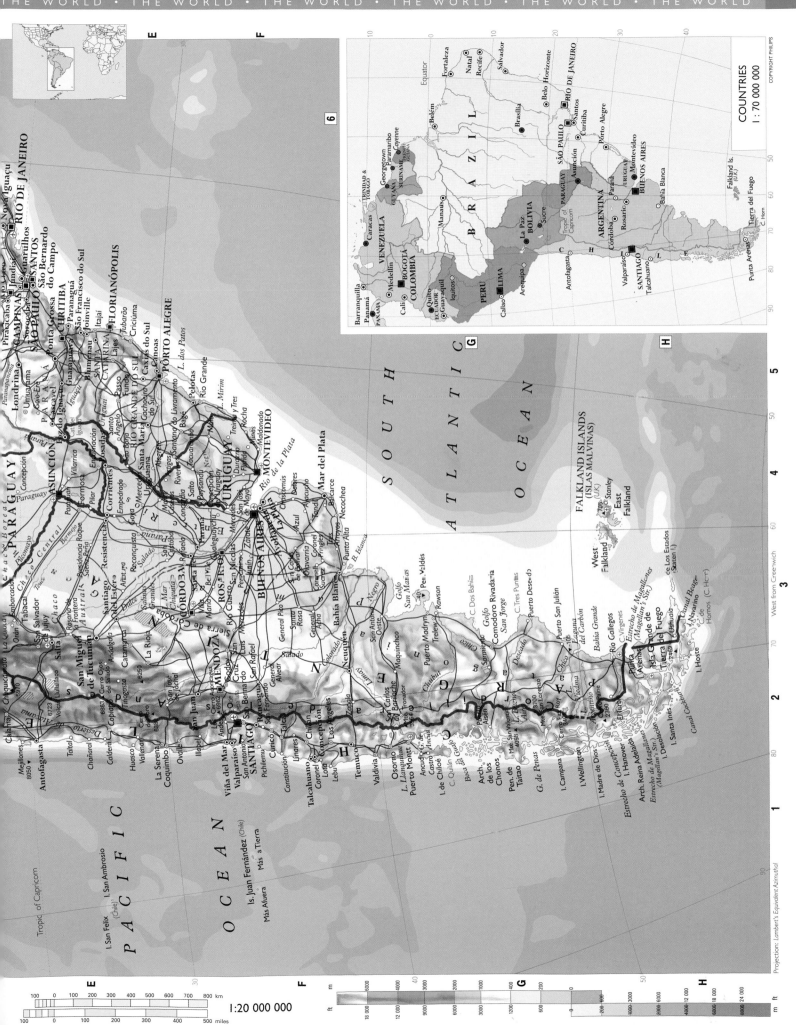

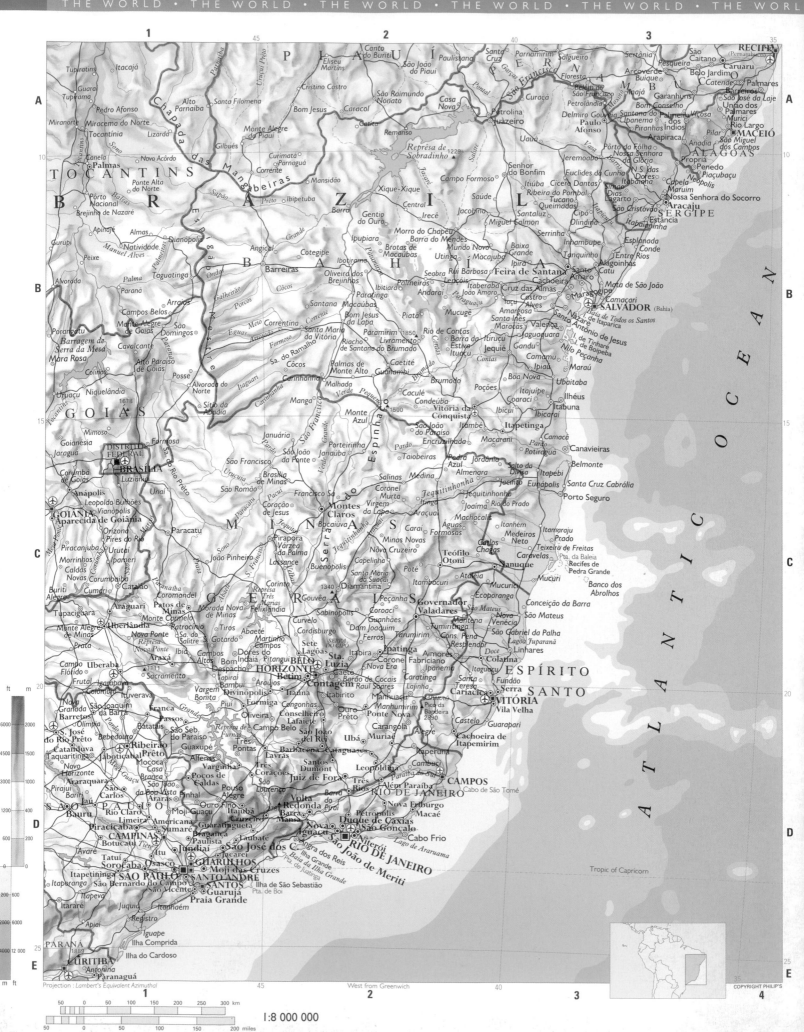

Projection : Lambert's Equivalent Azimuthal

West from Greenwich

1:8 000 000

COPYRIGHT PHILIP'S

50   0   50   100   150   200   250   300 km
50   0   50   100   150   200 miles

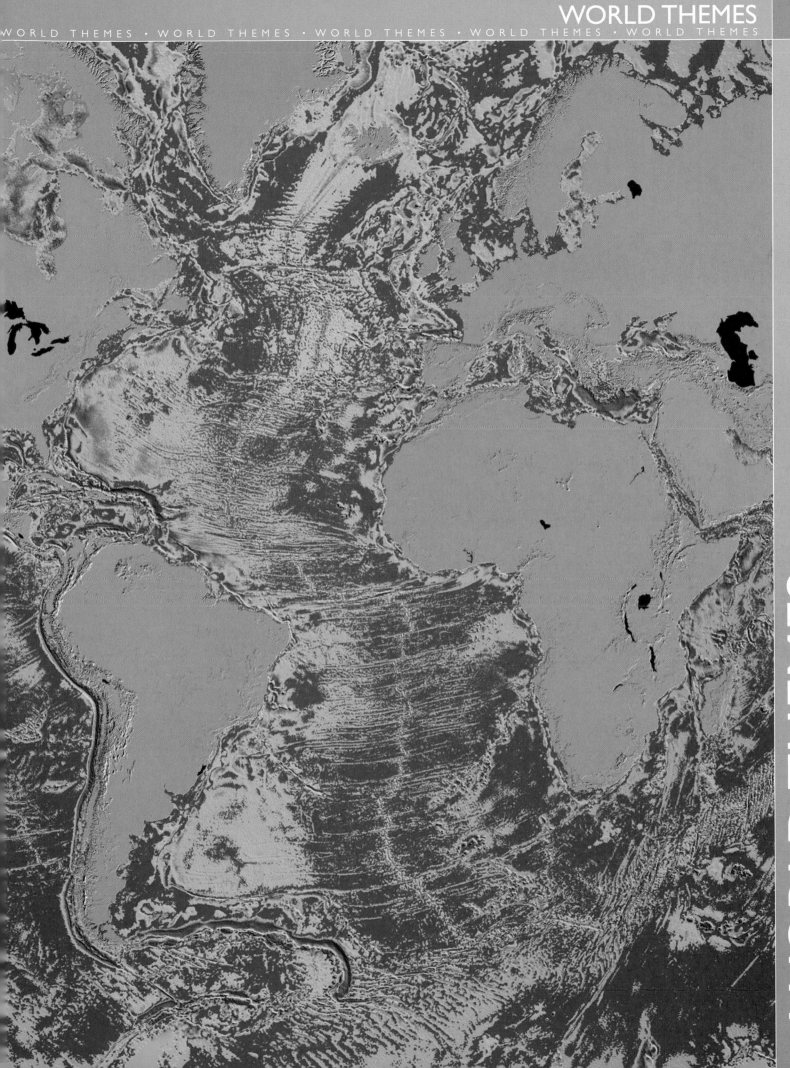

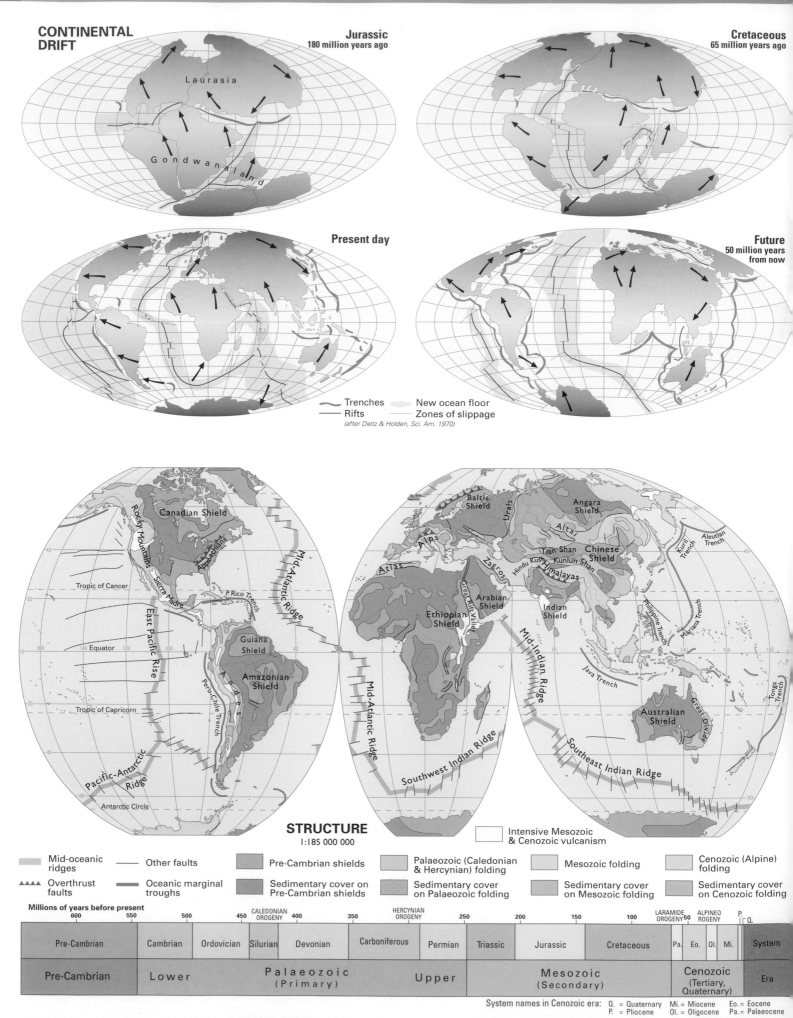

CONTINENTAL DRIFT

Jurassic
180 million years ago

Laurasia

Gondwanaland

Cretaceous
65 million years ago

Present day

Future
50 million years from now

— Trenches ░ New ocean floor
— Rifts ░ Zones of slippage
(after Dietz & Holden, Sci. Am. 1970)

Canadian Shield
Rocky Mountains
Appalachians
Sierra Madre
Tropic of Cancer
P. Rico Trench
Mid-Atlantic Ridge
East Pacific Rise
Equator
Guiana Shield
Andes
Amazonian Shield
Peru-Chile Trench
Tropic of Capricorn
Mid-Atlantic Ridge
Pacific-Antarctic Ridge
Antarctic Circle

Baltic Shield
Urals
Angara Shield
Altai
Alps
Tian Shan
Chinese Shield
Atlas
Zagros
Hindu Kush
Kunlun Shan
Himalayas
Aleutian Trench
Kuril Trench
Great Rift Valley
Arabian Shield
Ethiopian Shield
Indian Shield
Philippine Trench
Mariana Trench
Mid-Indian Ridge
Java Trench
Australian Shield
Great Divide
Tonga Trench
Southwest Indian Ridge
Southeast Indian Ridge

STRUCTURE
1:185 000 000

░ Intensive Mesozoic & Cenozoic vulcanism

▨ Mid-oceanic ridges	— Other faults	▨ Pre-Cambrian shields
▲▲▲ Overthrust faults	▬ Oceanic marginal troughs	▨ Sedimentary cover on Pre-Cambrian shields

░ Palaeozoic (Caledonian & Hercynian) folding
░ Sedimentary cover on Palaeozoic folding
░ Mesozoic folding
░ Sedimentary cover on Mesozoic folding
░ Cenozoic (Alpine) folding
░ Sedimentary cover on Cenozoic folding

Millions of years before present

600	550	500	CALEDONIAN OROGENY 450	400	350	HERCYNIAN OROGENY	250	200	150	100	LARAMIDE OROGENY 50	ALPINE OROGENY	P. Q.	
Pre-Cambrian	Cambrian	Ordovician	Silurian	Devonian	Carboniferous	Permian	Triassic	Jurassic		Cretaceous	Pa.	Eo.	Ol. Mi.	System
Pre-Cambrian	Lower		Palaeozoic (Primary)			Upper		Mesozoic (Secondary)			Cenozoic (Tertiary, Quaternary)			Era

System names in Cenozoic era: Q. = Quaternary Mi. = Miocene Eo. = Eocene
P. = Pliocene Ol. = Oligocene Pa. = Palaeocene

VOLCANOES AND PLATE TECTONICS

1:185 000 000

'Ring of Fire'

Constructive boundary
(plates moving apart)

Destructive boundary
(plates colliding)

Conservative boundary
(plates sliding past
each other)

7.2 ⤢ Direction of movement
along plate boundaries
(cm/year)

○ Submarine
volcanoes

✦ Geysers

△ Land volcanoes
active since 1700

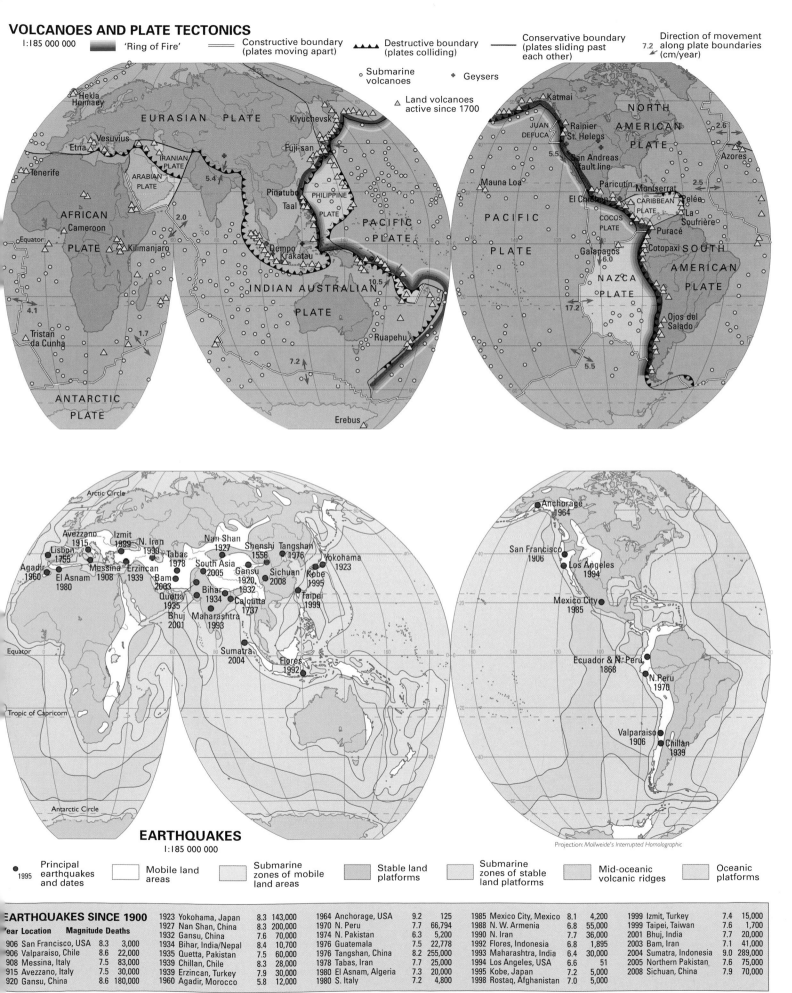

EARTHQUAKES

1:185 000 000

Projection: Mollweide's Interrupted Homolographic

● 1995 Principal
earthquakes
and dates

☐ Mobile land
areas

Submarine
zones of mobile
land areas

Stable land
platforms

Submarine
zones of stable
land platforms

Mid-oceanic
volcanic ridges

Oceanic
platforms

EARTHQUAKES SINCE 1900														
Year Location	Magnitude	Deaths	1923 Yokohama, Japan	8.3	143,000	1964 Anchorage, USA	9.2	125	1985 Mexico City, Mexico	8.1	4,200	1999 Izmit, Turkey	7.4	15,000
			1927 Nan Shan, China	8.3	200,000	1970 N. Peru	7.7	66,794	1988 N. W. Armenia	6.8	55,000	1999 Taipei, Taiwan	7.6	1,700
			1932 Gansu, China	7.6	70,000	1974 N. Pakistan	6.3	5,200	1990 N. Iran	7.7	36,000	2001 Bhuj, India	7.7	20,000
1906 San Francisco, USA	8.3	3,000	1934 Bihar, India/Nepal	8.4	10,700	1976 Guatemala	7.5	22,778	1992 Flores, Indonesia	7.5	1,895	2003 Bam, Iran	7.1	41,000
1906 Valparaiso, Chile	8.6	22,000	1935 Quetta, Pakistan	7.5	60,000	1976 Tangshan, China	8.2	255,000	1993 Maharashtra, India	6.4	30,000	2004 Sumatra, Indonesia	9.0	289,000
1908 Messina, Italy	7.5	83,000	1939 Chillan, Chile	8.3	28,000	1978 Tabas, Iran	7.7	25,000	1994 Los Angeles, USA	6.6	51	2005 Northern Pakistan	7.6	75,000
1915 Avezzano, Italy	7.5	30,000	1939 Erzincan, Turkey	7.9	30,000	1980 El Asnam, Algeria	7.3	20,000	1995 Kobe, Japan	7.2	5,000	2008 Sichuan, China	7.9	70,000
1920 Gansu, China	8.6	180,000	1960 Agadir, Morocco	5.8	12,000	1980 S. Italy	7.2	4,800	1998 Rostaq, Afghanistan	7.0	5,000			

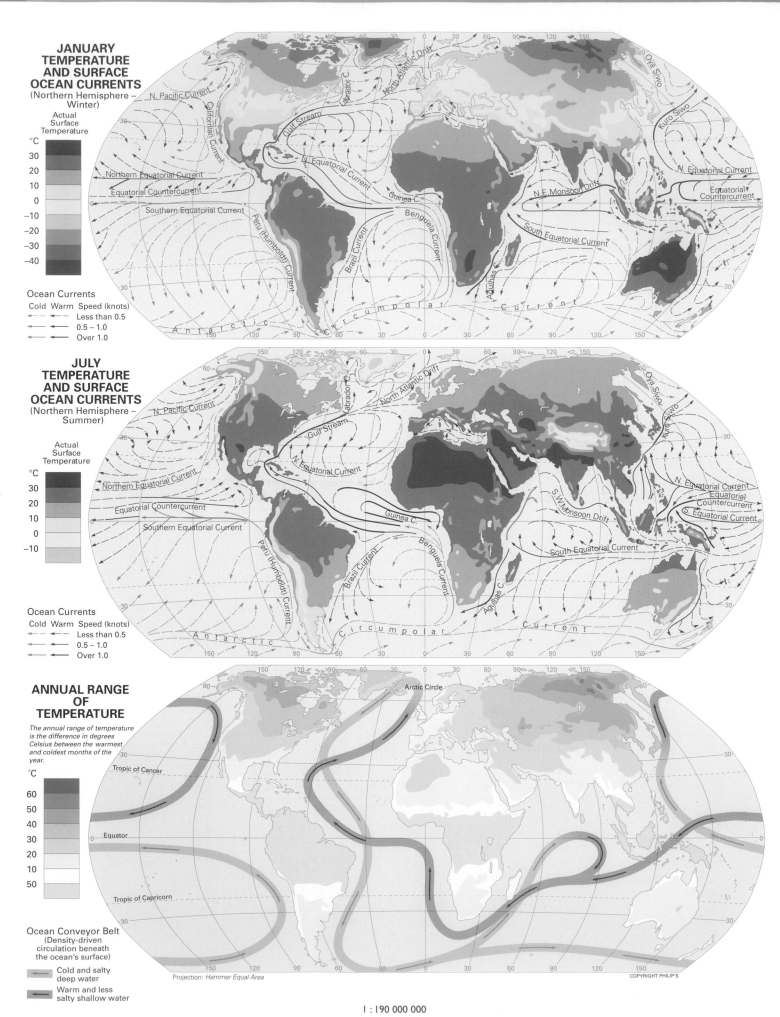

JANUARY TEMPERATURE AND SURFACE OCEAN CURRENTS
(Northern Hemisphere – Winter)

Actual Surface Temperature
°C
30
20
10
0
−10
−20
−30
−40

Ocean Currents
Cold Warm Speed (knots)
Less than 0.5
0.5 – 1.0
Over 1.0

JULY TEMPERATURE AND SURFACE OCEAN CURRENTS
(Northern Hemisphere – Summer)

Actual Surface Temperature
°C
30
20
10
0
−10

Ocean Currents
Cold Warm Speed (knots)
Less than 0.5
0.5 – 1.0
Over 1.0

ANNUAL RANGE OF TEMPERATURE

The annual range of temperature is the difference in degrees Celsius between the warmest and coldest months of the year.

°C
60
50
40
30
20
10
50

Ocean Conveyor Belt
(Density-driven circulation beneath the ocean's surface)

Cold and salty deep water

Warm and less salty shallow water

Projection: *Hammer Equal Area*

COPYRIGHT PHILIP'S

1 : 190 000 000

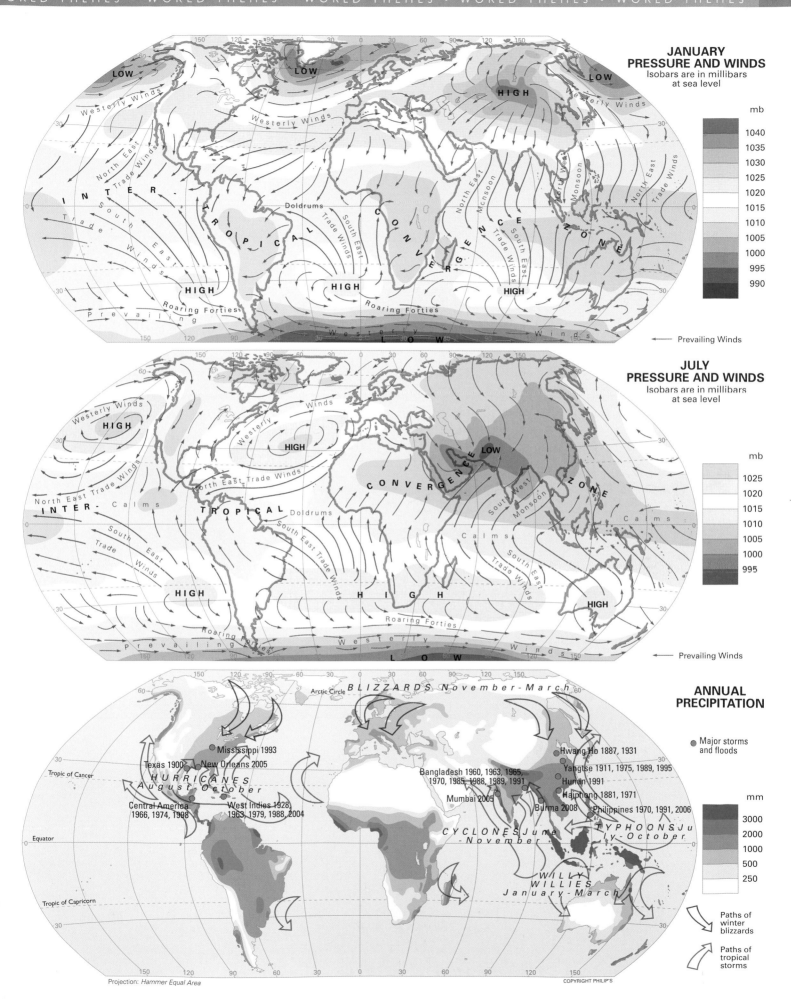

JANUARY PRESSURE AND WINDS
Isobars are in millibars at sea level

mb
1040
1035
1030
1025
1020
1015
1010
1005
1000
995
990

← Prevailing Winds

JULY PRESSURE AND WINDS
Isobars are in millibars at sea level

mb
1025
1020
1015
1010
1005
1000
995

← Prevailing Winds

ANNUAL PRECIPITATION

● Major storms and floods

mm
3000
2000
1000
500
250

Paths of winter blizzards

Paths of tropical storms

Projection: *Hammer Equal Area*   COPYRIGHT PHILIP'S

KEY TO CLIMATE REGIONS MAP

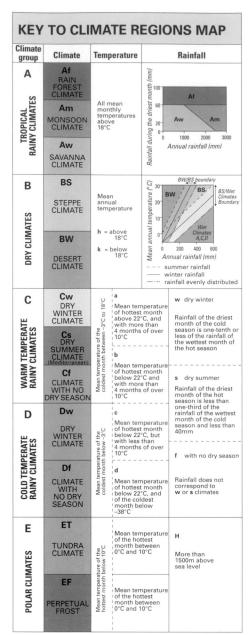

Climate group	Climate	Temperature	Rainfall
A TROPICAL RAINY CLIMATES	**Af** RAIN FOREST CLIMATE / **Am** MONSOON CLIMATE / **Aw** SAVANNA CLIMATE	All mean monthly temperatures above 18°C	*(Rainfall during the driest month graph: Af, Aw, Am)*
B DRY CLIMATES	**BS** STEPPE CLIMATE / **BW** DESERT CLIMATE	Mean annual temperature / h = above 18°C / k = below 18°C	*(BW/BS boundary graph: BW, BS, Wet Climates A,C,D)* summer rainfall / winter rainfall / rainfall evenly distributed
C WARM TEMPERATE RAINY CLIMATES	**Cw** DRY WINTER CLIMATE / **Cs** DRY SUMMER CLIMATE (Mediterranean) / **Cf** CLIMATE WITH NO DRY SEASON	a Mean temperature of hottest month above 22°C, and with more than 4 months of over 10°C / b Mean temperature below 22°C and with more than 4 months of over 10°C	w dry winter — Rainfall of the driest month of the cold season is one-tenth or less of the rainfall of the wettest month of the hot season / s dry summer — Rainfall of the driest month of the hot season is less than one-third of the rainfall of the wettest month of the cold season and less than 40mm
D COLD TEMPERATE RAINY CLIMATES	**Dw** DRY WINTER CLIMATE / **Df** CLIMATE WITH NO DRY SEASON	c Mean temperature of hottest month below 22°C, but with less than 4 months of over 10°C / d Mean temperature of hottest month below 22°C, and of the coldest month below −38°C	f with no dry season / Rainfall does not correspond to w or s climates
E POLAR CLIMATES	**ET** TUNDRA CLIMATE / **EF** PERPETUAL FROST	Mean temperature of the hottest month between 0°C and 10°C / Mean temperature of the hottest month below 0°C	H — More than 1500m above sea level

(Mean temperature of the coldest month between −3°C to 18°C; Mean temperature of the coldest month below −3°C; Mean temperature of the coldest month below −38°C)

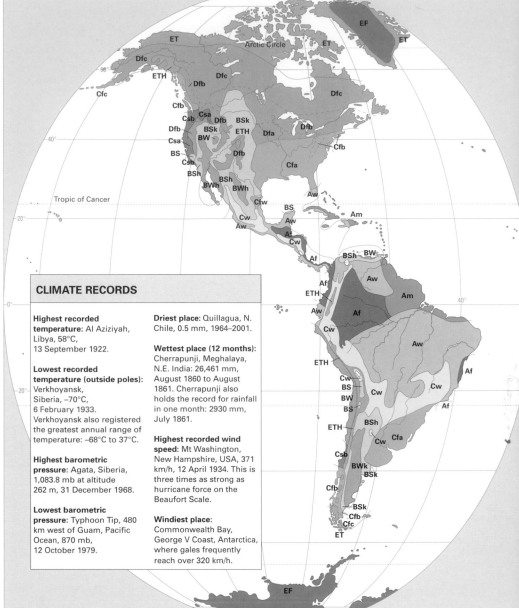

CLIMATE RECORDS

Highest recorded temperature: Al Aziziyah, Libya, 58°C, 13 September 1922.

Lowest recorded temperature (outside poles): Verkhoyansk, Siberia, −70°C, 6 February 1933. Verkhoyansk also registered the greatest annual range of temperature: −68°C to 37°C.

Highest barometric pressure: Agata, Siberia, 1,083.8 mb at altitude 262 m, 31 December 1968.

Lowest barometric pressure: Typhoon Tip, 480 km west of Guam, Pacific Ocean, 870 mb, 12 October 1979.

Driest place: Quillagua, N. Chile, 0.5 mm, 1964–2001.

Wettest place (12 months): Cherrapunji, Meghalaya, N.E. India: 26,461 mm, August 1860 to August 1861. Cherrapunji also holds the record for rainfall in one month: 2930 mm, July 1861.

Highest recorded wind speed: Mt Washington, New Hampshire, USA, 371 km/h, 12 April 1934. This is three times as strong as hurricane force on the Beaufort Scale.

Windiest place: Commonwealth Bay, George V Coast, Antarctica, where gales frequently reach over 320 km/h.

Projection: *Interrupted Mollweide's Homolographic*

THE MONSOON   1:90 000 000

Monthly rainfall

mm		mm
400		50
200		25
100		0

→ wind direction

━━ ITCZ (intertropical convergence zone)

In early March, which normally marks the end of the subcontinent's cool season and the start of the hot season, winds blow outwards from the mainland. But as the overhead sun and the ITCZ move northwards, the land is intensely heated, and a low-pressure system develops. The south-east trade winds, which are drawn across the Equator, change direction and are sucked into the interior to become south-westerly winds, bringing heavy rain. By November, the overhead sun and the ITCZ have again moved southwards and the wind directions are again reversed. Cool winds blow from the Asian interior to the sea, losing any moisture on the Himalayas before descending to the coast.

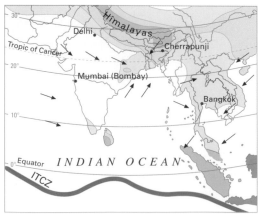

March – Start of the hot, dry season, the ITCZ is over the southern Indian Ocean.

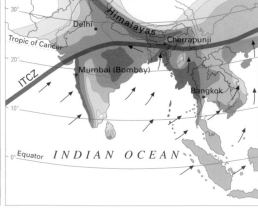

July – The rainy season, the ITCZ has migrated northwards; winds blow onshore.

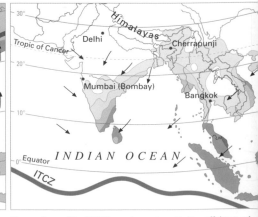

November – The ITCZ has returned south, the offshore winds are cool and dry.

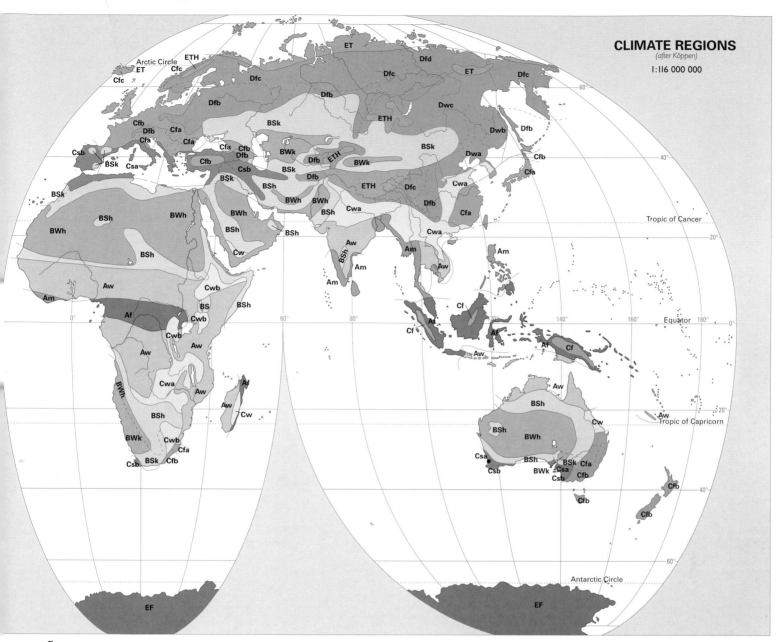

CLIMATE REGIONS
(after Köppen)

1:116 000 000

EL NIÑO

In a normal year, south-easterly trade winds drive surface waters westwards off the coast of South America, drawing cold, nutrient-rich water up from below. In an El Niño year, warm water from the west Pacific suppresses upwelling in the east, depriving the region of nutrients. The water is warmed by as much as 7°C, disturbing the tropical atmosphere circulation. During an intense El Niño, the south-east trade winds change direction and become equatorial westerlies, resulting in climatic extremes in many regions of the world, such as drought in parts of Australia and India, and heavy rainfall in south-eastern USA.

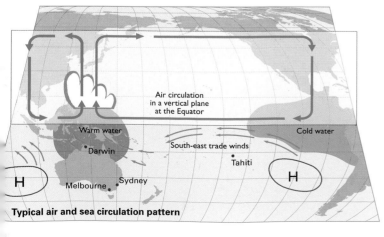

Typical air and sea circulation pattern

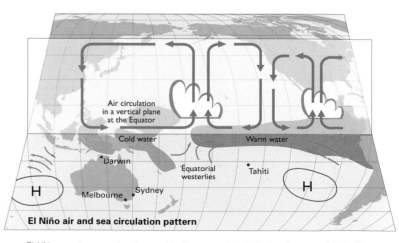

El Niño air and sea circulation pattern

El Niño events occur about every 4 to 7 years and typically last for around 12 to 18 months. El Niño usually results in reduced rainfall across northern and eastern Australia. This can lead to widespread and severe drought, as well as increased temperatures and bushfire risk. However, each El Niño event is unique in terms of its strength as well as its impact. It is measured by the Southern Oscillation Index (SOI) and the changes in ocean temperatures.

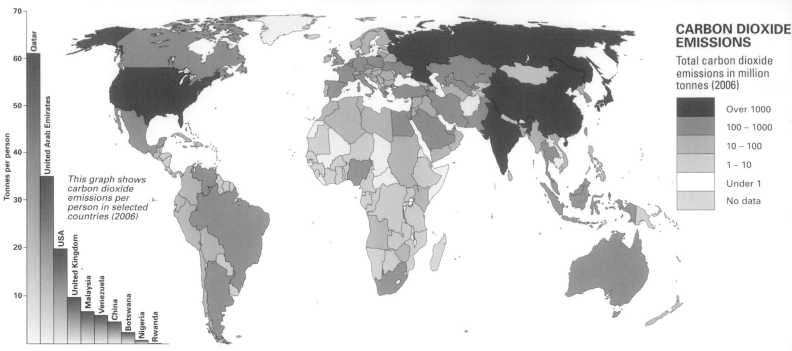

CARBON DIOXIDE EMISSIONS

Total carbon dioxide emissions in million tonnes (2006)

- Over 1000
- 100 – 1000
- 10 – 100
- 1 – 10
- Under 1
- No data

This graph shows carbon dioxide emissions per person in selected countries (2006)

Tonnes per person

Qatar / United Arab Emirates / USA / United Kingdom / Malaysia / Venezuela / China / Botswana / Nigeria / Rwanda

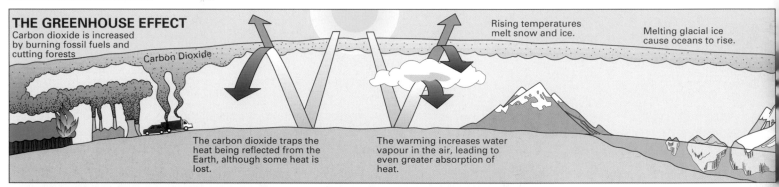

THE GREENHOUSE EFFECT

Carbon dioxide is increased by burning fossil fuels and cutting forests

Carbon Dioxide

The carbon dioxide traps the heat being reflected from the Earth, although some heat is lost.

Rising temperatures melt snow and ice.

The warming increases water vapour in the air, leading to even greater absorption of heat.

Melting glacial ice cause oceans to rise.

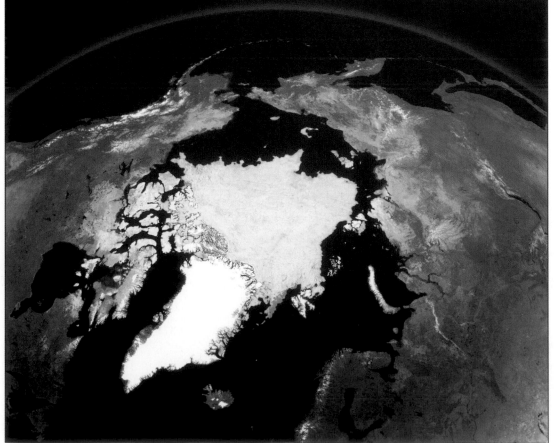

Arctic Ice Cap

This image shows the extent of sea-ice in the Arctic in September 2008. The sea-ice area expands and contracts seasonally and September, at the end of the northern hemisphere summer, represents its smallest extent. The year 2008 showed the biggest reduction in sea-ice since satellite surveillance began in 1979 and this is believed to be related to climate change and global warming. Although dramatic, the sea-ice itself is thought to be quite thin, on average about 3 m (10 ft) thick. Even large reductions would not in themselves involve any sea-level change since the ice is floating and displaces the sea water. One by-product of this is the opening-up of clear sea. This would enable shipping in the northern hemisphere to move between the Atlantic and Pacific Oceans using the much shorter routes around the north coasts of Canada and of Russia, rather than heading south to do this.

PREDICTED CHANGE IN TEMPERATURE

The difference between actual annual average surface air temperature, 1960–90, and predicted annual average surface air temperature, 2070–2100. This map shows the predicted increase, assuming a 'medium growth' of the global economy and assuming that no measures to combat the emission of greenhouse gases are taken.

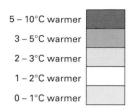

- 5 – 10°C warmer
- 3 – 5°C warmer
- 2 – 3°C warmer
- 1 – 2°C warmer
- 0 – 1°C warmer

Source: The Hadley Centre of Climate Prediction and Research, The Met. Office.

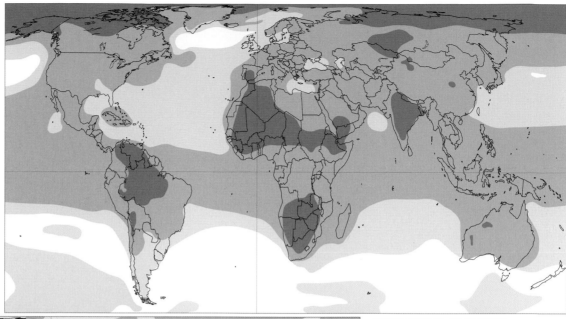

PREDICTED CHANGE IN PRECIPITATION

The difference between actual annual average precipitation, 1960–90, and predicted annual average precipitation, 2070–2100. It should be noted that these predicted annual mean changes mask quite significant seasonal detail.

- Over 2 mm more rain per day
- 1 – 2 mm more rain per day
- 0.5 – 1 mm more rain per day
- 0.2 – 0.5 mm more rain per day
- no change
- 0.2   0.5 mm less rain per day
- 0.5 – 1 mm less rain per day
- 1 – 2 mm less rain per day
- Over 2 mm less rain per day

DESERTIFICATION AND DEFORESTATION

- Existing deserts and dry areas
- Areas with a high risk of desertification
- Areas with a moderate risk of desertification
- Former extent of rainforest
- Existing rainforest

Deforestation 2000–2005

	Annual Actual Loss
Brazil	34,660 sq km
Indonesia	14,478 sq km
Russia	5,322 sq km
Mexico	2,600 sq km
Papua New Guinea	2,502 sq km

	% Loss 1990-2005
Nigeria	79%
Vietnam	78%
Cambodia	58%
Sri Lanka	35%
Indonesia	31%

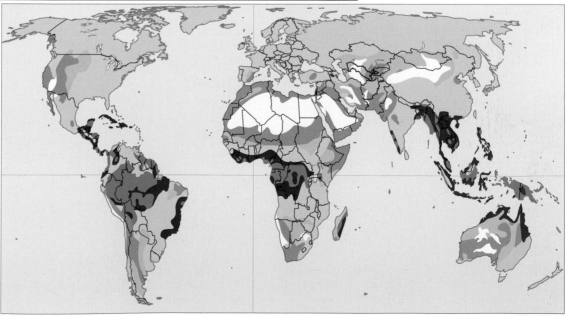

Projection: Eckert IV

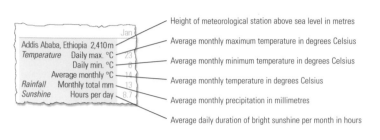

- Height of meteorological station above sea level in metres
- Average monthly maximum temperature in degrees Celsius
- Average monthly minimum temperature in degrees Celsius
- Average monthly temperature in degrees Celsius
- Average monthly precipitation in millimetres
- Average daily duration of bright sunshine per month in hours

Addis Ababa, Ethiopia	2,410m	Jan
Temperature	Daily max. °C	23
	Daily min. °C	6
	Average monthly °C	14
Rainfall	Monthly total mm	13
Sunshine	Hours per day	8.7

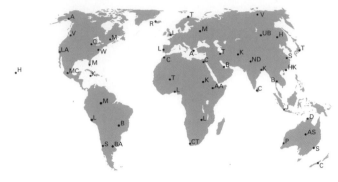

		Jan	Feb	Mar	Apr	May	June	July	Aug	Sept	Oct	Nov	Dec	Year
Addis Ababa, Ethiopia	**2,410m**													
Temperature	Daily max. °C	23	24	25	24	25	23	20	20	21	22	23	22	23
	Daily min. °C	6	7	9	10	9	10	11	11	10	7	5	5	8
	Average monthly °C	14	15	17	17	17	16	16	15	15	15	14	14	15
Rainfall	Monthly total mm	13	35	67	91	81	117	247	255	167	29	8	5	1,115
Sunshine	Hours per day	8.7	8.2	7.6	8.1	6.5	4.8	2.8	3.2	5.2	7.6	6.7	7	6.4
Alice Springs, Australia	**580m**													
Temperature	Daily max. °C	35	35	32	27	23	19	19	23	27	31	33	35	28
	Daily min. °C	21	20	17	12	8	5	4	6	10	15	18	20	13
	Average monthly °C	28	27	25	20	15	12	12	14	18	23	25	27	21
Rainfall	Monthly total mm	44	33	27	10	15	13	7	8	7	18	29	38	249
Sunshine	Hours per day	10.3	10.4	9.3	9.2	8	8	8.9	9.8	10	9.7	10.1	10	9.5
Anchorage, USA	**183m**													
Temperature	Daily max. °C	−7	−3	0	7	13	18	19	17	13	6	−2	−6	−6
	Daily min. °C	−15	−12	−9	−2	4	8	10	9	5	−2	−9	−14	−2
	Average monthly °C	−11	−7	−4	3	9	13	15	13	9	2	−5	−10	−4
Rainfall	Monthly total mm	20	18	13	11	13	25	47	64	64	47	28	24	374
Sunshine	Hours per day	2.4	4.1	6.6	8.3	8.3	9.2	8.5	6	4.4	3.1	2.6	1.6	5.4
Athens, Greece	**107m**													
Temperature	Daily max. °C	13	14	16	20	25	30	33	33	29	24	19	15	23
	Daily min. °C	6	7	8	11	16	20	23	23	19	15	12	8	14
	Average monthly °C	10	10	12	16	20	25	28	28	24	20	15	11	18
Rainfall	Monthly total mm	62	37	37	23	23	14	6	7	15	51	56	71	402
Sunshine	Hours per day	3.9	5.2	5.8	7.7	8.9	10.7	11.9	11.5	9.4	6.8	4.8	3.8	7.3
Bahrain City, Bahrain	**2m**													
Temperature	Daily max. °C	20	21	25	29	33	36	37	38	36	32	27	22	30
	Daily min. °C	14	15	18	22	25	29	31	32	29	25	22	16	23
	Average monthly °C	17	18	21	25	29	32	34	35	32	29	25	19	26
Rainfall	Monthly total mm	18	12	10	9	2	0	0	0	0	0.4	3	16	70
Sunshine	Hours per day	5.9	6.9	7.9	8.8	10.6	13.2	12.1	12	12	10.3	7.7	6.4	9.5
Bangkok, Thailand	**10m**													
Temperature	Daily max. °C	32	33	34	35	34	33	32	32	32	31	31	31	33
	Daily min. °C	20	23	24	26	25	25	25	24	24	24	23	20	24
	Average monthly °C	26	28	29	30	30	29	28	28	28	28	27	26	28
Rainfall	Monthly total mm	9	30	36	82	165	153	168	183	310	239	55	8	1,438
Sunshine	Hours per day	8.2	8	8	10	7.5	6.1	4.7	5.2	5.2	6.1	7.3	7.8	7
Brasilia, Brazil	**910m**													
Temperature	Daily max. °C	28	28	28	28	27	27	27	29	30	29	28	27	28
	Daily min. °C	18	18	18	17	15	13	13	14	16	18	18	18	16
	Average monthly °C	23	23	23	22	21	20	20	21	23	24	23	22	22
Rainfall	Monthly total mm	252	204	227	93	17	3	6	3	30	127	255	343	1,560
Sunshine	Hours per day	5.8	5.7	6	7.4	8.7	9.3	9.6	9.8	7.9	6.5	4.8	4.4	7.2
Buenos Aires, Argentina	**25m**													
Temperature	Daily max. °C	30	29	26	22	18	14	14	16	18	21	25	28	22
	Daily min. °C	17	17	16	12	9	5	6	6	8	10	14	16	11
	Average monthly °C	23	23	21	17	13	10	10	11	13	15	19	22	16
Rainfall	Monthly total mm	79	71	109	89	76	61	56	61	79	86	84	99	950
Sunshine	Hours per day	9.2	8.5	7.5	6.8	4.9	3.5	3.8	5.2	6	6.8	8.1	8.5	6.6
Cairo, Egypt	**75m**													
Temperature	Daily max. °C	19	21	24	28	32	35	35	35	33	30	26	21	28
	Daily min. °C	9	9	12	14	18	20	22	22	20	18	14	10	16
	Average monthly °C	14	15	18	21	25	28	29	28	26	24	20	16	22
Rainfall	Monthly total mm	4	4	3	1	2	1	0	0	1	1	3	7	27
Sunshine	Hours per day	6.9	8.4	8.7	9.7	10.5	11.9	11.7	11.3	10.4	9.4	8.3	6.4	9.5
Cape Town, South Africa	**44m**													
Temperature	Daily max. °C	26	26	25	23	20	18	17	18	19	21	24	25	22
	Daily min. °C	15	15	14	11	9	7	7	7	8	10	13	15	11
	Average monthly °C	21	20	20	17	14	13	12	12	14	16	18	20	16
Rainfall	Monthly total mm	12	19	17	42	67	98	68	76	36	45	12	13	505
Sunshine	Hours per day	11.4	10.2	9.4	7.7	6.1	5.7	6.4	6.6	7.6	8.6	10.2	10.9	8.4
Casablanca, Morocco	**59m**													
Temperature	Daily max. °C	17	18	20	21	22	24	26	26	26	24	21	18	22
	Daily min. °C	8	9	11	12	15	18	19	20	18	15	12	10	14
	Average monthly °C	13	13	15	16	18	21	23	23	22	20	17	14	18
Rainfall	Monthly total mm	78	61	54	37	20	3	0	1	6	28	58	94	440
Sunshine	Hours per day	5.2	6.3	7.3	9	9.4	9.7	10.2	9.7	9.1	7.4	5.9	5.3	7.9

		Jan	Feb	Mar	Apr	May	June	July	Aug	Sept	Oct	Nov	Dec	Year
Chicago, USA	**186m**													
Temperature	Daily max. °C	1	2	6	14	21	26	29	28	24	17	8	2	15
	Daily min. °C	−7	−6	−2	5	11	16	20	19	14	8	0	−5	−6
	Average monthly °C	−3	−2	2	9	16	21	24	23	19	13	4	−2	4
Rainfall	Monthly total mm	47	41	70	77	96	103	86	80	69	71	56	48	844
Sunshine	Hours per day	4	5	6.6	6.9	8.9	10.2	10	9.2	8.2	6.9	4.5	3.7	7
Christchurch, New Zealand	**5m**													
Temperature	Daily max. °C	21	21	19	17	13	11	10	11	14	17	19	21	16
	Daily min. °C	12	12	10	7	4	2	1	3	5	7	8	11	7
	Average monthly °C	16	16	15	12	9	6	6	7	9	12	13	16	11
Rainfall	Monthly total mm	56	46	43	46	76	69	61	58	51	51	51	61	669
Sunshine	Hours per day	7	6.5	5.6	4.7	4.3	3.9	4.1	4.7	5.6	6.1	6.9	6.3	5.5
Colombo, Sri Lanka	**10m**													
Temperature	Daily max. °C	30	31	31	31	30	30	29	29	30	29	29	30	30
	Daily min. °C	22	22	23	24	25	25	25	25	24	23	22	22	24
	Average monthly °C	26	26	27	28	28	27	27	27	27	27	26	26	27
Rainfall	Monthly total mm	101	66	118	230	394	220	140	102	174	348	333	142	2,368
Sunshine	Hours per day	7.9	9	8.1	7.2	6.4	5.4	6.1	6.3	6.2	6.5	6.4	7.8	6.9
Darwin, Australia	**30m**													
Temperature	Daily max. °C	32	32	33	33	33	31	31	32	33	34	34	33	33
	Daily min. °C	25	25	25	24	23	21	19	21	23	25	26	26	24
	Average monthly °C	29	29	29	29	28	26	25	26	28	29	30	29	28
Rainfall	Monthly total mm	405	309	279	77	8	2	0	1	15	48	108	214	1,466
Sunshine	Hours per day	5.8	5.8	6.6	9.8	9.3	10	9.9	10.4	10.1	9.4	9.6	6.8	8.6
Harbin, China	**175m**													
Temperature	Daily max. °C	−14	−9	0	12	21	26	29	27	20	12	−1	−11	9
	Daily min. °C	−26	−23	−12	−1	7	14	18	16	8	0	−12	−22	−3
	Average monthly °C	−20	−16	−6	6	14	20	23	22	14	6	−7	−17	3
Rainfall	Monthly total mm	4	6	17	23	44	92	167	119	52	36	12	5	577
Sunshine	Hours per day	6.4	7.8	8	7.8	8.3	8.6	8.6	8.2	7.2	6.9	6.1	5.7	7.5
Hong Kong, China	**35m**													
Temperature	Daily max. °C	18	18	20	24	28	30	31	31	30	27	24	20	25
	Daily min. °C	13	13	16	19	23	26	26	26	25	23	19	15	20
	Average monthly °C	16	15	18	22	25	28	28	28	27	25	21	17	23
Rainfall	Monthly total mm	30	60	70	133	332	479	286	415	364	33	46	17	2,265
Sunshine	Hours per day	4.7	3.5	3.1	3.8	5	5.4	6.8	6.5	6.6	7	6.2	5.5	5.3
Honolulu, Hawaii	**5m**													
Temperature	Daily max. °C	26	26	26	27	28	29	29	29	30	29	28	26	28
	Daily min. °C	19	19	19	20	21	22	23	23	23	22	21	20	21
	Average monthly °C	23	22	23	23	24	26	26	26	26	26	24	23	24
Rainfall	Monthly total mm	96	84	73	33	25	8	11	23	25	47	55	76	556
Sunshine	Hours per day	7.3	7.7	8.3	8.6	8.8	9.1	9.4	9.3	9.2	8.3	7.5	6.2	8.3
Jakarta, Indonesia	**10m**													
Temperature	Daily max. °C	29	29	30	31	31	31	31	31	31	31	30	29	30
	Daily min. °C	23	23	23	24	24	23	23	23	23	23	23	23	23
	Average monthly °C	26	26	27	27	27	27	27	27	27	27	27	26	27
Rainfall	Monthly total mm	300	300	211	147	114	97	64	43	66	112	142	203	1,799
Sunshine	Hours per day	6.1	6.5	7.7	8.5	8.4	8.5	9.1	9.5	9.6	9	7.7	7.1	8.1
Kabul, Afghanistan	**1,791m**													
Temperature	Daily max. °C	2	4	12	19	26	31	33	33	30	22	17	8	20
	Daily min. °C	−8	−6	1	6	11	13	16	15	11	6	1	−3	5
	Average monthly °C	−3	−1	6	13	18	22	25	24	20	14	9	3	12
Rainfall	Monthly total mm	28	61	72	117	33	1	7	1	0	1	37	14	372
Sunshine	Hours per day	5.9	6	5.7	6.8	10.1	11.5	11.4	11.2	9.8	9.4	7.8	6.1	8.5
Khartoum, Sudan	**380m**													
Temperature	Daily max. °C	32	33	37	40	42	41	38	36	38	39	35	32	37
	Daily min. °C	16	17	20	23	26	27	26	25	25	25	21	17	22
	Average monthly °C	24	25	28	32	34	34	32	30	32	32	28	25	30
Rainfall	Monthly total mm	0	0	0	1	7	5	56	80	28	2	0	0	179
Sunshine	Hours per day	10.6	11.2	10.4	10.8	10.4	10.1	8.6	8.6	9.6	10.3	10.8	10.6	10.2
Kingston, Jamaica	**35m**													
Temperature	Daily max. °C	30	30	30	31	31	32	32	32	32	31	31	31	31
	Daily min. °C	20	20	20	21	22	24	23	23	23	23	22	21	22
	Average monthly °C	25	25	25	26	26	28	28	28	27	27	26	26	26
Rainfall	Monthly total mm	23	15	23	31	102	89	38	91	99	180	74	36	801
Sunshine	Hours per day	8.3	8.8	8.7	8.7	8.3	7.8	8.5	8.5	7.6	7.3	8.3	7.7	8.2

Kolkata (Calcutta), India 5 m

		Jan	Feb	Mar	Apr	May	June	July	Aug	Sept	Oct	Nov	Dec	Year
Temperature	Daily max. °C	27	29	34	36	35	34	32	32	32	32	29	26	31
	Daily min. °C	13	15	21	24	25	26	26	26	26	23	18	13	21
	Average monthly °C	20	22	27	30	30	30	29	29	29	28	23	20	26
Rainfall	Monthly total mm	10	30	34	44	140	297	325	332	253	114	20	5	1,604
Sunshine	Hours per day	8.6	8.7	8.9	9	8.7	5.4	4.1	4.1	5.1	6.5	8.3	8.4	7.1

Lagos, Nigeria 40 m

		Jan	Feb	Mar	Apr	May	June	July	Aug	Sept	Oct	Nov	Dec	Year
Temperature	Daily max. °C	32	33	33	32	31	29	28	28	29	30	31	32	31
	Daily min. °C	22	23	23	23	23	22	22	21	22	22	23	22	22
	Average monthly °C	27	28	28	28	27	26	25	24	25	26	27	27	26
Rainfall	Monthly total mm	28	41	99	99	203	300	180	56	180	190	63	25	1,464
Sunshine	Hours per day	5.9	6.8	6.3	6.1	5.6	3.8	2.8	3.3	3	5.1	6.6	6.5	5.2

Lima, Peru 120 m

		Jan	Feb	Mar	Apr	May	June	July	Aug	Sept	Oct	Nov	Dec	Year
Temperature	Daily max. °C	28	29	29	27	24	20	20	19	20	22	24	26	24
	Daily min. °C	19	20	19	17	16	15	14	14	14	15	16	17	16
	Average monthly °C	24	24	24	22	20	17	17	16	17	18	20	21	20
Rainfall	Monthly total mm	1	1	1	1	5	5	8	8	8	3	3	1	45
Sunshine	Hours per day	6.3	6.8	6.9	6.7	4	1.4	1.1	1	1.1	2.5	4.1	5	3.9

Lisbon, Portugal 77 m

		Jan	Feb	Mar	Apr	May	June	July	Aug	Sept	Oct	Nov	Dec	Year
Temperature	Daily max. °C	14	15	17	20	21	25	27	28	26	22	17	15	21
	Daily min. °C	8	8	10	12	13	15	17	17	17	14	11	9	13
	Average monthly °C	11	12	14	16	17	20	22	23	21	18	14	12	17
Rainfall	Monthly total mm	111	76	109	54	44	16	3	4	33	62	93	103	708
Sunshine	Hours per day	4.7	5.9	6	8.3	9.1	10.6	11.4	10.7	8.4	6.7	5.2	4.6	7.7

London (Kew), UK 5 m

		Jan	Feb	Mar	Apr	May	June	July	Aug	Sept	Oct	Nov	Dec	Year
Temperature	Daily max. °C	6	7	10	13	17	20	22	21	19	14	10	7	14
	Daily min. °C	2	2	3	6	8	12	14	13	11	8	5	4	7
	Average monthly °C	4	5	7	9	12	16	18	17	15	11	8	5	11
Rainfall	Monthly total mm	54	40	37	37	46	45	57	59	49	57	64	48	593
Sunshine	Hours per day	1.7	2.3	3.5	5.7	6.7	7	6.6	6	5	3.3	1.9	1.4	4.3

Los Angeles, USA 30 m

		Jan	Feb	Mar	Apr	May	June	July	Aug	Sept	Oct	Nov	Dec	Year
Temperature	Daily max. °C	18	18	18	19	20	22	24	24	24	23	22	19	21
	Daily min. °C	7	8	9	11	13	15	17	17	16	14	11	9	12
	Average monthly °C	12	13	14	15	17	18	21	21	20	18	16	14	17
Rainfall	Monthly total mm	69	74	46	28	3	3	0	0	5	10	28	61	327
Sunshine	Hours per day	6.9	8.2	8.9	8.8	9.5	10.3	11.7	11	10.1	8.6	8.2	7.6	9.2

Lusaka, Zambia 1,154 m

		Jan	Feb	Mar	Apr	May	June	July	Aug	Sept	Oct	Nov	Dec	Year
Temperature	Daily max. °C	26	26	26	27	25	23	23	26	29	31	29	27	27
	Daily min. °C	17	17	16	15	12	10	9	11	15	18	18	17	15
	Average monthly °C	22	22	21	21	18	17	16	19	22	25	23	22	21
Rainfall	Monthly total mm	224	173	90	19	3	1	0	1	1	17	85	196	810
Sunshine	Hours per day	5.1	5.4	6.9	8.9	9	9	9.1	9.6	9.5	9	7	5.5	7.8

Manaus, Brazil 45 m

		Jan	Feb	Mar	Apr	May	June	July	Aug	Sept	Oct	Nov	Dec	Year
Temperature	Daily max. °C	31	31	31	31	31	31	32	33	34	34	33	32	32
	Daily min. °C	24	24	24	24	24	24	24	24	24	25	25	24	24
	Average monthly °C	28	28	28	27	28	28	28	29	29	29	29	28	28
Rainfall	Monthly total mm	278	278	300	287	193	99	61	41	62	112	165	220	2,096
Sunshine	Hours per day	3.9	4	3.6	3.9	5.4	6.9	7.9	8.2	7.5	6.6	5.9	4.9	5.7

Mexico City, Mexico 2,309 m

		Jan	Feb	Mar	Apr	May	June	July	Aug	Sept	Oct	Nov	Dec	Year
Temperature	Daily max. °C	21	23	26	27	26	25	23	24	23	22	21	21	24
	Daily min. °C	5	6	7	9	10	11	11	11	11	9	6	5	8
	Average monthly °C	13	15	16	18	18	18	17	17	17	16	14	13	16
Rainfall	Monthly total mm	8	4	9	23	57	111	160	149	119	46	16	7	709
Sunshine	Hours per day	7.3	8.1	8.5	8.1	7.8	7	6.2	6.4	5.6	6.3	7	7.3	7.1

Miami, USA 2 m

		Jan	Feb	Mar	Apr	May	June	July	Aug	Sept	Oct	Nov	Dec	Year
Temperature	Daily max. °C	24	25	27	28	30	31	32	32	31	29	27	25	28
	Daily min. °C	14	15	16	19	21	23	24	24	24	22	18	15	20
	Average monthly °C	19	20	21	23	25	27	28	28	27	25	22	20	24
Rainfall	Monthly total mm	51	48	58	99	163	188	170	178	241	208	71	43	1,518
Sunshine	Hours per day	7.7	8.3	8.7	9.4	8.9	8.5	8.7	8.4	7.1	6.5	7.5	7.1	8.1

Montreal, Canada 57 m

		Jan	Feb	Mar	Apr	May	June	July	Aug	Sept	Oct	Nov	Dec	Year
Temperature	Daily max. °C	–6	–4	2	11	18	23	26	25	20	14	5	–3	11
	Daily min. °C	–13	–11	–5	2	9	14	17	16	11	6	0	–9	3
	Average monthly °C	–9	–8	–2	6	13	19	22	20	16	10	3	–6	7
Rainfall	Monthly total mm	87	76	86	83	81	91	98	87	96	84	89	89	1,047
Sunshine	Hours per day	2.8	3.4	4.5	5.2	6.7	7.7	8.2	7.7	5.6	4.3	2.4	2.2	5.1

Moscow, Russia 156 m

		Jan	Feb	Mar	Apr	May	June	July	Aug	Sept	Oct	Nov	Dec	Year
Temperature	Daily max. °C	–6	–4	1	9	18	22	24	22	17	10	1	–5	9
	Daily min. °C	–14	–16	–11	–1	5	9	12	9	4	–2	–6	–12	–2
	Average monthly °C	–10	–10	–5	4	12	15	18	16	10	4	–2	–8	4
Rainfall	Monthly total mm	31	28	33	35	52	67	74	74	58	51	36	36	575
Sunshine	Hours per day	1	1.9	3.7	5.2	7.8	8.3	8.4	7.1	4.4	2.4	1	0.6	4.4

New Delhi, India 220 m

		Jan	Feb	Mar	Apr	May	June	July	Aug	Sept	Oct	Nov	Dec	Year
Temperature	Daily max. °C	21	24	29	36	41	39	35	34	34	34	28	23	32
	Daily min. °C	6	10	14	20	26	28	27	26	24	17	11	7	18
	Average monthly °C	14	17	22	28	33	34	31	30	29	26	20	15	25
Rainfall	Monthly total mm	25	21	13	8	13	77	178	184	123	10	2	11	665
Sunshine	Hours per day	7.7	8.2	8.2	8.7	9.2	7.9	6	6.3	6.9	9.4	8.7	8.3	8

Perth, Australia 60 m

		Jan	Feb	Mar	Apr	May	June	July	Aug	Sept	Oct	Nov	Dec	Year
Temperature	Daily max. °C	29	30	27	25	21	18	17	18	19	21	25	27	23
	Daily min. °C	17	18	16	14	12	10	9	9	10	11	14	16	13
	Average monthly °C	23	24	22	19	16	14	13	13	15	16	19	22	18
Rainfall	Monthly total mm	8	13	22	44	128	189	177	145	84	58	19	13	900
Sunshine	Hours per day	10.4	9.8	8.8	7.5	5.7	4.8	5.4	6	7.2	8.1	9.6	10.4	7.8

Reykjavik, Iceland 18 m

		Jan	Feb	Mar	Apr	May	June	July	Aug	Sept	Oct	Nov	Dec	Year
Temperature	Daily max. °C	2	3	5	6	10	13	15	14	12	8	5	4	8
	Daily min. °C	–3	–3	–1	1	4	7	9	8	6	3	0	–2	3
	Average monthly °C	0	0	2	4	7	10	12	11	9	5	3	1	5
Rainfall	Monthly total mm	89	64	62	56	42	42	50	56	67	94	78	79	779
Sunshine	Hours per day	0.8	2	3.6	4.5	5.9	6.1	5.8	5.4	3.5	2.3	1.1	0.3	3.7

Santiago, Chile 520 m

		Jan	Feb	Mar	Apr	May	June	July	Aug	Sept	Oct	Nov	Dec	Year
Temperature	Daily max. °C	30	29	27	24	19	15	15	17	19	22	26	29	23
	Daily min. °C	12	11	10	7	5	3	3	4	6	7	9	11	7
	Average monthly °C	21	20	18	15	12	9	9	10	12	15	17	20	15
Rainfall	Monthly total mm	3	3	5	13	64	84	76	56	31	15	8	5	363
Sunshine	Hours per day	10.8	8.9	8.5	5.5	3.6	3.3	3.3	3.6	4.8	6.1	8.7	10.1	6.4

Shanghai, China 5 m

		Jan	Feb	Mar	Apr	May	June	July	Aug	Sept	Oct	Nov	Dec	Year
Temperature	Daily max. °C	8	8	13	19	24	28	32	32	27	23	17	10	20
	Daily min. °C	–1	0	4	9	14	19	23	23	19	13	7	2	11
	Average monthly °C	3	4	8	14	19	23	27	27	23	18	12	6	15
Rainfall	Monthly total mm	48	59	84	94	94	180	147	142	130	71	51	36	1,136
Sunshine	Hours per day	4	3.7	4.4	4.8	5.4	4.7	6.9	7.5	5.3	5.6	4.7	4.5	5.1

Sydney, Australia 40 m

		Jan	Feb	Mar	Apr	May	June	July	Aug	Sept	Oct	Nov	Dec	Year
Temperature	Daily max. °C	26	26	25	22	19	17	17	18	20	22	24	25	22
	Daily min. °C	18	19	17	14	11	9	8	9	11	13	16	17	14
	Average monthly °C	22	22	21	18	15	13	12	13	16	18	20	21	18
Rainfall	Monthly total mm	89	101	127	135	127	117	117	76	74	71	74	74	1,182
Sunshine	Hours per day	7.5	7	6.4	6.1	5.7	5.3	6.1	7	7.3	7.5	7.5	7.5	6.8

Tehran, Iran 1,191 m

		Jan	Feb	Mar	Apr	May	June	July	Aug	Sept	Oct	Nov	Dec	Year
Temperature	Daily max. °C	9	11	16	21	29	30	37	36	29	24	16	11	22
	Daily min. °C	–1	1	4	10	16	20	23	23	18	12	6	1	11
	Average monthly °C	4	6	10	15	22	25	30	29	23	18	11	6	17
Rainfall	Monthly total mm	37	23	36	31	14	2	1	1	1	5	29	27	207
Sunshine	Hours per day	5.9	6.7	7.5	7.4	8.6	11.6	11.2	11	10.1	7.6	6.9	6.3	8.4

Timbuktu, Mali 269 m

		Jan	Feb	Mar	Apr	May	June	July	Aug	Sept	Oct	Nov	Dec	Year
Temperature	Daily max. °C	31	35	38	41	43	42	38	35	38	40	37	31	37
	Daily min. °C	13	16	18	22	26	27	25	24	24	23	18	14	21
	Average monthly °C	22	25	28	31	34	34	32	30	31	31	28	23	29
Rainfall	Monthly total mm	0	0	0	1	4	20	54	93	31	3	0	0	206
Sunshine	Hours per day	9.1	9.6	9.6	9.7	9.8	9.4	9.6	9	9.3	9.5	9.5	8.9	9.4

Tokyo, Japan 5 m

		Jan	Feb	Mar	Apr	May	June	July	Aug	Sept	Oct	Nov	Dec	Year
Temperature	Daily max. °C	9	9	12	18	22	25	29	30	27	20	16	11	19
	Daily min. °C	–1	–1	3	4	13	17	22	23	19	13	7	1	10
	Average monthly °C	4	4	8	11	18	21	25	26	23	17	11	6	14
Rainfall	Monthly total mm	48	73	101	135	131	182	146	147	217	220	101	61	1,562
Sunshine	Hours per day	6	5.9	5.7	6	6.2	5	5.8	6.6	4.5	4.4	4.8	5.4	5.5

Tromsø, Norway 100 m

		Jan	Feb	Mar	Apr	May	June	July	Aug	Sept	Oct	Nov	Dec	Year
Temperature	Daily max. °C	–2	–2	0	3	7	12	16	14	10	5	2	0	5
	Daily min. °C	–6	–6	–5	–2	1	6	9	8	5	1	–2	–4	0
	Average monthly °C	–4	–4	–3	0	4	9	13	11	7	3	0	–2	3
Rainfall	Monthly total mm	96	79	91	65	61	59	56	80	109	115	88	95	994
Sunshine	Hours per day	0.1	1.6	2.9	6.1	5.7	6.9	7.9	4.8	3.5	1.7	0.3	0	3.5

Ulan Bator, Mongolia 1,305 m

		Jan	Feb	Mar	Apr	May	June	July	Aug	Sept	Oct	Nov	Dec	Year
Temperature	Daily max. °C	–19	–13	–4	7	13	21	22	21	14	6	–6	–16	4
	Daily min. °C	–32	–29	–22	–8	–2	7	11	8	2	–8	–20	–28	–11
	Average monthly °C	–26	–21	–13	–1	6	14	16	14	8	–1	–13	–22	–4
Rainfall	Monthly total mm	1	1	2	5	10	28	76	51	23	5	5	2	209
Sunshine	Hours per day	6.4	7.8	8	7.8	8.3	8.6	8.6	8.2	7.2	6.9	6.1	5.7	7.5

Vancouver, Canada 5 m

		Jan	Feb	Mar	Apr	May	June	July	Aug	Sept	Oct	Nov	Dec	Year
Temperature	Daily max. °C	6	7	10	14	17	20	23	22	19	14	9	7	14
	Daily min. °C	0	1	3	5	8	11	13	12	10	7	3	2	6
	Average monthly °C	3	4	6	9	13	16	18	17	14	10	6	4	10
Rainfall	Monthly total mm	214	161	151	90	69	65	39	44	83	172	198	243	1,529
Sunshine	Hours per day	1.6	3	3.8	5.9	7.5	7.4	9.5	8.2	6	3.7	2	1.4	5

Verkhoyansk, Russia 137 m

		Jan	Feb	Mar	Apr	May	June	July	Aug	Sept	Oct	Nov	Dec	Year
Temperature	Daily max. °C	–47	–40	–20	–1	11	21	24	21	12	–8	–33	–42	–8
	Daily min. °C	–51	–48	–40	–25	–7	4	6	1	–6	–20	–39	–50	–23
	Average monthly °C	–49	–44	–30	–13	2	12	15	11	3	–14	–36	–46	–16
Rainfall	Monthly total mm	7	5	5	4	5	25	33	30	13	11	10	7	155
Sunshine	Hours per day	0	2.6	6.9	9.6	9.7	10	9.7	7.5	4.1	2.4	0.6	0	5.4

Washington, D.C., USA 22 m

		Jan	Feb	Mar	Apr	May	June	July	Aug	Sept	Oct	Nov	Dec	Year
Temperature	Daily max. °C	7	8	12	19	25	29	31	30	26	20	14	8	19
	Daily min. °C	–1	–1	2	8	13	18	21	20	16	10	4	–1	9
	Average monthly °C	3	3	7	13	19	24	26	25	21	15	9	4	14
Rainfall	Monthly total mm	84	68	96	85	103	88	108	120	100	78	75	75	1,080
Sunshine	Hours per day	4.4	5.7	6.7	7.4	8.2	8.8	8.6	8.2	7.5	6.5	5.3	4.5	6.8

Tropical Rain Forest

Tall broadleaved evergreen forest, trees 30–50m high with climbers and epiphytes forming continuous canopies. Associated with wet climate, 2–3000mm precipitation per year and high temperatures 24–28°C. High diversity of species, typically 100 per ha, including lianas, bamboo, palms, rubber, mahogany. Mangrove swamps form in coastal areas.

Subtropical and Temperate Rain Forest

Precipitation, which is less than in the Tropical Rain Forest, falls in the long wet season interspersed with a season of reduced rainfall and lower temperatures. As a result there are fewer species, thinner canopies, fewer lianas and denser ground level foliage. Vegetation consists of evergreen oak, laurel, bamboo, magnolia and tree ferns.

Monsoon Woodland and Open Jungle

Mostly deciduous trees, because of the long dry season and lower temperatures. Trees can reach 30m but are sparser than in the rain forests. There is less competition for light and thick jungle vegetation grows at lower levels. High species diversity includes lianas, bamboo, teak, sandalwood, sal and banyan.

This diagram shows the highly stratified nature of the tropical rain forest. Crowns of trees form numerous layers at different heights and the dense shade limits undergrowth.

Temperate Deciduous and Coniferous Forest

A transition zone between broadleaves and conifers. Broadleaves are better suited to the warmer, damper and flatter locations.

Coniferous Forest (Taiga or Boreal)

Forming a large continuous belt across Northern America and Eurasia with a uniformity in tree species. Characteristically trees are tall, conical with short branches and wax-covered needle-shaped leaves to retain moisture. Cold climate with prolonged harsh winters and cool summers where average temperatures are under 0°C for more than six months of the year Undergrowth is sparse with mosses and lichens. Tree species include pine, fir, spruce, larch, tamarisk.

Mountainous Forest, mainly Coniferous

Mild winters, high humidity and high levels of rainfall throughout the year provide habitat for dense needle-leaf evergreen forests and the largest trees in the world, up to 100m, including the Douglas fir, redwood and giant sequoia.

High Plateau Steppe and Tundra

Similar to arctic tundra with frozen ground for the majority of the year. Very sparse ground coverage of low, shallow-rooted herbs, small shrubs, mosses, lichens and heather interspersed with bare soil.

Arctic Tundra

Average temperatures are 0°C, precipitation is mainly snowfall and the ground remains frozen for 10 months of the year. Vegetation flourishes when the shallow surface layer melts in the long summer days. Underlying permafrost remains frozen and surface water cannot drain away, making conditions marshy. Consists of sedges, snow lichen, arctic meadow grass, cotton grasses and dwarf willow.

Polar and Mountainous Ice Desert

Areas of bare rock and ice with patches of rock-strewn lithosols, low in organic matter and low water content. In sheltered patches only a few mosses, lichens and low shrubs can grow, including woolly moss and purple saxifrage.

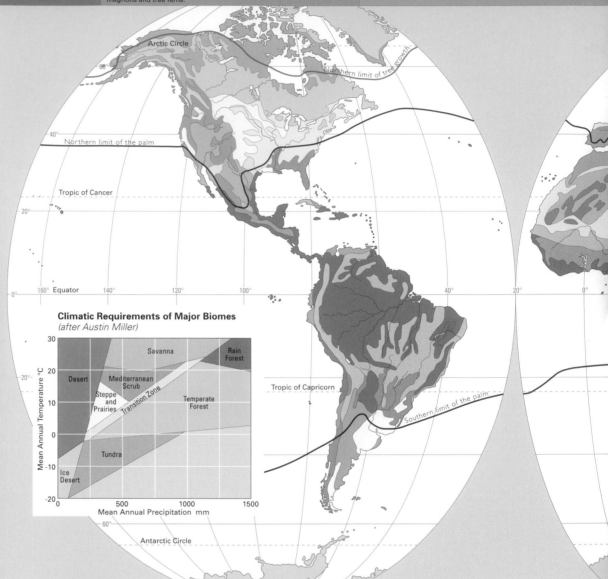

Climatic Requirements of Major Biomes
(after Austin Miller)

SOIL REGIONS
1:220 000 000

- Tundra soil
- Podzols
- Brown forest soil
- Lightly leached dry forest soil
- Red and yellow subtropical forest soil
- Reddish savanna soil and tropical red earths
- Laterites
- Chernozem
- Degraded chernozem
- Black savanna soil
- Chestnut steppe soil
- Desertic (arid) soil
- Alluvium
- Mountain and high plateau soils
- Oases soil
- Tropical and mangrove swamp

(after Glinka, Stremme, Marbut, and others)

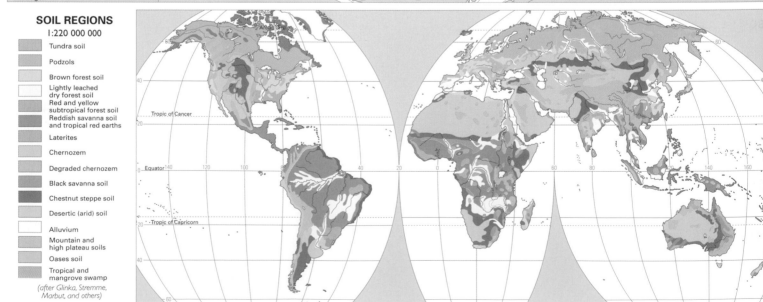

Projection: Interrupted Mollweide's Homolographic

Subtropical and Temperate Woodland, Scrub and Bush
Vast clearings with woody shrubs and tall grasses. Trees are fire-resistant and either deciduous or xerophytic because of long dry periods. Species include eucalyptus, acacia, mimosa and euphorbia.

Tropical Savanna with Low Trees and Bush
Tall, coarse grass with enough precipitation to support a scattering of short deciduous trees and thorn scrub. Vegetation consists of elephant grass, acacia, palms and baobab and is limited by aridity, grazing animals and periodic fires; trees have developed thick, woody bark, small leaves or thorns.

Tropical Savanna and Grassland
Areas with a hot climate and long dry season. Extensive areas of tall grasses often reach 3.5m with scattered fire and drought resistant bushes, low trees and thickets of elephant grass. Shrubs include acacia, baobab and palms.

BIOMES
Classified by Climax Vegetation
1:116 000 000

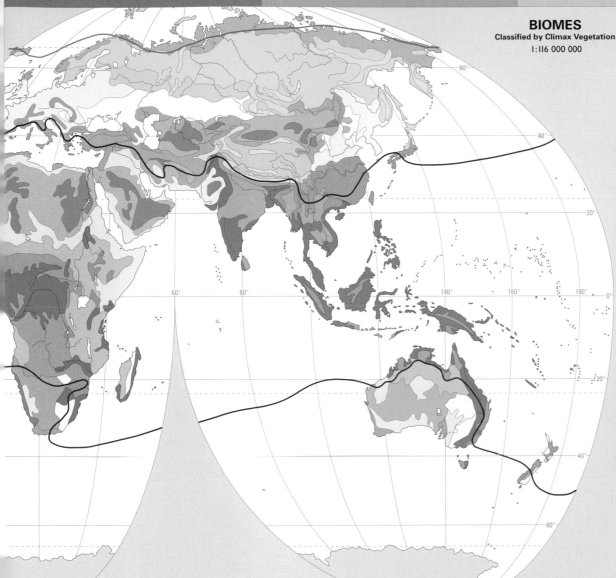

Dry Semi-desert with Shrub and Grass
Xerophytic shrubs with thin grass cover and few trees, limited by a long dry season and short, hot, rainy period. Sagebrush, bunch grass and acacia shrubs are common.

Desert Shrub
Scattered xerophytic plants able to withstand daytime extremes in temperature and long periods of drought. There is a large diversity of desert flora such as cacti, yucca, tamarisk, hard grass and artemisia.

Desert
Precipitation less than 250mm per year. Vegetation is very sparse, mainly bare rock, sand dunes and salt flats. Vegetation comprises a few xerophytic shrubs and ephemeral flowers.

Dry Steppe and Shrub
Semi-arid with cold, dry winters and hot summers. Bare soil with sparsely distributed short grasses and scattered shrubs and short trees. Species include acacia, artemisia, saksaul and tamarisk.

Temperate Grasslands, Prairie and Steppe
Continuous, tall, dense and deep-rooted swards of ancient grasslands, considered to be natural climax vegetation as determined by soil and climate. Average precipitation 250–750mm, with a long dry season, limits growth of trees and shrubs. Includes Stipa grass, buffalo grass, blue stems and loco weed.

Mediterranean Hardwood Forest and Scrub
Areas with hot and arid summers. Sparse evergreen trees are short and twisted with thick bark, interspersed with areas of scrub land. Trees have waxy leaves or thorns and deep root systems to resist drought. Many of the hardwood forests have been cleared by man, resulting in extensive scrub formation – maquis and chaparral. Species found are evergreen oak, stone pine, cork, olive and myrtle.

Temperate Deciduous Forest and Meadow
Areas of relatively high, well-distributed rainfall and temperature favourable for forest growth. The Tall broadleaved trees form a canopy in the summer, but shed their leaves in the winter. The undergrowth is sparse and poorly developed, but in the spring, herbs and flowers develop quickly. Diverse species, with up to 20 per ha, including oak, beech, birch, maple, ash, elm, chestnut and hornbeam. Many of these forests have been cleared for urbanization and farming.

SOIL DEGRADATION
1:220 000 000

Areas of Concern
- Areas of serious concern
- Areas of some concern
- Stable terrain
- Non-vegetated land

Causes of soil degradation (by region)
- Grazing practices
- Other agricultural practices
- Industrialization
- Deforestation
- Fuelwood collection

(after Wageningen)

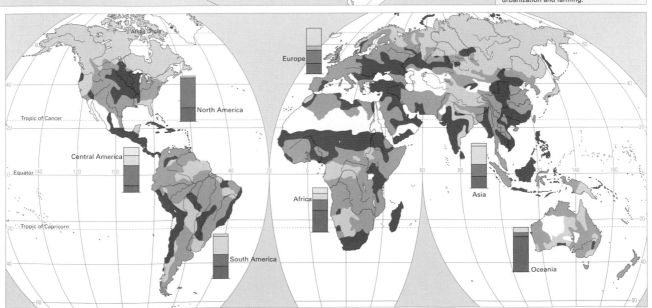

COPYRIGHT PHILIP'S

AGRICULTURAL PRODUCTION

Staple Crops

Wheat

China 17.2% | India 11.4% | USA 9.5% | Russia 7.4% | France 5.8% | Canada 4.5% | Germany 3.7%

World total (2006): 605,946,000 tonnes

Rice

China 28.0% | India 21.5% | Indonesia 8.6% | Bangladesh 6.9% | Vietnam 5.6% | Thailand 4.6% | Burma 4.0%

World total (2006): 634,606,000 tonnes

Cassava

Nigeria 20.2% | Brazil 11.8% | Thailand 10.0% | Indonesia 8.8% | Congo (D.R) 6.6% | Mozambique 5.1%

World total (2006): 226,337,000 tonnes

Barley

Russia 13.3% | Germany 8.8% | Ukraine 8.3% | France 7.6% | Canada 7.0% | Turkey 7.0%

World total (2006): 136,209,000 tonnes

Maize

USA 38.5% | China 20.9% | Brazil 6.1%

World total (2006): 695,228,000 tonnes

Potatoes

China 22.3% | Russia 12.2% | India 7.6% | USA 6.3% | Ukraine 6.2%

World total (2006): 315,100,000 tonnes

Soybeans

USA 38.6% | Brazil 23.6% | Argentina 18.3% | China 7.0%

World total (2006): 221,501,000 tonnes

Millet

India 31.8% | Nigeria 24.2% | Niger 10.1% | China 5.7%

World total (2006): 31,781,000 tonnes

Animal Products

Milk

India 14.6% | China 5.6% | Russia 4.9% | Pakistan 4.8% | Germany 4.4%

World total (2006): 653,789,000 tonnes

Eggs

China 40.6% | USA 8.6% | India 4.2% | Japan 4.0%

World total (2006): 62,089,000 tonnes

Chicken

USA 21.7% | China 14.6% | Brazil 11.9% | Mexico 3.4% | India 2.7%

World total (2006): 73,088,000 tonnes

Beef and Veal

USA 19.5% | Brazil 12.7% | China 11.8% | Argentina 4.9% | Australia 3.4% | Russia 2.9%

World total (2006): 61,033,000 tonnes

Pigmeat

China 46.9% | USA 9.0% | Germany 4.4% | Spain 3.1% | Brazil 2.9%

World total (2006): 106,383,000 tonnes

Sugars

Sugar Cane

Brazil 32.7% | India 20.2% | China 7.2% | Mexico 3.6% | Thailand 3.3% | Pakistan 3.2%

World total (2006): 1,393,365,000 tonnes

Sugar Beet

Russia 12.0% | France 11.7% | USA 11.3% | Ukraine 8.7% | Germany 8.1% | Turkey 5.9% | Poland 4.5% | Italy 4.2%

World total (2006): 256,407,000 tonnes

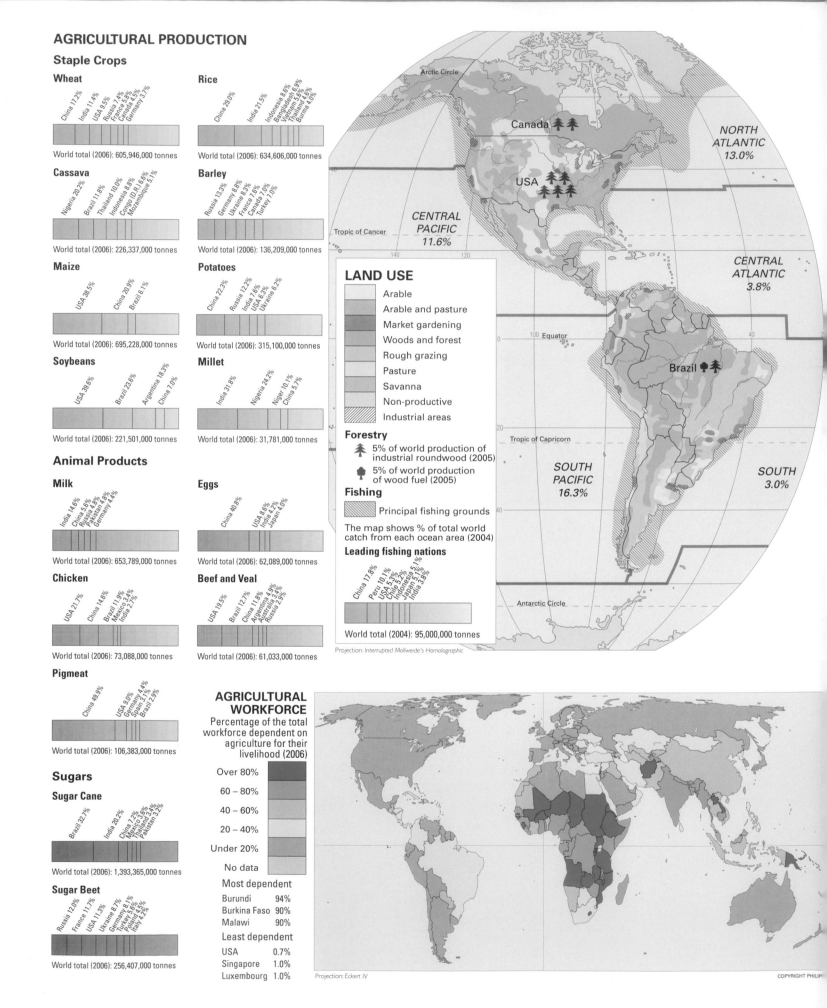

LAND USE

- Arable
- Arable and pasture
- Market gardening
- Woods and forest
- Rough grazing
- Pasture
- Savanna
- Non-productive
- Industrial areas

Forestry

🌲 5% of world production of industrial roundwood (2005)

🌳 5% of world production of wood fuel (2005)

Fishing

Principal fishing grounds

The map shows % of total world catch from each ocean area (2004)

Leading fishing nations

China 17.8% | Peru 10.1% | USA 5.3% | Chile 5.2% | Indonesia 5.1% | Japan 5.1% | India 3.8%

World total (2004): 95,000,000 tonnes

Projection: Interrupted Mollweide's Homolographic

NORTH ATLANTIC 13.0%

CENTRAL PACIFIC 11.6%

CENTRAL ATLANTIC 3.8%

SOUTH PACIFIC 16.3%

SOUTH 3.0%

Canada

USA

Brazil

Arctic Circle
Tropic of Cancer
Equator
Tropic of Capricorn
Antarctic Circle

AGRICULTURAL WORKFORCE

Percentage of the total workforce dependent on agriculture for their livelihood (2006)

- Over 80%
- 60 – 80%
- 40 – 60%
- 20 – 40%
- Under 20%
- No data

Most dependent

Burundi	94%
Burkina Faso	90%
Malawi	90%

Least dependent

USA	0.7%
Singapore	1.0%
Luxembourg	1.0%

Projection: Eckert IV

COPYRIGHT PHILIP

LAND USE, FORESTRY AND FISHING

1:110 000 000

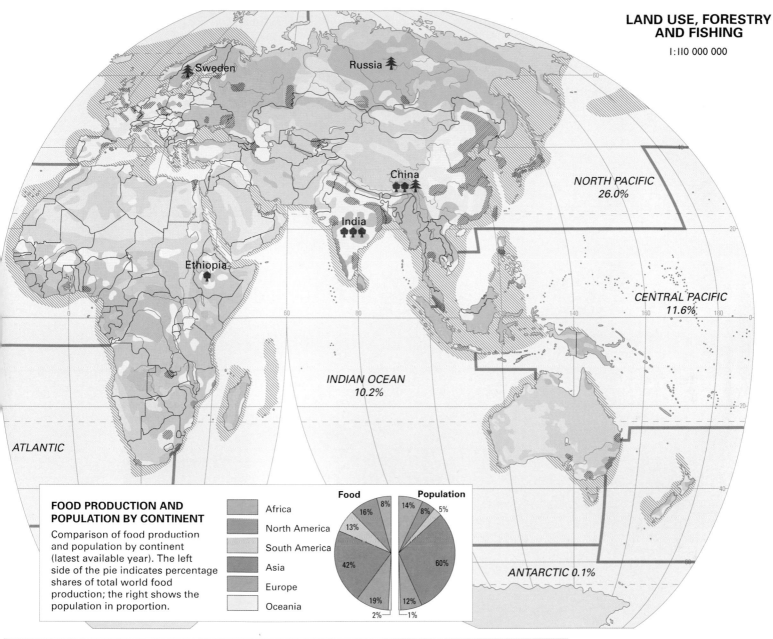

Sweden

Russia

China

India

Ethiopia

NORTH PACIFIC
26.0%

CENTRAL PACIFIC
11.6%

INDIAN OCEAN
10.2%

ATLANTIC

ANTARCTIC 0.1%

FOOD PRODUCTION AND POPULATION BY CONTINENT

Comparison of food production and population by continent (latest available year). The left side of the pie indicates percentage shares of total world food production; the right shows the population in proportion.

Africa
North America
South America
Asia
Europe
Oceania

Food
8%
16%
13%
42%
19%
2%

Population
14%
8%
5%
60%
12%
1%

DAILY FOOD CONSUMPTION

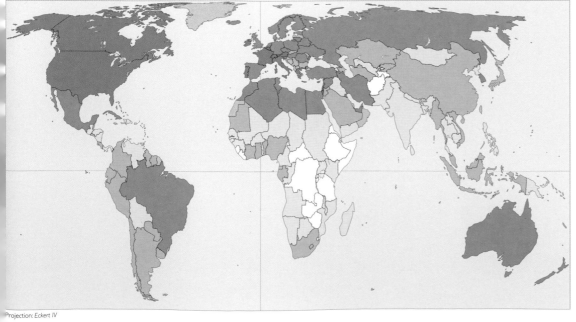

Average daily food intake in calories per person (2003)

Over 3,500

3,000 – 3,500

2,500 – 3,000

2,000 – 2,500

Under 2,000

No data

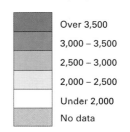

Top 5 countries		Bottom 5 countries	
USA	3,774	Eritrea	1,513
Portugal	3,741	Afghanistan	1,539
Greece	3,721	Congo (Dem. Rep.)	1,599
Luxembourg	3,701	Somalia	1,628
Austria	3,673	Burundi	1,648

UK 3,412

In 2008, the United Nations estimated that 923 million people were undernourished.

Projection: *Eckert IV*

ENERGY PRODUCTION BY REGION

Each square represents 1% of world primary energy production (2007)

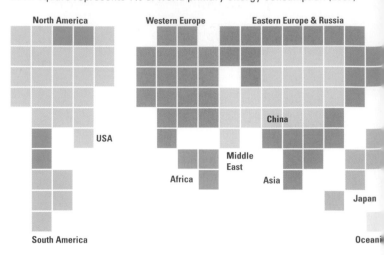

North America · **Western Europe** · **Eastern Europe & Russia**

USA · Japan · China · Middle East · Africa · Asia · South America · Oceania

ENERGY CONSUMPTION BY REGION

Each square represents 1% of world primary energy consumption (2007)

North America · **Western Europe** · **Eastern Europe & Russia**

USA · China · Middle East · Africa · Asia · Japan · South America · Oceania

ENERGY BALANCE

Difference between primary energy production and consumption in millions of tonnes of oil equivalent (MtOe) 2007

↑ **Energy surplus in MtOe**

- Over 35 surplus
- 1 – 35 surplus
- 1 deficit – 1 surplus (approx. balance)
- 1 – 35 deficit
- Over 35 deficit

↓ **Energy deficit in MtOe**

Fossil fuel production

	Principal	Secondary
Oilfields	●	●
Gasfields	▼	▽
Coalfields	△	△

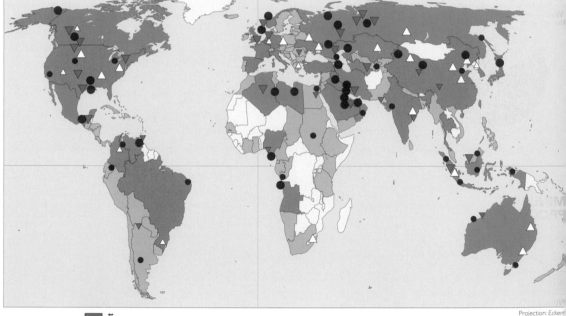

Projection: Eckert

OIL RESERVES

World oil reserves by region and country, thousand million tonnes (2006)

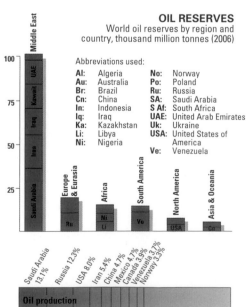

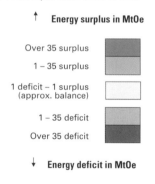

Abbreviations used:

Al:	Algeria	No:	Norway
Au:	Australia	Po:	Poland
Br:	Brazil	Ru:	Russia
Cn:	China	SA:	Saudi Arabia
In:	Indonesia	S Af:	South Africa
Iq:	Iraq	UAE:	United Arab Emirates
Ka:	Kazakhstan	Uk:	Ukraine
Li:	Libya	USA:	United States of America
Ni:	Nigeria	Ve:	Venezuela

Oil production

Saudi Arabia 13.1% · Russia 12.3% · USA 8.0% · Iran 5.4% · China 4.7% · Mexico 4.7% · Canada 3.9% · Venezuela 3.7% · Norway 3.3%

World total (2006): 3,914,000,000 tonnes

GAS RESERVES

World natural gas reserves by region and country, thousand million tonnes of oil equivalent (2006)

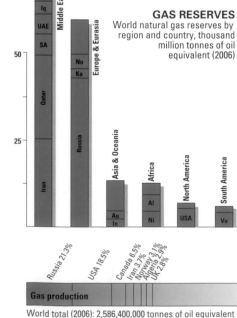

Gas production

Russia 21.3% · USA 18.5% · Canada 6.5% · Iran 3.7% · Norway 3.1% · Algeria 2.9% · UK 2.8%

World total (2006): 2,586,400,000 tonnes of oil equivalent

COAL RESERVES

World coal reserves by region and country, thousand million tonnes (2006, including lignite)

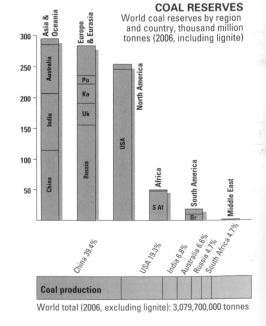

Coal production

China 39.4% · USA 19.3% · India 6.8% · Australia 6.6% · Russia 4.7% · South Africa 4.7%

World total (2006, excluding lignite): 3,079,700,000 tonnes

ELECTRICITY GENERATION
Percentage of electricity generated by source (2007)

- Over 75% from thermal
- 50 – 75% from thermal
- Over 75% from hydro
- 50 – 75% from hydro
- Over 50% from nuclear
- No dominant source
- No data
- ○ Selected geothermal plants
- ◆ Selected hydroelectric plants

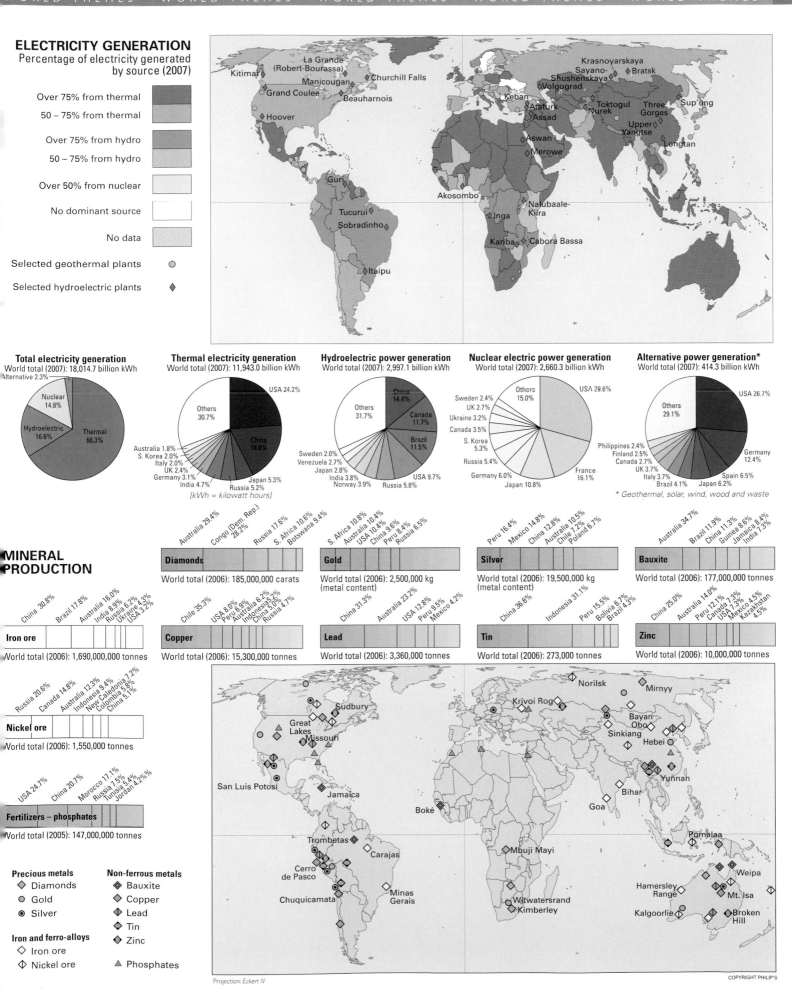

Total electricity generation
World total (2007): 18,014.7 billion kWh
- Alternative 2.3%
- Nuclear 14.8%
- Hydroelectric 16.6%
- Thermal 66.3%

Thermal electricity generation
World total (2007): 11,943.0 billion kWh
- USA 24.2%
- Others 30.7%
- China 18.6%
- Japan 5.3%
- Russia 5.2%
- India 4.7%
- Germany 3.1%
- UK 2.4%
- Italy 2.0%
- S. Korea 2.0%
- Australia 1.8%

[kWh = kilowatt hours]

Hydroelectric power generation
World total (2007): 2,997.1 billion kWh
- China 14.4%
- Canada 11.7%
- Brazil 11.5%
- USA 9.7%
- Russia 5.8%
- Norway 3.9%
- India 3.8%
- Japan 2.8%
- Venezuela 2.7%
- Sweden 2.0%
- Others 31.7%

Nuclear electric power generation
World total (2007): 2,660.3 billion kWh
- USA 29.6%
- France 16.1%
- Japan 10.8%
- Germany 6.0%
- Russia 5.4%
- S. Korea 5.3%
- Canada 3.5%
- Ukraine 3.2%
- UK 2.7%
- Sweden 2.4%
- Others 15.0%

Alternative power generation*
World total (2007): 414.3 billion kWh
- USA 26.7%
- Germany 12.4%
- Spain 6.5%
- Japan 6.2%
- Brazil 4.1%
- Italy 3.7%
- UK 3.7%
- Canada 3.4%
- Finland 2.5%
- Philippines 2.4%
- Others 29.1%

* Geothermal, solar, wind, wood and waste

MINERAL PRODUCTION

Iron ore
World total (2006): 1,690,000,000 tonnes
- China 30.8%
- Brazil 17.8%
- Australia 16.0%
- India 8.9%
- Russia 6.2%
- Ukraine 4.3%
- USA 3.2%

Diamonds
World total (2006): 185,000,000 carats
- Australia 29.4%
- Congo (Dem. Rep.) 28.2%
- Russia 17.6%
- S. Africa 10.6%
- Botswana 9.4%

Gold
World total (2006): 2,500,000 kg (metal content)
- S. Africa 10.8%
- Australia 10.4%
- USA 10.4%
- China 9.6%
- Peru 8.4%
- Russia 6.5%

Silver
World total (2006): 19,500,000 kg (metal content)
- Peru 16.4%
- Mexico 14.8%
- China 12.8%
- Australia 10.5%
- Chile 7.2%
- Poland 6.7%

Bauxite
World total (2006): 177,000,000 tonnes
- Australia 34.7%
- Brazil 11.9%
- China 11.3%
- Guinea 8.6%
- Jamaica 8.4%
- India 7.3%

Nickel ore
World total (2006): 1,550,000 tonnes
- Russia 20.6%
- Canada 14.8%
- Australia 12.3%
- Indonesia 9.4%
- New Caledonia 7.2%
- Colombia 5.8%
- China 5.1%

Copper
World total (2006): 15,300,000 tonnes
- Chile 35.3%
- USA 8.0%
- Peru 6.9%
- Australia 6.2%
- Indonesia 5.6%
- China 5.0%
- Russia 4.7%

Lead
World total (2006): 3,360,000 tonnes
- China 31.3%
- Australia 23.2%
- USA 12.8%
- Peru 9.5%
- Mexico 4.2%

Tin
World total (2006): 273,000 tonnes
- China 36.6%
- Indonesia 31.1%
- Peru 15.5%
- Bolivia 6.7%
- Brazil 4.3%

Zinc
World total (2006): 10,000,000 tonnes
- China 25.0%
- Australia 14.0%
- Peru 12.1%
- Canada 7.3%
- USA 7.3%
- Mexico 4.5%
- Kazakhstan 4.5%

Fertilizers – phosphates
World total (2005): 147,000,000 tonnes
- USA 24.7%
- China 20.7%
- Morocco 17.1%
- Russia 7.5%
- Tunisia 5.4%
- Jordan 4.2%

Precious metals
- ◇ Diamonds
- ○ Gold
- ◉ Silver

Iron and ferro-alloys
- ◇ Iron ore
- ◇ Nickel ore

Non-ferrous metals
- ◇ Bauxite
- ◇ Copper
- ◇ Lead
- ◇ Tin
- ◇ Zinc
- ▲ Phosphates

Projection: Eckert IV

COPYRIGHT PHILIP'S

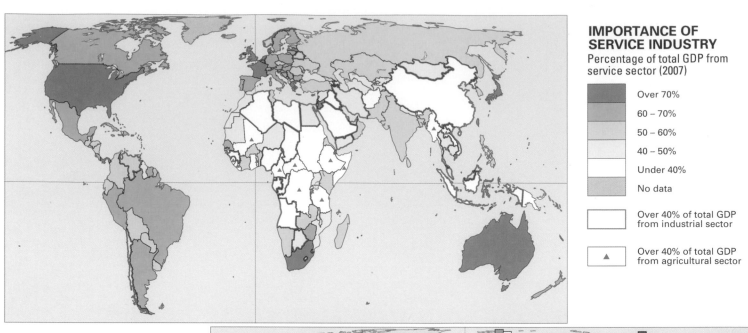

IMPORTANCE OF SERVICE INDUSTRY

Percentage of total GDP from service sector (2007)

- Over 70%
- 60 – 70%
- 50 – 60%
- 40 – 50%
- Under 40%
- No data

▢ Over 40% of total GDP from industrial sector

▲ Over 40% of total GDP from agricultural sector

LOCATION OF MANUFACTURING

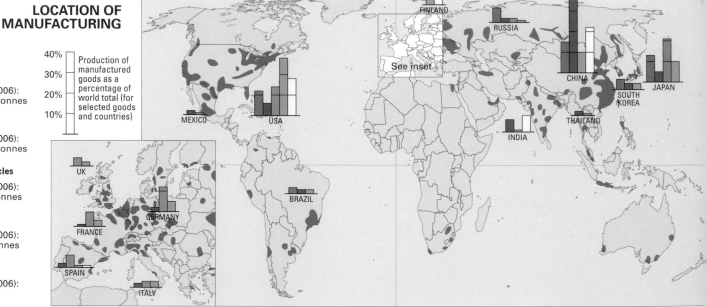

■ **Industrial regions**

■ **Steel**
World total (2006): 1,244 million tonnes

■ **Cement**
World total (2006): 2,310 million tonnes

■ **Motor vehicles**
World total (2006): 40.3 million tonnes

■ **Paper**
World total (2006): 365 million tonnes

□ **Textiles**
World total (2006): 24.6 million tonnes

Production of manufactured goods as a percentage of world total (for selected goods and countries)
40% 30% 20% 10%

See inset

EMPLOYMENT BY ECONOMIC ACTIVITY Selected countries (2005)

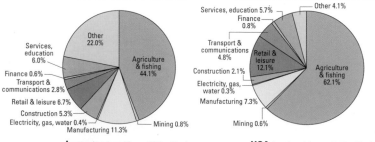

China (total workforce: 798.0 million)
- Agriculture & fishing 44.1%
- Other 22.0%
- Services, education 6.0%
- Finance 0.6%
- Transport & communications 2.8%
- Retail & leisure 6.7%
- Construction 5.3%
- Electricity, gas, water 0.4%
- Manufacturing 11.3%
- Mining 0.8%

Bangladesh (total workforce: 68.0 million)
- Agriculture & fishing 62.1%
- Services, education 5.7%
- Finance 0.8%
- Other 4.1%
- Transport & communications 4.8%
- Retail & leisure 12.1%
- Construction 2.1%
- Electricity, gas, water 0.3%
- Manufacturing 7.3%
- Mining 0.6%

Germany (total workforce: 36.6 million)
- Agriculture & fishing 2.4%
- Mining 0.3%
- Services, education 31.4%
- Manufacturing 22.0%
- Electricity, gas, water 0.9%
- Construction 6.6%
- Finance 13.2%
- Retail & leisure 17.9%
- Transport & communications 5.3%

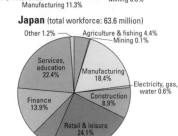

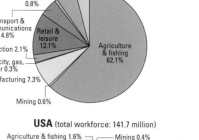

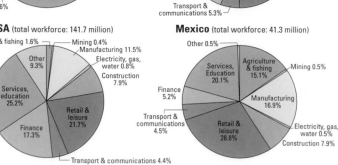

Japan (total workforce: 63.6 million)
- Agriculture & fishing 4.4%
- Mining 0.1%
- Other 1.2%
- Services, education 22.4%
- Manufacturing 18.4%
- Electricity, gas, water 0.6%
- Construction 8.9%
- Finance 13.9%
- Retail & leisure 24.1%
- Transport & communications 6.1%

USA (total workforce: 141.7 million)
- Agriculture & fishing 1.6%
- Mining 0.4%
- Manufacturing 11.5%
- Electricity, gas, water 0.8%
- Construction 7.9%
- Other 9.3%
- Services, education 25.2%
- Retail & leisure 21.7%
- Finance 17.3%
- Transport & communications 4.4%

Mexico (total workforce: 41.3 million)
- Other 0.5%
- Services, Education 20.1%
- Agriculture & fishing 15.1%
- Mining 0.5%
- Finance 5.2%
- Manufacturing 16.9%
- Transport & communications 4.5%
- Retail & leisure 28.8%
- Electricity, gas, water 0.5%
- Construction 7.9%

RESEARCH & DEVELOPMENT

Expenditure on R&D as a percentage of GDP (2005)

Country	Percentage
Israel	4.7
Sweden	3.9
Finland	3.5
Japan	3.2
South Korea	3.0
Switzerland	2.9
Iceland	2.8
USA	2.7
UK	2.6
Taiwan	2.5
Germany	2.5
Denmark	2.4
Austria	2.4
Singapore	2.4
France	2.1
Canada	2.0
Australia	1.8
Belgium	1.8
Netherlands	1.8
Luxembourg	1.6
Slovenia	1.5
Norway	1.5
Czech Republic	1.4
China	1.3
Ireland	1.3

WORLD TRADE

Percentage share of total world exports by value (2007)

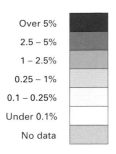

- Over 5%
- 2.5 – 5%
- 1 – 2.5%
- 0.25 – 1%
- 0.1 – 0.25%
- Under 0.1%
- No data

The members of 'G8', the inner circle of OECD, account for more than half the total. The majority of nations contribute less than one quarter of 1% to the worldwide total of exports; EU countries account for 35%; the Pacific Rim nations over 50%.

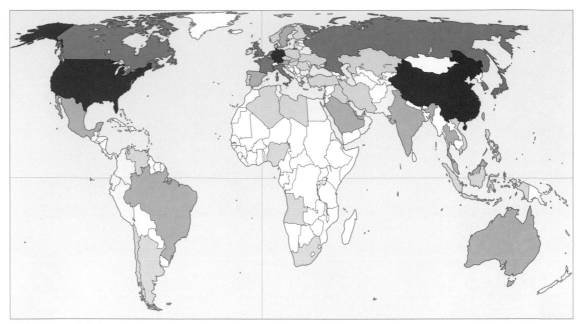

MAJOR EXPORTS Leading manufactured items and their exporters

Motor Vehicles
World total (2007): US$ 2,706,511 million

Germany 19%, Japan 14%, USA 9%, Canada 7%, France 7%, Spain 5%, Belgium 5%, S. Korea 4%, UK 4%, Mexico 4%, Italy 3%, China 2%, Sweden 2%, Other 15%

Telecommunications Gear
World total (2007): US$ 577,845 million

China 21%, UK 10%, Hong Kong 8%, S. Korea 8%, USA 6%, Japan 6%, Mexico 6%, Germany 6%, Singapore 3%, France 3%, Netherlands 3%, Malaysia 3%, Other 17%

Petrol Products
World total (2007): US$ 1,031,202 million

Russia 9%, Singapore 8%, Netherlands 7%, Saudi Arabia 5%, USA 5%, S. Korea 4%, Germany 4%, UK 4%, India 4%, Bahrain 3%, Italy 3%, France 3%, Other 37%

Computers
World total (2007): US$ 236,396 million

China 26%, USA 10%, Neth. 8%, Germany 7%, Singapore 7%, Malaysia 5%, Mexico 5%, S. Korea 4%, Ireland 4%, UK 4%, Japan 4%, Other 16%

Electrical Components
World total (2007): US$ 4,187,042 million

China 11%, USA 10%, Germany 8%, Japan 8%, Hong Kong 6%, Singapore 6%, Malaysia 4%, UK 4%, Mexico 4%, France 3%, Other 36%

Pharmaceuticals
World total (2007): US$ 1,042,778 million

Germany 16%, Belgium 14%, Switzerland 10%, USA 9%, UK 9%, France 9%, Ireland 7%, Italy 5%, Netherlands 3%, Sweden 3%, Other 15%

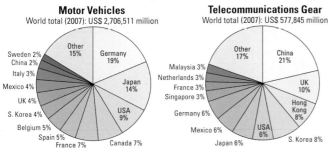

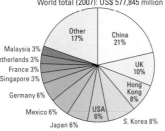

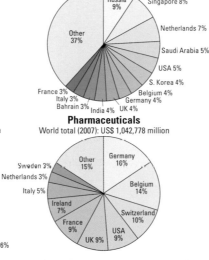

Top Container Ports

Total container traffic, in million TEU (2007)
('TEU' stands for Twenty-foot Equivalent Unit, the equivalent of a standard container)

Singapore, Shang'ai, Hong Kong, Shenzhen, Busan, Kaohsiung, Hamburg, Qingdao, Ningoo, Guanzhou

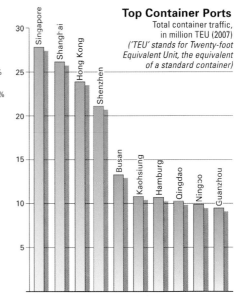

INTERNET AND TELECOMMUNICATIONS

Percentage of total population using the Internet (2007)

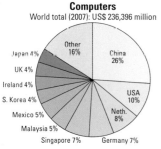

- Over 50%
- 25 – 50%
- 10 – 25%
- 1 – 10%
- Under 1%
- No data

Telecommunications

Trade in office machines and telecom equipment, percentage of world total (2007)

IMPORT EXPORT
40%
30%
20%
10%

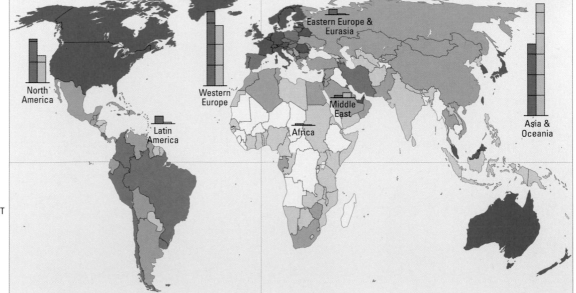

Eastern Europe & Eurasia

North America

Latin America

Western Europe

Middle East

Africa

Asia & Oceania

Projection: Eckert IV

COPYRIGHT PHILIP'S

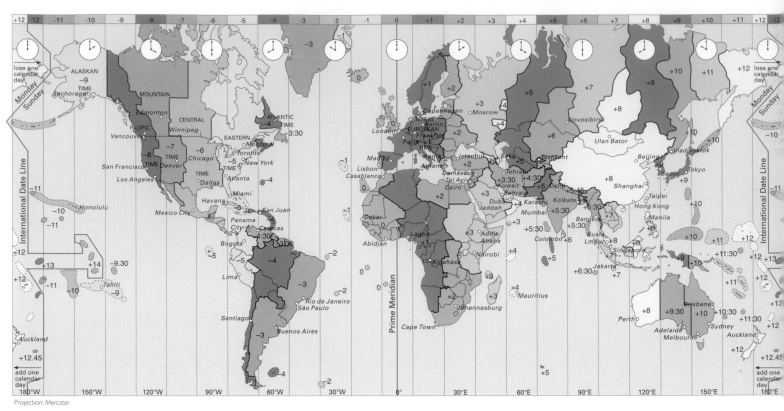

Projection: *Mercator*

TIME ZONES

Zones using UT (Universal Time)

Zones behind UT (Universal Time)

Zones ahead of UT (Universal Time)

Half-hour zones

10 Hours behind or ahead of UT (Universal Time)

- - - - - International boundaries
——— Time zone boundaries

——— Time-zone boundaries
——— International Date Line

Actual solar time, when it is noon at Greenwich, is shown at the top of the map.

Note: Certain time zones are affected by the incidence of daylight saving time in countries where it is adopted.
UT (Universal Time) has replaced GMT (Greenwich Mean Time)

AIR TRAVEL

Major airports
Number of passengers (international and domestic 2007)

○ Over 50 million
○ 25 – 50 million
○ 15 – 25 million
○ 10 – 15 million

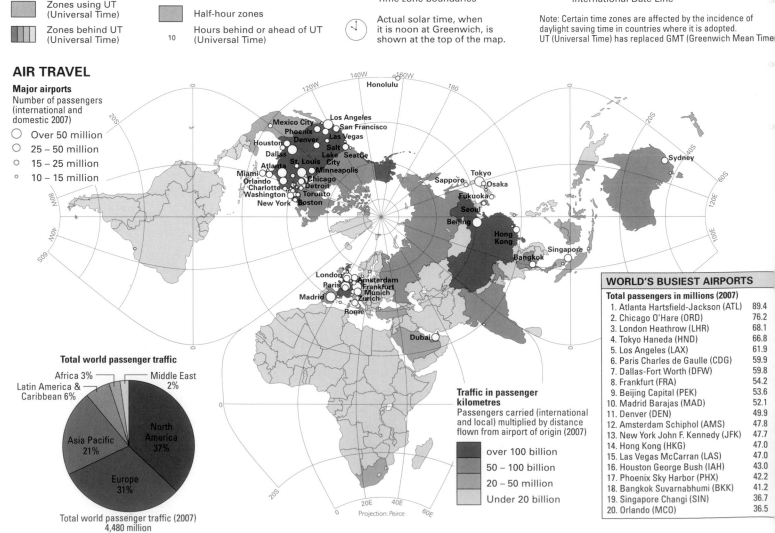

Total world passenger traffic

Africa 3%
Latin America & Caribbean 6%
Middle East 2%
North America 37%
Asia Pacific 21%
Europe 31%

Total world passenger traffic (2007)
4,480 million

Traffic in passenger kilometres
Passengers carried (international and local) multiplied by distance flown from airport of origin (2007)

over 100 billion
50 – 100 billion
20 – 50 million
Under 20 billion

Projection: *Peirce*

WORLD'S BUSIEST AIRPORTS

Total passengers in millions (2007)

1. Atlanta Hartsfield-Jackson (ATL)	89.4
2. Chicago O'Hare (ORD)	76.2
3. London Heathrow (LHR)	68.1
4. Tokyo Haneda (HND)	66.8
5. Los Angeles (LAX)	61.9
6. Paris Charles de Gaulle (CDG)	59.9
7. Dallas-Fort Worth (DFW)	59.8
8. Frankfurt (FRA)	54.2
9. Beijing Capital (PEK)	53.6
10. Madrid Barajas (MAD)	52.1
11. Denver (DEN)	49.9
12. Amsterdam Schiphol (AMS)	47.8
13. New York John F. Kennedy (JFK)	47.7
14. Hong Kong (HKG)	47.0
15. Las Vegas McCarran (LAS)	47.0
16. Houston George Bush (IAH)	43.0
17. Phoenix Sky Harbor (PHX)	42.2
18. Bangkok Suvarnabhumi (BKK)	41.2
19. Singapore Changi (SIN)	36.7
20. Orlando (MCO)	36.5

UNESCO WORLD HERITAGE SITES 2007

Total sites = 851 (660 cultural, 166 natural and 25 mixed)

Region	Cultural sites	Natural sites	Mixed sites
Africa	39	35	3
Arab States	59	3	1
Asia & Pacific	119	46	9
Europe & North America	380	57	10
Latin America & Caribbean	81	35	3

NB Some sites are trans-boundary, therefore the total figures may not add up

TOURIST EARNINGS

Countries receiving the most from overseas tourism, US$ million (2006)

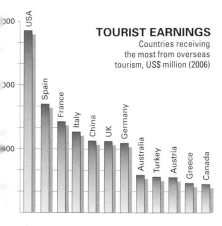

USA, Spain, France, Italy, China, UK, Germany, Australia, Turkey, Austria, Greece, Canada

TOURIST SPENDING

Countries spending the most on overseas tourism, US$ million (2006)

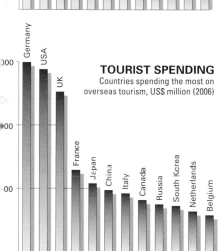

Germany, USA, UK, France, Japan, China, Italy, Canada, Russia, South Korea, Netherlands, Belgium

Europe at larger scale

Saimaa, Fjords, St Petersburg, Öland, Edinburgh, Dublin, Copenhagen, London, Amsterdam, Disneyland, Paris, Prague, Tatra, Brittany, Vienna, Budapest, Lourdes, Alps, Costa Brava, Black Sea Coast, Lisbon, Pyrenees, Venice, Florence, Barcelona, Côte d'Azur, Rome, Istanbul, Algarve, Balearic Islands, Pompeii, Aegean Is., Costa del Sol, Costa Blanca, Ionian Islands, Athens, Crete, Rhodes

Destinations

- ■ Cultural & historical centres
- ▫ Coastal resorts
- □ Ski resorts
- ▨ Centres of entertainment
- ▨ Places of pilgrimage
- ▨ Places of great natural beauty
- ▨ Other tourist destinations

Movement of tourists

- ⟹ More than 10 million
- ⟶ 5 – 10 million
- ⟶ 3 – 5 million
- ⟶ Less than 3 million

TOURIST DESTINATIONS

Projection: Peirce

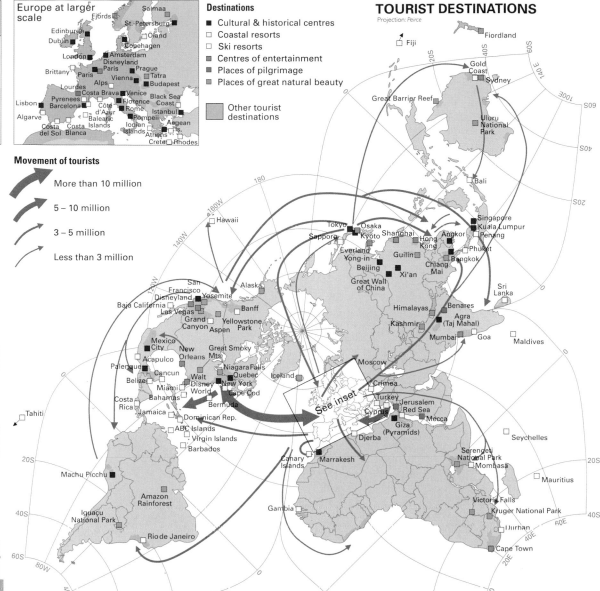

IMPORTANCE OF TOURISM

Tourism receipts as a percentage of Gross National Income (2005)

- 10% and over
- 5 – 10%
- 2.5 – 5%
- 1 – 2.5%
- Under 1%
- No data

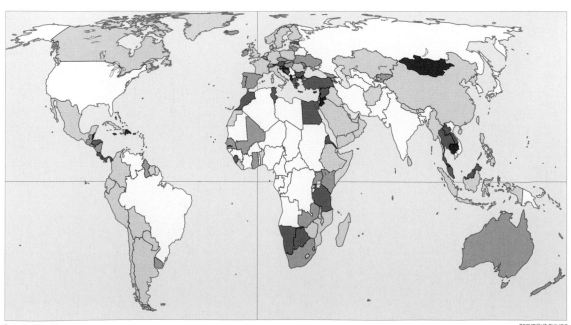

Tourist arrivals in millions (2006)

France	79.1
Spain	58.5
USA	51.1
China	49.6
Italy	41.1
UK	30.7

Projection: Eckert IV

WEALTH

The value of total production divided by the population (the Gross Domestic Product per capita, in 2007)

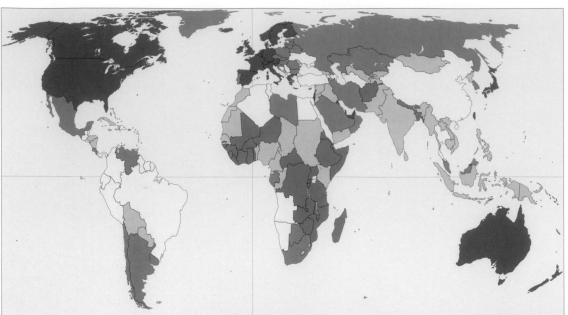

	Over 250% of world average
	100 – 250% of world average

World average U$10,000

	50 – 100% of world average
	15 – 50% of world average
	Under 15% of world average
	No data

Top 5 countries		Bottom 5 countries	
Lux'bourg	$80,800	Congo (D. Rep.)	$300
Norway	$55,600	Liberia	$500
Kuwait	$55,300	Zimbabwe	$500
UAE	$55,200	Comoros	$600
Singapore	$48,900	Guinea-Bissau	$600

UK $35,000

WATER SUPPLY

The percentage of total population with access to safe drinking water (2004)

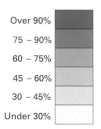

	Over 90%
	75 – 90%
	60 – 75%
	45 – 60%
	30 – 45%
	Under 30%

Least well-provided countries

Afghanistan	13%
Ethiopia	22%
Western Sahara	26%
Papua New Guinea	39%
Cambodia	41%
Somalia	42%

One person in eight in the world has no access to a safe water supply.

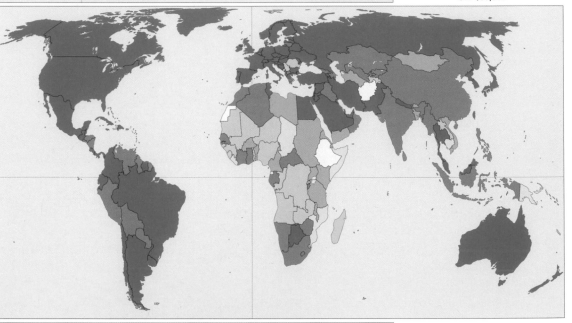

HUMAN DEVELOPMENT

The Human Development Index (HDI), calculated by the UN Development Programme (UNDP), gives a value to countries using indicators of life expectancy, education and standards of living in 2005. Higher values show more developed countries.

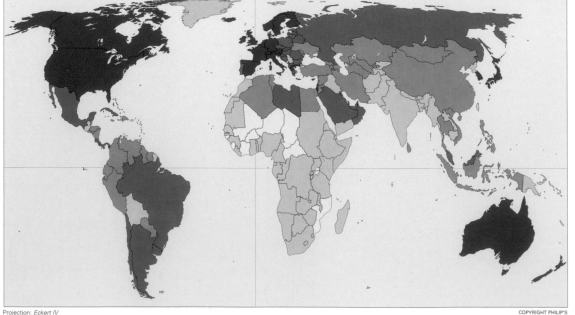

	Over 0.9
	0.8 – 0.9
	0.7 – 0.8
	0.4 – 0.7
	Under 0.4
	No data

Highest values		Lowest values	
Norway	0.968	Sierra Leone	0.336
Iceland	0.968	Burkina Faso	0.370
Australia	0.962	Niger	0.374
Canada	0.961	Guinea-Bissau	0.374
Ireland	0.959	Mali	0.380

UK 0.946

Projection: *Eckert IV*

COPYRIGHT PHILIP'S

HEALTH CARE

Number of qualified doctors
per 100,000 people (2004)

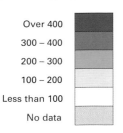

Over 400
300 – 400
200 – 300
100 – 200
Less than 100
No data

Countries with the most and least
doctors per 100,000 people

Most doctors		Least doctors	
Cuba	591	Malawi	2
Monaco	581	Tanzania	2
Belarus	455	Mozambique	3
Belgium	449	Ethiopia	3
Estonia	448	Burundi	3

UK = 230 doctors

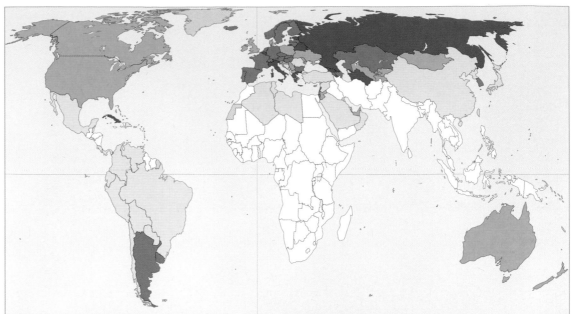

ILLITERACY

Percentage of adult total
population unable to read or
write (2005)

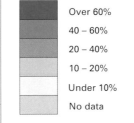

Over 60%
40 – 60%
20 – 40%
10 – 20%
Under 10%
No data

Countries with the highest
and lowest illiteracy rates

Highest (%)		Lowest (%)	
Burkina Faso	87	Australia	0
Niger	83	Denmark	0
Mali	81	Finland	0
Sierra Leone	69	Liechtenstein	0
Guinea	64	Luxembourg	0

UK 1%

GENDER DEVELOPMENT INDEX (GDI)

The Gender Development Index (GDI) shows
economic and social differences between
men and women by using various UNDP
indicators (2005). Countries with higher
values of GDI have more equality between
men and women.

Over 0.8
0.6 – 0.8
0.4 – 0.6
Under 0.4
No data

Highest values		Lowest values	
Iceland	0.962	Sierra Leone	0.320
Australia	0.960	Niger	0.355
Norway	0.957	Guinea-Bissau	0.355
Canada	0.956	Burkina Faso	0.354

UK = 0.944

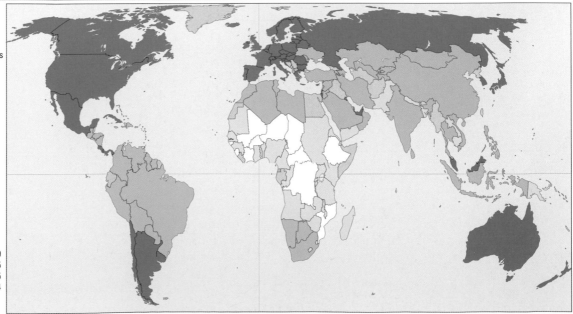

Projection: *Eckert IV*

AGE DISTRIBUTION PYRAMIDS

The bars represent the percentage of the total population (males plus females) in each age group. Developed countries such as New Zealand have populations spread evenly across age groups and usually a growing percentage of elderly people. Developing countries such as Kenya have the great majority of their people in the younger age groups, about to enter their most fertile years.

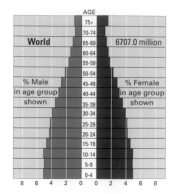

World — 6707.0 million

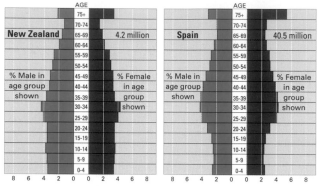

New Zealand — 4.2 million

Spain — 40.5 million

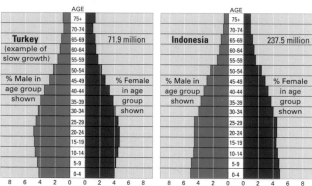

Turkey (example of slow growth) — 71.9 million

Indonesia — 237.5 million

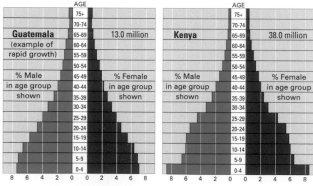

Guatemala (example of rapid growth) — 13.0 million

Kenya — 38.0 million

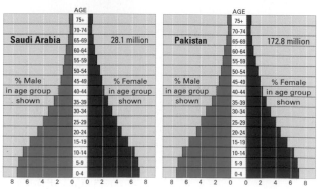

Saudi Arabia — 28.1 million

Pakistan — 172.8 million

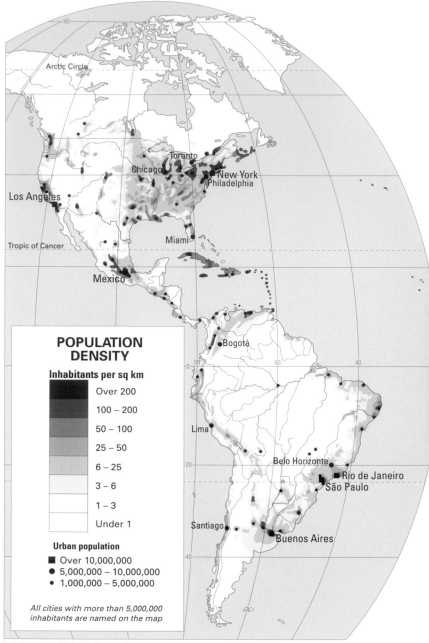

POPULATION DENSITY

Inhabitants per sq km

- Over 200
- 100 – 200
- 50 – 100
- 25 – 50
- 6 – 25
- 3 – 6
- 1 – 3
- Under 1

Urban population

- ■ Over 10,000,000
- ● 5,000,000 – 10,000,000
- • 1,000,000 – 5,000,000

All cities with more than 5,000,000 inhabitants are named on the map

Projection: Interrupted Mollweide's Homolographic

POPULATION CHANGE 1930–2020

Population totals are in millions

Figures in italics represent the percentage average annual increase for the period shown

	1930	1930–1960	1960	1960–1990	1990	1990–2020	2020
World	2,013	1.4%	3,019	1.9%	5,292	1.4%	8,062
Africa	1551	2.0%	2811	2.9%	6482	2.7%	1,441
North America	3512	1.3%	9921	1.1%	7644	0.6%	3277
Latin America*	91,07	1.8%	81,66	2.4%	83,10	1.6%	194,6
Asia	3355	1.5%	9425	2.1%	8498	1.4%	8051
Europe	1017	0.6%	1621	0.6%	2728	0.1%	4373
Oceania	6	1.4%	4	1.8%	8	1.1%	43
CIS†		0.7%		1.0%		0.6%	

* South America plus Central America, Mexico and the West Indies
† Commonwealth of Independent States, formerly the USSR

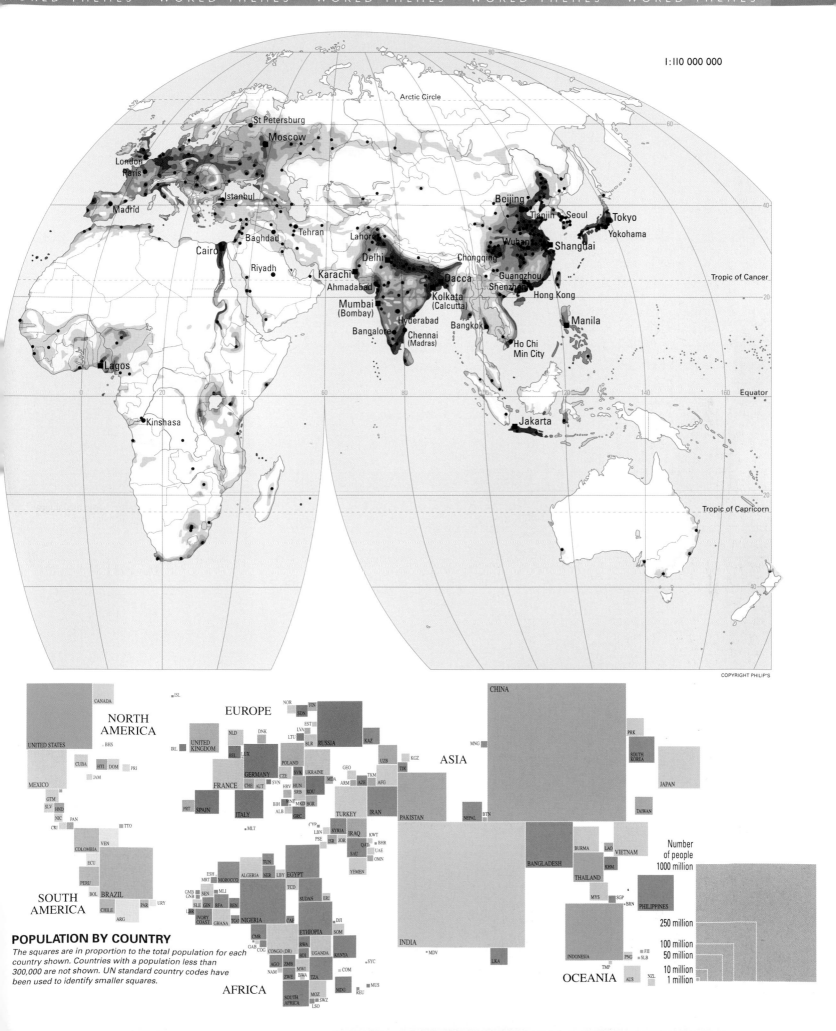

Arctic Circle

St Petersburg

Moscow

London
Paris

Madrid

Istanbul

Tehran

Baghdad

Cairo

Riyadh

Lahore

Delhi

Karachi

Ahmadabad

Mumbai
(Bombay)

Bangalore

Hyderabad

Chennai
(Madras)

Kolkata
(Calcutta)

Dacca

Bangkok

Ho Chi
Min City

Beijing

Tianjin   Seoul

Wuhan

Chongqing

Guangzhou

Shenzhen

Hong Kong

Shanghai

Tokyo

Yokohama

Manila

Lagos

Kinshasa

Jakarta

Tropic of Cancer

Equator

Tropic of Capricorn

1:110 000 000

COPYRIGHT PHILIP'S

POPULATION BY COUNTRY

The squares are in proportion to the total population for each
country shown. Countries with a population less than
300,000 are not shown. UN standard country codes have
been used to identify smaller squares.

NORTH
AMERICA

EUROPE

ASIA

CHINA

SOUTH
AMERICA

AFRICA

OCEANIA

Number
of people
1000 million

250 million

100 million

50 million

10 million

1 million

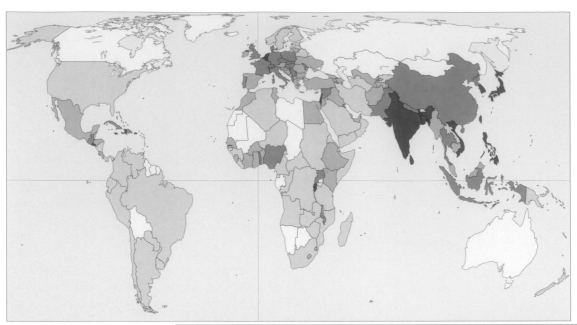

POPULATION DENSITY BY COUNTRY

Density of people per square kilometre (2008)

	Over 250
	100 – 250
	50 – 100
	10 – 50
	Under 10

Most and least densely populated countries

Most		Least	
Monaco	16,818	Chad	0.8
Singapore	6,650	W. Sahara	1.5
Gaza Strip	4,167	Mongolia	1.9
Maldives	1,286	Namibia	2.5
Malta	1,227	Australia	2.7

(UK = 249 people per square km)

POPULATION CHANGE

The projected population change for the years 2004–2050

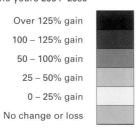

Over 125% gain	
100 – 125% gain	
50 – 100% gain	
25 – 50% gain	
0 – 25% gain	
No change or loss	

Based on estimates for the year 2050, below are listed the ten most populous nations in the world, in millions:

India	1,628	Pakistan	295
China	1,437	Bangladesh	280
USA	420	Brazil	221
Indonesia	308	Congo (Dem. Rep.)	181
Nigeria	307	Ethiopia	171

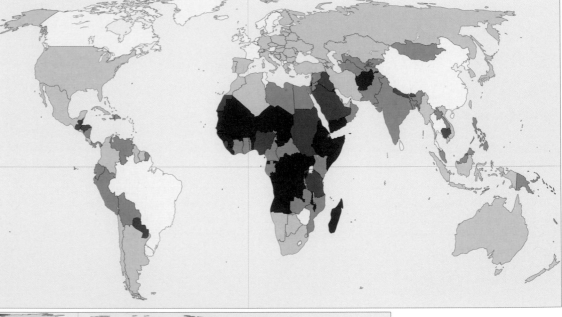

URBAN POPULATION

Percentage of total population living in towns and cities (2005)

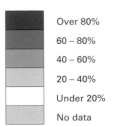

	Over 80%
	60 – 80%
	40 – 60%
	20 – 40%
	Under 20%
	No data

Countries that are the most and least urbanized (%)

Most urbanized		Least urbanized	
Singapore	100	Burundi	10
Kuwait	97	Bhutan	11
Belgium	97	Trinidad & Tob.	12

UK 89.6

In 2008, for the first time in history, more than half the world's population lived in urban areas.

Projection: *Eckert IV*

COPYRIGHT PHILIP'S

INFANT MORTALITY

Number of babies who died under the age of one, per 1,000 live births (2007)

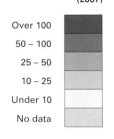

Over 100
50 – 100
25 – 50
10 – 25
Under 10
No data

Countries with the highest and lowest child mortality

Highest		Lowest	
Angola	184	Singapore	2
Sierra Leone	158	Sweden	3
Afghanistan	157	Hong Kong (China)	3
Liberia	150	Japan	3
Niger	117	Iceland	3

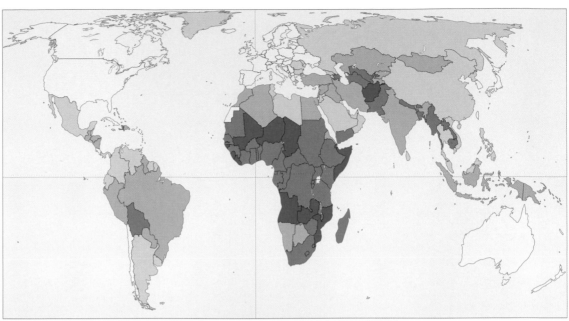

LIFE EXPECTANCY

The average expected lifespan of babies born in 2007

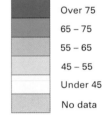

Over 75
65 – 75
55 – 65
45 – 55
Under 45
No data

Countries with the highest and lowest life expectancy at birth in years

Highest		Lowest	
Andorra	83.5	Mozambique	36.5
San Marino	81.2	Botswana	37.1
Japan	80.8	Zimbabwe	37.1
Singapore	80.2	Zambia	37.3
Australia	79.9	Angola	38.6

UK 78.7 years

FAMILY SIZE

Children born per woman (2007)

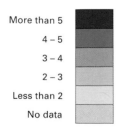

More than 5
4 – 5
3 – 4
2 – 3
Less than 2
No data

Countries with the largest and smallest family size

Largest		Smallest	
Mali	7.4	Hong Kong	1.0
Niger	7.4	Singapore	1.1
Uganda	6.8	Taiwan	1.1
Somalia	6.7	Lithuania	1.2
Afghanistan	6.6	Czech Rep.	1.2

UK = 1.7 children

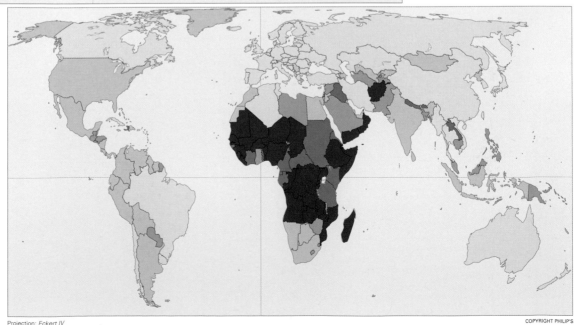

Projection: *Eckert IV*

COPYRIGHT PHILIP'S

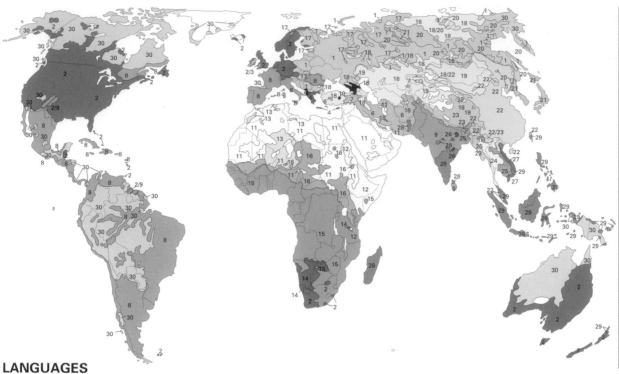

Languages of the World

Language can be classified by ancestry and structure. For example, the Romance and Germanic groups are both derived from an Indo-European language believed to have been spoken 5,000 years ago.

First-language speakers in millions (2005)
Mandarin Chinese 873, Spanish 322, English 309, Portuguese 230, Arabic 206, Hindi 181, Bengali 171, Russian 145, Japanese 122, German 95, Wu Chinese 77, Javanese 75, Telugu 70, Marathi 68, Vietnamese 67, Korean 67, Tamil 65, French 65, Italian 62, Punjabi 60.

Distribution of living languages
The figures refer to the number of languages currently in use in the regions shown
Asia 2,269
Africa 2,092
Pacific 1,310
The Americas 1,002
Europe 239

LANGUAGES

INDO-EUROPEAN FAMILY
1 Balto-Slavic group (incl. Russian, Ukrainian)
2 Germanic group (incl. English, German)
3 Celtic group
4 Greek
5 Albanian
6 Iranian group
7 Armenian
8 Romance group (incl. Spanish, Portuguese, French, Italian)
9 Indo-Aryan group (incl. Hindi, Bengali, Urdu, Punjabi, Marathi)
10 CAUCASIAN FAMILY

AFRO-ASIATIC FAMILY
11 Semitic group (incl. Arabic)
12 Kushitic group
13 Berber group

14 KHOISAN FAMILY

15 NIGER-CONGO FAMILY

16 NILO-SAHARAN FAMILY

17 URALIC FAMILY

ALTAIC FAMILY
18 Turkic group (incl. Turkish)
19 Mongolian group
20 Tungus-Manchu group
21 Japanese and Korean

SINO-TIBETAN FAMILY
22 Sinitic (Chinese) languages (incl. Mandarin, Wu, Yue)
23 Tibetic-Burmic languages

24 TAI FAMILY

AUSTRO-ASIATIC FAMILY
25 Mon-Khmer group
26 Munda group
27 Vietnamese

28 DRAVIDIAN FAMILY (incl. Telugu, Tamil)

29 AUSTRONESIAN FAMILY (incl. Malay-Indonesian, Javanese)

30 OTHER LANGUAGES

RELIGIONS

- Roman Catholicism
- Orthodox and other Eastern Churches
- Protestantism
- Sunni Islam
- Shiite Islam
- Buddhism
- Hinduism
- Confucianism
- Judaism
- Shintoism
- Tribal Religions

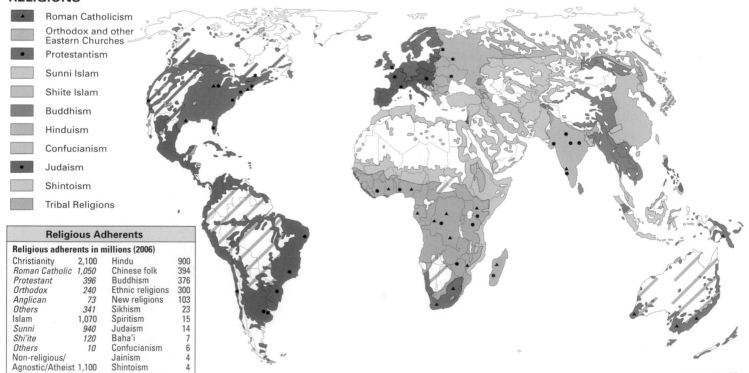

Religious Adherents

Religious adherents in millions (2006)

Christianity	2,100	Hindu	900
Roman Catholic	*1,050*	Chinese folk	394
Protestant	*396*	Buddhism	376
Orthodox	*240*	Ethnic religions	300
Anglican	*73*	New religions	103
Others	*341*	Sikhism	23
Islam	1,070	Spiritism	15
Sunni	*940*	Judaism	14
Shi'ite	*120*	Baha'i	7
Others	*10*	Confucianism	6
Non-religious/		Jainism	4
Agnostic/Atheist	1,100	Shintoism	4

United Nations

Created in 1945 to promote peace and co-operation and based in New York, the United Nations is the world's largest international organization, with 192 members and an annual budget of US $2.1 billion (2007). Each member of the General Assembly has one vote, while the five permanent members of the 15-nation Security Council – China, France, Russia, UK and USA – hold a veto. The Secretariat is the UN's principal administrative arm. The 54 members of the Economic and Social Council are responsible for economic, social, cultural, educational, health and related matters. The UN has 16 specialized agencies – based in Canada, France, Switzerland and Italy, as well as the USA – which help members in fields such as education (UNESCO), agriculture (FAO), medicine (WHO) and finance (IFC). By the end of 1994, all the original 11 trust territories of the Trusteeship Council had become independent.

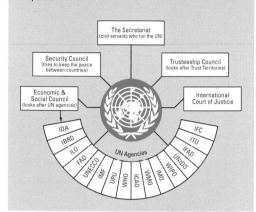

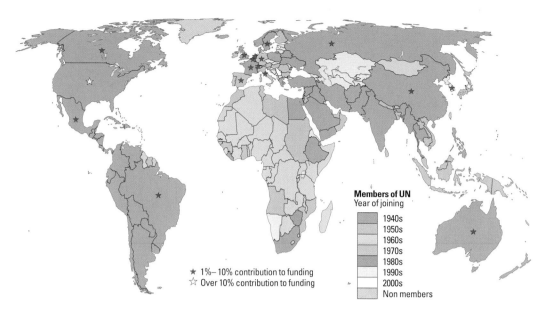

Members of UN
Year of joining

- 1940s
- 1950s
- 1960s
- 1970s
- 1980s
- 1990s
- 2000s
- Non members

★ 1%– 10% contribution to funding
☆ Over 10% contribution to funding

MEMBERSHIP OF THE UN In 1945 there were 51 members; by the end of 2006 membership had increased to 192 following the admission of East Timor, Switzerland and Montenegro. There are 2 independent states which are not members of the UN – Taiwan and the Vatican City. All the successor states of the former USSR had joined by the end of 1992. The official languages of the UN are Chinese, English, French, Russian, Spanish and Arabic.

FUNDING The UN regular budget for 2007 was US$ 2.1 billion. Contributions are assessed by the members' ability to pay, with the maximum 24% of the total (USA's share), the minimum 0.01%. The European Union pays over 37% of the budget.

PEACEKEEPING The UN has been involved in 65 peacekeeping operations worldwide since 1948.

International Organizations

ACP African-Caribbean-Pacific (formed in 1963). Members have economic ties with the EU.

APEC Asia-Pacific Economic Co-operation (formed in 1989). It aims to enhance economic growth and prosperity for the region and to strengthen the Asia-Pacific community. APEC is the only intergovernmental grouping in the world operating on the basis of non-binding commitments, open dialogue, and equal respect for the views of all participants. There are 21 member economies.

ARAB LEAGUE (formed in 1945). The League's aim is to promote economic, social, political and military co-operation. There are 22 member nations.

ASEAN Association of South-east Asian Nations (formed in 1967). Cambodia joined in 1999.

AU The African Union replaced the Organization of African Unity (formed in 1963) in 2002. Its 53 members represent over 94% of Africa's population. Arabic, French, Portuguese and English are recognized as working languages.

COLOMBO PLAN (formed in 1951). Its 25 members aim to promote economic and social development in Asia and the Pacific.

COMMONWEALTH The Commonwealth of Nations evolved from the British Empire. Pakistan was suspended in 1999, and Zimbabwe in 2002. In response to its continued suspension, Zimbabwe left the Commonwealth in December 2003. Pakistan was reinstated in 2004, but Fiji Islands was suspended in December 2006 following a military coup. It now comprises 16 Queen's realms, 31 republics and 6 indigenous monarchies, giving a total of 53 member states.

EU European Union (evolved from the European Community in 1993). Cyprus, the Czech Republic, Estonia, Hungary, Latvia, Lithuania, Malta, Poland, the Slovak Republic and Slovenia joined the EU in May 2004; Bulgaria and Romania joined in January 2007. The other members are Austria, Belgium, Denmark, Finland, France, Germany, Greece, Ireland, Italy, Luxembourg, Netherlands, Portugal, Spain, Sweden and the UK – together these 27 countries aim to integrate economies, co-ordinate social developments and bring about political union.

LAIA Latin American Integration Association (1980). Its aim is to promote freer regional trade.

NATO North Atlantic Treaty Organization (formed in 1949). It continues after 1991 despite the winding up of the Warsaw Pact. Bulgaria, Estonia, Latvia, Lithuania, Romania, the Slovak Republic and Slovenia became members in 2004.

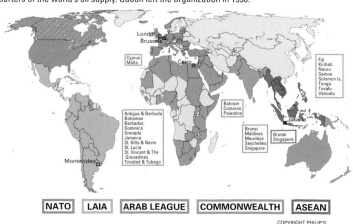

OAS | EU | AU | COLOMBO PLAN

OAS Organization of American States (formed in 1948). It aims to promote social and economic co-operation between developed countries of North America and developing nations of Latin America.

OECD Organization for Economic Co-operation and Development (formed in 1961). It comprises 30 major free-market economies. Poland, Hungary and South Korea joined in 1996, and the Slovak Republic in 2000. 'G8' is its 'inner group' of leading industrial nations, comprising Canada, France, Germany, Italy, Japan, Russia, UK and USA.

OPEC Organization of Petroleum Exporting Countries (formed in 1960). It controls about three-quarters of the world's oil supply. Gabon left the organization in 1996.

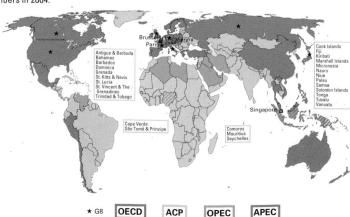

★ G8 | OECD | ACP | OPEC | APEC

NATO | LAIA | ARAB LEAGUE | COMMONWEALTH | ASEAN

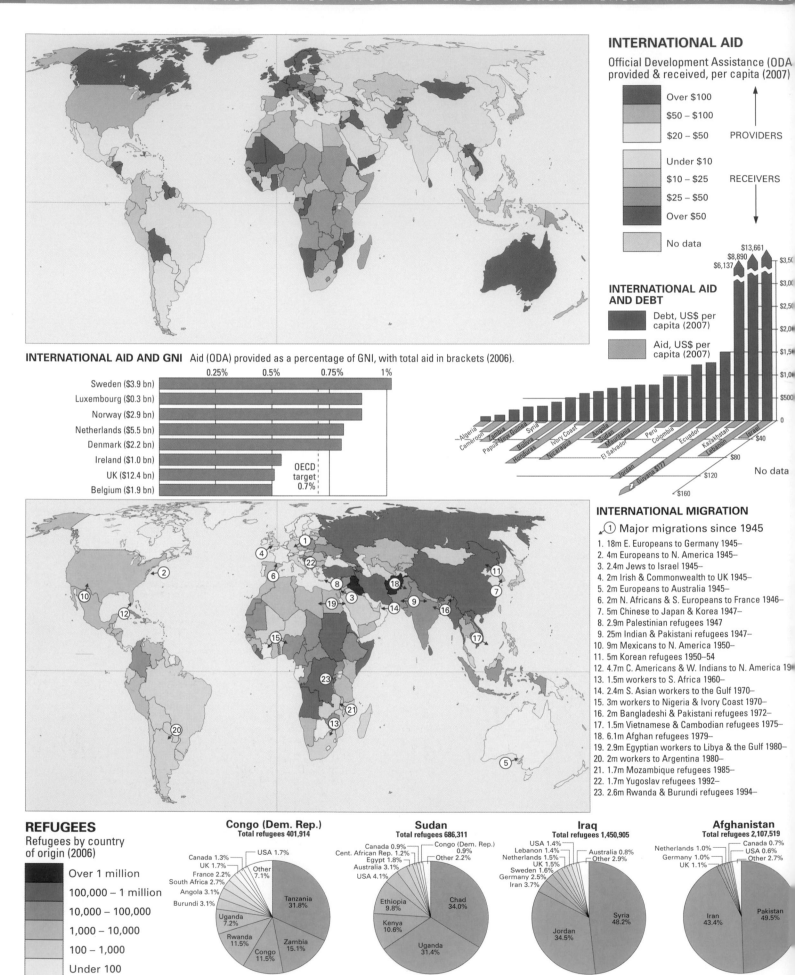

INTERNATIONAL AID

Official Development Assistance (ODA) provided & received, per capita (2007)

PROVIDERS
- Over $100
- $50 – $100
- $20 – $50

RECEIVERS
- Under $10
- $10 – $25
- $25 – $50
- Over $50

No data

INTERNATIONAL AID AND DEBT

- Debt, US$ per capita (2007)
- Aid, US$ per capita (2007)

$13,661 $8,890 $6,137

Algeria, Cameroon, Zambia, Papua New Guinea, Bolivia, Syria, Honduras, Nicaragua, Ivory Coast, El Salvador, Angola, Sudan, Mauritania, Peru, Colombia, Ecuador, Kazakhstan, Lebanon, Israel

Jordan $177, Guyana $177

$40, $80, $120, $160

No data

INTERNATIONAL AID AND GNI
Aid (ODA) provided as a percentage of GNI, with total aid in brackets (2006).

0.25%   0.5%   0.75%   1%

- Sweden ($3.9 bn)
- Luxembourg ($0.3 bn)
- Norway ($2.9 bn)
- Netherlands ($5.5 bn)
- Denmark ($2.2 bn)
- Ireland ($1.0 bn)
- UK ($12.4 bn)
- Belgium ($1.9 bn)

OECD target 0.7%

INTERNATIONAL MIGRATION

① Major migrations since 1945

1. 18m E. Europeans to Germany 1945–
2. 4m Europeans to N. America 1945–
3. 2.4m Jews to Israel 1945–
4. 2m Irish & Commonwealth to UK 1945–
5. 2m Europeans to Australia 1945–
6. 2m N. Africans & S. Europeans to France 1946–
7. 5m Chinese to Japan & Korea 1947–
8. 2.9m Palestinian refugees 1947
9. 25m Indian & Pakistani refugees 1947–
10. 9m Mexicans to N. America 1950–
11. 5m Korean refugees 1950–54
12. 4.7m C. Americans & W. Indians to N. America 19--
13. 1.5m workers to S. Africa 1960–
14. 2.4m S. Asian workers to the Gulf 1970–
15. 3m workers to Nigeria & Ivory Coast 1970–
16. 2m Bangladeshi & Pakistani refugees 1972–
17. 1.5m Vietnamese & Cambodian refugees 1975–
18. 6.1m Afghan refugees 1979–
19. 2.9m Egyptian workers to Libya & the Gulf 1980–
20. 2m workers to Argentina 1980–
21. 1.7m Mozambique refugees 1985–
22. 1.7m Yugoslav refugees 1992–
23. 2.6m Rwanda & Burundi refugees 1994–

REFUGEES
Refugees by country of origin (2006)

- Over 1 million
- 100,000 – 1 million
- 10,000 – 100,000
- 1,000 – 10,000
- 100 – 1,000
- Under 100

Congo (Dem. Rep.)
Total refugees 401,914
- USA 1.7%
- Canada 1.3%
- UK 1.7%
- France 2.2%
- South Africa 2.7%
- Angola 3.1%
- Burundi 3.1%
- Other 7.1%
- Uganda 7.2%
- Rwanda 11.5%
- Congo 11.5%
- Zambia 15.1%
- Tanzania 31.8%

Sudan
Total refugees 686,311
- Canada 0.9%
- Cent. African Rep. 1.2%
- Egypt 1.8%
- Australia 3.1%
- USA 4.1%
- Congo (Dem. Rep.) 0.9%
- Other 2.2%
- Ethiopia 9.8%
- Kenya 10.6%
- Uganda 31.4%
- Chad 34.0%

Iraq
Total refugees 1,450,905
- USA 1.4%
- Lebanon 1.4%
- Netherlands 1.5%
- UK 1.5%
- Sweden 1.6%
- Germany 2.5%
- Iran 3.7%
- Australia 0.8%
- Other 2.9%
- Jordan 34.5%
- Syria 48.2%

Afghanistan
Total refugees 2,107,519
- Netherlands 1.0%
- Germany 1.0%
- UK 1.1%
- Canada 0.7%
- USA 0.6%
- Other 2.7%
- Iran 43.4%
- Pakistan 49.5%

Projection: *Eckert IV*

COPYRIGHT PHILI

ARMED CONFLICTS

Armed conflict since 1994

 Countries with at least one armed conflict between 1994 and mid-2008

Countries in the top half of the Human Developement Index (HDI)

Countries in the bottom half of the HDI

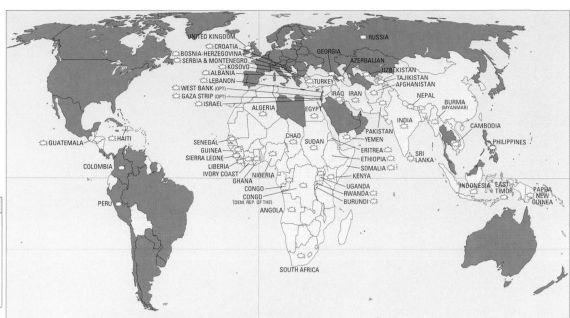

MAJOR WARS SINCE 1900	
War	**Total deaths**
Second World War (1939–45)	55,000,000
First World War (1914–18)	8,500,000
Korean War (1950–53)	4,000,000
Congolese Civil War (1998–)	3,800,000
Vietnam War (1965–73)	3,000,000
Sudanese Civil War (1983–2000)	2,000,000

SPREAD OF HIV/AIDS

Percentage of adults (15 – 49 years) living with HIV/AIDS (2007)

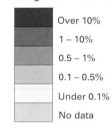

Over 10%

1 – 10%

0.5 – 1%

0.1 – 0.5%

Under 0.1%

No data

Total number of adults and children living with HIV/AIDS by region (2007)

Human Immunodeficiency Virus (HIV) is passed from one person to another and attacks the body's defence against illness. It develops into the Acquired Immunodeficiency Syndrome (AIDS) when a particularly severe illness, such as cancer, takes hold. The pandemic started just over 20 years ago and by 2007 33 millon people were living with HIV or AIDS.

TRAFFIC IN DRUGS

Countries producing illegal drugs

Cannabis

Opium poppy

Coca leaves

Cocaine

 Amphetamines

Major routes of drug trafficking

Opium

Coca leaves

Cocaine

Heroin

Cannabis

Amphetamines (usually used within producing countries)

 Conflicts relating to drug trafficking

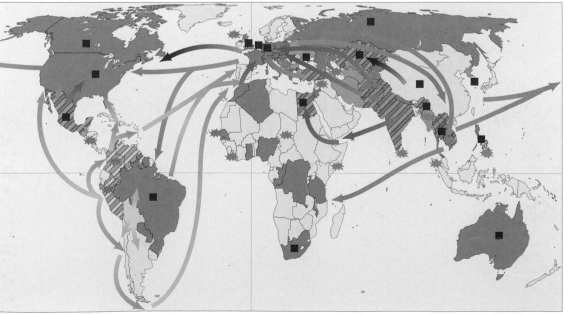

Projection: Eckert IV

COPYRIGHT PHILIP'S

	POPULATION							WEALTH					TRADE		
	Total population (millions 2008)	Population density (persons per km² 2008)	Life expectancy (years 2008)	Population change (average annual percentage 2008)	Birth rate (births per thousand people 2008)	Death rate (deaths per thousand people 2008)	Urban population (percentage of total 2006)	Gross National Income (million US$ 2007)	Gross National Income per capita (PPP US$ 2007)	GDP from agriculture (percentage of GDP 2007)	GDP from industry (percentage of GDP 2007)	GDP from services (percentage of GDP 2007)	Imports (US$ per capita 2008)	Exports (US$ per capita 2008)	Tourism receipts (US$ per capita 2005)
Afghanistan	32.7	51	44	2.6	46	20	22	10,137	250	31.0	26.0	43.0	148	10	–
Albania	3.6	126	78	0.5	15	5	45	10,456	6,580	20.6	19.9	59.5	1,346	393	239
Algeria	33.8	14	74	1.2	17	5	63	122,465	7,640	8.1	62.5	29.4	1,091	2,221	5
Angola	12.5	10	38	2.1	44	24	53	43,635	4,400	9.3	65.9	24.8	1,220	5,806	5
Argentina	40.5	15	74	1.1	18	7	90	238,853	12,990	9.2	34.1	56.7	1,479	1,802	69
Armenia	3.0	100	72	-0.1	13	8	64	7,925	5,900	17.2	36.4	46.4	1,182	408	45
Australia	21.0	3	82	1.2	13	7	88	755,795	33,340	2.5	26.4	71.1	8,914	8,519	831
Austria	8.2	98	79	0.1	9	10	66	355,088	38,140	1.9	30.6	67.5	22,366	19,915	1,886
Azerbaijan	8.2	94	66	0.7	18	8	52	21,872	6,260	6.0	62.6	31.4	914	4,668	8
Bahamas	0.3	22	66	0.6	17	9	90	4,476	14,920	3.0	7.0	90.0	8,003	2,247	6,897
Bahrain	0.7	1,080	75	1.3	17	4	96	14,022	34,310	0.3	43.6	56.1	22,343	27,386	1,234
Bangladesh	153.5	1,066	63	2.0	29	8	25	75,047	1,340	19.1	28.6	52.3	131	91	1
Barbados	0.3	654	73	0.4	12	9	52	4,842	16,140	6.0	16.0	78.0	5,287	1,283	2,550
Belarus	9.7	47	70	-0.4	10	14	72	40,897	10,740	8.4	41.5	50.1	3,777	3,279	24
Belgium	10.4	341	79	0.1	10	10	97	432,540	34,790	1.0	24.2	74.8	36,077	35,856	948
Belize	0.3	13	68	2.2	28	6	48	1,157	6,200	29.0	16.9	54.1	2,393	1,653	443
Benin	8.5	76	59	3.0	40	10	40	5,120	1,310	33.2	14.5	52.3	159	91	13
Bhutan	0.7	15	66	1.3	21	8	11	1,166	4,980	22.3	37.9	39.8	457	500	8
Bolivia	9.2	8	67	1.4	22	7	64	11,964	4,140	11.3	36.9	51.8	520	694	23
Bosnia-Herzegovina	4.6	90	78	0.7	9	9	45	14,302	7,700	10.2	23.8	66.0	2,596	1,107	126
Botswana	1.8	3	50	1.4	23	14	57	10,991	12,420	1.6	52.6	45.8	2,184	2,848	351
Brazil	196.3	23	72	1.2	19	6	84	1,133,030	9,370	5.5	28.5	66.0	897	1,019	21
Brunei	0.4	66	76	1.8	18	3	73	10,287	49,900	0.7	75.0	24.3	5,000	16,918	–
Bulgaria	7.3	66	73	-0.8	10	14	70	35,062	11,180	4.6	28.7	66.7	5,118	3,260	328
Burkina Faso	15.3	56	53	3.1	45	14	18	6,384	1,120	29.1	19.9	51.0	109	53	5
Burma (Myanmar)	47.8	70	63	0.8	17	9	30	10,516	220	40.9	19.7	39.4	75	129	2
Burundi	8.7	312	52	3.4	42	13	10	923	330	32.9	21.3	45.8	35	5	0
Cambodia	14.2	79	62	1.8	26	8	19	7,858	1,690	29.0	30.0	41.0	452	325	60
Cameroon	18.5	39	53	2.2	35	12	54	19,447	2,120	43.5	16.0	40.5	236	284	2
Canada	33.2	3	81	0.8	10	8	80	1,300,025	35,310	2.0	28.4	69.6	13,154	13,910	410
Cape Verde Is.	0.4	106	71	0.6	24	6	57	1,287	2,940	9.0	16.9	74.1	2,218	255	308
Central African Rep.	4.4	7	44	1.5	33	18	38	1,667	740	55.0	20.0	25.0	54	34	1
Chad	10.1	8	47	2.2	42	16	25	5,760	1,280	20.5	48.0	31.5	146	545	1
Chile	16.5	22	77	0.9	15	6	87	138,630	12,590	4.8	50.5	44.7	3,586	4,188	78
China	1330.0	139	73	0.6	14	7	40	3,120,891	5,370	10.6	49.2	40.2	869	1,102	22
Colombia	45.0	40	73	1.4	20	6	72	149,934	6,640	9.4	36.6	54.0	864	913	28
Comoros	0.7	337	63	2.8	36	8	36	425	1,150	40.0	4.0	56.0	204	46	14
Congo	3.9	11	54	2.7	42	12	60	5,797	2,750	5.6	57.1	37.3	698	2,310	5
Congo (Dem. Rep.)	66.5	28	54	3.2	43	12	32	8,573	290	55.0	11.0	34.0	34	24	0
Costa Rica	4.2	82	77	1.4	18	4	61	24,831	10,700	7.6	29.1	63.3	3,583	2,304	383
Croatia	4.5	79	75	-0.0	10	12	56	46,426	15,050	7.0	31.6	61.4	7,218	3,408	1,658
Cuba	11.4	103	77	0.3	11	7	76	13,338	1,170	4.4	22.8	72.8	1,030	307	168
Cyprus	0.8	86	78	0.5	13	8	69	19,617	26,370	2.6	19.1	78.3	10,861	1,913	2,911
Czech Republic	10.2	130	77	-0.1	9	11	74	149,378	22,020	2.6	38.7	58.7	14,225	14,755	454
Denmark	5.5	127	78	0.3	11	10	86	299,804	36,300	1.4	25.9	72.7	21,945	21,727	899
Djibouti	0.5	22	43	1.9	39	19	86	908	2,260	3.2	14.9	81.9	3,110	680	14
Dominican Republic	9.5	195	73	1.5	23	5	73	34,611	6,340	11.3	23.5	65.2	1,686	755	381
East Timor	1.1	74	67	2.1	27	6	26	1,604	3,080	32.2	12.8	55.0	184	9	–
Ecuador	13.9	49	77	0.9	22	4	62	41,148	7,040	6.6	33.9	59.5	1,194	1,396	36
Egypt	81.7	82	72	1.7	22	5	43	119,405	5,400	13.4	37.7	48.9	691	408	87
El Salvador	7.1	336	72	1.7	26	6	60	19,520	5,640	11.2	24.7	64.1	1,238	649	80
Equatorial Guinea	0.6	22	61	2.7	37	10	39	6,527	21,230	2.7	92.6	4.7	5,352	26,367	10
Eritrea	5.5	45	61	2.6	35	9	19	1,108	520	17.4	23.2	59.4	109	3	14
Estonia	1.3	29	73	-0.6	10	13	69	17,706	19,810	2.9	32.3	64.8	12,485	10,123	732
Ethiopia	82.5	73	55	3.2	44	12	16	17,565	780	45.9	12.9	41.2	75	17	2
Fiji	0.9	51	70	1.4	22	6	50	3,189	4,370	8.9	13.5	77.6	3,467	1,336	483
Finland	5.2	16	79	0.1	10	10	61	234,833	34,550	2.8	33.2	64.0	17,938	20,058	420
France	64.1	117	81	0.6	13	8	77	2,447,090	33,600	2.2	20.3	77.5	11,207	9,824	694
Gabon	1.5	6	54	2.0	36	13	83	8,876	13,080	5.7	57.3	37.0	1,887	6,495	11
Gambia, The	1.7	154	55	2.7	38	12	53	544	1,140	33.0	8.7	58.3	177	65	18
Gaza Strip (OPT)*	1.5	4,167	73	3.4	38	4	72	4,452	2,968	8.0	13.0	79.0	1,893	225	19
Georgia	4.6	66	77	-0.3	11	10	52	9,337	4,770	12.8	28.4	58.8	1,588	600	51
Germany	82.4	231	79	-0.0	8	11	75	3,197,029	33,530	0.9	30.1	69.0	14,587	18,568	354
Ghana	23.4	98	59	1.9	29	9	47	13,902	1,330	37.3	25.3	37.4	419	232	21
Greece	10.7	81	80	0.1	10	10	59	331,658	32,330	3.5	23.4	73.1	7,690	2,561	1,283

	ENERGY			LAND & AGRICULTURE					SOCIAL INDICATORS							
	Energy produced (tonnes of oil equivalent per capita 2007)	Energy consumed (tonnes of oil equivalent per capita 2007)	CO$_2$ emissions (tonnes per capita 2006)	Land area (thousand km²)	Arable and permanent crops (% of land area 2005)	Permanent pasture (% of land area 2005)	Forest (% of land area 2005)	Human development index (HDI value 2005)	Food intake (calories per capita per day 2003)	Doctors (per 100,000 people 2004)	Adults living with HIV/AIDS (percentage 2007)	Gender development index (GDI value 2005)	Adult illiteracy rate (percentage 2005)	Motor vehicles (per thousand people 2003)	Internet usage (per thousand people 2007)
Afghanistan	0.01	0.01	0.03	652	12	46	2	–	1,539	18.6	0.1	–	–	9	1.8
Albania	0.51	0.85	1.31	29	26	15	36	0.801	2,848	130.5	0.1	0.797	1	71	13.1
Algeria	5.87	1.17	2.83	2,382	3	13	1	0.733	3,022	113.1	0.1	0.720	30	88	10.5
Angola	6.39	0.34	1.77	1,247	3	43	56	0.446	2,083	7.7	2.1	0.439	33	18	0.8
Argentina	2.38	1.98	4.06	2,780	13	52	13	0.869	2,992	300.9	0.5	0.865	3	198	23.1
Armenia	0.39	1.68	3.48	30	20	30	12	0.775	2,268	358.8	0.1	0.772	1	–	5.8
Australia	14.04	6.91	20.58	7,741	6	51	21	0.962	3,054	247.4	0.2	0.960	1	624	55.0
Austria	1.53	4.68	9.32	84	18	22	47	0.948	3,673	337.8	0.2	0.934	1	501	52.2
Azerbaijan	5.18	2.19	4.94	87	25	33	13	0.746	2,575	354.7	0.1	0.743	1	45	12.8
Bahamas	0	5.59	16.48	14	1	0	84	0.845	2,755	105.4	3.0	0.841	–	342	39.3
Bahrain	18.26	17.35	38.44	0.7	8	6	0	0.866	–	108.7	0.1	0.857	14	322	35.3
Bangladesh	0.09	0.13	0.29	144	65	5	10	0.547	2,205	25.7	0.1	0.539	53	2	0.3
Barbados	0.27	1.76	5.34	0.4	40	5	5	0.892	3,091	120.6	1.2	0.887	–	338	57.0
Belarus	0.20	2.77	6.68	208	27	16	45	0.804	3,000	455.0	0.2	0.803	1	168	61.7
Belgium	1.19	6.61	14.22	31	26	16	22	0.946	3,584	449.4	0.2	0.940	1	470	50.2
Belize	0.54	1.35	3.44	23	4	2	59	0.778	2,869	104.6	2.1	–	25	161	10.9
Benin	0.01	0.12	0.34	113	25	5	24	0.437	2,548	4.5	0.1	0.422	65	2	1.9
Bhutan	0.30	0.26	0.49	47	4	9	64	0.579	–	5.1	0.1	–	53	–	1.7
Bolivia	1.72	0.60	1.38	1,099	3	31	49	0.695	2,235	121.8	0.2	0.691	13	56	11.0
Bosnia-Herzegovina	1.06	1.41	3.87	51	21	21	45	0.803	2,894	134.0	0.1	–	3	–	23.2
Botswana	0.37	0.92	2.39	582	1	45	22	0.654	2,151	39.8	23.9	0.639	19	38	4.4
Brazil	1.07	1.28	2.01	8,514	8	23	63	0.800	3,050	115.3	0.6	0.798	11	112	26.3
Brunei	60.87	11.08	26.89	6	4	1	84	0.894	2,855	100.6	–	0.886	7	397	42.5
Bulgaria	1.43	3.03	6.63	111	31	17	33	0.824	2,848	356.2	0.1	0.823	2	295	25.9
Burkina Faso	0	0.03	0.07	274	16	22	26	0.370	2,462	5.9	1.6	0.364	76	4	0.6
Burma (Myanmar)	0.27	0.23	0.27	677	16	1	52	0.583	2,937	35.5	0.7	–	10	6	0.1
Burundi	0	0.02	0.05	28	53	38	4	0.413	1,649	2.8	2.0	0.409	41	3	0.7
Cambodia	0	0.02	0.05	181	22	9	53	0.598	2,046	15.6	0.8	0.594	26	1	0.5
Cameroon	0.32	0.13	0.41	475	15	4	51	0.532	2,273	19.2	5.1	0.524	32	11	2.0
Canada	14.54	10.54	18.81	9,971	6	3	27	0.961	3,589	213.9	0.4	0.956	1	561	83.9
Cape Verde Is.	0	0.24	0.62	4	11	1	21	0.736	3,243	48.8	–	0.723	19	40	8.7
Central African Rep.	0.01	0.03	0.08	623	3	5	37	0.384	1,980	8.5	6.3	0.368	51	3	0.3
Chad	0.91	0.01	0.02	1,284	3	36	10	0.388	2,114	3.9	3.5	0.370	74	1	0.6
Chile	0.60	1.95	4.01	757	3	17	21	0.867	2,863	109.1	0.3	0.859	4	89	34.2
China	1.29	1.4	4.58	9,597	17	43	18	0.777	2,951	105.5	0.1	0.776	9	10	19.1
Colombia	2.03	0.75	1.42	1,139	3	37	48	0.791	2,585	135.0	0.6	0.789	7	28	27.3
Comoros	0	0.06	0.16	2	59	8	4	0.561	1,754	14.6	0.1	0.554	–	–	3.0
Congo	3.58	0.19	1.49	342	1	29	65	0.548	2,162	19.8	3.5	0.540	15	15	1.8
Congo (Dem. Rep.)	0.05	0.04	0.04	2,345	3	7	60	0.411	1,599	10.7	3.2	0.398	33	–	0.4
Costa Rica	0.56	1.08	1.41	51	10	46	39	0.846	2,876	132.5	0.4	0.842	5	103	36.3
Croatia	0.93	2.30	4.77	57	22	26	32	0.850	2,779	244.4	0.1	0.848	2	291	44.4
Cuba	0.31	0.87	2.52	111	34	26	21	0.838	3,152	590.5	0.1	0.839	–	1	11.5
Cyprus	0	3.79	11.37	9	15	0	13	0.903	3,255	234.2	0.1	0.899	3	393	48.2
Czech Republic	2.83	4.43	11.36	79	43	13	34	0.891	3,171	351.3	0.1	0.887	1	395	43.0
Denmark	5.52	4.00	10.85	43	53	8	11	0.949	3,439	292.5	0.1	0.944	1	431	64.0
Djibouti	0	1.34	4.12	23	0	57	0	0.516	2,220	18.1	3.1	0.507	–	3	2.2
Dominican Republic	0.04	0.73	1.89	49	33	44	28	0.779	2,347	187.6	1.1	0.773	13	100	17.9
East Timor	4.46	–	–	15	9	–	–	0.514	2,806	9.6	0.1	–	50	–	0.1
Ecuador	2.33	0.78	1.88	284	9	18	38	0.772	2,754	147.6	0.3	–	9	47	11.3
Egypt	1.03	0.81	1.92	1001	4	0	0	0.708	3,338	53.5	0.1	0.634	29	35	10.7
El Salvador	0.16	0.48	0.92	21	44	38	6	0.735	2,584	123.7	0.8	0.726	19	64	10.1
Equatorial Guinea	38.07	2.51	8.37	28	8	4	62	0.642	–	30.2	3.4	0.631	13	–	1.5
Eritrea	0	0.06	0.15	118	5	58	16	0.483	1,513	5.0	1.3	0.469	–	–	2.4
Estonia	2.30	4.46	14.06	45	14	5	49	0.860	3,002	447.5	1.3	0.858	0	321	59.3
Ethiopia	0.01	0.03	0.07	1,104	11	18	5	0.406	1,857	2.7	2.1	0.393	64	1	0.4
Fiji	0.19	0.71	1.47	18	16	10	45	0.762	2,894	33.7	0.1	0.757	–	126	8.7
Finland	2.11	6.36	11.15	338	7	0	72	0.952	3,100	316.5	0.1	0.947	1	434	68.7
France	2.11	4.70	6.60	552	36	18	28	0.952	3,654	336.7	0.4	0.950	1	495	51.4
Gabon	9.34	0.74	3.04	268	2	18	85	0.677	2,637	29.2	5.9	–	16	16	10.0
Gambia, The	–	0.07	0.19	11	26	46	48	0.502	2,273	10.9	0.9	0.670	–	6	5.9
Gaza Strip (OPT)*	–	–	–	0.4	–	–	–	0.731	2,180	–	–	0.496	8	–	24.0
Georgia	0.29	0.72	1.00	70	15	28	43	0.754	2,354	408.9	0.1	–	1	50	7.7
Germany	1.59	4.44	10.40	357	35	14	31	0.935	3,496	336.9	0.1	0.931	1	546	51.6
Ghana	0.08	0.18	0.32	239	28	37	28	0.553	2,667	15.2	1.9	0.549	42	11	2.8
Greece	0.95	3.47	10.02	132	29	36	28	0.926	3,721	438.0	0.2	0.922	4	414	23.7

	POPULATION						WEALTH					TRADE		
	Total population (millions 2008)	Population density (persons per km² 2008)	Life expectancy (years 2008)	Population change (average annual percentage 2008)	Birth rate (births per thousand people 2008)	Death rate (deaths per thousand people 2008)	Urban population (percentage of total 2006)	Gross National Income (million US$ 2006)	Gross National Income per capita (PPP US$ 2007)	GDP from agriculture (percentage of GDP 2007)	GDP from industry (percentage of GDP 2007)	GDP from services (percentage of GDP 2007)	Imports (US$ per capita 2008)	Exports (US$ per capita 2008)	Tourism receipts (US$ per capita 2005)
Guatemala	13.0	119	70	2.1	29	5	47	32,585	4,520	13.2	25.8	61.0	1,186	628	71
Guinea	9.8	40	57	2.5	38	11	33	3,722	1,120	22.4	40.9	36.7	142	123	3
Guinea-Bissau	1.5	42	48	2.0	36	16	30	331	470	62.0	12.0	26.0	133	89	1
Guyana	0.8	4	66	0.2	18	8	28	959	2,880	31.9	21.0	47.1	1,453	974	35
Haiti	8.9	322	58	2.5	36	10	38	5,366	1,150	28.0	20.0	52.0	235	55	11
Honduras	7.6	68	69	2.0	27	5	46	11,339	3,620	13.4	28.2	58.4	1,342	821	65
Hungary	9.9	107	73	-0.3	10	13	66	116,303	17,210	3.2	31.8	65.0	10,859	11,040	427
Iceland	0.3	3	81	0.8	14	7	93	16,826	33,960	5.0	26.5	68.5	21,810	22,820	1,363
India	1148.0	349	69	1.6	22	6	29	1,069,427	2,740	17.2	29.1	53.7	250	153	7
Indonesia	237.5	124	70	1.2	19	6	47	373,125	3,580	13.5	45.6	40.9	482	594	18
Iran	65.9	40	71	0.8	17	6	66	246,544	10,800	10.8	44.3	44.9	1,029	1,615	16
Iraq	28.2	65	70	2.6	31	5	68	–	–	5.0	68.0	27.0	1,324	2,350	0
Ireland	4.2	59	78	1.1	14	8	60	210,168	37,090	5.0	46.0	49.0	21,731	30,476	1,157
Israel	7.1	342	81	1.7	20	5	92	157,065	25,930	2.7	31.7	65.6	8,806	7,628	446
Italy	58.1	193	80	-0.0	8	11	68	1,991,284	29,850	2.0	26.7	71.3	9,756	9,744	609
Ivory Coast	20.2	63	55	2.2	33	11	45	17,543	1,590	27.9	21.9	50.2	393	592	4
Jamaica	2.8	255	74	0.8	20	6	53	9,923	6,210	5.2	32.9	61.9	2,568	918	552
Japan	127.3	337	82	-0.1	8	9	66	4,813,341	34,600	1.4	26.4	72.2	5,469	6,102	98
Jordan	6.2	67	79	2.3	20	3	82	16,282	5,160	3.6	10.1	86.3	2,524	1,052	244
Kazakhstan	15.3	6	68	0.4	16	9	57	78,281	9,700	5.8	39.4	54.8	2,453	4,351	45
Kenya	38.0	65	57	2.8	38	10	21	25,559	1,540	23.8	16.7	59.5	250	124	17
Korea, North	23.5	195	72	0.7	15	7	60	–	–	23.2	43.1	33.7	123	62	1
Korea, South	48.4	491	79	0.3	9	6	81	955,802	24,750	3.0	39.5	57.5	9,502	9,471	116
Kuwait	2.6	146	78	3.6	22	2	98	80,221	49,970	0.3	52.2	47.5	10,208	36,715	68
Kyrgyzstan	5.4	27	69	1.4	23	7	36	3,099	1,950	32.4	18.6	49.0	644	310	15
Laos	6.7	28	56	2.3	34	11	20	3,413	1,940	39.2	34.3	26.5	191	154	23
Latvia	2.2	35	72	-0.6	10	14	68	22,595	16,890	3.3	22.3	74.4	6,450	3,802	148
Lebanon	4.0	382	73	1.2	18	6	87	23,651	10,050	5.1	19.1	75.8	4,145	1,274	1,387
Lesotho	2.1	70	40	0.1	24	22	19	2,007	1,890	15.1	46.7	38.2	638	505	15
Liberia	3.3	30	41	3.7	43	21	45	554	290	76.9	5.4	17.7	2,165	363	2
Libya	6.2	4	77	2.2	26	3	85	55,473	14,710	1.5	61.7	36.8	3,329	10,666	37
Lithuania	3.6	55	75	-0.3	9	11	67	33,472	17,180	4.3	32.8	62.9	8,403	6,522	256
Luxembourg	0.5	188	79	1.2	12	8	83	36,420	63,590	0.4	13.6	86.0	56,240	41,560	7,232
Macedonia (FYROM)	2.1	81	74	0.3	12	9	68	7,052	8,510	11.4	27.2	61.4	3,173	2,094	40
Madagascar	20.0	34	63	3.0	38	8	27	6,331	920	26.0	15.9	58.1	127	66	2
Malawi	13.9	118	43	2.4	42	18	17	3,506	750	38.1	17.7	44.2	74	49	2
Malaysia	25.3	77	73	1.7	22	5	66	173,705	13,570	9.7	44.6	45.7	6,174	7,735	350
Mali	1.2	1	50	2.7	49	16	30	6,136	1,040	45.0	17.0	38.0	1,965	245	1
Malta	0.4	1,277	79	0.4	10	8	95	6,216	20,990	1.4	18.0	80.6	12,408	8,728	1,938
Mauritania	3.4	3	54	2.9	40	12	40	2,636	2,010	12.5	46.7	40.8	434	410	2
Mauritius	1.3	625	74	0.8	15	7	42	6,878	11,390	4.5	24.9	70.6	3,464	1,815	726
Mexico	110.0	56	76	1.1	20	5	76	878,020	12,580	3.7	34.1	62.2	2,781	2,673	110
Micronesia, Fed. States	0.1	153	71	-0.2	24	5	22	274	3,270	28.9	15.2	55.9	1,330	140	170
Moldova	4.3	128	71	-0.1	11	11	47	4,323	2,930	17.3	21.5	61.2	1,163	416	28
Mongolia	3.0	2	67	1.5	21	6	57	3,362	3,160	20.6	38.4	41.0	706	650	63
Montenegro	0.7	48	75	-0.9	11	9	52	3,109	10,290	–	–	–	860	244	2
Morocco	34.3	77	72	1.5	21	5	58	69,352	3,990	14.7	38.9	46.4	1,004	471	139
Mozambique	21.3	27	41	1.8	38	20	34	6,787	690	23.4	30.7	45.9	155	126	5
Namibia	2.1	3	50	0.9	23	14	35	6,970	5,120	10.4	36.2	53.4	1,695	1,419	17
Nepal	29.5	210	61	2.1	30	9	15	9,660	1,040	38.0	20.0	42.0	81	28	5
Netherlands	16.6	401	79	0.4	11	9	80	750,526	39,310	2.0	24.4	73.6	29,235	32,380	635
New Zealand	4.2	16	80	1.0	14	7	86	121,708	26,340	4.4	26.0	69.6	7,407	7,031	1,187
Nicaragua	5.8	45	71	1.8	24	4	59	5,519	2,520	17.0	26.1	56.9	910	549	3
Niger	13.3	11	44	2.9	50	20	17	3,992	630	39.0	17.0	44.0	60	32	4
Nigeria	146.3	158	47	2.0	37	17	47	137,091	1,770	18.0	50.9	31.1	317	568	9
Norway	4.6	14	80	0.4	11	9	77	360,036	53,320	2.4	40.7	56.9	20,263	38,609	747
Oman	3.3	16	74	3.2	35	4	72	27,887	19,740	2.1	37.2	60.7	4,036	10,273	15
Pakistan	172.8	215	64	2.0	28	8	35	141,009	2,570	20.4	26.6	53.0	205	119	5
Panama	3.3	42	77	1.5	21	5	70	18,423	10,610	6.2	16.1	77.7	4,600	3,142	24
Papua New Guinea	5.9	13	66	2.1	28	7	13	5,400	1,870	32.8	36.5	30.7	511	959	2
Paraguay	6.8	17	76	2.4	28	4	58	10,225	4,380	23.1	17.2	59.7	1,081	1,015	1
Peru	29.2	23	70	1.3	20	6	72	96,241	7,240	8.5	21.2	70.3	996	1,139	41
Philippines	96.1	320	71	2.0	26	5	62	142,623	3,730	14.7	31.6	53.7	660	531	24
Poland	38.5	123	75	-0.0	10	10	62	374,633	15,330	4.0	31.3	64.7	5,556	4,948	16
Portugal	10.7	116	78	0.3	10	11	57	201,079	20,890	3.0	25.6	71.4	8,217	5,402	746

	ENERGY			LAND & AGRICULTURE				SOCIAL INDICATORS							
	Energy produced (tonnes of oil equivalent per capita 2007)	Energy consumed (tonnes of oil equivalent per capita 2007)	CO2 emissions (tonnes per capita 2006)	Land area (thousand km2)	Arable and Permanent crops (% of land area 2005)	Permanent pasture (% of land area 2005)	Forest (% of land area 2005)	Human development index (HDI) value 2005	Food intake (calories per capita per day 2003)	Doctors (per 100,000 people 2004)	Adults living with HIV/AIDS (percentage 2007)	Gender development index (GDI) value 2005	Adult illiteracy rate (percentage 2005)	Motor vehicles (per thousand people 2003)	Internet usage (per thousand people 2007)
Guatemala	0.18	0.41	0.90	109	18	24	26	0.689	2,219	89.6	0.8	0.675	31	62	10.4
Guinea	0.01	0.06	0.14	246	6	43	28	0.456	2,409	11.5	1.6	0.446	71	2	0.5
Guinea-Bissau	0	0.10	0.28	36	19	39	78	0.374	2,024	12.2	1.8	0.355	–	–	2.5
Guyana	0	0.70	2.15	215	3	6	86	0.750	2,692	48.2	2.5	0.742	–	101	24.7
Haiti	0.01	0.08	0.21	28	40	18	3	0.529	2,086	25.0	2.2	–	–	19	11.5
Honduras	0.09	0.43	1.02	112	13	13	48	0.700	2,356	56.9	0.7	0.694	20	12	4.6
Hungary	0.99	2.86	5.88	93	52	11	20	0.874	3,483	332.9	0.1	0.872	1	274	42.2
Iceland	10.35	14.19	11.50	103	0	23	0	0.968	3,249	361.6	0.2	0.962	1	577	67.0
India	0.28	0.40	1.16	3,287	57	4	22	0.619	2,459	59.7	0.3	0.600	39	13	7.1
Indonesia	0.98	0.42	1.21	1,905	20	6	58	0.728	2,904	13.4	0.2	0.721	10	28	5.5
Iran	4.77	2.80	7.25	1,648	11	27	5	0.759	3,085	45.0	0.2	0.750	18	26	35.2
Iraq	4.05	1.16	3.69	438	14	9	2	–	2,197	65.8	0.1	–	–	47	0.2
Ireland	0.25	4.29	11.54	70	18	44	10	0.959	3,656	278.6	0.2	0.940	1	382	41.6
Israel	0.14	3.31	9.80	21	18	6	6	0.932	3,666	382.0	0.1	0.927	3	231	31.1
Italy	0.53	3.47	8.05	301	35	15	34	0.941	3,671	420.3	0.4	0.936	2	641	55.0
Ivory Coast	0.28	0.16	0.36	322	22	41	–	0.432	2,631	12.3	3.9	0.413	51	7	1.7
Jamaica	0.02	1.46	4.36	11	26	21	30	0.736	2,685	85.0	1.6	0.732	20	75	54.0
Japan	0.84	4.47	9.78	378	13	1	64	0.953	2,761	197.6	0.1	0.942	1	433	69.1
Jordan	0.05	1.31	3.37	89	3	8	1	0.773	2,674	203.0	0.1	0.760	9	67	18.6
Kazakhstan	9.39	4.89	14.02	2,725	8	69	5	0.794	2,677	353.9	0.1	0.792	1	77	12.4
Kenya	0.04	0.15	0.30	580	9	37	30	0.521	2,090	13.9	7.8	0.521	26	17	8.1
Korea, North	1.05	1.03	3.36	121	25	0	68	–	2,142	157.3		–	–	–	–
Korea, South	0.78	4.84	10.53	99	19	1	63	0.921	3,058	329.1	0.1	0.910	1	215	72.6
Kuwait	63.96	11.84	30.92	18	1	8	0	0.891	3,010	152.5	0.1	0.884	7	326	35.9
Kyrgyzstan	0.69	0.95	0.95	200	7	49	5	0.696	2,999	251.1	0.1	0.692	1	37	14.2
Laos	0.07	0.09	0.09	237	5	4	54	0.601	2,312	58.6	0.2	0.593	31	–	1.5
Latvia	0.30	1.98	3.84	65	18	10	47	0.855	2,938	300.8	0.8	0.853	1	280	52.1
Lebanon	0.04	1.32	3.69	10	31	2	4	0.772	3,196	325.3	0.1	0.759	–	417	24.2
Lesotho	0.02	0.07	0.11	30	11	67	0	0.549	2,638	4.9	23.2	0.541	18	–	3.3
Liberia	0	0.06	0.18	111	6	21	36	–	1,900	3.0	1.7	–	–	10	0
Libya	18.20	3.30	9.07	1,760	1	8	0	0.818	3,320	129.0	0.1	0.797	16	140	4.3
Lithuania	0.72	2.42	4.39	65	31	14	31	0.862	3,325	397.3	0.1	0.924	1	364	37.3
Luxembourg	0.13	10.06	26.28	3	2	2	–	0.944	3,701	266.2	0.2	–	1	641	71.8
Macedonia (FYROM)	0.69	1.35	3.50	26	24	25	36	0.801	2,655	219.1	0.1	0.795	4	167	33.3
Madagascar	0.01	0.06	0.14	587	6	41	20	0.533	2,005	29.1	0.1	0.530	29	5	0.6
Malawi	0.02	0.05	0.07	118	26	20	28	0.437	2,155	2.2	11.9	0.432	36	7	1.0
Malaysia	3.89	2.62	6.70	330	23	1	59	0.811	2,881	70.2	0.5	0.802	11	220	63.9
Mali	0.01	0.03	0.06	1,240	4	28	11	0.380	2,174	7.9	1.5	0.371	76	4	0.8
Malta	0	2.60	7.78	0.3	31	0	0	0.878	3,587	318.3	0.1	0.873	12	520	39.3
Mauritania	0.52	0.37	0.95	1,026	0	38	0	0.550	2,772	10.5	0.8	0.543	49	11	0.9
Mauritius	0.02	1.16	3.22	2	52	3	8	0.804	2,955	105.7	1.7	0.796	16	88	27.2
Mexico	2.41	1.71	4.05	1,958	14	42	29	0.829	3,145	198.0	0.3	0.820	8	133	21.0
Micronesia, Fed. States	0	–	–	0.7	51	16	0	–	–	59.8	–	–	–	–	13.9
Moldova	0.03	0.82	1.74	34	65	11	11	0.708	2,806	263.6	0.4	0.704	1	60	16.2
Mongolia	0.78	0.86	2.91	1,567	1	83	7	0.700	2,249	263.1	0.1	0.695	2	18	10.8
Montenegro	0	0	4.81	14	37	18	-	–	–	206.3	0.1	–	–	–	40.9
Morocco	0.02	0.38	1.04	447	21	47	7	0.646	3,052	51.5	0.1	0.621	48	57	21.6
Mozambique	0.26	0.28	0.24	802	6	56	39	0.384	2,079	2.7	12.5	0.373	61	9	1.0
Namibia	0.20	0.75	1.32	824	1	46	10	0.650	2,278	29.7	15.3	0.645	15	38	4.9
Nepal	0.02	0.06	0.11	147	17	12	27	0.534	2,453	20.9	0.5	0.520	51	6	1.2
Netherlands	4.02	6.27	15.79	42	28	29	11	0.953	3,362	314.9	0.2	0.951	1	439	90.5
New Zealand	4.03	5.27	9.38	271	13	52	30	0.943	3,219	236.6	0.1	0.935	1	632	81.6
Nicaragua	0.05	0.32	0.82	130	18	40	27	0.710	2,298	37.4	0.2	0.696	23	16	2.7
Niger	0.01	0.03	0.10	1,267	4	9	1	0.374	2,130	3.0	0.8	0.355	71	9	0.3
Nigeria	1.21	0.19	0.77	924	36	43	15	0.470	2,726	28.2	3.1	0.456	31	1	7.4
Norway	55.61	10.29	9.79	324	3	1	29	0.968	3,484	313.3	0.1	0.957	1	424	82.1
Oman	19.92	4.43	11.19	310	3	5	0	0.814	–	131.9	0.1	0.788	19	192	10.6
Pakistan	0.24	0.35	0.78	796	29	6	3	0.551	2,419	73.9	0.1	0.525	50	11	10.6
Panama	0.27	1.77	0.82	76	9	21	39	0.812	2,272	150.2	1.0	0.810	8	96	16.2
Papua New Guinea	0.46	0.32	0.58	463	2	0	68	0.530	2,175	5.2	1.5	0.529	43	21	1.9
Paraguay	2.03	1.64	1.05	407	8	55	59	0.755	2,565	110.7	0.6	0.744	7	66	4.2
Peru	0.43	0.54	0.81	1,285	3	21	51	0.773	2,571	116.7	0.5	0.769	12	30	26.6
Philippines	0.14	0.36	0.87	300	36	5	19	0.771	2,379	58.5	0.1	0.768	7	34	5.8
Poland	1.90	2.50	7.87	323	41	11	31	0.870	3,375	246.9	0.1	0.867	1	294	41.5
Portugal	0.37	2.56	5.82	89	25	16	40	0.897	3,741	342.3	0.5	0.895	6	734	33.3

	POPULATION							WEALTH					TRADE		
	Total population (millions 2008)	Population density (persons per km2, 2008)	Life expectancy (years 2008)	Population change (average annual percentage 2008)	Birth rate (births per thousand people 2008)	Death rate (deaths per thousand people 2008)	Urban population (percentage of total 2006)	Gross National Income (million US$ 2007)	Gross National Income per capita (PPP US$ 2007)	GDP from agriculture (percentage of GDP 2007)	GDP from industry (percentage of GDP 2007)	GDP from services (percentage of GDP 2007)	Imports (US$ per capita 2008)	Exports (US$ per capita 2008)	Tourism receipts (US$ per capita 2005)
Qatar	0.8	72	75	1.1	16	2	95	–	–	0.1	79.4	20.5	31,200	78,050	844
Romania	22.2	94	72	-0.1	11	12	54	132,502	10,980	8.1	36.0	55.9	4,148	2,691	47
Russia	140.7	8	66	-0.5	11	16	73	1,070,999	14,400	4.1	41.1	54.8	2,146	3,383	38
Rwanda	10.2	387	50	2.8	40	14	19	3,072	860	35.0	22.1	42.9	74	21	5
Saudi Arabia	28.1	14	76	2.0	29	2	81	373,490	22,910	3.1	61.6	35.3	3,822	11,733	226
Senegal	12.9	66	57	2.6	37	11	41	10,170	1,640	16.0	19.4	64.6	361	148	17
Serbia†	10.2	115	75	0.0	12	10	52	34,969	10,220	12.3	24.2	63.5	1,799	865	21
Sierra Leone	6.3	88	41	2.3	45	22	40	1,537	660	49.0	31.0	20.0	89	34	14
Singapore	4.6	6,650	82	1.1	9	5	100	148,992	48,520	0.0	33.2	66.8	66,870	75,978	1,276
Slovak Republic	5.5	112	75	0.1	11	10	56	63,324	19,340	2.6	33.4	64.0	14,502	14,385	224
Slovenia	2.0	99	77	-0.1	9	11	51	42,306	26,640	2.2	34.2	63.6	19,060	17,135	901
Solomon Is.	0.6	20	73	2.5	28	4	17	363	1,680	42.0	11.0	47.0	512	474	3
Somalia	9.6	15	49	2.8	44	16	33	1,248	130	65.0	10.0	25.0	83	31	–
South Africa	48.8	40	49	0.8	20	17	59	274,009	9,560	3.4	31.3	65.3	1,789	1,669	166
Spain	40.5	80	80	0.1	10	10	77	1,321,756	30,820	3.6	28.9	67.5	10,985	7,230	1,185
Sri Lanka	21.1	322	75	0.9	17	6	15	30,785	4,210	15.5	27.0	57.5	596	433	25
Sudan	40.2	16	50	2.1	34	14	40	37,031	1,880	32.9	31.1	36.0	193	339	2
Suriname	0.5	3	73	1.1	17	6	74	2,166	7,640	10.8	24.4	64.8	2,594	2,782	43
Swaziland	1.1	65	32	-0.4	27	31	24	2,951	4,930	11.9	45.1	43.0	1,798	1,664	86
Sweden	9.0	20	81	0.2	10	10	84	421,342	36,590	1.5	28.9	69.6	18,511	20,567	825
Switzerland	7.6	184	81	0.3	10	9	75	452,121	43,870	1.5	34.0	64.5	28,000	22,724	1,472
Syria	19.7	107	71	2.2	27	5	51	34,993	4,370	22.5	27.9	49.6	727	666	113
Taiwan	22.9	637	78	0.2	9	7	78	–	–	1.5	27.8	70.7	11,118	11,939	216
Tajikistan	7.2	50	65	1.9	27	7	25	3,103	1,710	23.0	29.4	47.6	528	233	0
Tanzania	40.2	43	51	2.1	35	13	24	16,287	1,200	27.0	22.7	50.3	147	62	15
Thailand	65.5	127	73	0.6	14	7	32	217,348	7,880	11.4	44.5	44.1	2,429	2,670	156
Togo	5.9	103	58	2.7	37	9	39	2,383	800	40.0	25.0	35.0	292	170	3
Trinidad & Tobago	1.2	240	71	-0.1	14	8	76	18,795	22,490	0.5	47.9	51.6	8,550	13,942	412
Tunisia	10.4	64	76	1.0	16	5	65	32,820	7,130	10.8	28.2	61.0	2,212	1,894	202
Turkey	71.9	92	73	1.0	16	6	67	592,850	12,350	8.5	28.6	62.9	2,848	1,972	258
Turkmenistan	5.2	11	69	1.6	25	6	46	22,620	4,350	10.7	38.8	50.5	1,018	1,901	9
Uganda	31.4	133	52	3.6	48	12	13	10,469	920	29.0	24.8	46.2	114	65	19
Ukraine	46.0	76	68	-0.7	10	16	68	118,445	6,810	9.3	31.7	59.0	1,794	1,411	67
United Arab Emirates	4.6	56	76	3.8	16	2	77	–	–	1.6	61.8	36.6	30,674	45,152	859
United Kingdom	60.9	249	79	0.3	11	10	90	2,608,513	33,800	0.9	22.8	76.3	10,603	7,696	506
USA	303.8	32	78	0.9	14	8	81	13,886,472	45,850	1.2	19.6	79.2	7,209	4,533	277
Uruguay	3.5	20	76	0.5	14	9	92	21,186	11,040	9.8	32.8	57.4	2,442	2,170	175
Uzbekistan	27.3	61	72	1.0	18	5	37	19,721	2,430	28.2	33.9	37.9	238	365	3
Venezuela	26.4	29	73	1.5	20	5	93	201,146	11,920	3.6	35.3	61.1	2,024	3,920	25
Vietnam	86.1	261	71	1.0	16	6	26	67,236	2,550	19.0	42.7	38.3	922	740	28
West Bank (OPT)*	2.4	411	74	2.2	26	4	72	4,452	1,855	8.0	13.0	79.0	542	141	
Western Sahara	0.4	2	54	2.9	40	12	94	–	–	–	–	–	–	–	
Yemen	23.0	44	62	3.5	42	8	27	19,421	2,200	9.4	52.4	38.2	401	401	12
Zambia	11.7	16	39	1.7	41	21	35	9,479	1,220	16.7	26.0	57.3	378	481	12
Zimbabwe	11.4	29	44	-0.8	32	17	35	4,466	392	18.1	22.6	59.3	205	158	

NOTES

SERBIA†
Kosovo separated from Serbia in February 2008.

OPT*
Occupied Palestinian Territory.

PER CAPITA
An amount divided by the total population of a country or the amount per person.

PPP
Purchasing Power Parity (PPP) is a method used to enable real comparisons to be made between countries when measuring wealth. The UN International Comparison Programme gives estimates of the PPP for each country, so it can be used as an indicator of real price levels for goods and services rather than using currency exchange rates (see GNI and GNI per capita).

POPULATION TOTAL
These are estimates of the mid-year total in 2008.

POPULATION DENSITY
The total population divided by the land area (both are recorded in the table above).

LIFE EXPECTANCY
The average age that a child born today is expected to live to, if mortality levels of today last throughout its lifetime.

BIRTH/DEATH RATES
These are 2008 estimates from the CIA World Factbook.

URBAN POPULATION
The urban population shows the percentage of the total population living in towns and cities (each country will differ with regard to the size or type of town that is defined as an urban area).

GNI
Gross National Income: this used to be referred to as GNP (Gross National Product) and is a good indication of a country's wealth. It is the income in US dollars from goods and services in a country for one year, including income from overseas.

GNI PER CAPITA
The GNI (see note) divided by the total population by using the PPP method (see note).

AGRICULTURE, INDUSTRY AND SERVICES
The percentage contributions that each of these three sectors makes to a country's GDP (see note).

IMPORTS AND EXPORTS
The total value of goods imported into a country and exported to other countries, given in US dollars ($) per capita.

TOURISM RECEIPTS
The amount of income generated from tourism in US dollars per capita.

	ENERGY			LAND & AGRICULTURE				SOCIAL INDICATORS							
	Energy produced (tonnes of oil equivalent per capita 2007)	Energy consumed (tonnes of oil equivalent per capita 2007)	CO$_2$ emissions (tonnes per capita 2006)	Land area (thousand km2)	Arable and Permanent crops (% of land area 2005)	Permanent pasture (% of land area 2005)	Forest (% of land area 2005)	Human development index (HDI value 2005)	Food intake (calories per capita per day 2003)	Doctors (per 100,000 people 2004)	Adults living with HIV/AIDS (percentage 2007)	Gender development index (GDI value 2005)	Adult illiteracy rate (percentage 2005)	Motor vehicles (per thousand people 2003)	Internet usage (per thousand people 2007)
Qatar	112.63	25.17	61.19	11	2	5	0	0.875	—	221.7	0.1	0.863	11	517	38.7
Romania	1.31	1.88	4.42	238	43	20	28	0.813	3,455	190.5	0.1	0.812	3	166	53.9
Russia	9.33	5.32	12.00	17,075	7	5	50	0.802	3,072	425.2	1.1	0.801	1	185	21.2
Rwanda	0	0.04	0.09	26	56	19	12	0.452	2,084	4.7	2.8	0.450	35	4	1.0
Saudi Arabia	22.85	6.38	15.70	2,150	2	79	1	0.812	2,845	137.5	0.1	0.783	17	372	22.5
Senegal	0.01	0.17	0.47	197	13	29	32	0.499	2,280	5.7	1.0	0.492	61	28	6.5
Serbia†	0.06	0	4.81	88	37	18	3	—	2,678	206.3	0.1	—	—	172	18.7
Sierra Leone	0	0.07	0.20	72	8	31	67	0.336	1,936	3.3	1.7	0.320	65	8	0.2
Singapore	0	11.90	31.41	0.7	1	0	3	0.922	—	140.0	0.2	—	8	101	68.2
Slovak Republic	1.42	3.76	7.01	49	29	11	42	0.863	2,889	317.9	0.1	0.860	1	252	43.1
Slovenia	1.79	4.04	8.77	20	10	15	55	0.917	3,001	225.3	0.1	0.914	1	446	64.7
Solomon Is.	0	0.12	0.38	29	3	1	91	0.602	2,265	12.7	—	—	23	—	1.4
Somalia	0	0.03	0.08	638	2	69	12	—	1,628	4.0	0.5	—	—	1	1.1
South Africa	3.40	2.93	10.04	1,221	13	69	7	0.674	2,956	77.0	18.1	0.667	18	145	11.6
Spain	0.86	4.03	9.22	498	37	21	29	0.949	3,371	329.5	0.5	0.944	1	455	48.7
Sri Lanka	0.04	0.27	0.61	66	30	7	30	0.743	2,385	54.5	0.1	0.735	9	34	3.7
Sudan	0.43	0.11	0.32	2,506	7	49	26	0.526	2,228	22.0	1.4	0.502	39	3	3.8
Suriname	2.58	2.61	4.31	163	0	0	90	0.774	2,652	44.9	2.4	0.767	10	204	9.3
Swaziland	0.22	0.39	0.91	17	11	71	30	0.547	2,322	15.8	26.1	0.529	20	40	3.7
Sweden	3.74	6.16	6.36	450	7	1	66	0.956	3,185	328.1	0.1	0.955	1	455	77.5
Switzerland	1.99	4.28	6.06	41	11	28	30	0.955	3,526	361.5	0.6	0.946	1	511	61.0
Syria	1.64	1.07	2.71	185	31	45	3	0.724	3,038	139.9	0.1	0.710	19	12	18.0
Taiwan	0.51	4.97	13.19	36	23	—	58	—	—	—	—	—	—	—	64.6
Tajikistan	0.58	0.96	1.06	143	8	23	3	0.673	1,828	203.3	0.3	0.669	1	22	0.3
Tanzania	0.01	0.05	0.12	945	6	40	44	0.467	1,975	2.3	6.2	0.464	31	4	1.0
Thailand	0.71	1.45	3.79	513	38	2	29	0.781	2,467	36.8	1.4	0.779	7	126	20.6
Togo	0	0.17	0.45	57	48	19	9	0.512	2,345	4.5	3.3	0.494	47	16	5.6
Trinidad & Tobago	39.45	18.65	44.32	5	24	2	50	0.814	2,732	78.8	1.5	0.808	2	220	40.8
Tunisia	0.66	0.82	2.06	164	32	31	3	0.766	3,238	134.1	0.1	0.750	26	87	16.8
Turkey	0.42	1.39	3.35	775	35	19	13	0.775	3,357	134.6	0.1	0.763	13	67	18.5
Turkmenistan	13.53	4.36	10.03	488	4	65	8	0.713	2,742	417.9	0.1	—	1	—	1.4
Uganda	0.01	0.03	0.06	241	37	26	21	0.505	2,410	8.3	5.4	0.501	33	6	6.6
Ukraine	1.78	3.14	7.05	604	58	14	17	0.788	3,054	295.1	1.6	0.785	1	114	21.6
United Arab Emirates	75.66	23.69	35.05	84	3	4	4	0.868	3,225	202.3	0.1	0.855	11	442	51.8
United Kingdom	3.25	4.04	9.66	242	24	46	11	0.946	3,412	230.0	0.2	0.944	1	439	66.1
USA	5.90	8.29	19.78	9,629	19	26	25	0.951	3,774	256.4	0.6	0.937	1	800	74.1
Uruguay	0.26	0.98	1.85	175	8	77	7	0.852	2,828	365.2	0.6	0.849	3	217	28.0
Uzbekistan	2.34	2.02	4.13	447	12	54	5	0.702	2,241	274.5	0.1	0.699	1	—	4.3
Venezuela	7.86	3.10	5.93	912	4	21	56	0.792	2,336	193.9	0.7	0.787	7	100	22.0
Vietnam	0.64	0.42	1.09	332	28	2	30	0.733	2,566	53.4	0.5	0.732	10	1	21.0
West Bank (OPT)*	0	0	—	6	—	—	—	0.731	2,180	—	—	—	—	—	14.0
Western Sahara	0	0.35	0.84	266	0	19	0	—	—	—	—	—	—	—	—
Yemen	0.91	0.31	0.84	528	3	30	1	0.508	2,038	32.5	0.1	0.472	46	50	1.4
Zambia	0.21	0.27	0.23	753	7	40	42	0.434	1,927	11.6	15.2	0.425	32	1	4.4
Zimbabwe	0.30	0.38	0.84	394	9	44	49	0.513	1,943	16.1	15.3	0.505	11	51	11.0

PRODUCTION AND CONSUMPTION OF ENERGY
The total amount of commercial energy produced or consumed in a country per capita (see note). It is expressed in metric tonnes of oil equivalent (an energy unit giving the heating value derived from one tonne of oil).

CARBON DIOXIDE EMISSIONS
The amount of carbon dioxide that each country produces per capita.

LAND AREA
This is the total land area of a country, less the area of major lakes and rivers, in square kilometres.

ARABLE AND PERMANENT CROPS
These figures give a percentage of the total land area that is used for crops and fruit (including temporary fallow land or meadows).

PERMANENT PASTURE
This is the percentage of land area that has permanent forage crops for cattle or horses, cultivated or wild. Some land may be classified both as permanent pasture or as forest (see Forest), especially areas of scrub or savanna.

FOREST
Natural/planted trees including cleared land that will be reforested in the near future as a percentage of the land area.

HUMAN DEVELOPMENT INDEX (HDI)
Produced by the UN Development Programme using indicators of life expectancy, knowledge and standards of living to give a value between 0 and 1 for each country. A high value shows a higher human development.

FOOD INTAKE
The amount of food (measured in calories) supplied, divided by the total population to show the amount each person consumes.

DOCTORS
The number of qualified doctors for every 100,000 people.

ADULTS LIVING WITH HIV/AIDS
The percentage of all adults (aged 15–49) who have the Human Immunodeficiency Virus or the Acquired Immunodeficiency Syndrome. The total number of adults and children with HIV/AIDS in 2007 was 32 million.

GENDER DEVELOPMENT INDEX (GDI)
Like the HDI (see note), the GDI uses the same UNDP indicators but gives a value between 0 and 1 to measure the social and economic differences between men and women. The higher the value, the more equality exists between men and women.

ILLITERACY
The percentage of all adult men and women (over 15 years) who cannot read or write simple sentences.

MOTOR VEHICLES AND INTERNET USAGE
These are good indicators of a country's development wealth. They are shown in total numbers per 1,000 people.

Each topic list is divided into continents and within a continent the items are listed in order of size. The bottom part of many of the lists is selective in order to give examples from as many different countries as possible. The figures are rounded as appropriate.

World, Continents, Oceans

	km^2	miles^2	%
The World	509,450,000	196,672,000	–
Land	149,450,000	57,688,000	29.3
Water	360,000,000	138,984,000	70.7
Asia	44,500,000	17,177,000	29.8
Africa	30,302,000	11,697,000	20.3
North America	24,241,000	9,357,000	16.2
South America	17,793,000	6,868,000	11.9
Antarctica	14,100,000	5,443,000	9.4
Europe	9,957,000	3,843,000	6.7
Australia & Oceania	8,557,000	3,303,000	5.7
Pacific Ocean	155,557,000	60,061,000	46.4
Atlantic Ocean	76,762,000	29,638,000	22.9
Indian Ocean	68,556,000	26,470,000	20.4
Southern Ocean	20,327,000	7,848,000	6.1
Arctic Ocean	14,056,000	5,427,000	4.2

Ocean Depths

Atlantic Ocean	m	ft
Puerto Rico (Milwaukee) Deep	8,605	28,232
Cayman Trench	7,680	25,197
Gulf of Mexico	5,203	17,070
Mediterranean Sea	5,121	16,801
Black Sea	2,211	7,254
North Sea	660	2,165
Indian Ocean	**m**	**ft**
Java Trench	7,450	24,442
Red Sea	2,635	8,454
Pacific Ocean	**m**	**ft**
Mariana Trench	11,022	36,161
Tonga Trench	10,882	35,702
Japan Trench	10,554	34,626
Kuril Trench	10,542	34,587
Arctic Ocean	**m**	**ft**
Molloy Deep	5,608	18,399

Mountains

Europe		m	ft
Elbrus	*Russia*	5,642	18,510
Dyka-Tau	*Russia*	5,205	17,076
Shkhara	*Russia/Georgia*	5,201	17,064
Koshtan-Tau	*Russia*	5,152	16,903
Kazbek	*Russia/Georgia*	5,047	16,558
Pushkin	*Russia/Georgia*	5,033	16,512
Katyn-Tau	*Russia/Georgia*	4,979	16,335
Shota Rustaveli	*Russia/Georgia*	4,860	15,945
Mont Blanc	*France/Italy*	4,808	15,774
Monte Rosa	*Italy/Switzerland*	4,634	15,203
Dom	*Switzerland*	4,545	14,911
Liskamm	*Switzerland*	4,527	14,852
Weisshorn	*Switzerland*	4,505	14,780
Taschorn	*Switzerland*	4,490	14,730
Matterhorn/Cervino	*Italy/Switzerland*	4,478	14,691
Grossglockner	*Austria*	3,797	12,457
Mulhacén	*Spain*	3,478	11,411
Zugspitze	*Germany*	2,962	9,718
Olympus	*Greece*	2,917	9,570
Galdhøpiggen	*Norway*	2,469	8,100
Kebnekaise	*Sweden*	2,117	6,946
Ben Nevis	*UK*	1,342	4,403
Asia		**m**	**ft**
Everest	*China/Nepal*	8,850	29,035
K2 (Godwin Austen)	*China/Kashmir*	8,611	28,251
Kanchenjunga	*India/Nepal*	8,598	28,208
Lhotse	*China/Nepal*	8,516	27,939
Makalu	*China/Nepal*	8,481	27,824
Cho Oyu	*China/Nepal*	8,201	26,906
Dhaulagiri	*Nepal*	8,167	26,795
Manaslu	*Nepal*	8,156	26,758
Nanga Parbat	*Kashmir*	8,126	26,660
Annapurna	*Nepal*	8,078	26,502
Gasherbrum	*China/Kashmir*	8,068	26,469
Xixabangma	*China*	8,012	26,286
Kangbachen	*India/Nepal*	7,902	25,925
Trivor	*Pakistan*	7,720	25,328
Pik Imeni Ismail Samani	*Tajikistan*	7,495	24,590
Demavend	*Iran*	5,604	18,386
Ararat	*Turkey*	5,165	16,945
Gunong Kinabalu	*Malaysia (Borneo)*	4,101	13,455
Fuji-San	*Japan*	3,776	12,388
Africa		**m**	**ft**
Kilimanjaro	*Tanzania*	5,895	19,340
Mt Kenya	*Kenya*	5,199	17,057
Ruwenzori	*Uganda/Congo (D.R.)*	5,109	16,762
Ras Dashen	*Ethiopia*	4,620	15,157
Meru	*Tanzania*	4,565	14,977
Karisimbi	*Rwanda/Congo (D.R.)*	4,507	14,787
Mt Elgon	*Kenya/Uganda*	4,321	14,176
Batu	*Ethiopia*	4,307	14,130
Toubkal	*Morocco*	4,165	13,665
Mt Cameroun	*Cameroon*	4,070	13,353
Oceania		**m**	**ft**
Puncak Jaya	*Indonesia*	5,029	16,499
Puncak Trikora	*Indonesia*	4,730	15,518
Puncak Mandala	*Indonesia*	4,702	15,427
Mt Wilhelm	*Papua New Guinea*	4,508	14,790
Mauna Kea	*USA (Hawaii)*	4,205	13,796
Mauna Loa	*USA (Hawaii)*	4,169	13,678
Aoraki Mt Cook	*New Zealand*	3,753	12,313
Mt Kosciuszko	*Australia*	2,228	7,310
North America		**m**	**ft**
Mt McKinley (Denali)	*USA (Alaska)*	6,194	20,321
Mt Logan	*Canada*	5,959	19,551
Pico de Orizaba	*Mexico*	5,610	18,405
Mt St Elias	*USA/Canada*	5,489	18,008
Popocatépetl	*Mexico*	5,452	17,887
Mt Foraker	*USA (Alaska)*	5,304	17,401
Iztaccihuatl	*Mexico*	5,286	17,342
Lucania	*Canada*	5,226	17,146
Mt Steele	*Canada*	5,073	16,644
Mt Bona	*USA (Alaska)*	5,005	16,420
Mt Whitney	*USA*	4,418	14,495
Tajumulco	*Guatemala*	4,220	13,845
Chirripó Grande	*Costa Rica*	3,837	12,589
Pico Duarte	*Dominican Rep.*	3,175	10,417
South America		**m**	**ft**
Aconcagua	*Argentina*	6,962	22,841
Bonete	*Argentina*	6,872	22,546
Ojos del Salado	*Argentina/Chile*	6,863	22,516
Pissis	*Argentina*	6,779	22,241
Mercedario	*Argentina/Chile*	6,770	22,211
Huascarán	*Peru*	6,768	22,204
Llullaillaco	*Argentina/Chile*	6,723	22,057
Nevado de Cachi	*Argentina*	6,720	22,047
Yerupaja	*Peru*	6,632	21,758
Sajama	*Bolivia*	6,520	21,391
Chimborazo	*Ecuador*	6,267	20,561
Pico Cristóbal Colón	*Colombia*	5,800	19,029
Pico Bolivar	*Venezuela*	5,007	16,427
Antarctica		**m**	**ft**
Vinson Massif		4,897	16,066
Mt Kirkpatrick		4,528	14,855

Rivers

Europe		km	miles
Volga	*Caspian Sea*	3,700	2,300
Danube	*Black Sea*	2,850	1,770
Ural	*Caspian Sea*	2,535	1,575
Dnieper	*Black Sea*	2,285	1,420
Kama	*Volga*	2,030	1,260
Don (Dnieper)	*Volga*	1,990	1,240
Petchora	*Arctic Ocean*	1,790	1,110
Oka	*Volga*	1,480	920
Dniester	*Black Sea*	1,400	870
Vyatka	*Kama*	1,370	850
Rhine	*North Sea*	1,320	820
North Dvina	*Arctic Ocean*	1,290	800
Elbe	*North Sea*	1,145	710
Asia		**km**	**miles**
Yangtse	*Pacific Ocean*	6,380	3,960
Yenisey–Angara	*Arctic Ocean*	5,550	3,445
Huang He	*Pacific Ocean*	5,464	3,395
Ob–Irtysh	*Arctic Ocean*	5,410	3,360
Mekong	*Pacific Ocean*	4,500	2,795
Amur	*Pacific Ocean*	4,442	2,760
Lena	*Arctic Ocean*	4,402	2,735
Irtysh	*Ob*	4,250	2,640
Yenisey	*Arctic Ocean*	4,090	2,540
Ob	*Arctic Ocean*	3,680	2,285
Indus	*Indian Ocean*	3,100	1,925
Brahmaputra	*Indian Ocean*	2,900	1,800
Syrdarya	*Aral Sea*	2,860	1,775
Salween	*Indian Ocean*	2,800	1,740
Euphrates	*Indian Ocean*	2,700	1,675
Amudarya	*Aral Sea*	2,540	1,575
Africa		**km**	**miles**
Nile	*Mediterranean*	6,670	4,140
Congo	*Atlantic Ocean*	4,670	2,900
Niger	*Atlantic Ocean*	4,180	2,595
Zambezi	*Indian Ocean*	3,540	2,200
Oubangi/Uele	*Congo (Dem. Rep.)*	2,250	1,400
Kasai	*Congo (Dem. Rep.)*	1,950	1,210
Shaballe	*Indian Ocean*	1,930	1,200
Orange	*Atlantic Ocean*	1,860	1,155
Cubango	*Okavango Delta*	1,800	1,120
Limpopo	*Indian Ocean*	1,770	1,100
Senegal	*Atlantic Ocean*	1,640	1,020
Australia		**km**	**miles**
Murray–Darling	*Southern Ocean*	3,750	2,330
Darling	*Murray*	3,070	1,905
Murray	*Southern Ocean*	2,575	1,600
Murrumbidgee	*Murray*	1,690	1,050
North America		**km**	**miles**
Mississippi–Missouri	*Gulf of Mexico*	5,971	3,710
Mackenzie	*Arctic Ocean*	4,240	2,630
Missouri	*Mississippi*	4,088	2,540
Mississippi	*Gulf of Mexico*	3,782	2,350
Yukon	*Pacific Ocean*	3,185	1,980
Rio Grande	*Gulf of Mexico*	3,030	1,880
Arkansas	*Mississippi*	2,340	1,450
Colorado	*Pacific Ocean*	2,330	1,445
Red	*Mississippi*	2,040	1,270
Columbia	*Pacific Ocean*	1,950	1,210
Saskatchewan	*Lake Winnipeg*	1,940	1,205
South America		**km**	**miles**
Amazon	*Atlantic Ocean*	6,450	4,010
Paraná–Plate	*Atlantic Ocean*	4,500	2,800
Purus	*Amazon*	3,350	2,080
Madeira	*Amazon*	3,200	1,990
São Francisco	*Atlantic Ocean*	2,900	1,800
Paraná	*Plate*	2,800	1,740
Tocantins	*Atlantic Ocean*	2,750	1,710
Orinoco	*Atlantic Ocean*	2,740	1,700
Paraguay	*Paraná*	2,550	1,580
Pilcomayo	*Paraná*	2,500	1,550
Araguaia	*Tocantins*	2,250	1,400

Lakes

Europe		km^2	miles^2
Lake Ladoga	*Russia*	17,700	6,800
Lake Onega	*Russia*	9,700	3,700
Saimaa system	*Finland*	8,000	3,100
Vänern	*Sweden*	5,500	2,100
Asia		**km^2**	**miles^2**
Caspian Sea	*Asia*	371,000	143,000
Lake Baikal	*Russia*	30,500	11,780
Tonlé Sap	*Cambodia*	20,000	7,700
Lake Balqash	*Kazakhstan*	18,500	7,100
Aral Sea	*Kazakhstan/Uzbekistan*	17,160	6,625
Africa		**km^2**	**miles^2**
Lake Victoria	*East Africa*	68,000	26,000
Lake Tanganyika	*Central Africa*	33,000	13,000
Lake Malawi/Nyasa	*East Africa*	29,600	11,430
Lake Chad	*Central Africa*	25,000	9,700
Lake Turkana	*Ethiopia/Kenya*	8,500	3,290
Lake Volta	*Ghana*	8,480	3,270
Australia		**km^2**	**miles^2**
Lake Eyre	*Australia*	8,900	3,400
Lake Torrens	*Australia*	5,800	2,200
Lake Gairdner	*Australia*	4,800	1,900
North America		**km^2**	**miles^2**
Lake Superior	*Canada/USA*	82,350	31,800
Lake Huron	*Canada/USA*	59,600	23,010
Lake Michigan	*USA*	58,000	22,400
Great Bear Lake	*Canada*	31,800	12,280
Great Slave Lake	*Canada*	28,500	11,000
Lake Erie	*Canada/USA*	25,700	9,900
Lake Winnipeg	*Canada*	24,400	9,400
Lake Ontario	*Canada/USA*	19,500	7,500
Lake Nicaragua	*Nicaragua*	8,200	3,200
South America		**km^2**	**miles^2**
Lake Titicaca	*Bolivia/Peru*	8,300	3,200
Lake Poopo	*Bolivia*	2,800	1,100

Islands

Europe		km^2	miles^2
Great Britain	*UK*	229,880	88,700
Iceland	*Atlantic Ocean*	103,000	39,800
Ireland	*Ireland/UK*	84,400	32,600
Novaya Zemlya (N.)	*Russia*	48,200	18,600
Sicily	*Italy*	25,500	9,800
Sardinia	*Italy*	23,950	9,250
Asia		**km^2**	**miles^2**
Borneo	*South-east Asia*	744,360	287,400
Sumatra	*Indonesia*	473,600	182,860
Honshu	*Japan*	230,500	88,980
Celebes	*Indonesia*	189,000	73,000
Java	*Indonesia*	126,700	48,900
Luzon	*Philippines*	104,700	40,400
Hokkaido	*Japan*	78,400	30,300
Africa		**km^2**	**miles^2**
Madagascar	*Indian Ocean*	587,040	226,660
Socotra	*Indian Ocean*	3,600	1,400
Réunion	*Indian Ocean*	2,500	965
Oceania		**km^2**	**miles^2**
New Guinea	*Indonesia/Papua NG*	821,030	317,000
New Zealand (S.)	*Pacific Ocean*	150,500	58,100
New Zealand (N.)	*Pacific Ocean*	114,700	44,300
Tasmania	*Australia*	67,800	26,200
New Caledonia	*Pacific Ocean*	16,650	6,470
North America		**km^2**	**miles^2**
Greenland	*Atlantic Ocean*	2,175,600	839,800
Baffin I.	*Canada*	508,000	196,100
Victoria I.	*Canada*	212,200	81,900
Ellesmere I.	*Canada*	212,000	81,800
Cuba	*Caribbean Sea*	110,860	42,800
Newfoundland	*Canada*	108,860	42,030
Banks I.	*Canada*	70,028	27,038
Hispaniola	*Dominican Rep./Haiti*	76,200	29,400
South America		**km^2**	**miles^2**
Tierra del Fuego	*Argentina/Chile*	47,000	18,100
Chiloé	*Chile*	8,480	3,275
Falkland I. (E.)	*Atlantic Ocean*	6,800	2,600

How to use the Index

The index contains the names of all the principal places and features shown on the maps. Each name is followed by an additional entry in italics giving the country or region within which it is located. The alphabetical order of names composed of two or more words is governed primarily by the first word and then by the second. This is an example of the rule:

Albert, L. *Africa*	1°30N 31°0E	**96** D6	
Albert Lea *U.S.A.*	43°39N 93°22W	**111** B8	
Albert Nile ➤ *Uganda*	3°36N 32°2E	**96** D6	
Alberta *Canada*	54°40N 115°0W	**108** D8	
Albertville *France*	45°40N 6°22E	**66** D7	

Physical features composed of a proper name (Erie) and a description (Lake) are positioned alphabetically by the proper name. The description is positioned after the proper name and is usually abbreviated:

Erie, L. *N. Amer.* 42°15N 81°0W **112** D7

Where a description forms part of a settlement or administrative name, however, it is always written in full and put in its true alphabetical position:

Mount Isa *Australia* 20°42S 139°26E **98** E6

Names beginning with M' and Mc are indexed as if they were spelled Mac. Names beginning St. are alphabetized under Saint, but Santa and San are spelled in full and are alphabetized accordingly. If the same place name occurs two or more times in the index and all are in the same country, each is followed by the name of the administrative subdivision in which it is located.

The geographical co-ordinates that follow each name in the index give the latitude and longitude of each place. The first co-ordinate indicates latitude – the distance north or south of the Equator. The second co-ordinate indicates longitude – the distance east or west of the Greenwich Meridian. Both latitude and longitude are measured in degrees and minutes (there are 60 minutes in a degree).

The latitude is followed by N(orth) or S(outh) and the longitude by E(ast) or W(est).

The number in bold type that follows the geographical co-ordinates refers to the number of the map page where that feature or place will be found. This is usually the largest scale at which the place or feature appears.

The letter and figure that are immediately after the page number give the grid square on the map page, within which the feature is situated. The letter represents the latitude and the figure the longitude. A lower-case letter immediately after the page number refers to an inset map on that page.

In some cases the feature itself may fall within the specified square, while the name is outside. This is usually the case only with features that are larger than a grid square.

Rivers are indexed to their mouths or confluences, and carry the symbol ➤ after their names. The following symbols are also used in the index: ■ country, ☑ overseas territory or dependency, □ first-order administrative area, △ national park, ✈ (LHR) principal airport (and location identifier).

Abbreviations used in the Index

Afghan. – Afghanistan
Ala. – Alabama
Alta. – Alberta
Amer. – America(n)
Arch. – Archipelago
Ariz. – Arizona
Ark. – Arkansas
Atl. Oc. – Atlantic Ocean
B. – Baie, Bahía, Bay, Bucht, Bugt
B.C. – British Columbia
Bangla. – Bangladesh
C. – Cabo, Cap, Cape, Coast
C.A.R. – Central African Republic
Calif. – California
Cent. – Central
Chan. – Channel
Colo. – Colorado
Conn. – Connecticut

Cord. – Cordillera
Cr. – Creek
D.C. – District of Columbia
Del. – Delaware
Dom. Rep. – Dominican Republic
E. – East
El Salv. – El Salvador
Eq. Guin. – Equatorial Guinea
Fla. – Florida
Falk. Is. – Falkland Is.
G. – Golfe, Golfo, Gulf
Ga. – Georgia
Hd. – Head
Hts. – Heights
I.(s). – Île, Ilha, Insel, Isla, Island, Isle(s)
Ill. – Illinois
Ind. – Indiana

Ind. Oc. – Indian Ocean
Ivory C. – Ivory Coast
Kans. – Kansas
Ky. – Kentucky
L. – Lac, Lacul, Lago, Lagoa, Lake, Limni, Loch, Lough
La. – Louisiana
Lux. – Luxembourg
Madag. – Madagascar
Man. – Manitoba
Mass. – Massachusetts
Md. – Maryland
Me. – Maine
Mich. – Michigan
Minn. – Minnesota
Miss. – Mississippi
Mo. – Missouri
Mont. – Montana
Mozam. – Mozambique

Mt.(s) – Mont, Monte, Monti, Montaña, Mountain
N. – Nord, Norte, North, Northern,
N.B. – New Brunswick
N.C. – North Carolina
N. Cal. – New Caledonia
N. Dak. – North Dakota
N.H. – New Hampshire
N.J. – New Jersey
N. Mex. – New Mexico
N.S. – Nova Scotia
N.S.W. – New South Wales
N.W.T. – North West Territory
N.Y. – New York
N.Z. – New Zealand
Nat. Park – National Park
Nebr. – Nebraska
Neths. – Netherlands

Nev. – Nevada
Nfld. – Newfoundland and Labrador
Nic. – Nicaragua
Okla. – Oklahoma
Ont. – Ontario
Oreg. – Oregon
P.E.I. – Prince Edward Island
Pa. – Pennsylvania
Pac. Oc. – Pacific Ocean
Papua N.G. – Papua New Guinea
Pen. – Peninsula, Péninsule
Phil. – Philippines
Pk. – Peak
Plat. – Plateau
Prov. – Province, Provincial
Pt. – Point
Pta. – Ponta, Punta
Pte. – Pointe

Qué. – Québec
Queens. – Queensland
R. – Rio, River
R.I. – Rhode Island
Ra.(s) – Range(s)
Reg. – Region
Rep. – Republic
Res. – Reserve, Reservoir
S. – San, South
Si. Arabia – Saudi Arabia
S.C. – South Carolina
S. Dak. – South Dakota
Sa. – Serra, Sierra
Sask. – Saskatchewan
Scot. – Scotland
Sd. – Sound
Sib. – Siberia
St. – Saint, Sankt, Sint
Str. – Strait, Stretto
Switz. – Switzerland

Tas. – Tasmania
Tenn. – Tennessee
Tex. – Texas
Trin. & Tob.. – Trinidad & Tobago
U.A.E. – United Arab Emirates
U.K. – United Kingdom
U.S.A. – United States of America
Va. – Virginia
Vic. – Victoria
Vol. – Volcano
Vt. – Vermont
W. – West
W. Va. – West Virginia
Wash. – Washington
Wis. – Wisconsin

A

Aachen *Germany*	50°45N 6°6E	**64** C4	
Aalborg *Denmark*	57°2N 9°54E	**63** F5	
Aarau *Switz.*	47°23N 8°4E	**64** E5	
Aare ➤ *Switz.*	47°33N 8°14E	**64** E5	
Aba *Nigeria*	5°10N 7°19E	**94** G7	
Abaco I. *Bahamas*	26°25N 77°10W	**115** B9	
Ābādān *Iran*	30°22N 48°20E	**86** D7	
Abaetetuba *Brazil*	1°40S 48°50W	**120** C5	
Abakan *Russia*	53°40N 91°10E	**77** D10	
Abancay *Peru*	13°35S 72°55W	**120** D2	
Abariringa *Kiribati*	2°50S 171°40W	**99** A16	
Abaya, L. *Ethiopia*	6°30N 37°50E	**89** F2	
Abbé, L. *Ethiopia*	11°8N 41°47E	**89** E3	
Abbeville *France*	50°6N 1°49E	**66** A4	
Abbey Town *U.K.*	54°51N 3°17W	**22** C2	
Abbot Ice Shelf *Antarctica*	73°0S 92°0W	**55** D16	
Abbots Bromley *U.K.*	52°50N 1°52W	**23** G5	
Abbotsbury *U.K.*	50°40N 2°37W	**24** E3	
Abéché *Chad*	13°50N 20°35E	**95** F10	
Abeokuta *Nigeria*	7°3N 3°19E	**94** G6	
Aberaeron *U.K.*	52°15N 4°15W	**26** A4	
Aberchirder *U.K.*	57°34N 2°37W	**19** G12	
Aberdare *U.K.*	51°43N 3°27W	**26** D7	
Aberdeen *U.K.*	57°9N 2°5W	**19** H13	
Aberdeen *S. Dak., U.S.A.*	45°28N 98°29W	**110** A7	
Aberdeen *Wash., U.S.A.*	46°59N 123°50W	**110** A2	
Aberdeenshire □ *U.K.*	57°17N 2°36W	**19** H12	
Aberdyfi *U.K.*	52°33N 4°3W	**26** B5	
Aberfeldy *U.K.*	56°37N 3°51W	**21** A8	
Aberfoyle *U.K.*	56°11N 4°23W	**20** B7	
Abergavenny *U.K.*	51°49N 3°1W	**26** D7	
Abergele *U.K.*	53°17N 3°35W	**26** A6	
Aberporth *U.K.*	52°8N 4°33W	**26** C4	
Abersoch *U.K.*	52°49N 4°30W	**26** B3	
Abersychan *U.K.*	51°44N 3°3W	**26** D7	
Abert, L. *U.S.A.*	42°38N 120°14W	**110** D2	
Abertillery *U.K.*	51°44N 3°8W	**26** D7	
Aberystwyth *U.K.*	52°25N 4°5W	**26** C5	
Abhā *Si. Arabia*	18°0N 42°34E	**89** D3	
Abidjan *Ivory C.*	5°26N 3°58W	**94** G5	
Abilene *U.S.A.*	32°28N 99°43W	**110** D7	
Abingdon *U.K.*	51°40N 1°17W	**24** C6	
Abitibi, L. *Canada*	48°40N 79°40W	**109** E12	
Abkhazia □ *Georgia*	43°12N 41°5E	**71** F7	
Abomey *Benin*	7°10N 2°5E	**94** G6	

Aboyne *U.K.*	57°4N 2°47W	**19** H12	
Abrolhos, Banco dos *Brazil*	18°0S 38°0W	**122** C3	
Absaroka Range *U.S.A.*	44°45N 109°50W	**110** B5	
Abu Dhabi *U.A.E.*	24°28N 54°22E	**87** E8	
Abu Hamed *Sudan*	19°32N 33°13E	**95** E12	
Abuja *Nigeria*	9°5N 7°32E	**94** G7	
Abunã *Brazil*	9°40S 65°20W	**120** C3	
Abunã ➤ *Brazil*	9°41S 65°20W	**120** C3	
Acaponeta *Mexico*	22°30N 105°22W	**114** C3	
Acapulco *Mexico*	16°51N 99°55W	**114** D5	
Acaraí, Serra *Brazil*	1°50N 57°50W	**120** B4	
Acarigua *Venezuela*	9°33N 69°12W	**120** B3	
Accomac *U.S.A.*	37°43N 75°40W	**113** G10	
Accra *Ghana*	5°35N 0°6W	**94** G5	
Accrington *U.K.*	53°45N 2°22W	**23** E4	
Aceh □ *Indonesia*	4°15N 97°30E	**82** D1	
Acharnes *Greece*	38°5N 23°44E	**69** E10	
Acheloos ➤ *Greece*	38°19N 21°7E	**69** E9	
Achill Hd. *Ireland*	53°58N 10°15W	**28** D1	
Achill I. *Ireland*	53°58N 10°1W	**28** D1	
Acklins I. *Bahamas*	22°30N 74°0W	**115** C10	
Acle *U.K.*	52°39N 1°33E	**25** A12	
Aconcagua, Cerro *Argentina*	32°39S 70°0W	**121** F3	
Acre □ *Brazil*	9°1S 71°0W	**120** C2	
Acre ➤ *Brazil*	8°45S 67°22W	**120** C3	
Acton Burnell *U.K.*	52°37N 2°41W	**23** G3	
Ad Dammām *Si. Arabia*	26°20N 50°5E	**86** E7	
Ad Dīwānīyah *Iraq*	32°0N 45°0E	**86** D6	
Adair, C. *Canada*	71°30N 71°34W	**109** B12	
Adak I. *U.S.A.*	51°45N 176°45W	**108** D2	
Adamaoua, Massif de l' *Cameroon*	7°20N 12°20E	**95** G8	
Adam's Bridge *Sri Lanka*	9°15N 79°40E	**84** Q11	
Adana *Turkey*	37°0N 35°16E	**71** G6	
Adare, C. *Antarctica*	71°0S 171°0E	**55** D11	
Addis Ababa *Ethiopia*	9°2N 38°42E	**89** F2	
Adelaide *Australia*	34°52S 138°30E	**98** G6	
Adelaide I. *Antarctica*	67°15S 68°30W	**55** C17	
Adelaide Pen. *Canada*	68°15N 97°30W	**108** B10	
Adélie, Terre *Antarctica*	68°0S 140°0E	**55** C10	
Aden *Yemen*	12°45N 45°0E	**89** E4	
Aden, G. of *Ind. Oc.*	12°30N 47°30E	**89** E4	
Adige ➤ *Italy*	45°9N 12°20E	**68** B5	
Adigrat *Ethiopia*	14°20N 39°26E	**89** E2	
Adirondack Mts. *U.S.A.*	44°0N 74°0W	**113** D10	
Adjuntas *Puerto Rico*	18°10N 66°43W	**115** d	
Admiralty Is. *Papua N. G.*	2°0S 147°0E	**102** H6	
Adour ➤ *France*	43°32N 1°32W	**66** E3	

Adrar *Mauritania*	20°30N 7°30W	**94** D3	
Adrar des Iforas *Africa*	19°40N 1°40E	**94** C5	
Adrian *U.S.A.*	41°54N 84°2W	**112** E5	
Adriatic Sea *Medit. S.*	43°0N 16°0E	**68** C6	
Adwa *Ethiopia*	14°15N 38°52E	**89** E2	
Adwick le Street *U.K.*	53°34N 1°10W	**23** E6	
Adygea □ *Russia*	45°0N 40°0E	**71** F7	
Ægean Sea *Medit. S.*	38°30N 25°0E	**69** E11	
Afghanistan ■ *Asia*	33°0N 65°0E	**87** C11	
Africa	10°0N 20°0E	**90** E6	
Afyon *Turkey*	38°45N 30°33E	**71** G5	
Agadez *Niger*	16°58N 7°59E	**94** E7	
Agadir *Morocco*	30°28N 9°55W	**94** B4	
Agartala *India*	23°50N 91°23E	**85** H17	
Agen *France*	44°12N 0°38E	**66** D4	
Agra *India*	27°17N 77°58E	**84** F10	
Ağrı *Turkey*	39°44N 43°3E	**71** G7	
Agrigento *Italy*	37°19N 13°34E	**68** F5	
Agua Prieta *Mexico*	31°18N 109°34W	**114** A3	
Aguadilla *Puerto Rico*	18°26N 67°10W	**115** d	
Aguascalientes *Mexico*	21°53N 102°18W	**114** C4	
Aguila, Punta *Puerto Rico*	17°57N 67°13W	**115** d	
Aguja, C. de la *Colombia*	11°18N 74°12W	**117** B3	
Agujereada, Pta. *Puerto Rico*	18°30N 67°8W	**115** d	
Agulhas, C. *S. Africa*	34°52S 20°0E	**97** L4	
Ahaggar *Algeria*	23°0N 6°30E	**94** D7	
Ahmadabad *India*	23°0N 72°40E	**84** H8	
Ahmadnagar *India*	19°7N 74°46E	**84** K9	
Ahmadpur East *Pakistan*	29°12N 71°10E	**84** E7	
Ahvāz *Iran*	31°20N 48°40E	**86** D7	
Ahvenanmaa *Finland*	60°15N 20°0E	**63** E8	
Ahwar *Yemen*	13°30N 46°40E	**89** E4	
Ailsa Craig *U.K.*	55°15N 5°6W	**20** D5	
Aimorés *Brazil*	19°30S 41°4W	**122** C2	
Aïn Témouchent *Algeria*	35°16N 1°8W	**94** A5	
Ainsdale *U.K.*	53°37N 3°2W	**23** E2	
Air *Niger*	18°30N 8°0E	**94** E7	
Air Force I. *Canada*	67°58N 74°5W	**109** C12	
Aird, The *U.K.*	57°25N 4°33W	**19** H8	
Airdrie *Canada*	51°18N 114°2W	**108** D8	
Airdrie *U.K.*	55°52N 3°57W	**21** C8	
Aire ➤ *U.K.*	53°43N 0°55W	**23** E7	
Aisgill *U.K.*	54°23N 2°21W	**22** D4	
Aisne ➤ *France*	49°26N 2°50E	**66** B5	
Aix-en-Provence *France*	43°32N 5°27E	**66** E6	
Aix-les-Bains *France*	45°41N 5°53E	**66** D6	
Aizawl *India*	23°40N 92°44E	**85** H18	
Aizuwakamatsu *Japan*	37°30N 139°56E	**81** E6	

Ajaccio *France*	41°55N 8°40E	**66** F8	
Ajanta Ra. *India*	20°28N 75°50E	**84** J9	
Ajaria □ *Georgia*	41°30N 42°0E	**71** F7	
Ajdābiyā *Libya*	30°54N 20°4E	**95** B10	
'Ajmān *U.A.E.*	25°25N 55°30E	**87** E8	
Ajmer *India*	26°28N 74°37E	**84** F9	
Aketi *Dem. Rep. of the Congo*	2°38N 23°47E	**96** D4	
Akhisar *Turkey*	38°56N 27°48E	**71** G4	
Akimiski I. *Canada*	52°50N 81°30W	**109** D11	
Akita *Japan*	39°45N 140°7E	**81** D7	
'Akko *Israel*	32°55N 35°4E	**86** C3	
Aklavik *Canada*	68°12N 135°0W	**108** C6	
Akola *India*	20°42N 77°2E	**84** J10	
Akpatok I. *Canada*	60°25N 68°8W	**109** C13	
Akranes *Iceland*	64°19N 22°5W	**63** B1	
Akron *U.S.A.*	41°5N 81°31W	**112** E7	
Aksai Chin *China*	35°15N 79°55E	**84** B11	
Aksaray *Turkey*	38°25N 34°2E	**71** G5	
Akşehir Gölü *Turkey*	38°30N 31°25E	**71** G5	
Aksu *China*	41°5N 80°10E	**78** C5	
Aksum *Ethiopia*	14°5N 38°40E	**89** E2	
Akure *Nigeria*	7°15N 5°5E	**94** G7	
Akureyri *Iceland*	65°40N 18°6W	**63** A2	
Ala-Iulia *Romania*	46°8N 23°39E	**65** E12	
Albacete *Spain*	39°0N 1°50W	**67** C5	
Albanel, L. *Canada*	50°55N 73°12W	**109** D12	
Albania ■ *Europe*	41°0N 20°0E	**69** D9	
Albany *Australia*	35°1S 117°58E	**98** H2	
Albany *Ga., U.S.A.*	31°35N 84°10W	**111** D10	
Albany *N.Y., U.S.A.*	42°39N 73°45W	**113** D11	
Albany *Oreg., U.S.A.*	44°38N 123°6W	**110** B2	
Albany ➤ *Canada*	52°17N 81°31W	**109** D11	
Albemarle Sd. *U.S.A.*	36°5N 76°0W	**111** C11	
Albert, L. *Africa*	1°30N 31°0E	**96** D6	
Albert Lea *U.S.A.*	43°39N 93°22W	**111** B8	
Albert Nile ➤ *Uganda*	3°36N 32°2E	**96** D6	
Alberta □ *Canada*	54°40N 115°0W	**108** D8	
Albertville *France*	45°40N 6°22E	**66** D7	
Albi *France*	43°56N 2°9E	**66** E5	
Albion *U.S.A.*	42°15N 84°45W	**112** D5	
Albrighton *U.K.*	52°38N 2°16W	**23** G4	
Albuquerque *U.S.A.*	35°5N 106°39W	**110** C5	
Albury *Australia*	36°3S 146°56E	**98** H8	
Alcalá de Henares *Spain*	40°28N 3°22W	**67** B4	
Alcester *U.K.*	52°14N 1°52W	**24** B5	
Alchevsk *Ukraine*	48°30N 38°45E	**71** E6	
Alcoy *Spain*	38°43N 0°30W	**67** C5	
Aldabra Is. *Seychelles*	9°22S 46°28E	**91** G8	
Aldan *Russia*	58°40N 125°30E	**77** D13	
Aldan ➤ *Russia*	63°28N 129°35E	**77** C13	
Aldbrough *U.K.*	53°49N 0°6W	**23** E8	
Aldbourne *U.K.*	51°29N 1°37W	**24** D5	
Aldbrough *U.K.*	53°49N 0°6W	**23** E8	
Aldeburgh *U.K.*	52°10N 1°37E	**25** B12	
Alderbury *U.K.*	51°3N 1°44W	**24** D5	

Al Qaṭīf *Si. Arabia*	26°35N 50°0E	**86** E7	
Al Qunfudhah *Si. Arabia*	19°3N 41°4E	**89** D3	
Alabama □ *U.S.A.*	33°0N 87°0W	**111** D9	
Alabama ➤ *U.S.A.*	31°8N 87°57W	**111** D9	
Alagoas □ *Brazil*	9°0S 36°0W	**122** A3	
Alagoinhas *Brazil*	12°7S 38°20W	**122** B3	
Alai Range *Asia*	39°45N 72°0E	**87** B13	
Alamogordo *U.S.A.*	32°54N 105°57W	**110** D5	
Alamosa *U.S.A.*	37°28N 105°52W	**110** C5	
Åland = Ahvenanmaa *Finland*	60°15N 20°0E	**63** E8	
Alanya *Turkey*	36°38N 32°0E	**71** G5	
Alaşehir *Turkey*	38°23N 28°30E	**71** G4	
Alaska □ *U.S.A.*	64°0N 154°0W	**108** C5	
Alaska, G. of *Pac. Oc.*	58°0N 145°0W	**108** D5	
Alaska Peninsula *U.S.A.*	56°0N 159°0W	**108** D4	
Alaska Range *U.S.A.*	62°50N 151°0W	**108** C4	

Alderley Edge   Babuyan Chan.

Alderley Edge U.K. 53°18N 2°13W 23 F4
Alderney U.K. 49°42N 2°11W 27 H9
Aldershot U.K. 51°15N 0°44W 25 D7
Aledo U.S.A. 41°12N 90°45W 112 E2
Alegrete Brazil 29°45S 56°0W 121 E4
Aleksandrovsk-Sakhalinskiy
Russia 50°50N 142°20E 79 A17
Além Paraíba Brazil 21°52S 42°41W 122 D2
Alençon France 48°27N 0°4E 66 B4
Alenquer Brazil 1°56S 54°46W 120 C4
'Alenuihāhā Channel
U.S.A. 20°30N 156°0W 110 H17
Aleppo Syria 36°10N 37°15E 86 B4
Alert Canada 83°2N 60°0W 109 A13
Alès France 44°9N 4°5E 66 D6
Alessándria Italy 44°54N 8°37E 68 B3
Ålesund Norway 62°28N 6°12E 63 E5
Aleutian Is. Pac. Oc. 52°0N 175°0W 102 B10
Aleutian Trench Pac. Oc. 48°0N 180°0E 102 C10
Alexander Arch. U.S.A. 56°0N 136°0W 108 D6
Alexander I. Antarctica 69°0S 70°0W 55 C17
Alexandria Egypt 31°13N 29°58E 95 B11
Alexandria U.K. 55°59N 4°35W 20 C6
Alexandria La., U.S.A. 31°18N 92°27W 111 D8
Alexandria Va., U.S.A. 38°49N 77°5W 112 F9
Alford Aberds., U.K. 57°14N 2°41W 19 H12
Alford Lincs., U.K. 53°15N 0°10E 23 F9
Alfreton U.K. 53°6N 1°24W 23 F6
Alfriston U.K. 50°48N 0°10E 25 E9
Algarve Portugal 36°58N 8°20W 67 D1
Algeciras Spain 36°9N 5°28W 67 D3
Algeria ■ Africa 28°30N 2°0E 94 C6
Algiers Algeria 36°42N 3°8E 94 A6
Algoa B. S. Africa 33°50S 25°45E 90 K6
Alicante Spain 38°23N 0°30W 67 C5
Alice Springs Australia 23°40S 133°50E 98 E5
Aligarh India 27°55N 78°10E 84 F11
Alipur Duar India 26°30N 89°35E 85 F16
Aliquippa U.S.A. 40°37N 80°15W 112 E5
Aliwal North S. Africa 30°45S 26°45E 97 L5
Alkmaar Neths. 52°37N 4°45E 64 B3
Allahabad India 25°25N 81°58E 85 G12
Allegan U.S.A. 42°32N 85°51W 112 D5
Allegheny → U.S.A. 40°27N 80°1W 112 E8
Allegheny Mts. U.S.A. 38°15N 80°10W 111 C11
Allègre, Pte. Guadeloupe 16°22N 61°46W 114 b
Allen → U.K. 54°58N 2°18W 22 C4
Allen, Bog of Ireland 53°15N 7°0W 31 B9
Allen, L. Ireland 54°8N 8°4W 28 C5
Allendale Town U.K. 54°53N 2°14W 22 C4
Allenheads U.K. 54°49N 2°12W 22 C4
Allentown U.S.A. 40°37N 75°29W 113 E10
Alleppey India 9°30N 76°28E 84 Q10
Alleynes B. Barbados 13°13N 59°39W 115 g
Alliance U.S.A. 42°6N 102°52W 110 B6
Allier → France 46°57N 3°4E 66 C5
Alligator Pond Jamaica 17°52N 77°34W 114 a
Alloa U.K. 56°7N 3°47W 21 B8
Allonby U.K. 54°46N 3°26W 22 C2
Alma U.S.A. 43°23N 84°39W 112 D5
Alma Ata Kazakhstan 43°15N 76°57E 78 C4
Almada Portugal 38°41N 9°8W 67 C1
Almelo Neths. 52°22N 6°42E 64 B4
Almería Spain 36°52N 2°27W 67 D4
Almondsbury U.K. 51°32N 2°34W 24 C3
Aln → U.K. 55°24N 1°37W 22 B6
Alness U.K. 57°41N 4°16W 19 G9
Alnmouth U.K. 55°24N 1°37W 22 B6
Alnwick U.K. 55°24N 1°42W 22 B5
Alor Indonesia 8°15S 124°30E 83 F6
Alor Setar Malaysia 6°7N 100°22E 82 C2
Alpena U.S.A. 45°4N 83°27W 112 C6
Alpes Maritimes Europe 44°10N 7°10E 66 D7
Alphington U.K. 50°42N 3°31W 27 F6
Alpine U.S.A. 30°22N 103°40W 110 D6
Alps Europe 46°30N 9°30E 64 E5
Alrewas U.K. 52°44N 1°44W 23 G5
Alsace □ France 48°15N 7°25E 66 B7
Alsager U.K. 53°6N 2°18W 23 F4
Alston U.K. 54°49N 2°25W 22 C4
Altai Mongolia 46°40N 92°45E 78 B7
Altamira Brazil 3°12S 52°10W 120 C4
Altamura Italy 40°49N 16°33E 68 D7
Altanbulag Mongolia 50°16N 106°30E 78 A10
Altarnun U.K. 50°35N 4°32W 27 F4
Altay China 47°48N 88°10E 78 B6
Altiplano Bolivia 17°0S 68°0W 120 D3
Alton U.K. 51°9N 0°59W 25 D7
Alton U.S.A. 38°53N 90°11W 112 F2
Alton Towers U.K. 52°59N 1°52W 23 G5
Altoona U.S.A. 40°31N 78°24W 112 E8
Altrincham U.K. 53°24N 2°21W 23 F4
Altun Shan China 38°30N 88°0E 78 D6
Altus U.S.A. 34°38N 99°20W 110 D7
Alucra Turkey 40°22N 38°47E 71 F6
Alvechurch U.K. 52°21N 1°57W 24 B5
Alwar India 27°38N 76°34E 84 F10
Alwinton U.K. 55°21N 2°7W 22 B4
Alxa Zuoqi China 38°50N 105°40E 78 D10
Alyth U.K. 56°38N 3°13W 19 J11
Amadjuak L. Canada 65°0N 71°8W 109 C12
Amagasaki Japan 34°42N 135°23E 81 F4
Amapá Brazil 2°5N 50°50W 120 B4
Amapá □ Brazil 1°40N 52°0W 120 B4
Amarillo U.S.A. 35°13N 101°50W 110 C6
Amasya Turkey 40°40N 35°50E 71 F6
Amazon = Amazonas →
S. Amer. 0°5S 50°0W 120 C4
Amazonas □ Brazil 5°0S 65°0W 120 C3
Amazonas → S. Amer. 0°5S 50°0W 120 C4
Ambala India 30°23N 76°56E 84 D10
Ambato Ecuador 1°5S 78°42W 120 C2
Ambergris Cay Belize 18°0N 87°55W 114 D7
Ambikapur India 23°15N 83°15E 85 H13
Ambilobé Madag. 13°10S 49°3E 97 G9
Amble U.K. 55°20N 1°36W 22 B5
Ambleside U.K. 54°26N 2°58E 22 C3
Ambon Indonesia 3°43S 128°12E 83 E7
Amchitka I. U.S.A. 51°32N 179°0E 108 D1
Amderma Russia 69°45N 61°30E 76 C7
Amdo China 32°20N 91°40E 78 E7

Ameca Mexico 20°33N 104°2W 114 C4
Ameland Neths. 53°27N 5°45E 64 B3
American Highland Antarctica 73°0S 75°0E 55 D6
American Samoa ☑ Pac. Oc. 14°20S 170°0W 99 C16
Americana Brazil 22°45S 47°20W 122 D1
Amersham U.K. 51°40N 0°36W 25 C7
Ames U.S.A. 42°2N 93°37W 111 B8
Amesbury U.K. 51°10N 1°46W 24 D5
Amherst Canada 45°48N 64°8W 109 E13
Amiens France 49°54N 2°16E 66 B5
Amirante Is. Seychelles 6°0S 53°0E 72 J7
Amlia I. U.S.A. 52°4N 173°30W 108 D2
Amlwch U.K. 53°24N 4°20W 26 A5
'Ammān Jordan 31°57N 35°52E 86 D3
Ammanford U.K. 51°48N 3°59W 26 D6
Amos Canada 48°35N 78°5W 109 E12
Ampleforth U.K. 54°13N 1°6W 22 D6
Ampthill U.K. 52°2N 0°30W 25 B8
Amravati India 20°55N 77°45E 84 J10
Amreli India 21°35N 71°17E 84 J7
Amritsar India 31°35N 74°57E 84 D9
Amroha India 28°53N 78°30E 84 E11
Amsterdam Neths. 52°23N 4°54E 64 B3
Amsterdam U.S.A. 42°56N 74°11W 113 D10
Amsterdam I. Ind. Oc. 38°30S 77°30E 53 F13
Amudarya → Uzbekistan 43°58N 59°34E 87 A9
Amund Ringnes I. Canada 78°20N 96°25W 109 B10
Amundsen Gulf Canada 71°0N 124°0W 108 B7
Amundsen Sea Antarctica 72°0S 115°0W 55 D15
Amuntai Indonesia 2°28S 115°25E 82 E5
Amur → Russia 52°56N 141°10E 77 D15
An Najaf Iraq 32°3N 44°15E 86 D5
An Uaimh Ireland 53°39N 6°41W 29 D8
Anaconda U.S.A. 46°8N 112°57W 110 A4
Anadyr Russia 64°35N 177°20E 77 C18
Anadyr, G. of Russia 64°0N 180°0E 77 C19
Anaheim U.S.A. 33°50N 117°55W 110 D3
Anambas, Kepulauan
Indonesia 3°20N 106°30E 82 D3
Anamur Turkey 36°8N 32°58E 71 G5
Anantapur India 14°39N 77°42E 84 M10
Anápolis Brazil 16°15S 48°50W 122 C1
Anār Iran 30°55N 55°13E 87 D8
Anatolia Turkey 39°0N 30°0E 71 G5
Añatuya Argentina 28°20S 62°50W 121 E3
Ancaster U.K. 52°59N 0°32W 23 G7
Ancholme → U.K. 53°40N 0°32W 23 E7
Anchorage U.S.A. 61°13N 149°54W 108 C5
Anci China 39°20N 116°40E 79 D12
Ancohuma Bolivia 16°0S 68°50W 120 D3
Ancona Italy 43°38N 13°30E 68 C5
Ancrum U.K. 55°31N 2°35W 21 D10
Ancud Chile 42°0S 73°50W 121 G2
Ancud, G. de Chile 42°0S 73°0W 121 G2
Anda China 46°24N 125°19E 79 B14
Andalgalá Argentina 27°40S 66°30W 121 E3
Andalucía □ Spain 37°35N 5°0W 67 D3
Andalusia U.S.A. 31°18N 86°29W 111 D9
Andaman Is. Ind. Oc. 12°30N 92°45E 53 D14
Anderson Alaska, U.S.A. 64°25N 149°15W 108 C5
Anderson Ind., U.S.A. 40°10N 85°41W 112 E5
Anderson S.C., U.S.A. 34°31N 82°39W 111 D10
Anderson → Canada 69°42N 129°0W 108 C7
Andes, Cord. de los S. Amer. 20°0S 68°0W 121 E3
Andhra Pradesh □ India 18°0N 79°0E 84 L11
Andijon Uzbekistan 41°10N 72°15E 87 A13
Andorra ■ Europe 42°30N 1°30E 66 E4
Andorra La Vella Andorra 42°31N 1°32E 66 E4
Andover U.K. 51°12N 1°29W 24 D6
Andradina Brazil 20°54S 51°23W 120 E4
Andreanof Is. U.S.A. 51°30N 176°0W 108 D2
Ándria Italy 41°13N 16°17E 68 D7
Andros Greece 37°50N 24°57E 69 F11
Andros I. Bahamas 24°30N 78°0W 115 C9
Anegada Br. Virgin Is. 18°45N 64°20W 115 e
Aneityum Vanuatu 20°12S 169°45E 99 E12
Angara → Russia 58°5N 94°20E 77 D10
Angarsk Russia 52°30N 104°0E 78 A9
Ånge Sweden 62°31N 15°35E 63 E7
Angel Falls Venezuela 5°57N 62°30W 120 B3
Angeles Phil. 15°9N 120°33E 83 A6
Ångermanälven → Sweden 64°0N 17°20E 63 E7
Angers France 47°30N 0°35W 66 C3
Anglesey □ U.K. 53°16N 4°18W 26 A5
Angoche Mozam. 16°8S 39°55E 97 H7
Angola ■ Africa 12°0S 18°0E 97 G3
Angoulême France 45°39N 0°10E 66 D4
Angoumois France 45°50N 0°25E 66 D3
Angra dos Reis Brazil 23°0S 44°10W 122 D2
Angren Uzbekistan 41°1N 70°12E 87 A12
Anguilla ☑ W. Indies 18°14N 63°5W 115 D12
Angus □ U.K. 56°46N 2°56W 19 J11
Angus, Braes of U.K. 56°51N 3°10W 19 J11
Anhui □ China 32°0N 117°0E 79 E12
Anjou France 47°20N 0°15W 66 C3
Ankang China 32°40N 109°1E 79 E10
Ankara Turkey 39°57N 32°54E 71 G5
Ann, C. U.S.A. 42°38N 70°35W 113 D12
Ann Arbor U.S.A. 42°17N 83°45W 112 D6
Annaba Algeria 36°50N 7°46E 94 A7
Annalee → Ireland 54°2N 7°24W 28 C7
Annan U.K. 54°59N 3°16W 21 E9
Annan → U.K. 54°58N 3°16W 21 E9
Annandale U.K. 55°10N 3°25W 21 D9
Annapolis U.S.A. 38°59N 76°30W 112 F9
Annapurna Nepal 28°34N 83°50E 85 E14
Annecy France 45°55N 6°8E 66 D7
Annfield Plain U.K. 54°52N 1°44W 22 C5
Anning China 24°55N 102°26E 78 G9
Anniston U.S.A. 33°39N 85°50W 111 D9
Annobón Atl. Oc. 1°25S 5°36E 90 G4
Annotto B. Jamaica 18°17N 76°45W 114 a
Anqing China 30°30N 117°3E 79 E12
Anshan China 41°5N 122°58E 79 C13
Anshun China 26°18N 105°57E 78 F10
Anstey U.K. 52°41N 1°12W 23 G6
Anstruther U.K. 56°14N 2°41W 21 B10
Antalaha Madag. 14°57S 50°20E 97 G10
Antalya Turkey 36°52N 30°45E 71 G5
Antalya Körfezi Turkey 36°15N 31°30E 71 G5
Antananarivo Madag. 18°55S 47°31E 97 H9

Antarctic Pen. Antarctica 67°0S 60°0W 55 C18
Antarctica 90°0S 0°0 55 E3
Anti Atlas Morocco 30°0N 8°30W 94 C4
Antibes France 43°34N 7°6E 66 E7
Anticosti, Î. d' Canada 49°30N 63°0W 109 E13
Antigo U.S.A. 45°9N 89°9W 112 C3
Antigonish Canada 45°38N 61°58W 109 E13
Antigua & Barbuda ■
W. Indies 17°20N 61°48W 115 D12
Antilles Cent. Amer. 15°0N 65°0W 104 H13
Antioch = Hatay Turkey 36°14N 36°10E 71 G6
Antioquia Colombia 6°40N 75°55W 120 B2
Antipodes Is. Pac. Oc. 49°45S 178°40E 102 M9
Antofagasta Chile 23°50S 70°30W 121 E2
Antrim U.K. 54°43N 6°14W 29 B9
Antrim □ U.K. 54°56N 6°25W 29 B9
Antrim, Mts. of U.K. 55°3N 6°14W 29 A9
Antsiranana Madag. 12°25S 49°20E 97 G9
Antsirabe Madag. 19°55S 47°2E 97 H9
Antwerp Belgium 51°13N 4°25E 64 C3
Anuradhapura Sri Lanka 8°22N 80°28E 84 Q12
Anxi China 40°30N 95°43E 78 C8
Anyang China 36°5N 114°21E 79 D11
Anzhero-Sudzhensk Russia 56°10N 86°0E 76 D9
Ânzio Italy 41°27N 12°37E 68 D5
Aomori Japan 40°45N 140°45E 81 C7
Aoraki Mount Cook N.Z. 43°36S 170°9E 99 J13
Aosta Italy 45°45N 7°20E 68 B2
Aozou, Couloir d' Chad 22°0N 19°0E 95 D9
Apalachee B. U.S.A. 30°0N 84°0W 111 E10
Apaporis → Colombia 1°23S 69°25W 120 C3
Aparecida de Goiânia Brazil 16°49S 49°14W 122 C1
Apatity Russia 67°34N 33°22E 70 A5
Apeldoorn Neths. 52°13N 5°57E 64 B3
Apia Samoa 13°50S 171°50W 99 C16
Apostle Is. U.S.A. 46°55N 90°40W 112 B2
Appalachian Mts. U.S.A. 38°0N 80°0W 112 G7
Appennini Italy 44°30N 10°0E 68 B4
Appleby-in-Westmorland
U.K. 54°35N 2°29W 22 C4
Applecross Forest U.K. 57°27N 5°40W 18 H6
Appledore Devon, U.K. 51°3N 4°13W 27 E5
Appledore Kent, U.K. 51°1N 0°47E 25 D10
Appleton U.S.A. 44°16N 88°25W 112 C3
Apure → Venezuela 7°37N 66°25W 120 B3
Apurimac → Peru 12°17S 73°56W 120 D2
Aqaba, G. of Red Sea 29°0N 34°40E 86 D3
Aqtaū Kazakhstan 43°39N 51°12E 71 F9
Aqtöbe Kazakhstan 50°17N 57°10E 71 D10
Aquitain, Bassin France 44°0N 0°30W 66 D3
Ar Ramādī Iraq 33°25N 43°20E 86 C5
Ara India 25°35N 84°32E 85 G14
'Arab, Bahr el → Sudan 9°0N 29°30E 95 G11
Arab, Shatt al → Asia 29°57N 48°34E 86 D7
Arabia 25°0N 45°0E 72 F6
Arabian Sea Ind. Oc. 16°0N 65°0E 72 G8
Aracaju Brazil 10°55S 37°4W 122 B3
Aracati Brazil 4°30S 37°44W 120 C6
Araçatuba Brazil 21°10S 50°30W 122 D1
Araçuaí Brazil 16°52S 42°4W 122 C2
Arad Romania 46°10N 21°20E 65 E11
Arafura Sea E. Indies 9°0S 135°0E 98 B5
Aragón □ Spain 41°25N 0°40W 67 B5
Araguacema Brazil 8°50S 49°20W 120 C5
Araguaia → Brazil 5°21S 48°41W 120 C5
Araguari Brazil 18°38S 48°11W 122 C1
Arāk Iran 34°0N 49°40E 86 C7
Arakan Coast Burma 19°0N 94°0E 85 K19
Arakan Yoma Burma 20°0N 94°40E 85 K19
Aral Kazakhstan 46°41N 61°45E 76 E7
Aral Sea Asia 44°30N 60°0E 76 E6
Aran I. Ireland 55°0N 8°30W 28 B4
Aran Is. Ireland 53°6N 9°38W 30 B3
Aransas Pass U.S.A. 27°55N 97°9W 111 E7
Arapiraca Brazil 9°45S 36°39W 122 A3
Araraquara Brazil 21°50S 48°0W 122 D1
Araras Brazil 22°22S 47°23W 122 D1
Ararat Turkey 39°50N 44°15E 71 G7
Araripe, Chapada do Brazil 7°20S 40°0W 120 C5
Aras, Rūd-e → Asia 40°5N 48°29E 86 A7
Arauca → Venezuela 7°24N 66°35W 120 B3
Arauca Venezuela 7°24N 66°35W 120 B3
Araxá Brazil 19°35S 46°55W 122 C1
Arbil Iraq 36°15N 44°5E 86 B6
Arbroath U.K. 56°34N 2°35W 21 B10
Arcachon France 44°40N 1°10W 66 D3
Arctic Bay Canada 73°1N 85°7W 109 B11
Arctic Ocean Arctic 78°0N 160°0W 54 B18
Ardabīl Iran 38°15N 48°18E 86 B7
Ardee Ireland 53°52N 6°33W 29 D8
Ardennes Belgium 49°50N 5°5E 64 D3
Arderin Ireland 53°2N 7°39W 31 B7
Ardgour U.K. 56°45N 5°25W 18 J7
Ardingly U.K. 51°3N 0°4W 25 D8
Ardmore U.S.A. 34°10N 97°8W 111 D7
Ardnamurchan □ U.K. 56°43N 6°0W 18 J5
Ardnamurchan, Pt. of U.K. 56°43N 6°14W 18 J5
Ardnave Pt. U.K. 55°53N 6°20W 20 C3
Ardrossan U.K. 55°39N 4°49W 20 C6
Ards Pen. U.K. 54°33N 5°34W 29 B10
Arecibo Puerto Rico 18°29N 66°43W 115 d
Arena, Pt. U.S.A. 38°57N 123°44W 110 C2
Arendal Norway 58°28N 8°46E 63 F5
Arequipa Peru 16°20S 71°30W 120 D2
Arezzo Italy 43°25N 11°53E 68 C4
Argentan France 48°45N 0°1W 66 B3
Argentina ■ S. Amer. 35°0S 66°0W 121 F3
Argentino, L. Argentina 50°10S 73°0W 121 H2
Argostoli Greece 38°11N 20°29E 69 E9
Argun → Russia 53°20N 121°28E 79 A13
Argyle, L. Australia 16°20S 128°40E 98 C4
Argyll □ U.K. 56°10N 5°20W 20 B5
Argyll & Bute □ U.K. 56°13N 5°28W 20 B5
Århus Denmark 56°8N 10°11E 63 F6
Ariana Tunisia 36°52N 10°12E 95 A8
Arica Chile 18°32S 70°20W 120 D2
Arinos → Brazil 10°25S 58°20W 120 C3
Aripuanã → Brazil 5°7S 60°25W 120 C3
Arisaig U.K. 56°55N 5°51W 18 J6
Arizona □ U.S.A. 34°0N 112°0W 110 D4
Arkaig, L. U.K. 56°59N 5°10W 18 J7

Arkansas □ U.S.A. 35°0N 92°30W 111 D8
Arkansas → U.S.A. 33°47N 91°4W 111 D8
Arkansas City U.S.A. 37°4N 97°2W 111 C7
Arkhangelsk Russia 64°38N 40°36E 70 B7
Arkle → U.K. 54°24N 1°56W 22 D5
Arklow Ireland 52°48N 6°10W 31 C10
Arlington U.S.A. 38°53N 77°7W 112 F9
Arlon Belgium 49°42N 5°49E 64 D3
Armagh U.K. 54°21N 6°39W 29 C8
Armagh □ U.K. 54°18N 6°37W 29 C8
Armavir Russia 45°2N 41°7E 71 E7
Armenia Colombia 4°35N 75°45W 120 B2
Armenia ■ Asia 40°20N 45°0E 71 F7
Arnaud → Canada 59°59N 69°46W 109 D13
Arnhem Neths. 51°58N 5°55E 64 C3
Arnhem, C. Australia 12°20S 137°30E 98 C6
Arnhem Land Australia 13°10S 134°30E 98 C5
Arno → Italy 43°41N 10°17E 68 C4
Arnold U.K. 53°1N 1°7W 23 F6
Arnprior Canada 45°26N 76°21W 112 C9
Arnside U.K. 54°12N 2°49W 22 D3
Arra Mts. Ireland 52°50N 8°22W 30 C6
Arran U.K. 55°34N 5°12W 20 C5
Arras France 50°17N 2°46E 66 A5
Arrecife Canary Is. 28°57N 13°37W 94 C3
Arrow, L. Ireland 54°3N 8°19W 28 C5
Artemovsk Ukraine 48°35N 38°0E 71 E6
Artigas Uruguay 30°20S 56°30W 121 F4
Artois France 50°20N 2°30E 66 A5
Artux China 39°40N 76°10E 78 D4
Artvin Turkey 41°14N 41°44E 71 F7
Aru, Kepulauan Indonesia 6°0S 134°30E 83 F8
Arua Uganda 3°1N 30°58E 96 D6
Aruanã Brazil 14°54S 51°10W 120 D4
Aruba ☑ W. Indies 12°30N 70°0W 115 E11
Arunachal Pradesh □ India 28°0N 95°0E 85 F19
Arundel U.K. 50°51N 0°33W 25 E7
Arusha Tanzania 3°20S 36°40E 96 E7
Aruwimi →
Dem. Rep. of the Congo 1°13N 23°36E 96 D4
Arvayheer Mongolia 46°15N 102°48E 78 B9
Arviat Canada 61°6N 93°59W 108 C10
Arxan China 47°11N 119°57E 79 B12
Arzamas Russia 55°27N 43°55E 70 C7
As Sulaymānīyah Iraq 35°35N 45°29E 86 C6
As Sulaymānīyah Si. Arabia 24°9N 47°18E 86 E6
As Suwayq Oman 23°51N 57°26E 89 C6
Aş Şuwayrah Iraq 32°55N 45°0E 86 C6
Asahikawa Japan 43°46N 142°22E 81 B8
Asama-Yama Japan 36°24N 138°31E 81 E6
Asamankese Ghana 5°50N 0°40W 94 G5
Asansol India 23°40N 87°1E 85 H15
Asbestos Canada 45°47N 71°58W 113 C12
Asbury Park U.S.A. 40°13N 74°1W 113 E10
Ascension I. Atl. Oc. 7°57S 14°23W 52 E9
Áscoli Piceno Italy 42°51N 13°34E 68 C5
Ascot U.K. 51°25N 0°40W 25 D7
Aseb Eritrea 13°0N 42°40E 89 E3
Asenovgrad Bulgaria 42°1N 24°51E 69 C11
Asfordby U.K. 52°47N 0°57W 23 G7
Ash Kent, U.K. 51°16N 1°17E 25 D11
Ash Surrey, U.K. 51°15N 0°43W 25 D7
Ashbourne U.K. 53°2N 1°43W 23 F5
Ashburton U.K. 50°30N 3°46W 27 F6
Ashby de la Zouch U.K. 52°46N 1°29W 23 G6
Ashdown Forest U.K. 51°3N 0°5E 25 D9
Asheville U.S.A. 35°36N 82°33W 111 C10
Ashford Derby, U.K. 53°14N 1°42W 23 F5
Ashford Kent, U.K. 51°8N 0°53E 25 D10
Ashington U.K. 55°11N 1°33W 22 B5
Ashkhabad Turkmenistan 38°0N 57°50E 87 B9
Ashland Ky., U.S.A. 38°28N 82°38W 112 F6
Ashland Ohio, U.S.A. 40°52N 82°19W 112 E6
Ashland Wis., U.S.A. 46°35N 90°53W 111 A8
Ashqelon Israel 31°42N 34°35E 86 D3
Ashtabula U.S.A. 41°52N 80°47W 112 E7
Ashton-in-Makerfield U.K. 53°30N 2°40W 23 F3
Ashton under Lyne U.K. 53°29N 2°6W 23 F4
Ashuanipi, L. Canada 52°45N 66°15W 109 D13
Ashwater U.K. 50°43N 4°19W 27 F5
Ashwick U.K. 51°13N 2°31W 24 D3
Asia 45°0N 75°0E 72 E9
Asinara Italy 41°4N 8°16E 68 D3
'Asir Si. Arabia 18°40N 42°30E 89 D3
Asir, Ras Somali Rep. 11°55N 51°10E 89 E5
Askrigg U.K. 54°19N 2°6W 22 D4
Aslackby U.K. 52°53N 0°24W 23 G8
Asmera Eritrea 15°19N 38°55E 89 D2
Aspatria U.K. 54°47N 3°19W 22 C2
Aspen U.S.A. 39°11N 106°49W 110 C5
Assal, L. Djibouti 11°40N 42°26E 89 E3
Assam □ India 26°0N 93°0E 85 G18
Assen Neths. 53°0N 6°35E 64 B4
Assiniboia Canada 49°40N 105°59W 108 E9
Assiniboine → Canada 49°53N 97°8W 108 E10
Assisi Italy 43°4N 12°37E 68 C5
Assynt U.K. 58°12N 5°12W 18 F7
Assynt, L. U.K. 58°10N 5°3W 18 F7
Astana Kazakhstan 51°10N 71°30E 76 D8
Asti Italy 44°54N 8°12E 68 B3
Astipálaia Greece 36°32N 26°22E 69 F12
Astoria U.S.A. 46°11N 123°50W 110 A2
Astrakhan Russia 46°25N 48°5E 71 E8
Asturias □ Spain 43°15N 6°0W 67 A3
Astwood Bank U.K. 52°15N 1°56W 24 B5
Asunción Paraguay 25°10S 57°30W 121 E4
Aswân Egypt 24°4N 32°57E 95 D12
Aswân High Dam Egypt 23°54N 32°54E 95 D12
Asyût Egypt 27°11N 31°4E 95 C12
At Tā'if Si. Arabia 21°5N 40°27E 89 C3
Atacama, Desierto de Chile 24°0S 69°20W 121 E3
Atatürk Baraji Turkey 38°28N 38°30E 71 G6
Atbara Sudan 17°42N 33°59E 95 E12
Atbara → Sudan 17°40N 33°56E 95 E12
Atchafalaya B. U.S.A. 29°25N 91°25W 111 E8
Athabasca Canada 54°45N 113°20W 108 D8
Athabasca → Canada 58°40N 110°50W 108 D8
Athabasca, L. Canada 59°15N 109°15W 108 D9

Athboy Ireland 53°37N 6°56W 29 D8
Athenry Ireland 53°18N 8°44W 30 B5
Athens Greece 37°58N 23°43E 69 F10
Athens Ga., U.S.A. 33°57N 83°23W 111 D10
Athens Ohio, U.S.A. 39°20N 82°6W 112 F6
Atherstone U.K. 52°35N 1°33W 23 G5
Atherton U.K. 53°32N 2°30W 23 F4
Athlone Ireland 53°25N 7°56W 30 B7
Atholl, Forest of U.K. 56°51N 3°50W 19 J10
Athos Greece 40°9N 24°22E 69 D11
Athy Ireland 53°0N 7°0W 31 B8
Atikokan Canada 48°45N 91°37W 112 A2
Atka I. U.S.A. 52°7N 174°30W 108 D2
Atlanta U.S.A. 33°45N 84°23W 111 D10
Atlantic City U.S.A. 39°21N 74°27W 113 F10
Atlantic Ocean 0°0 20°0W 50 F9
Atlas Saharien Algeria 33°30N 1°0E 94 B6
Atlin Canada 59°31N 133°41W 108 D6
Attawapiskat Canada 52°56N 82°24W 109 D11
Attawapiskat → Canada 52°57N 82°18W 109 D11
Attleborough U.K. 52°32N 1°1E 25 A11
Attu I. U.S.A. 52°55N 172°55E 108 D1
Atyraū Kazakhstan 47°5N 52°0E 71 E9
Au Sable → U.S.A. 44°25N 83°20W 112 C6
Aube → France 48°34N 3°43E 66 B5
Auburn Ind., U.S.A. 41°22N 85°4W 112 E5
Auburn N.Y., U.S.A. 42°56N 76°34W 112 D9
Aubusson France 45°57N 2°11E 66 D5
Auch France 43°39N 0°36E 66 E4
Auchterarder U.K. 56°18N 3°41W 21 B8
Auchtermuchty U.K. 56°18N 3°13W 21 B9
Auckland N.Z. 36°52S 174°46E 99 H13
Auckland Is. Pac. Oc. 50°40S 166°5E 102 N8
Aude → France 43°13N 3°14E 66 E5
Audlem U.K. 52°59N 2°30W 23 G4
Aughnacloy U.K. 54°25N 6°59W 29 C8
Augsburg Germany 48°25N 10°52E 64 D6
Augusta Australia 34°19S 115°9E 98 G2
Augusta U.S.A. 33°28N 81°58W 111 D10
Aunis France 46°5N 0°50W 66 C3
Aurangabad Bihar, India 24°45N 84°18E 85 G14
Aurangabad Maharashtra,
India 19°50N 75°23E 84 K9
Aurillac France 44°55N 2°26E 66 D5
Aurora Colo., U.S.A. 39°43N 104°49W 110 C6
Aurora Ill., U.S.A. 41°45N 88°19W 112 E3
Austin U.S.A. 30°17N 97°45W 110 D7
Australia ■ Oceania 23°0S 135°0E 98 E3
Australian Capital Territory □
Australia 35°30S 149°0E 98 H8
Austria ■ Europe 47°0N 14°0E 64 E8
Autun France 46°58N 4°17E 66 C6
Auvergne □ France 45°20N 3°15E 66 D5
Auvergne, Mts. d' France 45°20N 2°55E 66 D5
Auxerre France 47°48N 3°32E 66 C5
Avallon France 47°30N 3°53E 66 C5
Avaré Brazil 23°4S 48°58W 122 D1
Avebury U.K. 51°26N 1°50W 24 D5
Avellaneda Argentina 34°40S 58°22W 121 F4
Avellino Italy 40°54N 14°47E 68 D6
Aversa Italy 40°58N 14°12E 68 D6
Aveton Gifford U.K. 50°18N 3°50W 27 G6
Aviemore U.K. 57°12N 3°50W 19 H10
Avignon France 43°57N 4°50E 66 E6
Ávila Spain 40°39N 4°43W 67 B3
Avilés Spain 43°35N 5°57W 67 A3
Avoca → Ireland 52°48N 6°10W 31 C10
Avon → Bristol, U.K. 51°29N 2°41W 24 D3
Avon → Dorset, U.K. 50°44N 1°46W 24 E5
Avon → Warks., U.K. 52°0N 2°8W 24 B5
Avonmouth U.K. 51°30N 2°42W 24 C3
Avranches France 48°40N 1°20W 66 B3
Awasa Ethiopia 7°2N 38°28E 89 F2
Awash Ethiopia 9°1N 40°10E 89 F3
Awbārī, Idehan Libya 27°10N 11°30E 95 C8
Awe, L. U.K. 56°17N 5°16W 20 B5
Axbridge U.K. 51°17N 2°49W 24 D3
Axe → U.K. 50°42N 3°4W 27 F8
Axe Edge U.K. 53°14N 1°57W 23 F5
Axel Heiberg I. Canada 80°0N 90°0W 109 B11
Axholme, Isle of U.K. 53°32N 0°50W 23 E7
Axios → Greece 40°57N 22°35E 69 D10
Axminster U.K. 50°46N 3°0W 27 F8
Axmouth U.K. 50°42N 3°3W 27 F7
Ayacucho Argentina 37°5S 58°20W 121 F4
Ayacucho Peru 13°0S 74°0W 120 D2
Aydın Turkey 37°51N 27°51E 71 G4
Aydingkol Hu China 42°40N 89°15E 78 C6
Aylesbury U.K. 51°49N 0°49W 25 C7
Aylesford U.K. 51°18N 0°30E 25 D10
Aylmer, L. Canada 64°5N 108°30W 108 C8
Aylsham U.K. 52°48N 1°15E 25 A11
Aynho U.K. 52°0N 1°15W 24 C6
Ayr U.K. 55°28N 4°38W 20 D6
Ayr → U.K. 55°28N 4°38W 20 D6
Aysgarth U.K. 54°18N 2°1W 22 D4
Ayton Borders, U.K. 55°51N 2°6W 21 C11
Ayton N. Yorks., U.K. 54°15N 0°28W 22 D8
Ayvalık Turkey 39°20N 26°46E 71 G4
Az Zarqā Jordan 32°5N 36°4E 86 C4
Az Zāwiyah Libya 32°52N 12°56E 95 B8
Azad Kashmir □ Pakistan 33°50N 73°50E 84 B8
Azamgarh India 26°5N 83°13E 85 F13
Azare Nigeria 11°55N 10°10E 94 F8
Azerbaijan ■ Asia 40°20N 48°0E 71 F8
Azores Atl. Oc. 38°0N 27°0W 91 C1
Azov Russia 47°3N 39°25E 71 E6
Azov, Sea of Europe 46°0N 36°30E 71 E6
Azuero, Pen. de Panama 7°30N 80°30W 115 F8
Azul Argentina 36°42S 59°43W 121 F4

B

Bab el Mandeb Red Sea 12°35N 43°25E 89 E3
Bābā, Koh-i- Afghan. 34°30N 67°0E 84 B5
Babine L. Canada 54°48N 126°0W 108 D7
Bābol Iran 36°40N 52°50E 87 B8
Babruysk Belarus 53°10N 29°15E 65 B15
Babuyan Chan. Phil. 18°40N 121°30E 83 A6

Babylon — **Big Belt Mts.**

Babylon Iraq 32°34N 44°22E 86 C6
Bac Lieu Vietnam 9°17N 105°43E 82 C3
Bacabal Brazil 4°15S 44°45W 120 C5
Bacău Romania 46°35N 26°55E 65 E14
Back → Canada 65°10N 104°0W 108 C9
Bacolod Phil. 10°40N 122°57E 83 B6
Bacton U.K. 52°52N 1°27E 25 A11
Bacup U.K. 53°42N 2°11W 23 E4
Bad Axe U.S.A. 43°48N 83°0W 112 D6
Badagara India 11°35N 75°40E 84 P9
Badajoz Spain 38°50N 6°59W 67 C2
Badakhshān □ Afghan. 36°30N 71°0E 87 B12
Badalona Spain 41°26N 2°15E 67 B7
Baden-Württemberg □
  Germany 48°20N 8°40E 64 D5
Badenoch U.K. 56°59N 4°15W 19 J9
Bādghīs □ Afghan. 35°0N 63°0E 87 C10
Badlands U.S.A. 43°55N 102°30W 110 B6
Baffin B. N. Amer. 72°0N 64°0W 109 B13
Baffin I. Canada 68°0N 75°0W 109 C12
Bafoulabé Mali 13°50N 10°55W 94 F3
Bafoussam Cameroon 5°28N 10°25E 96 C2
Bafra Turkey 41°34N 35°54E 71 F6
Bagamoyo Tanzania 6°28S 38°55E 96 F7
Bagé Brazil 31°20S 54°15W 121 F4
Baggy Pt. U.K. 51°8N 4°16W 27 E5
Baghdād Iraq 33°20N 44°23E 86 C6
Baghlān Afghan. 32°12N 68°46E 87 B12
Bagshot U.K. 51°22N 0°41W 25 D7
Baguio Phil. 16°26N 120°34E 83 A6
Bahamas ■ N. Amer. 24°0N 75°0W 115 C10
Baharampur India 24°2N 88°27E 85 G16
Bahawalpur Pakistan 29°24N 71°40E 84 E7
Bahía = Salvador Brazil 13°0S 38°30W 122 B3
Bahía □ Brazil 12°0S 42°0W 122 B2
Bahía, Is. de la Honduras 16°45N 86°15W 114 D7
Bahía Blanca Argentina 38°35S 62°13W 121 F3
Bahir Dar Ethiopia 11°37N 37°10E 89 E2
Bahraich India 27°38N 81°37E 85 F12
Bahrain ■ Asia 26°0N 50°35E 87 E7
Baia Mare Romania 47°40N 23°35E 65 E12
Baicheng China 45°38N 122°42E 79 B13
Baie-Comeau Canada 49°12N 68°10W 109 E13
Baie-St-Paul Canada 47°28N 70°32W 113 B12
Baie Verte Canada 49°55N 56°12W 109 E14
Ba'iji Iraq 35°0N 43°30E 86 C5
Baikal, L. Russia 53°0N 108°0E 77 D11
Baildon U.K. 53°51N 1°46W 23 E5
Bain → U.K. 53°6N 0°12W 23 F8
Bainbridge U.K. 54°18N 2°6W 22 D4
Baiyin China 36°45N 104°14E 78 D9
Baja, Pta. Mexico 29°58N 115°49W 114 B1
Baja California Mexico 31°10N 115°12W 114 A1
Baker, L. Canada 64°0N 96°0W 108 C10
Baker City U.S.A. 44°47N 117°50W 110 B3
Baker I. Pac. Oc. 0°10N 176°35W 99 A15
Baker Lake Canada 64°20N 96°3W 108 C10
Bakers Dozen Is. Canada 56°45N 78°45W 109 D12
Bakersfield U.S.A. 35°23N 119°1W 110 C3
Bakewell U.K. 53°13N 1°40W 23 F5
Baku Azerbaijan 40°29N 49°56E 71 F8
Bala U.K. 52°54N 3°36W 26 B6
Bala, L. U.K. 52°53N 3°37W 26 B6
Balabac Str. E. Indies 7°53N 117°5E 82 C5
Balaghat Ra. India 18°50N 76°30E 84 K10
Balaklava Ukraine 44°30N 33°30E 71 F5
Balakovo Russia 52°4N 47°55E 70 D8
Balashov Russia 51°30N 43°10E 71 D7
Balaton Hungary 46°50N 17°40E 65 E9
Balbi, Mt. Papua N. G. 5°55S 154°58E 99 B10
Balbina, Represa de Brazil 2°0S 59°30W 120 C4
Balbriggan Ireland 53°37N 6°11W 29 D9
Balcarce Argentina 38°0S 58°10W 121 F4
Balderton U.K. 53°3N 0°47W 23 F7
Baldock U.K. 52°0N 0°11W 25 C8
Baldoyle Ireland 53°24N 6°8W 31 B10
Baldwin U.S.A. 43°54N 85°51W 112 D5
Baldy Peak U.S.A. 33°54N 109°34W 110 D5
Balearic Is. Spain 39°30N 3°0E 67 C7
Baleine → Canada 58°15N 67°40W 109 D13
Baleshare U.K. 57°31N 7°22W 18 G3
Baleshwar India 21°35N 87°3E 85 J15
Bali Indonesia 8°20S 115°0E 82 F4
Balıkesir Turkey 39°39N 27°53E 71 G4
Balikpapan Indonesia 1°10S 116°55E 82 E5
Balkan Mts. Bulgaria 43°15N 23°0E 69 C10
Balkanabat Turkmenistan 39°30N 54°22E 87 B8
Balkhash, L. Kazakhstan 46°0N 74°50E 76 E8
Ballachulish U.K. 56°41N 5°8W 18 J7
Ballaghaderreen Ireland 53°55N 8°34W 28 D4
Ballantrae U.K. 55°6N 4°59W 20 D6
Ballarat Australia 37°33S 143°50E 98 H7
Ballater U.K. 57°3N 3°3W 19 H11
Balleny Is. Antarctica 66°30S 163°0E 55 C11
Ballina Australia 54°7N 9°9W 28 C3
Ballinasloe Ireland 53°20N 8°13W 30 B6
Ballinrobe Ireland 53°38N 9°13W 28 D3
Ballinskelligs B. Ireland 51°48N 10°13W 30 E2
Ballybunion Ireland 52°31N 9°40W 30 C3
Ballycastle U.K. 55°12N 6°15W 29 A9
Ballyclare U.K. 54°46N 6°0W 29 B10
Ballyhaunis Ireland 53°46N 8°46W 28 D4
Ballyhoura Mts. Ireland 52°18N 8°33W 30 D5
Ballymena U.K. 54°52N 6°17W 29 B9
Ballymoney U.K. 55°5N 6°31W 29 A8
Ballymote Ireland 54°5N 8°31W 28 C4
Ballynahinch U.K. 54°24N 5°54W 29 C10
Ballyquintin Pt. U.K. 54°20N 5°30W 29 C11
Ballyshannon Ireland 54°30N 8°11W 28 B5
Balmoral Forest U.K. 57°0N 3°15W 19 H11
Balrampur India 27°30N 82°20E 85 F13
Balsas → Mexico 17°55N 102°10W 114 D4
Baltic Sea Europe 57°0N 19°0E 63 F7
Baltimore Ireland 51°29N 9°22W 30 F3
Baltimore U.S.A. 39°17N 76°36W 112 F9
Baluchistan □ Pakistan 27°30N 65°0E 84 F4
Bam Iran 29°7N 58°14E 87 D9
Bamako Mali 12°34N 7°55W 94 F4
Bambari C.A.R. 5°40N 20°35E 96 C4

Bamberg Germany 49°54N 10°54E 64 D6
Bamburgh U.K. 55°37N 1°43W 22 A5
Bamenda Cameroon 5°57N 10°11E 96 C2
Bamford U.K. 53°22N 1°41W 23 F5
Bāmīān □ Afghan. 35°0N 67°0E 87 C11
Bampton Devon, U.K. 50°59N 3°29W 27 F7
Bampton Oxon., U.K. 51°44N 1°32W 24 C5
Banaba Kiribati 0°45S 169°50E 102 H8
Bananal, I. do Brazil 11°30S 50°30W 120 D4
Banbridge U.K. 54°22N 6°16W 29 C9
Banbury U.K. 52°4N 1°20W 24 B6
Banchory U.K. 57°3N 2°29W 19 H13
Bancroft Canada 45°3N 77°51W 112 C9
Banda India 25°30N 80°26E 84 G12
Banda, Kepulauan Indonesia 4°37S 129°50E 83 E7
Banda Aceh Indonesia 5°35N 95°20E 82 C1
Banda Sea Indonesia 6°0S 130°0E 83 F7
Bandar-e Abbās Iran 27°15N 56°15E 87 E9
Bandar-e Anzalī Iran 37°30N 49°30E 86 B7
Bandar-e Ma'shur Iran 30°35N 49°10E 86 D7
Bandar-e Torkeman Iran 37°0N 54°10E 87 B8
Bandar Lampung Indonesia 5°20S 105°10E 82 F3
Bandar Seri Begawan Brunei 4°52N 115°0E 82 C4
Bandeira, Pico da Brazil 20°26S 41°47W 122 D2
Banderas, B. de Mexico 20°40N 105°25W 104 G9
Bandırma Turkey 40°20N 28°0E 71 F4
Bandon Ireland 51°44N 8°44W 30 E5
Bandon → Ireland 51°43N 8°37W 30 E5
Bandundu
  Dem. Rep. of the Congo 3°15S 17°22E 96 E3
Bandung Indonesia 6°54S 107°36E 82 F3
Banes Cuba 21°0N 75°42W 115 C9
Banff Canada 51°10N 115°34W 108 D8
Banff U.K. 57°40N 2°33W 19 G12
Bangalore India 12°59N 77°40E 84 N10
Bangassou C.A.R. 4°55N 23°7E 96 D4
Banggai, Kepulauan Indonesia 1°40S 123°30E 83 E6
Bangka Indonesia 2°0S 105°50E 82 E3
Bangkok Thailand 13°45N 100°35E 82 B2
Bangladesh ■ Asia 24°0N 90°0E 85 H17
Bangor Down, U.K. 54°40N 5°40W 29 B10
Bangor Gwynedd, U.K. 53°14N 4°8W 26 A5
Bangui C.A.R. 4°23N 18°35E 96 D3
Bangweulu, L. Zambia 11°0S 30°0E 96 G6
Banham U.K. 52°27N 1°2E 25 B11
Bani Dom. Rep. 18°16N 70°22W 115 D10
Banja Luka Bos.-H. 44°49N 17°11E 68 B7
Banjarmasin Indonesia 3°20S 114°35E 82 E4
Banjul Gambia 13°28N 16°40W 94 F2
Bankend U.K. 55°1N 3°33W 21 D8
Banks I. Canada 73°15N 121°30W 108 B7
Banks Is. Vanuatu 13°50S 167°30E 99 C12
Bann → U.K. 55°8N 6°41W 29 A8
Bannockburn U.K. 56°5N 3°55W 21 B8
Bannu Pakistan 33°0N 70°18E 84 C7
Banská Bystrica Slovak Rep. 48°46N 19°14E 65 D10
Bantry Ireland 51°41N 9°27W 30 E4
Bantry B. Ireland 51°37N 9°44W 30 E3
Banwell U.K. 51°19N 2°52W 24 D3
Banyak, Kepulauan Indonesia 2°10N 97°10E 82 D1
Banyuwangi Indonesia 8°13S 114°21E 82 F4
Baoding China 38°50N 115°28E 79 D12
Baoji China 34°20N 107°5E 78 E10
Baoshan China 25°10N 99°5E 78 D8
Baotou China 40°32N 110°2E 79 C11
Ba'qūbah Iraq 33°45N 44°50E 86 C6
Bar Harbor U.S.A. 44°23N 68°13W 113 C13
Bar-le-Duc France 48°47N 5°10E 66 B6
Baraboo U.S.A. 43°28N 89°45W 112 D3
Baracoa Cuba 20°20N 74°30W 115 C10
Barahona Dom. Rep. 18°13N 71°7W 115 D10
Barail Range India 25°15N 93°20E 85 G18
Barakaldo Spain 43°18N 2°59W 67 A4
Baranof I. U.S.A. 57°0N 135°0W 108 D6
Baranovichi Belarus 53°10N 26°0E 65 B14
Barbacena Brazil 21°15S 43°56W 122 D2
Barbados ■ W. Indies 13°10N 59°30W 115 g
Barberton U.S.A. 41°1N 81°39W 112 E7
Barcelona Spain 41°22N 2°10E 67 B7
Barcelona Venezuela 10°10N 64°40W 120 A3
Barceloneta Puerto Rico 18°27N 66°32W 115 d
Barddhaman India 23°14N 87°39E 85 H15
Bardīyah Libya 31°45N 25°5E 95 B10
Bardney U.K. 53°13N 0°19W 23 F8
Bardsey I. U.K. 52°45N 4°47W 26 B4
Bardstown U.S.A. 37°49N 85°28W 112 G5
Bareilly India 28°22N 79°27E 84 E11
Barents Sea Arctic 73°0N 39°0E 54 B9
Barford U.K. 52°16N 1°35W 24 B5
Bargoed U.K. 51°42N 3°15W 26 D7
Barham U.K. 51°12N 1°11E 25 D11
Barhi India 24°15N 85°25E 85 G14
Bari Italy 41°8N 16°51E 68 D7
Bari Doab Pakistan 30°20N 73°0E 84 D8
Barīm Yemen 12°39N 43°25E 90 E8
Barinas Venezuela 8°36N 70°15W 120 B2
Baring, C. Canada 70°0N 117°30W 108 C8
Barisal Bangla. 22°45N 90°20E 85 H17
Barisal □ Bangla. 22°45N 90°20E 85 H17
Barkly Tableland Australia 17°50S 136°40E 98 D6
Barlborough U.K. 53°17N 1°17W 23 F6
Barlby U.K. 53°48N 1°2W 23 E6
Barlee, L. Australia 29°15S 119°30E 98 F2
Barletta Italy 41°19N 16°17E 68 D7
Barmby Moor U.K. 53°56N 0°48W 23 E7
Barmer India 25°45N 71°20E 84 G7
Barmoor Castle U.K. 55°39N 1°59W 22 A5
Barmouth U.K. 52°44N 4°4W 26 B5
Barnard Castle U.K. 54°33N 1°55W 22 C5
Barnaul Russia 53°20N 83°40E 76 D9
Barnet □ U.K. 51°38N 0°9W 25 C8
Barnetby le Wold U.K. 53°34N 0°24W 23 E8
Barnoldswick U.K. 53°55N 2°11W 23 E4
Barnsley U.K. 53°34N 1°27W 23 E6
Barnstaple U.K. 51°5N 4°4W 27 E5
Barotseland Zambia 15°0S 24°0E 97 H4
Barques, Pt. Aux U.S.A. 44°4N 82°58W 112 C6

Barra Brazil 11°5S 43°10W 122 B2
Barra U.K. 57°0N 7°29W 18 J2
Barra, Sd. of U.K. 57°4N 7°25W 18 H3
Barra do Corda Brazil 5°30S 45°10W 120 C5
Barra do Piraí Brazil 22°30S 43°50W 122 D2
Barra Hd. U.K. 56°47N 7°40W 18 J2
Barra Mansa Brazil 22°35S 44°12W 122 D2
Barrancabermeja Colombia 7°0N 73°50W 120 B2
Barranquilla Colombia 11°0N 74°50W 120 A2
Barreiras Brazil 12°8S 45°0W 122 B2
Barreiro Portugal 38°39N 9°5W 67 C1
Barreiros Brazil 8°49S 35°12W 122 A3
Barretos Brazil 20°30S 48°35W 122 D1
Barrhead U.K. 55°48N 4°23W 20 C7
Barrie Canada 44°24N 79°40W 109 E12
Barrow U.S.A. 71°18N 156°47W 108 B4
Barrow → Ireland 52°25N 6°58W 31 D9
Barrow, Pt. U.S.A. 71°23N 156°29W 104 B4
Barrow-in-Furness U.K. 54°7N 3°14W 22 D2
Barrow upon Humber U.K. 53°41N 0°23W 23 E8
Barrowford U.K. 53°51N 2°14W 23 E4
Barry U.K. 51°24N 3°16W 27 F7
Barry I. U.K. 51°23N 3°16W 27 F7
Barry's Bay Canada 45°29N 77°41W 112 C9
Barstow U.S.A. 34°54N 117°1W 110 D3
Bartlesville U.S.A. 36°45N 95°59W 111 C7
Barton U.K. 54°29N 1°38W 22 D5
Barton upon Humber U.K. 53°41N 0°25W 23 E8
Barú, Volcan Panama 8°55N 82°35W 115 F8
Baruun-Urt Mongolia 46°46N 113°15E 79 B11
Barwell U.K. 52°35N 1°21W 23 G6
Barysaw Belarus 54°17N 28°28E 65 A15
Bashkortostan □ Russia 54°0N 57°0E 70 D10
Basilan Phil. 6°35N 122°0E 83 C6
Basildon U.K. 51°34N 0°28E 25 C9
Basingstoke U.K. 51°15N 1°5W 24 D6
Baskatong, Rés. Canada 46°46N 75°50W 113 B10
Basle Switz. 47°35N 7°35E 64 E4
Basque Provinces = País Vasco □
  Spain 42°50N 2°45W 67 A4
Basra Iraq 30°30N 47°50E 86 D6
Bass Rock U.K. 56°5N 2°38W 21 B10
Bass Str. Australia 39°15S 146°30E 98 H8
Bassas da India Ind. Oc. 22°0S 39°0E 97 J7
Basse-Pointe Martinique 14°52N 61°8W 114 c
Basse-Terre Guadeloupe 16°0N 61°44W 114 b
Bassein Burma 16°45N 94°30E 85 L19
Bassenthwaite L. U.K. 54°40N 3°14W 22 C2
Basses, Pte. des Guadeloupe 15°52N 61°17W 114 b
Basseterre St. Kitts & Nevis 17°17N 62°43W 115 D12
Basti India 26°52N 82°55E 85 F13
Bastia France 42°40N 9°30E 66 E8
Baston U.K. 52°43N 0°21W 23 G8
Bata Eq. Guin. 1°57N 9°50E 96 D1
Batabanó, G. de Cuba 22°30N 82°30W 115 C8
Batangas Phil. 13°35N 121°10E 83 B6
Batatais Brazil 20°54S 47°37W 122 D1
Batavia U.S.A. 43°0N 78°11W 112 D8
Batdambang Cambodia 13°7N 103°12E 82 B2
Bath U.K. 51°23N 2°22W 24 D4
Bath Maine, U.S.A. 43°55N 69°49W 113 D13
Bath N.Y., U.S.A. 42°20N 77°19W 112 D9
Bathgate U.K. 55°54N 3°39W 21 C8
Bathsheba Barbados 13°13N 59°32W 115 g
Bathurst Australia 33°25S 149°31E 98 G8
Bathurst Canada 47°37N 65°43W 109 E13
Bathurst, C. Canada 70°34N 128°0W 108 B7
Bathurst I. Canada 76°0N 100°30W 104 B9
Bathurst Inlet Canada 66°50N 108°1W 108 C9
Batley U.K. 53°43N 1°38W 23 E5
Batman Turkey 37°55N 41°5E 71 G7
Batna Algeria 35°34N 6°15E 94 A7
Baton Rouge U.S.A. 30°27N 91°11W 111 D8
Batticaloa Sri Lanka 7°43N 81°45E 84 R12
Battle U.K. 50°55N 0°30E 25 E9
Battle Creek U.S.A. 42°19N 85°11W 112 D5
Batu, Kepulauan Indonesia 0°30S 98°25E 82 E1
Batu Pahat Malaysia 1°50N 102°56E 82 D2
Batumi Georgia 41°39N 41°44E 71 F7
Bauld, C. Canada 51°38N 55°26W 109 D14
Bauru Brazil 22°10S 49°0W 122 D1
Bavaria = Bayern □ Germany 48°50N 12°0E 64 D6
Bawdsey U.K. 52°1N 1°27E 25 B11
Bawtry U.K. 53°26N 1°2W 23 F6
Bay City U.S.A. 43°36N 83°54W 112 D6
Bayamo Cuba 20°20N 76°40W 115 C9
Bayamón Puerto Rico 18°24N 66°9W 115 d
Bayan Har Shan China 34°0N 98°0E 78 E8
Bayanhongor Mongolia 46°8N 102°43E 78 B9
Baydhabo Somali Rep. 3°8N 43°30E 89 G3
Bayern □ Germany 48°50N 12°0E 64 D6
Bayeux France 49°17N 0°42W 66 B3
Bayonne France 43°30N 1°28W 66 E3
Beachley U.K. 51°37N 2°39W 24 D4
Beachy Hd. U.K. 50°44N 0°15E 25 E9
Beacon U.S.A. 41°30N 73°58W 113 E11
Beaconsfield U.K. 51°36N 0°38W 25 C7
Beadnell U.K. 55°33N 1°38W 22 A5
Beagle, Canal S. Amer. 55°0S 68°30W 121 H3
Beaminster U.K. 50°48N 2°44W 24 E3
Bear → U.S.A. 41°30N 112°8W 110 B4
Bear I. Arctic 74°30N 19°0E 54 B8
Bear I. Ireland 51°38N 9°50W 30 E3
Bear L. U.S.A. 41°59N 111°21W 110 B4
Beardmore Glacier Antarctica 84°30S 170°0E 55 E11
Beardstown U.S.A. 40°1N 90°26W 112 E2
Béarn France 43°20N 0°30W 66 E3
Bearsden U.K. 55°55N 4°21W 20 C7
Bearsted U.K. 51°16N 0°35E 25 D10
Beatrice U.S.A. 40°16N 96°45W 111 B7
Beattock U.K. 55°19N 3°28W 21 D8
Beauce, Plaine de la France 48°10N 1°45E 66 B4
Beaufort Sea Arctic 72°0N 140°0W 104 B5
Beaufort West S. Africa 32°18S 22°36E 97 L4
Beauharnois Canada 45°20N 73°52W 113 C11
Beaulieu U.K. 50°48N 1°27W 24 E5
Beauly → U.K. 57°29N 4°27W 19 H9
Beauly U.K. 57°30N 4°28W 19 H9

Beauly Firth U.K. 57°30N 4°20W 19 H9
Beaumaris U.K. 53°16N 4°6W 26 A5
Beaumont U.S.A. 30°5N 94°6W 111 D8
Beaune France 47°2N 4°50E 66 C6
Beauvais France 49°25N 2°8E 66 B5
Beaver → Canada 55°26N 107°45W 108 D9
Beaver Creek Canada 63°0N 141°0W 108 C5
Beaver Dam U.S.A. 43°28N 88°50W 112 D3
Beaver Falls U.S.A. 40°46N 80°20W 112 E7
Beaver I. U.S.A. 45°40N 85°33W 112 C5
Beawar India 26°3N 74°18E 84 F9
Bebedouro Brazil 21°0S 48°25W 122 D1
Bebington U.K. 53°22N 3°0W 23 F3
Beccles U.K. 52°27N 1°35E 25 B12
Béchar Algeria 31°38N 2°18W 94 B5
Beckermet U.K. 54°27N 3°30W 22 D1
Beckfoot U.K. 54°50N 3°24W 22 C2
Beckingham U.K. 53°24N 0°50W 23 F7
Beckley U.S.A. 37°47N 81°11W 112 G7
Bedale U.K. 54°18N 1°36W 22 D5
Beddgelert U.K. 53°1N 4°6W 26 A5
Bedford U.K. 52°8N 0°28W 25 B8
Bedford Ind., U.S.A. 38°52N 86°29W 112 F4
Bedford Va., U.S.A. 37°20N 79°31W 112 G8
Bedford □ U.K. 52°4N 0°28W 25 B8
Bedford Level U.K. 52°32N 0°7W 25 A8
Bedlington U.K. 55°8N 1°35W 22 B5
Bedworth U.K. 52°29N 1°28W 24 B6
Beef I. Br. Virgin Is. 18°26N 64°30W 115 e
Beeford U.K. 53°58N 0°17W 23 E8
Beer U.K. 50°41N 3°6W 27 F7
Be'er Sheva Israel 31°15N 34°48E 86 D3
Beeston U.K. 52°56N 1°14W 23 G6
Bei Jiang → China 23°2N 112°58E 79 G11
Bei Shan China 41°30N 96°0E 78 C8
Bei'an China 48°10N 126°20E 79 B14
Beighton U.K. 53°21N 1°20W 23 F6
Beihai China 21°28N 109°6E 79 G10
Beijing China 39°53N 116°21E 79 D12
Beira Mozam. 19°50S 34°52E 97 H6
Beirut Lebanon 33°53N 35°31E 86 C3
Beitbridge Zimbabwe 22°12S 30°0E 97 J6
Beith U.K. 55°45N 4°38W 20 C6
Béja Tunisia 36°43N 9°12E 95 A7
Bejaïa Algeria 36°42N 5°2E 94 A7
Békéscsaba Hungary 46°40N 21°5E 65 E11
Bela Pakistan 26°12N 66°20E 84 F5
Belarus ■ Europe 53°30N 27°0E 70 D4
Belau = Palau ■ Palau 7°30N 134°30E 102 G5
Belbroughton U.K. 52°24N 2°7W 24 B4
Belcher Chan. Canada 77°15N 95°0W 109 B11
Belcher Is. Canada 56°15N 78°45W 109 D12
Beledweyne Somali Rep. 4°30N 45°5E 89 G4
Belém Brazil 1°20S 48°30W 120 C5
Belep, Îs. N. Cal. 19°45S 163°40E 99 D11
Belfast U.K. 54°37N 5°56W 29 B10
Belfast U.S.A. 44°26N 69°1W 113 C13
Belfast □ U.K. 54°40N 5°50W 29 B10
Belford U.K. 55°36N 1°49W 22 A5
Belfort France 47°38N 6°50E 66 C7
Belgaum India 15°55N 74°35E 84 M9
Belgium ■ Europe 50°30N 5°0E 64 C3
Belgorod Russia 50°35N 36°35E 71 D6
Belgrade Serbia 44°50N 20°37E 69 B9
Belitung Indonesia 3°10S 107°50E 82 E3
Belize ■ Cent. Amer. 17°0N 88°30W 114 D7
Belize City Belize 17°25N 88°10W 114 D7
Bell Peninsula Canada 63°50N 82°0W 109 C11
Bell Ville Argentina 32°40S 62°40W 121 F3
Bella Coola Canada 52°25N 126°40W 108 D7
Bellaire U.S.A. 40°1N 80°45W 112 E7
Bellary India 15°10N 76°56E 84 M10
Belle-Île France 47°20N 3°10W 66 C2
Belle Isle Canada 51°57N 55°25W 109 D14
Belle Isle, Str. of Canada 51°30N 56°30W 109 D14
Bellefontaine U.S.A. 40°22N 83°46W 112 E6
Belleplaine Barbados 13°15N 59°34W 115 g
Belleville Canada 44°10N 77°23W 109 E12
Belleville U.S.A. 38°31N 89°59W 112 F3
Bellingham U.K. 55°9N 2°16W 22 B4
Bellingham U.S.A. 48°46N 122°29W 110 A2
Bellingshausen Sea Antarctica 66°0S 80°0W 55 C17
Bellinzona Switz. 46°11N 9°1E 64 E5
Belmonte Brazil 16°0S 39°0W 122 C3
Belmopan Belize 17°18N 88°30W 114 D7
Belmullet Ireland 54°14N 9°58W 28 C2
Belo Horizonte Brazil 19°55S 43°56W 122 C2
Belo Jardim Brazil 8°20S 36°26W 122 A3
Belogorsk Russia 51°0N 128°20E 77 D13
Beloit U.S.A. 42°31N 89°2W 112 D3
Belomorsk Russia 64°35N 34°54E 70 B5
Beloretsk Russia 53°58N 58°24E 70 D10
Beloye, L. Russia 60°10N 37°35E 70 B6
Belper U.K. 53°2N 1°29W 23 F6
Belsay U.K. 55°6N 1°51W 22 B5
Belton N. Lincs., U.K. 53°33N 0°48W 23 E7
Belton Norfolk, U.K. 52°35N 1°40E 25 A12
Beltsy Moldova 47°48N 27°58E 65 E14
Belturbet Ireland 54°6N 7°26W 28 B6
Belukha Russia 49°50N 86°50E 78 B6
Belvidere U.S.A. 42°15N 88°50W 112 D3
Bembridge U.K. 50°41N 1°5W 24 E6
Bemidji U.S.A. 47°28N 94°53W 111 A8
Ben Cruachan U.K. 56°26N 5°8W 20 B5
Ben Dearg U.K. 57°47N 4°56W 19 G8
Ben Hope U.K. 58°25N 4°36W 19 F8
Ben Lawers U.K. 56°32N 4°14W 20 A7
Ben Lomond U.K. 56°11N 4°38W 20 B6
Ben Macdhui U.K. 57°4N 3°40W 19 H10
Ben Mhor U.K. 57°15N 7°18W 18 H3
Ben More Argyll & Bute, U.K. 56°26N 6°1W 20 B3
Ben More Stirling, U.K. 56°23N 4°32W 20 B6
Ben More Assynt U.K. 58°8N 4°52W 19 F8
Ben Nevis U.K. 56°48N 5°1W 18 J7
Ben Vorlich U.K. 56°21N 4°14W 20 B7
Ben Wyvis U.K. 57°40N 4°35W 19 G8
Benares = Varanasi India 25°22N 83°0E 85 G13
Benbecula U.K. 57°26N 7°21W 18 H3
Bend U.S.A. 44°4N 121°19W 110 B2

Benderloch U.K. 56°30N 5°22W 20 A5
Bendigo Australia 36°40S 144°15E 98 H7
Benevento Italy 41°8N 14°45E 68 D6
Bengal, Bay of Ind. Oc. 15°0N 90°0E 85 M17
Bengbu China 32°58N 117°20E 79 E12
Benghazi Libya 32°11N 20°3E 95 B10
Bengkulu Indonesia 3°50S 102°12E 82 E2
Benguela Angola 12°37S 13°25E 97 G2
Beni → Bolivia 10°23S 65°24W 120 D3
Beni Mellal Morocco 32°21N 6°21W 94 B4
Beni Suef Egypt 29°5N 31°6E 95 C12
Benidorm Spain 38°33N 0°9W 67 C5
Benin ■ Africa 10°0N 2°0E 94 G6
Benin, Bight of W. Afr. 5°0N 3°0E 94 H6
Benin City Nigeria 6°20N 5°31E 94 G7
Benington U.K. 53°0N 0°5E 23 F9
Benjamin Constant Brazil 4°40S 70°15W 120 C2
Benoni S. Africa 26°11S 28°18E 97 K5
Benson U.K. 51°37N 1°6W 24 C6
Bentley Hants., U.K. 51°12N 0°52W 25 D7
Bentley S. Yorks., U.K. 53°33N 1°9W 23 E6
Bentley Subglacial Trench Antarctica 80°0S 115°0W 55 E14
Benton U.S.A. 38°0N 88°55W 112 G3
Benton Harbor U.S.A. 42°6N 86°27W 112 D4
Benue → Nigeria 7°48N 6°46E 94 G7
Benxi China 41°20N 123°48E 79 C13
Beppu Japan 33°15N 131°30E 81 G2
Berber Sudan 18°0N 34°0E 95 E12
Berbera Somali Rep. 10°30N 45°2E 89 E4
Berbérati C.A.R. 4°15N 15°40E 96 D3
Berbice → Guyana 6°20N 57°32W 120 B4
Berdyansk Ukraine 46°45N 36°50E 71 E6
Berdychiv Ukraine 49°57N 28°30E 71 E4
Bere Alston U.K. 50°29N 4°13W 27 G5
Bere Regis U.K. 50°45N 2°14W 24 E4
Berea U.S.A. 37°34N 84°17W 112 G5
Berens → Canada 52°25N 97°0W 108 D10
Berezina → Belarus 52°33N 30°14E 70 D5
Berezniki Russia 59°24N 56°46E 70 C10
Bérgamo Italy 45°41N 9°43E 68 B3
Bergen Norway 60°20N 5°20E 63 E5
Bergerac France 44°51N 0°30E 66 D4
Bering Sea Pac. Oc. 58°0N 171°0W 104 D2
Bering Strait Pac. Oc. 65°30N 169°0W 108 C3
Berkeley U.K. 51°41N 2°27W 24 C4
Berkhamsted U.K. 51°45N 0°33W 25 C7
Berkner I. Antarctica 79°30S 50°0W 55 D18
Berkshire Downs U.K. 51°33N 1°29W 24 C6
Berlin Germany 52°31N 13°23E 64 B7
Berlin U.S.A. 44°28N 71°11W 113 C12
Bermejo → Argentina 26°51S 58°23W 121 E4
Bermuda ☑ Atl. Oc. 32°18N 64°45W 52 C6
Bern Switz. 46°57N 7°28E 64 E4
Berneray U.K. 57°43N 7°11W 18 G3
Berry France 46°50N 2°0E 66 C5
Berry Hd. U.K. 50°24N 3°29W 27 G7
Bertraghboy B. Ireland 53°22N 9°54W 30 B3
Berwick U.S.A. 41°3N 76°14W 112 E9
Berwick-upon-Tweed U.K. 55°46N 2°0W 22 A5
Berwyn Mts. U.K. 52°54N 3°26W 26 B7
Besançon France 47°15N 6°2E 66 C7
Bessarabiya Moldova 47°0N 28°10E 65 E15
Bessemer U.S.A. 46°29N 90°3W 112 B2
Bethel U.S.A. 60°48N 161°45W 108 C3
Bethesda U.K. 53°10N 4°3W 26 A5
Bethlehem S. Africa 28°14S 28°18E 97 K5
Bethlehem U.S.A. 40°37N 75°23W 113 E10
Béthune France 50°30N 2°38E 66 A5
Betim Brazil 19°58S 44°7W 122 C2
Bettiah India 26°48N 84°33E 85 F14
Betul India 21°58N 77°59E 84 J10
Betws-y-Coed U.K. 53°5N 3°48W 26 A6
Beverley U.K. 53°51N 0°26W 23 E8
Bewdley U.K. 52°23N 2°19W 24 B4
Bexhill U.K. 50°51N 0°29E 25 E9
Bexley □ U.K. 51°27N 0°9E 25 D9
Beyneu Kazakhstan 45°18N 55°9E 71 E10
Beypazarı Turkey 40°10N 31°56E 71 F5
Beyşehir Gölü Turkey 37°41N 31°33E 71 G5
Béziers France 43°20N 3°12E 66 E5
Bhagalpur India 25°10N 87°0E 85 G15
Bhaktapur Nepal 27°38N 85°24E 85 F14
Bhanrer Ra. India 23°40N 79°45E 84 H11
Bharatpur India 27°15N 77°30E 84 F10
Bharuch India 21°47N 73°0E 84 J8
Bhatpara India 22°50N 88°25E 85 H16
Bhavnagar India 21°45N 72°10E 84 J8
Bhilainagar-Durg India 21°13N 81°26E 85 J12
Bhilwara India 25°25N 74°38E 84 G9
Bhima → India 16°25N 77°17E 84 L10
Bhiwandi India 19°20N 73°0E 84 K8
Bhiwani India 28°50N 76°9E 84 E10
Bhopal India 23°20N 77°30E 84 H10
Bhubaneshwar India 20°15N 85°50E 85 J14
Bhuj India 23°15N 69°49E 84 H6
Bhusawal India 21°3N 75°46E 84 J9
Bhutan ■ Asia 27°25N 90°30E 85 F17
Biała Podlaska Poland 52°4N 23°6E 65 B12
Białystok Poland 53°10N 23°10E 65 B12
Biarritz France 43°29N 1°33W 66 E3
Bibury U.K. 51°45N 1°49W 24 C5
Bicester U.K. 51°54N 1°9W 24 C6
Bicton U.K. 52°44N 2°48W 23 G3
Bida Nigeria 9°3N 5°58E 94 G7
Biddeford U.S.A. 43°30N 70°28W 113 D12
Biddenden U.K. 51°7N 0°40E 25 D10
Biddulph U.K. 53°7N 2°10W 23 F4
Bideford U.K. 51°1N 4°13W 27 E5
Bideford Bay U.K. 51°5N 4°20W 27 E5
Bidford-on-Avon U.K. 52°11N 1°50W 24 B5
Bié Plateau Angola 12°0S 16°0E 97 G3
Biel Switz. 47°8N 7°14E 64 E4
Bielefeld Germany 52°1N 8°33E 64 B5
Biella Italy 45°46N 8°3E 68 B3
Bielsko-Biała Poland 49°50N 19°2E 65 D10
Bien Hoa Vietnam 10°57N 106°49E 82 B3
Bienville, L. Canada 55°5N 72°40W 109 D12
Big Belt Mts. U.S.A. 46°30N 111°25W 110 A4

Big Rapids U.S.A. 43°42N 85°29W 112 D5
Big Sioux → U.S.A. 42°29N 96°27W 111 B7
Big Spring U.S.A. 32°15N 101°28W 110 D6
Big Trout L. Canada 53°40N 90°0W 109 D11
Bigbury U.K. 50°18N 3°53W 27 G6
Bigbury B. U.K. 50°16N 3°54W 27 G6
Biggar Canada 52°4N 108°0W 108 D9
Biggar U.K. 55°38N 3°32W 21 C8
Biggleswade U.K. 52°5N 0°14W 25 B8
Bighorn → U.S.A. 46°10N 107°28W 110 A5
Bighorn Mts. U.S.A. 44°25N 107°0W 110 B5
Bihar India 25°5N 85°40E 85 G14
Bihar □ India 25°0N 86°0E 85 G15
Bijagós, Arquipélago dos
  Guinea-Biss. 11°15N 16°10W 94 F2
Bijapur India 16°50N 75°55E 84 L9
Bikaner India 28°2N 73°18E 84 E8
Bikin Russia 46°50N 134°20E 79 B15
Bikini Atoll Marshall Is. 12°0N 167°30E 102 F8
Bila Tserkva Ukraine 49°45N 30°10E 65 D16
Bilaspur India 22°2N 82°15E 85 H13
Bilbao Spain 43°16N 2°56W 67 A4
Bilecik Turkey 40°5N 30°5E 71 F5
Bilhorod-Dnistrovskyy
  Ukraine 46°11N 30°23E 71 E5
Billericay U.K. 51°38N 0°26E 25 C9
Billesdon U.K. 52°38N 0°54W 23 G7
Billingham U.K. 54°36N 1°17W 22 C6
Billinghay U.K. 53°5N 0°15W 23 E8
Billings U.S.A. 45°47N 108°30W 110 A5
Billingshurst U.K. 51°2N 0°27W 25 D8
Bilma Niger 18°50N 13°30E 95 E8
Biloxi U.S.A. 30°24N 88°53W 111 D9
Bilston U.K. 52°34N 2°4W 23 G4
Bimini Is. Bahamas 25°42N 79°25W 115 B9
Binbrook U.K. 53°26N 0°10W 23 E8
Bingham U.K. 52°57N 0°58W 23 G7
Binghamton U.S.A. 42°6N 75°55W 113 D10
Bingley U.K. 53°51N 1°50W 23 E5
Bioko Eq. Guin. 3°30N 8°40E 96 D1
Biratnagar Nepal 26°27N 87°17E 85 F15
Birchington U.K. 51°22N 1°19E 25 D11
Birdlip U.K. 51°50N 2°5W 24 C4
Birkdale U.K. 53°38N 3°1W 23 E2
Birkenhead U.K. 53°23N 3°2W 23 F2
Birmingham U.K. 52°29N 1°52W 23 G5
Birmingham U.S.A. 33°31N 86°48W 111 D9
Birmingham Int. ✈ (BHX)
  U.K. 52°26N 1°45W 23 H5
Birnin Kebbi Nigeria 12°32N 4°12E 94 F6
Birobidzhan Russia 48°50N 132°50E 79 B15
Birr Ireland 53°6N 7°54W 30 B7
Birtley Northumberland, U.K. 55°6N 2°12W 22 B4
Birtley Tyne & W., U.K. 54°54N 1°34W 22 C5
Biscay, B. of Atl. Oc. 45°0N 2°0W 66 D1
Bishkek Kyrgyzstan 42°54N 74°46E 78 C3
Bishop Auckland U.K. 54°39N 1°40W 22 C5
Bishop's Castle U.K. 52°30N 2°59W 23 H3
Bishop's Cleeve U.K. 51°57N 2°3W 24 C4
Bishop's Frome U.K. 52°8N 2°29W 24 B4
Bishop's Nympton U.K. 51°0N 3°47W 27 F6
Bishop's Stortford U.K. 51°52N 0°10E 25 C9
Bishop's Waltham U.K. 50°57N 1°11W 24 E6
Bishopsteignton U.K. 50°33N 3°33W 27 F6
Bishopstoke U.K. 50°58N 1°19W 24 E6
Biskra Algeria 34°50N 5°44E 94 B7
Bismarck U.S.A. 46°48N 100°47W 110 A6
Bismarck Arch. Papua N. G. 2°30S 150°0E 98 A9
Bissau Guinea-Biss. 11°45N 15°45W 94 F2
Bitola Macedonia 41°1N 21°20E 69 D9
Bitterfontein S. Africa 31°1S 18°32E 97 L3
Bitterroot Range U.S.A. 46°0N 114°20W 110 A4
Bitton U.K. 51°25N 2°27W 24 D4
Biu Nigeria 10°40N 12°3E 95 F8
Biwa-Ko Japan 35°15N 136°10E 81 F5
Biysk Russia 52°40N 85°0E 76 D9
Bizerte Tunisia 37°15N 9°50E 95 A7
Blaby U.K. 52°35N 1°10W 23 G6
Black → U.S.A. 35°38N 91°20W 111 C8
Black Combe U.K. 54°16N 3°20W 22 C2
Black Esk → U.K. 55°12N 3°11W 21 D9
Black Forest = Schwarzwald
  Germany 48°30N 8°20E 64 D5
Black Hd. Ireland 53°9N 9°16W 30 B4
Black Hd. U.K. 50°0N 5°7W 27 H3
Black Hills U.S.A. 44°0N 103°45W 110 B6
Black Isle U.K. 57°35N 4°16W 19 G9
Black Mts. U.K. 51°55N 3°7W 26 D7
Black Range U.S.A. 33°15N 107°50W 110 D5
Black River Jamaica 18°0N 77°50W 114 a
Black River Falls U.S.A. 44°18N 90°51W 112 C2
Black Rock Barbados 13°7N 59°37W 115 g
Black Sea Eurasia 43°30N 35°0E 71 F6
Blackburn U.K. 53°45N 2°29W 23 E4
Blackdown Hills U.K. 50°57N 3°15W 24 E2
Blackmoor Vale U.K. 50°54N 2°28W 24 E4
Blackpool U.K. 53°49N 3°3W 23 E2
Blackrock Ireland 53°18N 6°11W 31 B10
Blacksburg U.S.A. 37°14N 80°25W 112 G7
Blacksod B. Ireland 54°6N 10°0W 28 C1
Blackwater → Meath, Ireland 53°39N 6°41W 29 D8
Blackwater → Waterford,
  Ireland 52°4N 7°52W 30 D7
Blackwater → Armagh, U.K. 54°31N 6°35W 29 B8
Blackwater → Essex, U.K. 51°44N 0°53E 25 C10
Blaenau Ffestiniog U.K. 53°0N 3°56W 26 B6
Blaenavon U.K. 51°46N 3°6W 26 D7
Blagdon U.K. 51°20N 2°43W 24 D4
Blagoevgrad Bulgaria 42°2N 23°5E 69 C10
Blagoveshchensk Russia 50°20N 127°30E 79 A14
Blair Atholl U.K. 56°46N 3°50W 19 J10
Blairgowrie U.K. 56°35N 3°21W 21 A9
Blakeney Gloucs., U.K. 51°46N 2°28W 24 C4
Blakeney Norfolk, U.K. 52°58N 1°1E 25 A11
Blanc, Mont Europe 45°48N 6°50E 66 D7
Blanca, B. Argentina 39°10S 61°30W 121 F3
Blanca Peak U.S.A. 37°35N 105°29W 110 C5
Blanco, C. Costa Rica 9°34N 85°8W 104 J11
Blanco, C. U.S.A. 42°51N 124°34W 110 B2
Blandford Forum U.K. 50°51N 2°9W 24 E4
Blanquilla Venezuela 11°51N 64°37W 115 E12

Blantyre Malawi 15°45S 35°0E 97 H6
Blarney Ireland 51°56N 8°33W 30 E5
Blaydon U.K. 54°58N 1°42W 22 C5
Blean U.K. 51°18N 1°3E 25 D11
Bleasdale Moors U.K. 53°55N 2°35W 23 E3
Blenheim N.Z. 41°38S 173°57E 99 J13
Bletchingdon U.K. 51°51N 1°15W 24 C6
Bletchley U.K. 51°59N 0°44W 25 C7
Blida Algeria 36°30N 2°49E 94 A6
Blisworth U.K. 52°10N 0°56W 25 B7
Blitar Indonesia 8°5S 112°11E 82 F4
Blockley U.K. 52°1N 1°44W 24 B5
Bloemfontein S. Africa 29°6S 26°7E 97 K5
Blofield U.K. 52°38N 1°26E 25 A11
Blois France 47°35N 1°20E 66 C4
Bloody Foreland Ireland 55°10N 8°17W 28 A5
Bloomington Ill., U.S.A. 40°28N 89°0W 112 E3
Bloomington Ind., U.S.A. 39°10N 86°32W 112 F4
Bloomsburg U.S.A. 41°0N 76°27W 112 E9
Bloxham U.K. 52°1N 1°21W 24 B6
Blue Mountain Pk. Jamaica 18°3N 76°36W 114 a
Blue Mt. U.S.A. 40°30N 76°30W 112 E9
Blue Mts. Jamaica 18°3N 76°36W 114 a
Blue Nile → Sudan 15°38N 32°31E 95 E12
Blue Ridge U.S.A. 36°40N 80°50W 111 C10
Blue Stack Mts. Ireland 54°42N 8°12W 28 B5
Bluefield U.S.A. 37°15N 81°17W 112 G7
Bluefields Nic. 12°20N 83°50W 115 E8
Blumenau Brazil 27°0S 49°0W 121 E5
Blundeston U.K. 52°33N 1°42E 25 A12
Blyth Northumberland, U.K. 55°8N 1°31W 22 B5
Blyth Notts., U.K. 53°22N 1°3W 23 F6
Blyth → U.K. 55°8N 1°33W 22 B5
Blyth Bridge U.K. 55°42N 3°22W 21 C9
Blyton U.K. 53°27N 0°42W 23 F7
Bo S. Leone 7°55N 11°50W 94 G3
Bo Hai China 39°0N 119°0E 79 D12
Boa Vista Brazil 2°48N 60°30W 120 B3
Bobcaygeon Canada 44°33N 78°33W 112 C8
Bobo-Dioulasso Burkina Faso 11°8N 4°13W 94 F5
Bóbr → Poland 52°4N 15°4E 64 B8
Bochum Germany 51°28N 7°13E 64 C4
Boddam U.K. 59°56N 1°17W 18 C15
Boden Sweden 65°50N 21°42E 63 D8
Bodiam U.K. 51°0N 0°34E 25 D10
Bodinnick U.K. 50°20N 4°38W 27 G4
Bodmin U.K. 50°28N 4°43W 27 G4
Bodmin Moor U.K. 50°33N 4°36W 27 F4
Bodø Norway 67°17N 14°24E 63 D6
Bodrog → Hungary 48°11N 21°22E 65 D11
Bodrum Turkey 37°3N 27°30E 71 G4
Bogalusa U.S.A. 30°47N 89°52W 111 D9
Bogda Shan China 43°35N 89°40E 78 C6
Boggeragh Mts. Ireland 52°2N 8°55W 30 D5
Bognor Regis U.K. 50°47N 0°40W 25 E7
Bogor Indonesia 6°36S 106°48E 82 F3
Bogotá Colombia 4°34N 74°0W 120 B2
Bogra Bangla. 24°51N 89°22E 85 G16
Böhmerwald Germany 49°8N 13°14E 64 D7
Bohol Sea Phil. 9°0N 124°0E 83 C6
Boise U.S.A. 43°37N 116°13W 110 B3
Bole China 44°55N 81°37E 78 B5
Bolivar, Pico Venezuela 8°32N 71°2W 115 F10
Bolivia ■ S. Amer. 17°6S 64°0W 120 D3
Bollington U.K. 53°18N 2°6W 23 F4
Bolney U.K. 50°59N 0°12W 25 E8
Bologna Italy 44°29N 11°20E 68 B4
Bologoye Russia 57°55N 34°5E 70 C5
Bolsena, L. di Italy 42°36N 11°56E 68 C4
Bolsover U.K. 53°14N 1°16W 23 F6
Bolt Head U.K. 50°12N 3°48W 27 G6
Bolt Tail U.K. 50°14N 3°52W 27 G6
Bolton U.K. 53°35N 2°26W 23 E4
Bolton Abbey U.K. 53°59N 1°53W 23 E5
Bolton by Bowland U.K. 53°56N 2°20W 23 E4
Bolton le Sands U.K. 54°6N 2°48W 22 D3
Bolu Turkey 40°45N 31°35E 71 F5
Bolvadin Turkey 38°45N 31°4E 71 G5
Bolzano Italy 46°31N 11°22E 68 A4
Bom Despacho Brazil 19°43S 45°15W 122 C1
Bom Jesus da Lapa Brazil 13°15S 43°25W 122 B1
Boma Dem. Rep. of the Congo 5°50S 13°4E 96 F2
Bombala Australia 36°56S 149°15E 98 H8
Bombay = Mumbai India 18°56N 72°50E 84 K8
Bomu → C.A.R. 4°40N 22°30E 96 D4
Bon, C. Tunisia 37°1N 11°2E 95 A8
Bonaire Neth. Ant. 12°10N 68°15W 115 E11
Bonar Bridge U.K. 57°54N 4°20W 19 G9
Bonavista Canada 48°40N 53°5W 109 E14
Bonchester Bridge U.K. 55°24N 2°39W 21 D10
Bonchurch U.K. 50°37N 1°11W 24 E6
Bo'ness U.K. 56°1N 3°37W 21 B8
Bongor Chad 10°35N 15°20E 95 F9
Bongos, Massif des C.A.R. 8°40N 22°25E 96 C4
Bonifacio France 41°24N 9°10E 66 F8
Bonn Germany 50°46N 7°6E 64 C4
Bonny, Bight of Africa 3°30N 9°20E 96 D1
Bonnyrigg U.K. 55°53N 3°6W 21 C9
Boonville U.S.A. 38°3N 87°16W 112 F4
Boosaaso Somali Rep. 11°12N 49°18E 89 E4
Boot U.K. 54°24N 3°13W 22 D2
Boothia, Gulf of Canada 71°0N 90°0W 109 B11
Boothia Pen. Canada 71°0N 94°0W 108 B10
Bootle Cumb., U.K. 54°18N 3°22W 22 D2
Bootle Mersey., U.K. 53°28N 3°1W 23 F2
Borås Sweden 57°43N 12°56E 63 F6
Borborema, Planalto da Brazil 7°0S 37°0W 117 D7
Bordeaux France 44°50N 0°36W 66 D3
Borden I. Canada 78°30N 111°30W 109 B8
Borden Pen. Canada 73°0N 83°0W 109 B11
Bordon U.K. 51°8N 0°52W 25 D7
Borehamwood U.K. 51°40N 0°15W 25 C8
Boreland U.K. 55°12N 3°16W 21 D9
Borger U.S.A. 35°39N 101°24W 110 C6
Borhoyn Tal Mongolia 43°50N 111°58E 79 C11
Borisoglebsk Russia 51°27N 42°5E 71 D7
Borkou Chad 18°15N 18°50E 95 E9
Borneo E. Indies 1°0N 115°0E 82 D5
Bornholm Denmark 55°10N 15°0E 63 F7

Borohoro Shan China 44°6N 83°10E 78 C5
Boroughbridge U.K. 54°6N 1°24W 22 D6
Borovichi Russia 58°25N 33°55E 70 C5
Borrowdale U.K. 54°31N 3°10W 22 C2
Borth U.K. 52°29N 4°2W 26 C5
Borūjerd Iran 33°55N 48°50E 86 C7
Borzya Russia 50°24N 116°31E 79 A12
Bosbury U.K. 52°5N 2°26W 24 B4
Boscastle U.K. 50°41N 4°42W 27 F4
Boscobelle Barbados 13°17N 59°35W 115 g
Bose China 23°53N 106°35E 78 G10
Bosham U.K. 50°49N 0°51W 25 E7
Bosnia-Herzegovina ■ Europe 44°0N 18°0E 69 B7
Bosporus Turkey 41°5N 29°3E 71 F4
Bossangoa C.A.R. 6°35N 17°30E 96 C3
Bosten Hu China 41°55N 87°40E 78 C6
Boston U.K. 52°59N 0°2W 23 G8
Boston U.S.A. 42°22N 71°3W 113 D12
Bothel U.K. 54°45N 3°15W 22 C2
Bothnia, G. of Europe 62°0N 20°0E 63 E8
Botletle → Botswana 20°10S 23°15E 97 J4
Botoşani Romania 47°42N 26°41E 65 E14
Botswana ■ Africa 22°0S 24°0E 97 J4
Bottesford U.K. 52°57N 0°47W 23 G7
Botucatu Brazil 22°55S 48°30W 122 D1
Bou Saâda Algeria 35°11N 4°9E 94 A6
Bouaké Ivory C. 7°40N 5°2W 94 G4
Bouar C.A.R. 6°0N 15°40E 96 C3
Bouârfa Morocco 32°32N 1°58W 94 B5
Bougainville I. Papua N. G. 6°0S 155°0E 99 B10
Bouillante Guadeloupe 16°8N 61°46W 114 b
Boulder U.S.A. 40°1N 105°17W 110 B5
Boulogne-sur-Mer France 50°42N 1°36E 66 A4
Bounty Is. Pac. Oc. 48°0S 178°30E 102 M9
Bourbonnais France 46°28N 3°0E 66 C5
Bourg-en-Bresse France 46°13N 5°12E 66 C6
Bourges France 47°9N 2°25E 66 C5
Bourgogne □ France 47°0N 4°50E 66 C6
Bourke Australia 30°8S 145°55E 98 G8
Bourne U.K. 52°47N 0°22W 23 G8
Bournemouth U.K. 50°43N 1°52W 24 E5
Bourton-on-the-Water U.K. 51°52N 1°45W 24 C5
Bouvet I. Antarctica 54°26S 3°24E 52 G10
Bovey Tracey U.K. 50°36N 3°41W 27 F6
Bow → Canada 49°57N 111°41W 108 D8
Bowes U.K. 54°32N 1°59W 22 C5
Bowland, Forest of U.K. 54°0N 2°30W 23 E3
Bowling Green Ky., U.S.A. 36°59N 86°27W 112 G4
Bowling Green Ohio, U.S.A. 41°23N 83°39W 112 E6
Bowmore U.K. 55°45N 6°17W 20 C3
Bowness-on-Solway U.K. 54°57N 3°12W 22 C2
Bowness-on-Windermere
  U.K. 54°22N 2°55W 22 D3
Box U.K. 51°25N 2°15W 24 D4
Box Hill U.K. 51°15N 0°16W 25 D8
Boyle Ireland 53°59N 8°18W 28 D5
Boyne → Ireland 53°43N 6°15W 29 D9
Boyoma, Chutes
  Dem. Rep. of the Congo 0°35N 25°23E 90 F6
Bozeat U.K. 52°14N 0°40W 25 B7
Bozeman U.S.A. 45°41N 111°2W 110 A4
Bozoum C.A.R. 6°25N 16°35E 96 C3
Brač Croatia 43°20N 16°40E 68 C7
Bracadale, L. U.K. 57°20N 6°30W 18 H4
Bracebridge Canada 45°2N 79°19W 112 C8
Bracebridge Heath U.K. 53°12N 0°32W 23 F7
Bräcke Sweden 62°45N 15°26E 63 E7
Brackley U.K. 52°2N 1°8W 24 B6
Bracknell U.K. 51°25N 0°43W 25 D7
Bradford U.K. 53°47N 1°45W 23 E5
Bradford U.S.A. 41°58N 78°38W 112 E8
Bradford on Avon U.K. 51°21N 2°14W 24 D4
Brading U.K. 50°41N 1°8W 24 E6
Bradwell-on-Sea U.K. 51°43N 0°56E 25 C10
Bradworthy U.K. 50°53N 4°24W 27 F5
Braemar U.K. 57°2N 3°26W 19 H11
Braga Portugal 41°35N 8°25W 67 B1
Bragança Brazil 1°0S 47°2W 120 C5
Bragança Paulista Brazil 22°55S 46°32W 122 D1
Brahmanbaria Bangla. 23°58N 91°15E 85 H17
Brahmani → India 20°39N 86°46E 85 J15
Brahmapur India 19°15N 84°54E 85 K14
Brahmaputra → Asia 23°40N 90°35E 85 H16
Braich-y-pwll U.K. 52°47N 4°46W 26 B4
Brăila Romania 45°19N 27°59E 65 F14
Brailsford U.K. 52°58N 1°35W 23 G5
Brainerd U.S.A. 46°22N 94°12W 111 A8
Braintree U.K. 51°53N 0°34E 25 C10
Bramford U.K. 52°4N 1°7E 25 B11
Brampton Canada 43°45N 79°45W 112 D8
Brampton Cambs., U.K. 52°20N 0°14W 25 B8
Brampton Cumb., U.K. 54°57N 2°44W 22 C3
Brancaster U.K. 52°58N 0°38E 25 A10
Branco → Brazil 1°20S 61°50W 120 C3
Brandenburg Germany 52°25N 12°33E 64 B7
Brandenburg □ Germany 52°50N 13°0E 64 B6
Branderburgh U.K. 57°43N 3°17W 19 G11
Brandon Canada 49°50N 99°57W 108 E10
Brandon Durham, U.K. 54°46N 1°37W 22 C5
Brandon Suffolk, U.K. 52°27N 0°38E 25 B10
Brandon B. Ireland 52°17N 10°8W 30 D2
Brandon Mt. Ireland 52°15N 10°15W 30 D2
Branston U.K. 53°12N 0°27W 23 F7
Brantford Canada 43°10N 80°15W 112 D7
Bras d'Or L. Canada 45°50N 60°50W 113 C17
Brasília Brazil 15°47S 47°55W 122 C1
Braşov Romania 45°38N 25°35E 65 F13
Bratislava Slovak Rep. 48°10N 17°7E 65 D9
Bratsk Russia 56°10N 101°30E 77 D11
Bratsk Res. Russia 56°15N 101°45E 77 D11
Brattleboro U.S.A. 42°51N 72°34W 113 D11
Braunschweig Germany 52°15N 10°31E 64 B6
Braunton U.K. 51°7N 4°10W 27 E5
Bray Ireland 53°13N 6°7W 31 B10
Bray U.K. 51°30N 0°41W 25 D7
Brazil ■ S. Amer. 12°0S 50°0W 120 D4
Brazilian Highlands Brazil 18°0S 46°30W 117 E6
Brazos → U.S.A. 28°53N 95°23W 111 E7
Brazzaville Congo 4°9S 15°12E 96 E3

Breadalbane U.K. 56°30N 4°15W 20 A7
Breage U.K. 50°6N 5°20W 27 G3
Breamish → U.K. 55°35N 2°2W 22 A4
Brechin U.K. 56°44N 2°39W 19 J12
Breckland U.K. 52°30N 0°40E 25 B10
Brecon U.K. 51°57N 3°23W 26 D7
Brecon Beacons U.K. 51°53N 3°26W 26 D7
Brecon Beacons △ U.K. 51°50N 3°30W 26 D6
Breda Neths. 51°35N 4°45E 64 C3
Brede U.K. 50°56N 0°36E 25 E10
Bredon Hill U.K. 52°3N 2°2W 24 B4
Bregenz Austria 47°30N 9°45E 64 E5
Breiðafjörður Iceland 65°15N 23°15W 63 A1
Bremen Germany 53°4N 8°47E 64 B5
Bremerhaven Germany 53°33N 8°36E 64 B5
Bremerton U.S.A. 47°34N 122°37W 110 A2
Brendon Hills U.K. 51°6N 3°25W 24 D2
Brennerpass Austria 47°2N 11°30E 64 E6
Brent □ U.K. 51°33N 0°16W 25 C8
Brentwood U.K. 51°37N 0°19E 25 C9
Bréscia Italy 45°33N 10°15E 68 B4
Bressay U.K. 60°9N 1°6W 18 B15
Brest Belarus 52°10N 23°40E 65 B12
Brest France 48°24N 4°31W 66 B1
Bretagne □ France 48°10N 3°0W 66 B2
Breton Sd. U.S.A. 29°35N 89°15W 111 E9
Brewer U.S.A. 44°48N 68°46W 113 C13
Brewood U.K. 52°41N 2°9W 23 G4
Briançon France 44°54N 6°39E 66 D7
Bridestowe U.K. 50°41N 4°7W 27 F5
Bridge U.K. 51°15N 1°8E 25 D11
Bridgefield Barbados 13°9N 59°36W 115 g
Bridgend U.K. 51°30N 3°34W 26 D7
Bridgeport U.S.A. 41°11N 73°12W 113 E11
Bridgeton U.S.A. 39°26N 75°14W 113 F10
Bridgetown Barbados 13°6N 59°37W 115 g
Bridgewater Canada 44°25N 64°31W 109 E13
Bridgnorth U.K. 52°32N 2°25W 23 G4
Bridgwater U.K. 51°8N 2°59W 24 D3
Bridgwater B. U.K. 51°15N 3°15W 24 D2
Bridlington U.K. 54°5N 0°12W 22 D8
Bridlington B. U.K. 54°4N 0°10W 23 D8
Bridport U.K. 50°44N 2°45W 24 E3
Brierfield U.K. 53°49N 2°14W 23 E4
Brierley Hill U.K. 52°29N 2°6W 23 H4
Brigg U.K. 53°34N 0°28W 23 E8
Brigham City U.S.A. 41°31N 112°1W 110 B4
Brighouse U.K. 53°42N 1°46W 23 E5
Brighstone U.K. 50°38N 1°23W 24 E6
Brightlingsea U.K. 51°49N 1°2E 25 C11
Brighton U.K. 50°49N 0°7W 25 E8
Brigstock U.K. 52°27N 0°36W 25 B7
Brill U.K. 51°49N 1°1W 24 C6
Brimfield U.K. 52°18N 2°41W 24 B3
Bríndisi Italy 40°39N 17°55E 69 D7
Brinklow U.K. 52°25N 1°22W 24 B6
Brinkworth U.K. 51°33N 1°59W 24 C5
Brisbane Australia 27°25S 153°2E 98 F9
Bristol U.K. 51°26N 2°35W 24 D3
Bristol B. U.S.A. 58°0N 160°0W 108 D4
Bristol Channel U.K. 51°18N 4°30W 27 E5
Briston U.K. 52°51N 1°4E 25 A11
British Columbia □ Canada 55°0N 125°15W 108 D7
British Isles Europe 54°0N 4°0W 56 E5
British Virgin Is. ☑ W. Indies 18°30N 64°30W 115 e
Brittany = Bretagne □ France 48°10N 3°0W 66 B2
Brive-la-Gaillarde France 45°10N 1°32E 66 D4
Brixham U.K. 50°23N 3°31W 27 G6
Brixworth U.K. 52°20N 0°54W 25 B7
Brize Norton U.K. 51°46N 1°34W 24 C5
Brno Czech Rep. 49°10N 16°35E 65 D9
Broad B. U.K. 58°14N 6°18W 18 F5
Broad Chalke U.K. 51°2N 1°56W 24 D5
Broad Haven Ireland 54°20N 9°55W 28 C2
Broad Law U.K. 55°30N 3°21W 21 C9
Broad Sd. U.K. 49°55N 6°21W 27 H1
Broadclyst U.K. 50°46N 3°27W 27 F7
Broadhembury U.K. 50°49N 3°18W 27 F7
Broadstairs U.K. 51°21N 1°27E 25 D11
Broadway U.K. 52°2N 1°50W 24 B5
Broadwindsor U.K. 50°48N 2°47W 24 E3
Brochet Canada 57°53N 101°40W 108 D9
Brock I. Canada 77°52N 114°19W 109 B8
Brocken Germany 51°47N 10°37E 64 C6
Brockenhurst U.K. 50°49N 1°34W 24 E5
Brockville Canada 44°35N 75°41W 113 C10
Brockworth U.K. 51°51N 2°9W 24 C4
Brodeur Pen. Canada 72°30N 88°10W 109 B11
Brodick U.K. 55°35N 5°9W 20 C5
Broken Hill Australia 31°58S 141°29E 98 G7
Bromfield U.K. 52°24N 2°45W 23 H3
Bromham U.K. 51°23N 2°1W 24 D4
Bromley □ U.K. 51°24N 0°2E 25 D9
Brompton U.K. 54°21N 1°25W 22 D6
Bromsgrove U.K. 52°21N 2°2W 24 B4
Bromyard U.K. 52°11N 2°30W 24 B4
Brookings U.S.A. 44°19N 96°48W 111 B7
Brooks Canada 50°35N 111°55W 108 D8
Brooks Range U.S.A. 68°0N 152°0W 108 C5
Broom, L. U.K. 57°55N 5°15W 18 G7
Broome Australia 18°0S 122°15E 98 D3
Broomhill U.K. 55°18N 1°36W 22 B5
Brora U.K. 58°0N 3°52W 19 F10
Brora → U.K. 58°0N 3°51W 19 F10
Broseley U.K. 52°37N 2°29W 23 G4
Brosna → Ireland 53°14N 7°58W 30 B7
Brothertoft U.K. 53°0N 0°7W 23 F8
Brotton U.K. 54°35N 0°56W 22 C7
Brough Cumb., U.K. 54°32N 2°18W 22 C4
Brough E. Riding, U.K. 53°44N 0°36W 23 E7
Brough Hd. U.K. 59°8N 3°20W 19 D11
Broughton Borders, U.K. 55°37N 3°24W 21 C9
Broughton N. Lincs., U.K. 53°34N 0°34W 23 E7
Broughton Northants., U.K. 52°23N 0°46W 25 B7
Broughton-in-Furness U.K. 54°17N 3°13W 22 D2
Broughty Ferry U.K. 56°29N 2°51W 21 A10
Brown Willy U.K. 50°35N 4°37W 27 F4
Brownhills U.K. 52°38N 1°54W 23 G5
Brownsville U.S.A. 25°54N 97°30W 111 E7
Brownwood U.S.A. 31°43N 98°59W 110 D7

Broxburn U.K. 55°56N 3°28W 21 C9
Bruay-la-Buissière France 50°29N 2°33E 66 A5
Bruce, Mt. Australia 22°37S 118°8E 98 E2
Brue → U.K. 51°13N 2°59W 24 D3
Brugge Belgium 51°13N 3°13E 64 C2
Brumado Brazil 14°14S 41°40W 122 B2
Brunei ■ Asia 4°50N 115°0E 82 D4
Brunswick Maine, U.S.A. 43°55N 69°58W 113 D13
Brunton U.K. 55°2N 2°6W 22 B4
Brussels Belgium 50°51N 4°21E 64 C3
Bruton U.K. 51°7N 2°27W 24 D4
Bryan Ohio, U.S.A. 41°28N 84°33W 112 E5
Bryan Tex., U.S.A. 30°40N 96°22W 111 D7
Bryansk Russia 53°13N 34°25E 70 D5
Bryher U.K. 49°57N 6°22W 27 H1
Brynamman U.K. 51°49N 3°51W 26 D6
Brynmawr U.K. 51°48N 3°10W 26 D7
Bucaramanga Colombia 7°0N 73°0W 120 B2
Buchan U.K. 57°32N 2°21W 19 G13
Buchan Ness U.K. 57°29N 1°46W 19 H14
Buchanan Liberia 5°57N 10°2W 94 G3
Bucharest Romania 44°27N 26°10E 65 F14
Buckden U.K. 52°18N 0°14W 25 B8
Buckfastleigh U.K. 50°28N 3°48W 27 G6
Buckhannon U.S.A. 39°0N 80°8W 112 F7
Buckhaven U.K. 56°11N 3°3W 21 B9
Buckie U.K. 57°41N 2°58W 19 G12
Buckingham Canada 45°37N 75°24W 113 C10
Buckingham U.K. 51°59N 0°57W 25 C7
Buckinghamshire □ U.K. 51°53N 0°55W 25 C7
Buckland Brewer U.K. 50°58N 4°15W 27 F5
Buckland Newton U.K. 50°50N 2°26W 24 E4
Buckley U.K. 53°10N 3°5W 26 A7
Budapest Hungary 47°29N 19°3E 65 E10
Bude U.K. 50°49N 4°34W 27 F4
Bude B. U.K. 50°49N 4°35W 27 F4
Budleigh Salterton U.K. 50°37N 3°19W 27 F7
Buena Vista U.S.A. 37°44N 79°21W 112 G8
Buenaventura Colombia 3°53N 77°4W 120 B2
Buenos Aires Argentina 34°36S 58°22W 121 F4
Buenos Aires, L. Argentina 46°35S 72°30W 121 G2
Buffalo N.Y., U.S.A. 42°53N 78°53W 112 D8
Buffalo Wyo., U.S.A. 44°21N 106°42W 110 B5
Bug → Poland 52°31N 21°5E 65 B11
Bug → Ukraine 46°59N 31°58E 71 E5
Bugle U.K. 50°24N 4°47W 27 G4
Bugulma Russia 54°33N 52°48E 70 D9
Buguruslan Russia 53°39N 52°26E 70 D9
Builth Wells U.K. 52°9N 3°25W 26 C7
Buir Nur Mongolia 47°50N 117°42E 79 B12
Bujumbura Burundi 3°16S 29°18E 96 E5
Bukavu Dem. Rep. of the Congo 2°20S 28°52E 96 E5
Bukhara Uzbekistan 39°48N 64°25E 87 B11
Bukittinggi Indonesia 0°20S 100°20E 82 E2
Bulawayo Zimbabwe 20°7S 28°32E 97 J5
Bulford U.K. 51°11N 1°45W 24 D5
Bulgan Mongolia 48°45N 103°34E 78 B9
Bulgaria ■ Europe 42°35N 25°30E 69 C11
Bullhead City U.S.A. 35°8N 114°32W 110 C4
Bunbury Australia 33°20S 115°35E 98 G2
Bunclody Ireland 52°39N 6°40W 31 C9
Buncrana Ireland 55°8N 7°27W 28 A7
Bundaberg Australia 24°54S 152°22E 98 E9
Bundi India 25°30N 75°35E 84 G9
Bundoran Ireland 54°28N 8°16W 28 B5
Bungay U.K. 52°27N 1°28E 25 B11
Buntingford U.K. 51°56N 0°0 25 C9
Bunwell U.K. 52°30N 1°9E 25 A11
Buon Ma Thuot Vietnam 12°40N 108°3E 82 B3
Bûr Safâga Egypt 26°43N 33°57E 95 C12
Buraydah Si. Arabia 26°20N 43°59E 86 E5
Burbage Derby, U.K. 53°15N 1°55W 23 F5
Burbage Leics., U.K. 52°32N 1°21W 23 G6
Burbage Wilts., U.K. 51°21N 1°39W 24 D5
Burco Somali Rep. 9°32N 45°32E 89 F4
Burdur Turkey 37°45N 30°17E 71 G5
Bure → U.K. 52°38N 1°43E 25 A12
Burford U.K. 51°49N 1°38W 24 C5
Burgas Bulgaria 42°33N 27°29E 69 C12
Burgess Hill U.K. 50°58N 0°6W 25 E8
Burgh le Marsh U.K. 53°9N 0°15E 23 F9
Burghead U.K. 57°43N 3°30W 19 G11
Burgos Spain 42°21N 3°41W 67 A4
Burgundy = Bourgogne □
  France 47°0N 4°50E 66 C6
Burhanpur India 21°18N 76°14E 84 J10
Burica, Pta. Costa Rica 8°3N 82°51W 104 J11
Burkina Faso ■ Africa 12°0N 1°0W 94 F5
Burley Hants., U.K. 50°49N 1°43W 24 E5
Burley W. Yorks., U.K. 53°54N 1°45W 23 E5
Burley U.S.A. 42°32N 113°48W 110 B4
Burlington Colo., U.S.A. 39°18N 102°16W 110 C6
Burlington Iowa, U.S.A. 40°49N 91°14W 111 B81
Burlington Vt., U.S.A. 44°29N 73°12W 113 C11
Burlington Wis., U.S.A. 42°41N 88°17W 112 D3
Burma ■ Asia 21°0N 96°30E 85 J20
Burnham Market U.K. 52°57N 0°44E 25 A10
Burnham-on-Crouch U.K. 51°38N 0°49E 25 C10
Burnham-on-Sea U.K. 51°14N 3°0W 24 D2
Burnie Australia 41°4S 145°56E 98 J8
Burnley U.K. 53°47N 2°14W 23 E4
Burnmouth U.K. 55°50N 2°4W 21 C11
Burns U.S.A. 43°35N 119°3W 110 B3
Burnside → Canada 66°51N 108°4W 108 C9
Burntisland U.K. 56°3N 3°14W 21 B9
Burqin China 47°43N 87°0E 78 B6
Burray U.K. 58°51N 2°54W 19 D12
Burren △ Ireland 53°1N 8°58W 30 B4
Burrow Hd. U.K. 54°41N 4°24W 20 E7
Burry Port U.K. 51°41N 4°15W 26 D5
Bursa Turkey 40°15N 29°5E 71 F4
Burstwick U.K. 53°44N 0°8W 23 E8
Burton U.K. 54°11N 2°43W 22 D3
Burton Agnes U.K. 54°4N 0°17W 23 D8
Burton Bradstock U.K. 50°42N 2°43W 24 E3
Burton Fleming U.K. 54°8N 0°20W 22 D8
Burton Latimer U.K. 52°22N 0°41W 25 B7
Burton upon Stather U.K. 53°39N 0°41W 23 E7

Burton upon Trent   Chesterfield Inlet

Burton upon Trent *U.K.* 52°48N 1°38W 23 G5
Buru *Indonesia* 3°30S 126°30E 83 E7
Burundi ■ *Africa* 3°15S 30°0E 96 E5
Burwash *U.K.* 50°59N 0°23E 25 E9
Burwell *U.K.* 52°17N 0°20E 25 B9
Burwick *U.K.* 58°45N 2°58W 19 E12
Bury *U.K.* 53°35N 2°17W 23 E4
Bury St. Edmunds *U.K.* 52°15N 0°43E 25 B10
Buryatia □ *Russia* 53°0N 110°0E 77 D11
Busan *S. Korea* 35°5N 129°0E 79 D14
Büshehr *Iran* 28°55N 50°55E 87 D7
Bushey *U.K.* 51°38N 0°22W 25 C8
Busto Arsizio *Italy* 45°37N 8°51E 68 B3
Buta *Dem. Rep. of the Congo* 2°50N 24°53E 96 D4
Butare *Rwanda* 2°31S 29°52E 96 E5
Butaritari *Kiribati* 3°30N 174°0E 102 G9
Bute *U.K.* 55°48N 5°2W 20 C5
Bute, Kyles of *U.K.* 55°55N 5°10W 20 C5
Butembo *Dem. Rep. of the Congo* 0°9N 29°18E 96 D5
Butha Qi *China* 48°0N 122°32E 79 B13
Butler *U.S.A.* 40°52N 79°54W 112 E8
Buton *Indonesia* 5°0S 122°45E 83 E6
Butte *U.S.A.* 46°0N 112°32W 110 A4
Buttermere *U.K.* 54°32N 3°16W 22 C2
Butterworth *Malaysia* 5°24N 100°23E 82 C2
Buttevant *Ireland* 52°14N 8°40W 30 D6
Butuan *Phil.* 8°57N 125°33E 83 C7
Buurhakaba *Somali Rep.* 3°12N 44°20E 89 G3
Buxton *U.K.* 53°16N 1°54W 23 F5
Buyant-Uhaa *Mongolia* 44°55N 110°11E 79 C11
Buzău *Romania* 45°10N 26°50E 65 F14
Buzuluk *Russia* 52°48N 52°12E 70 D9
Bydgoszcz *Poland* 53°10N 18°0E 65 B9
Byfield *U.K.* 52°10N 1°14W 24 B6
Bylot I. *Canada* 73°13N 78°34W 109 B12
Byrranga Ra. *Russia* 75°0N 100°0E 77 B11
Bytom *Poland* 50°25N 18°54E 65 C10

C

Ca Mau *Vietnam* 9°7N 105°8E 82 C3
Cabanatuan *Phil.* 15°30N 120°58E 83 A6
Cabedelo *Brazil* 7°0S 34°50W 120 C6
Cabimas *Venezuela* 10°23N 71°25W 120 A2
Cabinda *Angola* 5°33S 12°11E 96 F2
Cabinda □ *Angola* 5°0S 12°30E 96 F2
Cabo Frio *Brazil* 22°51S 42°3W 122 D2
Cabo San Lucas *Mexico* 22°53N 109°54W 114 C3
Cabonga, Réservoir *Canada* 47°20N 76°40W 109 E12
Cabora Bassa Dam *Mozam.* 15°20S 32°50E 97 H6
Cabot Str. *Canada* 47°15N 59°40W 109 E14
Čačak *Serbia* 43°54N 20°20E 69 C9
Cáceres *Brazil* 16°5S 57°40W 120 D4
Cáceres *Spain* 39°26N 6°23W 67 C2
Cachimbo, Serra do *Brazil* 9°30S 55°30W 120 C4
Cachoeira *Brazil* 12°30S 39°0W 122 D3
Cachoeira do Sul *Brazil* 30°3S 52°53W 121 F4
Cachoeiro de Itapemirim
 Brazil 20°51S 41°7W 122 D2
Cader Idris *U.K.* 52°42N 3°53W 26 B6
Cadillac *U.S.A.* 44°15N 85°24W 112 C5
Cádiz *Spain* 36°30N 6°20W 67 D2
Cádiz, G. de *Spain* 36°40N 7°0W 67 D2
Caen *France* 49°10N 0°22W 66 B3
Caenby Corner *U.K.* 53°24N 0°33W 23 F7
Caernarfon *U.K.* 53°8N 4°16W 26 A5
Caernarfon B. *U.K.* 53°4N 4°40W 26 A4
Caerphilly *U.K.* 51°35N 3°13W 27 D7
Caersws *U.K.* 52°31N 3°26W 26 B7
Caeté *Brazil* 19°55S 43°40W 122 C2
Caetité *Brazil* 13°50S 42°32W 122 B2
Cagayan de Oro *Phil.* 8°30N 124°40E 83 C6
Cágliari *Italy* 39°13N 9°7E 68 E3
Caguas *Puerto Rico* 18°14N 66°2W 115 d
Caha Mts. *Ireland* 51°45N 9°40W 30 E3
Caher *Ireland* 52°22N 7°56W 30 D7
Cahersiveen *Ireland* 51°56N 10°14W 30 E2
Cahore Pt. *Ireland* 52°33N 6°12W 31 C10
Cahors *France* 44°27N 1°22E 66 D4
Cairn Gorm *U.K.* 57°7N 3°39W 19 H10
Cairngorm Mts. *U.K.* 57°6N 3°42W 19 H10
Cairngorms △ *U.K.* 57°10N 3°50W 19 H10
Cairnryan *U.K.* 54°59N 5°1W 20 E5
Cairns *Australia* 16°57S 145°45E 98 D8
Cairnsmore of Fleet *U.K.* 54°59N 4°20W 20 F7
Cairo *Egypt* 30°2N 31°13E 95 B12
Cairo *U.S.A.* 37°0N 89°11W 112 G3
Caister-on-Sea *U.K.* 52°40N 1°43E 25 A12
Caistor *U.K.* 53°30N 0°18W 23 F8
Caithness *U.K.* 58°25N 3°35W 19 F10
Caithness, Ord of *U.K.* 58°8N 3°36W 19 F10
Caja de Muertos, I.
 Puerto Rico 17°54N 66°32W 115 d
Cajamarca *Peru* 7°5S 78°28W 120 C2
Calabar *Nigeria* 4°57N 8°20E 94 H7
Calábria □ *Italy* 39°0N 16°30E 68 E7
Calais *France* 50°57N 1°56E 66 A4
Calais *U.S.A.* 45°11N 67°17W 113 C14
Calama *Chile* 22°30S 68°55W 121 E3
Calamian Group *Phil.* 11°50N 119°55E 83 B5
Calanscio, Sarīr *Libya* 27°30N 21°30E 95 C10
Calapan *Phil.* 13°25N 121°7E 83 B6
Calbayog *Phil.* 12°4N 124°38E 83 B6
Calcutta = Kolkata *India* 22°34N 88°21E 85 H16
Caldbeck *U.K.* 54°45N 3°3W 22 C2
Calder → *U.K.* 53°44N 1°22W 23 E6
Calder Bridge *U.K.* 54°27N 3°29W 22 C2
Caldera *Chile* 27°5S 70°55W 121 E2
Caldew → *U.K.* 54°54N 2°56W 22 C3
Caldwell *U.S.A.* 43°40N 116°41W 110 B3
Caledonian Canal *U.K.* 57°29N 4°15W 19 H9
Calgary *Canada* 51°0N 114°10W 108 D8
Cali *Colombia* 3°25N 76°35W 120 B2
Calicut *India* 11°15N 75°43E 84 P9
California □ *U.S.A.* 37°30N 119°30W 110 C2
California, G. de *Mexico* 27°0N 111°0W 114 B2
Callan *Ireland* 52°32N 7°24W 31 C8
Callander *U.K.* 56°15N 4°13W 20 B7
Callao *Peru* 12°3S 77°8W 120 D2
Calne *U.K.* 51°26N 2°0W 24 D5

Calshot *U.K.* 50°48N 1°19W 24 E6
Calstock *U.K.* 50°30N 4°13W 27 F5
Caltanissetta *Italy* 37°29N 14°4E 68 F6
Calvi *France* 42°34N 8°45E 66 E8
Calvinia *S. Africa* 31°28S 19°45E 97 L3
Cam → *U.K.* 52°21N 0°16E 25 B9
Cam Ranh *Vietnam* 11°54N 109°12E 82 B3
Camagüey *Cuba* 21°20N 77°55W 115 C9
Camargue *France* 43°34N 4°34E 66 E6
Camberley *U.K.* 51°20N 0°44W 25 D7
Cambo *U.K.* 55°10N 1°57W 22 B5
Cambodia ■ *Asia* 12°15N 105°0E 82 B3
Camborne *U.K.* 50°12N 5°19W 27 G3
Cambrai *France* 50°11N 3°14E 66 A5
Cambrian Mts. *U.K.* 52°3N 3°57W 26 C6
Cambridge *U.K.* 52°12N 0°8E 25 B9
Cambridge *Jamaica* 18°18N 77°54W 114 a
Cambridge *Mass., U.S.A.* 42°23N 71°7W 113 D12
Cambridge *Md., U.S.A.* 38°34N 76°5W 113 F9
Cambridge *Ohio, U.S.A.* 40°2N 81°35W 112 E7
Cambridge Bay *Canada* 69°10N 105°0W 108 C9
Cambridgeshire □ *U.K.* 52°25N 0°7W 25 B8
Camden *Ark., U.S.A.* 33°35N 92°50W 111 D8
Camden *N.J., U.S.A.* 39°55N 75°7W 113 F10
Camden □ *U.K.* 51°32N 0°8W 25 C8
Camel → *U.K.* 50°31N 4°51W 27 F4
Camelford *U.K.* 50°37N 4°42W 27 F4
Cameroon ■ *Africa* 6°0N 12°30E 96 C2
Cameroun, Mt. *Cameroon* 4°13N 9°10E 96 D1
Cametá *Brazil* 2°12S 49°30W 120 C5
Camocim *Brazil* 2°55S 40°50W 120 C5
Campana, I. *Chile* 48°20S 75°20W 121 G2
Campánia □ *Italy* 41°0N 14°30E 68 D6
Campbell I. *Pac. Oc.* 52°30S 169°0E 102 N8
Campbell River *Canada* 50°5N 125°20W 108 D7
Campbellsville *U.S.A.* 37°21N 85°20W 112 G5
Campbellton *Canada* 47°57N 66°43W 109 E13
Campbeltown *U.K.* 55°26N 5°36W 20 D4
Campeche *Mexico* 19°51N 90°32W 114 D6
Campeche, Golfo de *Mexico* 19°30N 93°0W 114 D6
Campina Grande *Brazil* 7°20S 35°47W 120 C6
Campinas *Brazil* 22°50S 47°0W 122 D1
Campo Belo *Brazil* 20°52S 45°16W 122 D1
Campo Grande *Brazil* 20°25S 54°40W 120 E4
Campos *Brazil* 21°50S 41°20W 122 D2
Campos Belos *Brazil* 13°10S 47°3W 122 B1
Camrose *Canada* 53°0N 112°50W 108 D8
Can Tho *Vietnam* 10°2N 105°46E 82 B3
Canada ■ *N. Amer.* 60°0N 100°0W 108 D10
Canadian → *U.S.A.* 35°28N 95°3W 111 C7
Canadian Shield *Canada* 53°0N 75°0W 104 D12
Çanakkale *Turkey* 40°8N 26°24E 71 F4
Canandaigua *U.S.A.* 42°54N 77°17W 112 D9
Cananea *Mexico* 31°0N 110°18W 114 A2
Canaries *St. Lucia* 13°55N 61°4W 115 f
Canary Is. *Atl. Oc.* 28°30N 16°0W 94 C2
Canaveral, C. *U.S.A.* 28°27N 80°32W 111 E10
Canavieiras *Brazil* 15°39S 39°0W 122 B3
Canberra *Australia* 35°15S 149°8E 98 H8
Cancún *Mexico* 21°8N 86°44W 114 C7
Cangzhou *China* 38°19N 116°52E 79 D12
Caniapiscau → *Canada* 56°40N 69°30W 109 D13
Caniapiscau, L. *Canada* 54°10N 69°55W 109 D13
Çankırı *Turkey* 40°40N 33°37E 71 F5
Canna *U.K.* 57°3N 6°33W 18 H4
Canna, Sd. of *U.K.* 57°1N 6°30W 18 H4
Cannanore *India* 11°53N 75°27E 84 P9
Cannes *France* 43°32N 7°1E 66 E7
Cannington *U.K.* 51°9N 3°4W 24 D2
Cannock *U.K.* 52°41N 2°1W 23 G4
Cannock Chase *U.K.* 52°44N 2°4W 23 G4
Canoas *Brazil* 29°56S 51°11W 121 E4
Canon City *U.S.A.* 38°27N 105°14W 110 C5
Canonbie *U.K.* 55°5N 2°58W 21 D10
Canora *Canada* 51°40N 102°30W 108 D9
Canso *Canada* 45°20N 61°0W 113 C17
Canterbury *U.K.* 51°16N 1°6E 25 D11
Canton = Guangzhou *China* 23°6N 113°13E 79 G11
Canton *Ill., U.S.A.* 40°33N 90°2W 112 E2
Canton *N.Y., U.S.A.* 44°36N 75°10W 113 C10
Canton *Ohio, U.S.A.* 40°48N 81°23W 112 E7
Canvey *U.K.* 51°31N 0°37E 25 C10
Cap-de-la-Madeleine
 Canada 46°22N 72°31W 113 B11
Cap-Haïtien *Haiti* 19°40N 72°20W 115 D10
Cap Pt. *St. Lucia* 14°7N 60°57W 115 f
Cape Breton I. *Canada* 46°0N 60°30W 113 C17
Cape Charles *U.S.A.* 37°16N 76°1W 113 G10
Cape Coast *Ghana* 5°5N 1°15W 94 G5
Cape Coral *U.S.A.* 26°33N 81°57W 111 E10
Cape Fear → *U.S.A.* 33°53N 78°1W 111 D11
Cape Girardeau *U.S.A.* 37°19N 89°32W 112 G3
Cape May *U.S.A.* 38°56N 74°56W 113 F10
Cape Town *S. Africa* 33°55S 18°22E 97 L3
Cape Verde Is. ■ *Atl. Oc.* 16°0N 24°0W 91 E1
Cape York Peninsula
 Australia 12°0S 142°30E 98 C7
Capela *Brazil* 10°30S 37°0W 122 B3
Capesterre-Belle-Eau
 Guadeloupe 16°4N 61°36W 114 b
Capesterre-de-Marie-Galante
 Guadeloupe 15°53N 61°14W 114 b
Capreol *Canada* 46°43N 80°56W 112 B7
Capri *Italy* 40°33N 14°14E 68 D6
Caprivi Strip *Namibia* 18°0S 23°0E 97 H4
Caquetá → *Colombia* 1°15S 69°15W 120 C3
Caracas *Venezuela* 10°30N 66°55W 120 A3
Caracol *Brazil* 9°15S 43°22W 122 B2
Carangola *Brazil* 20°44S 42°5W 122 D2
Caratasca, L. de *Honduras* 15°20N 83°40W 115 D8
Caratinga *Brazil* 19°50S 42°10W 122 C2
Caravelas *Brazil* 17°45S 39°15W 122 C3
Caravelle, Presqu'île de la
 Martinique 14°46N 60°48W 114 c
Carbón, L. del *Argentina* 49°35S 68°21W 121 G3
Carbondale *Ill., U.S.A.* 37°44N 89°13W 112 G3
Carbondale *Pa., U.S.A.* 41°35N 75°30W 113 E10

Carbonear *Canada* 47°42N 53°13W 109 E14
Carcassonne *France* 43°13N 2°20E 66 E5
Carcross *Canada* 60°13N 134°45W 108 C6
Cardamon Hills *India* 9°30N 77°15E 84 Q10
Cardiff *U.K.* 51°29N 3°10W 27 E7
Cardigan *U.K.* 52°5N 4°40W 26 C4
Cardigan B. *U.K.* 52°30N 4°30W 26 B4
Cardington *U.K.* 52°6N 0°25W 25 B8
Cardston *Canada* 49°15N 113°20W 108 E8
Cariacica *Brazil* 20°16S 40°25W 122 D2
Caribbean Sea *W. Indies* 15°0N 75°0W 115 E10
Cariboo Mts. *Canada* 53°0N 121°0W 108 D7
Caribou *U.S.A.* 46°52N 68°1W 113 B13
Caribou Mts. *Canada* 59°12N 115°40W 108 D8
Carinhanha *Brazil* 14°15S 44°46W 122 B2
Carinhanha → *Brazil* 14°20S 43°47W 122 B2
Carinthia = Kärnten □
 Austria 46°52N 13°30E 64 E8
Carisbrooke *U.K.* 50°41N 1°19W 24 E6
Cark *U.K.* 54°11N 2°58W 22 D3
Carleton Place *Canada* 45°8N 76°9W 113 C9
Carleton Rode *U.K.* 52°30N 1°7E 25 A11
Carlingford L. *U.K.* 54°3N 6°9W 29 B9
Carlinville *U.S.A.* 39°17N 89°53W 112 F3
Carlisle *U.K.* 54°54N 2°56W 22 C3
Carlisle *U.S.A.* 40°12N 77°12W 112 E9
Carlisle B. *Barbados* 13°5N 59°37W 115 g
Carlops *U.K.* 55°47N 3°20W 21 C9
Carlow *Ireland* 52°50N 6°56W 31 C9
Carlow □ *Ireland* 52°43N 6°50W 31 C9
Carlsbad *U.S.A.* 32°25N 104°14W 110 D6
Carlton *U.K.* 52°59N 1°5W 23 G6
Carlton Colville *U.K.* 52°27N 1°43E 25 B12
Carlton Miniott *U.K.* 54°12N 1°22W 22 D6
Carluke *U.K.* 55°45N 3°50W 21 C8
Carmacks *Canada* 62°5N 136°16W 108 C6
Carmarthen *U.K.* 51°52N 4°19W 26 D5
Carmarthen B. *U.K.* 51°40N 4°30W 26 D4
Carmarthenshire □ *U.K.* 51°55N 4°13W 26 D5
Carmaux *France* 44°3N 2°10E 66 D5
Carn Ban *U.K.* 57°7N 4°15W 19 H9
Carn Eige *U.K.* 57°17N 5°8W 18 H7
Carnarvon *Australia* 24°51S 113°42E 98 E1
Carnarvon *S. Africa* 30°56S 22°8E 97 L4
Carndonagh *Ireland* 55°16N 7°15W 29 A7
Carnegie, L. *Australia* 26°5S 122°30E 98 F3
Carnforth *U.K.* 54°7N 2°45W 22 D3
Carno *U.K.* 52°34N 3°30W 26 B6
Carnoustie *U.K.* 56°30N 2°42W 21 B10
Carnsore Pt. *Ireland* 52°10N 6°22W 31 D10
Caro *U.S.A.* 43°29N 83°24W 112 D6
Carolina *Puerto Rico* 18°23N 65°58W 115 d
Caroline I. *Kiribati* 9°58S 150°13W 103 H12
Caroline Is. *Micronesia* 8°0N 150°0E 102 G6
Carondelet Reef *Kiribati* 5°33S 173°50E 99 D16
Caroní → *Venezuela* 8°21N 62°43W 120 B3
Carpathians *Europe* 49°30N 21°0E 65 D11
Carpentaria, G. of *Australia* 14°0S 139°0E 98 C6
Carpentras *France* 44°3N 5°2E 66 D6
Carpi *Italy* 44°47N 10°53E 68 B4
Carrara *Italy* 44°5N 10°6E 68 B4
Carrauntoohill *Ireland* 52°0N 9°45W 30 E3
Carrick-on-Shannon *Ireland* 53°57N 8°5W 28 D5
Carrick on Suir *Ireland* 52°21N 7°24W 31 D8
Carrickfergus *U.K.* 54°43N 5°49W 29 B10
Carrickmacross *Ireland* 53°59N 6°43W 29 D8
Carrollton *U.S.A.* 39°18N 90°24W 112 F2
Carron → *U.K.* 57°53N 4°22W 19 G9
Carron, L. *U.K.* 57°22N 5°35W 18 H7
Carson City *U.S.A.* 39°10N 119°46W 110 C3
Carson Sink *U.S.A.* 39°50N 118°25W 110 C3
Cartagena *Colombia* 10°25N 75°33W 120 A2
Cartagena *Spain* 37°38N 0°59W 67 D5
Cartago *Colombia* 4°45N 75°55W 120 B2
Carthage *Tunisia* 36°52N 10°20E 95 A8
Cartmel *U.K.* 54°12N 2°57W 22 D3
Cartwright *Canada* 53°41N 56°58W 109 D14
Caruaru *Brazil* 8°15S 35°55W 122 A3
Carúpano *Venezuela* 10°39N 63°15W 120 A3
Casa Grande *U.S.A.* 32°53N 111°45W 110 D4
Casa Nova *Brazil* 9°25S 41°5W 122 A2
Casablanca *Morocco* 33°36N 7°36W 94 B4
Cascade Ra. *U.S.A.* 47°0N 121°30W 110 B2
Cascavel *Ceará, Brazil* 4°7S 38°14W 120 C6
Cascavel *Paraná, Brazil* 24°57S 53°28W 121 E4
Caserta *Italy* 41°4N 14°20E 68 D6
Casiquiare → *Venezuela* 2°1N 67°7W 120 B3
Casper *U.S.A.* 42°51N 106°19W 110 B5
Caspian Depression *Eurasia* 47°0N 48°0E 71 E8
Caspian Sea *Eurasia* 43°0N 50°0E 71 F9
Cassiar Mts. *Canada* 59°30N 130°30W 108 D6
Castellammare di Stábia *Italy* 40°42N 14°29E 68 D6
Castelló de la Plana *Spain* 39°58N 0°3W 67 C5
Castelsarrasin *France* 44°2N 1°7E 66 E4
Castilla-La Mancha □ *Spain* 39°30N 3°30W 67 C4
Castilla y Leon □ *Spain* 42°0N 5°0W 67 B3
Castle Acre *U.K.* 52°42N 0°42E 25 A10
Castle Cary *U.K.* 51°6N 2°31W 24 D3
Castle Donington *U.K.* 52°51N 1°20W 23 G6
Castle Douglas *U.K.* 54°56N 3°56W 21 E8
Castlebar *Ireland* 53°52N 9°18W 28 D2
Castlebay *U.K.* 56°57N 7°31W 18 J2
Castleblaney *Ireland* 54°7N 6°44W 29 C8
Castlederg *U.K.* 54°42N 7°35W 28 B6
Castleford *U.K.* 53°43N 1°21W 23 E6
Castlemaine Harbour *Ireland* 52°8N 9°50W 30 D3
Castlepollard *Ireland* 53°41N 7°19W 28 D7
Castlerea *Ireland* 53°46N 8°29W 28 D5
Castleside *U.K.* 54°50N 1°52W 22 C5
Castleton *Derby, U.K.* 53°22N 1°46W 23 F5
Castleton *N. Yorks., U.K.* 54°28N 0°57W 22 C7
Castletown *I. of Man* 54°5N 4°38W 29 C12
Castletown Bearhaven *Ireland* 51°39N 9°55W 30 E3
Castres *France* 43°37N 2°13E 66 E5
Castries *St. Lucia* 14°2N 60°58W 115 f
Castro *Chile* 42°30S 73°50W 121 G2
Castro Alves *Brazil* 12°46S 39°33W 122 B3

Cat I. *Bahamas* 24°30N 75°30W 115 C9
Cataguases *Brazil* 21°23S 42°39W 122 D2
Catalão *Brazil* 18°10S 47°57W 122 C1
Cataluña □ *Spain* 41°40N 1°15E 67 B6
Catamarca *Argentina* 28°30S 65°50W 121 E3
Catanduanes *Phil.* 13°50N 124°20E 83 B6
Catanduva *Brazil* 21°5S 48°58W 122 D1
Catánia *Italy* 37°30N 15°6E 68 F6
Catanzaro *Italy* 38°54N 16°35E 68 E7
Catcleugh *U.K.* 55°20N 2°24W 22 B4
Caterham *U.K.* 51°15N 0°4W 25 D8
Catoche, C. *Mexico* 21°35N 87°5W 114 C7
Caton *U.K.* 54°5N 2°42W 22 D3
Catsfield *U.K.* 50°54N 0°28E 25 E9
Catskill *U.S.A.* 42°14N 73°52W 113 D11
Catskill Mts. *U.S.A.* 42°10N 74°25W 113 D10
Catterick *U.K.* 54°23N 1°37W 22 D5
Catterick Camp *U.K.* 54°22N 1°42W 22 D5
Catton *U.K.* 54°55N 2°15W 22 C4
Cauca → *Colombia* 8°54N 74°28W 120 B2
Caucaia *Brazil* 3°40S 38°35W 120 C6
Caucasus Mountains *Eurasia* 42°50N 44°0E 71 F7
Caulkerbush *U.K.* 54°54N 3°41W 21 E9
Caura → *Venezuela* 7°38N 64°53W 120 B3
Cauvery → *India* 11°9N 78°52E 84 P11
Cavan *Ireland* 54°0N 7°22W 28 D7
Cavan □ *Ireland* 54°1N 7°16W 29 C7
Caviana, I. *Brazil* 0°10N 50°10W 120 B4
Cawood *U.K.* 53°50N 1°8W 23 E6
Cawston *U.K.* 52°47N 1°9E 25 A11
Caxias *Brazil* 4°55S 43°20W 120 C5
Caxias do Sul *Brazil* 29°10S 51°10W 121 E4
Cayenne *Fr. Guiana* 5°5N 52°18W 120 B4
Cayey *Puerto Rico* 18°7N 66°10W 115 d
Cayman Is. □ *W. Indies* 19°40N 80°30W 115 D8
Cayman Trench *Caribbean* 17°0N 83°0W 115 D8
Cayuga L. *U.S.A.* 42°41N 76°41W 112 D9
Ceanannus Mor *Ireland* 53°44N 6°53W 29 D8
Ceará □ *Brazil* 5°0S 40°0W 120 C6
Cebu *Phil.* 10°18N 123°54E 83 B6
Cedar City *U.S.A.* 37°41N 113°4W 110 C4
Cedar L. *Canada* 53°10N 100°0W 108 D10
Cedar Rapids *U.S.A.* 41°59N 91°40W 111 B81
Cefalù *Italy* 38°2N 14°1E 68 E6
Cegléd *Hungary* 47°11N 19°47E 65 E10
Celaya *Mexico* 20°31N 100°37W 114 C4
Celebes Sea *Indonesia* 3°0N 123°0E 83 D6
Celina *U.S.A.* 40°33N 84°35W 112 E5
Celtic Sea *Atl. Oc.* 50°9N 9°34W 62 F2
Cemaes *U.K.* 53°24N 4°27W 26 A5
Central, Cordillera *Colombia* 5°0N 75°0W 117 C3
Central, Cordillera *Puerto Rico* 18°8N 66°35W 115 d
Central African Rep. ■ *Africa* 7°0N 20°0E 96 C4
Central America *America* 12°0N 85°0W 104 H11
Central Bedfordshire □ *U.K.* 52°5N 0°20W 25 B8
Central Makran Range
 Pakistan 26°30N 64°15E 84 F4
Central Russian Uplands
 Europe 54°0N 36°0E 56 E13
Central Siberian Plateau
 Russia 65°0N 105°0E 72 B12
Centralia *Ill., U.S.A.* 38°32N 89°8W 112 F3
Centralia *Wash., U.S.A.* 46°43N 122°58W 110 A2
Cephalonia = Kefalonia
 Greece 38°15N 20°30E 69 E9
Ceredigion □ *U.K.* 52°16N 4°15W 26 C5
Cerignola *Italy* 41°17N 15°53E 68 D6
Cerne Abbas *U.K.* 50°49N 2°29W 24 E4
Cerrigydrudion *U.K.* 53°1N 3°35W 26 A6
Cerro de Pasco *Peru* 10°45S 76°10W 120 D2
Cesena *Italy* 44°8N 12°15E 68 B5
České Budějovice *Czech Rep.* 48°55N 14°25E 64 D8
Çeşme *Turkey* 38°20N 26°23E 71 G4
Ceuta *N. Afr.* 35°52N 5°18W 67 E3
Ceve-i-Ra *Fiji* 21°46S 174°31E 99 E13
Cévennes *France* 44°10N 3°50E 66 D5
Chacewater *U.K.* 50°15N 5°11W 27 G3
Chachapoyas *Peru* 6°15S 77°50W 120 C2
Chaco Austral *S. Amer.* 27°0S 61°30W 121 E3
Chaco Boreal *S. Amer.* 22°0S 60°0W 121 E4
Chaco Central *S. Amer.* 24°0S 61°0W 121 E3
Chad ■ *Africa* 15°0N 17°15E 95 F8
Chad, L. *Chad* 13°30N 14°30E 95 F8
Chadron *U.S.A.* 42°50N 103°0W 110 B6
Chagford *U.K.* 50°40N 3°50W 27 F6
Chaghcharān *Afghan.* 34°31N 65°15E 87 C11
Chagos Arch. ☑ *Ind. Oc.* 6°0S 72°0E 73 J9
Chāh Gay Hills *Afghan.* 29°30N 64°0E 87 D10
Chakradharpur *India* 22°45N 85°40E 85 H14
Chaleur B. *Canada* 47°55N 65°30W 113 B15
Chalisgaon *India* 20°30N 75°10E 84 J9
Challenger Deep *Pac. Oc.* 11°30N 142°0E 102 F6
Chalon-sur-Saône *France* 46°48N 4°50E 66 C6
Châlons-en-Champagne
 France 48°58N 4°20E 66 B6
Chambal → *India* 26°29N 79°15E 84 F11
Chambersburg *U.S.A.* 39°56N 77°40W 112 F9
Chambéry *France* 45°34N 5°55E 66 D6
Chamonix-Mont Blanc *France* 45°55N 6°51E 66 D7
Champagne *France* 48°40N 4°20E 66 B6
Champaign *U.S.A.* 40°7N 88°15W 112 E3
Champlain, L. *U.S.A.* 44°40N 73°20W 113 C11
Chañaral *Chile* 26°23S 70°40W 121 E2
Chancery Lane *Barbados* 13°3N 59°30W 115 g
Chandigarh *India* 30°43N 76°47E 84 D10
Chandler's Ford *U.K.* 50°59N 1°22W 24 E6
Chandpur *Bangla.* 23°8N 90°45E 85 H17
Chandrapur *India* 19°57N 79°25E 84 K11
Changbai Shan *China* 42°20N 129°0E 79 C14
Changchun *China* 43°57N 125°17E 79 C14
Changde *China* 29°4N 111°35E 79 F11
Changhua *Taiwan* 24°2N 120°30E 79 G13
Changji *China* 44°1N 87°19E 78 C6
Changsha *China* 28°12N 113°0E 79 F11
Changzhi *China* 36°10N 113°6E 79 D11
Changzhou *China* 31°47N 119°58E 79 E12
Chania *Greece* 35°30N 24°4E 69 G11
Channel Is. *U.K.* 49°19N 2°24W 27 J9
Channel Is. *U.S.A.* 33°40N 119°15W 110 D2

Channel-Port aux Basques
 Canada 47°30N 59°9W 109 E14
Chantrey Inlet *Canada* 67°48N 96°20W 108 C10
Chaoyang *China* 41°35N 120°22E 79 C13
Chaozhou *China* 23°42N 116°32E 79 G12
Chapala, L. de *Mexico* 20°15N 103°0W 114 C4
Chapayevsk *Russia* 53°0N 49°40E 70 D8
Chapel en le Frith *U.K.* 53°20N 1°54W 23 F5
Chapel St. Leonards *U.K.* 53°13N 0°20E 23 F9
Chapleau *Canada* 47°50N 83°24W 109 E11
Charaña *Bolivia* 17°30S 69°25W 120 D3
Chard *U.K.* 50°52N 2°58W 24 E3
Chari → *Chad* 12°58N 14°31E 95 F8
Chārīkār *Afghan.* 35°0N 69°10E 87 C12
Charing *U.K.* 51°12N 0°49E 25 D10
Charlbury *U.K.* 51°53N 1°28W 24 C6
Charleroi *Belgium* 50°24N 4°27E 64 C3
Charles, C. *U.S.A.* 37°7N 75°58W 113 G10
Charles City *U.S.A.* 43°4N 92°41W 111 B81
Charleston *Ill., U.S.A.* 39°30N 88°10W 112 F3
Charleston *Mo., U.S.A.* 36°55N 89°21W 112 G3
Charleston *S.C., U.S.A.* 32°46N 79°56W 111 D11
Charleston *W. Va., U.S.A.* 38°21N 81°38W 112 F7
Charlestown *Ireland* 53°58N 8°48W 28 D4
Charlestown of Aberlour
 U.K. 57°28N 3°14W 19 H11
Charleville *Australia* 26°24S 146°15E 98 F8
Charleville-Mézières *France* 49°44N 4°40E 66 B6
Charlevoix *U.S.A.* 45°19N 85°16W 112 C5
Charlotte *Mich., U.S.A.* 42°34N 84°50W 112 D5
Charlotte *N.C., U.S.A.* 35°13N 80°50W 111 C10
Charlotte Amalie
 U.S. Virgin Is. 18°21N 64°56W 115 e
Charlotte Harbor *U.S.A.* 26°57N 82°4W 111 E10
Charlottesville *U.S.A.* 38°2N 78°30W 112 F8
Charlottetown *Canada* 46°14N 63°8W 113 B16
Charlton I. *Canada* 52°0N 79°20W 109 D12
Charlton Kings *U.K.* 51°53N 2°3W 24 C4
Charminster *U.K.* 50°44N 2°28W 24 E4
Charmouth *U.K.* 50°44N 2°54W 24 E3
Charnwood Forest *U.K.* 52°44N 1°17W 23 G6
Charolles *France* 46°27N 4°16E 66 C6
Charters Towers *Australia* 20°5S 146°13E 98 E8
Chartham *U.K.* 51°14N 1°1E 25 D11
Chartres *France* 48°29N 1°30E 66 B4
Chascomús *Argentina* 35°30S 58°0W 121 F4
Châteaubriant *France* 47°43N 1°23W 66 C3
Châteaulin *France* 48°11N 4°8W 66 B1
Châteauroux *France* 46°50N 1°40E 66 C4
Châteaux, Pte. des *Guadeloupe* 16°15N 61°10W 114 b
Châtellerault *France* 46°50N 0°30E 66 C4
Chatham *N.B., Canada* 47°2N 65°28W 109 E13
Chatham *Ont., Canada* 42°24N 82°11W 112 D6
Chatham *U.K.* 51°22N 0°32E 25 D10
Chatham Is. *Pac. Oc.* 44°0S 176°40W 99 J15
Chatsworth *U.K.* 53°13N 1°36W 23 F5
Chattahoochee → *U.S.A.* 30°54N 84°57W 104 F11
Chattanooga *U.S.A.* 35°3N 85°19W 111 C9
Chatteris *U.K.* 52°28N 0°2E 25 B9
Chatton *U.K.* 55°35N 2°0W 22 A5
Chaumont *France* 48°7N 5°8E 66 B6
Chaykovskiy *Russia* 56°47N 54°9E 70 C9
Cheadle *Gt. Man., U.K.* 53°23N 2°12W 23 F4
Cheadle *Staffs., U.K.* 52°59N 1°58W 23 G5
Cheb *Czech Rep.* 50°9N 12°28E 64 C7
Cheboksary *Russia* 56°8N 47°12E 70 C8
Cheboygan *U.S.A.* 45°39N 84°29W 112 C5
Chech, Erg *Africa* 25°0N 2°15W 94 D5
Chechenia □ *Russia* 43°30N 45°29E 71 F8
Chedabucto B. *Canada* 45°25N 61°8W 113 C17
Cheddar *U.K.* 51°17N 2°46W 24 D3
Cheddleton *U.K.* 53°4N 2°2W 23 F4
Cheduba I. *Burma* 18°45N 93°40E 85 K18
Chegutu *Zimbabwe* 18°10S 30°14E 97 H6
Chełm *Poland* 51°8N 23°30E 65 C12
Chelmer → *U.K.* 51°44N 0°30E 25 C10
Chelmsford *U.K.* 51°44N 0°29E 25 C9
Cheltenham *U.K.* 51°54N 2°4W 24 C4
Chelyabinsk *Russia* 55°10N 61°24E 76 D7
Chelyuskin, C. *Russia* 77°30N 103°0E 77 B11
Chemnitz *Germany* 50°51N 12°54E 64 C7
Chenab → *Pakistan* 30°23N 71°2E 84 D7
Chengde *China* 40°59N 117°58E 79 C12
Chengdu *China* 30°38N 104°2E 78 E9
Chengjiang *China* 24°39N 103°0E 78 G9
Chennai *India* 13°8N 80°19E 84 N12
Chepstow *U.K.* 51°38N 2°41W 26 D8
Cher → *France* 47°21N 0°29E 66 C4
Cherbourg *France* 49°39N 1°40W 66 B3
Cheremkhovo *Russia* 53°8N 103°1E 78 A9
Cherepovets *Russia* 59°5N 37°55E 70 C6
Chergui, Chott ech *Algeria* 34°21N 0°25E 94 B6
Cheriton □ *U.K.* 51°3N 1°8W 24 D6
Cheriton Fitzpaine *U.K.* 50°51N 3°35W 27 F6
Cherkasy *Ukraine* 49°27N 32°4E 71 E5
Cherkessk *Russia* 44°15N 42°5E 71 F7
Cherni[h]iv *Ukraine* 51°28N 31°20E 70 D5
Chernivtsi *Ukraine* 48°15N 25°52E 65 D13
Chernobyl *Ukraine* 51°20N 30°15E 65 C16
Cherokee *U.S.A.* 42°45N 95°33W 111 B7
Cherrapunji *India* 25°17N 91°47E 85 G17
Cherski Ra. *Russia* 65°0N 143°0E 77 C15
Chertsey *U.K.* 51°23N 0°30W 25 D7
Chervonohrad *Ukraine* 50°25N 24°10E 71 D3
Cherwell → *U.K.* 51°44N 1°14W 24 C6
Chesapeake B. *U.S.A.* 38°0N 76°10W 112 F9
Chesha B. *Russia* 67°20N 47°0E 70 A8
Chesham *U.K.* 51°43N 0°36W 25 C7
Cheshire East □ *U.K.* 53°15N 2°15W 23 F4
Cheshire West and Chester □
 U.K. 53°15N 2°40W 23 F3
Cheshunt *U.K.* 51°43N 0°1W 25 C8
Chesil Beach *U.K.* 50°37N 2°33W 24 E4
Chester *U.K.* 53°12N 2°53W 23 F3
Chester *U.S.A.* 39°51N 75°22W 113 F10
Chester-le-Street *U.K.* 54°51N 1°34W 22 C5
Chesterfield *U.K.* 53°15N 1°25W 23 F6
Chesterfield, Îs. *N. Cal.* 19°52S 158°15E 99 D13
Chesterfield Inlet *Canada* 63°30N 90°45W 108 C10

Chesuncook L. Culebra

Chesuncook L. *U.S.A.* 46°0N 69°21W **113** B13
Chetumal *Mexico* 18°30N 88°20W **114** D7
Chetwynd *Canada* 55°45N 121°36W **108** D7
Cheviot, The *U.K.* 55°29N 2°9W **22** B4
Cheviot Hills *U.K.* 55°20N 2°30W **22** B3
Chew Bahir *Ethiopia* 4°40N 36°50E **89** G2
Chew Magna *U.K.* 51°22N 2°37W **24** D3
Cheyenne *U.S.A.* 41°8N 104°49W **110** B6
Cheyenne → *U.S.A.* 44°41N 101°18W **110** B6
Chhapra *India* 25°48N 84°44E **85** G14
Chhattisgarh □ *India* 22°0N 82°0E **85** J12
Chi → *Thailand* 15°11N 104°43E **82** A3
Chiai *Taiwan* 23°29N 120°25E **79** G13
Chiávari *Italy* 44°19N 9°19E **68** B3
Chiba *Japan* 35°30N 140°7E **81** F7
Chibougamau *Canada* 49°56N 74°24W **109** E12
Chibougamau, L. *Canada* 49°50N 74°20W **113** A10
Chic-Chocs, Mts. *Canada* 48°55N 66°0W **113** A14
Chicago *U.S.A.* 41°52N 87°38W **112** E4
Chichagof I. *U.S.A.* 57°30N 135°30W **108** D6
Chichester *U.K.* 50°50N 0°47W **25** E7
Chickasha *U.S.A.* 35°3N 97°58W **110** C7
Chiclayo *Peru* 6°42S 79°50W **120** C2
Chico *U.S.A.* 39°44N 121°50W **110** C2
Chico → *Chubut, Argentina* 44°0S 67°0W **121** G3
Chico → *Santa Cruz, Argentina* 50°0S 68°30W **121** G3
Chicopee *U.S.A.* 42°9N 72°37W **113** D11
Chicoutimi *Canada* 48°28N 71°5W **113** A12
Chiddingfold *U.K.* 51°7N 0°37W **25** D7
Chidley, C. *Canada* 60°23N 64°26W **109** C13
Chieti *Italy* 42°21N 14°10E **68** C6
Chifeng *China* 42°18N 118°58E **79** C12
Chihuahua *Mexico* 28°38N 106°5W **114** B3
Chilapa *Mexico* 17°36N 99°10W **114** D5
Chilaw *Sri Lanka* 7°30N 79°50E **84** R11
Childress *U.S.A.* 34°25N 100°13W **110** D6
Chile ■ *S. Amer.* 35°0S 72°0W **121** F2
Chilham *U.K.* 51°15N 0°59E **25** D10
Chililabombwe *Zambia* 12°18S 27°43E **97** G5
Chilka L. *India* 19°40N 85°25E **85** K14
Chillán *Chile* 36°40S 72°10W **121** F2
Chillicothe *Ill., U.S.A.* 40°55N 89°29W **112** E3
Chillicothe *Ohio, U.S.A.* 39°20N 82°59W **112** F6
Chilliwack *Canada* 49°10N 121°54W **108** E7
Chiloé, I. de *Chile* 42°30S 73°50W **121** G2
Chilpancingo *Mexico* 17°33N 99°30W **114** D5
Chiltern Hills *U.K.* 51°40N 0°53W **25** D7
Chilton *U.S.A.* 44°2N 88°10W **112** C3
Chilung *Taiwan* 25°3N 121°45E **79** F13
Chilwa, L. *Malawi* 15°15S 35°40E **97** H7
Chimborazo *Ecuador* 1°29S 78°55W **120** C2
Chimbote *Peru* 9°0S 78°35W **120** C2
Chin □ *Burma* 22°0N 93°0E **85** J18
Chin Hills *Burma* 22°30N 93°30E **85** H18
China ■ *Asia* 30°0N 110°0E **79** E11
China, Great Plain of *Asia* 35°0N 115°0E **72** C13
Chinandega *Nic.* 12°35N 87°12W **114** E7
Chincha Alta *Peru* 13°25S 76°7W **120** D2
Chindwin → *Burma* 21°26N 95°15E **85** J19
Chingola *Zambia* 12°31S 27°53E **97** G5
Chinhoyi *Zimbabwe* 17°20S 30°8E **97** H6
Chiniot *Pakistan* 31°45N 73°0E **84** D8
Chinon *France* 47°10N 0°15E **66** C4
Chióggia *Italy* 45°13N 12°17E **68** B5
Chipata *Zambia* 13°38S 32°28E **97** G6
Chipman *Canada* 46°6N 65°53W **113** B15
Chippenham *U.K.* 51°27N 2°6W **24** D4
Chippewa Falls *U.S.A.* 44°56N 91°24W **112** C2
Chipping Campden *U.K.* 52°3N 1°45W **24** B5
Chipping Norton *U.K.* 51°56N 1°32W **24** C5
Chipping Ongar *U.K.* 51°42N 0°15E **25** C9
Chipping Sodbury *U.K.* 51°33N 2°23W **24** C4
Chiquinquira *Colombia* 5°37N 73°50W **120** B2
Chirbury *U.K.* 52°35N 3°4W **23** G2
Chirchiq *Uzbekistan* 41°29N 69°35E **87** A12
Chiredzi *Zimbabwe* 21°0S 31°38E **97** J6
Chirnside *U.K.* 55°48N 2°12W **21** C11
Chisasibi *Canada* 53°50N 79°0W **109** D12
Chiseldon *U.K.* 51°31N 1°44W **24** C5
Chistopol *Russia* 55°25N 50°38E **70** C9
Chita *Russia* 52°0N 113°35E **79** A11
Chitral *Pakistan* 35°50N 71°56E **84** B7
Chittagong *Bangla.* 22°19N 91°48E **85** H17
Chittagong □ *Bangla.* 24°5N 91°0E **85** G17
Chitungwiza *Zimbabwe* 18°0S 31°6E **97** H6
Choiseul *St. Lucia* 13°47N 61°3W **115** f
Choiseul *Solomon Is.* 7°0S 156°40E **99** B10
Chōkai-San *Japan* 39°6N 140°3E **81** D7
Cholet *France* 47°4N 0°52W **66** C3
Chollerton *U.K.* 55°4N 2°7W **22** B4
Cholsey *U.K.* 51°35N 1°8W **24** C6
Choluteca *Honduras* 13°20N 87°14W **114** E7
Chon Buri *Thailand* 13°21N 101°1E **82** B2
Ch'ŏngjin *N. Korea* 41°47N 129°50E **79** C14
Chongqing *China* 29°35N 106°25E **78** F10
Chongqing Shi □ *China* 30°0N 108°0E **78** F10
Chonos, Arch. de los *Chile* 45°0S 75°0W **121** G2
Chorley *U.K.* 53°39N 2°38W **23** E3
Chorzów *Poland* 50°18N 18°57E **65** C10
Choybalsan *Mongolia* 48°4N 114°30E **79** B11
Christchurch *N.Z.* 43°33S 172°47E **99** J13
Christchurch *U.K.* 50°44N 1°47W **24** E5
Christmas I. *Ind. Oc.* 10°30S 105°40E **102** J2
Chubut → *Argentina* 43°20S 65°5W **121** G3
Chudleigh *U.K.* 50°36N 3°36W **27** F6
Chudskoye, L. *Russia* 58°13N 27°30E **70** C4
Chukchi Sea *Russia* 68°0N 175°0W **77** C19
Chukot Ra. *Russia* 68°0N 175°0E **77** C18
Chulmleigh *U.K.* 50°54N 3°51W **27** F6
Chuncheon *S. Korea* 37°58N 127°44E **79** D14
Chuquicamata *Chile* 22°15S 69°0W **121** E3
Chur *Switz.* 46°52N 9°32E **64** E5
Church Stretton *U.K.* 52°32N 2°48W **23** G3
Churchdown *U.K.* 51°52N 2°10W **24** C4
Churchill *Canada* 58°47N 94°11W **108** D10
Churchill → *Man., Canada* 58°47N 94°12W **108** D10
Churchill → *Nfld. & L., Canada* 53°19N 60°10W **109** D13
Churchill, C. *Canada* 58°46N 93°12W **108** D10
Churchill Falls *Canada* 53°36N 64°19W **109** D13

Churchill L. *Canada* 55°55N 108°20W **108** D9
Churchill Pk. *Canada* 58°10N 125°10W **108** D7
Churu *India* 28°20N 74°50E **84** E9
Chuska Mts. *U.S.A.* 36°15N 108°50W **110** C5
Chusovoy *Russia* 58°22N 57°50E **70** C10
Chuvashia □ *Russia* 55°30N 47°0E **70** C8
Cicero *U.S.A.* 41°51N 87°44W **112** E4
Ciechanów *Poland* 52°52N 20°38E **65** B11
Ciego de Ávila *Cuba* 21°50N 78°50W **115** C9
Cienfuegos *Cuba* 22°10N 80°30W **115** C8
Cilo Dağı *Turkey* 37°28N 43°55E **71** G7
Cimarron → *U.S.A.* 36°10N 96°16W **111** C7
Cincinnati *U.S.A.* 39°9N 84°27W **112** F5
Cinderford *U.K.* 51°49N 2°30W **24** C3
Cinto, Mte. *France* 42°24N 8°54E **66** E8
Circle *U.S.A.* 65°50N 144°4W **108** C5
Circleville *U.S.A.* 39°36N 82°57W **112** F6
Cirebon *Indonesia* 6°45S 108°32E **82** F3
Cirencester *U.K.* 51°43N 1°57W **24** C5
Ciudad Acuña *Mexico* 29°18N 100°55W **114** B4
Ciudad Bolívar *Venezuela* 8°5N 63°36W **120** B3
Ciudad del Carmen *Mexico* 18°38N 91°50W **114** D6
Ciudad Guayana *Venezuela* 8°0N 62°30W **120** B3
Ciudad Guzmán *Mexico* 19°41N 103°29W **114** D4
Ciudad Juárez *Mexico* 31°44N 106°29W **114** A3
Ciudad Madero *Mexico* 22°19N 97°50W **114** C5
Ciudad Mante *Mexico* 22°44N 98°59W **114** C5
Ciudad Obregón *Mexico* 27°29N 109°56W **114** B3
Ciudad Real *Spain* 38°59N 3°55W **67** C4
Ciudad Valles *Mexico* 21°59N 99°1W **114** C5
Ciudad Victoria *Mexico* 23°44N 99°8W **114** C5
Civitavécchia *Italy* 42°6N 11°48E **68** C4
Cizre *Turkey* 37°19N 42°10E **71** G7
Clackmannan *U.K.* 56°7N 3°45W **21** B8
Clacton-on-Sea *U.K.* 51°47N 1°11E **25** C11
Claire, L. *Canada* 58°35N 112°5W **108** D8
Clara *Ireland* 53°21N 7°37W **28** E6
Clare *U.K.* 52°4N 0°34E **25** B10
Clare □ *Ireland* 52°45N 9°0W **30** C4
Clare → *Ireland* 53°20N 9°2E **28** E3
Clare I. *Ireland* 53°49N 10°0W **28** D1
Claremont *U.S.A.* 43°23N 72°20W **113** D11
Clarence → *Australia* 29°25S 153°22E **98** F9
Clarence → *N.Z.* 42°10S 173°56E **99** K14
Clarence I. *Antarctica* 61°10S 54°0W **55** C18
Clarion Fracture Zone *Pac. Oc.* 20°0N 120°0W **104** H7
Clark Fork → *U.S.A.* 48°9N 116°15W **110** A3
Clarksburg *U.S.A.* 39°17N 80°30W **112** F7
Clarksdale *U.S.A.* 34°12N 90°35W **111** D8
Clarksville *U.S.A.* 36°32N 87°21W **111** C9
Claverley *U.K.* 52°32N 2°18W **23** G4
Clay Cross *U.K.* 53°10N 1°25W **23** F6
Claydon *U.K.* 52°7N 1°8E **25** B11
Clear, C. *Ireland* 51°25N 9°32W **30** E3
Clear I. *Ireland* 51°26N 9°30W **30** F4
Clearfield *U.S.A.* 41°2N 78°27W **112** E8
Clearwater *U.S.A.* 27°59N 82°48W **111** E10
Cleator Moor *U.K.* 54°32N 3°30W **22** C2
Clee Hills *U.K.* 52°26N 2°35W **23** H3
Cleethorpes *U.K.* 53°33N 0°3W **23** E8
Cleeve Cloud *U.K.* 51°56N 2°0W **24** C5
Clent Hills *U.K.* 52°25N 2°4W **24** B4
Cleobury Mortimer *U.K.* 52°22N 2°28W **23** H4
Clermont-Ferrand *France* 45°46N 3°4E **66** D5
Clevedon *U.K.* 51°26N 2°52W **24** D3
Cleveland *Miss., U.S.A.* 33°45N 90°43W **111** D8
Cleveland *Ohio, U.S.A.* 41°29N 81°41W **112** E7
Cleveland Hills *U.K.* 54°25N 1°11W **22** C6
Clew B. *Ireland* 53°50N 9°49W **28** D2
Cley *U.K.* 52°57N 1°2E **25** A11
Clifden *Ireland* 53°29N 10°1W **28** E1
Cliffe *U.K.* 51°28N 0°31E **25** D10
Clifford *U.K.* 52°7N 3°6W **24** B2
Clinton *Iowa, U.S.A.* 41°51N 90°12W **112** E2
Clinton *Okla., U.S.A.* 35°31N 98°58W **110** C7
Clinton Colden L. *Canada* 63°58N 107°27W **108** C9
Clipperton, I. *Pac. Oc.* 10°18N 109°13W **103** F17
Clipston *U.K.* 52°27N 0°58W **25** B7
Clitheroe *U.K.* 53°53N 2°22W **23** E4
Clogher Hd. *Ireland* 53°48N 6°14W **29** D9
Cloghran *Ireland* 53°27N 6°14W **31** B10
Clonakilty *Ireland* 51°37N 8°53W **30** E5
Clonakilty B. *Ireland* 51°35N 8°51W **30** E5
Cloncurry → *Australia* 18°37S 140°40E **98** E7
Clondalkin *Ireland* 53°19N 6°25N **31** B10
Clones *Ireland* 54°11N 7°15W **29** C7
Clonmel *Ireland* 52°21N 7°42W **31** D7
Clontarf *Ireland* 53°22N 6°11W **31** B10
Cloughton *U.K.* 54°20N 0°26W **22** C8
Clovelly *U.K.* 51°0N 4°25W **27** F5
Clovis *U.S.A.* 34°24N 103°12W **110** D6
Clowne *U.K.* 53°16N 1°17W **23** F6
Cluj-Napoca *Romania* 46°47N 23°38E **65** E12
Clun Forest *U.K.* 52°27N 3°7W **23** H2
Clunbury *U.K.* 52°25N 2°55W **23** H3
Clwyd → *U.K.* 53°19N 3°31W **26** A6
Clyde → *U.K.* 55°55N 4°30W **20** C6
Clyde, Firth of *U.K.* 55°22N 5°1W **20** D5
Clyde River *Canada* 70°30N 68°30W **109** B13
Clydebank *U.K.* 55°54N 4°23W **20** C7
Clydesdale *U.K.* 55°43N 3°51W **21** C8
Coalbrookdale *U.K.* 52°39N 2°30W **23** G4
Coalisland *U.K.* 54°33N 6°42W **29** B8
Coalville *U.K.* 52°44N 1°23W **23** G6
Coamo *Puerto Rico* 18°5N 66°22W **115** d
Coast Mts. *Canada* 55°0N 129°20W **108** D7
Coast Ranges *U.S.A.* 39°0N 123°0W **110** B2
Coatbridge *U.K.* 55°52N 4°6W **20** C7
Coaticook *Canada* 45°10N 71°46W **113** C12
Coats I. *Canada* 62°30N 83°0W **109** C11
Coats Land *Antarctica* 77°0S 25°0W **55** D1
Coatzacoalcos *Mexico* 18°7N 94°25W **114** D6
Cobán *Guatemala* 15°30N 90°21W **114** D6
Cobar *Australia* 31°27S 145°48E **98** G8
Cóbh *Ireland* 51°51N 8°17W **30** E6
Cobija *Bolivia* 11°0S 68°50W **120** D3
Cobourg *Canada* 43°58N 78°10W **112** D8
Cochabamba *Bolivia* 17°26S 66°10W **120** D3
Cochin *India* 9°58N 76°20E **84** Q10
Cochrane *Canada* 49°0N 81°0W **109** E11
Cockburn, Canal *Chile* 54°30S 72°0W **121** H2
Cockburn I. *Canada* 45°55N 83°22W **112** C6

Cockburn Town *Bahamas* 24°2N 74°31W **115** C10
Cockerham *U.K.* 53°58N 2°49W **23** E3
Cockermouth *U.K.* 54°40N 3°22W **22** C2
Cockfield *U.K.* 52°10N 0°48E **25** B10
Cockpit Country, The *Jamaica* 18°15N 77°45W **114** a
Coco → *Cent. Amer.* 15°0N 83°8W **115** E8
Coco, I. del *Pac. Oc.* 5°25N 87°55W **114** F7
Cod, C. *U.S.A.* 42°5N 70°10W **113** D12
Coddenham *U.K.* 52°9N 1°8E **25** B11
Codó *Brazil* 4°30S 43°55W **120** C5
Cody *U.S.A.* 44°32N 109°3W **110** B5
Coeur d'Alene *U.S.A.* 47°41N 116°46W **110** A3
Coggeshall *U.K.* 51°52N 0°42E **25** C10
Cognac *France* 45°41N 0°20W **66** D3
Coigach *U.K.* 57°59N 5°14W **18** G7
Coigach, Rubha *U.K.* 58°6N 5°26W **18** F7
Coimbatore *India* 11°2N 76°59E **84** P10
Coimbra *Portugal* 40°15N 8°27W **67** B1
Colatina *Brazil* 19°32S 40°37W **122** C2
Colchester *U.K.* 51°54N 0°55E **25** C10
Cold Fell *U.K.* 54°53N 2°36W **22** C3
Coldstream *U.K.* 55°39N 2°15W **21** C11
Colebrook *U.S.A.* 44°54N 71°30W **113** C12
Colebrooke *U.K.* 50°47N 3°44W **27** F6
Coleford *U.K.* 51°47N 2°36W **24** C3
Coleraine *U.K.* 55°8N 6°41W **29** A8
Coleshill *U.K.* 52°30N 1°41W **23** G5
Colgrave Sd. *U.K.* 60°36N 0°58N **18** A16
Colima *Mexico* 19°14N 103°43W **114** D4
Colima, Nevado de *Mexico* 19°33N 103°38W **114** D4
Coll *U.K.* 56°39N 6°34W **20** J4
Collier Law *U.K.* 54°47N 1°59W **22** C5
Collin *U.K.* 55°4N 3°31W **21** D8
Collingbourne Kingston *U.K.* 51°18N 1°40W **24** D5
Collingham *U.K.* 53°8N 0°46W **23** F7
Collingwood *Canada* 44°29N 80°13W **112** C7
Collooney *Ireland* 54°11N 8°29W **28** C5
Colmar *France* 48°5N 7°20E **66** B7
Colne *U.K.* 53°51N 2°9W **23** E4
Colne → *Bucks., U.K.* 51°27N 0°32W **25** D7
Colne → *Essex, U.K.* 51°51N 0°58E **25** C10
Cologne *Germany* 50°56N 6°57E **64** C4
Colombia ■ *S. Amer.* 3°45N 73°0W **120** B2
Colombian Basin *Caribbean* 14°0N 76°0W **104** H12
Colombo *Sri Lanka* 6°56N 79°58E **84** R11
Colonsay *U.K.* 56°5N 6°12W **20** B3
Colorado □ *U.S.A.* 39°30N 105°30W **110** C5
Colorado → *Argentina* 39°50S 62°8W **121** F3
Colorado → *N. Amer.* 31°45N 114°40W **110** D4
Colorado → *U.S.A.* 28°36N 95°59W **111** E7
Colorado Plateau *U.S.A.* 37°0N 111°0W **110** C4
Colorado Springs *U.S.A.* 38°50N 104°49W **110** C6
Colsterworth *U.K.* 52°49N 0°37W **23** G7
Coltishall *U.K.* 52°44N 1°21E **25** A11
Columbia *Mo., U.S.A.* 38°57N 92°20W **111** C81
Columbia *S.C., U.S.A.* 34°0N 81°2W **111** D10
Columbia *Tenn., U.S.A.* 35°37N 87°2W **111** C9
Columbia → *N. Amer.* 46°15N 124°5W **110** A2
Columbia, C. *Canada* 83°6N 69°57W **104** A4
Columbia, District of □ *U.S.A.* 38°55N 77°0W **112** F9
Columbia Plateau *U.S.A.* 44°0N 117°30W **110** B3
Columbus *Ga., U.S.A.* 32°28N 84°59W **111** D10
Columbus *Ind., U.S.A.* 39°13N 85°55W **112** F5
Columbus *Miss., U.S.A.* 33°30N 88°25W **111** D9
Columbus *Nebr., U.S.A.* 41°26N 97°22W **111** B7
Columbus *Ohio, U.S.A.* 39°58N 83°0W **112** F6
Colville → *U.S.A.* 70°25N 150°30W **108** B4
Colwell *U.K.* 55°5N 2°4W **22** B4
Colwich *U.K.* 52°48N 1°58W **23** G5
Colwyn Bay *U.K.* 53°18N 3°44W **26** A6
Colyton *U.K.* 50°44N 3°5W **27** F7
Comayagua *Honduras* 14°25N 87°37W **114** E7
Combe Martin *U.K.* 51°12N 4°3W **27** E5
Comber *U.K.* 54°33N 5°45W **29** B10
Comeragh Mts. *Ireland* 52°18N 7°34W **31** D7
Comilla *Bangla.* 23°28N 91°10E **85** H17
Comitán *Mexico* 16°15N 92°8W **114** D6
Committee B. *Canada* 68°30N 86°30W **109** C11
Como *Italy* 45°47N 9°5E **68** B3
Como, Lago di *Italy* 46°0N 9°11E **68** B3
Comodoro Rivadavia *Argentina* 45°50S 67°40W **121** G3
Comoros ■ *Ind. Oc.* 12°10S 44°15E **91** H8
Compass Mt. *S. Africa* 31°45S 24°32E **90** K6
Compiègne *France* 49°24N 2°50E **66** B5
Conakry *Guinea* 9°29N 13°49W **94** G3
Conceição da Barra *Brazil* 18°35S 39°45W **122** C3
Concepción *Chile* 36°50S 73°0W **121** F2
Concepción *Paraguay* 23°22S 57°26W **121** E4
Concepción, Est. de *Chile* 50°30N 74°55W **121** H2
Concepción del Oro *Mexico* 24°38N 101°25W **114** C4
Concepción del Uruguay *Argentina* 32°35S 58°20W **121** F4
Conception, Pt. *U.S.A.* 34°27N 120°28W **110** D2
Conchos → *Mexico* 29°35N 104°25W **114** B4
Concord *Calif., U.S.A.* 37°59N 122°2W **110** C2
Concord *N.H., U.S.A.* 43°12N 71°32W **113** D12
Concordia *Argentina* 31°20S 58°2W **121** F4
Concordia *U.S.A.* 39°34N 97°40W **110** C7
Condeúba *Brazil* 14°52S 42°0W **122** D2
Condover *U.K.* 52°39N 2°44W **23** G3
Congleton *U.K.* 53°10N 2°13W **23** F4
Congo → *Africa* 1°0S 16°0E **96** E3
Congo → *Africa* 6°4S 12°24E **96** F2
Congo, Dem. Rep. of the ■ *Africa* 3°0S 23°0E **96** E4
Congo Basin *Africa* 0°10S 24°30E **96** E4
Congresbury *U.K.* 51°22N 2°48W **24** D3
Coningsby *U.K.* 53°7N 0°10W **23** F8
Conisbrough *U.K.* 53°29N 1°14W **23** F6
Coniston *Canada* 46°29N 80°51W **112** B7
Coniston *U.K.* 54°22N 3°5W **22** C2
Coniston Water *U.K.* 54°20N 3°5W **22** C2
Conn, L. *Ireland* 54°3N 9°15W **28** C3
Connacht □ *Ireland* 53°43N 9°12W **28** D3
Connah's Quay *U.K.* 53°13N 3°4W **26** A7
Conneaut *U.S.A.* 41°57N 80°34W **112** E7
Connecticut □ *U.S.A.* 41°30N 72°45W **113** E11
Connecticut → *U.S.A.* 41°16N 72°20W **113** E11

Connellsville *U.S.A.* 40°1N 79°35W **112** E8
Connemara *Ireland* 53°29N 9°45W **28** D2
Connemara △ *Ireland* 53°32N 9°52W **28** D2
Connersville *U.S.A.* 39°39N 85°8W **112** F5
Conselheiro Lafaiete *Brazil* 20°40S 43°48W **122** D2
Consett *U.K.* 54°51N 1°50W **22** C5
Constance, L. *Europe* 47°35N 9°25E **64** E5
Constanța *Romania* 44°14N 28°38E **65** F15
Constantine *Algeria* 36°25N 6°42E **94** A7
Constitución *Chile* 35°20S 72°30W **121** F2
Contagem *Brazil* 19°56S 44°3W **122** C2
Contas → *Brazil* 14°17S 39°1W **122** B3
Contwoyto L. *Canada* 65°42N 110°50W **108** C8
Conway *Ark., U.S.A.* 35°5N 92°26W **111** C8
Conway *N.H., U.S.A.* 43°59N 71°7W **113** D12
Conwy *U.K.* 53°17N 3°50W **26** A6
Conwy □ *U.K.* 53°10N 3°44W **26** A6
Conwy → *U.K.* 53°17N 3°50W **26** A6
Coober Pedy *Australia* 29°1S 134°43E **98** F6
Cook Inlet *U.S.A.* 60°0N 152°0W **108** D4
Cook Is. *Pac. Oc.* 17°0S 160°0W **103** J12
Cook Strait *N.Z.* 41°15S 174°29E **99** J13
Cookstown *U.K.* 54°39N 6°45W **29** B8
Cooktown *Australia* 15°30S 145°16E **98** D8
Coondapoor *India* 13°42N 74°40E **84** N9
Coos Bay *U.S.A.* 43°22N 124°13W **110** B2
Cootehill *Ireland* 54°4N 7°5W **29** C7
Copenhagen *Denmark* 55°40N 12°26E **63** F6
Copiapó *Chile* 27°30S 70°20W **121** E2
Copper Harbor *U.S.A.* 47°28N 87°53W **112** B4
Coppermine → *Canada* 67°49N 116°4W **108** C8
Coquet → *U.K.* 55°20N 1°32W **22** B5
Coquet I. *U.K.* 55°20N 1°36W **22** B5
Coquimbo *Chile* 30°0S 71°20W **121** E2
Coracora *Peru* 15°5S 73°45W **120** D2
Coral Harbour *Canada* 64°8N 83°10W **109** C11
Coral Sea *Pac. Oc.* 15°0S 150°0E **98** C9
Corbin *U.S.A.* 36°57N 84°6W **112** G5
Corbridge *U.K.* 54°58N 2°0W **22** C5
Corby *U.K.* 52°30N 0°41W **25** A7
Corby Glen *U.K.* 52°49N 0°30W **23** G7
Cordele *U.S.A.* 31°58N 83°47W **111** D10
Córdoba *Argentina* 31°20S 64°10W **121** F3
Córdoba *Mexico* 18°53N 96°56W **114** D5
Córdoba *Spain* 37°50N 4°50W **67** D3
Córdoba, Sierra de *Argentina* 31°10S 64°25W **121** F3
Cordova *U.S.A.* 60°33N 145°45W **108** C5
Corfe Castle *U.K.* 50°38N 2°3W **24** E4
Corfe Mullen *U.K.* 50°46N 2°1W **24** E4
Corfu *Greece* 39°38N 19°50E **69** E8
Corinth *Greece* 37°56N 22°55E **69** F10
Corinth *U.S.A.* 34°56N 88°31W **111** D9
Corinth, G. of *Greece* 38°16N 22°30E **69** E10
Corinto *Brazil* 18°20S 44°30W **122** C2
Cork *Ireland* 51°54N 8°29W **30** E6
Cork □ *Ireland* 51°57N 8°40W **30** E5
Cork Harbour *Ireland* 51°47N 8°16W **30** E6
Corner Brook *Canada* 48°57N 57°58W **109** E14
Corning *U.S.A.* 42°9N 77°3W **112** D9
Cornwall *Canada* 45°2N 74°44W **113** C10
Cornwall □ *U.K.* 50°26N 4°40W **27** G2
Cornwall, C. *U.K.* 50°8N 5°43W **27** G2
Cornwall I. *Canada* 77°37N 94°38W **109** B10
Cornwallis I. *Canada* 75°8N 95°0W **109** B10
Coro *Venezuela* 11°25N 69°41W **120** A3
Corocoro *Bolivia* 17°15S 68°28W **120** D3
Coromandel Coast *India* 12°30N 81°0E **84** N12
Coronation Gulf *Canada* 68°25N 110°0W **108** B8
Coronel *Chile* 37°0S 73°10W **121** F2
Coronel Fabriciano *Brazil* 19°31S 42°38W **122** C2
Coronel Pringles *Argentina* 38°0S 61°30W **121** F3
Coronel Suárez *Argentina* 37°30S 61°52W **121** F3
Coropuna, Nevado *Peru* 15°30S 72°41W **120** D2
Corpus Christi *U.S.A.* 27°47N 97°24W **110** E7
Corraun Pen. *Ireland* 53°54N 9°54W **28** D2
Corrib, L. *Ireland* 53°27N 9°16W **30** B4
Corrientes *Argentina* 27°30S 58°45W **121** E4
Corrientes, C. *Colombia* 5°30N 77°34W **120** B2
Corrientes, C. *Mexico* 20°25N 105°42W **114** C3
Corringham *U.K.* 53°25N 0°41W **23** F7
Corry *U.S.A.* 41°55N 79°39W **112** E8
Corse, C. *France* 43°1N 9°25E **66** E8
Corsham *U.K.* 51°27N 2°10W **24** D4
Corsica □ *France* 42°0N 9°0E **66** F8
Corsicana *U.S.A.* 32°6N 96°28W **111** D7
Corsley *U.K.* 51°13N 2°14W **24** D4
Corte *France* 42°19N 9°11E **66** E8
Cortez *U.S.A.* 37°21N 108°35W **110** C5
Cortland *U.S.A.* 42°36N 76°11W **113** D9
Corton *U.K.* 52°31N 1°45E **25** A12
Çorum *Turkey* 40°30N 34°57E **71** F5
Corumbá *Brazil* 19°0S 57°30W **120** D4
Corunna = La Coruña *Spain* 43°20N 8°25W **67** A1
Corvallis *U.S.A.* 44°34N 123°16W **110** B2
Corve → *U.K.* 52°22N 2°43W **23** H3
Coseley *U.K.* 52°33N 2°9W **23** G4
Cosenza *Italy* 39°18N 16°15E **68** E7
Cosham *U.K.* 50°51N 1°2W **24** E6
Coshocton *U.S.A.* 40°16N 81°51W **112** E7
Costa Blanca *Spain* 38°25N 0°10W **67** C5
Costa Brava *Spain* 41°30N 3°0E **67** B7
Costa Cálida *Spain* 37°30N 1°30W **67** D5
Costa Daurada *Spain* 41°12N 1°15E **67** B6
Costa de la Luz *Spain* 36°15N 5°58W **67** D2
Costa del Azahar *Spain* 39°39N 0°13W **67** B6
Costa del Sol *Spain* 36°30N 4°30W **67** D3
Costa Rica ■ *Cent. Amer.* 10°0N 84°0W **115** F8
Costa Verde *Spain* 43°22N 4°14W **67** A3
Costessey *U.K.* 52°40N 1°13E **25** A11
Cotabato *Phil.* 7°14N 124°15E **83** C6
Côte d'Azur *France* 43°25N 7°10E **66** E7
Côte-d'Ivoire = Ivory Coast ■ *Africa* 7°30N 5°0W **94** G4
Coteau du Missouri *U.S.A.* 47°0N 100°0W **110** A6
Cotentin *France* 49°15N 1°30W **66** B3
Cotherstone *U.K.* 54°35N 1°59W **22** C5
Cotonou *Benin* 6°20N 2°25E **94** G6
Cotopaxi *Ecuador* 0°40S 78°30W **120** C2

Cotswold Hills *U.K.* 51°42N 2°10W **24** C4
Cottbus *Germany* 51°45N 14°20E **64** C8
Cottenham *U.K.* 52°18N 0°9E **25** B9
Coudersport *U.S.A.* 41°46N 78°1W **112** E8
Council Bluffs *U.S.A.* 41°16N 95°52W **111** B7
Courantyne → *S. Amer.* 5°55N 57°5W **120** B4
Courtenay *Canada* 49°45N 125°0W **108** E7
Cove *U.K.* 56°0N 4°51W **20** B6
Coventry *U.K.* 52°25N 1°28W **24** B6
Cover → *U.K.* 54°17N 1°47W **22** D5
Coverack *U.K.* 50°1N 5°7W **27** G3
Covington *U.S.A.* 39°5N 84°30W **112** F5
Cowal *U.K.* 56°5N 5°8W **20** B5
Cowbridge *U.K.* 51°27N 3°27W **27** E7
Cowdenbeath *U.K.* 56°7N 3°21W **21** B9
Cowes *U.K.* 50°45N 1°18W **24** E6
Cowfold *U.K.* 50°59N 0°16W **25** E8
Cowpen *U.K.* 55°8N 1°32W **22** B5
Cox's Bazar *Bangla.* 21°26N 91°59E **85** J17
Cozumel, Isla *Mexico* 20°30N 86°40W **114** C7
Crab Hill *Barbados* 13°19N 59°38W **115** g
Cradock *S. Africa* 32°8S 25°36E **97** L5
Craig *U.S.A.* 40°31N 107°33W **110** B5
Craigavon *U.K.* 54°27N 6°23W **29** C9
Crail *U.K.* 56°16N 2°37W **21** B10
Craiova *Romania* 44°21N 23°48E **65** F12
Cramlington *U.K.* 55°6N 1°34W **22** B5
Cranborne *U.K.* 50°55N 1°54W **24** E5
Cranborne Chase *U.K.* 50°56N 2°6W **24** E4
Cranbrook *Canada* 49°30N 115°46W **108** E8
Cranbrook *U.K.* 51°6N 0°34E **25** D10
Crandon *U.S.A.* 45°34N 88°54W **112** C3
Crane, The *Barbados* 13°6N 59°27W **115** g
Cranleigh *U.K.* 51°8N 0°28W **25** D8
Cranwell *U.K.* 53°3N 0°27W **23** F8
Crateús *Brazil* 5°10S 40°39W **120** C5
Crato *Brazil* 7°10S 39°25W **120** C6
Craven Arms *U.K.* 52°26N 2°50W **23** H3
Crawfordsville *U.S.A.* 40°2N 86°54W **112** E4
Crawley *U.K.* 51°7N 0°11W **25** D8
Credenhill *U.K.* 52°5N 2°48W **24** B3
Crediton *U.K.* 50°47N 3°40W **27** F6
Cree → *Canada* 58°57N 105°47W **108** D9
Cree → *U.K.* 54°55N 4°25W **20** E7
Cree L. *Canada* 57°30N 106°30W **108** D9
Cremona *Italy* 45°7N 10°2E **68** B4
Cres *Croatia* 44°58N 14°25E **68** B6
Crete *Greece* 35°15N 25°0E **69** G11
Créteil *France* 48°47N 2°27E **66** B5
Creuse → *France* 47°0N 0°34E **66** C4
Crewe *U.K.* 53°6N 2°26W **23** F4
Crewkerne *U.K.* 50°53N 2°48W **24** E3
Crianlarich *U.K.* 56°24N 4°37W **20** B6
Criccieth *U.K.* 52°55N 4°13W **26** B5
Crick *U.K.* 52°22N 1°8W **24** B6
Crickhowell *U.K.* 51°52N 3°8W **26** D7
Cricklade *U.K.* 51°38N 1°50W **24** C5
Crieff *U.K.* 56°22N 3°50W **21** B8
Criffell *U.K.* 54°56N 3°39W **21** E8
Crimea □ *Ukraine* 45°30N 33°10E **71** E5
Crimean Pen. *Ukraine* 45°0N 34°0E **71** F5
Crișul Alb → *Romania* 46°42N 21°17E **65** E11
Crișul Negru → *Romania* 46°42N 21°16E **65** E11
Croagh Patrick *Ireland* 53°46N 9°40W **28** D2
Croatia ■ *Europe* 45°20N 16°0E **68** B7
Croglin *U.K.* 54°50N 2°39W **22** C3
Crohy Hd. *Ireland* 54°55N 8°26W **28** B5
Croker, C. *Australia* 10°58S 132°35E **98** C5
Cromarty *U.K.* 57°40N 4°2W **19** G9
Cromarty Firth *U.K.* 57°40N 4°15W **19** G9
Cromdale, Hills of *U.K.* 57°20N 3°28W **19** H11
Cromer *U.K.* 52°56N 1°17E **25** A11
Crondall *U.K.* 51°14N 0°51W **25** D7
Crook *U.K.* 54°43N 1°45W **22** C5
Crooked I. *Bahamas* 22°50N 74°10W **115** C10
Crooklands *U.K.* 54°16N 2°42W **22** D3
Crosby *Cumb., U.K.* 54°45N 3°25W **22** C2
Crosby *Mersey., U.K.* 53°30N 3°3W **23** F2
Crosby Ravensworth *U.K.* 54°33N 2°35W **22** C4
Cross Fell *U.K.* 54°43N 2°28W **22** C4
Cross Sound *U.S.A.* 58°0N 135°0W **108** D6
Crosshaven *Ireland* 51°47N 8°17W **30** E6
Crossmaglen *U.K.* 54°5N 6°36W **29** C8
Crotone *Italy* 39°5N 17°8E **68** E7
Crouch → *U.K.* 51°37N 0°53E **25** C10
Crow Hd. *Ireland* 51°35N 10°9W **30** E2
Crow Sound *U.K.* 49°56N 6°16W **27** H1
Crowborough *U.K.* 51°3N 0°11E **25** D9
Crowland *U.K.* 52°41N 0°10W **23** G8
Crowle *U.K.* 53°36N 0°49W **23** E7
Crowsnest Pass *Canada* 49°40N 114°40W **108** E8
Croyde *U.K.* 51°7N 4°14W **27** E5
Croydon □ *U.K.* 51°22N 0°5W **25** D8
Crozet, Is. *Ind. Oc.* 46°27S 52°0E **53** G12
Cruden Bay *U.K.* 57°25N 1°52W **19** H14
Crudgington *U.K.* 52°46N 2°32W **23** G3
Crummock Water *U.K.* 54°33N 3°18W **22** C2
Cruz Bay *U.S. Virgin Is.* 18°20N 64°48W **115** e
Cruz das Almas *Brazil* 12°0S 39°6W **122** D3
Cruzeiro *Brazil* 22°33S 45°0W **122** D1
Cruzeiro do Sul *Brazil* 7°35S 72°35W **120** C3
Crystal Falls *U.S.A.* 46°5N 88°20W **112** B3
Cuando → *Angola* 17°30S 23°15E **97** H4
Cuango = Kwango → *Dem. Rep. of the Congo* 3°14S 17°22E **96** E3
Cuanza → *Angola* 9°21S 13°9E **96** F2
Cuauhtémoc *Mexico* 28°25N 106°52W **114** B3
Cuba ■ *W. Indies* 22°0N 79°0W **115** C9
Cubango → *Africa* 18°50S 22°25E **97** H4
Cuckfield *U.K.* 51°1N 0°8W **25** D8
Cúcuta *Colombia* 7°54N 72°31W **120** B2
Cuddalore *India* 11°46N 79°45E **84** P11
Cuenca *Ecuador* 2°50S 79°9W **120** C2
Cuenca *Spain* 40°5N 2°10W **67** B4
Cuernavaca *Mexico* 18°55N 99°15W **114** D5
Cuiabá *Brazil* 15°30S 56°0W **120** D4
Cuillin Hills *U.K.* 57°13N 6°15W **18** H5
Cuillin Sd. *U.K.* 57°4N 6°20W **18** H5
Cuito → *Angola* 18°1S 20°48E **97** H4
Culebra *Puerto Rico* 18°19N 65°18W **115** d

Culiacán Mexico 24°50N 107°23W 114 C3
Cullen U.K. 57°42N 2°49W 19 G12
Cullompton U.K. 50°51N 3°24W 27 F7
Culm → U.K. 50°46N 3°31W 27 F6
Culpeper U.S.A. 38°30N 78°0W 112 F7
Cumaná Venezuela 10°30N 64°5W 120 A3
Cumberland U.S.A. 39°39N 78°46W 112 F8
Cumberland ☐ U.K. 37°9N 88°25W 111 C9
Cumberland Pen. Canada 67°0N 64°0W 109 C13
Cumberland Plateau U.S.A. 36°0N 85°0W 111 C10
Cumberland Sd. Canada 65°30N 66°0W 109 C13
Cumbernauld U.K. 55°57N 3°58W 21 C8
Cumbrae Is. U.K. 55°46N 4°54W 20 C6
Cumbria ☐ U.K. 54°42N 2°52W 22 C3
Cumbrian Mts. U.K. 54°30N 3°0W 22 D2
Cummertrees U.K. 54°59N 3°20W 21 E9
Cumnock U.K. 55°28N 4°17W 20 D7
Cumnor U.K. 51°44N 1°19W 24 C6
Cumwhinton U.K. 54°52N 2°50W 22 C3
Cunene → Angola 17°20S 11°50E 97 H2
Cúneo Italy 44°23N 7°32E 68 B2
Cunnamulla Australia 28°2S 145°38E 98 F8
Cunninghame U.K. 55°38N 4°35W 20 C6
Cupar U.K. 56°19N 3°1W 21 B9
Curaçao Neth. Ant. 12°10N 69°0W 115 E11
Curicó Chile 34°55S 71°20W 121 F2
Curitiba Brazil 25°20S 49°10W 122 E1
Curlew Mts. Ireland 54°0N 8°20W 28 D5
Curry Rivel U.K. 51°1N 2°52W 24 D3
Curvelo Brazil 18°45S 44°27W 122 C2
Cuttack India 20°25N 85°57E 85 J14
Cuxhaven Germany 53°51N 8°41E 64 B5
Cuyahoga Falls U.S.A. 41°8N 81°29W 112 E7
Cuyuni → Guyana 6°23N 58°41W 120 B4
Cuzco Peru 13°32S 72°0W 120 D2
Cwmbran U.K. 51°39N 3°2W 26 D7
Cyclades Greece 37°0N 24°30E 69 F11
Cynthiana U.S.A. 38°23N 84°18W 112 F5
Cyprus ■ Asia 35°0N 33°0E 86 C3
Cyrenaica Libya 27°0N 23°0E 95 C10
Czech Rep. ■ Europe 50°0N 15°0E 64 D8
Częstochowa Poland 50°49N 19°7E 65 C10

D
Da Lat Vietnam 11°56N 108°25E 82 B3
Da Nang Vietnam 16°4N 108°13E 82 A3
Da Qaidam China 37°50N 95°15E 78 D8
Da Yunhe → China 34°25N 120°5E 79 E12
Daba Shan China 32°0N 109°0E 79 E10
Dabie Shan China 31°20N 115°20E 79 E12
Dadra & Nagar Haveli ☐ India 20°5N 73°0E 84 J8
Dadu Pakistan 26°45N 67°45E 84 F5
Daegu S. Korea 35°50N 128°37E 79 D14
Daejeon S. Korea 36°20N 127°28E 79 D14
Dagestan ☐ Russia 42°30N 47°0E 71 F8
Dagupan Phil. 16°3N 120°20E 83 A6
Dahod India 22°50N 74°15E 84 H9
Dahongliutan China 35°45N 79°20E 78 D4
Daingean Ireland 53°18N 7°17W 31 B8
Dajarra Australia 21°42S 139°30E 98 E6
Dakar Senegal 14°34N 17°29W 94 F2
Dakhla W. Sahara 23°50N 15°53W 94 D2
Dakhla, El Wâhât el Egypt 25°30N 28°50E 95 C11
Dalandzadgad Mongolia 43°27N 104°30E 78 C9
Dalbeattie U.K. 54°56N 3°50W 21 E8
Dalhart U.S.A. 36°4N 102°31W 110 C6
Dalhousie Canada 48°5N 66°26W 113 A14
Dali China 25°40N 100°10E 78 F9
Dalian China 38°50N 121°40E 79 D13
Daliang Shan China 28°0N 102°45E 78 F9
Dalkeith U.K. 55°54N 3°4W 21 C9
Dalkey Ireland 53°16N 6°6W 31 B10
Dallas U.S.A. 32°47N 96°48W 111 E7
Dalles, The U.S.A. 45°36N 121°10W 110 A2
Dalmatia Croatia 43°20N 17°0E 68 C7
Dalmellington U.K. 55°19N 4°23W 20 D7
Daloa Ivory C. 7°0N 6°30W 94 G4
Dalry U.K. 55°42N 4°43W 20 C6
Dalrymple, L. Australia 20°40S 147°0E 98 E8
Dalton Dumf. & Gall., U.K. 55°4N 3°24W 21 D9
Dalton N. Yorks., U.K. 54°28N 1°32W 22 D5
Dalton-in-Furness U.K. 54°10N 3°11W 22 D2
Daly Waters Australia 16°15S 133°24E 98 D5
Daman India 20°25N 72°57E 84 J8
Damanhûr Egypt 31°0N 30°30E 95 B12
Damaraland Namibia 20°0S 15°0E 97 H2
Damascus Syria 33°30N 36°18E 86 C4
Damerham U.K. 50°56N 1°51W 24 E5
Dampier Australia 20°41S 116°42E 98 E2
Danakil Desert Ethiopia 12°45N 41°0E 89 E3
Danbury U.S.A. 41°24N 73°28W 113 E11
Dandong China 40°10N 124°20E 79 C13
Danube → Europe 45°20N 29°40E 65 F15
Danville Ill., U.S.A. 40°8N 87°37W 112 E4
Danville Ky., U.S.A. 37°39N 84°46W 112 G5
Danville Va., U.S.A. 36°36N 79°23W 111 C11
Daqing China 46°35N 125°0E 79 B13
Dar Banda Africa 8°0N 23°0E 90 F6
Dar es Salaam Tanzania 6°50S 39°12E 96 F7
Darbhanga India 26°15N 85°55E 85 F14
Dardanelles Turkey 40°17N 26°32E 69 D12
Darent → U.K. 51°28N 0°14E 25 D9
Dârfûr Sudan 13°40N 24°0E 95 F10
Darhan Mongolia 49°37N 106°21E 78 B10
Darién, G. del Colombia 9°0N 77°0W 120 B2
Darjiling India 27°3N 88°18E 85 F16
Darling → Australia 34°4S 141°54E 98 G7
Darling Ra. Australia 32°30S 116°20E 98 G2
Darlington U.K. 54°32N 1°33W 22 C5
Darmstadt Germany 49°51N 8°39E 64 D5
Darnah Libya 32°45N 22°45E 95 B10
Darnley, C. Antarctica 68°0S 69°0E 55 C6
Darnley B. Canada 69°30N 123°30W 108 C7
Dart → U.K. 50°24N 3°39W 27 G6
Dartford U.K. 51°26N 0°13E 25 D9
Dartington U.K. 50°27N 3°43W 27 G6
Dartmoor U.K. 50°38N 3°57W 27 F6
Dartmoor △ U.K. 50°37N 3°59W 27 F6
Dartmouth Canada 44°40N 63°30W 113 C16

Dartmouth U.K. 50°21N 3°36W 27 G6
Darton U.K. 53°35N 1°31W 23 E5
Darwen U.K. 53°42N 2°29W 23 E4
Darwin Australia 12°25S 130°51E 98 C5
Dashen, Ras Ethiopia 13°8N 38°26E 89 E2
Dashoguz Turkmenistan 41°49N 59°58E 87 A9
Dasht → Pakistan 25°10N 61°40E 84 G2
Datong China 40°6N 113°18E 79 C11
Daugava → Latvia 57°4N 24°3E 63 F9
Daugavpils Latvia 55°53N 26°32E 63 F9
Dauphin Canada 51°9N 100°5W 108 D9
Dauphiné France 45°15N 5°25E 66 D6
Davangere India 14°25N 75°55E 84 M9
Davao Phil. 7°0N 125°40E 83 C7
Davenport U.S.A. 41°32N 90°35W 112 E2
Daventry U.K. 52°16N 1°10W 24 B6
David Panama 8°30N 82°30W 115 F8
Davis Str. N. Amer. 65°0N 58°0W 104 C14
Dawlish U.K. 50°35N 3°28W 27 F7
Dawna Ra. Burma 16°30N 98°30E 85 L21
Dawros Hd. Ireland 54°50N 8°33W 28 B4
Dawson City Canada 64°10N 139°30W 108 C6
Dawson Creek Canada 55°45N 120°15W 108 D7
Dax France 43°44N 1°3W 66 E3
Daxian China 31°15N 107°23E 78 E10
Daxue Shan China 30°30N 101°30E 78 E9
Dayr az Zawr Syria 35°20N 40°5E 86 C5
Dayton U.S.A. 39°45N 84°12W 112 F5
Daytona Beach U.S.A. 29°13N 81°1W 111 E10
De Aar S. Africa 30°39S 24°0E 97 L4
De Pere U.S.A. 44°27N 88°4W 112 D3
Dead Sea Asia 31°30N 35°30E 86 D3
Deal U.K. 51°13N 1°25E 25 D11
Dean, Forest of U.K. 51°45N 2°33W 24 C3
Dearham U.K. 54°44N 3°25W 22 C2
Dease → Canada 59°56N 128°32W 108 D7
Dease Lake Canada 58°25N 130°6W 108 D6
Death Valley U.S.A. 36°15N 116°50W 110 C3
Deben → U.K. 52°0N 1°25E 25 B11
Debenham U.K. 52°14N 1°12E 25 B11
Debre Markos Ethiopia 10°20N 37°40E 89 E2
Debre Tabor Ethiopia 11°50N 38°26E 89 E2
Debrecen Hungary 47°33N 21°42E 65 E11
Decatur Ala., U.S.A. 34°36N 86°59W 111 D9
Decatur Ill., U.S.A. 39°51N 88°57W 112 F3
Decatur Ind., U.S.A. 40°50N 84°56W 112 E5
Deccan India 18°0N 79°0E 84 L11
Deddington U.K. 51°59N 1°18W 24 C6
Dee → Aberds., U.K. 57°9N 2°5W 19 H13
Dee → Dumf. & Gall., U.K. 54°51N 4°3W 20 E7
Dee → Wales, U.K. 53°22N 3°17W 26 A7
Deeping Fen U.K. 52°45N 0°15W 23 G8
Deeping St. Nicholas U.K. 52°44N 0°12W 23 G8
Deer Lake Canada 49°11N 57°27W 109 E14
Defiance U.S.A. 41°17N 84°22W 112 E5
Dehra Dun India 30°20N 78°4E 84 D11
DeKalb U.S.A. 41°56N 88°46W 112 E3
Del Rio U.S.A. 29°22N 100°54W 110 E6
Delabole U.K. 50°37N 4°46W 27 F4
Delaware U.S.A. 40°18N 83°4W 112 E6
Delaware ☐ U.S.A. 39°0N 75°20W 113 F10
Delaware → U.S.A. 39°15N 75°20W 113 F10
Delaware B. U.S.A. 39°0N 75°10W 111 C12
Delgado, C. Mozam. 10°45S 40°40E 96 G8
Delhi India 28°39N 77°13E 84 E10
Delice Turkey 39°54N 34°2E 71 G5
Delicias Mexico 28°13N 105°28W 114 B3
Déline Canada 65°11N 123°25W 108 C7
Delphos U.S.A. 40°51N 84°21W 112 E5
Delta Junction U.S.A. 64°2N 145°44W 108 C5
Demanda, Sierra de la Spain 42°15N 3°0W 67 A4
Demavend Iran 35°56N 52°10E 87 C8
Deming U.S.A. 32°16N 107°46W 110 D5
Demopolis U.S.A. 32°31N 87°50W 111 D9
Den Helder Neths. 52°57N 4°45E 64 B3
Denbigh U.K. 53°12N 3°25W 26 A7
Denbighshire ☐ U.K. 53°8N 3°22W 26 A7
Denby Dale U.K. 53°34N 1°40W 23 E5
Denham, Mt. Jamaica 18°13N 77°32W 114 a
Denia Spain 38°49N 0°8E 67 C6
Denizli Turkey 37°42N 29°2E 71 G4
Denmark ■ Europe 55°45N 10°0E 63 F6
Denmark Str. Atl. Oc. 66°0N 30°0W 104 C17
Dennery St. Lucia 13°55N 60°54W 115 f
Denny U.K. 56°1N 3°55W 21 B8
Denpasar Indonesia 8°39S 115°13E 82 F5
Dent U.K. 54°17N 2°27W 22 D4
Denton Gt. Man., U.K. 53°27N 2°9W 23 F4
Denton Lincs., U.K. 52°53N 0°43W 23 G7
Denton U.K. 33°13N 97°8W 111 D7
D'Entrecasteaux Is. Papua N. G. 9°0S 151°0E 98 B9
Denver U.S.A. 39°42N 104°59W 110 C6
Deoghar India 24°30N 86°42E 85 G15
Deolali India 19°58N 73°50E 84 K8
Deosai Mts. Pakistan 35°40N 75°0E 84 B9
Dera Ghazi Khan Pakistan 30°5N 70°43E 84 D7
Dera Ismail Khan Pakistan 31°50N 70°50E 84 D7
Derbent Russia 42°5N 48°15E 71 F8
Derby Australia 17°18S 123°38E 98 D3
Derby U.K. 52°56N 1°28W 23 G6
Derbyshire ☐ U.K. 53°11N 1°38W 23 F5
Dereham U.K. 52°41N 0°57E 25 A10
Derg → U.K. 54°44N 7°26W 28 B7
Derg, L. Ireland 53°0N 8°20W 30 C6
Deridder U.S.A. 30°51N 93°17W 111 D8
Derry = Londonderry U.K. 55°0N 7°20W 28 A7
Derrynasaggart Mts. Ireland 51°58N 9°15W 30 E4
Derryveagh Mts. Ireland 54°56N 8°11W 28 B5
Derwent → Derby, U.K. 52°57N 1°28W 23 G6
Derwent → N. Yorks., U.K. 53°45N 0°58W 23 E7
Derwent → Tyne & W., U.K. 54°58N 1°41W 22 C5
Derwent Water U.K. 54°35N 3°9W 22 C2
Des Moines U.S.A. 41°35N 93°37W 111 B8
Des Moines → U.S.A. 40°23N 91°25W 111 B8
Desborough U.K. 52°27N 0°49W 23 G7
Deschutes → U.S.A. 45°38N 120°55W 110 A2
Dese Ethiopia 11°5N 39°40E 89 E2
Deseado → Argentina 47°45S 65°54W 121 G3
Desford U.K. 52°37N 1°17W 23 G6
Desolación, I. Chile 53°0S 74°0W 121 H2

Dessau Germany 51°51N 12°14E 64 C7
Detour, Pt. U.S.A. 45°40N 86°40W 112 C4
Detroit U.S.A. 42°19N 83°12W 112 D6
Deutsche Bucht Germany 54°15N 8°0E 64 A5
Deventer Neths. 52°15N 6°10E 64 B4
Deveron → U.K. 57°41N 2°32W 19 G12
Devils Lake U.S.A. 48°7N 98°52W 110 A7
Devizes U.K. 51°22N 1°58W 24 D5
Devon ☐ U.K. 50°50N 3°40W 27 F6
Devon I. Canada 75°10N 85°0W 109 B11
Devonport U.K. 50°22N 4°11W 27 G5
Dewey Puerto Rico 18°18N 65°18W 115 d
Dewsbury U.K. 53°42N 1°37W 23 E5
Dexter U.S.A. 36°48N 89°57W 112 G3
Deyang China 31°3N 104°27E 78 E9
Dezfūl Iran 32°20N 48°30E 86 C7
Dezhneva, C. Russia 66°5N 169°40W 77 C20
Dezhou China 37°26N 116°18E 79 D12
Dhahran Si. Arabia 26°10N 50°7E 86 E7
Dhaka Bangla. 23°43N 90°26E 85 H17
Dhaka ☐ Bangla. 24°25N 90°25E 85 G17
Dhamār Yemen 14°30N 44°20E 89 E3
Dhamtari India 20°42N 81°35E 85 J12
Dhanbad India 23°50N 86°30E 85 H15
Dharwad India 15°30N 75°4E 84 M9
Dhaulagiri Nepal 28°39N 83°28E 85 E13
Dhenkanal India 20°45N 85°35E 85 J14
Dhuburi India 26°2N 89°59E 85 F16
Dhule India 20°58N 74°50E 84 J9
Diamantina Brazil 18°17S 43°40W 122 C2
Diamantina → Australia 26°45S 139°10E 98 F6
Diamantino Brazil 14°30S 56°30W 120 D4
Dibrugarh India 27°29N 94°55E 85 F19
Dickinson U.S.A. 46°53N 102°47W 110 A6
Didcot U.K. 51°36N 1°14W 24 C6
Diefenbaker, L. Canada 51°0N 106°55W 108 D9
Dieppe France 49°54N 1°4E 66 B4
Digby Canada 44°38N 65°50W 109 E13
Digne-les-Bains France 44°5N 6°12E 66 D7
Dijon France 47°20N 5°3E 66 C6
Dikson Russia 73°40N 80°5E 76 B9
Dili E. Timor 8°39S 125°34E 83 F7
Dillingham U.S.A. 59°3N 158°28W 108 D4
Dimitrovgrad Bulgaria 42°5N 25°35E 69 C11
Dimitrovgrad Russia 54°14N 49°39E 70 D8
Dinajpur Bangla. 25°33N 88°43E 85 G16
Dinan France 48°28N 2°2W 66 B2
Dinant Belgium 50°16N 4°55E 64 C3
Dinaric Alps Croatia 44°0N 16°30E 68 C7
Dingle Ireland 52°9N 10°17W 30 D2
Dingle B. Ireland 52°3N 10°20W 30 D2
Dingwall U.K. 57°36N 4°26W 19 G9
Dipolog Phil. 8°36N 123°20E 83 C6
Dire Dawa Ethiopia 9°35N 41°45E 89 F3
Dirranbandi Australia 28°33S 148°17E 98 F8
Disappointment, C. U.S.A. 46°18N 124°5W 110 A2
Disappointment, L. Australia 23°20S 122°40E 98 E3
Diss U.K. 52°23N 1°7E 25 B11
Distington U.K. 54°36N 3°32W 22 C1
District of Columbia ☐ U.S.A. 38°55N 77°0W 112 F9
Ditchingham U.K. 52°28N 1°28E 25 B11
Ditchling Beacon U.K. 50°54N 0°6W 25 E8
Dittisham U.K. 50°22N 3°37W 27 G6
Ditton Priors U.K. 52°30N 2°34W 23 H3
Diu India 20°46N 70°58E 84 J7
Divinópolis Brazil 20°10S 44°54W 122 D2
Dixon U.S.A. 41°50N 89°29W 112 E3
Dixon Entrance U.S.A. 54°30N 132°0W 108 D6
Diyarbakır Turkey 37°55N 40°18E 71 G7
Dizzard Pt. U.K. 50°44N 4°40W 27 F4
Djerba, Î. de Tunisia 33°50N 10°48E 95 B8
Djerid, Chott Tunisia 33°42N 8°30E 94 B7
Djibouti Djibouti 11°30N 43°5E 89 E3
Djibouti ■ Africa 12°0N 43°0E 89 E3
Djourab, Erg du Chad 16°40N 18°50E 95 E9
Dmitri Laptev Str. Russia 73°0N 140°0E 77 B15
Dnepropetrovsk Ukraine 48°30N 35°0E 71 E6
Dnieper → Ukraine 46°30N 32°18E 71 E5
Dniester → Ukraine 46°18N 30°17E 65 E16
Dniprodzerzhynsk Ukraine 48°32N 34°37E 71 E5
Doba Chad 8°40N 16°50E 95 G9
Doberai, Jazirah Indonesia 1°25S 133°0E 83 E8
Dobrich Bulgaria 43°37N 27°49E 69 C12
Dobruja Europe 44°30N 28°15E 65 F15
Docking U.K. 52°54N 0°38E 25 A10
Doddington Cambs., U.K. 52°30N 0°3E 25 B9
Doddington Northumberland, U.K. 55°33N 1°54W 22 A5
Dodecanese Greece 36°35N 27°0E 69 F12
Dodge City U.S.A. 37°45N 100°1W 110 C6
Dodman Pt. U.K. 50°13N 4°48W 27 G4
Dodoma Tanzania 6°8S 35°45E 96 F7
Doha Qatar 25°15N 51°35E 87 E7
Dolbeau-Mistassini Canada 48°53N 72°14W 109 E12
Dole France 47°7N 5°31E 66 C6
Dolgarrog U.K. 53°11N 3°50W 26 A6
Dolgellau U.K. 52°45N 3°53W 26 B6
Dolo Ethiopia 4°11N 42°3E 89 G3
Dolomites Italy 46°23N 11°51E 68 A4
Dolores Argentina 36°20S 57°40W 121 F4
Dolphin and Union Str. Canada 69°5N 114°45W 108 C8
Dolphinton U.K. 55°42N 3°25W 21 C9
Dolton U.K. 50°53N 4°2W 27 F5
Dominica ■ W. Indies 15°20N 61°20W 115 D12
Dominican Rep. ■ W. Indies 19°0N 70°30W 115 D10
Don → Russia 47°4N 39°18E 71 E6
Don → Aberds., U.K. 57°11N 2°5W 19 H13
Don → S. Yorks., U.K. 53°41N 0°52W 23 E7
Don Figuero Mts. Jamaica 18°5N 77°36W 114 a
Donaghadee U.K. 54°39N 5°33W 29 B10
Doncaster U.K. 53°32N 1°6W 23 E6
Dondra Head Sri Lanka 5°55N 80°40E 84 S12
Donegal Ireland 54°39N 8°5W 28 B5
Donegal ☐ Ireland 54°53N 8°0W 28 B5
Donegal B. Ireland 54°31N 8°49W 28 B4
Donets → Russia 47°33N 40°55E 71 E7
Donetsk Ukraine 48°0N 37°45E 71 E6
Dong Hoi Vietnam 17°29N 106°36E 82 A3

Dongguan China 22°58N 113°44E 79 G11
Dongola Sudan 19°9N 30°22E 95 E12
Dongting Hu China 29°18N 112°45E 79 F11
Donhead U.K. 51°1N 2°7W 24 D4
Donington U.K. 52°54N 0°12W 23 G8
Donna Nook U.K. 53°29N 0°8E 23 F9
Donostia-San Sebastián Spain 43°17N 1°58W 67 A5
Doon → U.K. 55°27N 4°39W 20 D6
Dorchester Dorset, U.K. 50°42N 2°27W 24 E4
Dorchester Oxon., U.K. 51°39N 1°10W 24 C6
Dorchester, C. Canada 65°27N 77°27W 109 C12
Dordogne → France 45°2N 0°36W 66 D3
Dordrecht Neths. 51°48N 4°39E 64 C3
Dores do Indaiá Brazil 19°27S 45°36W 122 C1
Dorking U.K. 51°14N 0°19W 25 D8
Dornie U.K. 57°17N 5°31W 18 H6
Dornoch U.K. 57°53N 4°2W 19 G9
Dornoch Firth U.K. 57°51N 4°4W 19 G9
Döröö Nuur Mongolia 48°0N 93°0E 78 B7
Dorset ☐ U.K. 50°45N 2°26W 24 E4
Dorstone U.K. 52°3N 2°59W 24 B3
Dortmund Germany 51°30N 7°28E 64 C4
Dos Bahías, C. Argentina 44°58S 65°32W 121 E3
Dos Hermanas Spain 37°16N 5°55W 67 D3
Dothan U.S.A. 31°13N 85°24W 111 D9
Douai France 50°21N 3°4E 66 A5
Douala Cameroon 4°0N 9°45E 96 D1
Douarnenez France 48°6N 4°21W 66 B1
Doubs → France 46°53N 5°1E 66 C6
Douglas I. of Man 54°10N 4°28W 29 C13
Douglas U.S.A. 31°21N 109°33W 110 D5
Dounreay U.K. 58°35N 3°44W 19 E10
Dourados Brazil 22°9S 54°50W 120 E4
Douro → Europe 41°8N 8°40W 67 B1
Dove → Derby, U.K. 52°51N 1°36W 23 G5
Dove → N. Yorks., U.K. 54°15N 0°55W 22 D7
Dove Dale U.K. 53°7N 1°46W 23 F5
Dover U.K. 51°7N 1°19E 25 D11
Dover Del., U.S.A. 39°10N 75°32W 113 F10
Dover N.H., U.S.A. 43°12N 70°56W 113 D12
Dover, Str. of Europe 51°0N 1°30E 62 F7
Dover-Foxcroft U.S.A. 45°11N 69°13W 113 C13
Doveridge U.K. 52°54N 1°49W 23 G5
Dovey → U.K. 52°32N 4°0W 26 B5
Dovrefjell Norway 62°15N 9°33E 63 E5
Down ☐ U.K. 54°23N 6°2W 29 C9
Downham U.K. 52°26N 0°14E 25 B9
Downham Market U.K. 52°37N 0°23E 25 A9
Downpatrick U.K. 54°20N 5°43W 29 C10
Downpatrick Hd. Ireland 54°20N 9°21W 28 C3
Downton U.K. 50°59N 1°44W 24 E5
Drâa, Oued → Morocco 28°40N 11°10W 94 C3
Draguignan France 43°32N 6°27E 66 E7
Drake Passage S. Ocean 58°0S 68°0W 55 B17
Drakensberg S. Africa 31°0S 28°0E 97 L5
Drammen Norway 59°42N 10°12E 63 F6
Drava → Croatia 45°33N 18°55E 69 B8
Dresden Germany 51°3N 13°44E 64 C7
Dreux France 48°44N 1°23E 66 B4
Driffield U.K. 54°0N 0°26W 23 D8
Drina → Bos.-H. 44°53N 19°21E 69 B8
Drobeta-Turnu Severin Romania 44°39N 22°41E 65 F12
Drogheda Ireland 53°43N 6°22W 29 D9
Drohobych Ukraine 49°20N 23°30E 71 E3
Droichead Nua Ireland 53°11N 6°48W 31 B9
Droitwich U.K. 52°16N 2°8W 24 B4
Dromore West Ireland 54°15N 8°52W 28 C4
Dromore U.K. 54°31N 7°28W 28 C7
Dronfield U.K. 53°19N 1°27W 23 F6
Dronning Maud Land Antarctica 72°30S 12°0E 55 D3
Drumheller Canada 51°25N 112°40W 108 D8
Drummond I. U.S.A. 46°1N 83°39W 112 C5
Drummondville Canada 45°55N 72°25W 113 C11
Druridge B. U.K. 55°17N 1°32W 22 B5
Dry Harbour Mts. Jamaica 18°19N 77°24W 114 a
Dryden Canada 49°47N 92°50W 108 E10
Drygalski I. Antarctica 66°0S 92°0E 55 C7
Du Quoin U.S.A. 38°1N 89°14W 112 F3
Duarte, Pico Dom. Rep. 19°2N 70°59W 115 D10
Dubai U.A.E. 25°18N 55°20E 87 E8
Dubawnt → Canada 64°33N 100°6W 108 C9
Dubawnt L. Canada 63°8N 101°28W 108 C9
Dubbo Australia 32°11S 148°35E 98 G8
Dublin Ireland 53°21N 6°15W 31 B10
Dublin U.S.A. 32°32N 82°54W 111 D10
Dublin ☐ Ireland 53°24N 6°20W 31 B10
Dublin ✈ (DUB) Ireland 53°26N 6°15W 31 B10
DuBois U.S.A. 41°7N 78°46W 112 E8
Dubrovnik Croatia 42°39N 18°6E 69 C8
Dubuque U.S.A. 42°30N 90°41W 112 D2
Duddington U.K. 52°36N 0°32W 23 G7
Duddon → U.K. 54°12N 3°15W 22 D2
Dudinka Russia 69°30N 86°13E 77 C9
Dudley U.K. 52°31N 2°5W 23 G4
Duffield U.K. 52°59N 1°29W 23 G6
Dufftown U.K. 57°27N 3°8W 19 H11
Dugi Otok Croatia 44°0N 15°3E 68 C6
Duisburg Germany 51°26N 6°45E 64 C4
Dukinfield U.K. 53°28N 2°6W 23 F4
Dulce → Argentina 30°32S 62°33W 121 F3
Duluth U.S.A. 46°47N 92°6W 112 B1
Dulverton U.K. 51°2N 3°33W 27 E6
Dumaguete Phil. 9°17N 123°15E 83 C6
Dumbarton U.K. 55°57N 4°33W 20 C6
Dumfries U.K. 55°4N 3°37W 21 D8
Dumfries & Galloway ☐ U.K. 55°9N 3°58W 21 D8
Dumyât Egypt 31°24N 31°48E 95 B12
Dún Laoghaire Ireland 53°17N 6°8W 31 B10
Dunbar U.K. 56°0N 2°31W 21 B10
Dunblane U.K. 56°11N 3°58W 21 B8
Duncan U.S.A. 34°30N 97°57W 110 D7
Duncansby Head U.K. 58°38N 3°1W 19 E11
Dunchurch U.K. 52°21N 1°17W 24 B6
Dundalk Ireland 54°1N 6°24W 29 B9
Dundalk Bay Ireland 53°55N 6°15W 29 D9
Dundee U.K. 56°28N 2°59W 21 B10
Dundrum Ireland 53°18N 6°14W 31 B10
Dundrum U.K. 54°16N 5°52W 29 C10
Dundrum B. U.K. 54°13N 5°47W 29 C10
Dunedin N.Z. 45°50S 170°33E 99 K13

Dunfermline U.K. 56°5N 3°27W 21 B9
Dungannon U.K. 54°31N 6°46W 29 B8
Dungarvan Ireland 52°5N 7°37W 31 D7
Dungarvan Harbour Ireland 52°4N 7°35W 31 D7
Dungeness U.K. 50°54N 0°59E 25 E10
Dunhua China 43°20N 128°14E 79 C14
Dunhuang China 40°8N 94°36E 78 C7
Dunkeld U.K. 56°34N 3°35W 21 A8
Dunkerque France 51°2N 2°20E 66 A5
Dunkery Beacon U.K. 51°9N 3°36W 27 E6
Dunkirk U.S.A. 42°29N 79°20W 112 D8
Dunleer Ireland 53°50N 6°24W 29 D9
Dunmanway Ireland 51°43N 9°6W 30 E4
Dunmore U.S.A. 41°25N 75°38W 113 E10
Dunnet Hd. U.K. 58°40N 3°21W 19 E11
Dunoon U.K. 55°57N 4°56W 20 C6
Duns U.K. 55°47N 2°20W 21 C11
Dunsford U.K. 50°41N 3°42W 27 F6
Dunstable U.K. 51°53N 0°32W 25 C7
Dunster U.K. 51°11N 3°27W 24 D2
Dunstone U.K. 52°46N 2°7W 23 G4
Dunvegan U.K. 57°27N 6°35W 18 H4
Duque de Caxias Brazil 22°46S 43°18W 122 D2
Durance → France 43°55N 4°45E 66 E6
Durango Mexico 24°3N 104°39W 114 C4
Durango U.S.A. 37°16N 107°53W 110 C5
Durant U.S.A. 33°59N 96°25W 111 D7
Durazno Uruguay 33°25S 56°31W 121 F4
Durban S. Africa 29°49S 31°1E 97 K6
Düren Germany 50°48N 6°29E 64 C4
Durgapur India 23°30N 87°20E 85 H15
Durham U.K. 54°47N 1°34W 22 C5
Durham U.S.A. 35°59N 78°54W 111 C11
Durham ☐ U.K. 54°42N 1°45W 22 C5
Durlston Hd. U.K. 50°36N 1°57W 24 E5
Durness U.K. 58°34N 4°45W 19 E8
Durrës Albania 41°19N 19°28E 69 D8
Durrington U.K. 51°12N 1°47W 24 D5
Durrow Ireland 52°51N 7°24W 31 C8
Dursey I. Ireland 51°36N 10°12W 30 E2
Dursley U.K. 51°40N 2°21W 24 C4
Dushanbe Tajikistan 38°33N 68°48E 87 B12
Düsseldorf Germany 51°14N 6°47E 64 C4
Dutch Harbor U.S.A. 53°53N 166°32W 108 D3
Duyun China 26°18N 107°29E 78 F10
Dvina, N. → Russia 64°32N 40°30E 70 B7
Dvina B. Russia 65°0N 39°0E 70 B6
Dwarka India 22°18N 69°8E 84 H6
Dyce U.K. 57°13N 2°12W 19 H13
Dyer, C. Canada 66°37N 61°16W 109 C13
Dyersburg U.S.A. 36°3N 89°23W 111 C9
Dyfi → U.K. 52°32N 4°3W 26 B5
Dymchurch U.K. 51°1N 1°0E 25 D11
Dymock U.K. 51°59N 2°26W 24 C4
Dzerzhinsk Russia 56°14N 43°30E 70 C7
Dzhankoy Ukraine 45°40N 34°20E 71 E5
Dzhugdzhur Ra. Russia 57°30N 138°0E 77 D14
Dzungarian Basin China 44°30N 86°0E 78 C6
Dzüünmod Mongolia 47°45N 106°58E 78 B10

E
Eagle U.S.A. 64°47N 141°12W 108 C5
Eagle L. U.S.A. 46°20N 69°22W 113 B13
Eagle Pass U.S.A. 28°43N 100°30W 110 E6
Eagle River U.S.A. 45°55N 89°15W 112 B3
Eaglesfield U.K. 55°4N 3°12W 21 D9
Eakring U.K. 53°9N 0°58W 23 F7
Ealing ☐ U.K. 51°31N 0°20W 25 C8
Earby U.K. 53°55N 2°7W 23 E4
Eardisley U.K. 52°8N 3°1W 24 B2
Earith U.K. 52°22N 0°2E 25 B9
Earl Shilton U.K. 52°35N 1°18W 23 G6
Earl Soham U.K. 52°14N 1°18E 25 B11
Earls Barton U.K. 52°16N 0°45W 25 B7
Earl's Colne U.K. 51°56N 0°43E 25 C10
Earlston U.K. 55°39N 2°40W 21 C10
Earn → U.K. 56°21N 3°18W 21 B9
Earn, L. U.K. 56°23N 4°13W 20 B7
Earsdon U.K. 55°3N 1°29W 22 B6
Easebourne U.K. 51°0N 0°43W 25 E7
Easington Durham, U.K. 54°47N 1°21W 22 C6
Easington E. Riding, U.K. 53°39N 0°6E 23 E9
Easington Colliery U.K. 54°48N 1°19W 22 C6
Easingwold U.K. 54°8N 1°11W 22 D6
East Ayrshire ☐ U.K. 55°26N 4°11W 20 C7
East Bengal Bangla. 24°0N 90°0E 85 H17
East Bergholt U.K. 51°59N 1°2E 25 C11
East Beskids Europe 49°20N 22°0E 65 D11
East Brent U.K. 51°15N 2°56W 24 D3
East C. = Dezhneva, C. Russia 66°5N 169°40W 77 C20
East China Sea Asia 30°0N 126°0E 79 F14
East Cowes U.K. 50°45N 1°16W 24 E6
East Falkland Falk. Is. 51°30S 58°30W 121 H4
East Fen U.K. 53°4N 0°5E 23 F9
East Grinstead U.K. 51°7N 0°0 25 D9
East Harling U.K. 52°26N 0°56E 25 B10
East Ilsley U.K. 51°33N 1°16W 24 C6
East Indies Asia 0°0 120°0E 72 J14
East Kilbride U.K. 55°47N 4°11W 20 C7
East Lansing U.S.A. 42°44N 84°29W 112 D5
East London S. Africa 33°0S 27°55E 97 L5
East Lothian ☐ U.K. 55°58N 2°44W 21 C10
East Markham U.K. 53°15N 0°53W 23 F7
East Moor U.K. 53°16N 1°34W 23 F5
East Pt. Br. Virgin Is. 18°40N 64°18W 115 e
East Pt. Canada 46°27N 61°58W 113 C17
East St. Louis U.S.A. 38°37N 90°9W 112 F3
East Sea = Japan, Sea of Asia 40°0N 135°0E 81 D4
East Siberian Sea Russia 73°0N 160°0E 77 B17
East Sussex ☐ U.K. 50°56N 0°19E 25 E9
East Timor ■ Asia 8°50S 126°0E 83 F7
East Wittering U.K. 50°46N 0°52W 25 E7
East Woodhay U.K. 51°21N 1°25W 24 D6
Eastbourne U.K. 50°46N 0°18E 25 E9
Eastchurch U.K. 51°24N 0°53E 25 D10
Eastern Desert Egypt 27°30N 32°30E 95 C12
Eastern Ghats India 14°0N 78°50E 84 N11
Eastern Group Fiji 17°0S 178°30W 99 D15

Eastleigh   Frederikshavn

Eastleigh *U.K.*	50°58N 1°21W	**24** E6
Eastmain *Canada*	52°10N 78°30W	**109** D12
Eastmain → *Canada*	52°27N 78°26W	**109** D12
Eastnor *U.K.*	52°2N 2°23W	**24** B4
Easton *Dorset, U.K.*	50°33N 2°26W	**24** E4
Easton *Northants., U.K.*	52°37N 0°31W	**25** A7
Easton *Md., U.S.A.*	38°47N 76°5W	**113** F9
Easton *Pa., U.S.A.*	40°41N 75°13W	**113** E10
Easton-in-Gordano *U.K.*	51°28N 2°42W	**24** D3
Eastport *U.S.A.*	44°56N 67°0W	**113** C14
Eastry *U.K.*	51°14N 1°19E	**25** D11
Eastwood *U.K.*	53°1N 1°18W	**23** F6
Eaton *U.K.*	52°51N 0°49W	**23** G7
Eaton Socon *U.K.*	52°14N 0°17W	**25** B8
Eau Claire *U.S.A.*	44°49N 91°30W	**112** C2
Eau Claire, L. à l' *Canada*	56°10N 74°25W	**109** D12
Ebberston *U.K.*	54°14N 0°37W	**22** D7
Ebbw Vale *U.K.*	51°46N 3°12W	**26** D7
Eberswalde-Finow *Germany*	52°50N 13°49E	**64** B7
Ebetsu *Japan*	43°7N 141°34E	**81** B7
Ebinur Hu *China*	44°55N 82°55E	**78** C5
Ebolowa *Cameroon*	2°55N 11°10E	**96** D2
Ebro → *Spain*	40°43N 0°54E	**67** B6
Ecclefechan *U.K.*	55°4N 3°16W	**21** D9
Eccleshall *U.K.*	52°52N 2°15W	**23** G4
Ech Chéliff *Algeria*	36°10N 1°20E	**94** A6
Echo Bay *Canada*	66°5N 117°55W	**108** C8
Eckington *U.K.*	53°18N 1°22W	**23** F6
Eclipse Sd. *Canada*	72°38N 79°0W	**109** B12
Ecuador ■ *S. Amer.*	2°0S 78°0W	**120** C2
Ed Damazin *Sudan*	11°46N 34°21E	**95** F12
Eday *U.K.*	59°11N 2°47W	**19** D12
Eddrachillis B. *U.K.*	58°17N 5°14W	**18** F7
Eddystone *U.K.*	50°11N 4°16W	**27** G5
Eden → *U.K.*	54°57N 3°1W	**22** C2
Edenbridge *U.K.*	51°12N 0°5E	**25** D9
Edenderry *Ireland*	53°21N 7°4W	**31** B8
Edfu *Egypt*	24°55N 32°49E	**95** D12
Edge Hill *U.K.*	52°8N 1°26W	**24** B6
Edinburgh *U.K.*	55°57N 3°13W	**21** C9
Edinburgh ✈ (EDI) *U.K.*	55°54N 3°22W	**21** C9
Edington *U.K.*	51°17N 2°5W	**24** D4
Edirne *Turkey*	41°40N 26°34E	**71** F4
Edmonton *Canada*	53°30N 113°30W	**108** D8
Edmundbyers *U.K.*	54°50N 1°58W	**22** C5
Edmundston *Canada*	47°23N 68°20W	**109** E13
Edremit *Turkey*	39°34N 27°0E	**86** B1
Edson *Canada*	53°35N 116°28W	**108** D8
Edward, L. *Africa*	0°25S 29°40E	**96** E5
Edward VII Land *Antarctica*	80°0S 150°0W	**55** E13
Edwards Plateau *U.S.A.*	30°45N 101°20W	**110** D6
Effingham *U.S.A.*	39°7N 88°33W	**112** F3
Égadi, Ísole *Italy*	37°55N 12°16E	**68** F5
Eganville *Canada*	45°32N 77°5W	**112** A9
Eger *Hungary*	47°53N 20°27E	**65** E11
Egham *U.K.*	51°25N 0°32W	**25** D7
Eglinton I. *Canada*	75°48N 118°30W	**109** B8
Egremont *U.K.*	54°29N 3°32W	**22** D1
Eğridir *Turkey*	37°52N 30°51E	**71** G5
Eğridir Gölü *Turkey*	37°53N 30°50E	**71** G5
Egton *U.K.*	54°28N 0°44W	**22** D7
Egypt ■ *Africa*	28°0N 31°0E	**95** C12
Eifel *Germany*	50°15N 6°50E	**64** C4
Eigg *U.K.*	56°54N 6°10W	**18** J5
Eil, L. *U.K.*	56°51N 5°16W	**18** J7
Eindhoven *Neths.*	51°26N 5°28E	**64** C3
Eire = Ireland ■ *Europe*	53°50N 7°52W	**62** E2
Eivissa *Spain*	38°54N 1°26E	**67** C6
Ekaterinburg *Russia*	56°50N 60°30E	**76** D7
Ekibastuz *Kazakhstan*	51°50N 75°10E	**76** D8
El Aaiún *W. Sahara*	27°9N 13°12W	**94** C3
El Alamein *Egypt*	30°48N 28°58E	**95** B11
El Centro *U.S.A.*	32°48N 115°34W	**110** D3
El Djouf *Mauritania*	20°0N 9°0W	**94** D4
El Dorado *U.S.A.*	33°12N 92°40W	**111** D8
El Faiyûm *Egypt*	29°19N 30°50E	**95** C12
El Fâsher *Sudan*	13°33N 25°26E	**95** F11
El Fuerte *Mexico*	26°25N 108°39W	**114** B3
El Geneina *Sudan*	13°27N 22°45E	**95** F10
El Geziza □ *Sudan*	15°0N 33°0E	**95** F12
El Gîza *Egypt*	30°0N 31°12E	**95** C12
El Istiwa'iya *Sudan*	5°0N 28°0E	**95** G11
El Jadida *Morocco*	33°11N 8°17W	**94** B4
El Khârga *Egypt*	25°30N 30°33E	**95** C12
El Mahalla el Kubra *Egypt*	31°0N 31°0E	**95** B12
El Mansûra *Egypt*	31°0N 31°19E	**95** B12
El Minyâ *Egypt*	28°7N 30°33E	**95** C12
El Obeid *Sudan*	13°8N 30°10E	**95** F12
El Oued *Algeria*	33°20N 6°58E	**94** B7
El Paso *U.S.A.*	31°45N 106°29W	**110** D5
El Puerto de Santa María *Spain*	36°36N 6°13W	**67** D2
El Reno *U.S.A.*	35°32N 97°57W	**110** C7
El Salvador ■ *Cent. Amer.*	13°50N 89°0W	**114** E7
El Tigre *Venezuela*	8°44N 64°15W	**120** B3
El Uqsur *Egypt*	25°41N 32°38E	**95** C12
Elat *Israel*	29°30N 34°56E	**86** D3
Elâzığ *Turkey*	38°37N 39°14E	**71** G6
Elba *Italy*	42°46N 10°17E	**68** C4
Elbasan *Albania*	41°9N 20°9E	**69** D9
Elbe → *Europe*	53°50N 9°0E	**64** B5
Elbert, Mt. *U.S.A.*	39°7N 106°27W	**110** C5
Elbeuf *France*	49°17N 1°2E	**66** B4
Elbląg *Poland*	54°10N 19°25E	**65** A10
Elbrus *Russia*	43°21N 42°30E	**71** F7
Elburz Mts. *Iran*	36°0N 52°0E	**87** B8
Elche *Spain*	38°15N 0°42W	**67** C5
Elda *Spain*	38°29N 0°47W	**67** C5
Eldoret *Kenya*	0°30N 35°17E	**96** D7
Elektrostal *Russia*	55°41N 38°32E	**70** C6
Elemi Triangle *Africa*	5°0N 35°20E	**96** D7
Elephant Butte Res. *U.S.A.*	33°9N 107°11W	**110** D5
Elephant I. *Antarctica*	61°0S 55°0W	**55** C18
Eleuthera *Bahamas*	25°0N 76°20W	**115** C9
Elgin *U.K.*	57°39N 3°19W	**19** G11
Elgin *U.S.A.*	42°2N 88°17W	**112** D3
Elgon, Mt. *Africa*	1°10N 34°30E	**96** D6
Elham *U.K.*	51°9N 1°8E	**25** D11
Elishaw *U.K.*	55°15N 2°14W	**22** B4
Elista *Russia*	46°16N 44°14E	**71** E7

Elizabeth *U.S.A.*	40°39N 74°12W	**113** E10
Elizabeth City *U.S.A.*	36°18N 76°14W	**111** C11
Elizabethtown *U.S.A.*	37°42N 85°52W	**112** G5
Elkhart *U.S.A.*	41°41N 85°58W	**112** E5
Elkins *U.S.A.*	38°55N 79°51W	**112** F8
Elko *U.S.A.*	40°50N 115°46W	**110** B3
Elland *U.K.*	53°41N 1°50W	**23** E5
Ellef Ringnes I. *Canada*	78°30N 102°2W	**109** B9
Ellen → *U.K.*	54°44N 3°30W	**22** C2
Ellensburg *U.S.A.*	46°59N 120°34W	**110** A2
Ellerton *Barbados*	13°7N 59°33W	**115** g
Ellesmere *U.K.*	52°55N 2°53W	**23** G3
Ellesmere I. *Canada*	79°30N 80°0W	**109** B12
Ellesmere Port *U.K.*	53°17N 2°54W	**23** F3
Ellington *U.K.*	55°14N 1°33W	**22** B5
Elliot Lake *Canada*	46°25N 82°35W	**109** E11
Ellon *U.K.*	57°22N 2°4W	**19** H13
Ellsworth Land *Antarctica*	76°0S 89°0W	**55** D16
Elmalı *Turkey*	36°44N 29°56E	**71** G4
Elmira *U.S.A.*	42°6N 76°48W	**112** D9
Elmswell *U.K.*	52°15N 0°55E	**25** B10
Eluru *India*	16°48N 81°8E	**85** L12
Ely *U.K.*	52°24N 0°16E	**25** B9
Ely *U.S.A.*	39°15N 114°54W	**110** C4
Elyria *U.S.A.*	41°22N 82°7W	**112** E6
eMalahleni *S. Africa*	25°51S 29°14E	**97** K5
Emämrüd *Iran*	36°30N 55°0E	**87** B8
Embarcación *Argentina*	23°10S 64°0W	**121** E3
Embleton *U.K.*	55°29N 1°38W	**22** B5
Emden *Germany*	53°21N 7°12E	**64** B4
Emerald *Australia*	37°56S 145°29E	**98** E8
Emmen *Neths.*	52°48N 6°57E	**64** B4
Emmonak *U.S.A.*	62°47N 164°31W	**108** C3
Empalme *Mexico*	27°58N 110°51W	**114** B2
Empangeni *S. Africa*	28°50S 31°52E	**97** K6
Empedrado *Argentina*	28°0S 58°46W	**121** E4
Emporia *U.S.A.*	38°25N 96°11W	**111** C7
Emporium *U.S.A.*	41°31N 78°14W	**112** E8
Empty Quarter = Rub' al Khālī *Si. Arabia*	19°0N 48°0E	**89** D4
Ems → *Germany*	53°20N 7°12E	**64** B4
En Nahud *Sudan*	12°45N 28°25E	**95** F11
Enard B. *U.K.*	58°5N 5°20W	**18** F7
Encarnación *Paraguay*	27°15S 55°50W	**121** E4
Encounter B. *Australia*	35°45S 138°45E	**98** H6
Ende *Indonesia*	8°45S 121°40E	**83** F6
Enderbury *Kiribati*	3°8S 171°5W	**102** H10
Enderby *U.K.*	52°36N 1°13W	**23** G6
Enderby Land *Antarctica*	66°0S 53°0E	**55** C5
Endicott *U.S.A.*	42°6N 76°4W	**113** D9
Enewetak Atoll *Marshall Is.*	11°30N 162°15E	**102** F8
Enez *Turkey*	40°45N 26°5E	**71** F4
Enfer, Pte. d' *Martinique*	14°22N 60°54W	**114** c
Enfield □ *U.K.*	51°38N 0°5W	**25** C8
Engadin *Switz.*	46°45N 10°10E	**64** E6
Engels *Russia*	51°28N 46°6E	**71** D8
Enggano *Indonesia*	5°20S 102°40E	**82** F2
England □ *U.K.*	53°0N 2°0W	**62** E6
English → *Canada*	49°12N 91°5W	**108** D10
English Channel *Europe*	50°0N 2°0W	**62** F6
Enid *U.S.A.*	36°24N 97°53W	**110** C7
Ennadai L. *Canada*	60°58N 101°20W	**108** C9
Ennedi *Chad*	17°15N 22°0E	**95** E10
Ennerdale Water *U.K.*	54°32N 3°24W	**22** C2
Ennis *Ireland*	52°51N 8°59W	**30** C5
Enniscorthy *Ireland*	52°30N 6°34W	**31** D9
Enniskillen *U.K.*	54°21N 7°39W	**28** C6
Ennistimon *Ireland*	52°57N 9°17W	**30** C4
Enns → *Austria*	48°14N 14°32E	**64** D8
Enschede *Neths.*	52°13N 6°53E	**64** B4
Ensenada *Mexico*	31°52N 116°37W	**114** A1
Enshi *China*	30°18N 109°29E	**79** E10
Enstone *U.K.*	51°55N 1°27W	**24** C6
Entebbe *Uganda*	0°4N 32°28E	**96** D6
Entre Ríos □ *Argentina*	30°30S 58°30W	**121** F4
Enugu *Nigeria*	6°30N 7°30E	**94** G7
Eólie, Ís. *Italy*	38°30N 14°57E	**68** E6
Épernay *France*	49°3N 3°56E	**66** B5
Épinal *France*	48°10N 6°27E	**66** B7
Epping *U.K.*	51°41N 0°7E	**25** C9
Epping Forest *U.K.*	51°40N 0°5E	**25** C9
Epsom *U.K.*	51°19N 0°16W	**25** D8
Epworth *U.K.*	53°32N 0°48W	**23** E7
Equatorial Guinea ■ *Africa*	2°0N 8°0E	**96** D1
Er Rachidia *Morocco*	31°58N 4°20W	**94** B5
Erciyaş Dağı *Turkey*	38°30N 35°30E	**86** B3
Erdenet *Mongolia*	49°2N 104°5E	**78** B9
Erebus, Mt. *Antarctica*	77°35S 167°0E	**55** D11
Ereğli *Konya, Turkey*	37°31N 34°4E	**71** G5
Ereğli *Zonguldak, Turkey*	41°15N 31°24E	**71** F5
Erfurt *Germany*	50°58N 11°2E	**64** C6
Ergeni Lowlands *Russia*	47°0N 44°0E	**71** E7
Eriboll, L. *U.K.*	58°30N 4°42W	**19** E8
Erie *U.S.A.*	42°8N 80°5W	**112** D7
Erie, L. *N. Amer.*	42°15N 81°0W	**112** D7
Eriskay *U.K.*	57°4N 7°18W	**18** H3
Eritrea ■ *Africa*	14°0N 38°30E	**89** D2
Erlangen *Germany*	49°36N 11°0E	**64** D6
Ermoupoli *Greece*	37°28N 24°57E	**69** F11
Ernakulam *India*	9°59N 76°22E	**84** Q10
Erne → *Ireland*	54°30N 8°16W	**28** C5
Erne, Lower L. *U.K.*	54°28N 7°47W	**28** C6
Erne, Upper L. *U.K.*	54°14N 7°32W	**28** C6
Erode *India*	11°24N 77°45E	**84** P10
Erramala Hills *India*	15°30N 78°15E	**84** M11
Errigal *Ireland*	55°2N 8°6W	**28** A5
Erris Hd. *Ireland*	54°19N 10°0W	**28** C1
Erromango *Vanuatu*	18°45S 169°5E	**99** D12
Erzgebirge *Germany*	50°27N 12°55E	**64** C7
Erzincan *Turkey*	39°57N 39°30E	**71** G6
Erzurum *Turkey*	39°57N 41°15E	**71** G7
Esbjerg *Denmark*	55°29N 8°29E	**63** F5
Escada *Brazil*	8°22S 35°8W	**122** A3
Escanaba *U.S.A.*	45°45N 87°4W	**112** C4
Esch-sur-Alzette *Lux.*	49°32N 6°0E	**64** D3
Escrick *U.K.*	53°53N 1°2W	**23** E6
Escuinapa de Hidalgo *Mexico*	22°50N 105°50W	**114** C3
Escuintla *Guatemala*	14°20N 90°48W	**114** E6
Eşfahān *Iran*	32°39N 51°43E	**87** C7

Esha Ness *U.K.*	60°29N 1°38W	**18** B14
Esk → *Cumb., U.K.*	54°20N 3°24W	**22** D2
Esk → *Dumf. & Gall., U.K.*	54°58N 3°2W	**21** E9
Esk → *N. Yorks., U.K.*	54°30N 0°37W	**22** D7
Eskdale *U.K.*	55°12N 3°4W	**21** D9
Esker Siding *Canada*	53°53N 66°25W	**109** D13
Eskilstuna *Sweden*	59°22N 16°32E	**63** F7
Eskişehir *Turkey*	39°50N 30°30E	**71** G5
Eslāmābād-e Gharb *Iran*	34°10N 46°30E	**86** C6
Esna *Egypt*	25°17N 32°30E	**95** C12
Esperance *Australia*	33°45S 121°55E	**98** G3
Esperanza *Puerto Rico*	18°6N 65°28W	**115** d
Espinhaço, Serra do *Brazil*	17°30S 43°30W	**122** C2
Espírito Santo □ *Brazil*	20°0S 40°45W	**122** C2
Espíritu Santo *Vanuatu*	15°15S 166°50E	**99** D12
Espoo *Finland*	60°12N 24°40E	**63** E8
Essaouira *Morocco*	31°32N 9°42W	**94** B4
Essen *Germany*	51°28N 7°2E	**64** C4
Essequibo → *Guyana*	6°50N 58°30W	**120** B4
Essex □ *U.K.*	51°54N 0°27E	**25** C9
Esslingen *Germany*	48°44N 9°18E	**64** D5
Estados, I. de Los *Argentina*	54°40S 64°30W	**121** H3
Estância *Brazil*	11°16S 37°26W	**122** B3
Estevan *Canada*	49°10N 102°59W	**108** E9
Eston *U.K.*	54°34N 1°8W	**22** C6
Estonia ■ *Europe*	58°30N 25°30E	**63** F8
Estrela, Serra da *Portugal*	40°10N 7°45W	**67** B2
Estrondo, Serra do *Brazil*	7°20S 48°0W	**122** B1
Etawah *India*	26°48N 79°6E	**84** F11
Etchingham *U.K.*	51°0N 0°26E	**25** D9
Ethiopia ■ *Africa*	8°0N 40°0E	**89** F3
Ethiopian Highlands *Ethiopia*	10°0N 37°0E	**89** F2
Etive, L. *U.K.*	56°29N 5°10W	**20** B5
Etna *Italy*	37°50N 14°55E	**68** F6
Eton *U.K.*	51°30N 0°36W	**25** C7
Etosha Pan *Namibia*	18°40S 16°30E	**97** H3
Ettington *U.K.*	52°8N 1°35W	**24** B5
Ettrick Forest *U.K.*	55°30N 3°0W	**21** C9
Ettrick Water → *U.K.*	55°31N 2°55W	**21** C10
Euclid *U.S.A.*	41°34N 81°32W	**112** E7
Eugene *U.S.A.*	44°5N 123°4W	**110** B2
Euphrates → *Asia*	31°0N 47°25E	**86** D6
Eureka *Canada*	80°0N 85°56W	**109** B11
Eureka *U.S.A.*	40°47N 124°9W	**110** B2
Europa, Île *Ind. Oc.*	22°20S 40°22E	**97** J8
Europa, Picos de *Spain*	43°10N 4°49W	**67** A3
Europe	50°0N 20°0E	**56** E10
Eurotunnel Terminal *U.K.*	51°6N 1°10E	**25** D11
Euxton *U.K.*	53°41N 2°41W	**23** E3
Evanston *Ill., U.S.A.*	42°3N 87°40W	**112** D4
Evanston *Wyo., U.S.A.*	41°16N 110°58W	**110** B4
Evansville *U.S.A.*	37°58N 87°35W	**112** G4
Evercreech *U.K.*	51°9N 2°30W	**24** D4
Everest, Mt. *Nepal*	28°5N 86°58E	**85** C15
Everett *U.S.A.*	47°59N 122°12W	**110** A2
Everglades, The *U.S.A.*	25°50N 81°0W	**111** E10
Evesham *U.K.*	52°6N 1°56W	**24** B5
Evia *Greece*	38°30N 24°0E	**69** E11
Évora *Portugal*	38°33N 7°57W	**67** C2
Évreux *France*	49°3N 1°8E	**66** B4
Evros → *Greece*	41°40N 26°34E	**69** D12
Ewe, L. *U.K.*	57°49N 5°38W	**18** G6
Ewell *U.K.*	51°20N 0°14W	**25** D8
Ewhurst *U.K.*	51°9N 0°25W	**25** D8
Exe → *U.K.*	50°41N 3°29W	**27** F7
Exeter *U.K.*	50°43N 3°31W	**27** F6
Exminster *U.K.*	50°40N 3°29W	**27** F7
Exmoor □ *U.K.*	51°12N 3°45W	**27** E6
Exmoor △ *U.K.*	51°8N 3°42W	**27** E6
Exmouth *U.K.*	50°37N 3°25W	**27** F7
Exton *U.K.*	52°42N 0°38W	**23** G7
Extremadura □ *Spain*	39°30N 6°5W	**67** C2
Eyam *U.K.*	53°17N 1°40W	**23** F5
Eyasi, L. *Tanzania*	3°30S 35°0E	**96** E6
Eye *Cambs., U.K.*	52°37N 0°11W	**25** A8
Eye *Suffolk, U.K.*	52°19N 1°9E	**25** B11
Eye Pen. *U.K.*	58°13N 6°10W	**18** F5
Eyemouth *U.K.*	55°52N 2°5W	**21** C11
Eynsham *U.K.*	51°47N 1°22W	**24** C6
Eyre, L. *Australia*	29°30S 137°26E	**98** F6
Eyre Pen. *Australia*	33°30S 136°17E	**98** G6

F

F.Y.R.O.M. = Macedonia ■ *Europe*	41°53N 21°40E	**69** D9
Faenza *Italy*	44°17N 11°53E	**68** B4
Fair Hd. *U.K.*	55°14N 6°9W	**29** A9
Fair Isle *U.K.*	59°32N 1°38W	**18** C14
Fairbanks *U.S.A.*	64°51N 147°43W	**108** C5
Fairfield *U.S.A.*	38°23N 88°22W	**112** F3
Fairford *U.K.*	51°43N 1°46W	**24** C5
Fairlight *U.K.*	50°52N 0°40E	**25** E10
Fairmont *U.S.A.*	39°29N 80°9W	**112** F7
Faisalabad *Pakistan*	31°30N 73°5E	**84** D8
Faizabad *India*	26°45N 82°10E	**85** F13
Fajardo *Puerto Rico*	18°20N 65°39W	**115** d
Fakenham *U.K.*	52°51N 0°51E	**25** A10
Falcon Res. *U.S.A.*	26°34N 99°10W	**110** E7
Faldingworth *U.K.*	53°21N 0°24W	**23** F8
Falkirk *U.K.*	56°0N 3°47W	**21** C8
Falkland *U.K.*	56°16N 3°12W	**21** B9
Falkland Is. □ *Atl. Oc.*	51°30S 59°0W	**121** H4
Fall River *U.S.A.*	41°43N 71°10W	**113** E12
Falmouth *Jamaica*	18°30N 77°40W	**114** a
Falmouth *U.K.*	50°9N 5°5W	**27** G3
Falmouth B. *U.K.*	50°6N 5°5W	**27** G3
Falsa, Pta. *Mexico*	27°51N 115°3W	**104** G8
Falstone *U.K.*	55°11N 2°26W	**22** B4
Falun *Sweden*	60°37N 15°37E	**63** E7
Famagusta *Cyprus*	35°8N 33°55E	**86** C3
Fanad Hd. *Ireland*	55°17N 7°38W	**28** A6
Fannich, L. *U.K.*	57°38N 4°59W	**19** G8
Fano *Italy*	43°50N 13°1E	**68** C5
Far East *Asia*	40°0N 130°0E	**72** E14
Farāh *Afghan.*	32°20N 62°7E	**87** C10
Farasān *Si. Arabia*	16°45N 41°55E	**89** D3
Fareham *U.K.*	50°51N 1°11W	**24** E6
Farewell C. *Greenland*	59°48N 43°55W	**104** D15

Farghona *Uzbekistan*	40°23N 71°19E	**76** E7
Fargo *U.S.A.*	46°53N 96°48W	**111** A7
Faridabad *India*	28°26N 77°19E	**84** E10
Faringdon *U.K.*	51°39N 1°34W	**24** C5
Farmington *U.S.A.*	36°44N 108°12W	**110** C5
Farmville *U.S.A.*	37°18N 78°24W	**112** G8
Farne Is. *U.K.*	55°38N 1°37W	**22** A5
Farnham *U.K.*	51°13N 0°47W	**25** D7
Farnworth *U.K.*	53°34N 2°25W	**23** E4
Faro *Canada*	62°11N 133°22W	**108** C6
Faro *Portugal*	37°2N 7°55W	**67** D2
Faroe Is. □ *Atl. Oc.*	62°0N 7°0W	**57** C4
Fārs □ *Iran*	29°30N 55°0E	**87** D8
Fāryāb □ *Afghan.*	36°0N 65°0E	**87** B11
Faslane *U.K.*	56°5N 4°49W	**20** B6
Fataka *Solomon Is.*	11°55S 170°12E	**99** C12
Fatehgarh *India*	27°25N 79°35E	**84** F11
Fatehpur *Raj., India*	28°0N 74°40E	**84** F9
Fatehpur *Ut. P., India*	25°56N 81°13E	**85** G12
Fauldhouse *U.K.*	55°50N 3°43W	**21** C8
Faversham *U.K.*	51°19N 0°56E	**25** D10
Fawley *U.K.*	50°50N 1°20W	**24** E6
Fayetteville *Ark., U.S.A.*	36°4N 94°10W	**111** C8
Fayetteville *N.C., U.S.A.*	35°3N 78°53W	**111** D11
Fazeley *U.K.*	52°37N 1°40W	**23** G5
Fazilka *India*	30°27N 74°2E	**84** D9
Fdérik *Mauritania*	22°40N 12°45W	**94** D3
Feale → *Ireland*	52°27N 9°37W	**30** D3
Fear, C. *U.S.A.*	33°50N 77°58W	**111** D11
Fécamp *France*	49°45N 0°22E	**66** B4
Fehmarn *Germany*	54°27N 11°7E	**64** A6
Feira de Santana *Brazil*	12°15S 38°57W	**122** B3
Felipe Carrillo Puerto *Mexico*	19°38N 88°3W	**114** D7
Felixstowe *U.K.*	51°58N 1°23E	**25** C11
Felton *U.K.*	55°18N 1°42W	**22** B5
Feltwell *U.K.*	52°30N 0°32E	**25** B10
Fenny Bentley *U.K.*	53°3N 1°45W	**23** F5
Fenny Compton *U.K.*	52°10N 1°23W	**24** B6
Fenny Stratford *U.K.*	52°0N 0°44W	**25** C7
Fens, The *U.K.*	52°38N 0°2W	**25** A8
Fenyang *China*	37°18N 111°48E	**79** D11
Feodosiya *Ukraine*	45°2N 35°16E	**71** E6
Fergus Falls *U.S.A.*	46°17N 96°4W	**111** A7
Ferkéssédougou *Ivory C.*	9°35N 5°6W	**94** G4
Fermanagh □ *U.K.*	54°21N 7°40W	**28** C6
Fermont *Canada*	52°47N 67°5W	**109** D13
Fermoy *Ireland*	52°9N 8°16W	**30** D6
Fernhurst *U.K.*	51°3N 0°43W	**25** D7
Ferrara *Italy*	44°50N 11°35E	**68** B4
Ferret, C. *France*	44°38N 1°15W	**66** D3
Ferrol *Spain*	43°29N 8°15W	**67** A1
Ferryhill *U.K.*	54°41N 1°33W	**22** C5
Fès *Morocco*	34°0N 5°0W	**94** B5
Fethiye *Turkey*	36°36N 29°6E	**71** G4
Fetlar *U.K.*	60°36N 0°52W	**18** A16
Feuilles → *Canada*	58°47N 70°4W	**109** D12
Feyẕābād *Afghan.*	37°7N 70°33E	**87** B12
Fezzan *Libya*	27°0N 13°0E	**95** C8
Ffestiniog *U.K.*	52°57N 3°55W	**26** B6
Fianarantsoa *Madag.*	21°26S 47°5E	**97** J9
Fife □ *U.K.*	56°16N 3°1W	**21** B9
Fife Ness *U.K.*	56°17N 2°35W	**21** B10
Figeac *France*	44°37N 2°2E	**66** D5
Figueres *Spain*	42°18N 2°58E	**67** A7
Fiji ■ *Pac. Oc.*	17°20S 179°0E	**99** D14
Filby *U.K.*	52°40N 1°39E	**25** A12
Filey *U.K.*	54°12N 0°18W	**22** D8
Filey B. *U.K.*	54°12N 0°15W	**22** D8
Filton *U.K.*	51°30N 2°34W	**24** C3
Fincham *U.K.*	52°38N 0°30E	**25** A9
Findhorn → *U.K.*	57°38N 3°38W	**19** G10
Findlay *U.S.A.*	41°2N 83°39W	**112** E6
Findon *U.K.*	52°21N 0°39W	**25** B7
Fingal's Cave *U.K.*	56°27N 6°21W	**20** B3
Finglas *Ireland*	53°23N 6°19W	**31** B10
Finike *Turkey*	36°21N 30°10E	**86** B2
Finland ■ *Europe*	63°0N 27°0E	**63** E9
Finland, G. of *Europe*	60°0N 26°0E	**63** F9
Finlay → *Canada*	57°0N 125°10W	**108** D7
Finn → *Ireland*	54°51N 7°28W	**28** B7
Firozabad *India*	27°10N 78°25E	**84** F11
Firozpur *India*	30°55N 74°40E	**84** D9
Fish → *Namibia*	28°7S 17°10E	**97** K3
Fishguard *U.K.*	52°0N 4°58W	**26** D4
Fishtoft *U.K.*	52°58N 0°1E	**23** G9
Fisterra, C. *Spain*	42°50N 9°19W	**67** A1
Fitchburg *U.S.A.*	42°35N 71°48W	**113** D12
Flagstaff *U.S.A.*	35°12N 111°39W	**110** C4
Flamborough *U.K.*	54°7N 0°7W	**22** D8
Flamborough Hd. *U.K.*	54°7N 0°5E	**22** D8
Flandre *Europe*	50°50N 2°30E	**64** C2
Flathead L. *U.S.A.*	47°51N 114°8W	**110** A4
Flattery, C. *U.S.A.*	48°23N 124°29W	**110** A2
Fleet *U.K.*	51°17N 0°50W	**25** D7
Fleetwood *U.K.*	53°55N 3°1W	**23** E2
Flensburg *Germany*	54°47N 9°27E	**64** A5
Flers *France*	48°47N 0°33W	**66** B3
Flimby *U.K.*	54°42N 3°30W	**22** C2
Flin Flon *Canada*	54°46N 101°53W	**108** D9
Flinders → *Australia*	17°36S 140°36E	**98** D7
Flinders I. *Australia*	40°0S 148°0E	**98** H8
Flinders Ranges *Australia*	31°30S 138°30E	**98** G6
Flint *U.K.*	53°15N 3°8W	**26** A7
Flint *U.S.A.*	43°1N 83°41W	**112** D6
Flint → *U.S.A.*	30°57N 84°34W	**111** D10
Flint I. *Kiribati*	11°26S 151°48W	**103** J12
Flintshire □ *U.K.*	53°17N 3°17W	**26** A7
Flitwick *U.K.*	52°0N 0°30W	**25** C8
Flodden *U.K.*	55°37N 2°8W	**22** A4
Flora *U.S.A.*	38°40N 88°29W	**112** F3
Florence *Italy*	43°46N 11°15E	**68** C4
Florence *U.S.A.*	34°12N 79°46W	**111** D11
Florencia *Colombia*	1°36N 75°36W	**120** C2
Flores *Indonesia*	8°35S 121°0E	**83** F6
Flores Sea *Indonesia*	6°30S 120°0E	**83** F6
Florianópolis *Brazil*	27°30S 48°30W	**121** E5
Florida *Uruguay*	34°7S 56°10W	**121** F4
Florida □ *U.S.A.*	28°0N 82°0W	**111** E10
Florida, Straits of *U.S.A.*	25°0N 80°0W	**115** C9

Florida Keys *U.S.A.*	24°40N 81°0W	**111** F10
Florø *Norway*	61°35N 5°1E	**63** E5
Fly → *Papua N. G.*	8°25S 143°0E	**98** B7
Fochabers *U.K.*	57°37N 3°6W	**19** G11
Focşani *Romania*	45°41N 27°15E	**65** F14
Fóggia *Italy*	41°27N 15°34E	**68** D6
Foix *France*	42°58N 1°38E	**66** E4
Foligno *Italy*	42°57N 12°42E	**68** C5
Folkestone *U.K.*	51°5N 1°12E	**25** D11
Fond-du-Lac *Canada*	59°19N 107°12W	**108** D9
Fond du Lac *U.S.A.*	43°47N 88°27W	**112** D3
Fongafale *Tuvalu*	8°31S 179°13E	**99** B14
Fonseca, G. de *Cent. Amer.*	13°10N 87°40W	**104** H11
Fontainebleau *France*	48°24N 2°40E	**66** B5
Fontenay-le-Comte *France*	46°28N 0°48W	**66** C3
Fordham *U.K.*	52°19N 0°23E	**25** B9
Fordingbridge *U.K.*	50°56N 1°47W	**24** E5
Forel, Mt. *Greenland*	66°52N 36°55W	**54** C6
Forest Row *U.K.*	51°5N 0°3E	**25** D9
Forfar *U.K.*	56°39N 2°53W	**19** J12
Forlì *Italy*	44°13N 12°3E	**68** B5
Formartine *U.K.*	57°20N 2°15W	**19** H13
Formby *U.K.*	53°34N 3°4W	**23** E2
Formby Pt. *U.K.*	53°33N 3°6W	**23** E2
Formentera *Spain*	38°43N 1°27E	**67** C6
Formiga *Brazil*	20°27S 45°25W	**122** D1
Formosa *Argentina*	26°15S 58°10W	**121** E4
Formosa *Brazil*	15°32S 47°20W	**122** C1
Forres *U.K.*	57°37N 3°37W	**19** G10
Forsayth *Australia*	18°33S 143°34E	**98** D7
Fort Albany *Canada*	52°15N 81°35W	**109** D11
Fort Augustus *U.K.*	57°9N 4°42W	**19** H8
Fort Chipewyan *Canada*	58°42N 111°8W	**108** D8
Fort Collins *U.S.A.*	40°35N 105°5W	**110** B5
Fort-Coulonge *Canada*	45°50N 76°45W	**112** C9
Fort-de-France *Martinique*	14°36N 61°2W	**114** c
Fort Dodge *U.S.A.*	42°30N 94°11W	**111** B8
Fort Good Hope *Canada*	66°14N 128°40W	**108** C7
Fort Kent *U.S.A.*	47°15N 68°36W	**113** B13
Fort Lauderdale *U.S.A.*	26°7N 80°8W	**111** E10
Fort Liard *Canada*	60°14N 123°30W	**108** C7
Fort MacKay *Canada*	57°12N 111°41W	**108** D8
Fort Macleod *Canada*	49°45N 113°30W	**108** E8
Fort McMurray *Canada*	56°44N 111°7W	**108** D8
Fort McPherson *Canada*	67°30N 134°55W	**108** C6
Fort Morgan *U.S.A.*	40°15N 103°48W	**110** B6
Fort Myers *U.S.A.*	26°39N 81°52W	**111** E10
Fort Nelson *Canada*	58°50N 122°44W	**108** D7
Fort Nelson → *Canada*	59°32N 124°0W	**108** D7
Fort Peck L. *U.S.A.*	48°0N 106°26W	**110** A5
Fort Providence *Canada*	61°3N 117°40W	**108** C8
Fort Resolution *Canada*	61°10N 113°40W	**108** C8
Fort St. John *Canada*	56°15N 120°50W	**108** D7
Fort Scott *U.S.A.*	37°50N 94°42W	**111** C8
Fort Shevchenko *Kazakhstan*	44°35N 50°23E	**71** F9
Fort Simpson *Canada*	61°45N 121°15W	**108** C7
Fort Smith *Canada*	60°0N 111°51W	**108** B8
Fort Smith *U.S.A.*	35°23N 94°25W	**111** C8
Fort Stockton *U.S.A.*	30°53N 102°53W	**110** D6
Fort Wayne *U.S.A.*	41°4N 85°9W	**112** E5
Fort William *U.K.*	56°49N 5°7W	**18** J7
Fort Worth *U.S.A.*	32°43N 97°19W	**111** D7
Fort Yukon *U.S.A.*	66°34N 145°16W	**108** C5
Fortaleza *Brazil*	3°45S 38°35W	**120** C6
Forth → *U.K.*	56°9N 3°50W	**21** B8
Forth, Firth of *U.K.*	56°5N 2°55W	**21** B10
Fortrose *U.K.*	57°35N 4°9W	**19** G9
Foshan *China*	23°6N 113°9E	**79** G11
Fostoria *U.S.A.*	41°10N 83°25W	**112** E6
Fothergill *U.K.*	54°43N 3°29W	**22** C2
Fotheringhay *U.K.*	52°32N 0°27W	**25** B8
Fougères *France*	48°21N 1°14W	**66** B3
Foula *U.K.*	60°10N 2°5W	**62** A5
Foulness I. *U.K.*	51°36N 0°55E	**25** C10
Foulness Pt. *U.K.*	51°37N 0°58E	**25** C10
Foulsham *U.K.*	52°48N 0°59E	**25** A10
Fountainhall *U.K.*	55°44N 2°53W	**21** C10
Fouta Djallon *Guinea*	11°20N 12°10W	**94** F3
Fovant *U.K.*	51°4N 2°0W	**24** D5
Fowey *U.K.*	50°20N 4°39W	**27** G4
Fownhope *U.K.*	52°0N 2°36W	**24** B3
Foxe Basin *Canada*	66°0N 77°0W	**109** C12
Foxe Chan. *Canada*	65°0N 80°0W	**109** C12
Foxe Pen. *Canada*	65°0N 76°0W	**109** C12
Foyle → *U.K.*	55°3N 7°15W	**29** A7
Foyle, Lough *U.K.*	55°7N 7°4W	**29** A7
Foynes *Ireland*	52°37N 9°7W	**30** D4
Foz do Iguaçu *Brazil*	25°30S 54°30W	**121** E4
Fraddon *U.K.*	50°23N 4°58W	**27** G4
Framlingham *U.K.*	52°14N 1°21E	**25** B11
Franca *Brazil*	20°33S 47°30W	**122** D1
France ■ *Europe*	47°0N 3°0E	**66** C5
Franceville *Gabon*	1°40S 13°32E	**96** E2
Franche-Comté □ *France*	46°50N 5°55E	**66** C6
Francis Case, L. *U.S.A.*	43°4N 98°34W	**110** B7
Francistown *Botswana*	21°7S 27°33E	**97** J5
François L. *Canada*	54°0N 125°30W	**108** D7
Frankfort *Ind., U.S.A.*	40°17N 86°31W	**112** E4
Frankfort *Ky., U.S.A.*	38°12N 84°52W	**112** F5
Frankfurt *Brandenburg, Germany*	52°20N 14°32E	**64** B8
Frankfurt *Hessen, Germany*	50°7N 8°41E	**64** C5
Fränkische Alb *Germany*	49°10N 11°23E	**64** D6
Franklin *N.H., U.S.A.*	43°27N 71°39W	**113** D12
Franklin *Pa., U.S.A.*	41°24N 79°50W	**112** E8
Franklin B. *Canada*	69°45N 126°0W	**108** C7
Franklin D. Roosevelt L. *U.S.A.*	48°18N 118°9W	**110** A3
Franklin L. *U.S.A.*	40°25N 115°22W	**110** B3
Franklin Mts. *Canada*	65°0N 125°0W	**108** C7
Franklin Str. *Canada*	72°0N 96°0W	**108** B10
Frant *U.K.*	51°5N 0°16E	**25** D9
Franz Josef Land *Russia*	82°0N 55°0E	**54** A10
Fraser → *Canada*	49°7N 123°11W	**108** D7
Fraserburgh *U.K.*	57°42N 2°1W	**19** G13
Frederick *U.S.A.*	39°25N 77°25W	**112** F9
Fredericksburg *U.S.A.*	38°18N 77°28W	**112** F9
Fredericktown *U.S.A.*	37°34N 90°18W	**112** G2
Fredericton *Canada*	45°57N 66°40W	**113** C14
Frederikshavn *Denmark*	57°28N 10°31E	**63** F6

Fredonia   Guadix

Fredonia U.S.A. 42°26N 79°20W **112 D8**
Fredrikstad Norway 59°13N 10°57E **63 F6**
Free State □ S. Africa 28°30S 27°0E **97 K5**
Freeport Bahamas 26°30N 78°47W **115 B9**
Freeport Ill., U.S.A. 42°17N 89°36W **112 D3**
Freeport Tex., U.S.A. 28°57N 95°21W **111 E7**
Freetown S. Leone 8°30N 13°17W **94 G3**
Freiburg Germany 47°59N 7°51E **64 E4**
Fréjus France 43°25N 6°44E **66 E7**
Fremont U.S.A. 41°21N 83°7W **112 E6**
French Creek → U.S.A. 41°24N 79°50W **112 E8**
French Guiana ☑ S. Amer. 4°0N 53°0W **120 B4**
French Polynesia ☑ Pac. Oc. 20°0S 145°0W **103 J13**
Frenchman Cr. →
    N. Amer. 48°31N 107°10W **110 A5**
Freshwater U.K. 50°41N 1°31W **24 E5**
Fresnillo Mexico 23°10N 102°53W **114 C4**
Fresno U.S.A. 36°44N 119°47W **110 C3**
Fria, C. Namibia 18°0S 12°0E **90 H5**
Fridaythorpe U.K. 54°2N 0°39W **23 D7**
Friedrichshafen Germany 47°39N 9°30E **64 E5**
Frimley U.K. 51°19N 0°44W **25 D7**
Frinton-on-Sea U.K. 51°49N 1°15E **25 C11**
Frio, C. Brazil 22°50S 41°50W **117 F6**
Frizington U.K. 54°33N 3°28W **22 C2**
Frobisher B. Canada 62°30N 66°0W **109 C13**
Frobisher L. Canada 56°20N 108°15W **108 D9**
Frodsham U.K. 53°18N 2°43W **23 F3**
Frome U.K. 51°14N 2°19W **24 D4**
Frome → U.K. 50°41N 2°6W **24 E4**
Front Range U.S.A. 40°25N 105°45W **110 B5**
Front Royal U.S.A. 38°55N 78°12W **112 F8**
Frutal Brazil 20°0S 49°0W **122 C1**
Frýdek-Místek Czech Rep. 49°40N 18°20E **65 D10**
Fuchū Japan 34°34N 133°14E **81 F3**
Fuengirola Spain 36°32N 4°41W **67 D3**
Fuerte → Mexico 25°54N 109°22W **114 B3**
Fuerteventura Canary Is. 28°30N 14°0W **94 C3**
Fuhai China 47°2N 87°25E **78 B6**
Fuji Japan 35°9N 138°39E **81 F6**
Fuji-San Japan 35°22N 138°44E **81 F6**
Fujian □ China 26°0N 118°0E **79 F12**
Fujin China 47°16N 132°1E **79 B15**
Fukui Japan 36°5N 136°10E **81 E5**
Fukuoka Japan 33°39N 130°21E **81 G2**
Fukushima Japan 37°44N 140°28E **81 E7**
Fukuyama Japan 34°35N 133°20E **81 F3**
Fulda Germany 50°32N 9°40E **64 C5**
Fulda → Germany 51°25N 9°39E **64 C5**
Fulton U.S.A. 43°19N 76°25W **112 D9**
Fulwood U.K. 53°47N 2°40W **23 E3**
Funabashi Japan 35°45N 140°0E **81 F7**
Funchal Madeira 32°38N 16°54W **94 B2**
Fundy, B. of Canada 45°0N 66°0W **113 C15**
Furnas, Represa de Brazil 20°50S 45°30W **122 D1**
Furneaux Group Australia 40°10S 147°50E **98 J8**
Fürth Germany 49°28N 10°59E **64 D6**
Fury and Hecla Str. Canada 69°56N 84°0W **109 C11**
Fushun China 41°50N 123°56E **79 C13**
Fustic Barbados 13°16N 59°38W **115 g**
Fuxin China 42°5N 121°48E **79 C13**
Fuyang China 33°0N 115°48E **79 E12**
Fuyu Heilongjiang, China 47°49N 124°27E **79 B13**
Fuyu Jilin, China 45°12N 124°43E **79 B13**
Fuyun China 47°0N 89°28E **78 B6**
Fuzhou China 26°5N 119°16E **79 F12**
Fylingdales Moor U.K. 54°25N 0°41W **22 D7**
Fyn Denmark 55°20N 10°30E **63 F6**
Fyne, L. U.K. 55°59N 5°23W **20 C5**

G

Gaalkacyo Somali Rep. 6°30N 47°30E **89 F4**
Gabès Tunisia 33°53N 10°2E **95 B8**
Gabès, G. de Tunisia 34°0N 10°30E **95 B8**
Gabon ■ Africa 0°10S 10°0E **96 E2**
Gaborone Botswana 24°45S 25°57E **97 J5**
Gabrovo Bulgaria 42°52N 25°19E **69 C11**
Gachsārān Iran 30°15N 50°45E **87 D7**
Gadarwara India 22°50N 78°50E **84 H11**
Gadsden U.S.A. 34°1N 86°1W **111 D9**
Gafsa Tunisia 34°24N 8°43E **95 B7**
Gagnoa Ivory C. 6°56N 5°16W **94 G4**
Gagnon Canada 51°50N 68°5W **109 D13**
Gainesville Fla., U.S.A. 29°40N 82°20W **111 E10**
Gainesville Ga., U.S.A. 34°18N 83°50W **111 D10**
Gainford U.K. 54°34N 1°43W **22 C5**
Gainsborough U.K. 53°24N 0°46W **23 F7**
Gairdner, L. Australia 31°30S 136°0E **98 G6**
Gairloch U.K. 57°43N 5°41W **18 G6**
Gairloch, L. U.K. 57°43N 5°45W **18 G6**
Galapagos Ecuador 0°0 91°0W **117 D1**
Galashiels U.K. 55°37N 2°49W **21 C10**
Galați Romania 45°27N 28°2E **65 F15**
Galdhøpiggen Norway 61°38N 8°18E **63 E5**
Galena U.S.A. 64°44N 156°56W **108 C4**
Galesburg U.S.A. 40°57N 90°22W **112 E2**
Galgate U.K. 53°59N 2°46W **23 E3**
Galicia □ Spain 42°43N 7°45W **67 A2**
Galilee, Sea of Israel 32°45N 35°35E **86 C3**
Galina Pt. Jamaica 18°24N 76°58W **114 a**
Gallan Hd. U.K. 58°15N 7°2W **18 F3**
Galle Sri Lanka 6°5N 80°10E **84 R12**
Galley Hd. Ireland 51°32N 8°55W **30 E5**
Gallinas, Pta. Colombia 12°28N 71°40W **120 A2**
Gallipoli Italy 38°49N 82°12W **112 F6**
Gällivare Sweden 67°9N 20°40E **63 D8**
Galloway U.K. 55°1N 4°29W **20 D7**
Galloway, Mull of U.K. 54°39N 4°52W **20 E6**
Gallup U.S.A. 35°32N 108°45W **110 C5**
Galmpton U.K. 50°23N 3°35W **27 G6**
Galston U.K. 55°36N 4°24W **20 D7**
Galty Mts. Ireland 52°22N 8°10W **30 D6**
Galtymore Ireland 52°21N 8°11W **30 D6**
Galveston U.S.A. 29°18N 94°48W **111 E8**
Galway Ireland 53°17N 9°3W **30 B4**
Galway □ Ireland 53°22N 9°1W **30 B4**
Galway B. Ireland 53°13N 9°10W **30 B4**
Gambia ■ W. Afr. 13°25N 16°0W **94 F2**
Gambia → W. Afr. 13°28N 16°34W **94 F2**

Gamlingay U.K. 52°10N 0°11W **25 B8**
Gan Jiang → China 29°15N 116°0E **79 F12**
Gananoque Canada 44°20N 76°10W **113 C9**
Gäncä Azerbaijan 40°45N 46°20E **71 F8**
Gand = Gent Belgium 51°2N 3°42E **64 C2**
Gandak → India 25°39N 85°13E **85 G14**
Gander Canada 48°58N 54°35W **109 E14**
Gandhi Sagar India 24°40N 75°40E **84 G9**
Gandia Spain 38°58N 0°9W **67 C5**
Ganganagar India 29°56N 73°56E **84 E8**
Gangdisê Shan China 31°20N 81°0E **78 E5**
Ganges → India 23°20N 90°30E **85 H17**
Gangneung S. Korea 37°45N 128°54E **79 D14**
Gangtok India 27°20N 88°37E **85 F16**
Gannett Peak U.S.A. 43°11N 109°39W **110 B5**
Gansu □ China 36°0N 104°0E **78 D9**
Ganzhou China 25°51N 114°56E **79 F11**
Gao Mali 16°15N 0°5W **94 E5**
Gap France 44°33N 6°5E **66 D7**
Gar China 32°10N 79°58E **78 E4**
Garanhuns Brazil 8°50S 36°30W **122 A3**
Garboldisham U.K. 52°23N 0°57E **25 B10**
Garda, L. di Italy 45°40N 10°41E **68 B4**
Garden City U.S.A. 37°58N 100°53W **110 C6**
Gardēz Afghan. 33°37N 69°9E **87 C12**
Gare L. U.K. 56°1N 4°50W **20 B6**
Garforth U.K. 53°47N 1°24W **23 E6**
Gargrave U.K. 53°59N 2°7W **23 E4**
Garioch U.K. 57°18N 2°40W **19 H12**
Garissa Kenya 0°25S 39°40E **96 E7**
Garonne → France 45°2N 0°36W **66 D3**
Garoowe Somali Rep. 8°25N 48°33E **89 F4**
Garoua Cameroon 9°19N 13°21E **95 G8**
Garron Pt. U.K. 55°3N 5°59W **29 A10**
Garry → U.K. 56°44N 3°47W **19 J10**
Garry, L. Canada 65°58N 100°18W **108 C9**
Garsdale Head U.K. 54°20N 2°20W **22 D4**
Garstang U.K. 53°55N 2°46W **23 E3**
Gary U.S.A. 41°36N 87°20W **112 E4**
Garzê China 31°38N 100°1E **78 E8**
Gascogne France 43°45N 0°20E **66 E4**
Gascogne, G. de Europe 44°0N 2°0W **66 D2**
Gashua Nigeria 12°54N 11°0E **95 F8**
Gaspé Canada 48°52N 64°30W **109 E13**
Gaspé, C. de Canada 48°48N 64°7W **113 A15**
Gaspésie, Pén. de la Canada 48°45N 65°40W **113 A15**
Gata, Sierra de Spain 40°20N 6°45W **67 B2**
Gatehouse of Fleet U.K. 54°53N 4°12W **20 E7**
Gateshead U.K. 54°57N 1°35W **22 C5**
Gatineau Canada 45°29N 75°39W **113 C10**
Gatineau → Canada 45°27N 75°42W **113 C10**
Gatley U.K. 53°24N 2°15W **23 F4**
Gatwick, London ✈ (LGW)
    U.K. 51°10N 0°11W **25 D8**
Gävle Sweden 60°40N 17°9E **63 E7**
Gawilgarh Hills India 21°15N 76°45E **84 J10**
Gawthwaite U.K. 54°16N 3°8W **22 D2**
Gaxun Nur China 42°22N 100°30E **78 C9**
Gaya India 24°47N 85°4E **85 G14**
Gaylord U.S.A. 45°2N 84°41W **112 C5**
Gayton U.K. 52°45N 0°36E **25 A10**
Gaywood U.K. 52°46N 0°26E **25 A9**
Gaza Gaza Strip 31°30N 34°28E **86 D3**
Gaza Strip ■ Asia 31°29N 34°25E **86 D3**
Gaziantep Turkey 37°6N 37°23E **71 G6**
Gdańsk Poland 54°22N 18°40E **65 A10**
Gdynia Poland 54°35N 18°33E **65 A10**
Gebze Turkey 40°47N 29°25E **71 F4**
Gedaref Sudan 14°2N 35°28E **95 F13**
Gedney U.K. 52°48N 0°4E **23 G9**
Gedser Denmark 54°35N 11°55E **63 G6**
Geelong Australia 38°10S 144°22E **98 H7**
Gejiu China 23°20N 103°10E **78 G9**
Gela Italy 37°4N 14°15E **68 F6**
Gelibolu Turkey 40°28N 26°43E **71 F4**
Gelsenkirchen Germany 51°32N 7°6E **64 C4**
General Acha Argentina 37°20S 64°38W **121 F3**
General Alvear Argentina 35°0S 67°40W **121 F3**
General Pico Argentina 35°45S 63°50W **121 F3**
General Santos Phil. 6°5N 125°14E **83 C7**
Geneva Switz. 46°12N 6°9E **64 E4**
Geneva U.S.A. 42°52N 76°59W **112 D9**
Geneva, L. = Léman, L. Europe 46°26N 6°30E **64 E4**
Gennargentu, Mti. del Italy 40°1N 9°19E **68 D3**
Genoa Italy 44°25N 8°57E **68 B3**
Génova, G. di Italy 44°0N 9°0E **68 C3**
Gent Belgium 51°2N 3°42E **64 C2**
George S. Africa 33°58S 22°29E **97 L4**
George → Canada 58°49N 66°10W **109 D13**
George, L. U.S.A. 29°17N 81°36W **111 E10**
George Town Cayman Is. 19°20N 81°24W **115 D8**
George Town Malaysia 5°25N 100°20E **82 C2**
George V Land Antarctica 69°0S 148°0E **55 C10**
Georgetown Guyana 6°50N 58°12W **120 B4**
Georgetown Ky., U.S.A. 38°13N 84°33W **112 F5**
Georgetown S.C., U.S.A. 33°23N 79°17W **111 D10**
Georgia □ U.S.A. 32°50N 83°15W **111 D10**
Georgia ■ Asia 42°0N 43°0E **71 F7**
Georgia, Str. of N. Amer. 49°25N 124°0W **104 E7**
Georgian B. Canada 45°15N 81°0W **112 C7**
Georgiyevsk Russia 44°12N 43°28E **71 F7**
Gera Germany 50°53N 12°4E **64 C7**
Geraldton Australia 28°48S 114°32E **98 F1**
Germany ■ Europe 51°0N 10°0E **64 C6**
Germiston S. Africa 26°13S 28°10E **97 K5**
Gerrans B. U.K. 50°12N 4°57W **27 G4**
Gerrards Cross U.K. 51°35N 0°33W **25 C7**
Getafe Spain 40°18N 3°43W **67 B4**
Ghadāmis Libya 30°11N 9°29E **95 B7**
Ghaghara → India 25°45N 84°40E **85 G14**
Ghana ■ W. Afr. 8°0N 1°0W **94 G5**
Ghardaïa Algeria 32°20N 3°37E **94 B6**
Gharyān Libya 32°10N 13°0E **95 B8**
Ghats, Eastern India 14°0N 78°50E **84 N11**
Ghats, Western India 14°0N 75°0E **84 N9**
Ghazâl, Bahr el → Chad 13°0N 15°47E **95 F9**
Ghazâl, Bahr el → Sudan 9°31N 30°25E **95 G12**
Ghaziabad India 28°42N 77°26E **84 E10**
Ghazipur India 25°38N 83°35E **85 G13**
Ghaznī Afghan. 33°30N 68°28E **87 C12**

Ghent = Gent Belgium 51°2N 3°42E **64 C2**
Ghowr □ Afghan. 34°0N 64°20E **87 C11**
Giants Causeway U.K. 55°16N 6°29W **29 A9**
Gibraltar ☑ Europe 36°7N 5°22W **67 D3**
Gibraltar, Str. of Medit. S. 35°55N 5°40W **67 E3**
Gibraltar Pt. U.K. 53°6N 0°19E **23 F9**
Gibson Desert Australia 24°0S 126°0E **98 E4**
Gifu Japan 35°30N 136°45E **81 F5**
Giggleswick U.K. 54°5N 2°17W **22 D4**
Gigha U.K. 55°42N 5°44W **20 C4**
Gijón Spain 43°32N 5°42E **67 A3**
Gila → U.S.A. 32°43N 114°33W **110 D4**
Gīlān □ Iran 37°0N 50°0E **86 B7**
Gilbert Is. Kiribati 1°0N 172°0E **102 G9**
Gilgit India 35°50N 74°15E **84 B9**
Gillam Canada 56°20N 94°40W **108 D10**
Gillette U.S.A. 44°18N 105°30W **110 B5**
Gillingham Dorset, U.K. 51°2N 2°18W **24 D4**
Gillingham Medway, U.K. 51°23N 0°33E **25 D10**
Gilsland U.K. 55°0N 2°34W **22 C3**
Gimie, Mt. St. Lucia 13°54N 61°0W **115 f**
Girdle Ness U.K. 57°9N 2°3W **19 H13**
Giresun Turkey 40°55N 38°30E **71 F6**
Girga Egypt 26°17N 31°55E **95 C12**
Girona Spain 41°58N 2°46E **67 B7**
Gironde → France 45°32N 1°7W **66 D3**
Girvan U.K. 55°14N 4°51W **20 D6**
Gisborne N.Z. 38°39S 178°5E **99 H14**
Gisburn U.K. 53°56N 2°16W **23 E4**
Gitega Burundi 3°26S 29°56E **96 E5**
Gizhiga Russia 62°3N 160°30E **77 C17**
Gjoa Haven Canada 68°38N 95°53W **108 C10**
Glace Bay Canada 46°11N 59°58W **113 B18**
Glacier Nat. Park △ U.S.A. 48°42N 113°48W **110 A4**
Gladstone Australia 23°52S 151°16E **98 E9**
Gladstone U.S.A. 45°51N 87°1W **112 C4**
Gladwin U.S.A. 43°59N 84°29W **112 D5**
Glamorgan, Vale of □ U.K. 51°28N 3°25W **27 F7**
Glanaruddery Mts. Ireland 52°20N 9°27W **30 D4**
Glanton U.K. 55°26N 1°54W **22 B5**
Glasgow U.K. 55°51N 4°15W **20 C7**
Glasgow Ky., U.S.A. 37°0N 85°55W **112 G5**
Glasgow Mont., U.S.A. 48°12N 106°38W **110 A5**
Glasgow Int. ✈ (GLA) U.K. 55°51N 4°21W **20 C7**
Glasnevin U.K. 53°22N 6°15W **31 B10**
Glastonbury U.K. 51°9N 2°43W **24 D3**
Glazov Russia 58°9N 52°40E **70 C9**
Glemsford U.K. 52°6N 0°40E **25 B10**
Glen → U.K. 52°51N 0°7W **23 G8**
Glen Affric U.K. 57°17N 5°1W **18 H7**
Glen Almond U.K. 56°28N 3°50W **21 B8**
Glen Coe U.K. 56°40N 5°0W **18 J7**
Glen Etive U.K. 56°37N 5°0W **20 A5**
Glen Garry Highl., U.K. 57°3N 5°7W **18 H7**
Glen Garry Perth & Kinr., U.K. 56°47N 4°5W **19 J9**
Glen Mor U.K. 57°9N 4°37W **18 H8**
Glen Moriston U.K. 57°11N 4°52W **19 H8**
Glen Orchy U.K. 56°27N 4°52W **20 B6**
Glen Orrin U.K. 57°31N 4°45W **19 G8**
Glen Oykel U.K. 58°5N 4°50W **19 F8**
Glen Roy U.K. 56°56N 4°50W **19 J8**
Glen Shee U.K. 56°50N 3°28W **19 J11**
Glen Shiel U.K. 57°9N 5°18W **18 H7**
Glen Spean U.K. 56°53N 4°40W **19 J8**
Glendale Ariz., U.S.A. 33°32N 112°11W **110 D4**
Glendale Calif., U.S.A. 34°9N 118°15W **110 D3**
Glendive U.S.A. 47°7N 104°43W **110 A6**
Gleneagles U.K. 56°17N 3°43W **21 B8**
Glenfinnan U.K. 56°53N 5°27W **18 J7**
Glengarriff Ireland 51°45N 9°34W **30 E3**
Glenkens, The U.K. 55°12N 4°12W **20 D7**
Glenluce U.K. 54°52N 4°48W **20 E6**
Glennallen U.S.A. 62°7N 145°33W **108 C5**
Glennamaddy Ireland 53°37N 8°33W **28 D4**
Glenrothes U.K. 56°12N 3°10W **21 B9**
Glens Falls U.S.A. 43°19N 73°39W **113 D11**
Glenties Ireland 54°49N 8°16W **28 B5**
Glenveagh △ Ireland 55°3N 8°1W **28 A5**
Gliwice Poland 50°22N 18°41E **65 C10**
Globe U.S.A. 33°24N 110°47W **110 D4**
Głogów Poland 51°37N 16°5E **64 C9**
Glomma → Norway 59°12N 10°57E **63 F6**
Glossop U.K. 53°27N 1°56E **23 F5**
Gloucester U.K. 51°53N 2°15W **24 C4**
Gloucestershire □ U.K. 51°46N 2°15W **24 C4**
Gloversville U.S.A. 43°3N 74°21W **113 D10**
Gniezno Poland 52°30N 17°35E **65 B9**
Gnosall U.K. 52°48N 2°14W **23 G4**
Goa India 15°33N 73°59E **84 M8**
Goa □ India 15°33N 73°59E **84 M8**
Goat Fell U.K. 55°38N 5°11W **20 C5**
Gobi Asia 44°0N 110°0E **79 C11**
Godalming U.K. 51°11N 0°36W **25 D7**
Godavari → India 16°25N 82°18E **85 L13**
Goderich Canada 43°45N 81°41W **112 D7**
Godhra India 22°49N 73°40E **84 H8**
Godmanchester U.K. 52°20N 0°11W **25 B8**
Godoy Cruz Argentina 32°56S 68°52W **121 F3**
Gods → Canada 56°22N 92°51W **108 D10**
Gods L. Canada 54°40N 94°15W **108 D10**
Godshill U.K. 50°38N 1°15W **24 E6**
Godstone U.K. 51°14N 0°3W **25 D8**
Gogama Canada 47°35N 81°43W **112 B7**
Goiânia Brazil 16°43S 49°20W **122 C1**
Goiás Brazil 15°55S 50°10W **120 D4**
Goiás □ Brazil 12°10S 48°0W **120 D5**
Goio-Erê Brazil 24°10S 53°1W **121 E4**
Gold Coast Australia 28°0S 153°25E **98 F9**
Gold Coast W. Afr. 4°0N 1°40W **94 H5**
Golden Vale Ireland 52°33N 8°17W **30 D6**
Goldsboro U.S.A. 35°23N 77°59W **111 C11**
Golmud China 36°25N 94°53E **78 D7**
Golspie U.K. 57°58N 3°59W **19 G10**
Goma Dem. Rep. of the Congo 1°37S 29°10E **96 E5**
Gomel Belarus 52°28N 31°0E **65 B16**
Gomera Canary Is. 28°7N 17°14W **94 C2**
Gómez Palacio Mexico 25°34N 103°30W **114 B4**
Gonābād Iran 34°15N 58°45E **87 C9**
Gonaïves Haiti 19°20N 72°42W **115 D10**

Gonda India 27°9N 81°58E **85 F12**
Gonder Ethiopia 12°39N 37°30E **89 E2**
Gongga Shan China 29°40N 101°55E **78 F9**
Gonghe China 36°18N 100°32E **78 D9**
Good Hope, C. of S. Africa 34°24S 18°30E **97 L3**
Goodrich U.K. 51°52N 2°37W **24 C3**
Goodwood U.K. 50°53N 0°44W **25 E7**
Goole U.K. 53°42N 0°53W **23 E7**
Goose L. U.S.A. 41°56N 120°26W **110 B2**
Gorakhpur India 26°47N 83°23E **85 F13**
Gordon U.K. 55°41N 2°34W **21 C10**
Gore Ethiopia 8°12N 35°32E **89 F2**
Gorebridge U.K. 55°50N 3°2W **21 C9**
Gorey Ireland 52°41N 6°18W **31 C10**
Gorgān Iran 36°55N 54°30E **87 B8**
Goring U.K. 51°31N 1°7W **24 C6**
Goring-by-Sea U.K. 50°49N 0°24W **25 E8**
Gorleston U.K. 52°35N 1°44E **25 A12**
Görlitz Germany 51°9N 14°58E **64 C8**
Gorno-Altay □ Russia 51°0N 86°0E **76 D9**
Gorontalo Indonesia 0°35N 123°5E **83 D6**
Gorzów Wielkopolski Poland 52°43N 15°15E **64 B8**
Gosberton U.K. 52°52N 0°10W **23 G8**
Gosforth U.K. 54°26N 3°27W **22 D2**
Gosport U.K. 50°48N 1°9W **24 E6**
Göta kanal Sweden 58°30N 15°58E **63 F7**
Götaland Sweden 57°30N 14°30E **63 F6**
Göteborg Sweden 57°43N 11°59E **63 F6**
Gotha Germany 50°56N 10°42E **64 C6**
Gothenburg = Göteborg Sweden 57°43N 11°59E **63 F6**
Gotland Sweden 57°30N 18°33E **63 F7**
Gotō-Rettō Japan 32°55N 129°5E **81 G1**
Göttingen Germany 51°31N 9°55E **64 C5**
Gouda Neths. 52°1N 4°42E **64 B3**
Goudhurst U.K. 51°6N 0°29E **25 D9**
Gouin, Rés. Canada 48°35N 74°40E **113 A10**
Goulburn Australia 34°44S 149°44E **98 G8**
Goulimine Morocco 28°56N 10°0W **94 C3**
Goundam Mali 16°27N 3°40W **94 E5**
Gourock U.K. 55°57N 4°49W **20 C6**
Governador Valadares Brazil 18°15S 41°57W **122 C2**
Gower U.K. 51°35N 4°10W **27 D5**
Gowna, L. Ireland 53°51N 7°34W **28 D6**
Goya Argentina 29°10S 59°10W **121 E4**
Gozo Malta 36°3N 14°15E **68 a**
Graaff-Reinet S. Africa 32°13S 24°32E **97 L4**
Gracias a Dios, C. Honduras 15°0N 83°10W **115 E8**
Grafham Water U.K. 52°19N 0°18W **25 B8**
Grafton Australia 29°38S 152°58E **98 F9**
Grafton U.S.A. 48°25N 97°25W **111 A7**
Graham Land Antarctica 65°0S 64°0W **55 C17**
Grahamstown S. Africa 33°19S 26°31E **97 L5**
Grain Coast W. Afr. 4°20N 10°0W **94 H3**
Grainthorpe U.K. 53°27N 0°5E **23 F9**
Grampian Mts. U.K. 56°50N 4°0W **19 J9**
Gran Canaria Canary Is. 27°55N 15°35W **94 C2**
Gran Chaco S. Amer. 25°0S 61°0W **121 E3**
Gran Sasso d'Itália Italy 42°27N 13°42E **68 C5**
Granada Nic. 11°58N 86°0W **114 E7**
Granada Spain 37°10N 3°35W **67 D4**
Granard Ireland 53°47N 7°30W **28 D6**
Granby Canada 45°25N 72°45W **109 E12**
Grand → U.S.A. 45°40N 100°45W **110 A6**
Grand Bahama I. Bahamas 26°40N 78°30W **115 B9**
Grand-Bourg Guadeloupe 15°53N 61°19W **114 b**
Grand Canyon U.S.A. 36°3N 112°9W **110 C4**
Grand Canyon Nat. Park △ U.S.A. 36°15N 112°30W **110 C4**
Grand Cayman Cayman Is. 19°20N 81°20W **115 D8**
Grand Erg de Bilma Niger 18°30N 14°0E **95 E8**
Grand Falls Canada 47°3N 67°44W **109 E13**
Grand Falls-Windsor Canada 48°56N 55°40W **109 E14**
Grand Forks U.S.A. 47°55N 97°3W **111 A7**
Grand Haven U.S.A. 43°4N 86°13W **112 D4**
Grand Island U.S.A. 40°55N 98°21W **110 B7**
Grand Junction U.S.A. 39°4N 108°33W **110 C5**
Grand Manan I. Canada 44°45N 66°52W **113 C14**
Grand-Mère Canada 46°36N 72°40W **113 C11**
Grand Rapids Canada 53°12N 99°19W **108 D10**
Grand Rapids U.S.A. 42°58N 85°40W **112 D4**
Grand St-Bernard, Col du Europe 45°50N 7°10E **64 F4**
Grand Teton U.S.A. 43°54N 110°50W **110 B4**
Grande → Bolivia 15°51S 64°39W **120 D3**
Grande → Brazil 11°30S 44°30W **122 B2**
Grande, B. Argentina 50°30S 68°20W **121 H3**
Grande, Rio → N. Amer. 25°58N 97°9W **111 E7**
Grande Baleine → Canada 55°16N 77°47W **109 D12**
Grande Prairie Canada 55°10N 118°50W **108 D8**
Grande-Terre Guadeloupe 16°20N 61°25W **114 b**
Grande Vigie, Pte. de la Guadeloupe 16°32N 61°27W **114 b**
Grange-over-Sands U.K. 54°12N 2°54W **22 D3**
Grangemouth U.K. 56°1N 3°42W **21 B8**
Grangeville U.S.A. 45°56N 116°7W **110 A3**
Grantham U.K. 52°55N 0°38W **23 G7**
Grantown-on-Spey U.K. 57°20N 3°36W **19 H10**
Grants Pass U.S.A. 42°26N 123°19W **110 B2**
Granville U.S.A. 43°24N 73°16W **113 D11**
Grasmere U.K. 54°28N 3°1W **22 D2**
Grasse France 43°38N 6°56E **66 E7**
Grassington U.K. 54°5N 1°59W **22 D5**
Graulhet France 43°45N 1°59E **66 E4**
Gravesend U.K. 51°26N 0°22E **25 D9**
Grayling → Canada 59°21N 125°0W **108 D7**
Grayrigg U.K. 54°23N 2°39W **22 D3**
Grays U.K. 51°28N 0°21E **25 D9**
Graz Austria 47°4N 15°27E **64 E8**
Great Australian Bight Australia 33°30S 130°0E **98 G5**
Great Ayton U.K. 54°30N 1°8W **22 D6**
Great Baddow U.K. 51°43N 0°31E **25 C10**
Great Barrier Reef Australia 18°0S 146°50E **98 D8**
Great Basin U.S.A. 40°0N 117°0W **110 B3**
Great Bear → Canada 65°0N 126°0W **108 C7**

Great Bear L. Canada 65°30N 120°0W **108 B7**
Great Bend U.S.A. 38°22N 98°46W **110 C7**
Great Bentley U.K. 51°51N 1°4E **25 C11**
Great Bernera U.K. 58°14N 6°50W **18 F4**
Great Blasket I. Ireland 52°6N 10°32W **30 D1**
Great Britain Europe 54°0N 2°15W **62 D5**
Great Broughton U.K. 54°26N 1°9W **22 D6**
Great Camanoe Br. Virgin Is. 18°30N 64°35W **115 e**
Great Chesterford U.K. 52°4N 0°13E **25 B9**
Great Clifton U.K. 54°39N 3°29W **22 C2**
Great Dividing Ra. Australia 23°0S 146°0E **98 E8**
Great Dunmow U.K. 51°52N 0°23E **25 C9**
Great Exuma I. Bahamas 23°30N 75°50W **115 C9**
Great Falls U.S.A. 47°30N 111°17W **110 A4**
Great Harwood U.K. 53°47N 2°24W **23 E4**
Great Inagua I. Bahamas 21°0N 73°20W **115 C10**
Great Karoo S. Africa 31°55S 21°0E **97 L4**
Great Khingan Mts. China 48°0N 121°0E **79 B13**
Great Lakes N. Amer. 46°0N 84°0W **104 E11**
Great Malvern U.K. 52°7N 2°18W **24 B4**
Great Massingham U.K. 52°47N 0°40E **25 A10**
Great Missenden U.K. 51°42N 0°41W **25 C7**
Great Ormes Head U.K. 53°20N 3°52W **26 A5**
Great Ouse → U.K. 52°48N 0°21E **25 A9**
Great Pedro Bluff Jamaica 17°51N 77°44W **114 a**
Great Plains N. Amer. 47°0N 105°0W **110 A6**
Great Salt Desert Iran 34°30N 55°0E **87 C8**
Great Salt L. U.S.A. 41°15N 112°40W **110 B4**
Great Salt Lake Desert U.S.A. 40°50N 113°30W **110 B4**
Great Sandy Desert Australia 21°0S 124°0E **98 E3**
Great Sandy Desert U.S.A. 43°35N 120°15W **110 B2**
Great Shefford U.K. 51°28N 1°28W **24 D6**
Great Shelford U.K. 52°9N 0°8E **25 B9**
Great Shunner Fell U.K. 54°22N 2°14W **22 D4**
Great Skellig Ireland 51°47N 10°33W **30 E1**
Great Slave L. Canada 61°23N 115°38W **108 C8**
Great Snow Mt. Canada 57°26N 124°0W **108 D7**
Great Torrington U.K. 50°57N 4°9W **27 F5**
Great Victoria Desert Australia 29°30S 126°30E **98 F4**
Great Wall of China China 38°30N 109°30E **79 D10**
Great Waltham U.K. 51°47N 0°28E **25 C9**
Great Whernside U.K. 54°10N 1°58W **22 D5**
Great Yarmouth U.K. 52°37N 1°44E **25 A12**
Greater Antilles W. Indies 17°40N 74°0W **115 D10**
Greater London □ U.K. 51°31N 0°6W **25 C8**
Greater Manchester □ U.K. 53°30N 2°15W **23 E4**
Greater Sunda Is. Indonesia 7°0S 112°0E **82 F4**
Greatham U.K. 54°39N 1°14W **22 C6**
Greece ■ Europe 40°0N 23°0E **69 E9**
Greeley U.S.A. 40°25N 104°42W **110 B6**
Greely Fd. Canada 80°30N 85°0W **109 A11**
Green → Ky., U.S.A. 37°54N 87°30W **112 G4**
Green → Utah, U.S.A. 38°11N 109°53W **110 C5**
Green B. U.S.A. 45°0N 87°30W **112 C4**
Green Bay U.S.A. 44°31N 88°0W **112 C4**
Green Hammerton U.K. 54°1N 1°18W **23 D6**
Green River U.S.A. 38°12N 109°28W **110 B5**
Greencastle U.S.A. 39°38N 86°52W **112 F4**
Greenfield Ind., U.S.A. 39°47N 85°46W **112 F5**
Greenfield Mass., U.S.A. 42°35N 72°36W **113 D11**
Greenhead U.K. 54°59N 2°30W **22 C3**
Greenland ☑ N. Amer. 66°0N 45°0W **54 C5**
Greenland Sea Arctic 73°0N 10°0W **54 B7**
Greenlaw U.K. 55°43N 2°27W **21 C11**
Greenock U.K. 55°57N 4°46W **20 C6**
Greenodd U.K. 54°14N 3°4W **22 D2**
Greenore Ireland 54°2N 6°8W **29 B9**
Greenore Pt. Ireland 52°14N 6°19W **31 D10**
Greensboro U.S.A. 36°4N 79°48W **111 C11**
Greensburg Ind., U.S.A. 39°20N 85°29W **112 F5**
Greensburg Pa., U.S.A. 40°18N 79°33W **112 E8**
Greenstone Pt. U.K. 57°55N 5°37W **18 G6**
Greenville Ala., U.S.A. 31°50N 86°38W **111 D9**
Greenville Maine, U.S.A. 45°28N 69°35W **113 C13**
Greenville Mich., U.S.A. 43°11N 85°15W **112 D5**
Greenville Miss., U.S.A. 33°24N 91°4W **111 D8**
Greenville Ohio, U.S.A. 40°6N 84°38W **112 E5**
Greenville S.C., U.S.A. 34°51N 82°24W **111 D10**
Greenwich □ U.K. 51°29N 0°1E **25 D9**
Greenwood U.S.A. 33°31N 90°11W **111 D8**
Gremikha Russia 67°59N 39°47E **70 A6**
Grenada ■ W. Indies 12°10N 61°40W **115 E12**
Grenoble France 45°12N 5°42E **66 D6**
Greta → U.K. 54°9N 2°37W **22 D3**
Gretna U.K. 55°0N 3°3W **21 D9**
Gretna Green U.K. 55°1N 3°3W **21 D9**
Gretton U.K. 52°33N 0°40W **25 A7**
Grey, Ra. Australia 27°0S 143°30E **98 F7**
Greymouth N.Z. 42°29S 171°13E **99 J13**
Greystoke U.K. 54°41N 2°51W **22 C3**
Greystones Ireland 53°9N 6°5W **31 B10**
Griffith Australia 34°18S 146°2E **98 G8**
Grimsay U.K. 57°29N 7°14W **18 H3**
Grimsby U.K. 53°34N 0°5W **23 E8**
Gris-Nez, C. France 50°52N 1°35E **66 A4**
Grise Fiord Canada 76°25N 82°57W **109 B11**
Grizebeck U.K. 54°16N 3°10W **22 D2**
Groningen Neths. 53°15N 6°35E **64 B4**
Groote Eylandt Australia 14°0S 136°40E **98 D6**
Gros Islet St. Lucia 14°5N 60°58W **115 f**
Gros Piton St. Lucia 13°49N 61°5W **115 f**
Gros Piton Pt. St. Lucia 13°49N 61°5W **115 f**
Grosseto Italy 42°46N 11°8E **68 C4**
Grossglockner Austria 47°5N 12°40E **64 E7**
Groundhog → Canada 48°45N 82°58W **112 A6**
Groznyy Russia 43°20N 45°45E **71 F8**
Grudziądz Poland 53°30N 18°47E **65 B10**
Gruinard B. U.K. 57°56N 5°35W **18 G6**
Guadalajara Mexico 20°40N 103°20W **114 C4**
Guadalajara Spain 40°37N 3°12W **67 B4**
Guadalcanal Solomon Is. 9°32S 160°12E **99 B11**
Guadalete → Spain 36°35N 6°13W **67 D2**
Guadalquivir → Spain 36°47N 6°22W **67 D2**
Guadalupe, I. Pac. Oc. 29°0N 118°50W **104 G8**
Guadarrama, Sierra de Spain 41°0N 4°0W **67 B4**
Guadeloupe ☑ W. Indies 16°20N 61°40W **114 b**
Guadiana → Portugal 37°14N 7°22W **67 D2**
Guadix Spain 37°18N 3°11W **67 D4**

Guafo, Boca del

Guafo, Boca del Chile 43°35S 74°0'W 121 G2
Guajará-Mirim Brazil 10°50S 65°20'W 120 D3
Guajira, Pen. de la Colombia 12°0'N 72°0'W 120 A2
Gualeguaychú Argentina 33°3S 59°31'W 121 F4
Guam ☑ Pac. Oc. 13°27'N 144°45E 102 F6
Guamúchil Mexico 25°28'N 108°6'W 114 B3
Guana I. Br. Virgin Is. 18°30'N 64°30'W 115 e
Guanajuato Mexico 21°1'N 101°15'W 114 C4
Guane Cuba 22°10'N 84°7'W 115 C8
Guangdong ☐ China 23°0'N 113°0E 79 G11
Guangxi Zhuang ☐ China 24°0'N 109°0E 79 G10
Guangyuan China 32°26'N 105°51E 78 E10
Guangzhou China 23°6'N 113°13E 79 G11
Guanica Puerto Rico 17°58'N 66°55'W 115 d
Guantánamo Cuba 20°10'N 75°14'W 115 C9
Guantánamo B. Cuba 19°59'N 75°10'W 115 D9
Guaporé → Brazil 11°55S 65°4'W 120 D3
Guaqui Bolivia 16°41S 68°54'W 120 D3
Guarapuava Brazil 25°20S 51°30'W 121 E4
Guaratinguetá Brazil 22°49S 45°9'W 122 D1
Guarulhos Brazil 23°29S 46°33'W 122 D1
Guatemala Guatemala 14°40'N 90°22'W 114 E6
Guatemala ■ Cent. Amer. 15°40'N 90°30'W 114 D6
Guatemala Trench Pac. Oc. 14°0'N 95°0'W 104 H10
Guaviare → Colombia 4°3'N 67°44'W 120 B3
Guaxupé Brazil 21°10S 47°5'W 122 D1
Guayama Puerto Rico 17°59'N 66°7'W 115 d
Guayaquil Ecuador 2°15S 79°52'W 120 C2
Guayaquil, G. de Ecuador 3°10S 81°0'W 120 C1
Guaymas Mexico 27°56'N 110°54'W 114 B2
Gubkin Russia 51°17'N 37°32E 71 D6
Guelph Canada 43°35'N 80°20'W 112 D7
Guéret France 46°11'N 1°51E 66 C4
Guernsey U.K. 49°26'N 2°35'W 27 J8
Guestling Green U.K. 50°53'N 0°39E 25 E9
Guiana Highlands S. Amer. 5°10'N 60°40'W 117 C4
Guidónia-Montecélio Italy 42°1'N 12°45E 68 C5
Guildford U.K. 51°14'N 0°34'W 25 D7
Guilin China 25°18'N 110°15E 79 F11
Guinea ■ W. Afr. 10°20'N 11°30'W 94 F3
Guinea, Gulf of Atl. Oc. 3°0'N 2°30E 90 F4
Guinea-Bissau ■ Africa 12°0'N 15°0'W 94 F3
Güines Cuba 22°50'N 82°0'W 115 C8
Guingamp France 48°34'N 3°10'W 66 B2
Guisborough U.K. 54°33'N 1°4'W 22 C6
Guiyang China 26°32'N 106°40E 78 F10
Guizhou ☐ China 27°0'N 107°0E 78 F10
Gujarat ☐ India 23°20'N 71°0E 84 H7
Gujranwala Pakistan 32°10'N 74°12E 84 C9
Gujrat Pakistan 32°40'N 74°2E 84 C9
Gulbarga India 17°20'N 76°50E 84 L10
Gulf, The = Persian Gulf Asia 27°0'N 50°0E 87 E7
Gulfport U.S.A. 30°22'N 89°6'W 111 D9
Gulu Uganda 2°48'N 32°17E 96 D6
Guna India 24°40'N 77°19E 84 G10
Gunnison → U.S.A. 39°4'N 108°35'W 110 C5
Gunsan S. Korea 35°59'N 126°45E 79 D14
Guntur India 16°23'N 80°30E 85 L12
Gurbantüngüt Desert China 45°8'N 87°20E 78 B6
Gurgueia → Brazil 6°50S 43°24'W 120 C5
Guri, Embalse de Venezuela 7°50'N 62°52'W 120 B3
Gurkha Nepal 28°5'N 84°40E 85 E14
Gurnard's Hd. U.K. 50°11'N 5°37'W 27 G2
Gürün Turkey 38°43'N 37°15E 71 G6
Gurupi Brazil 11°43S 49°4'W 122 B1
Gurupi → Brazil 1°13S 46°6'W 120 C5
Gurvan Sayhan Uul Mongolia 43°50'N 104°0E 78 C9
Gusau Nigeria 12°12'N 6°40E 94 F7
Guwahati India 26°10'N 91°45E 85 E17
Guyana ■ S. Amer. 5°0'N 59°0'W 120 B4
Guyenne France 44°30'N 0°40E 66 D4
Gwadar Pakistan 25°10'N 62°18E 84 G3
Gwalchmai U.K. 53°16'N 4°25'W 26 A5
Gwalior India 26°12'N 78°10E 84 F11
Gwanda Zimbabwe 20°55S 29°0E 97 J5
Gwangju S. Korea 35°9'N 126°54E 79 D14
Gweebarra B. Ireland 54°51'N 8°23'W 28 B5
Gweedore Ireland 55°3'N 8°13'W 28 A5
Gweek U.K. 50°5'N 5°13'W 27 G3
Gwennap U.K. 50°12'N 5°11'W 27 G3
Gweru Zimbabwe 19°28S 29°45E 97 H5
Gwynedd ☐ U.K. 52°52'N 4°10'W 26 B6
Gyaring Hu China 34°50'N 97°40E 78 E8
Gympie Australia 26°11S 152°38E 98 F9
Győr Hungary 47°41'N 17°40E 65 E9
Gyumri Armenia 40°47'N 43°50E 71 F7

H

Ha'apai Group Tonga 19°47S 174°27'W 99 D16
Haarlem Neths. 52°23'N 4°39E 64 B3
Habahe China 48°3'N 86°23E 78 B6
Hachinohe Japan 40°30'N 141°29E 81 C7
Hackney ☐ U.K. 51°33'N 0°3'W 25 C8
Hackthorpe U.K. 54°34'N 2°42'W 22 C3
Ḥadd, Ra's al Oman 22°35'N 59°50E 87 F9
Haddenham U.K. 51°46'N 0°55'W 25 C7
Haddington U.K. 55°57'N 2°47'W 21 C10
Hadejia Nigeria 12°30'N 10°5E 94 F7
Hadleigh U.K. 52°3'N 0°58E 25 B10
Hadlow U.K. 51°13'N 0°22E 25 D9
Hadramawt Yemen 15°30'N 49°30E 89 D4
Hadrian's Wall U.K. 55°0'N 2°30'W 22 B4
Haeju N. Korea 38°3'N 125°45E 79 D14
Hafizabad Pakistan 32°5'N 73°40E 84 C8
Hagen Germany 51°21'N 7°27E 64 C4
Hagerstown U.S.A. 39°39'N 77°43'W 112 F9
Hags Hd. Ireland 52°57'N 9°28'W 30 C4
Hague, C. de la France 49°44'N 1°56'W 66 B3
Hague, The Neths. 52°7'N 4°17E 64 B3
Haguenau France 48°49'N 7°47E 66 B7
Haifa Israel 32°46'N 35°0E 86 C3
Haikou China 20°1'N 110°16E 79 E11
Ḥā'il Si. Arabia 27°28'N 41°45E 86 E5
Hailar China 49°10'N 119°38E 79 B12
Hailey U.S.A. 43°31'N 114°19'W 110 B4
Haileybury Canada 47°30'N 79°38'W 112 B8
Hailsham U.K. 50°52'N 0°16E 25 E9
Hailun China 47°28'N 126°50E 79 B14

Hainan ☐ China 19°0'N 109°30E 79 H10
Haines Junction Canada 60°45'N 137°30'W 108 C6
Hainton U.K. 53°21'N 0°14'W 23 F8
Haiphong Vietnam 20°47'N 106°41E 78 G10
Haiti ■ W. Indies 19°0'N 72°30'W 115 D10
Haji Ibrahim Iraq 36°40'N 44°30E 86 B6
Hajjah Yemen 15°42'N 43°36E 89 D3
Hakkoda-San Japan 40°39'N 140°53E 81 C7
Hakodate Japan 41°45'N 140°44E 81 C7
Haku-San Japan 36°9'N 136°46E 81 E5
Halaib Triangle Africa 22°30'N 35°20E 95 D13
Halberstadt Germany 51°54'N 11°3E 64 C6
Halberton U.K. 50°54'N 3°25'W 27 F7
Halden Norway 59°9'N 11°23E 63 F6
Haldia India 22°5'N 88°3E 85 H16
Haldwani India 29°31'N 79°30E 84 E11
Halesowen U.K. 52°27'N 2°3'W 23 H4
Halesworth U.K. 52°20'N 1°31E 25 B12
Halifax Canada 44°38'N 63°35'W 113 C16
Halifax U.K. 53°43'N 1°52'W 23 E5
Halkirk U.K. 58°30'N 3°29'W 19 E11
Hall Beach Canada 68°46'N 81°12'W 109 C11
Hall Pen. Canada 63°30'N 66°0'W 109 C13
Halle Germany 51°30'N 11°56E 64 C6
Hallow U.K. 52°14'N 2°15'W 24 B4
Halls Creek Australia 18°16S 127°38E 98 D4
Hallworthy U.K. 50°39'N 4°35'W 27 F4
Halmahera Indonesia 0°40'N 128°0E 83 D7
Halmstad Sweden 56°41'N 12°52E 63 F6
Halstead U.K. 51°57'N 0°40E 25 C10
Haltwhistle U.K. 54°58'N 2°26'W 22 C4
Hamadān Iran 34°52'N 48°32E 86 C7
Ḥamāh Syria 35°5'N 36°40E 86 C4
Hamamatsu Japan 34°45'N 137°45E 81 F5
Hamar Norway 60°48'N 11°7E 63 E6
Hambantota Sri Lanka 6°10'N 81°10E 84 R12
Hambledon U.K. 50°55'N 1°5'W 24 E6
Hambleton Hills U.K. 54°17'N 1°12'W 22 D6
Hamburg Germany 53°33'N 9°59E 64 B5
Hämeenlinna Finland 61°0'N 24°28E 63 E8
Hameln Germany 52°6'N 9°21E 64 B5
Hamersley Ra. Australia 22°0S 117°45E 98 E2
Hamhŭng N. Korea 39°54'N 127°30E 79 D14
Hami China 42°55'N 93°25E 78 C7
Hamilton Canada 43°15'N 79°50'W 112 D8
Hamilton N.Z. 37°47S 175°19E 99 H14
Hamilton U.K. 55°46'N 4°2'W 20 C7
Hamilton U.S.A. 39°24'N 84°34'W 112 F5
Hamilton Inlet Canada 54°0'N 57°30'W 109 D14
Hamm Germany 51°40'N 7°50E 64 C4
Hammerfest Norway 70°39'N 23°41E 63 C8
Hammersmith and Fulham ☐ U.K. 51°30'N 0°14'W 25 D8
Hammond U.S.A. 41°38'N 87°30'W 112 E4
Hammonton U.S.A. 39°39'N 74°48'W 113 F10
Hampshire ☐ U.K. 51°7'N 1°23'W 24 D6
Hampshire Downs U.K. 51°15'N 1°10'W 24 D6
Hampton in Arden U.K. 52°26'N 1°41'W 23 H5
Han Shui → China 30°34'N 114°17E 79 E11
Hancock U.S.A. 47°8'N 88°35'W 112 B3
Handan China 36°35'N 114°28E 79 D11
Hanford U.S.A. 36°20'N 119°39'W 110 C3
Hangayn Nuruu Mongolia 47°30'N 99°0E 78 B8
Hangzhou China 30°18'N 120°11E 79 E13
Hangzhou Wan China 30°15'N 120°45E 79 E13
Hankö Finland 59°50'N 22°57E 63 F8
Hanna Canada 51°40'N 111°54'W 108 D8
Hannibal U.S.A. 39°42'N 91°22'W 111 C8
Hanningfield Res. U.K. 51°40'N 0°31E 25 D10
Hannover Germany 52°22'N 9°46E 64 B5
Hanoi Vietnam 21°5'N 105°55E 78 G10
Hanover U.S.A. 39°48'N 76°59'W 112 F9
Hanover, I. Chile 51°0S 74°50'W 121 H2
Hans Lollik I. U.S. Virgin Is. 18°24'N 64°53'W 115 e
Hanzhong China 33°10'N 107°1E 78 E10
Haora India 22°34'N 88°18E 85 H16
Haparanda Sweden 65°52'N 24°8E 63 D8
Happy Valley-Goose Bay Canada 53°15'N 60°20'W 109 D13
Har Hu China 38°20'N 97°38E 78 D8
Har Us Nuur Mongolia 48°0'N 92°0E 78 B7
Ḥaraḍ Si. Arabia 24°22'N 49°0E 86 E7
Harare Zimbabwe 17°43S 31°2E 97 H6
Harbin China 45°48'N 126°40E 79 B14
Harbor Beach U.S.A. 43°51'N 82°39'W 112 D6
Hardangerfjorden Norway 60°5'N 6°0E 63 E5
Hardy, Pte. St. Lucia 14°6'N 60°56'W 115 f
Harer Ethiopia 9°20'N 42°8E 89 F3
Harewood U.K. 53°54'N 1°30'W 23 E6
Hargeisa Somali Rep. 9°30'N 44°2E 89 F3
Haridwar India 29°58'N 78°9E 84 E11
Haringey ☐ U.K. 51°34'N 0°5'W 25 C8
Haringhata → Bangla. 22°0'N 89°58E 85 J16
Ḥarīrūd → Asia 37°24'N 60°38E 87 B10
Harlech U.K. 52°52'N 4°6'W 26 B5
Harleston U.K. 52°24'N 1°18E 25 B11
Harlingen U.S.A. 26°12'N 97°42'W 110 E7
Harlow U.K. 51°46'N 0°8E 25 C9
Harney L. U.S.A. 43°14'N 119°8'W 110 B3
Härnösand Sweden 62°38'N 17°55E 63 E7
Haroldswick U.K. 60°48'N 0°50'W 18 A16
Harpenden U.K. 51°49'N 0°21'W 25 C8
Harricana → Canada 50°56'N 79°32'W 109 D12
Harrietsham U.K. 51°14'N 0°41E 25 D10
Harrington U.K. 54°37'N 3°33'W 22 C1
Harris U.K. 57°50'N 6°55'W 18 G4
Harris, Sd. of U.K. 57°44'N 7°6'W 18 G3
Harrisburg U.S.A. 40°16'N 76°53'W 112 E9
Harrisonburg U.S.A. 38°27'N 78°52'W 112 F8
Harrisville U.S.A. 44°39'N 83°17'W 112 C6
Harrogate U.K. 53°59'N 1°32'W 23 E6
Harrow ☐ U.K. 51°35'N 0°21'W 25 C8
Hart U.S.A. 43°42'N 86°22'W 112 D4
Hartest U.K. 52°8'N 0°40E 25 B10
Hartford Conn., U.S.A. 41°46'N 72°41'W 113 E11
Hartford Ky., U.S.A. 37°27'N 86°55'W 112 G4
Hartford Wis., U.S.A. 43°19'N 88°22'W 112 D3
Hartland U.K. 50°59'N 4°29'W 27 F5
Hartland Pt. U.K. 51°1'N 4°32'W 27 E4

Hartlebury U.K. 52°20'N 2°14'W 24 B4
Hartlepool U.K. 54°42'N 1°13'W 22 C6
Hartley U.K. 55°5'N 1°28'W 22 B6
Hartpury U.K. 51°55'N 2°17'W 24 C4
Harvey U.S.A. 41°36'N 87°50'W 112 E4
Harwell U.K. 51°36'N 1°17'W 24 C6
Harwich U.K. 51°56'N 1°17E 25 C11
Haryana ☐ India 29°0'N 76°10E 84 E10
Harz Germany 51°38'N 10°44E 64 C6
Haslemere U.K. 51°5'N 0°43'W 25 D7
Haslingden U.K. 53°42'N 2°19'W 23 E4
Hasa Si. Arabia 25°50'N 49°0E 86 E7
Hastings U.K. 50°51'N 0°35E 25 E10
Hastings U.S.A. 40°35'N 98°23'W 110 B7
Hat Yai Thailand 7°1'N 100°27E 82 C2
Hatay Turkey 36°14'N 36°10E 71 G6
Hatfield U.K. 51°46'N 0°13'W 25 C8
Hatgal Mongolia 50°26'N 100°9E 78 A9
Hatherleigh U.K. 50°49'N 4°5'W 27 F5
Hathersage U.K. 53°20'N 1°39'W 23 F5
Hathras India 27°36'N 78°6E 84 F11
Hatia Bangla. 22°30'N 91°5E 85 H17
Hatteras, C. U.S.A. 35°14'N 75°32'W 111 C11
Hattiesburg U.S.A. 31°20'N 89°17'W 111 D9
Haugesund Norway 59°23'N 5°13E 63 F5
Haughley U.K. 52°14'N 0°57E 25 B10
Haut Atlas Morocco 32°30'N 5°0'W 94 B4
Hauts Plateaux Algeria 35°0'N 1°0E 94 B6
Havana = La Habana Cuba 23°8'N 82°22'W 115 C8
Havant U.K. 50°51'N 0°58'W 25 E7
Havasu, L. U.S.A. 34°18'N 114°28'W 110 D4
Havel → Germany 52°50'N 12°3E 64 B7
Haverfordwest U.K. 51°48'N 4°58'W 26 D4
Haverhill U.K. 52°5'N 0°28E 25 B9
Haverhill U.S.A. 42°47'N 71°5'W 113 D12
Haverigg U.K. 54°13'N 3°17'W 22 D2
Havering ☐ U.K. 51°34'N 0°13E 25 C9
Havre U.S.A. 48°33'N 109°41'W 110 A5
Havre-St.-Pierre Canada 50°18'N 63°33'W 109 D13
Hawai'i U.S.A. 19°30'N 155°30'W 110 J17
Hawai'i ☐ U.S.A. 19°30'N 156°30'W 110 H16
Hawaiian Is. Pac. Oc. 20°30'N 156°0'W 103 E12
Hawes U.K. 54°19'N 2°12'W 22 D4
Haweswater U.K. 54°31'N 2°47'W 22 C3
Hawick U.K. 55°26'N 2°47'W 21 D10
Hawkchurch U.K. 50°48'N 2°56'W 24 E3
Hawkesbury Canada 45°37'N 74°37'W 113 C10
Hawkesbury Upton U.K. 51°35'N 2°19'W 24 C4
Hawkhurst U.K. 51°2'N 0°32E 25 D10
Hawkshead U.K. 54°23'N 2°59'W 22 D3
Haworth U.K. 53°50'N 1°58'W 23 E5
Hawsker U.K. 54°27'N 0°34'W 22 D7
Haxby U.K. 54°1'N 1°4'W 23 D6
Hay Australia 34°30S 144°51E 98 G8
Hay → Canada 60°50'N 116°26'W 108 C8
Hay-on-Wye U.K. 52°5'N 3°8'W 26 C7
Hay River Canada 60°51'N 115°44'W 108 C8
Haydon Bridge U.K. 54°58'N 2°14'W 22 C4
Hayes → Canada 57°3'N 92°12'W 108 D10
Hayle U.K. 50°11'N 5°26'W 27 G3
Hays U.S.A. 38°53'N 99°20'W 110 C7
Hayton U.K. 54°55'N 2°45'W 22 C3
Hayward U.S.A. 46°1'N 91°29'W 112 B2
Haywards Heath U.K. 51°0'N 0°5'W 25 E8
Hazar Turkmenistan 39°34'N 53°16E 71 G9
Hazard U.S.A. 37°15'N 83°12'W 112 G6
Hazaribag India 23°58'N 85°26E 85 H14
Heacham U.K. 52°54'N 0°29E 25 A9
Headcorn U.K. 51°10'N 0°38E 25 D10
Heanor U.K. 53°1'N 1°21'W 23 F6
Heard I. Ind. Oc. 53°6'S 72°36E 53 G13
Hearst Canada 49°40'N 83°41'W 109 E11
Heathfield U.K. 50°58'N 0°16E 25 E9
Heathrow, London ✈ (LHR) U.K. 51°28'N 0°27'W 25 D8
Hebburn U.K. 54°59'N 1°32'W 22 C5
Hebden Bridge U.K. 53°45'N 2°0'W 23 E5
Hebei ☐ China 39°0'N 116°0E 79 D12
Hebrides U.K. 57°30'N 7°0'W 18 H4
Hebrides, Sea of the U.K. 57°5'N 7°0'W 18 H4
Hebron Canada 58°5'N 62°30'W 109 D13
Hecate Str. Canada 53°10'N 130°30'W 108 D6
Hechi China 24°40'N 108°2E 78 G10
Hechuan China 30°2'N 106°12E 78 E10
Heckington U.K. 52°59'N 0°17'W 23 G8
Hednesford U.K. 52°43'N 1°59'W 23 G5
Hedon U.K. 53°44'N 0°12'W 23 E8
Heerlen Neths. 50°55'N 5°58E 64 C3
Hefei China 31°52'N 117°18E 79 E12
Hegang China 47°20'N 130°19E 79 B15
Heidelberg Germany 49°24'N 8°42E 64 D5
Heihe China 50°10'N 127°30E 79 A14
Heilbronn Germany 49°9'N 9°13E 64 D5
Heilongjiang ☐ China 48°0'N 126°0E 79 B14
Heimaey Iceland 63°26'N 20°17'W 63 B1
Hekou China 22°30'N 103°59E 78 G9
Helena U.S.A. 46°36'N 112°2'W 110 A4
Helensburgh U.K. 56°1'N 4°43'W 20 B6
Helgoland Germany 54°10'N 7°53E 64 A4
Hellifield U.K. 54°1'N 2°12'W 23 D4
Helmand → Afghan. 31°12'N 61°34E 87 D10
Helmsdale U.K. 58°7'N 3°39'W 19 F10
Helmsley U.K. 54°15'N 1°1'W 22 D6
Helperby U.K. 54°8'N 1°19'W 22 D6
Helsby U.K. 53°17'N 2°46'W 23 F3
Helsingborg Sweden 56°3'N 12°42E 63 F6
Helsinki Finland 60°10'N 24°55E 63 E9
Helston U.K. 50°6'N 5°17'W 27 G3
Helvellyn U.K. 54°32'N 3°1'W 22 C2
Helwân Egypt 29°50'N 31°20E 95 C12
Hemel Hempstead U.K. 51°44'N 0°28'W 25 C8
Hempton U.K. 52°50'N 0°49E 25 A10
Hemsworth U.K. 53°37'N 1°21'W 23 E6
Hemyock U.K. 50°55'N 3°15'W 27 F7
Henan ☐ China 34°0'N 114°0E 79 E11
Henderson Ky., U.S.A. 37°50'N 87°35'W 112 G4
Henderson Nev., U.S.A. 36°2'N 114°59'W 110 D4
Henfield U.K. 50°56'N 0°16'W 25 E8
Hengduan Shan China 27°30'N 99°0E 78 F8
Hengyang China 26°59'N 112°22E 79 F11

Henley-in-Arden U.K. 52°18'N 1°46'W 24 B5
Henley-on-Thames U.K. 51°32'N 0°54'W 25 C7
Henlopen, C. U.S.A. 38°48'N 75°6'W 113 F10
Henlow U.K. 52°2'N 0°17'W 25 B8
Henrietta Maria, C. Canada 55°9'N 82°20'W 109 D11
Henstridge U.K. 50°58'N 2°24'W 24 E4
Hentiyn Nuruu Mongolia 48°30'N 108°30E 79 B10
Herāt Afghan. 34°20'N 62°7E 87 C10
Hereford U.K. 52°4'N 2°43'W 24 B3
Herefordshire ☐ U.K. 52°8'N 2°40'W 24 B3
Herford Germany 52°7'N 8°39E 64 B5
Herlen → Asia 48°48'N 117°0E 79 B12
Herm U.K. 49°30'N 2°28'W 27 J9
Herma Ness U.K. 60°50'N 0°54'W 18 A16
Hermosillo Mexico 29°10'N 111°0'W 114 B2
Hernád → Hungary 47°56'N 21°8E 65 D11
Herne Bay U.K. 51°21'N 1°8E 25 D11
Herstmonceux U.K. 50°53'N 0°20E 25 E9
Hertford U.K. 51°48'N 0°4'W 25 C8
Hertfordshire ☐ U.K. 51°51'N 0°5'W 25 C8
's-Hertogenbosch Neths. 51°42'N 5°17E 64 C3
Hessen ☐ Germany 50°30'N 9°0E 64 C5
Hessle U.K. 53°44'N 0°24'W 23 E8
Hethersett U.K. 52°36'N 1°10E 25 A11
Hetton-le-Hole U.K. 54°50'N 1°26'W 22 C6
Hexham U.K. 54°58'N 2°4'W 22 C4
Heybridge U.K. 51°45'N 0°42E 25 C10
Heysham U.K. 54°3'N 2°53'W 22 D3
Heytesbury U.K. 51°11'N 2°6'W 24 D4
Heywood U.K. 53°35'N 2°12'W 23 E4
Heze China 35°14'N 115°20E 79 D12
Hibbing U.S.A. 47°25'N 92°56'W 111 A8
Hickman U.S.A. 36°34'N 89°11'W 112 G3
Hidalgo del Parral Mexico 26°56'N 105°40'W 114 B3
Hierro Canary Is. 27°44'N 18°0'W 94 C2
Higashiōsaka Japan 34°39'N 135°37E 81 F4
High Bentham U.K. 54°7'N 2°28'W 22 D4
High Ercall U.K. 52°45'N 2°35'W 23 G3
High Hesket U.K. 54°48'N 2°49'W 22 C3
High Level Canada 58°31'N 117°8'W 108 D8
High Pike U.K. 54°42'N 3°4'W 22 C2
High Prairie Canada 55°30'N 116°30'W 108 D8
High River Canada 50°30'N 113°50'W 108 D8
High Veld Africa 27°0S 27°0E 90 J6
High Willhays U.K. 50°40'N 4°0'W 27 F5
High Wycombe U.K. 51°37'N 0°45'W 25 C7
Higham Ferrers U.K. 52°19'N 0°35'W 25 B7
Highbridge U.K. 51°13'N 2°58'W 24 D3
Highclere U.K. 51°20'N 1°21'W 24 D6
Highland ☐ U.K. 57°17'N 4°21'W 19 H8
Highley U.K. 52°27'N 2°23'W 23 H4
Hightae U.K. 55°6'N 3°26'W 21 D9
Highworth U.K. 51°37'N 1°43'W 24 C5
Hiiumaa Estonia 58°50'N 22°45E 63 F8
Ḥijāz Si. Arabia 24°0'N 40°0E 86 E4
Hildesheim Germany 52°9'N 9°56E 64 B5
Hilgay U.K. 52°34'N 0°24E 25 A9
Hillaby, Mt. Barbados 13°12'N 59°35'W 115 g
Hillcrest Barbados 13°13'N 59°31'W 115 g
Hillingdon ☐ U.K. 51°32'N 0°27'W 25 C8
Hillsborough U.K. 54°28'N 6°5'W 29 C9
Hillsdale U.S.A. 41°56'N 84°38'W 112 E5
Hilo U.S.A. 19°44'N 155°5'W 110 J17
Hilpsford Pt. U.K. 54°3'N 3°12'W 22 D2
Hilversum Neths. 52°14'N 5°10E 64 B3
Himachal Pradesh ☐ India 31°30'N 77°0E 84 D10
Himalaya Asia 29°0'N 84°0E 85 E14
Himeji Japan 34°50'N 134°40E 81 F4
Hinckley U.K. 52°33'N 1°22'W 23 G6
Hinderwell U.K. 54°32'N 0°45'W 22 C7
Hindhead U.K. 51°7'N 0°43'W 25 D7
Hindley U.K. 53°33'N 2°35'W 23 E3
Hindu Kush Asia 36°0'N 71°0E 87 C12
Hingham U.K. 52°35'N 1°0E 25 A10
Hingoli India 19°41'N 77°15E 84 K10
Hinkley Pt. U.K. 51°12'N 3°8'W 24 D2
Hinstock U.K. 52°50'N 2°27'W 23 G4
Hinton U.S.A. 37°40'N 80°54'W 112 G7
Hios Greece 38°27'N 26°9E 69 E12
Hirosaki Japan 40°34'N 140°28E 81 C7
Hiroshima Japan 34°24'N 132°30E 81 F3
Hisar India 29°12'N 75°45E 84 E9
Hispaniola W. Indies 19°0'N 71°0'W 115 D10
Histon U.K. 52°15'N 0°7E 25 B9
Hitachi Japan 36°36'N 140°39E 81 E7
Hitchin U.K. 51°58'N 0°16'W 25 C8
Hjälmaren Sweden 59°18'N 15°40E 63 F7
Hkakabo Razi Burma 28°25'N 97°23E 85 E20
Ho Chi Minh City Vietnam 10°58'N 106°40E 82 B3
Hoare B. Canada 65°17'N 62°30'W 109 C13
Hobart Australia 42°50S 147°21E 98 J8
Hobbs U.S.A. 32°42'N 103°8'W 110 D6
Hodder → U.K. 53°57'N 2°27'W 23 E4
Hoddesdon U.K. 51°45'N 0°1'W 25 C8
Hodge → U.K. 54°16'N 0°56'W 22 D7
Hodgson Canada 51°13'N 97°36'W 108 D10
Hódmezővásárhely Hungary 46°28'N 20°22E 65 E11
Hodna, Chott el Algeria 35°26'N 4°43E 94 A6
Hoek van Holland Neths. 52°0'N 4°7E 64 B3
Hoff U.K. 54°34'N 2°31'W 22 C3
Hōfu Japan 34°3'N 131°34E 81 F2
Hog's Back U.K. 51°13'N 0°38'W 25 D7
Hoh Xil Shan China 36°30'N 89°0E 78 D6
Hoher Rhön Germany 50°24'N 9°58E 64 C5
Hohhot China 40°52'N 111°40E 79 C11
Hokkaidō ☐ Japan 43°30'N 143°0E 81 B8
Holbeach U.K. 52°48'N 0°1E 23 G9
Holbeach Marsh U.K. 52°52'N 0°5E 23 G9
Holderness U.K. 53°45'N 0°5'W 23 E8
Holetown Barbados 13°11'N 59°38'W 115 g
Holguín Cuba 20°50'N 76°20'W 115 C9
Holkham U.K. 52°57'N 0°48E 25 A10
Holland U.S.A. 42°47'N 86°7'W 112 D4
Holland Fen U.K. 53°0'N 0°8'W 23 G8
Holland on Sea U.K. 51°48'N 1°13E 25 C11
Holman Canada 70°44'N 117°44'W 108 A8
Holme U.K. 53°50'N 0°46'W 23 E7
Holmes Chapel U.K. 53°12'N 2°21'W 23 F4
Holmfirth U.K. 53°35'N 1°46'W 23 E5

Holstebro Denmark 56°22'N 8°37E 63 F5
Holsworthy U.K. 50°48'N 4°22'W 27 F5
Holt U.K. 52°55'N 1°6E 25 A11
Holy I. Anglesey, U.K. 53°17'N 4°37'W 26 A4
Holy I. Northumberland, U.K. 55°40'N 1°47'W 22 A5
Holyhead U.K. 53°18'N 4°38'W 26 A4
Holywell U.K. 53°16'N 3°14'W 26 A7
Home B. Canada 68°40'N 67°10'W 109 C13
Homer U.S.A. 59°39'N 151°33'W 108 D4
Homs Syria 34°40'N 36°45E 86 C4
Honduras ■ Cent. Amer. 14°40'N 86°30'W 114 E7
Honduras, G. of Caribbean 16°50'N 87°0'W 114 D7
Hønefoss Norway 60°10'N 10°18E 63 E6
Honey L. U.S.A. 40°15'N 120°19'W 110 B2
Hong Kong ☐ China 22°11'N 114°14E 79 a
Hongjiang China 27°7'N 109°59E 79 F10
Hongshui He → China 23°48'N 109°30E 79 G10
Hongze Hu China 33°15'N 118°35E 79 E12
Honiara Solomon Is. 9°27S 159°57E 99 B10
Honington U.K. 52°59'N 0°35'W 23 G7
Honiton U.K. 50°47'N 3°11'W 27 F7
Honolulu U.S.A. 21°19'N 157°52'W 103 E12
Honshū Japan 36°0'N 138°0E 81 F6
Hoo U.K. 51°25'N 0°35E 25 D10
Hood, Mt. U.S.A. 45°23'N 121°42'W 110 A2
Hook U.K. 51°17'N 0°57'W 25 D7
Hook Hd. Ireland 52°7'N 6°56'W 31 D9
Hooper Bay U.S.A. 61°32'N 166°6'W 108 C3
Hoopeston U.S.A. 40°28'N 87°40'W 112 E4
Hoorn Neths. 52°38'N 5°4E 64 B3
Hoover Dam U.S.A. 36°1'N 114°44'W 110 C4
Hope U.K. 53°22'N 1°43'W 23 F5
Hope, Pt. U.S.A. 68°21'N 166°47'W 104 C3
Hopedale Canada 55°28'N 60°13'W 109 D13
Horden U.K. 54°46'N 1°19'W 22 C6
Horley U.K. 51°10'N 0°10'W 25 D8
Horlivka Ukraine 48°19'N 38°5E 71 E6
Hormozgān ☐ Iran 27°30'N 56°0E 87 E9
Hormuz, Str. of The Gulf 26°30'N 56°30E 87 E9
Horn, C. = Hornos, C. de Chile 55°50S 67°30'W 121 H3
Horn, Is. Wall. & F. Is. 14°16S 178°6'W 99 C15
Horn Head Ireland 55°14'N 8°0'W 28 A6
Hornavan Sweden 66°15'N 17°30E 63 D7
Horncastle U.K. 53°13'N 0°7'W 23 F8
Horndean U.K. 50°55'N 1°1'W 24 E6
Hornell U.S.A. 42°20'N 77°40'W 112 D9
Hornepayne Canada 49°14'N 84°48'W 112 A5
Horningsham U.K. 51°10'N 2°15'W 24 D4
Hornos, C. de Chile 55°50S 67°30'W 121 H3
Hornsea U.K. 53°55'N 0°11'W 23 E8
Horqin Youyi Qianqi China 46°5'N 122°3E 79 B13
Horsforth U.K. 53°50'N 1°39'W 23 E5
Horsham Australia 36°44S 142°13E 98 H7
Horsham U.K. 51°4'N 0°20'W 25 D8
Horsham St. Faith U.K. 52°43'N 1°14E 25 A11
Horsted Keynes U.K. 51°2'N 0°1'W 25 D8
Horton → Canada 69°56'N 126°52'W 108 C7
Horton in Ribblesdale U.K. 54°9'N 2°17'W 22 D4
Horwich U.K. 53°36'N 2°33'W 23 E3
Hoste, I. Chile 55°0S 69°0'W 121 H3
Hot Springs Ark., U.S.A. 34°31'N 93°3'W 111 D8
Hot Springs S. Dak., U.S.A. 43°26'N 103°29'W 110 B6
Hotan China 37°25'N 79°55E 78 D4
Houghton U.S.A. 47°7'N 88°34'W 112 B3
Houghton L. U.S.A. 44°21'N 84°44'W 112 C5
Houghton-le-Spring U.K. 54°51'N 1°28'W 22 C6
Houghton Regis U.K. 51°54'N 0°32'W 25 C7
Houlton U.S.A. 46°8'N 67°51'W 113 B14
Houma U.S.A. 29°36'N 90°43'W 111 E8
Hounslow ☐ U.K. 51°28'N 0°21'W 25 D8
Hourn, L. U.K. 57°7'N 5°35'W 18 H6
Houston U.S.A. 29°45'N 95°21'W 111 E7
Hove U.K. 50°50'N 0°10'W 25 E8
Hoveton U.K. 52°43'N 1°25E 25 A11
Hovingham U.K. 54°11'N 0°58'W 22 D7
Hövsgöl Nuur Mongolia 51°0'N 100°30E 78 A9
Howden U.K. 53°45'N 0°52'W 23 E7
Howe, C. Australia 37°30S 150°0E 98 H9
Howell U.S.A. 42°36'N 83°56'W 112 D6
Howland I. Pac. Oc. 0°48'N 176°38'W 102 G10
Howth Ireland 53°23'N 6°4'W 31 B10
Howth Hd. Ireland 53°22'N 6°4'W 31 B10
Hoxne U.K. 52°21'N 1°12E 25 B11
Hoy U.K. 58°50'N 3°15'W 19 E11
Høyanger Norway 61°13'N 6°4E 63 E5
Hoylake U.K. 53°24'N 3°10'W 23 F2
Hradec Králové Czech Rep. 50°15'N 15°50E 64 C8
Hrodna Belarus 53°42'N 23°52E 65 E10
Hron → Slovak Rep. 47°49'N 18°45E 65 E10
Hsinchu Taiwan 24°48'N 120°58E 79 G13
Huacho Peru 11°10S 77°35'W 120 D2
Huai He → China 33°0'N 118°30E 79 E12
Huaibei China 34°0'N 116°48E 79 E12
Huaihua China 27°32'N 109°57E 79 F10
Huainan China 32°38'N 116°58E 79 E12
Huallaga → Peru 5°15S 75°30'W 120 C2
Huambo Angola 12°42S 15°54E 97 G3
Huancavelica Peru 12°50S 75°5'W 120 D2
Huancayo Peru 12°5S 75°12'W 120 D2
Huang He → China 37°55'N 118°50E 79 D12
Huangshan China 29°42'N 118°25E 79 F12
Huangshi China 30°10'N 115°3E 79 E12
Huánuco Peru 9°55S 76°15'W 120 C2
Huaraz Peru 9°30S 77°32'W 120 C2
Huascarán, Nevado Peru 9°7S 77°37'W 120 C2
Huasco Chile 28°30S 71°15'W 121 E2
Huatabampo Mexico 26°50'N 109°38'W 114 B3
Hubei ☐ China 31°0'N 112°0E 79 E11
Hubli India 15°22'N 75°15E 84 M9
Hucknall U.K. 53°3'N 1°13'W 23 F6
Huddersfield U.K. 53°39'N 1°47'W 23 E5
Hudiksvall Sweden 61°43'N 17°10E 63 E7
Hudson → U.S.A. 40°42'N 74°2'W 113 E10
Hudson Bay Canada 60°0'N 86°0'W 109 D11
Hudson Falls U.S.A. 43°18'N 73°35'W 113 D11
Hudson Str. Canada 62°0'N 70°0'W 109 C13
Hue Vietnam 16°30'N 107°35E 82 A3
Huelva Spain 37°18'N 6°57'W 67 D2

Huelva

Huesca
Karamay

Huesca Spain 42°8N 0°25W 67 A5
Hugh Town U.K. 49°55N 6°19W 27 H1
Hughenden Australia 20°52S 144°10E 98 E7
Hugli → India 21°56N 88°4E 85 J16
Huila, Nevado del Colombia 3°0N 76°0W 120 B2
Huize China 26°24N 103°15E 78 F9
Hull = Kingston upon Hull U.K. 53°45N 0°21W 23 E8
Hull Canada 45°26N 75°43W 113 C10
Hull → U.K. 53°44N 0°20W 23 E8
Hullavington U.K. 51°32N 2°8W 24 C4
Hulme End U.K. 53°8N 1°50W 23 F5
Hulun Nur China 49°0N 117°30E 79 B12
Humacao Puerto Rico 18°9N 65°50W 115 d
Humaitá Brazil 7°35S 63°1W 120 C3
Humber → U.K. 53°42N 0°27W 23 E8
Humber, Mouth of the U.K. 53°32N 0°8E 23 E9
Humboldt Canada 52°15N 105°9W 108 D9
Humboldt → U.S.A. 39°59N 118°36W 110 B3
Humphreys Peak U.S.A. 35°21N 111°41W 110 C4
Humshaugh U.K. 55°3N 2°8W 22 B4
Húnaflói Iceland 65°50N 20°50W 63 A1
Hunan □ China 27°30N 112°0E 79 F11
Hungary ■ Europe 47°20N 19°20E 65 E10
Hungary, Plain of Europe 47°0N 20°0E 56 F10
Hungerford U.K. 51°25N 1°31W 24 D5
Hŭngnam N. Korea 39°49N 127°45E 79 D14
Hunmanby U.K. 54°10N 0°20W 22 D8
Hunsrück Germany 49°56N 7°27E 64 D4
Hunstanton U.K. 52°56N 0°29E 25 A9
Huntingdon U.K. 52°20N 0°11W 25 B8
Huntingdon Ind., U.S.A. 40°53N 85°30W 112 E5
Huntington W. Va., U.S.A. 38°25N 82°27W 112 F6
Huntly U.K. 57°27N 2°47W 19 H12
Huntsville Canada 45°20N 79°14W 109 E12
Huntsville Ala., U.S.A. 34°44N 86°35W 111 D9
Huntsville Tex., U.S.A. 30°43N 95°33W 111 D7
Hurghada Egypt 27°15N 33°50E 95 C12
Hurley U.K. 46°27N 90°11W 112 B2
Huron U.S.A. 44°22N 98°13W 110 B7
Huron, L. U.S.A. 44°30N 82°40W 112 C6
Hursley U.K. 51°2N 1°23W 24 D6
Hurstbourne Tarrant U.K. 51°17N 1°26W 24 D6
Hurstpierpoint U.K. 50°56N 0°11W 25 E8
Húsavík Iceland 66°3N 17°21W 63 A2
Husband's Bosworth U.K. 52°28N 1°4W 23 H6
Hutchinson U.S.A. 38°5N 97°56W 110 C7
Huyton U.K. 53°25N 2°51W 23 F3
Huzhou China 30°51N 120°8E 79 E13
Hvar Croatia 43°11N 16°28E 68 C7
Hwang Ho = Huang He → China 37°55N 118°50E 79 D12
Hwange Zimbabwe 18°18S 26°30E 97 H5
Hyargas Nuur Mongolia 49°0N 93°0E 78 B7
Hyde U.K. 53°27N 2°4W 23 F4
Hyderabad India 17°22N 78°29E 84 L11
Hyderabad Pakistan 25°23N 68°24E 84 G6
Hyères France 43°8N 6°9E 66 E7
Hyères, Îs. d' France 43°0N 6°20E 66 E7
Hyndman Peak U.S.A. 43°45N 114°8W 110 B4
Hythe U.K. 51°4N 1°5E 25 D11

Ialomița → Romania 44°42N 27°51E 65 F14
Iași Romania 47°10N 27°40E 65 E14
Ibadan Nigeria 7°22N 3°58E 94 G6
Ibagué Colombia 4°20N 75°20W 120 B2
Ibarra Ecuador 0°21N 78°7W 120 B2
Ibb Yemen 14°2N 44°10E 89 E3
Iberian Peninsula Europe 40°0N 5°0W 56 H5
Ibiá Brazil 19°30S 46°30W 122 C1
Ibiapaba, Sa. da Brazil 4°0S 41°30W 120 C5
Ibicaraí Brazil 14°51S 39°36W 122 B3
Ibiza = Eivissa Spain 38°54N 1°26E 67 C6
Ibotirama Brazil 12°13S 43°12W 122 B2
Ibstock U.K. 52°42N 1°24W 23 G6
Ica Peru 14°0S 75°48W 120 D2
Içá → Brazil 2°55S 67°58W 120 C3
İçel Turkey 36°51N 34°36E 71 G5
Iceland ■ Europe 64°45N 19°0W 63 B2
Ichihara Japan 35°28N 140°5E 81 F7
Ichinomiya Japan 35°18N 136°48E 81 F5
Icy C. U.S.A. 70°20N 161°52W 104 B3
Idaho □ U.S.A. 45°0N 115°0W 110 B4
Idaho Falls U.S.A. 43°30N 112°2W 110 B4
Idar-Oberstein Germany 49°43N 7°16E 64 D4
Idle → U.K. 53°27N 0°49W 23 F7
Idlib Syria 35°55N 36°36E 86 C4
Idmiston U.K. 51°9N 1°42W 24 D5
Ife Nigeria 7°30N 4°31E 94 G6
Iforas, Adrar des Africa 19°40N 1°40E 94 C5
Igarapava Brazil 20°3S 47°47W 122 D1
Igarka Russia 67°30N 86°33E 76 C9
Iglésias Italy 39°19N 8°32E 68 E3
Iglulik Canada 69°20N 81°49W 109 C11
Ignace Canada 49°30N 91°40W 112 A2
Igoumenitsa Greece 39°32N 20°18E 69 E9
Iguaçu → Brazil 25°36S 54°36W 121 E4
Iguaçu, Cat. del Brazil 25°41S 54°26W 121 E4
Iguala Mexico 18°21N 99°32W 114 D5
Iguatu Brazil 6°20S 39°18W 120 C6
Iguidi, Erg Africa 27°0N 7°0W 94 C4
Iisalmi Finland 63°32N 27°10E 63 E9
Ijebu-Ode Nigeria 6°47N 3°58E 94 G6
IJsselmeer Neths. 52°45N 5°20E 64 B3
Ikare Nigeria 7°32N 5°40E 94 G7
Ikaria Greece 37°35N 26°10E 69 F12
Ikeda Japan 34°1N 133°48E 81 F3
Ilagan Phil. 17°7N 121°53E 83 A6
Ilām Iran 33°36N 46°36E 86 C6
Ilchester U.K. 51°0N 2°41W 24 D3
Île-de-France □ France 49°0N 2°20E 66 B5
Ilebo Dem. Rep. of the Congo 4°17S 20°55E 96 E4
Ilesha Nigeria 7°37N 4°40E 94 G6
Ilfracombe U.K. 51°12N 4°8W 27 E5
Ilhéus Brazil 14°49S 39°2W 122 B3
Ili → Kazakhstan 45°53N 77°10E 76 E8
Iliamna L. U.S.A. 59°30N 155°0W 108 D4

Iligan Phil. 8°12N 124°13E 83 C6
Ilkeston U.K. 52°58N 1°19W 23 G6
Ilkley U.K. 53°56N 1°48W 23 E5
Illapel Chile 32°0S 71°10W 121 F2
Iller → Germany 48°23N 9°58E 64 D6
Illimani Bolivia 16°30S 67°50W 120 D3
Illinois □ U.S.A. 40°15N 89°30W 111 B9
Illinois → U.S.A. 38°58N 90°28W 111 C8
Ilmen, L. Russia 58°15N 31°10E 70 C5
Ilminster U.K. 50°55N 2°55W 24 E3
Iloilo Phil. 10°45N 122°33E 83 B6
Ilorin Nigeria 8°30N 4°35E 94 G6
Imabari Japan 34°4N 133°0E 81 F3
Imandra, L. Russia 67°30N 33°0E 70 A5
Imatra Finland 61°12N 28°48E 63 E9
imeni Ismail Samani, Pik Tajikistan 39°0N 72°2E 87 B13
Immingham U.K. 53°37N 0°13W 23 E8
Ímola Italy 44°20N 11°42E 68 D4
Imperatriz Brazil 5°30S 47°29W 120 C5
Impéria Italy 43°53N 8°3E 68 C3
Imphal India 24°48N 93°56E 85 G18
In Salah Algeria 27°10N 2°32E 94 C6
Inari Finland 68°54N 27°1E 63 D9
Inarijärvi Finland 69°0N 28°0E 63 D9
İnce Burun Turkey 42°7N 34°56E 71 F5
Incheon S. Korea 37°27N 126°40E 79 D14
Incomáti → Mozam. 25°46S 32°43E 97 K6
Indalsälven → Sweden 62°36N 17°30E 63 E7
India ■ Asia 20°0N 78°0E 84 K11
Indian Ocean 5°0S 75°0E 53 E13
Indiana U.S.A. 40°37N 79°9W 112 E8
Indiana □ U.S.A. 40°0N 86°0W 112 E4
Indiana → U.S.A. 39°46N 86°9W 112 F4
Indigirka → Russia 70°48N 148°54E 77 B15
Indira Gandhi Canal India 28°0N 72°0E 84 F8
Indo-China Asia 15°0N 102°0E 72 G12
Indonesia ■ Asia 5°0S 115°0E 82 F5
Indore India 22°42N 75°53E 84 H9
Indre → France 47°16N 0°11E 66 C4
Indus → Pakistan 24°20N 67°47E 84 G5
Inebolu Turkey 41°55N 33°40E 71 F5
Ingatestone U.K. 51°40N 0°24E 25 C9
Ingleborough U.K. 54°10N 2°22W 22 D4
Ingleton U.K. 54°10N 2°27W 22 D4
Ingolstadt Germany 48°46N 11°26E 64 D6
Ingraj Bazar India 24°58N 88°10E 85 G16
Ingushetia □ Russia 43°20N 44°50E 71 F8
Inishbofin Ireland 53°37N 10°13W 28 D1
Inisheer Ireland 53°3N 9°32W 30 B3
Inishfree B. Ireland 55°4N 8°23W 28 A5
Inishkea North Ireland 54°9N 10°11W 28 C1
Inishkea South Ireland 54°7N 10°12W 28 C1
Inishmaan Ireland 53°5N 9°35W 30 B3
Inishmore Ireland 53°8N 9°45W 30 B3
Inishowen Pen. Ireland 55°14N 7°15W 29 A7
Inishshark Ireland 53°37N 10°16W 28 D1
Inishtrahull Ireland 55°26N 7°13W 29 A7
Inishturk Ireland 53°42N 10°7W 28 D1
Inishvickillane Ireland 52°3N 10°37W 30 D1
Inkberrow U.K. 52°13N 1°58W 24 B5
Inland Sea Japan 34°20N 133°30E 81 F3
Inn → Austria 48°35N 13°28E 64 D7
Inner Hebrides U.K. 57°0N 6°30W 18 J4
Inner Mongolia □ China 42°0N 112°0E 79 C11
Inner Sound U.K. 57°30N 5°55W 18 H6
Innerleithen U.K. 55°37N 3°4W 21 C9
Innsbruck Austria 47°16N 11°23E 64 E6
Inowrocław Poland 52°50N 18°12E 65 B10
Insein Burma 16°50N 96°5E 85 L20
Inta Russia 66°5N 60°8E 70 A11
Interlaken Switz. 46°41N 7°50E 64 E4
Inukjuak Canada 58°25N 78°15W 109 D12
Inuvik Canada 68°16N 133°40W 108 C6
Inveraray U.K. 56°14N 5°5W 20 B5
Inverbervie U.K. 56°51N 2°17W 19 J13
Invercargill N.Z. 46°24S 168°24E 99 K12
Invergordon U.K. 57°41N 4°10W 19 G9
Inverkeithing U.K. 56°2N 3°24W 21 B9
Inverness U.K. 57°29N 4°13W 19 H9
Inverurie U.K. 57°17N 2°23W 19 H13
Ioannina Greece 39°42N 20°47E 69 E9
Iona U.K. 56°20N 6°25W 20 B3
Ionia U.S.A. 42°59N 85°4W 112 D5
Ionian Is. Greece 38°40N 20°0E 69 E9
Ionian Sea Medit. S. 37°30N 17°30E 69 E7
Ios Greece 36°41N 25°20E 69 F11
Iowa □ U.S.A. 42°18N 93°30W 111 B8
Iowa City U.S.A. 41°40N 91°32W 111 B81
Ipameri Brazil 17°44S 48°9W 122 C1
Ipatinga Brazil 19°32S 42°30W 122 C2
Ipiales Colombia 0°50N 77°37W 120 B2
Ipoh Malaysia 4°35N 101°5E 82 D2
Ipswich Australia 27°35S 152°40E 98 F9
Ipswich U.K. 52°4N 1°10E 25 B11
Iqaluit Canada 63°44N 68°31W 109 C13
Iquique Chile 20°19S 70°5W 120 E2
Iquitos Peru 3°45S 73°10W 120 C2
Iraklio Greece 35°20N 25°12E 69 G11
Iran ■ Asia 33°0N 53°0E 87 C8
Irapuato Mexico 20°41N 101°28W 114 C4
Iraq ■ Asia 33°0N 44°0E 86 C5
Irazú, Vol. Costa Rica 10°10N 84°20W 115 E8
Irchester U.K. 52°18N 0°39W 25 B7
Ireland ■ Europe 53°50N 7°52W 62 E2
Ireland's Eye Ireland 53°24N 6°4W 31 B10
Iringa Tanzania 7°48S 35°43E 96 F7
Irish Sea Europe 53°38N 4°48W 62 E4
Irkutsk Russia 52°18N 104°20E 78 A9
Irlam U.K. 53°26N 2°26W 23 F4
Iron Gate Europe 44°44N 22°30E 65 F12
Iron Mountain U.S.A. 45°49N 88°4W 112 C3
Ironbridge U.K. 52°38N 2°30W 23 G3
Ironton U.S.A. 38°32N 82°41W 112 F6
Ironwood U.S.A. 46°27N 90°9W 112 B2
Irrawaddy → Burma 15°50N 95°6E 85 M19
Irt → U.K. 54°23N 3°26W 22 D2
Irthlingborough U.K. 52°20N 0°37W 25 B7
Irtysh → Russia 61°4N 68°52E 76 C7
Irún Spain 43°20N 1°52W 67 A5

Irvine U.K. 55°37N 4°41W 20 C6
Irvinestown U.K. 54°28N 7°39W 28 C6
Isabela Puerto Rico 18°30N 67°2W 115 d
Ísafjörður Iceland 66°5N 23°9W 63 A1
Isar → Germany 48°48N 12°57E 64 D7
Íschia Italy 40°44N 13°57E 68 D5
Isère → France 44°59N 4°51E 66 D6
Ishim → Russia 57°45N 71°10E 76 D8
Ishinomaki Japan 38°32N 141°20E 81 D7
Ishpeming U.S.A. 46°29N 87°40W 112 B4
Isiro Dem. Rep. of the Congo 2°53N 27°40E 96 D5
Iskenderun Turkey 36°32N 36°10E 71 G6
Isla → U.K. 56°32N 3°20W 21 A9
Islamabad Pakistan 33°40N 73°10E 84 C8
Island L. Canada 53°47N 94°25W 108 D10
Island Pond U.S.A. 44°49N 71°53W 113 C12
Islay U.K. 55°46N 6°10W 20 C2
Isleham U.K. 52°21N 0°25E 25 B9
Islington □ U.K. 51°33N 0°6W 26 C8
Islip U.K. 51°50N 1°12W 24 C6
Ismâ'iliya Egypt 30°37N 32°18E 95 B12
Isparta Turkey 37°47N 30°30E 71 G5
Israel ■ Asia 32°0N 34°50E 86 C3
İstanbul Turkey 41°0N 28°58E 71 F4
Istra Croatia 45°10N 14°0E 68 B5
Istria Croatia 45°10N 14°0E 68 B5
Itaberaba Brazil 12°32S 40°18W 122 B2
Itabira Brazil 19°37S 43°13W 122 C2
Itabuna Brazil 14°48S 39°16W 122 B3
Itacoatiara Brazil 3°8S 58°25W 120 C4
Itaipú, Represa de Brazil 25°30S 54°30W 117 F5
Itajaí Brazil 27°50S 48°39W 121 E5
Itajubá Brazil 22°24S 45°30W 122 D1
Italy ■ Europe 42°0N 13°0E 68 C5
Itaperuna Brazil 21°10S 41°54W 122 D2
Itapetinga Brazil 15°15S 40°15W 122 C2
Itapetininga Brazil 23°36S 48°7W 122 D1
Itapicuru → Brazil 11°47S 37°32W 122 B3
Itararé Brazil 24°6S 49°23W 122 D1
Itaúna Brazil 20°4S 44°34W 122 D2
Itchen → U.K. 50°55N 1°22W 24 E6
Ithaca U.S.A. 42°27N 76°30W 112 D9
Itháki Greece 38°25N 20°40E 69 E9
Ittoqqortoormiit Greenland 70°20N 23°0W 54 B6
Itu Brazil 23°17S 47°15W 122 D1
Ivanava Belarus 52°7N 25°29E 65 B13
Ivano-Frankivsk Ukraine 48°40N 24°40E 65 D13
Ivanovo Russia 57°5N 41°0E 70 C7
Ivinghoe U.K. 51°50N 0°37W 25 C7
Ivory Coast ■ Africa 7°30N 5°0W 94 G4
Ivujivik Canada 62°24N 77°55W 109 C12
Ivybridge U.K. 50°23N 3°56W 27 G6
Iwaki Japan 37°3N 140°55E 81 E7
Iwakuni Japan 34°15N 132°8E 81 F3
Iwo Nigeria 7°39N 4°9E 94 G6
Ixworth U.K. 52°18N 0°51E 25 B10
Izhevsk Russia 56°51N 53°14E 70 C9
Izmayil Ukraine 45°22N 28°46E 71 E4
İzmir Turkey 38°25N 27°8E 71 G4
İznik Gölü Turkey 40°27N 29°30E 71 F4
Izumi-Sano Japan 34°23N 135°18E 81 F4

Jabalpur India 23°9N 79°58E 84 H11
Jaboatão Brazil 8°7S 35°1W 120 C6
Jaboticabal Brazil 21°15S 48°17W 122 D1
Jacareí Brazil 23°20S 46°0W 122 D1
Jackson Barbados 13°7N 59°36W 115 g
Jackson Ky., U.S.A. 37°33N 83°23W 112 G6
Jackson Mich., U.S.A. 42°15N 84°24W 112 D5
Jackson Miss., U.S.A. 32°18N 90°12W 111 D8
Jackson Mo., U.S.A. 37°23N 89°40W 112 G3
Jackson Tenn., U.S.A. 35°37N 88°49W 111 C9
Jacksonville Fla., U.S.A. 30°20N 81°39W 111 D10
Jacksonville Ill., U.S.A. 39°44N 90°14W 112 F2
Jacmel Haiti 18°14N 72°32W 115 D10
Jacobabad Pakistan 28°20N 68°29E 84 E6
Jacobina Brazil 11°11S 40°30W 122 B2
Jade U.K. Taiwan 23°25N 120°52E 79 G13
Jaén Spain 37°44N 3°43W 67 D4
Jaffna Sri Lanka 9°45N 80°2E 84 Q12
Jahrom Iran 28°30N 53°31E 87 D8
Jaipur India 27°0N 75°50E 84 F9
Jakarta Indonesia 6°9S 106°52E 82 F3
Jalālābād Afghan. 34°30N 70°29E 87 C12
Jalgaon India 21°0N 75°42E 84 J9
Jalna India 19°48N 75°38E 84 K9
Jalpaiguri India 26°32N 88°46E 85 F16
Jaluit I. Marshall Is. 6°0N 169°30E 102 G8
Jamaame Somali Rep. 0°4N 42°44E 89 G3
Jamaica ■ W. Indies 18°10N 77°30W 114 a
Jamalpur Bangla. 24°52N 89°56E 85 G16
Jamalpur India 25°18N 86°28E 85 G15
Jambi Indonesia 1°38S 103°30E 82 E2
James → U.S.A. 42°52N 97°18W 111 B7
James B. Canada 54°0N 80°0W 109 D12
Jamestown N. Dak., U.S.A. 46°54N 98°42W 110 A7
Jamestown N.Y., U.S.A. 42°6N 79°14W 112 D8
Jammu India 32°43N 74°54E 84 C9
Jammu & Kashmir □ India 34°25N 77°0E 84 B10
Jamnagar India 22°30N 70°6E 84 H7
Jamshedpur India 22°44N 86°12E 85 H15
Jan Mayen Arctic 71°0N 9°0W 54 B7
Janaúba Brazil 15°48S 43°19W 122 C2
Janesville U.S.A. 42°41N 89°1W 112 D3
Januária Brazil 15°25S 44°25W 122 C2
Jaora India 23°40N 75°10E 84 H9
Japan ■ Asia 36°0N 136°0E 81 F5
Japan, Sea of Asia 40°0N 135°0E 81 D4
Japan Trench Pac. Oc. 32°0N 142°0E 102 D6
Japurá → Brazil 3°8S 65°46W 120 C3
Jari → Brazil 1°9S 51°54W 120 C4
Jarrow U.K. 54°59N 1°28W 22 C6
Jarvis I. Pac. Oc. 0°15S 160°5W 103 H12
Jāsk Iran 25°38N 57°45E 87 E9
Jasper Canada 52°55N 118°5W 108 D8
Jaú Brazil 22°10S 48°30W 122 D1
Jauja Peru 11°45S 75°15W 120 D2

Jaunpur India 25°46N 82°44E 85 G13
Java Indonesia 7°0S 110°0E 82 F3
Java Sea Indonesia 4°35S 107°15E 82 E3
Java Trench Ind. Oc. 9°0S 105°0E 82 F3
Jawhar Somali Rep. 2°48N 45°30E 89 G4
Jebel, Bahr el → Sudan 9°30N 30°25E 95 G12
Jedburgh U.K. 55°29N 2°33W 21 D10
Jedda Si. Arabia 21°29N 39°10E 86 F4
Jeffersonville U.S.A. 38°17N 85°44W 112 F5
Jeju-do S. Korea 33°29N 126°34E 79 E14
Jelenia Góra Poland 50°50N 15°45E 64 C8
Jelgava Latvia 56°41N 23°49E 63 F8
Jena Germany 50°54N 11°35E 64 C6
Jeonju S. Korea 35°50N 127°4E 79 D14
Jequié Brazil 13°51S 40°5W 122 B2
Jequitinhonha Brazil 16°30S 41°0W 122 C2
Jequitinhonha → Brazil 15°51S 38°53W 122 C3
Jérémie Haiti 18°40N 74°10W 115 D10
Jerez de la Frontera Spain 36°41N 6°7W 67 D2
Jersey U.K. 49°11N 2°7W 27 J9
Jersey City U.S.A. 40°42N 74°4W 113 E10
Jerseyville U.S.A. 39°7N 90°20W 112 F2
Jerusalem Israel/West Bank 31°47N 35°10E 86 D3
Jervaulx U.K. 54°16N 1°43W 22 D5
Jessore Bangla. 23°10N 89°10E 85 H16
Jhang Maghiana Pakistan 31°15N 72°22E 84 D8
Jhansi India 25°30N 78°36E 84 G11
Jharkhand □ India 24°0N 85°50E 85 H14
Jhelum Pakistan 33°0N 73°45E 84 C8
Jhelum → Pakistan 31°20N 72°10E 84 D8
Jiamusi China 46°40N 130°26E 79 B15
Ji'an China 27°6N 114°59E 79 F11
Jiangsu □ China 33°0N 120°0E 79 E12
Jiangxi □ China 27°30N 116°0E 79 F12
Jiaxing China 30°49N 120°45E 79 E13
Jihlava → Czech Rep. 48°55N 16°36E 65 D9
Jijiga Ethiopia 9°20N 42°50E 89 F3
Jilib Somali Rep. 0°29N 42°46E 89 G3
Jilin China 43°44N 126°30E 79 C14
Jilin □ China 44°0N 127°0E 79 C14
Jima Ethiopia 7°40N 36°47E 89 F2
Jiménez Mexico 27°8N 104°54W 114 B4
Jinan China 36°38N 117°1E 79 D12
Jinchang China 38°30N 102°10E 78 D9
Jincheng China 35°29N 112°50E 79 D11
Jingdezhen China 29°20N 117°11E 79 F12
Jinggu China 23°35N 100°41E 78 G9
Jingmen China 31°0N 112°10E 79 E11
Jinhua China 29°8N 119°38E 79 F12
Jining Nei Monggol Zizhiqu, China 41°5N 113°0E 79 C11
Jining Shandong, China 35°22N 116°34E 79 D12
Jinja Uganda 0°25N 33°12E 96 D6
Jinxi China 40°52N 120°50E 79 C13
Jinzhong China 37°42N 112°46E 79 D11
Jinzhou China 41°5N 121°3E 79 C13
Jipijapa Ecuador 1°0S 80°40W 120 C1
Jishou China 28°21N 109°43E 79 F10
Jiujiang China 29°42N 115°58E 79 F12
Jiwani Pakistan 25°1N 61°44E 87 E10
Jixi China 45°20N 130°50E 79 B15
Jīzān Si. Arabia 17°0N 42°20E 89 D3
Jizzax Uzbekistan 40°6N 67°50E 87 A11
João Pessoa Brazil 7°10S 34°52W 120 C6
Jodhpur India 26°23N 73°8E 84 F8
Joensuu Finland 62°37N 29°49E 63 E9
Johannesburg S. Africa 26°11S 28°2E 97 K5
John Crow Mts. Jamaica 18°5N 76°25W 114 a
John Day → U.S.A. 45°44N 120°39W 110 A2
John o' Groats U.K. 58°38N 3°4W 19 E11
Johnson City U.S.A. 36°19N 82°21W 111 C10
Johnston I. Pac. Oc. 17°10N 169°8W 103 F11
Johnstone U.K. 55°49N 4°31W 20 C6
Johnstown U.S.A. 40°20N 78°55W 112 E8
Johor Bahru Malaysia 1°28N 103°46E 82 D2
Joinville Brazil 26°15S 48°55W 121 E5
Joliet U.S.A. 41°32N 88°5W 112 E3
Joliette Canada 46°3N 73°24W 109 E12
Jolo Phil. 6°0N 121°0E 83 C6
Jones Sound Canada 76°0N 85°0W 109 B11
Jonesboro U.S.A. 35°50N 90°42W 111 C8
Jönköping Sweden 57°45N 14°8E 63 F6
Jonquière Canada 48°27N 71°14W 113 A12
Joplin U.S.A. 37°6N 94°31W 111 C8
Jordan ■ Asia 31°0N 36°0E 86 D4
Jordan → Asia 31°48N 35°32E 86 D3
Jos Nigeria 9°53N 8°51E 94 G7
Joseph Bonaparte G. Australia 14°35S 128°50E 98 C4
Jost Van Dyke I. Br. Virgin Is. 18°29N 64°47W 115 e
Jotunheimen Norway 61°35N 8°25E 63 E5
Jowzjān □ Afghan. 36°10N 66°0E 87 B11
Juan de Fuca, Str. of. N. Amer. 48°15N 124°0W 110 A2
Juan Fernández, Arch. de Pac. Oc. 33°50S 80°0W 103 L20
Juàzeiro Brazil 9°30S 40°30W 122 A2
Juàzeiro do Norte Brazil 7°10S 39°18W 120 C6
Jūbā Sudan 4°50N 31°35E 95 H12
Juba → Somali Rep. 1°30N 42°35E 89 G3
Juchitán de Zaragoza Mexico 16°26N 95°1W 114 D5
Juiz de Fora Brazil 21°43S 43°19W 122 D2
Juliaca Peru 15°25S 70°10W 120 D2
Julianatop Suriname 3°40N 56°30W 120 B4
Jullundur India 31°20N 75°40E 84 D9
Junagadh India 21°30N 70°30E 84 J7
Jundiaí Brazil 24°30S 47°0W 122 D1
Juneau U.S.A. 58°18N 134°25W 108 D6
Junín Argentina 34°33S 60°57W 121 F3
Jur, Nahr el → Sudan 8°45N 29°15E 95 G11
Jura Europe 46°40N 6°5E 66 C7
Jura U.K. 56°0N 5°50W 20 C4
Jura, Sd. of U.K. 55°57N 5°45W 20 C4
Juruá → Brazil 2°37S 65°44W 120 C3
Juruena → Brazil 7°20S 58°3W 120 C4
Juticalpa Honduras 14°40N 86°12W 114 E7
Jutland Denmark 56°25N 9°30E 63 F5
Juventud, I. de la Cuba 21°40N 82°40W 115 C8
Jyväskylä Finland 62°14N 25°50E 63 E9

K

K2 Pakistan 35°58N 76°32E 84 B10
Kabardino-Balkaria □ Russia 43°30N 43°30E 71 F7
Kābul Afghan. 34°28N 69°11E 87 C12
Kabwe Zambia 14°30S 28°29E 97 G5
Kachchh, Gulf of India 22°50N 69°15E 84 H6
Kachchh, Rann of India 24°0N 70°0E 84 H7
Kachin □ Burma 26°0N 97°30E 85 G20
Kaçkar Turkey 40°45N 41°10E 71 F7
Kadavu Fiji 19°0S 178°15E 99 E14
Kade Ghana 6°7N 0°56W 94 G5
Kadoma Zimbabwe 18°20S 29°52E 97 H5
Kaduna Nigeria 10°30N 7°21E 94 F7
Kaesŏng N. Korea 37°58N 126°35E 79 D14
Kafue → Zambia 15°30S 29°0E 97 H5
Kaga Bandoro C.A.R. 7°0N 19°10E 96 C3
Kagera → Uganda 0°57S 31°47E 96 E6
Kagoshima Japan 31°35N 130°33E 81 H2
Kaho'olawe U.S.A. 20°33N 156°37W 110 H16
Kahramanmaraş Turkey 37°37N 36°53E 71 G6
Kai, Kepulauan Indonesia 5°55S 132°45E 83 F8
Kaieteur Falls Guyana 5°1N 59°10W 120 B4
Kaifeng China 34°48N 114°21E 79 E11
Kailua Kona U.S.A. 19°39N 155°59W 110 J17
Kainji Res. Nigeria 10°1N 4°40E 94 F6
Kairouan Tunisia 35°45N 10°5E 95 A8
Kaiserslautern Germany 49°26N 7°45E 64 D4
Kaitaia N.Z. 35°8S 173°17E 99 H13
Kaiyuan China 23°40N 103°12E 78 G9
Kajaani Finland 64°17N 27°46E 63 E9
Kajabbi Australia 20°0S 140°1E 98 E7
Kakamega Kenya 0°20N 34°46E 96 D6
Kakhovka Res. Ukraine 47°5N 34°0E 71 E5
Kakinada India 16°57N 82°11E 85 L13
Kalaallit Nunaat = Greenland ☑ N. Amer. 66°0N 45°0W 54 C5
Kalahari Africa 24°0S 21°30E 97 J4
Kalamata Greece 37°3N 22°10E 69 F10
Kalamazoo U.S.A. 42°17N 85°35W 112 D5
Kalamazoo → U.S.A. 42°40N 86°10W 112 D4
Kalemie Dem. Rep. of the Congo 5°55S 29°9E 96 F5
Kalgoorlie-Boulder Australia 30°40S 121°22E 98 G3
Kalimantan Indonesia 0°0 114°0E 82 E4
Kálimnos Greece 37°0N 27°0E 69 F12
Kaliningrad Russia 54°42N 20°32E 63 F8
Kalispell U.S.A. 48°12N 114°19W 110 A4
Kalisz Poland 51°45N 18°8E 65 C10
Kalkaska U.S.A. 44°44N 85°11W 112 C5
Kallsjön Sweden 63°38N 13°0E 63 E6
Kalmar Sweden 56°40N 16°20E 63 F7
Kalmykia □ Russia 46°5N 46°1E 71 E8
Kaluga Russia 54°35N 36°10E 70 D6
Kalutara Sri Lanka 6°35N 80°0E 84 R12
Kalyan India 19°15N 73°9E 84 K8
Kama → Russia 55°45N 52°0E 70 C9
Kamchatka Pen. Russia 57°0N 160°0E 77 D16
Kamensk Uralskiy Russia 56°25N 62°2E 76 D7
Kamina Dem. Rep. of the Congo 8°45S 25°0E 96 F5
Kamloops Canada 50°40N 120°20W 108 D7
Kampala Uganda 0°20N 32°30E 96 D6
Kampong Saom Cambodia 10°38N 103°30E 82 B2
Kamyanets-Podilskyy Ukraine 48°45N 26°40E 65 D14
Kamyshin Russia 50°10N 45°24E 71 D8
Kananga Dem. Rep. of the Congo 5°55S 22°18E 96 F4
Kanash Russia 55°30N 47°32E 70 C8
Kanawha → U.S.A. 38°50N 82°9W 112 F6
Kanazawa Japan 36°30N 136°38E 81 E5
Kanchenjunga Nepal 27°50N 88°10E 85 F16
Kanchipuram India 12°52N 79°45E 84 N11
Kandahār Afghan. 31°32N 65°43E 87 D11
Kandalaksha Russia 67°9N 32°30E 70 A5
Kandalaksha, G. of Russia 66°0N 35°0E 70 A6
Kandi Benin 11°7N 2°55E 94 F6
Kandy Sri Lanka 7°18N 80°43E 84 R12
Kane U.S.A. 41°40N 78°49W 112 E8
Kane Basin Greenland 79°1N 70°0W 104 B12
Käne'ohe U.S.A. 21°25N 157°48W 110 H16
Kangaroo I. Australia 35°45S 137°0E 98 H6
Kangiqsualujjuaq Canada 58°30N 65°59W 109 D13
Kangiqsujuaq Canada 61°30N 72°0W 109 C12
Kangirsuk Canada 60°0N 70°0W 109 D13
Kanin Pen. Russia 68°0N 45°0E 70 A8
Kankakee U.S.A. 41°7N 87°52W 112 E4
Kankakee → U.S.A. 41°23N 88°15W 112 E3
Kankan Guinea 10°23N 9°15W 94 F4
Kannyakumari India 8°3N 77°40E 84 Q10
Kano Nigeria 12°2N 8°30E 94 F7
Kanpur India 26°28N 80°20E 84 F12
Kansas □ U.S.A. 38°30N 99°0W 110 C7
Kansas → U.S.A. 39°7N 94°37W 111 C8
Kansas City U.S.A. 39°6N 94°35W 111 C8
Kansk Russia 56°20N 95°37E 77 D10
Kanturk Ireland 52°11N 8°54W 30 D5
Kanye Botswana 24°55S 25°28E 97 J5
Kaohsiung Taiwan 22°35N 120°16E 79 G13
Kaolack Senegal 14°5N 16°8W 94 F2
Kapa'a U.S.A. 22°5N 159°19W 110 G15
Kapiri Mposhi Zambia 13°59S 28°43E 97 G5
Kāpīsā □ Afghan. 35°0N 69°20E 87 C12
Kaposvár Hungary 46°25N 17°47E 65 E9
Kaptai L. Bangla. 22°40N 92°20E 85 H18
Kapuas → Indonesia 0°25S 109°20E 82 E3
Kapuskasing Canada 49°25N 82°30W 112 A6
Kara Bogaz Gol Turkmenistan 41°0N 53°30E 87 A8
Kara Kum Turkmenistan 39°30N 60°0E 87 B8
Kara Sea Russia 75°0N 70°0E 76 B7
Karabük Turkey 41°12N 32°37E 71 F5
Karachey-Cherkessia □ Russia 43°40N 41°30E 71 F7
Karachi Pakistan 24°50N 67°0E 84 G5
Karaganda Kazakhstan 49°50N 73°10E 78 B3
Karagiye Depression Kazakhstan 43°27N 51°45E 71 F9
Karakalpakstan □ Uzbekistan 43°0N 58°0E 87 A9
Karakoram Pakistan 35°30N 77°0E 84 B10
Karaman Turkey 37°14N 33°13E 71 G5
Karamay China 45°30N 84°58E 78 B5

Karatax Shan   Ladock

Karatax Shan *China* 35°57N 81°0E 78 D5
Karayazı *Turkey* 39°41N 42°9E 71 G7
Karbalā' *Iraq* 32°36N 44°3E 86 C6
Karelia □ *Russia* 65°30N 32°30E 70 A5
Kariba, L. *Zimbabwe* 16°40S 28°25E 97 H5
Kariba Dam *Zimbabwe* 16°30S 28°35E 97 H5
Karimata, Str. of *Indonesia* 2°0S 108°40E 82 E3
Karlovac *Croatia* 45°31N 15°36E 68 B6
Karlskrona *Sweden* 56°10N 15°35E 63 F7
Karlsruhe *Germany* 49°0N 8°23E 64 D5
Karlstad *Sweden* 59°23N 13°30E 63 F6
Karnak *Egypt* 25°43N 32°39E 95 C12
Karnal *India* 29°42N 77°2E 84 E10
Karnataka □ *India* 13°15N 77°0E 84 N10
Kärnten □ *Austria* 46°52N 13°30E 64 E8
Karpathos *Greece* 35°37N 27°10E 69 G12
Kars *Turkey* 40°40N 43°5E 71 F7
Karwar *India* 14°55N 74°13E 84 M9
Kasai → *Dem. Rep. of the Congo* 3°30S 16°10E 96 E3
Kasaragod *India* 12°30N 74°58E 84 N9
Kāshān *Iran* 34°5N 51°30E 87 C7
Kashi *China* 39°30N 76°2E 78 D4
Kasongo *Dem. Rep. of the Congo* 4°30S 26°33E 96 E5
Kassalâ *Sudan* 15°30N 36°0E 95 E13
Kassel *Germany* 51°18N 9°26E 64 C5
Kastamonu *Turkey* 41°25N 33°43E 71 F5
Kasur *Pakistan* 31°5N 74°25E 84 D9
Katanga □ *Dem. Rep. of the Congo* 8°0S 25°0E 96 F4
Kathiawar *India* 22°20N 71°0E 84 H7
Kathmandu *Nepal* 27°45N 85°20E 85 F14
Katihar *India* 25°34N 87°36E 85 G15
Katima Mulilo *Namibia* 17°28S 24°13E 97 H4
Katiola *Ivory C.* 8°10N 5°10W 94 G4
Katowice *Poland* 50°17N 19°5E 65 C10
Katrine, L. *U.K.* 56°15N 4°30W 20 B7
Katsina *Nigeria* 13°0N 7°32E 94 F7
Kattegat *Denmark* 56°40N 11°20E 63 F6
Kaua'i *U.S.A.* 22°3N 159°30W 110 H15
Kauai Channel *U.S.A.* 21°45N 158°50W 110 H15
Kaukauna *U.S.A.* 44°17N 88°17W 112 C3
Kaunakakai *U.S.A.* 21°6N 157°1W 110 H16
Kaunas *Lithuania* 54°54N 23°54E 63 G8
Kavala *Greece* 40°57N 24°28E 69 D11
Kavieng *Papua N. G.* 2°36S 150°51E 98 A9
Kawagoe *Japan* 35°55N 139°29E 81 F6
Kawaguchi *Japan* 35°52N 139°45E 81 F6
Kawardha *India* 22°0N 81°17E 85 J12
Kawasaki *Japan* 35°31N 139°43E 81 F6
Kawawachikamach *Canada* 54°48N 66°50W 109 D13
Kayah □ *Burma* 19°15N 97°15E 85 K20
Kayes *Mali* 14°25N 11°30W 94 F3
Kayin □ *Burma* 18°0N 97°30E 85 L20
Kayseri *Turkey* 38°45N 35°30E 71 G6
Kazan *Russia* 55°50N 49°10E 70 C8
Kazan-Rettō *Pac. Oc.* 25°0N 141°0E 102 E6
Kazanlŭk *Bulgaria* 42°38N 25°20E 69 C11
Kea *Greece* 37°35N 24°22E 69 F11
Kea *U.K.* 50°14N 5°6W 27 G3
Keady *U.K.* 54°15N 6°42W 29 C8
Kearney *U.S.A.* 40°42N 99°5W 110 B7
Keban *Turkey* 38°50N 38°50E 71 G6
Keban Barajı *Turkey* 38°41N 38°33E 71 G6
Kebnekaise *Sweden* 67°53N 18°33E 63 D7
Kebri Dehar *Ethiopia* 6°45N 44°17E 89 F3
Kebumen *Indonesia* 7°42S 109°40E 82 F3
Kecskemét *Hungary* 46°57N 19°42E 65 E10
Kediri *Indonesia* 7°51S 112°1E 82 F4
Keelby *U.K.* 53°35N 0°16W 23 E8
Keele *U.K.* 53°0N 2°17W 23 F4
Keene *U.S.A.* 42°56N 72°17W 113 D11
Keeper Hill *Ireland* 52°45N 8°16W 30 C6
Keetmanshoop *Namibia* 26°35S 18°8E 97 K3
Kefalonia *Greece* 38°15N 20°30E 69 E9
Keflavík *Iceland* 64°2N 22°35W 63 B1
Kegworth *U.K.* 52°50N 1°17W 23 G6
Keighley *U.K.* 53°52N 1°54W 23 E5
Keith *U.K.* 57°32N 2°57W 19 G12
Keld *U.K.* 54°24N 2°10W 22 D4
Kelkit → *Turkey* 40°45N 36°32E 71 F6
Kellett, C. *Canada* 72°0N 126°0W 109 B7
Kellogg *U.S.A.* 47°32N 116°7W 110 A3
Kelowna *Canada* 49°50N 119°25W 108 D8
Kelsale *U.K.* 52°14N 1°31E 25 B12
Kelsall *U.K.* 53°13N 2°43W 23 F3
Kelso *U.K.* 55°36N 2°26W 21 C11
Kelvedon *U.K.* 51°50N 0°43E 25 C10
Kem *Russia* 65°0N 34°38E 70 B5
Kemble *U.K.* 51°40N 1°59W 24 C5
Kemerovo *Russia* 55°20N 86°5E 76 D9
Kemi *Finland* 65°44N 24°34E 63 D8
Kemijoki → *Finland* 65°47N 24°32E 63 D8
Kemp Land *Antarctica* 69°0S 55°0E 55 C5
Kempsey *U.K.* 52°8N 2°12W 24 B4
Kempston *U.K.* 52°7N 0°30W 25 B8
Kempten *Germany* 47°45N 10°17E 64 E6
Kenai *U.S.A.* 60°33N 151°16W 108 C4
Kendal *U.K.* 54°20N 2°44W 22 D3
Kendari *Indonesia* 3°50S 122°30E 83 E6
Kenema *S. Leone* 7°50N 11°14W 94 G3
Kenilworth *U.K.* 52°21N 1°34W 24 B5
Kenitra *Morocco* 34°15N 6°40W 94 B4
Kenmare *Ireland* 51°53N 9°36W 30 E3
Kenmare River *Ireland* 51°48N 9°51W 30 E3
Kennet → *U.K.* 51°27N 0°57W 25 D7
Kennewick *U.S.A.* 46°12N 119°7W 110 A3
Kenninghall *U.K.* 52°26N 1°0E 25 B11
Kenogami → *Canada* 51°6N 84°28W 109 D11
Kenora *Canada* 49°47N 94°29W 108 E10
Kenosha *U.S.A.* 42°35N 87°49W 112 D4
Kent *U.S.A.* 41°9N 81°22W 112 E7
Kent □ *U.K.* 51°12N 0°40E 25 D10
Kent Pen. *Canada* 68°30N 107°0W 108 C9
Kentisbeare *U.K.* 50°51N 3°20W 27 F7
Kenton *U.S.A.* 40°39N 83°37W 112 E6
Kentucky □ *U.S.A.* 37°0N 84°0W 112 G5
Kentucky → *U.S.A.* 38°41N 85°11W 112 F5
Kentville *Canada* 45°6N 64°29W 109 E13
Kenya ■ *Africa* 1°0N 38°0E 96 D7

Kenya, Mt. *Kenya* 0°1S 37°18E 96 E7
Kerala □ *India* 11°0N 76°15E 84 P10
Kerch *Ukraine* 45°20N 36°20E 71 E6
Kerguelen *Ind. Oc.* 49°15S 69°10E 53 G13
Kericho *Kenya* 0°22S 35°15E 96 E7
Kerinci *Indonesia* 1°40S 101°15E 82 E2
Kermadec Is. *Pac. Oc.* 30°0S 178°15W 99 G15
Kermadec Trench *Pac. Oc.* 30°30S 176°0W 99 G15
Kermān *Iran* 30°15N 57°1E 87 D9
Kermānshāh *Iran* 34°23N 47°0E 86 C6
Kerrera *U.K.* 56°24N 5°33W 20 B4
Kerrobert *Canada* 51°56N 109°8W 108 D9
Kerry □ *Ireland* 52°7N 9°35W 30 D3
Kerry Hd. *Ireland* 52°25N 9°56W 30 D3
Kessingland *U.K.* 52°26N 1°43E 25 B12
Keswick *U.K.* 54°36N 3°8W 22 C2
Ketchikan *U.S.A.* 55°21N 131°39W 108 D6
Kettering *U.K.* 52°24N 0°43W 25 B7
Kettle Ness *U.K.* 54°33N 0°42W 22 C7
Kettlewell *U.K.* 54°9N 2°3W 22 C4
Kewaunee *U.S.A.* 44°27N 87°31W 112 C4
Keweenaw B. *U.S.A.* 47°0N 88°15W 112 B3
Keweenaw Pen. *U.S.A.* 47°15N 88°15W 112 B3
Keweenaw Pt. *U.S.A.* 47°25N 87°43W 112 B4
Kexby *U.K.* 53°22N 0°42W 23 F7
Key West *U.S.A.* 24°33N 81°48W 111 F10
Keyingham *U.K.* 53°43N 0°7W 23 E8
Keymer *U.K.* 50°55N 0°7W 25 E8
Keynsham *U.K.* 51°24N 2°29W 24 D4
Keyser *U.S.A.* 39°26N 78°59W 112 F8
Keyworth *U.K.* 52°52N 1°5W 23 G6
Khabarovsk *Russia* 48°30N 135°5E 79 B16
Khairpur *Pakistan* 27°32N 68°49E 84 F6
Khambhat *India* 22°23N 72°33E 84 H8
Khambhat, G. of *India* 20°45N 72°30E 84 J8
Khamis Mushayt *Si. Arabia* 18°18N 42°44E 89 D3
Khandyga *Russia* 62°42N 135°35E 77 C14
Khanewal *Pakistan* 30°20N 71°55E 84 D7
Khanka, L. *Asia* 45°0N 132°24E 79 C15
Kharagpur *India* 22°20N 87°25E 85 H15
Kharg *Iran* 29°15N 50°28E 86 D7
Khârga, El Wâhât el *Egypt* 25°10N 30°35E 95 C12
Kharkov *Ukraine* 49°58N 36°20E 71 E6
Khartoum *Sudan* 15°31N 32°35E 95 E12
Khaskovo *Bulgaria* 41°56N 25°30E 69 D11
Khatanga *Russia* 72°0N 102°20E 77 B11
Khemisset *Morocco* 33°50N 6°1W 94 B4
Khenchela *Algeria* 35°28N 7°11E 94 A7
Kherson *Ukraine* 46°35N 32°35E 71 E5
Khmelnytskyy *Ukraine* 49°23N 27°0E 65 D14
Khojak Pass *Afghan.* 30°51N 66°34E 87 D11
Kholm *Afghan.* 36°45N 67°40E 87 B11
Khon Kaen *Thailand* 16°30N 102°47E 82 A2
Khorramābād *Iran* 33°30N 48°25E 86 C7
Khorramshahr *Iran* 30°29N 48°15E 86 D7
Khouribga *Morocco* 32°58N 6°57W 94 B4
Khŭjand *Tajikistan* 40°17N 69°37E 87 B12
Khulna *Bangla.* 22°45N 89°34E 85 H16
Khulna □ *Bangla.* 22°25N 89°35E 85 H16
Khunjerab Pass *Asia* 36°40N 75°25E 84 A9
Khushab *Pakistan* 32°20N 72°20E 84 C8
Khuzdar *Pakistan* 27°52N 66°30E 84 F5
Khvoy *Iran* 38°35N 45°0E 86 B6
Khyber Pass *Afghan.* 34°10N 71°8E 84 B7
Kibworth Beauchamp *U.K.* 52°33N 0°59W 23 G7
Kicking Horse Pass *Canada* 51°28N 116°16W 108 D8
Kidderminster *U.K.* 52°24N 2°15W 24 B4
Kidlington *U.K.* 51°50N 1°15W 24 C6
Kidsgrove *U.K.* 53°5N 2°14W 23 F4
Kidstones *U.K.* 54°13N 2°2W 22 D4
Kidwelly *U.K.* 51°44N 4°18W 26 D5
Kiel *Germany* 54°19N 10°8E 64 A6
Kiel Canal = Nord-Ostsee-Kanal *Germany* 54°12N 9°32E 64 A5
Kielce *Poland* 50°52N 20°42E 65 C11
Kielder *U.K.* 55°14N 2°35W 22 B3
Kieler Bucht *Germany* 54°35N 10°25E 64 A6
Kiev *Ukraine* 50°30N 30°28E 65 C16
Kigali *Rwanda* 1°59S 30°4E 96 E6
Kigoma-Ujiji *Tanzania* 4°55S 29°36E 96 E5
Kikwit *Dem. Rep. of the Congo* 5°0S 18°45E 96 E3
Kilauea *U.S.A.* 19°25N 155°17W 110 J17
Kilbirnie *U.K.* 55°46N 4°41W 20 C6
Kilbrannan Sd. *U.K.* 55°37N 5°26W 20 C5
Kildare *Ireland* 53°9N 6°55W 31 B9
Kildare □ *Ireland* 53°10N 6°50W 31 B9
Kilfinnane *Ireland* 52°21N 8°28W 30 D6
Kilham *U.K.* 54°4N 0°23W 22 D8
Kilifi *Kenya* 3°40S 39°48E 96 E7
Kilimanjaro *Tanzania* 3°7S 37°20E 96 E7
Kilindini *Kenya* 4°4S 39°40E 96 E7
Kilkee *Ireland* 52°41N 9°39W 30 C3
Kilkeel *U.K.* 54°4N 6°0W 29 C10
Kilkenny *Ireland* 52°39N 7°15W 31 C8
Kilkenny □ *Ireland* 52°35N 7°15W 31 C8
Kilkhampton *U.K.* 50°52N 4°31W 27 F4
Kilkieran B. *Ireland* 53°20N 9°41W 30 B3
Killala *Ireland* 54°13N 9°12W 28 C3
Killala B. *Ireland* 54°16N 9°8W 28 C3
Killaloe *Ireland* 52°48N 8°28W 30 C6
Killarney *Ireland* 52°4N 9°30W 30 D4
Killarney △ *Ireland* 52°0N 9°33W 30 E3
Killary Harbour *Ireland* 53°38N 9°52W 28 D2
Killeen *U.S.A.* 31°7N 97°44W 110 D7
Killin *U.K.* 56°28N 4°19W 20 B5
Killiney *Ireland* 53°15N 6°7W 31 B10
Killinghall *U.K.* 54°2N 1°33W 22 D5
Killorglin *Ireland* 52°6N 9°47W 30 D3
Killybegs *Ireland* 54°38N 8°26W 28 B5
Kilmarnock *U.K.* 55°37N 4°29W 20 C7
Kilrush *Ireland* 52°38N 9°29W 30 C4
Kilsby *U.K.* 52°20N 1°10W 24 B6
Kilsyth *U.K.* 55°59N 4°3W 20 C7
Kilwa Kivinje *Tanzania* 8°45S 39°25E 96 F7
Kilwinning *U.K.* 55°39N 4°43W 20 C6
Kimberley *Australia* 16°20S 127°0E 98 D4
Kimberley *S. Africa* 28°43S 24°46E 97 K4
Kimbolton *U.K.* 52°18N 0°24W 25 B8
Kimch'aek *N. Korea* 40°40N 129°10E 79 C14
Kimmirut *Canada* 62°50N 69°50W 109 C13

Kimry *Russia* 56°55N 37°15E 70 C6
Kinabalu, Gunung *Malaysia* 6°0N 116°0E 82 C5
Kincardine *Canada* 44°10N 81°40W 112 C7
Kincardine *Aberds., U.K.* 56°57N 2°25W 19 J13
Kincardine *Fife, U.K.* 56°4N 3°43W 21 B8
Kinder Scout *U.K.* 53°24N 1°52W 23 F5
Kindersley *Canada* 51°30N 109°10W 108 D9
Kindia *Guinea* 10°0N 12°52W 94 F3
Kindu *Dem. Rep. of the Congo* 2°55S 25°50E 96 E5
Kineshma *Russia* 57°30N 42°5E 70 C7
Kineton *U.K.* 52°10N 1°31W 24 B5
King George I. *Antarctica* 60°0S 60°0W 55 C18
King George Is. *Canada* 57°20N 80°30W 109 D11
King I. *Australia* 39°50S 144°0E 98 H7
King William I. *Canada* 69°10N 97°25W 108 C10
Kingman *U.S.A.* 35°12N 114°4W 110 C4
King's Lynn *U.K.* 52°45N 0°24E 25 A9
King's Sutton *U.K.* 52°2N 1°15W 24 B6
King's Worthy *U.K.* 51°6N 1°17W 24 D6
Kingsbridge *U.K.* 50°17N 3°47W 27 G6
Kingsbury *U.K.* 52°34N 1°40W 23 G5
Kingscourt *Ireland* 53°55N 6°48W 29 D8
Kingskerswell *U.K.* 50°29N 3°35W 27 G6
Kingsland *U.K.* 52°15N 2°48W 24 B3
Kingsteignton *U.K.* 50°33N 3°36W 27 F6
Kingston *Canada* 44°14N 76°30W 109 E12
Kingston *Jamaica* 18°0N 76°50W 114 a
Kingston *N.Y., U.S.A.* 41°56N 73°59W 113 E10
Kingston *Pa., U.S.A.* 41°16N 75°54W 113 E10
Kingston upon Hull *U.K.* 53°45N 0°21W 23 E8
Kingston-upon-Thames □ *U.K.* 51°24N 0°17W 25 D8
Kingstown *St. Vincent* 13°10N 61°10W 115 E12
Kingsville *U.S.A.* 27°31N 97°52W 110 E7
Kingswear *U.K.* 50°21N 3°35W 27 G6
Kingswood *U.K.* 51°27N 2°31W 24 D3
Kington *U.K.* 52°13N 3°1W 24 B2
Kingussie *U.K.* 57°6N 4°2W 19 H8
Kinlochleven *U.K.* 56°43N 5°0W 18 J7
Kinnairds Hd. *U.K.* 57°43N 2°1W 19 G13
Kinngait *Canada* 64°14N 76°32W 109 C12
Kinross *U.K.* 56°13N 3°25W 21 B9
Kinsale *Ireland* 51°42N 8°31W 30 E5
Kinsale, Old Hd. of *Ireland* 51°37N 8°33W 30 E5
Kinshasa *Dem. Rep. of the Congo* 4°20S 15°15E 96 E3
Kintore *U.K.* 57°14N 2°20W 19 H13
Kintyre *U.K.* 55°30N 5°35W 20 D4
Kintyre, Mull of *U.K.* 55°17N 5°47W 20 D4
Kinver *U.K.* 52°27N 2°13W 24 B3
Kippure *Ireland* 53°11N 6°21W 31 B10
Kirensk *Russia* 57°50N 107°55E 77 D11
Kirgiz Steppe *Eurasia* 50°0N 55°0E 71 E10
Kiribati ■ *Pac. Oc.* 3°0S 180°0E 102 H10
Kırıkkale *Turkey* 39°51N 33°32E 71 G5
Kiritimati *Kiribati* 1°58N 157°27W 103 G12
Kirkbean *U.K.* 54°55N 3°36W 21 E9
Kirkbride *U.K.* 54°54N 3°12W 22 C2
Kirkburton *U.K.* 53°37N 1°42W 23 E5
Kirkby *U.K.* 53°30N 2°54W 23 F3
Kirkby-in-Ashfield *U.K.* 53°6N 1°14W 23 F6
Kirkby Lonsdale *U.K.* 54°12N 2°36W 22 D3
Kirkby Malzeard *U.K.* 54°10N 1°37W 22 D5
Kirkby Stephen *U.K.* 54°29N 2°21W 22 D4
Kirkby Thore *U.K.* 54°37N 2°32W 22 C4
Kirkbymoorside *U.K.* 54°17N 0°56W 22 D7
Kirkcaldy *U.K.* 56°7N 3°9W 21 B9
Kirkcudbright *U.K.* 54°50N 4°2W 20 E7
Kirkham *U.K.* 53°47N 2°53W 23 E3
Kirkintilloch *U.K.* 55°56N 4°8W 20 C7
Kirkland Lake *Canada* 48°9N 80°2W 109 E11
Kırklareli *Turkey* 41°44N 27°15E 86 A1
Kirkoswald *U.K.* 54°46N 2°41W 22 C3
Kirksville *U.S.A.* 40°12N 92°35W 111 B8
Kirkūk *Iraq* 35°30N 44°21E 86 C6
Kirkwall *U.K.* 58°59N 2°58W 19 E12
Kirkwhelpington *U.K.* 55°9N 1°59W 22 B5
Kirov *Russia* 58°35N 49°40E 70 C8
Kirovohrad *Ukraine* 48°35N 32°20E 71 E5
Kirriemuir *U.K.* 56°41N 3°1W 19 J11
Kırşehir *Turkey* 39°14N 34°5E 71 G5
Kirthar Range *Pakistan* 27°0N 67°0E 84 F5
Kirtlington *U.K.* 51°53N 1°15W 24 C6
Kirton *U.K.* 52°56N 0°3W 23 G8
Kirton in Lindsey *U.K.* 53°29N 0°34W 23 F7
Kiruna *Sweden* 67°52N 20°15E 63 D8
Kiryū *Japan* 36°24N 139°20E 81 E6
Kisangani *Dem. Rep. of the Congo* 0°35N 25°15E 96 D5
Kiselevsk *Russia* 54°5N 86°39E 76 D9
Kishanganj *India* 26°3N 88°14E 85 F16
Kishinev *Moldova* 47°2N 28°50E 65 E15
Kisii *Kenya* 0°40S 34°45E 96 E6
Kislovodsk *Russia* 43°50N 42°45E 71 F7
Kismaayo *Somali Rep.* 0°22S 42°32E 89 H3
Kisumu *Kenya* 0°3S 34°45E 96 E6
Kitakyūshū *Japan* 33°50N 130°50E 81 G2
Kitale *Kenya* 1°0N 35°0E 96 D7
Kitami *Japan* 43°48N 143°54E 81 B8
Kitchener *Canada* 43°27N 80°29W 112 D7
Kithnos *Greece* 37°26N 24°27E 69 F11
Kitimat *Canada* 54°3N 128°38W 108 D7
Kittanning *U.S.A.* 40°49N 79°31W 112 E8
Kitwe *Zambia* 12°54S 28°13E 97 G5
Kivu, L. *Dem. Rep. of the Congo* 1°48S 29°0E 96 E5
Kizil Irmak → *Turkey* 41°44N 35°58E 71 F6
Kizlyar *Russia* 43°51N 46°40E 71 F8
Kladno *Czech Rep.* 50°10N 14°7E 64 C8
Klagenfurt *Austria* 46°38N 14°20E 64 E8
Klaipėda *Lithuania* 55°43N 21°10E 63 F8
Klamath → *U.S.A.* 41°33N 124°5W 110 B2
Klamath Falls *U.S.A.* 42°13N 121°46W 110 B2
Klang *Malaysia* 3°2N 101°26E 82 D2
Klarälven → *Sweden* 59°23N 13°32E 63 F6
Klerksdorp *S. Africa* 26°53S 26°38E 97 K5
Kluane L. *Canada* 61°15N 138°40W 108 C6
Klyuchevskaya, Gora *Russia* 55°50N 160°30E 77 D17
Knaresborough *U.K.* 54°1N 1°28W 23 D6
Knebworth *U.K.* 51°52N 0°11W 25 C8

Knighton *U.K.* 52°21N 3°3W 26 C7
Knock *Ireland* 53°48N 8°55W 28 D4
Knockmealdown Mts. *Ireland* 52°14N 7°56W 30 D7
Knossós *Greece* 35°16N 25°10E 69 G11
Knottingley *U.K.* 53°43N 1°16W 23 E6
Knowle *U.K.* 52°24N 1°44W 23 H5
Knoxville *U.S.A.* 35°58N 83°55W 111 C10
Knoydart *U.K.* 57°3N 5°33W 18 H6
Knutsford *U.K.* 53°18N 2°21W 23 F4
Kōbe *Japan* 34°41N 135°13E 81 F4
Koblenz *Germany* 50°21N 7°36E 64 C4
Koch Bihar *India* 26°22N 89°29E 85 F16
Kōchi *Japan* 33°30N 133°35E 81 G3
Kodiak *U.S.A.* 57°47N 152°24W 108 D4
Kodiak I. *U.S.A.* 57°30N 152°45W 108 D4
Koforidua *Ghana* 6°3N 0°17W 94 G5
Kōfu *Japan* 35°40N 138°30E 81 F6
Kogalym *Russia* 62°16N 74°29E 76 C8
Kohat *Pakistan* 33°40N 71°29E 84 C7
Kohima *India* 25°35N 94°10E 85 G19
Kohtla-Järve *Estonia* 59°20N 27°20E 63 F9
Kokkola *Finland* 63°50N 23°8E 63 E8
Koko Kyunzu *Burma* 14°7N 93°22E 85 M18
Kokomo *U.S.A.* 40°29N 86°8W 112 E4
Kökshetaü *Kazakhstan* 53°20N 69°25E 76 D7
Koksoak → *Canada* 58°30N 68°10W 109 D13
Kola Pen. *Russia* 67°30N 38°0E 70 A6
Kolar Gold Fields *India* 12°58N 78°16E 84 N11
Kolguyev *Russia* 69°20N 48°30E 70 A8
Kolhapur *India* 16°43N 74°15E 84 L9
Kolkata *India* 22°34N 88°21E 85 H16
Kolomna *Russia* 55°8N 38°45E 70 C6
Kolomyya *Ukraine* 48°31N 25°2E 71 E4
Kolpino *Russia* 59°44N 30°39E 70 C5
Kolwezi *Dem. Rep. of the Congo* 10°40S 25°25E 96 G5
Kolyma → *Russia* 69°30N 161°0E 77 C17
Kolyma Ra. *Russia* 63°0N 157°0E 77 C16
Komatsu *Japan* 36°25N 136°30E 81 E5
Komi □ *Russia* 64°0N 55°0E 70 B10
Kompong Cham *Cambodia* 12°0N 105°30E 82 B3
Komsomolsk-na-Amur *Russia* 50°30N 137°0E 77 D14
Konar □ *Afghan.* 34°30N 71°3E 87 C12
Kondūz *Afghan.* 36°50N 68°50E 87 B12
Kongur Shan *China* 38°34N 75°18E 78 D4
Konin *Poland* 52°12N 18°15E 65 B10
Konosha *Russia* 61°0N 40°5E 70 B7
Konotop *Ukraine* 51°12N 33°7E 71 D5
Konqi He → *China* 41°0N 86°0E 78 C6
Konya *Turkey* 37°52N 32°35E 71 G5
Kootenay L. *Canada* 49°45N 116°50W 108 E8
Kopet Dagh *Asia* 38°0N 58°0E 87 B9
Korçë *Albania* 40°37N 20°50E 69 D9
Korčula *Croatia* 42°56N 16°57E 68 C7
Kordestān □ *Iran* 36°0N 47°0E 86 C6
Kordofân *Sudan* 13°0N 29°0E 95 F11
Korea, North ■ *Asia* 40°0N 127°0E 79 D14
Korea, South ■ *Asia* 36°0N 128°0E 79 D14
Korea Bay *Asia* 39°0N 124°0E 79 D13
Korea Strait *Asia* 34°0N 129°30E 79 E14
Korhogo *Ivory C.* 9°29N 5°28W 94 G4
Kōriyama *Japan* 37°24N 140°23E 81 E7
Korla *China* 41°45N 86°4E 78 C6
Koror *Palau* 7°20N 134°28E 102 G5
Körös → *Hungary* 46°43N 20°12E 65 E11
Korosten *Ukraine* 50°54N 28°36E 71 D4
Kortrijk *Belgium* 50°50N 3°17E 64 C2
Koryak Ra. *Russia* 61°0N 171°0E 77 C18
Kos *Greece* 36°50N 27°15E 69 F12
Kościuszko, Mt. *Australia* 36°27S 148°16E 98 H8
Košice *Slovak Rep.* 48°42N 21°15E 65 D11
Kosovo ■ *Europe* 42°30N 21°0E 69 C9
Kôsti *Sudan* 13°8N 32°43E 95 F12
Kostroma *Russia* 57°50N 40°58E 70 C7
Koszalin *Poland* 54°11N 16°8E 64 A9
Kota *India* 25°14N 75°49E 84 G9
Kota Bharu *Malaysia* 6°7N 102°14E 82 C2
Kota Kinabalu *Malaysia* 6°0N 116°4E 82 C5
Kotabumi *Indonesia* 4°49S 104°54E 82 E2
Kotelnich *Russia* 58°22N 48°24E 70 C8
Kotka *Finland* 60°28N 26°58E 63 E9
Kotlas *Russia* 61°17N 46°43E 70 B8
Kotor *Montenegro* 42°25N 18°47E 69 C8
Kotri *Pakistan* 25°22N 68°22E 84 G6
Kotuy → *Russia* 71°54N 102°6E 77 B11
Kotzebue *U.S.A.* 66°53N 162°39W 108 C3
Kotzebue Sound *U.S.A.* 66°20N 163°0W 104 C3
Koudougou *Burkina Faso* 12°10N 2°20W 94 F5
Koumra *Chad* 8°50N 17°35E 95 G9
Kovel *Ukraine* 51°11N 24°38E 70 D3
Kovrov *Russia* 56°25N 41°25E 70 C7
Kowloon *China* 22°19N 114°11E 79 a
Koyukuk → *U.S.A.* 64°55N 157°32W 104 C4
Kozáni *Greece* 40°19N 21°47E 69 D9
Kpalimé *Togo* 6°57N 0°44E 94 G6
Kra, Isthmus of *Thailand* 10°15N 99°30E 82 B1
Kragujevac *Serbia* 44°2N 20°56E 69 B9
Krakatoa *Indonesia* 6°10S 105°20E 82 F3
Kraków *Poland* 50°4N 19°57E 65 C10
Kraljevo *Serbia* 43°44N 20°41E 69 C9
Kramatorsk *Ukraine* 48°50N 37°30E 71 E6
Krasnodar *Russia* 45°5N 39°0E 71 E6
Krasnokamensk *Russia* 50°3N 118°0E 77 D12
Krasnokamsk *Russia* 58°4N 55°48E 70 C10
Krasnoturinsk *Russia* 59°46N 60°12E 70 C11
Krasnoyarsk *Russia* 56°8N 93°0E 77 D10
Krasnyy Luch *Ukraine* 48°13N 39°0E 71 E6
Krefeld *Germany* 51°20N 6°33E 64 C4
Kremenchuk *Ukraine* 49°5N 33°25E 71 E5
Kribi *Cameroon* 2°57N 9°56E 96 D1
Krishna → *India* 15°57N 80°59E 85 M12
Kristiansand *Norway* 58°8N 8°1E 63 F5
Kristiansund *Norway* 63°7N 7°45E 63 E5
Krivoy Rog *Ukraine* 47°51N 33°20E 71 E5
Krk *Croatia* 45°8N 14°40E 68 B6
Kronshtadt *Russia* 59°57N 29°51E 70 B4
Kroonstad *S. Africa* 27°43S 27°19E 97 K5
Kropotkin *Russia* 45°28N 40°28E 71 E7
Krosno *Poland* 49°42N 21°46E 65 D11
Krugersdorp *S. Africa* 26°5S 27°46E 97 K5

Kruševac *Serbia* 43°35N 21°28E 69 C9
Ksar el Kebir *Morocco* 35°0N 6°0W 94 B4
Kuala Belait *Malaysia* 4°35N 114°11E 82 D4
Kuala Lumpur *Malaysia* 3°9N 101°41E 82 D2
Kuala Terengganu *Malaysia* 5°20N 103°8E 82 C2
Kuantan *Malaysia* 3°49N 103°20E 82 D2
Kuching *Malaysia* 1°33N 110°25E 82 D4
Kudymkar *Russia* 59°1N 54°39E 70 C9
Kugluktuk *Canada* 67°50N 115°5W 108 C8
Kuito *Angola* 12°22S 16°55E 97 G3
Kŭlob *Tajikistan* 37°55N 69°50E 87 B12
Kuma → *Russia* 44°55N 47°0E 71 F8
Kumagaya *Japan* 36°9N 139°22E 81 E6
Kumamoto *Japan* 32°45N 130°45E 81 G2
Kumanovo *Macedonia* 42°9N 21°42E 69 C9
Kumasi *Ghana* 6°41N 1°38W 94 G5
Kumba *Cameroon* 4°36N 9°24E 96 D1
Kumbakonam *India* 10°58N 79°25E 84 P11
Kumertau *Russia* 52°45N 55°57E 70 D10
Kumtag Desert *China* 39°40N 92°0E 78 C7
Kungur *Russia* 57°25N 56°57E 70 C10
Kunlun Shan *Asia* 36°0N 86°30E 78 D6
Kunming *China* 25°1N 102°41E 78 F9
Kuopio *Finland* 62°53N 27°35E 63 E9
Kupang *Indonesia* 10°19S 123°39E 83 F6
Kuqa *China* 41°35N 82°30E 78 C5
Kür → *Azerbaijan* 39°29N 49°15E 71 G8
Kurdistan *Asia* 37°20N 43°30E 86 B5
Kure *Japan* 34°14N 132°32E 81 F3
Kurgan *Russia* 55°26N 65°18E 76 D7
Kuril Is. *Russia* 45°0N 150°0E 77 E16
Kuril-Kamchatka Trench *Pac. Oc.* 44°0N 153°0E 102 C7
Kurnool *India* 15°45N 78°0E 84 M11
Kursk *Russia* 51°42N 36°11E 70 D6
Kuruktag *China* 41°0N 89°0E 78 C6
Kurume *Japan* 33°15N 130°30E 81 G2
Kushiro *Japan* 43°0N 144°25E 81 B9
Kushtia *Bangla.* 23°55N 89°5E 85 H16
Kuskokwim → *U.S.A.* 60°5N 162°25W 104 C3
Kuskokwim B. *U.S.A.* 59°45N 162°25W 108 D3
Kütahya *Turkey* 39°30N 30°2E 71 G5
Kutaisi *Georgia* 42°19N 42°40E 71 F7
Kuujjuaq *Canada* 58°6N 68°15W 109 D13
Kuujjuarapik *Canada* 55°20N 77°35W 109 D12
Kuwait *Kuwait* 29°30N 48°0E 86 D7
Kuwait ■ *Asia* 29°30N 47°30E 86 D6
Kuybyshev Res. *Russia* 55°2N 49°30E 70 C8
Kuznetsk *Russia* 53°12N 46°40E 70 D8
Kuzomen *Russia* 66°22N 36°50E 70 A6
KwaMashu *S. Africa* 29°45S 30°58E 97 K6
KwaZulu Natal □ *S. Africa* 29°0S 30°0E 97 K6
Kwekwe *Zimbabwe* 18°58S 29°48E 97 H5
Kyle of Lochalsh *U.K.* 57°17N 5°44W 18 H6
Kyoga, L. *Uganda* 1°35N 33°0E 96 D6
Kyōto *Japan* 35°0N 135°45E 81 F4
Kyrenia *Cyprus* 35°20N 33°20E 86 C3
Kyrgyzstan ■ *Asia* 42°0N 75°0E 76 E8
Kyūshū *Japan* 33°0N 131°0E 81 G2
Kyustendil *Bulgaria* 42°16N 22°41E 69 C10
Kyzyl Kum *Uzbekistan* 42°30N 65°0E 87 A10
Kyzyl-Orda *Kazakhstan* 44°48N 65°28E 76 E7

L

La Alcarria *Spain* 40°31N 2°45W 67 B4
La Barra *Nic.* 12°54N 83°33W 115 E8
La Ceiba *Honduras* 15°40N 86°50W 114 D7
La Coruña *Spain* 43°20N 8°25W 67 A1
La Crosse *U.S.A.* 43°48N 91°15W 112 D2
La Désirade *Guadeloupe* 16°18N 61°3W 114 b
La Grande *U.S.A.* 45°20N 118°5W 110 A3
La Grande → *Canada* 53°50N 79°0W 109 D12
La Grange *U.S.A.* 33°2N 85°2W 111 D10
La Habana *Cuba* 23°8N 82°22W 115 C8
La Junta *U.S.A.* 37°59N 103°33W 110 C6
La Línea de la Concepción *Spain* 36°15N 5°23W 67 D3
La Loche *Canada* 56°29N 109°26W 108 D9
La Mancha *Spain* 39°10N 2°54W 67 C4
La Oroya *Peru* 11°32S 75°54W 120 D2
La Palma *Canary Is.* 28°40N 17°50W 94 C2
La Paz *Bolivia* 16°20S 68°10W 120 D3
La Paz *Mexico* 24°10N 110°18W 114 C2
La Perouse Str. *Asia* 45°40N 142°0E 102 C6
La Plata *Argentina* 35°0S 57°55W 121 F4
La Quiaca *Argentina* 22°5S 65°35W 121 E3
La Rioja *Argentina* 29°20S 67°0W 121 E3
La Rioja □ *Spain* 42°20N 2°20W 67 A4
La Roche-sur-Yon *France* 46°40N 1°25W 66 C3
La Rochelle *France* 46°10N 1°9W 66 C3
La Romana *Dom. Rep.* 18°27N 68°57W 115 D11
La Ronge *Canada* 55°5N 105°20W 108 D9
La Sarre *Canada* 48°45N 79°15W 112 A8
La Serena *Chile* 29°55S 71°10W 121 E2
La Seyne-sur-Mer *France* 43°7N 5°52E 66 E6
La Spézia *Italy* 44°7N 9°50E 68 B3
La Tortuga *Venezuela* 11°0N 65°22W 120 A3
La Trinité *Martinique* 14°45N 60°58W 114 c
La Tuque *Canada* 47°30N 72°50W 109 E12
La Vega *Dom. Rep.* 19°20N 70°30W 115 D10
Labé *Guinea* 11°24N 12°16W 94 F3
Labinsk *Russia* 44°40N 40°48E 71 F7
Laborie *St. Lucia* 13°45N 61°2W 115 f
Labrador *Canada* 53°20N 61°0W 109 D13
Labrador City *Canada* 52°57N 66°55W 109 D13
Labrador Sea *Atl. Oc.* 57°0N 54°0W 109 D14
Labuan *Malaysia* 5°21N 115°13E 82 C5
Lac La Biche *Canada* 54°45N 111°58W 108 D8
Lac-Mégantic *Canada* 45°35N 70°53W 113 C12
Laccadive Is. = Lakshadweep Is. *India* 10°0N 72°30E 72 G9
Laceby *U.K.* 53°33N 0°10W 23 E8
Lacock *U.K.* 51°24N 2°7W 24 D4
Lacombe *Canada* 52°30N 113°44W 108 D8
Laconia *U.S.A.* 43°32N 71°28W 113 D12
Ladakh Ra. *India* 34°0N 78°0E 84 C11
Ladder Hills *U.K.* 57°13N 3°16W 19 H11
Ladock *U.K.* 50°19N 4°58W 27 G4

Ladoga, L. **Lydham**

Ladoga, L. Russia	61°15N 30°30E	70 B5
Ladysmith S. Africa	28°32S 29°46E	97 K5
Ladysmith U.S.A.	45°28N 91°12W	112 C2
Lae Papua N. G.	6°40S 147°2E	98 B8
Lafayette Ind., U.S.A.	40°25N 86°54W	112 E4
Lafayette La., U.S.A.	30°14N 92°1W	111 D8
Lafia Nigeria	8°30N 8°34E	94 G7
Lagan → U.K.	54°36N 5°55W	29 B10
Lagarto Brazil	10°54S 37°41W	122 B3
Lagdo, L. de Cameroon	8°40N 14°0E	95 G8
Laghouat Algeria	33°50N 2°59E	94 B6
Lagos Nigeria	6°25N 3°27E	94 G6
Lagos Portugal	37°5N 8°41W	67 D1
Lahore Pakistan	31°32N 74°22E	84 D9
Lahti Finland	60°58N 25°40E	63 E9
Lairg U.K.	58°2N 4°24W	19 F9
Laizhou China	37°8N 119°57E	79 D12
Lake Charles U.S.A.	30°14N 93°13W	111 D8
Lake City U.S.A.	30°11N 82°38W	111 D10
Lake District △ U.K.	54°30N 3°21W	22 C2
Lake Havasu City U.S.A.	34°27N 114°22W	110 D4
Lakeland U.S.A.	28°3N 81°57W	111 E10
Lakenheath U.K.	52°25N 0°32E	25 B10
Lakewood U.S.A.	41°28N 81°47W	112 E7
Lakshadweep Is. India	10°0N 72°30E	72 G9
Lamar U.S.A.	38°5N 102°37W	110 C6
Lambaréné Gabon	0°41S 10°12E	96 E2
Lambay I. Ireland	53°29N 6°1W	31 B10
Lamberhurst U.K.	51°5N 0°24E	25 D9
Lambeth □ U.K.	51°28N 0°6W	25 D8
Lambley U.K.	54°56N 2°30W	22 C4
Lambourn U.K.	51°30N 1°32W	24 C5
Lamesa U.S.A.	32°44N 101°58W	110 D6
Lammermuir U.K.	55°50N 2°25W	21 C11
Lammermuir Hills U.K.	55°50N 2°40W	21 C10
Lamon B. Phil.	14°30N 122°20E	83 B6
Lampedusa Medit. S.	35°36N 12°40E	68 G5
Lampeter U.K.	52°7N 4°4W	26 C5
Lamu Kenya	2°16S 40°55E	96 E8
Lanark U.K.	55°40N 3°47W	21 C8
Lancashire □ U.K.	53°50N 2°48W	23 E3
Lancaster U.K.	54°3N 2°48W	22 D3
Lancaster N.H., U.S.A.	44°29N 71°34W	113 C12
Lancaster Pa., U.S.A.	40°2N 76°19W	112 E9
Lancaster Wis., U.S.A.	42°51N 90°43W	112 D2
Lancaster Sd. Canada	74°13N 84°0W	109 B11
Lanchester U.K.	54°50N 1°44W	22 C5
Lancing U.K.	50°49N 0°19W	25 E8
Landes France	44°0N 1°0W	66 D3
Landkey U.K.	51°3N 4°0W	27 E6
Land's End U.K.	50°4N 5°44W	27 G2
Langholm U.K.	55°9N 3°0W	21 D10
Langport U.K.	51°2N 2°50W	24 D3
Langreo Spain	43°18N 5°40W	67 A3
Langres France	47°52N 5°20E	66 C6
Langres, Plateau de France	47°45N 5°3E	66 C6
Langsa Indonesia	4°30N 97°57E	82 D1
Langstrothdale Chase U.K.	54°14N 2°13W	22 D4
Langtoft U.K.	52°42N 0°20W	23 G8
Langtree U.K.	50°55N 4°13W	27 F5
Languedoc France	43°58N 3°55E	66 E5
Lannion France	48°46N 3°29W	66 B2
L'Annonciation Canada	46°25N 74°55W	113 B10
L'Anse U.S.A.	46°45N 88°27W	112 B31
L'Anse la Raye St. Lucia	13°55N 61°3W	115 f
Lansing U.S.A.	42°44N 84°33W	112 D5
Lanzarote Canary Is.	29°0N 13°40W	94 C3
Lanzhou China	36°1N 103°52E	78 D9
Laoag Phil.	18°7N 120°34E	83 A6
Laois □ Ireland	52°57N 7°36W	31 C7
Laon France	49°33N 3°35E	66 B5
Laos ■ Asia	17°45N 105°0E	82 A3
Lapeer U.S.A.	43°3N 83°19W	112 D6
Lapford U.K.	50°51N 3°48W	27 F6
Lapland Europe	68°7N 24°0E	63 D8
LaPorte U.S.A.	41°36N 86°43W	112 E4
Laptev Sea Russia	76°0N 125°0E	77 B13
L'Áquila Italy	42°22N 13°22E	68 C5
Laramie U.S.A.	41°19N 105°35W	110 B5
Laramie Mts. U.S.A.	42°0N 105°30W	110 B5
Laredo U.S.A.	27°30N 99°30W	110 E7
Largs U.K.	55°47N 4°52W	20 C6
Larisa Greece	39°36N 22°27E	69 E10
Larnaca Cyprus	34°55N 33°38E	86 C3
Larne U.K.	54°51N 5°51W	29 B10
Larne L. U.K.	54°50N 5°48W	29 B10
Larrimah Australia	15°35S 133°12E	98 D5
Larsen Ice Shelf Antarctica	67°0S 62°0W	55 C17
Larvik Norway	59°4N 10°2E	63 F6
Las Cruces U.S.A.	32°19N 106°47W	110 D5
Las Palmas Canary Is.	28°7N 15°26W	94 C2
Las Tunas Cuba	20°58N 76°59W	115 C9
Las Vegas N. Mex., U.S.A.	35°36N 105°13W	110 C5
Las Vegas Nev., U.S.A.	36°10N 115°8W	110 C3
Lashio Burma	22°56N 97°45E	85 H20
Lassen Pk. U.S.A.	40°29N 121°30W	110 B2
Lastoursville Gabon	0°55S 12°38E	96 E2
Latacunga Ecuador	0°50S 78°35W	120 C2
Latakia Syria	35°30N 35°45E	86 C3
Latina Italy	41°28N 12°52E	68 D5
Latvia ■ Europe	56°50N 24°0E	63 F8
Lauder U.K.	55°43N 2°43W	21 C10
Lauderdale U.K.	55°44N 2°41W	21 C10
Launceston Australia	41°24S 147°8E	98 J8
Launceston U.K.	50°38N 4°22W	27 F5
Laune → Ireland	52°7N 9°47W	30 D3
Laurel U.S.A.	31°41N 89°8W	111 D9
Laurencekirk U.K.	56°50N 2°28W	19 J13
Laurentian Plateau Canada	52°0N 70°0W	104 E12
Lausanne Switz.	46°32N 6°38E	64 E4
Lavagh More Ireland	54°46N 8°6W	28 B5
Laval Canada	45°33N 73°42W	113 C11
Laval France	48°4N 0°48W	66 B3
Lavendon U.K.	52°11N 0°39W	25 B7
Lavenham U.K.	52°6N 0°48E	25 B10
Lavras Brazil	21°20S 45°0W	122 D2
Lawrence Kans., U.S.A.	38°58N 95°14W	111 C7
Lawrence Mass., U.S.A.	42°43N 71°10W	113 D12
Lawton U.S.A.	34°37N 98°25W	110 D7
Laxey U.K.	54°14N 4°23W	29 C13
Laxfield U.K.	52°18N 1°22E	25 B11
Laxford, L. U.K.	58°24N 5°6W	18 F7
Lazio □ Italy	42°10N 12°30E	68 C5
Lazonby U.K.	54°46N 2°42W	22 C3
Le Creusot France	46°48N 4°24E	66 C6
Le François Martinique	14°38N 60°57W	114 c
Le Gosier Guadeloupe	16°14N 61°29W	114 b
Le Havre France	49°30N 0°5E	66 B4
Le Lamentin Martinique	14°35N 61°2W	114 c
Le Mans France	48°0N 0°10E	66 C4
Le Marin Martinique	14°27N 60°55W	114 c
Le Moule Guadeloupe	16°20N 61°22W	114 b
Le Prêcheur Martinique	14°50N 61°12W	114 c
Le Puy-en-Velay France	45°3N 3°52E	66 D5
Le Robert Martinique	14°40N 60°56W	114 c
Le St-Esprit Martinique	14°34N 60°56W	114 c
Lea → U.K.	53°22N 0°45W	23 F7
Lea U.K.	51°31N 0°1E	25 C9
Leadenham U.K.	53°3N 0°35W	23 F7
Leamington Canada	42°3N 82°36W	112 D6
Leane, L. Ireland	52°2N 9°32W	30 D3
Leatherhead U.K.	51°18N 0°20W	25 D8
Leavenworth U.S.A.	39°19N 94°55W	111 C8
Lebanon Ind., U.S.A.	40°3N 86°28W	112 E4
Lebanon Ky., U.S.A.	37°34N 85°15W	112 G5
Lebanon Pa., U.S.A.	40°20N 76°26W	112 E9
Lebanon ■ Asia	34°0N 36°0E	86 C3
Lebu Chile	37°40S 73°47W	121 F2
Lecce Italy	40°23N 18°11E	69 D8
Lechlade U.K.	51°42N 1°41W	24 C5
Ledbury U.K.	52°2N 2°25W	24 B4
Lee → Ireland	51°53N 8°56W	30 E5
Lee-on-the-Solent U.K.	50°48N 1°12W	24 E6
Leech L. U.S.A.	47°10N 94°24W	111 A8
Leeds U.K.	53°48N 1°33W	23 E5
Leek U.K.	53°7N 2°1W	23 F4
Leeuwarden Neths.	53°15N 5°48E	64 B3
Leeuwin, C. Australia	34°20S 115°9E	98 G2
Leeward Is. Atl. Oc.	16°30N 63°30W	115 D12
Lefkada Greece	38°40N 20°43E	69 E9
Leganés Spain	40°19N 3°45W	67 B4
Legazpi Phil.	13°10N 123°45E	83 B6
Legionowo Poland	52°25N 20°50E	65 B11
Legnica Poland	51°12N 16°10E	64 C9
Leicester U.K.	52°38N 1°8W	23 G6
Leicestershire □ U.K.	52°41N 1°17W	23 G6
Leiden Neths.	52°9N 4°30E	64 B3
Leigh Gt. Man., U.K.	53°30N 2°32W	23 E3
Leigh Hereford, U.K.	52°11N 2°20W	24 B4
Leighton Buzzard U.K.	51°54N 0°38W	25 C7
Leine → Germany	52°43N 9°36E	64 B5
Leinster □ Ireland	53°3N 7°8W	31 B8
Leinster, Mt. Ireland	52°37N 6°46W	31 C9
Leintwardine U.K.	52°22N 2°51W	24 B3
Leipzig Germany	51°18N 12°22E	64 C7
Leiston U.K.	52°12N 1°36E	25 B12
Leith U.K.	55°59N 3°11W	21 C9
Leith Hill U.K.	51°11N 0°22W	25 D8
Leitholm U.K.	55°41N 2°20W	21 C11
Leitrim Ireland	54°0N 8°5W	28 C5
Leitrim □ Ireland	54°8N 8°0W	28 C5
Leixlip Ireland	53°22N 6°30W	31 B9
Leizhou Pen. China	21°0N 110°0E	79 G11
Lelant U.K.	50°11N 5°28W	27 G3
Léman, L. Europe	46°26N 6°30E	64 E4
Lena → Russia	72°52N 126°40E	77 B13
Lenham U.K.	51°14N 0°44E	25 D10
Leninsk-Kuznetskiy Russia	54°44N 86°10E	76 D9
Lennox Hills U.K.	56°3N 4°12W	20 B7
Lens France	50°26N 2°50E	66 A5
Leominster U.K.	52°14N 2°43W	24 B3
Leominster U.S.A.	42°32N 71°46W	113 D12
León Mexico	21°6N 101°41W	114 C4
León Nic.	12°20N 86°51W	114 E7
León Spain	42°38N 5°34W	67 A3
Leonora Australia	28°49S 121°19E	98 F3
Leopoldina Brazil	21°28S 42°40W	122 D2
Lerwick U.K.	60°9N 1°9W	18 B15
Les Cayes Haiti	18°15N 73°46W	115 D10
Les Sables-d'Olonne France	46°30N 1°45W	66 C3
Lesbos Greece	39°10N 26°20E	69 E12
Lesbury U.K.	55°25N 1°36W	22 B5
Leshan China	29°33N 103°41E	78 F9
Leskovac Serbia	43°0N 21°58E	69 C9
Lesosibirsk Russia	58°14N 92°29E	77 D10
Lesotho ■ Africa	29°40S 28°0E	97 K5
Lesser Antilles W. Indies	15°0N 61°0W	115 E12
Lesser Slave L. Canada	55°30N 115°25W	108 D8
Lesser Sunda Is. Indonesia	8°0S 120°0E	83 F6
Leszno Poland	51°50N 16°30E	65 C9
Letchworth U.K.	51°59N 0°13W	25 C8
Lethbridge Canada	49°45N 112°45W	108 E8
Leti, Kepulauan Indonesia	8°10S 128°0E	83 F7
Leticia Colombia	4°9S 70°0W	120 C2
Letterkenny Ireland	54°57N 7°45W	28 B6
Leuchars U.K.	56°24N 2°53W	21 B10
Leuven Belgium	50°52N 4°42E	64 C3
Leven E. Riding, U.K.	53°53N 0°18W	23 E8
Leven Fife, U.K.	56°12N 3°0W	21 B10
Leven → U.K.	54°31N 1°19W	22 C6
Leven, L. Highl., U.K.	56°42N 5°6W	18 J7
Leven, L. Perth & Kinr., U.K.	56°12N 3°22W	21 B9
Lévis Canada	46°48N 71°9W	113 C12
Lewes U.K.	50°52N 0°1E	25 E9
Lewis U.K.	58°9N 6°40W	18 F5
Lewis, Butt of U.K.	58°31N 6°16W	18 E5
Lewisham □ U.K.	51°27N 0°1W	25 D9
Lewisporte Canada	49°15N 55°3W	109 E14
Lewiston Idaho, U.S.A.	46°25N 117°1W	110 A3
Lewiston Maine, U.S.A.	44°6N 70°13W	113 C12
Lewistown Mont., U.S.A.	47°4N 109°26W	110 A5
Lewistown Pa., U.S.A.	40°36N 77°34W	112 E9
Lexington U.S.A.	38°3N 84°30W	112 F5
Lexington Park U.S.A.	38°16N 76°27W	112 F9
Leyburn U.K.	54°19N 1°48W	22 D5
Leyland U.K.	53°42N 2°43W	23 E3
Leysdown on Sea U.K.	51°24N 0°56E	25 D10
Leyte Phil.	11°0N 125°0E	83 B6
Lhasa China	29°25N 90°58E	78 F7
Lhazê China	29°5N 87°38E	78 F6
L'Hospitalet de Llobregat Spain	41°21N 2°6E	67 B7
Lianyungang China	34°40N 119°11E	79 E12
Liaodong Pen. China	40°0N 122°30E	79 D13
Liaoning □ China	41°40N 122°30E	79 C13
Liaoyang China	41°15N 122°58E	79 C13
Liaoyuan China	42°58N 125°2E	79 C14
Liard → Canada	61°51N 121°18W	108 C7
Liberal U.S.A.	37°3N 100°55W	110 C6
Liberec Czech Rep.	50°47N 15°7E	64 C8
Liberia ■ W. Afr.	6°30N 9°30W	94 G4
Libourne France	44°55N 0°14W	66 D3
Libreville Gabon	0°25N 9°26E	96 D1
Libya ■ N. Afr.	27°0N 17°0E	95 C9
Libyan Desert Africa	25°0N 25°0E	95 C10
Libyan Plateau Egypt	30°40N 26°30E	95 B11
Lichfield U.K.	52°41N 1°49W	23 G5
Liddesdale U.K.	55°14N 2°50W	21 D10
Liechtenstein ■ Europe	47°8N 9°35E	64 E5
Liège Belgium	50°38N 5°35E	64 C3
Liepāja Latvia	56°30N 21°0E	63 F8
Liffey → Ireland	53°21N 6°13W	31 B10
Lifford Ireland	54°51N 7°29W	28 B7
Liguria □ Italy	44°30N 8°50E	68 B3
Ligurian Sea Medit. S.	43°20N 9°0E	68 C3
Lihu'e U.S.A.	21°59N 159°23W	110 H15
Lijiang China	26°55N 100°20E	78 F9
Likasi Dem. Rep. of the Congo	10°55S 26°48E	96 G5
Lille France	50°38N 3°3E	66 A5
Lillehammer Norway	61°8N 10°30E	63 E6
Lilleshall U.K.	52°44N 2°23W	23 G4
Lilongwe Malawi	14°0S 33°48E	97 G6
Lima Peru	12°3S 77°2W	120 D2
Lima U.S.A.	40°44N 84°6W	112 E5
Limassol Cyprus	34°42N 33°1E	86 C3
Limavady U.K.	55°3N 6°56W	29 A8
Limay → Argentina	39°0S 68°0W	121 F3
Limbe Cameroon	4°1N 9°10E	96 D1
Limeira Brazil	22°35S 47°28W	122 D1
Limerick Ireland	52°40N 8°37W	30 D5
Limerick □ Ireland	52°30N 8°50W	30 D5
Limfjorden Denmark	56°55N 9°0E	63 F5
Limnos Greece	39°50N 25°5E	69 E11
Limoges France	45°50N 1°15E	66 D4
Limón Costa Rica	10°0N 83°2W	115 F8
Limousin France	45°30N 1°30E	66 D4
Limoux France	43°4N 2°12E	66 E5
Limpopo → Africa	25°5S 33°30E	97 K6
Linares Chile	35°50S 71°40W	121 F2
Linares Mexico	24°52N 99°34W	114 C5
Linares Spain	38°10N 3°40W	67 C4
Linchuan China	27°57N 116°15E	79 F12
Lincoln U.K.	53°14N 0°32W	23 F7
Lincoln Ill., U.S.A.	40°9N 89°22W	112 E3
Lincoln Maine, U.S.A.	45°22N 68°30W	113 C13
Lincoln Nebr., U.S.A.	40°49N 96°41W	111 B7
Lincoln Sea Arctic	84°0N 55°0W	54 A5
Lincolnshire □ U.K.	53°14N 0°32W	23 F7
Lincolnshire Wolds U.K.	53°26N 0°13W	23 F8
Lindale U.K.	54°14N 2°53W	22 D3
Lindesnes Norway	57°58N 7°3E	63 F5
Lindsay Canada	44°22N 78°43W	112 C8
Linfen China	36°3N 111°30E	79 D11
Lingfield U.K.	51°11N 0°0	25 D8
Lingga, Kepulauan Indonesia	0°10S 104°30E	82 E2
Linhai China	28°50N 121°8E	79 F13
Linhares Brazil	19°25S 40°4W	122 C2
Linhe China	40°48N 107°20E	78 C10
Linkinhorne U.K.	50°32N 4°24W	27 F5
Linköping Sweden	58°28N 15°36E	63 F7
Linnhe, L. U.K.	56°36N 5°25W	20 A5
Linqing China	36°50N 115°42E	79 D12
Linslade U.K.	51°54N 0°41W	25 C7
Linstead Jamaica	18°8N 77°2W	114 a
Linton U.K.	52°6N 0°17E	25 B9
Linton U.S.A.	39°2N 87°10W	112 F4
Linxia China	35°36N 103°10E	78 D9
Linyi China	35°5N 118°21E	79 D12
Linz Austria	48°18N 14°18E	64 D8
Lion, G. du France	43°10N 4°0E	66 E6
Lipa Phil.	13°57N 121°10E	83 B6
Lipari Italy	38°26N 14°58E	68 E6
Lipetsk Russia	52°37N 39°35E	70 D6
Lippe → Germany	51°39N 6°36E	64 C4
Lisbon Portugal	38°42N 9°8W	67 C1
Lisburn U.K.	54°31N 6°3W	29 B9
Liscannor B. Ireland	52°55N 9°24W	30 C4
Lisianski I. U.S.A.	26°2N 174°0W	102 E10
Lisieux France	49°10N 0°12E	66 B4
Liskeard U.K.	50°27N 4°29W	27 G5
Liski Russia	51°3N 39°30E	71 D6
Lismore Australia	28°44S 153°21E	98 F9
Lismore Ireland	52°8N 7°55W	30 D7
Liss U.K.	51°3N 0°54W	25 D7
Listowel Canada	43°44N 80°58W	112 D7
Listowel Ireland	52°27N 9°29W	30 D4
Litani → Lebanon	33°20N 35°15E	86 C3
Litcham U.K.	52°44N 0°47E	25 A10
Litchfield U.S.A.	39°11N 89°39W	112 F3
Litherland U.K.	53°29N 2°59W	23 F3
Lithuania ■ Europe	55°30N 24°0E	63 F8
Little Current Canada	45°55N 82°0W	112 C7
Little Khingan Mts. China	49°0N 127°0E	79 B14
Little Minch U.K.	57°35N 6°45W	18 G4
Little Missouri → U.S.A.	47°36N 102°25W	110 A6
Little Ouse → U.K.	52°22N 1°12E	25 B11
Little Rock U.S.A.	34°45N 92°17W	111 D8
Little Walsingham U.K.	52°54N 0°52E	25 A10
Littlehampton U.K.	50°49N 0°32W	25 E7
Littleport U.K.	52°27N 0°19E	25 B9
Littlestone-on-Sea U.K.	50°58N 0°58E	25 E10
Liupanshui China	26°38N 104°48E	78 F9
Liuwa Plain Zambia	14°20S 22°30W	97 G4
Liuzhou China	24°22N 109°22E	79 G10
Liverpool Canada	44°5N 64°41W	109 E13
Liverpool U.K.	53°25N 3°0W	23 F3
Livingston U.K.	55°54N 3°30W	21 C9
Livingston U.S.A.	45°40N 110°34W	110 A4
Livingstone Zambia	17°46S 25°52E	97 H5
Livonia U.S.A.	42°23N 83°23W	112 D6
Livorno Italy	43°33N 10°19E	68 C4
Lizard U.K.	49°58N 5°13W	27 H3
Lizard Pt. U.K.	49°57N 5°13W	27 H3
Ljubljana Slovenia	46°4N 14°33E	64 E8
Ljungan → Sweden	62°18N 17°23E	63 E7
Ljusdal Sweden	61°46N 16°3E	63 E7
Llandeilo U.K.	51°53N 3°59W	26 D6
Llandovery U.K.	51°59N 3°48W	26 D6
Llandrindod Wells U.K.	52°14N 3°22E	26 C7
Llandudno U.K.	53°19N 3°50W	26 A6
Llanelli U.K.	51°41N 4°10W	26 D5
Llanerchymedd U.K.	53°20N 4°23W	26 A5
Llanfair Caereinion U.K.	52°39N 3°20W	26 B7
Llanfair Talhaiarn U.K.	53°13N 3°37W	26 A6
Llanfairfechan U.K.	53°15N 3°58W	26 A6
Llangefni U.K.	53°15N 4°18W	26 A5
Llangollen U.K.	52°58N 3°11W	26 B7
Llanidloes U.K.	52°27N 3°31W	26 C6
Llanllyfni U.K.	53°2N 4°17W	26 A5
Llano Estacado U.S.A.	33°30N 103°0W	110 D6
Llanos S. Amer.	5°0N 71°35W	120 B2
Llanquihue, L. Chile	41°10S 72°50W	121 G2
Llanrhystyd U.K.	52°19N 4°7W	26 C5
Llantrisant U.K.	51°32N 3°22W	27 D7
Llantwit-Major U.K.	51°24N 3°29W	27 E7
Llanwrtyd Wells U.K.	52°7N 3°38W	26 C6
Llanybloedwel U.K.	52°48N 3°8W	26 B7
Llanymynech U.K.	52°47N 3°5W	26 B7
Lleida Spain	41°37N 0°39E	67 B6
Lleyn Peninsula U.K.	52°51N 4°36W	26 B4
Llobregat → Spain	41°19N 2°5E	67 B7
Lloret de Mar Spain	41°41N 2°53E	67 B7
Lloydminster Canada	53°17N 110°0W	108 D9
Llullaillaco, Volcán S. Amer.	24°43S 68°30W	121 E3
Lobatse Botswana	25°12S 25°40E	97 K5
Lobito Angola	12°18S 13°35E	97 G2
Loch Lomond and the Trossachs △ U.K.	56°10N 4°40W	20 B6
Lochaber U.K.	56°59N 5°1W	18 J7
Lochcarrbriggs U.K.	55°7N 3°35W	21 D8
Lochboisdale U.K.	57°9N 7°20W	18 H3
Loches France	47°7N 1°0E	66 C4
Lochgelly U.K.	56°7N 3°19W	21 B9
Lochgilphead U.K.	56°2N 5°26W	20 B5
Lochinver U.K.	58°9N 5°14W	18 F7
Lochmaben U.K.	55°8N 3°27W	21 D9
Lochmaddy U.K.	57°36N 7°10W	18 G3
Lochnagar U.K.	56°57N 3°15W	19 J11
Lochy, L. U.K.	57°0N 4°53W	19 J8
Lock Haven U.S.A.	41°8N 77°28W	112 E9
Lockerbie U.K.	55°7N 3°21W	21 D9
Loddon U.K.	52°32N 1°31E	25 A12
Lodwar Kenya	3°7N 35°36E	96 D7
Łódź Poland	51°45N 19°27E	65 C10
Lofoten Norway	68°30N 13°59E	63 D6
Loftus U.K.	54°34N 0°53W	22 C7
Logan Ohio, U.S.A.	39°32N 82°25W	112 F6
Logan Utah, U.S.A.	41°44N 111°50W	110 B4
Logan W. Va., U.S.A.	37°51N 81°59W	112 G7
Logan, Mt. Canada	60°34N 140°23W	108 C5
Logansport U.S.A.	40°45N 86°22W	112 E4
Logroño Spain	42°28N 2°27W	67 A4
Lohardaga India	23°27N 84°45E	85 H14
Loir → France	47°33N 0°32W	66 C3
Loire → France	47°16N 2°10W	66 C2
Loja Ecuador	3°59S 79°16W	120 C2
Lokoja → Dem. Rep. of the Congo	0°46N 24°16E	96 D4
Lombárdia □ Italy	45°40N 9°30E	68 B3
Lomblen Indonesia	8°30S 123°32E	83 F6
Lombok Indonesia	8°45S 116°30E	82 F5
Lomé Togo	6°9N 1°20E	94 G6
Lomela → Dem. Rep. of the Congo	0°15S 20°40E	96 E4
Lomond, L. U.K.	56°8N 4°38W	20 B6
Łomza Poland	53°10N 22°2E	65 B12
London Canada	42°59N 81°15W	112 D7
London U.K.	51°30N 0°3W	25 D8
London Gatwick ✈ (LGW) U.K.	51°10N 0°11W	25 D8
London Heathrow ✈ (LHR) U.K.	51°28N 0°27W	25 D8
London Stansted ✈ (STN) U.K.	51°54N 0°14E	25 C9
Londonderry U.K.	55°0N 7°20W	28 A7
Londonderry □ U.K.	55°0N 7°20W	28 A7
Londonderry, C. Australia	13°45S 126°55E	98 C4
Londrina Brazil	23°18S 51°10W	121 E4
Long, L. U.K.	56°4N 4°50W	20 B6
Long Beach U.S.A.	33°46N 118°11W	110 D3
Long Bennington U.K.	52°59N 0°44W	23 G7
Long Branch U.S.A.	40°18N 74°0W	113 E11
Long Clawson U.K.	52°51N 0°55W	23 G7
Long Crendon U.K.	51°46N 0°59W	25 C7
Long Eaton U.K.	52°53N 1°15W	23 G6
Long I. Bahamas	23°20N 75°10W	115 C9
Long I. Ireland	51°30N 9°34W	30 F3
Long I. U.S.A.	40°45N 73°30W	113 E11
Long Itchington U.K.	52°16N 1°22W	24 B6
Long Melford U.K.	52°4N 0°45E	25 B10
Long Mynd, The U.K.	52°35N 2°50W	23 G4
Long Preston U.K.	54°2N 2°14W	23 D4
Long Sutton U.K.	52°47N 0°7E	23 G9
Long Xuyen Vietnam	10°19N 105°28E	82 B3
Longford Ireland	53°43N 7°49W	28 D6
Longford □ Ireland	53°42N 7°45W	28 D6
Longframlington U.K.	55°18N 1°47W	22 B5
Longhoughton U.K.	55°26N 1°37W	22 B6
Longlac Canada	49°45N 86°25W	112 A4
Longreach Australia	23°28S 144°14E	98 E7
Longridge U.K.	53°50N 2°35W	23 E3
Longton U.K.	53°44N 2°48W	23 E3
Longtown Cumb., U.K.	55°1N 2°58W	22 B3
Longtown Hereford, U.K.	51°58N 2°59W	24 C3
Longueuil Canada	45°31N 73°29W	113 C11
Longview Tex., U.S.A.	32°30N 94°44W	111 D8
Longview Wash., U.S.A.	46°8N 122°57W	110 A2
Longyan China	25°10N 117°0E	79 F12
Lons-le-Saunier France	46°40N 5°31E	66 C6
Looe U.K.	50°22N 4°28W	27 G5
Loop Hd. Ireland	52°34N 9°56W	30 C3
Lop China	37°3N 80°11E	78 D5
Lop Nur China	40°20N 90°10E	78 C7
Lopez, C. Gabon	0°47S 8°40E	90 G4
Lorain U.S.A.	41°28N 82°11W	112 E6
Loralai Pakistan	30°20N 68°41E	84 D6
Lorca Spain	37°41N 1°42W	67 D5
Lord Howe I. Pac. Oc.	31°33S 159°6E	99 G10
Lord Howe Rise Pac. Oc.	30°0S 162°30E	99 H12
Lordsburg U.S.A.	32°21N 108°43W	110 D5
Lorestän □ Iran	33°30N 48°40E	86 C7
Lorient France	47°45N 3°23W	66 C2
Lorn U.K.	56°26N 5°10W	20 B5
Lorn, Firth of U.K.	56°20N 5°40W	20 B4
Lorraine □ France	48°53N 6°0E	66 B7
Los Alamos U.S.A.	35°53N 106°19W	110 C5
Los Andes Chile	32°50S 70°40W	121 F2
Los Angeles Chile	37°28S 72°23W	121 F2
Los Angeles U.S.A.	34°4N 118°15W	110 D3
Los Mochis Mexico	25°45N 108°57W	114 B3
Los Roques Is. Venezuela	11°50N 66°45W	120 A3
Lošinj Croatia	44°30N 14°30E	68 B6
Lossiemouth U.K.	57°42N 3°17W	19 G11
Lostwithiel U.K.	50°24N 4°41W	27 G4
Lot → France	44°18N 0°20E	66 D4
Lota Chile	37°5S 73°10W	121 F2
Loubomo Congo	4°9S 12°47E	96 E2
Loughborough U.K.	52°47N 1°11W	23 G6
Loughed I. Canada	77°26N 105°6W	109 B9
Loughrea Ireland	53°12N 8°33W	30 B5
Loughros More B. Ireland	54°48N 8°32W	28 B4
Louis XIV, Pte. Canada	54°37N 79°45W	109 D12
Louisa U.S.A.	38°7N 82°36W	112 F6
Louisiade Arch. Papua N. G.	11°10S 153°0E	98 C9
Louisiana □ U.S.A.	30°50N 92°0W	111 D8
Louisville U.S.A.	38°15N 85°46W	112 F5
Lourdes France	43°6N 0°3W	66 E3
Louth Ireland	53°58N 6°32W	29 D8
Louth U.K.	53°22N 0°1W	23 F8
Louth □ Ireland	53°56N 6°34W	29 D8
Lovech Bulgaria	43°8N 24°42E	69 C11
Lowell U.S.A.	42°38N 71°19W	113 D12
Lower Beeding U.K.	51°2N 0°15W	25 D8
Lower Saxony = Niedersachsen □ Germany	52°50N 9°0E	64 B5
Lower Tunguska → Russia	65°48N 88°4E	77 C9
Lowestoft U.K.	52°29N 1°45E	25 B12
Lowick U.K.	55°39N 1°57W	22 A5
Lowther Hills U.K.	55°20N 3°40W	21 D8
Lowville U.S.A.	43°47N 75°29W	113 D10
Loyauté, Îs. N. Cal.	20°50S 166°30E	99 E12
Lualaba → Dem. Rep. of the Congo	0°26N 25°20E	96 D5
Luanda Angola	8°50S 13°15E	96 F2
Luangwa → Zambia	14°25S 30°25E	97 G6
Luanshya Zambia	13°3S 28°28E	97 G5
Luapula → Africa	9°26S 28°33E	96 G5
Lubango Angola	14°55S 13°30E	97 G2
Lubbock U.S.A.	33°35N 101°51W	110 D6
Lübeck Germany	53°52N 10°40E	64 B6
Lublin Poland	51°12N 22°38E	65 C12
Lubumbashi Dem. Rep. of the Congo	11°40S 27°28E	97 G5
Lucan Ireland	53°22N 6°28W	31 B10
Lucania, Mt. Canada	61°1N 140°27W	108 C5
Lucca Italy	43°50N 10°29E	68 C4
Luce Bay U.K.	54°45N 4°48W	20 E6
Lucea Jamaica	18°27N 78°10W	114 a
Lucena Phil.	13°56N 121°37E	83 B6
Lucknow India	26°50N 81°0E	85 F12
Lüda = Dalian China	38°50N 121°40E	79 D13
Lüderitz Namibia	26°41S 15°8E	97 K3
Ludgershall U.K.	51°15N 1°37W	24 D5
Ludhiana India	30°57N 75°56E	84 D9
Ludington U.S.A.	43°57N 86°27W	112 D4
Ludlow U.K.	52°22N 2°42W	23 G4
Ludwigsburg Germany	48°53N 9°11E	64 D5
Ludwigshafen Germany	49°29N 8°26E	64 D5
Lufkin U.S.A.	31°21N 94°44W	111 D8
Luga Russia	58°40N 29°55E	70 C4
Lugano Switz.	46°1N 8°57E	64 E5
Lugansk Ukraine	48°38N 39°15E	71 E6
Lugnaquillia Ireland	52°58N 6°28W	31 C10
Lugo Spain	43°2N 7°35W	67 A2
Lugwardine U.K.	52°4N 2°39W	24 B3
Luing U.K.	56°14N 5°39W	20 B4
Luleå Sweden	65°35N 22°10E	63 D8
Luleälven → Sweden	65°35N 22°10E	63 D8
Lundy U.K.	51°10N 4°41W	27 E4
Lune → U.K.	54°0N 2°51W	23 D3
Lüneburger Heide Germany	53°10N 10°12E	64 B6
Lunéville France	48°36N 6°30E	64 D7
Luni → India	24°41N 71°14E	84 G7
Luofu Dem. Rep. of the Congo	0°10S 29°15E	96 E5
Luoyang China	34°40N 112°26E	79 E11
Luquillo, Sierra de Puerto Rico	18°20N 65°47W	115 d
Luray U.S.A.	38°40N 78°28W	112 F8
Lurgan U.K.	54°28N 6°19W	29 C9
Lusaka Zambia	15°28S 28°16E	97 H5
Lüt, Dasht-e Iran	31°30N 58°0E	87 D9
Lutherstadt Wittenberg Germany	51°53N 12°39E	64 C7
Luton U.K.	51°53N 0°24W	25 C7
Lutsel K'e Canada	62°24N 110°44W	108 C8
Lutsk Ukraine	50°50N 25°15E	65 C13
Lutterworth U.K.	52°28N 1°12W	23 H6
Luvua → Dem. Rep. of the Congo	6°50S 27°30E	96 F5
Luxembourg Lux.	49°37N 6°9E	64 D4
Luxembourg ■ Europe	49°45N 6°0E	64 D4
Luxor = El Uqsur Egypt	25°41N 32°38E	95 C12
Luzern Switz.	47°3N 8°18E	64 E5
Luzhou China	28°52N 105°20E	78 F10
Luziânia Brazil	16°20S 48°0W	122 C1
Luzon Phil.	16°0N 121°0E	83 A6
Lvov Ukraine	49°50N 24°0E	65 D13
Lyakhov Is. Russia	73°40N 141°0E	77 B15
Lybster U.K.	58°18N 3°15W	19 F11
Lydd U.K.	50°57N 0°55E	25 E10
Lydford U.K.	50°38N 4°8W	27 F5
Lydham U.K.	52°31N 2°58W	23 G3

Lyme B. *U.K.* 50°42N 2°53W **24 E3**
Lyme Regis *U.K.* 50°43N 2°57W **24 E3**
Lyminge *U.K.* 51°7N 1°6E **25 D11**
Lymington *U.K.* 50°45N 1°32W **24 E5**
Lymm *U.K.* 53°23N 2°29W **23 F4**
Lympne *U.K.* 51°4N 1°2E **25 D11**
Lynchburg *U.S.A.* 37°25N 79°9W **112 G8**
Lyndhurst *U.K.* 50°52N 1°35W **24 E5**
Lyneham *U.K.* 51°30N 1°58W **24 C5**
Lynmouth *U.K.* 51°13N 3°49W **27 E6**
Lynn Lake *Canada* 56°51N 101°3W **108 D9**
Lynton *U.K.* 51°13N 3°50W **27 E6**
Lyonnais *France* 45°45N 4°15E **66 D6**
Lyons *France* 45°46N 4°50E **66 D6**
Lysva *Russia* 58°7N 57°49E **70 C10**
Lysychansk *Ukraine* 48°55N 38°30E **71 E6**
Lytchett Minster *U.K.* 50°44N 2°4W **24 E4**
Lytham St. Anne's *U.K.* 53°45N 3°0W **23 E2**
Lythe *U.K.* 54°31N 0°41W **22 C7**
Lyubertsy *Russia* 55°40N 37°51E **70 C6**

M

Ma-ubin *Burma* 16°44N 95°39E **85 L19**
Ma'ân *Jordan* 30°12N 35°44E **86 D3**
Maas → *Neths.* 51°45N 4°32E **64 C3**
Maastricht *Neths.* 50°50N 5°40E **64 C3**
Mablethorpe *U.K.* 53°20N 0°15E **23 F9**
Macaé *Brazil* 22°20S 41°43W **122 D2**
McAlester *U.S.A.* 34°56N 95°46W **111 D7**
McAllen *U.S.A.* 26°12N 98°14W **110 E7**
MacAlpine L. *Canada* 66°32N 102°45W **108 C9**
Macapá *Brazil* 0°5N 51°4W **120 B4**
Macau *Brazil* 5°15S 36°40W **120 C6**
Macau *China* 22°12N 113°33E **79 a**
Macclesfield *U.K.* 53°15N 2°8W **23 F4**
M'Clintock Chan. *Canada* 72°0N 102°0W **108 B9**
M'Clure Str. *Canada* 75°0N 119°0W **109 B8**
McComb *U.S.A.* 31°15N 90°27W **111 D8**
McCook *U.S.A.* 40°12N 100°38W **110 B6**
McDonald Is. *Ind. Oc.* 53°0S 73°0E **53 G13**
MacDonnell Ranges *Australia* 23°40S 133°0E **98 E5**
Macduff *U.K.* 57°40N 2°31W **19 G12**
Macedonia □ *Greece* 40°39N 22°0E **69 D10**
Macedonia ■ *Europe* 41°53N 21°40E **69 D9**
Maceió *Brazil* 9°40S 35°41W **122 A3**
Macgillycuddy's Reeks *Ireland* 51°58N 9°45W **30 E3**
Mach *Pakistan* 29°50N 67°20E **84 E5**
Machakos *Kenya* 1°30S 37°15E **96 E7**
Machala *Ecuador* 3°20S 79°57W **120 C2**
Machars, The *U.K.* 54°46N 4°30W **20 E6**
Machias *U.S.A.* 44°43N 67°28W **113 C14**
Machilipatnam *India* 16°12N 81°8E **85 L12**
Machrihanish *U.K.* 55°25N 5°43W **20 D4**
Machu Picchu *Peru* 13°8S 72°30W **120 D2**
Machynlleth *U.K.* 52°35N 3°50W **26 B6**
Mackay *Australia* 21°8S 149°11E **98 E8**
Mackay, L. *Australia* 22°30S 129°0E **98 E4**
McKeesport *U.S.A.* 40°20N 79°51W **112 E8**
Mackenzie *Canada* 55°20N 123°5W **108 D7**
Mackenzie → *Canada* 69°10N 134°20W **108 C6**
Mackenzie Bay *Canada* 69°0N 137°30W **104 C6**
Mackenzie King I. *Canada* 77°45N 111°0W **109 B8**
Mackenzie Mts. *Canada* 64°0N 130°0W **108 B6**
Mackinaw City *U.S.A.* 45°47N 84°44W **112 C5**
McKinley, Mt. *U.S.A.* 63°4N 151°0W **108 C4**
McKinley Sea *Arctic* 82°0N 0°0 **54 A7**
McMinnville *U.S.A.* 45°13N 123°12W **110 A2**
McMurdo Sd. *Antarctica* 77°0S 170°0E **55 D11**
Macomb *U.S.A.* 40°27N 90°40W **112 E2**
Mâcon *France* 46°19N 4°50E **66 C6**
Macon *U.S.A.* 32°51N 83°38W **111 D10**
McPherson *U.S.A.* 38°22N 97°40W **110 C7**
Macquarie Is. *Pac. Oc.* 54°36S 158°55E **102 N7**
Macroom *Ireland* 51°54N 8°57W **30 E5**
Madagascar ■ *Africa* 20°0S 47°0E **97 J9**
Madang *Papua N. G.* 5°12S 145°49E **98 B8**
Madeira *Atl. Oc.* 32°50N 17°0W **94 B2**
Madeira → *Brazil* 3°22S 58°45W **120 C4**
Madeleine, Îs. de la *Canada* 47°30N 61°40W **113 B17**
Madeley *U.K.* 53°0N 2°20W **23 F4**
Madhya Pradesh □ *India* 22°50N 78°0E **84 H11**
Madison *Ind., U.S.A.* 38°44N 85°23W **112 F5**
Madison *S. Dak., U.S.A.* 44°0N 97°7W **111 B7**
Madison *Wis., U.S.A.* 43°4N 89°24W **112 D3**
Madisonville *U.S.A.* 37°20N 87°30W **112 G4**
Madiun *Indonesia* 7°38S 111°32E **82 F4**
Madley *U.K.* 52°2N 2°51W **24 B3**
Madras = Chennai *India* 13°8N 80°19E **84 N12**
Madre, L. *U.S.A.* 25°15N 97°30W **104 G10**
Madre de Dios → *Bolivia* 10°59S 66°8W **120 D3**
Madre de Dios, I. *Chile* 50°20S 75°10W **121 H2**
Madre del Sur, Sierra *Mexico* 17°30N 100°0W **104 H10**
Madre Occidental, Sierra *Mexico* 27°0N 107°0W **114 B3**
Madre Oriental, Sierra *Mexico* 25°0N 100°0W **114 C5**
Madrid *Spain* 40°24N 3°42W **67 B4**
Madura *Indonesia* 7°30S 114°0E **82 F4**
Madurai *India* 9°55N 78°10E **84 Q11**
Maebashi *Japan* 36°24N 139°4E **81 E6**
Maesteg *U.K.* 51°36N 3°40W **27 D6**
Mafeking *S. Africa* 25°50S 25°38E **97 K5**
Mafia I. *Tanzania* 7°45S 39°50E **96 F7**
Magadan *Russia* 59°38N 150°50E **77 D16**
Magallanes, Estrecho de *Chile* 52°30S 75°0W **121 H2**
Magangué *Colombia* 9°14N 74°45W **120 B2**
Magdalena → *Colombia* 11°6N 74°51W **120 A2**
Magdeburg *Germany* 52°7N 11°38E **64 B6**
Magee, I. *U.K.* 54°48N 5°43W **29 B10**
Magelang *Indonesia* 7°29S 110°13E **82 F4**
Magellan's Str. = Magallanes, Estrecho de *Chile* 52°30S 75°0W **121 H2**
Maggiore, Lago *Italy* 45°57N 8°39E **68 B3**
Maggotty *Jamaica* 18°9N 77°46W **114 a**
Maghâgha *Egypt* 28°38N 30°50E **95 C12**
Magherafelt *U.K.* 54°45N 6°37W **29 B8**
Maghreb *N. Afr.* 32°0N 4°0W **90 C3**
Maghull *U.K.* 53°31N 2°57W **23 E3**
Magnetic Pole (North) *Arctic* 82°42N 114°24W **54 A2**
Magnetic Pole (South) *Antarctica* 64°8S 138°8E **55 C9**
Magnitogorsk *Russia* 53°27N 59°4E **70 D10**
Magog *Canada* 45°18N 72°9W **113 C11**
Magwe *Burma* 20°10N 95°0E **85 J19**
Mahābād *Iran* 36°50N 45°45E **86 B6**
Mahajanga *Madag.* 15°40S 46°25E **97 H9**
Mahakam → *Indonesia* 0°35S 117°17E **82 E5**
Mahalapye *Botswana* 23°1S 26°51E **97 J5**
Maḩallāt *Iran* 33°55N 50°30E **87 C7**
Mahanadi → *India* 20°20N 86°25E **85 J15**
Maharashtra □ *India* 20°30N 75°30E **84 J9**
Mahdia *Tunisia* 35°28N 11°0E **95 A8**
Mahesana *India* 23°39N 72°26E **84 H8**
Mahilyow *Belarus* 53°55N 30°18E **65 B16**
Mai-Ndombe, L. *Dem. Rep. of the Congo* 2°0S 18°20E **96 E3**
Maiden Bradley *U.K.* 51°9N 2°17W **24 D4**
Maiden Newton *U.K.* 50°46N 2°34W **24 E3**
Maidenhead *U.K.* 51°31N 0°42W **25 C7**
Maidstone *U.K.* 51°16N 0°32E **25 D10**
Maiduguri *Nigeria* 12°0N 13°20E **95 F8**
Main → *Germany* 50°0N 8°18E **64 C5**
Main → *U.K.* 54°48N 6°18W **29 B9**
Maine *France* 48°20N 0°15W **66 C3**
Maine □ *U.S.A.* 45°20N 69°0W **113 C13**
Maine → *Ireland* 52°9N 9°45W **30 D3**
Mainland *Orkney, U.K.* 58°59N 3°8W **19 E11**
Mainland *Shet., U.K.* 60°15N 1°22W **18 B15**
Mainz *Germany* 50°1N 8°14E **64 C5**
Maiquetía *Venezuela* 10°36N 66°57W **120 A3**
Majorca = Mallorca *Spain* 39°30N 3°0E **67 C7**
Majuro *Marshall Is.* 7°9N 171°12E **102 G9**
Makale *Indonesia* 3°6S 119°51E **83 E5**
Makasar, Str. of *Indonesia* 1°0S 118°20E **83 E5**
Makgadikgadi Salt Pans *Botswana* 20°40S 25°45E **97 J5**
Makhachkala *Russia* 43°0N 47°30E **71 F8**
Makhado *S. Africa* 23°1S 29°43E **97 J5**
Makran Coast Range *Pakistan* 25°40N 64°0E **84 G4**
Makurdi *Nigeria* 7°43N 8°35E **94 G7**
Mal B. *Ireland* 52°50N 9°30W **30 C4**
Malabar Coast *India* 11°0N 75°0E **84 P9**
Malacca, Straits of *Indonesia* 3°0N 101°0E **82 D2**
Málaga *Spain* 36°43N 4°23W **67 D3**
Malahide *Ireland* 53°26N 6°9W **31 B10**
Malaita *Solomon Is.* 9°0S 161°0E **99 B11**
Malakâl *Sudan* 9°33N 31°40E **95 G12**
Malakula *Vanuatu* 16°15S 167°30E **99 D12**
Malang *Indonesia* 7°59S 112°45E **82 F4**
Malanje *Angola* 9°36S 16°17E **96 F3**
Mälaren *Sweden* 59°30N 17°10E **63 F7**
Malatya *Turkey* 38°25N 38°20E **71 G6**
Malawi ■ *Africa* 11°55S 34°0E **97 G6**
Malawi, L. *Africa* 12°30S 34°30E **97 G6**
Malay Pen. *Asia* 7°25N 100°0E **72 H12**
Malāyer *Iran* 34°19N 48°51E **86 C7**
Malaysia ■ *Asia* 5°0N 110°0E **82 D4**
Malden *U.S.A.* 36°34N 89°57W **112 G3**
Malden I. *Kiribati* 4°3S 155°1W **103 H12**
Maldives ■ *Ind. Oc.* 5°0N 73°0E **73 H9**
Maldon *U.K.* 51°44N 0°42E **25 C10**
Maldonado *Uruguay* 34°59S 55°0W **121 F4**
Malegaon *India* 20°30N 74°38E **84 J9**
Malham Tarn *U.K.* 54°6N 2°10W **22 D4**
Malheur L. *U.S.A.* 43°20N 118°48W **110 B3**
Mali ■ *Africa* 17°0N 3°0W **94 E5**
Malin Hd. *Ireland* 55°23N 7°23W **28 A7**
Malin Pen. *Ireland* 55°20N 7°17W **29 A7**
Malindi *Kenya* 3°12S 40°5E **96 E8**
Mallaig *U.K.* 57°0N 5°50W **18 H6**
Mallawi *Egypt* 27°44N 30°44E **95 C12**
Mallorca *Spain* 39°30N 3°0E **67 C7**
Mallow *Ireland* 52°8N 8°39W **30 D5**
Malmesbury *U.K.* 51°35N 2°5W **24 C4**
Malmö *Sweden* 55°36N 12°59E **63 F6**
Malone *U.S.A.* 44°51N 74°18W **113 C10**
Malpas *U.K.* 53°1N 2°45W **23 F3**
Malpelo, I. de *Colombia* 4°3N 81°35W **115 G8**
Malta ■ *Europe* 35°55N 14°26E **68 a**
Maltby *U.K.* 53°25N 1°12W **23 F6**
Malton *U.K.* 54°8N 0°49W **22 D7**
Malvinas, Is. = Falkland Is. ☑ *Atl. Oc.* 51°30S 59°0W **121 H4**
Mamoré → *Bolivia* 10°23S 65°53W **120 D3**
Mamoudzou *Mayotte* 12°48S 45°14E **91 H8**
Man *Ivory C.* 7°30N 7°40W **94 G4**
Man, I. of *U.K.* 54°15N 4°30W **29 C12**
Manacles, The *U.K.* 50°2N 5°4W **27 G3**
Manado *Indonesia* 1°29N 124°51E **83 D6**
Managua *Nic.* 12°6N 86°20W **114 E7**
Manas *China* 44°17N 86°10E **78 C6**
Manatí *Puerto Rico* 18°26N 66°29W **115 d**
Manaus *Brazil* 3°0S 60°0W **120 C3**
Manby *U.K.* 53°21N 0°6E **23 F9**
Manchester *U.K.* 53°29N 2°12W **23 F4**
Manchester *U.S.A.* 42°59N 71°28W **113 D12**
Manchester Int. ✕ (MAN) *U.K.* 53°21N 2°17W **23 F4**
Manchuria *China* 45°0N 125°0E **79 C14**
Manchurian Plain *China* 47°0N 124°0E **72 D14**
Mandal *Norway* 58°2N 7°25E **63 F5**
Mandalay *Burma* 22°0N 96°4E **85 J20**
Mandalgovi *Mongolia* 45°45N 106°10E **78 B10**
Mandan *U.S.A.* 46°50N 100°54W **110 A6**
Mandaue *Phil.* 10°20N 123°56E **83 B6**
Mandeville *Jamaica* 18°2N 77°31W **114 a**
Mandla *India* 22°39N 80°30E **85 H12**
Mandsaur *India* 24°3N 75°8E **84 G9**
Mandvi *India* 22°51N 69°22E **84 H6**
Manea *U.K.* 52°29N 0°10E **25 B9**
Manfalût *Egypt* 27°20N 30°52E **95 C12**
Manfredónia *Italy* 41°38N 15°55E **68 D6**
Mangabeiras, Chapada das *Brazil* 10°0S 46°30W **122 B1**
Mangalore *India* 12°55N 74°47E **84 N9**
Mangnai *China* 37°52N 91°43E **78 D7**
Mangole *Indonesia* 1°50S 125°55E **83 E6**
Mangotsfield *U.K.* 51°29N 2°30W **24 D4**
Manhattan *U.S.A.* 39°11N 96°35W **111 C7**
Manhuaçu *Brazil* 20°15S 42°2W **122 D2**
Manica *Mozam.* 18°58S 32°59E **97 H6**
Manicoré *Brazil* 5°48S 61°16W **120 C3**
Manicouagan → *Canada* 49°30N 68°30W **109 E13**
Manicouagan, Rés. *Canada* 51°5N 68°40W **109 D13**
Manihiki *Cook Is.* 10°24S 161°1W **103 J11**
Manila *Phil.* 14°35N 120°58E **83 B6**
Manipur □ *India* 25°0N 94°0E **85 G19**
Manisa *Turkey* 38°38N 27°30E **71 G4**
Manistee *U.S.A.* 44°15N 86°19W **112 C4**
Manistee → *U.S.A.* 44°15N 86°21W **112 C4**
Manistique *U.S.A.* 45°57N 86°15W **112 C4**
Manitoba □ *Canada* 53°30N 97°0W **108 D10**
Manitoba, L. *Canada* 51°0N 98°45W **108 D10**
Manitou Is. *U.S.A.* 45°8N 86°0W **112 C4**
Manitoulin I. *Canada* 45°40N 82°30W **112 C6**
Manitowoc *U.S.A.* 44°5N 87°40W **112 C4**
Manizales *Colombia* 5°5N 75°32W **120 B2**
Mankato *U.S.A.* 44°10N 94°0W **111 B8**
Mannar *Sri Lanka* 9°1N 79°54E **84 Q11**
Mannar, G. of *Asia* 8°30N 79°0E **84 Q11**
Mannheim *Germany* 49°29N 8°29E **64 D5**
Manning *Canada* 56°53N 117°39W **108 D8**
Manningtree *U.K.* 51°56N 1°5E **25 C11**
Manokwari *Indonesia* 0°54S 134°0E **83 E8**
Manosque *France* 43°49N 5°47E **66 E6**
Manresa *Spain* 41°48N 1°50E **67 B6**
Mansel I. *Canada* 62°0N 80°0W **109 C12**
Mansfield *U.K.* 53°9N 1°11W **23 F6**
Mansfield *U.S.A.* 40°45N 82°31W **112 E6**
Mansfield Woodhouse *U.K.* 53°11N 1°12W **23 F6**
Manta *Ecuador* 1°0S 80°40W **120 C1**
Mantes-la-Jolie *France* 48°58N 1°41E **66 B4**
Mantiqueira, Serra da *Brazil* 22°0S 44°0W **117 F6**
Manton *U.K.* 52°38N 0°41W **23 G7**
Manton *U.S.A.* 44°25N 85°24W **112 C5**
Mántova *Italy* 45°9N 10°48E **68 B4**
Manuel Alves → *Brazil* 11°19S 48°28W **122 B1**
Manzai *Pakistan* 32°12N 70°15E **84 C7**
Manzanillo *Cuba* 20°20N 77°31W **115 C9**
Manzanillo *Mexico* 19°3N 104°20W **114 D4**
Manzhouli *China* 49°35N 117°25E **79 B12**
Maó *Spain* 39°53N 4°16E **67 C8**
Maoming *China* 21°50N 110°54E **79 G11**
Mapam Yumco *China* 30°45N 81°28E **78 E5**
Maputo *Mozam.* 25°58S 32°32E **97 K6**
Maputo B. *Mozam.* 25°50S 32°45E **90 J7**
Maquinchao *Argentina* 41°15S 68°50W **121 G3**
Maquoketa *U.S.A.* 42°4N 90°40W **112 D2**
Mar *U.K.* 57°11N 2°53W **19 H12**
Mar, Serra do *Brazil* 25°30S 49°0W **117 F6**
Mar Chiquita, L. *Argentina* 30°40S 62°50W **121 F3**
Mar del Plata *Argentina* 38°0S 57°30W **121 F4**
Mara Rosa *Brazil* 14°1S 49°11W **122 B1**
Marabá *Brazil* 5°20S 49°5W **120 C5**
Maracá, I. de *Brazil* 2°10N 50°30W **120 B4**
Maracaibo *Venezuela* 10°40N 71°37W **120 A2**
Maracaibo, L. de *Venezuela* 9°40N 71°30W **120 B2**
Maracay *Venezuela* 10°15N 67°28W **120 A3**
Maradi *Niger* 13°29N 7°20E **94 F7**
Maragogipe *Brazil* 12°46S 38°55W **122 B3**
Marajó, I. de *Brazil* 1°0S 49°30W **120 C5**
Maranguape *Brazil* 3°55S 38°50W **120 C6**
Maranhão □ *Brazil* 5°0S 46°0W **120 C5**
Marañón → *Peru* 4°30S 73°35W **120 C2**
Marazion *U.K.* 50°7N 5°29W **27 G3**
Marbella *Spain* 36°30N 4°57W **67 D3**
March *U.K.* 52°33N 0°5E **25 A9**
Marche *France* 46°5N 1°20E **66 C4**
Marcus I. *Pac. Oc.* 24°20N 153°58E **102 E7**
Mardan *Pakistan* 34°20N 72°0E **84 B8**
Marden *U.K.* 52°7N 2°42W **24 B3**
Mardin *Turkey* 37°20N 40°43E **71 G7**
Maree, L. *U.K.* 57°40N 5°26W **18 G7**
Mareham le Fen *U.K.* 53°8N 0°4W **23 F8**
Marfleet *U.K.* 53°45N 0°17W **23 E8**
Margarita, I. de *Venezuela* 11°0N 64°0W **120 A3**
Margate *U.K.* 51°23N 1°23E **25 D11**
Marghilon *Uzbekistan* 40°27N 71°42E **87 A12**
Mārgow, Dasht-e *Afghan.* 30°40N 62°30E **87 D10**
Mari El □ *Russia* 56°30N 48°0E **70 C8**
Mariana Trench *Pac. Oc.* 13°0N 145°0E **102 F6**
Marías, Is. *Mexico* 21°25N 106°28W **114 C3**
Maribor *Slovenia* 46°36N 15°40E **64 E8**
Marie Byrd Land *Antarctica* 79°30S 125°0W **55 D14**
Marie-Galante *Guadeloupe* 15°56N 61°16W **114 b**
Mariental *Namibia* 24°36S 18°0E **97 J3**
Marietta *U.S.A.* 39°25N 81°27W **112 F7**
Marília *Brazil* 22°13S 50°0W **120 E4**
Marinette *U.S.A.* 45°6N 87°38W **112 C4**
Marion *Ill., U.S.A.* 37°44N 88°56W **112 G3**
Marion *Ind., U.S.A.* 40°32N 85°40W **112 E5**
Marion *Ohio, U.S.A.* 40°35N 83°8W **112 E6**
Mariupol *Ukraine* 47°5N 37°31E **71 E6**
Marka *Somali Rep.* 1°48N 44°50E **89 G3**
Markam *China* 29°42N 98°38E **78 F8**
Market Bosworth *U.K.* 52°38N 1°24W **23 G6**
Market Deeping *U.K.* 52°41N 0°19W **23 G8**
Market Drayton *U.K.* 52°54N 2°29W **23 G4**
Market Harborough *U.K.* 52°29N 0°55W **23 H7**
Market Lavington *U.K.* 51°17N 1°58W **24 D5**
Market Rasen *U.K.* 53°24N 0°20W **23 F8**
Market Weighton *U.K.* 53°52N 0°40W **23 E7**
Markfield *U.K.* 52°42N 1°17W **23 G6**
Markham, Mt. *Antarctica* 83°0S 164°0E **55 E11**
Marks Tey *U.K.* 51°52N 0°49E **25 C10**
Marlborough *U.K.* 51°25N 1°43W **24 D5**
Marlborough Downs *U.K.* 51°27N 1°53W **24 D5**
Marlow *U.K.* 51°34N 0°46W **25 C7**
Marmara, Sea of *Turkey* 40°45N 28°15E **71 F4**
Marmaris *Turkey* 36°50N 28°14E **86 B2**
Marmora *Canada* 44°28N 77°41W **112 C9**
Marne → *France* 48°47N 2°29E **66 B5**
Marnhull *U.K.* 50°57N 2°19W **24 E4**
Maroua *Cameroon* 10°40N 14°20E **95 F8**
Marple *U.K.* 53°24N 2°4W **23 F4**
Marquette *U.S.A.* 46°33N 87°24W **112 B4**
Marquis *St. Lucia* 14°2N 60°54W **115 f**
Marquises, Îs. *French Polynesia* 9°30S 140°0W **103 H14**
Marrakesh *Morocco* 31°9N 8°0W **94 B4**
Marree *Australia* 29°39S 138°1E **98 F6**
Marsá Matrûh *Egypt* 31°19N 27°9E **95 B11**
Marsabit *Kenya* 2°18N 38°0E **96 D7**
Marsala *Italy* 37°48N 12°26E **68 F5**
Marseilles *France* 43°18N 5°23E **66 E6**
Marsh I. *U.S.A.* 29°34N 91°53W **111 E8**
Marshall *U.S.A.* 32°33N 94°23W **111 D8**
Marshall Is. ■ *Pac. Oc.* 9°0N 171°0E **102 G9**
Marshfield *U.K.* 51°28N 2°19W **24 D4**
Marshfield *U.S.A.* 44°40N 90°10W **112 C2**
Marske by the Sea *U.K.* 54°36N 1°0W **22 C7**
Marston Moor *U.K.* 53°58N 1°17W **23 E6**
Martaban *Burma* 16°30N 97°35E **85 L20**
Martaban, G. of *Burma* 16°5N 96°30E **85 L20**
Martapura *Indonesia* 3°22S 114°47E **82 E4**
Martham *U.K.* 52°42N 1°37E **25 A12**
Martha's Vineyard *U.S.A.* 41°25N 70°38W **113 E12**
Martigues *France* 43°24N 5°4E **66 E6**
Martinique ☑ *W. Indies* 14°40N 61°0W **114 c**
Martin's Bay *Barbados* 13°12N 59°29W **115 g**
Martinsburg *U.S.A.* 39°27N 77°58W **112 F9**
Martinsville *U.S.A.* 39°26N 86°25W **112 F4**
Martley *U.K.* 52°15N 2°21W **24 B4**
Martock *U.K.* 50°58N 2°46W **24 E3**
Marwar *India* 25°43N 73°45E **84 G8**
Mary *Turkmenistan* 37°40N 61°50E **87 B10**
Maryborough *Australia* 25°31S 152°37E **98 F9**
Maryland □ *U.S.A.* 39°0N 76°30W **112 F9**
Maryport *U.K.* 54°44N 3°28W **22 C2**
Marystown *Canada* 47°10N 55°10W **109 E14**
Marytavy *U.K.* 50°36N 4°7W **27 F5**
Marzūq *Libya* 25°53N 13°57E **95 C8**
Masai Steppe *Tanzania* 4°30S 36°30E **96 E7**
Masan *S. Korea* 35°11N 128°32E **79 D14**
Masandam, Ra's *Oman* 26°30N 56°30E **89 B6**
Masaya *Nic.* 12°0N 86°7W **114 E7**
Masbate *Phil.* 12°21N 123°36E **83 B6**
Mascara *Algeria* 35°26N 0°6E **94 A6**
Maseru *Lesotho* 29°18S 27°30E **97 K5**
Masham *U.K.* 54°14N 1°39W **22 D5**
Mashhad *Iran* 36°20N 59°35E **87 B9**
Mashonaland *Zimbabwe* 16°30S 31°0E **97 H6**
Maşīrah, Jazīrat *Oman* 21°0N 58°50E **89 C6**
Masjed Soleyman *Iran* 31°55N 49°18E **86 D7**
Mask, L. *Ireland* 53°36N 9°22W **28 D3**
Mason City *U.S.A.* 43°9N 93°12W **111 B8**
Massa *Italy* 44°1N 10°9E **68 B4**
Massachusetts □ *U.S.A.* 42°30N 72°0W **113 D11**
Massawa *Eritrea* 15°35N 39°25E **89 D2**
Massena *U.S.A.* 44°56N 74°54W **113 C10**
Massiah Street *Barbados* 13°9N 59°29W **115 g**
Massif Central *France* 44°55N 3°0E **66 D5**
Massillon *U.S.A.* 40°48N 81°32W **112 E7**
Masurian Lakes *Poland* 53°50N 21°0E **65 B11**
Masvingo *Zimbabwe* 20°8S 30°49E **97 J6**
Mata-Utu *Wall. & F. Is.* 13°17S 176°8W **99 C15**
Matabeleland *Zimbabwe* 18°0S 27°0E **97 H5**
Matadi *Dem. Rep. of the Congo* 5°52S 13°31E **96 F2**
Matagalpa *Nic.* 13°0N 85°58W **114 E7**
Matagami *Canada* 49°45N 77°34W **109 E12**
Matagami, L. *Canada* 49°50N 77°40W **109 E12**
Matagorda I. *U.S.A.* 28°15N 96°30W **111 E7**
Matamoros *Mexico* 25°32N 103°15W **114 B5**
Matane *Canada* 48°50N 67°33W **109 E13**
Matanzas *Cuba* 23°0N 81°40W **115 C8**
Matara *Sri Lanka* 5°58N 80°30E **84 S12**
Mataró *Spain* 41°32N 2°29E **67 B7**
Matehuala *Mexico* 23°39N 100°39W **114 C4**
Mateke Hills *Zimbabwe* 21°48S 31°0E **97 J6**
Matera *Italy* 40°40N 16°36E **68 D7**
Mathura *India* 27°30N 77°40E **84 F10**
Mati *Phil.* 6°55N 126°15E **83 C7**
Matlock *U.K.* 53°9N 1°33W **23 F5**
Mato Grosso □ *Brazil* 14°0S 55°0W **120 D4**
Mato Grosso, Planalto do *Brazil* 15°0S 55°0W **120 D4**
Mato Grosso do Sul □ *Brazil* 18°0S 55°0W **120 D4**
Matopo Hills *Zimbabwe* 20°36S 28°20E **97 J5**
Maţruḩ *Oman* 23°37N 58°30E **87 F9**
Matsue *Japan* 35°25N 133°10E **81 F3**
Matsumoto *Japan* 36°15N 138°0E **81 E6**
Matsusaka *Japan* 34°34N 136°32E **81 F5**
Matsuyama *Japan* 33°45N 132°45E **81 G3**
Mattagami → *Canada* 50°43N 81°29W **109 D11**
Mattancheri *India* 9°50N 76°15E **84 Q10**
Mattawa *Canada* 46°20N 78°45W **112 B8**
Matterhorn *Switz.* 45°58N 7°39E **64 F4**
Matthew, Î. *N. Cal.* 22°29S 171°15E **99 E13**
Mattoon *U.S.A.* 39°29N 88°23W **112 F3**
Maturín *Venezuela* 9°45N 63°11W **120 B3**
Maubeuge *France* 50°17N 3°57E **66 A6**
Maudin Sun *Burma* 16°0N 94°30E **85 M19**
Maui *U.S.A.* 20°48N 156°20W **110 H16**
Maumee → *U.S.A.* 41°42N 83°28W **112 E6**
Maumturk Mts. *Ireland* 53°32N 9°42W **28 D2**
Maun *Botswana* 20°0S 23°26E **97 H4**
Mauna Kea *U.S.A.* 19°50N 155°28W **110 J17**
Mauna Loa *U.S.A.* 19°30N 155°35W **110 J17**
Mauritania ■ *Africa* 20°50N 10°0W **94 E3**
Mauritius ■ *Ind. Oc.* 20°0S 57°0E **91 J9**
Mawgan *U.K.* 50°4N 5°13W **27 G3**
Maxwellheugh *U.K.* 55°35N 2°26W **21 C11**
May, I. of *U.K.* 56°11N 2°32W **21 B10**
May Pen *Jamaica* 17°58N 77°15W **114 a**
Mayaguana *Bahamas* 22°30N 72°44W **115 C10**
Mayagüez *Puerto Rico* 18°12N 67°9W **115 d**
Maybole *U.K.* 55°21N 4°42W **20 D6**
Mayfield *E. Sussex, U.K.* 51°1N 0°17E **25 D9**
Mayfield *Staffs., U.K.* 53°1N 1°47W **23 F5**
Mayfield *U.S.A.* 36°44N 88°38W **112 G3**
Maykop *Russia* 44°35N 40°10E **71 F7**
Maynooth *Ireland* 53°23N 6°34W **31 B9**
Mayo *Canada* 63°38N 135°57W **108 C6**
Mayo □ *Ireland* 53°53N 9°3W **28 D3**
Mayon Volcano *Phil.* 13°15N 123°41E **83 B6**
Mayotte ☑ *Ind. Oc.* 12°50S 45°10E **97 G9**
Maysville *U.S.A.* 38°39N 83°46W **112 F6**
Māzandarān □ *Iran* 36°30N 52°0E **87 B8**
Mazar *China* 36°32N 77°1E **78 D4**
Mazār-e Sharīf *Afghan.* 36°41N 67°0E **87 B11**
Mazaruni → *Guyana* 6°25N 58°35W **120 B4**
Mazatlán *Mexico* 23°13N 106°25W **114 C3**
Mazyr *Belarus* 51°59N 29°15E **70 D4**
Mbabane *Swaziland* 26°18S 31°6E **97 K6**
Mbaïki *C.A.R.* 3°53N 18°1E **96 D3**
Mbala *Zambia* 8°46S 31°24E **96 F6**
Mbale *Uganda* 1°8N 34°12E **96 D6**
Mbandaka *Dem. Rep. of the Congo* 0°1N 18°18E **96 D3**
Mbanza Ngungu *Dem. Rep. of the Congo* 5°12S 14°53E **96 F2**
Mbeya *Tanzania* 8°54S 33°29E **96 F6**
Mbour *Senegal* 14°22N 16°54W **94 F2**
Mbuji-Mayi *Dem. Rep. of the Congo* 6°9S 23°40E **96 F4**
Mdantsane *S. Africa* 32°56S 27°46E **97 L5**
Mead, L. *U.S.A.* 36°0N 114°44W **110 C4**
Meadow Lake *Canada* 54°10N 108°26W **108 D9**
Meadville *U.S.A.* 41°39N 80°9W **112 E7**
Meaford *Canada* 44°36N 80°35W **112 C7**
Mealsgate *U.K.* 54°47N 3°13W **22 C2**
Mearns, Howe of the *U.K.* 56°52N 2°26W **19 J13**
Measham *U.K.* 52°43N 1°31W **23 G5**
Meath □ *Ireland* 53°40N 6°57W **29 D8**
Meaux *France* 48°58N 2°50E **66 B5**
Mecca *Si. Arabia* 21°30N 39°54E **86 F4**
Mechelen *Belgium* 51°2N 4°29E **64 C3**
Mecklenburg *Germany* 53°33N 11°40E **64 B7**
Mecklenburger Bucht *Germany* 54°20N 11°40E **64 A6**
Medan *Indonesia* 3°40N 98°38E **82 D1**
Médéa *Algeria* 36°12N 2°50E **94 A6**
Medellín *Colombia* 6°15N 75°35W **120 B2**
Medford *Oreg., U.S.A.* 42°19N 122°52W **110 B2**
Medford *Wis., U.S.A.* 45°9N 90°20W **112 C2**
Medicine Hat *Canada* 50°0N 110°45W **108 E8**
Medina *Si. Arabia* 24°35N 39°52E **86 E4**
Mediterranean Sea *Europe* 35°0N 15°0E **90 C5**
Médoc *France* 45°10N 0°50W **66 D3**
Medstead *U.K.* 51°8N 1°3W **24 D6**
Medvezhyegorsk *Russia* 63°0N 34°25E **70 B5**
Medway → *U.K.* 51°27N 0°46E **25 D10**
Meekatharra *Australia* 26°32S 118°29E **98 F2**
Meerut *India* 29°1N 77°42E **84 E10**
Meghalaya □ *India* 25°50N 91°0E **85 G17**
Meghna → *Bangla.* 22°50N 90°50E **85 H17**
Megisti *Greece* 36°8N 29°34E **86 B2**
Meighen I. *Canada* 80°0N 99°30W **109 B10**
Meiktila *Burma* 20°53N 95°54E **85 J19**
Meizhou *China* 24°16N 116°6E **79 G12**
Mejillones *Chile* 23°10S 70°30W **121 E2**
Mekele *Ethiopia* 13°33N 39°30E **89 E2**
Mekhtar *Pakistan* 30°30N 69°15E **84 D6**
Meknès *Morocco* 33°57N 5°33W **94 B4**
Mekong → *Asia* 9°30N 106°15E **82 C3**
Melaka *Malaysia* 2°15N 102°15E **82 D2**
Melanesia *Pac. Oc.* 4°0S 155°0E **102 H7**
Melbourn *U.K.* 52°4N 0°0 **25 B9**
Melbourne *Australia* 37°48S 144°58E **98 H8**
Melbourne *U.K.* 52°50N 1°25W **23 G6**
Melekeok *Palau* 7°27N 134°38E **102 G5**
Mélèzes → *Canada* 57°40N 69°29W **109 D13**
Melfort *Canada* 52°50N 104°37W **108 D9**
Melilla *N. Afr.* 35°21N 2°57W **67 E4**
Melitopol *Ukraine* 46°50N 35°22E **71 E6**
Melksham *U.K.* 51°23N 2°8W **24 D4**
Melmerby *U.K.* 54°45N 2°35W **22 C3**
Melrhir, Chott *Algeria* 34°13N 6°30E **94 B7**
Melrose *U.K.* 55°36N 2°43W **21 C10**
Melsonby *U.K.* 54°29N 1°42W **22 D5**
Melton Constable *U.K.* 52°52N 1°2E **25 A11**
Melton Mowbray *U.K.* 52°47N 0°54W **23 G7**
Melun *France* 48°32N 2°39E **66 B5**
Melville *Canada* 50°55N 102°50W **108 D9**
Melville I. *Australia* 11°30S 131°0E **98 C5**
Melville I. *Canada* 75°30N 112°0W **109 B8**
Melville Pen. *Canada* 68°0N 84°0W **109 C11**
Memphis *U.S.A.* 35°8N 90°2W **111 C9**
Menai Bridge *U.K.* 53°14N 4°10W **26 A5**
Menai Strait *U.K.* 53°11N 4°13W **26 A5**
Mende *France* 44°31N 3°30E **66 D5**
Mendip Hills *U.K.* 51°17N 2°40W **24 D3**
Mendlesham *U.K.* 52°16N 1°6E **25 B11**
Mendocino, C. *U.S.A.* 40°26N 124°25W **110 B2**
Mendota *U.S.A.* 41°33N 89°7W **112 E3**
Mendoza *Argentina* 32°50S 68°52W **121 F3**
Mengzi *China* 23°20N 103°22E **78 G9**
Menominee *U.S.A.* 45°6N 87°37W **112 C4**
Menominee → *U.S.A.* 45°6N 87°35W **112 C4**
Menomonie *U.S.A.* 44°53N 91°55W **112 C2**
Menorca *Spain* 40°0N 4°0E **67 C8**
Mentawai, Kepulauan *Indonesia* 2°0S 99°0E **82 E1**
Merced *U.S.A.* 37°18N 120°29W **110 C2**
Mercedes *Corrientes, Argentina* 29°10S 58°5W **121 E4**
Mercedes *San Luis, Argentina* 33°40S 65°21W **121 F3**
Mercedes *Uruguay* 33°12S 58°0W **121 F4**
Mercy, C. *Canada* 65°0N 63°30W **109 C13**
Mere *U.K.* 51°6N 2°16W **24 D4**
Mergui *Burma* 12°26N 98°34E **82 B1**
Mérida *Mexico* 20°58N 89°37W **114 C7**
Mérida *Spain* 38°55N 6°25W **67 C2**
Mérida *Venezuela* 8°24N 71°8W **120 B2**
Mérida, Cord. de *Venezuela* 9°0N 71°0W **117 C3**
Meriden *U.K.* 52°26N 1°38W **23 H5**
Meriden *U.S.A.* 41°32N 72°48W **113 E11**
Meridian *U.S.A.* 32°22N 88°42W **111 D9**
Merowe Dam *Sudan* 18°47N 32°3E **95 E12**
Merrick *U.K.* 55°8N 4°28W **20 D7**
Merrill *U.S.A.* 45°11N 89°41W **112 C3**
Merritt *Canada* 50°10N 120°45W **108 D7**
Merse *U.K.* 55°43N 2°16W **21 C11**
Mersea I. *U.K.* 51°47N 0°58E **25 C10**
Mersey → *U.K.* 53°25N 3°1W **23 F2**
Merseyside □ *U.K.* 53°31N 3°2W **23 E2**
Merthyr Tydfil *U.K.* 51°45N 3°22W **26 D7**
Merton □ *U.K.* 51°25N 0°11W **25 D8**
Meru *Kenya* 0°3N 37°40E **96 D7**

Meru Tanzania 3°15S 36°46E 96 E7
Mesa U.S.A. 33°25N 111°50W 110 D4
Mesopotamia Iraq 33°30N 44°0E 86 C5
Messina Italy 38°11N 15°34E 68 E6
Messina, Str. di Italy 38°15N 15°35E 68 F6
Mestre, Espigão Brazil 12°30S 46°10W 122 B1
Meta → S. Amer. 6°12N 67°28W 120 B3
Meta Incognita Pen. Canada 62°45N 68°30W 109 C13
Metheringham U.K. 53°9N 0°23W 23 F8
Methwold U.K. 52°32N 0°33E 25 A10
Metlakatla U.S.A. 55°8N 131°35W 108 D6
Metropolis U.S.A. 37°9N 88°44W 112 G3
Metz France 49°8N 6°10E 66 B7
Meuse → Europe 50°45N 5°41E 64 C3
Mevagissey U.K. 50°16N 4°48W 27 G4
Mevagissey B. U.K. 50°17N 4°47W 27 G4
Mexborough U.K. 53°30N 1°15W 23 E6
Mexiana, I. Brazil 0°0 49°30W 120 B5
Mexicali Mexico 32°40N 115°30W 114 A1
Mexican Plateau Mexico 25°0N 104°0W 104 G9
México Mexico 19°24N 99°9W 114 D5
Mexico ■ Cent. Amer. 25°0N 105°0W 114 C4
Mexico, G. of Cent. Amer. 25°0N 90°0W 114 C7
Meymaneh Afghan. 35°53N 64°38E 87 C11
Mezen → Russia 65°44N 44°22E 70 A7
Mezhdurechensk Russia 53°41N 88°3E 76 D9
Miami U.S.A. 25°46N 80°11W 111 E10
Miāndowāb Iran 37°0N 46°5E 86 B6
Mīāneh Iran 37°30N 47°40E 86 B6
Mianwali Pakistan 32°38N 71°28E 84 C7
Mianyang China 31°22N 104°47E 78 E9
Miass Russia 54°59N 60°6E 70 D11
Micheldever U.K. 51°9N 1°14W 24 D6
Michigan □ U.S.A. 44°0N 85°0W 112 B4
Michigan, L. U.S.A. 44°0N 87°0W 112 C4
Michipicoten I. Canada 47°40N 85°40W 112 B5
Michurinsk Russia 52°58N 40°27E 70 D7
Mickle Fell U.K. 54°37N 2°18W 22 C4
Mickleover U.K. 52°55N 1°33W 23 G5
Mickleton U.K. 54°36N 2°2W 22 C4
Micoud St. Lucia 13°49N 60°54W 115 f
Micronesia Pac. Oc. 11°0N 160°0E 102 G7
Micronesia, Federated States of ■ Pac. Oc. 9°0N 150°0E 102 G7
Middelburg S. Africa 31°30S 25°0E 97 L5
Middle East Asia 35°0N 40°0E 72 E5
Middleham U.K. 54°17N 1°48W 22 C5
Middlemarsh U.K. 50°51N 2°28W 24 E4
Middlesbrough U.K. 54°35N 1°13W 22 C6
Middleton Gt. Man., U.K. 53°33N 2°12W 23 E4
Middleton Norfolk, U.K. 52°43N 0°29E 25 A9
Middleton Cheney U.K. 52°4N 1°16W 24 B6
Middleton in Teesdale U.K. 54°38N 2°4W 22 C4
Middleton on the Wolds U.K. 53°56N 0°35W 23 E7
Middletown U.K. 54°17N 6°51W 29 C8
Middletown N.Y., U.S.A. 41°27N 74°25W 113 E10
Middletown Ohio, U.S.A. 39°31N 84°24W 112 F5
Middlewich U.K. 53°12N 2°28W 23 F4
Middlezoy U.K. 51°6N 2°54W 24 D7
Midhurst U.K. 50°59N 0°44W 25 E7
Midi, Canal du → France 43°45N 1°21E 66 E4
Midland Canada 44°45N 79°50W 112 C8
Midland Mich., U.S.A. 43°37N 84°14W 112 D5
Midland Tex., U.S.A. 32°0N 102°3W 110 D6
Midleton Ireland 51°55N 8°10W 30 E6
Midsomer Norton U.K. 51°17N 2°28W 24 D4
Midway Is. Pac. Oc. 28°13N 177°22W 102 E10
Midwest U.S.A. 42°0N 90°0W 111 C9
Mieres Spain 43°18N 5°48W 67 A3
Mikhaylovka Russia 50°3N 43°5E 71 D7
Milan Italy 45°28N 9°10E 68 B3
Milborne Port U.K. 50°58N 2°28W 24 E4
Mildenhall U.K. 52°21N 0°32E 25 B10
Mildura Australia 34°13S 142°9E 98 G7
Miles City U.S.A. 46°25N 105°51W 110 A5
Milford U.S.A. 38°55N 75°26W 113 F10
Milford Haven U.K. 51°42N 5°7W 26 D3
Milford on Sea U.K. 50°43N 1°35W 24 E5
Milḥ, Baḥr al Iraq 32°40N 43°35E 86 C5
Milk → U.S.A. 48°4N 106°19W 110 A5
Millau France 44°8N 3°4E 66 D5
Millbrook U.K. 50°20N 4°14W 27 G5
Millet St. Lucia 13°55N 60°59W 115 f
Millinocket U.S.A. 45°39N 68°43W 113 C13
Millom U.K. 54°13N 3°16W 22 D2
Milltown Malbay Ireland 52°52N 9°24W 30 C4
Millville U.S.A. 39°24N 75°2W 113 F10
Milngavie U.K. 55°56N 4°19W 20 C7
Milnthorpe U.K. 54°14N 2°45W 22 D3
Milos Greece 36°44N 24°25E 69 F11
Milton Abbot U.K. 50°35N 4°16W 27 F5
Milton Keynes U.K. 52°1N 0°44W 25 B7
Milverton U.K. 51°1N 3°16W 24 D2
Milwaukee U.S.A. 43°2N 87°54W 112 D4
Min Jiang → Fujian, China 26°0N 119°35E 79 F12
Min Jiang → Sichuan, China 28°45N 104°40E 78 F9
Minas Uruguay 34°20S 55°10W 121 F4
Minas Gerais □ Brazil 18°50S 46°0W 122 C1
Minatitlán Mexico 17°59N 94°31W 114 D6
Minchinhampton U.K. 51°42N 2°11W 24 C4
Mindanao Phil. 8°0N 125°0E 83 C6
Mindoro Phil. 13°0N 121°0E 83 B6
Mindoro Str. Phil. 12°30N 120°30E 83 B6
Minehead U.K. 51°12N 3°29W 24 D2
Mineral Wells U.S.A. 32°48N 98°7W 110 D7
Minfeng China 37°4N 82°46E 78 D5
Minginish U.K. 57°14N 6°15W 18 H5
Mingulay U.K. 56°49N 7°39W 18 J2
Minna Nigeria 9°37N 6°30E 94 G7
Minneapolis U.S.A. 44°57N 93°16W 111 B8
Minnesota □ U.S.A. 46°0N 94°15W 111 A8
Minorca = Menorca Spain 40°0N 4°0E 67 C8
Minot U.S.A. 48°14N 101°18W 110 A6
Minsk Belarus 53°52N 27°30E 65 B14
Minster Kent, U.K. 51°20N 1°20E 25 D11
Minster Kent, U.K. 51°25N 0°50E 25 D10
Minsterley U.K. 52°39N 2°54W 23 G3
Minto, L. Canada 57°13N 75°0W 109 D12
Miramichi B. Canada 47°15N 65°0W 113 B15

Mirim, L. S. Amer. 32°45S 52°50W 121 F4
Mirnyy Russia 62°33N 113°53E 77 C12
Mirpur Khas Pakistan 25°30N 69°0E 84 G6
Mirtoo Sea Greece 37°0N 23°20E 69 F10
Mirzapur India 25°10N 82°34E 85 G13
Mishan China 45°37N 131°48E 79 B15
Mishawaka U.S.A. 41°40N 86°11W 112 E4
Miskolc Hungary 48°7N 20°50E 65 D11
Misool Indonesia 1°52S 130°10E 83 E8
Mişrātah Libya 32°24N 15°3E 95 B9
Missinaibi → Canada 50°43N 81°29W 109 D11
Mississippi □ U.S.A. 33°0N 90°0W 111 D9
Mississippi → U.S.A. 29°9N 89°15W 111 E9
Mississippi River Delta U.S.A. 29°10N 89°15W 111 E9
Missoula U.S.A. 46°52N 114°1W 110 A4
Missouri □ U.S.A. 38°25N 92°30W 111 C8
Missouri → U.S.A. 38°49N 90°7W 111 C8
Mistassini, L. Canada 51°0N 73°30W 109 D12
Misterton Notts., U.K. 53°27N 0°50W 23 F7
Misterton Somst., U.K. 50°52N 2°47W 24 E3
Mitcheldean U.K. 51°51N 2°28W 24 C4
Mitchell U.S.A. 43°43N 98°2W 110 B7
Mitchell → Australia 15°12S 141°35E 98 D7
Mitchell, Mt. U.S.A. 35°46N 82°16W 104 F11
Mitchelstown Ireland 52°15N 8°16W 30 D6
Mito Japan 36°20N 140°30E 81 E7
Mitrovica Kosovo 42°54N 20°52E 69 C9
Mitú Colombia 1°15N 70°13W 120 B2
Mitumba, Mts. Dem. Rep. of the Congo 7°0S 27°30E 96 F5
Miyakonojō Japan 31°40N 131°5E 81 H2
Miyazaki Japan 31°56N 131°30E 81 H2
Mizen Hd. Cork, Ireland 51°27N 9°50W 30 F3
Mizen Hd. Wicklow, Ireland 52°51N 6°4W 31 C10
Mizoram □ India 23°30N 92°40E 85 H18
Mjøsa Norway 60°40N 11°0E 63 E6
Mljet Croatia 42°43N 17°30E 68 C7
Mo i Rana Norway 66°20N 14°7E 63 D6
Moab U.S.A. 38°35N 109°33W 110 C5
Moate Ireland 53°24N 7°44W 28 D7
Mobaye C.A.R. 4°25N 21°5E 96 D4
Moberly U.S.A. 39°25N 92°26W 111 C81
Mobile U.S.A. 30°41N 88°3W 111 D9
Mobridge U.S.A. 45°32N 100°26W 110 A6
Moçâmedes Mozam. 15°3S 40°42E 97 H8
Mochudi Botswana 24°27S 26°7E 97 J5
Mocoa Colombia 1°7N 76°35W 120 B2
Mococa Brazil 21°28S 47°0W 122 D1
Mocuba Mozam. 16°54S 36°57E 97 H7
Modbury U.K. 50°21N 3°55W 27 G6
Módena Italy 44°40N 10°55E 68 B4
Modesto U.S.A. 37°39N 121°0W 110 C2
Moffat U.K. 55°21N 3°27W 21 D9
Mogadishu Somali Rep. 2°2N 45°25E 89 G4
Mogi-Mirim Brazil 22°29S 47°0W 122 D1
Mohammedia Morocco 33°44N 7°21W 94 B4
Moher, Cliffs of Ireland 52°58N 9°27W 30 C4
Moidart U.K. 56°49N 5°41W 18 J6
Moidart, L. U.K. 56°47N 5°52W 18 J6
Moisie → Canada 50°14N 66°5W 109 D13
Mojave Desert U.S.A. 35°0N 116°30W 110 D3
Moji das Cruzes Brazil 23°31S 46°11W 122 D1
Mokpo S. Korea 34°50N 126°25E 79 E14
Mold U.K. 53°9N 3°8W 26 A7
Molde Norway 62°45N 7°9E 63 E5
Moldova ■ Europe 47°0N 28°0E 65 E15
Mole → U.K. 51°24N 0°21W 25 D8
Molepolole Botswana 24°28S 25°28E 97 J5
Mollendo Peru 17°0S 72°0W 120 D2
Moloka'i U.S.A. 21°8N 157°0W 110 H16
Molopo → Africa 28°30S 20°12E 97 K4
Molucca Sea Indonesia 0°0 125°0E 83 E6
Moluccas Indonesia 1°0S 127°0E 83 E7
Mombasa Kenya 4°3S 39°40E 96 E7
Mompós Colombia 9°14N 74°26W 120 B2
Mon □ Burma 16°0N 97°30E 85 L20
Mona Passage W. Indies 18°30N 67°45W 115 D11
Monach Is. U.K. 57°32N 7°40W 18 G2
Monaco ■ Europe 43°46N 7°23E 66 E7
Monadhliath Mts. U.K. 57°10N 4°4W 19 H9
Monaghan Ireland 54°15N 6°57W 29 C8
Monaghan □ Ireland 54°11N 6°56W 29 C8
Monar, L. U.K. 57°26N 5°8W 18 H7
Monar Forest U.K. 57°27N 5°10W 18 H7
Monasterevin Ireland 53°8N 7°4W 31 B8
Monavullagh Mts. Ireland 52°14N 7°35W 31 D7
Mönchengladbach Germany 51°11N 6°27E 64 C4
Monclova Mexico 26°54N 101°25W 114 B4
Moncton Canada 46°7N 64°51W 113 B15
Moneague Jamaica 18°16N 77°7W 114 a
Moneymore U.K. 54°41N 6°40W 29 C8
Mongolia ■ Asia 47°0N 103°0E 78 B9
Mongolia, Plateau of Asia 45°0N 105°0E 72 D12
Mongu Zambia 15°16S 23°12E 97 H4
Monifieth U.K. 56°30N 2°48W 21 B10
Monmouth U.K. 51°48N 2°42W 26 D5
Monmouth U.S.A. 40°55N 90°39W 112 E2
Monmouthshire □ U.K. 51°48N 2°54W 26 D5
Monnow → U.K. 51°49N 2°43W 24 C3
Monroe La., U.S.A. 32°30N 92°7W 111 D8
Monroe Mich., U.S.A. 41°55N 83°24W 112 E6
Monroe Wis., U.S.A. 42°36N 89°38W 112 D3
Monrovia Liberia 6°18N 10°47W 94 G3
Mons Belgium 50°27N 3°58E 64 C2
Mont-de-Marsan France 43°54N 0°31W 66 E3
Mont-Laurier Canada 46°35N 75°30W 109 E12
Montana Bulgaria 43°27N 23°16E 69 C10
Montaña Peru 6°0S 73°0W 120 C2
Montana □ U.S.A. 47°0N 110°0W 110 A5
Montargis France 47°59N 2°43E 66 C5
Montauban France 44°2N 1°21E 66 D4
Montbéliard France 47°31N 6°48E 66 C7
Montceau-les-Mines France 46°40N 4°23E 66 C6
Monte Azul Brazil 15°9S 42°53W 122 C2
Monte-Carlo Monaco 43°44N 7°25E 66 E7
Monte Caseros Argentina 30°10S 57°50W 121 F4
Monte Cristi Dom. Rep. 19°52N 71°39W 115 D10
Montego Bay Jamaica 18°28N 77°55W 114 a
Montélimar France 44°33N 4°45E 66 D6

Montello U.S.A. 43°48N 89°20W 112 D3
Montemorelos Mexico 25°12N 99°49W 114 B5
Montenegro ■ Europe 42°40N 19°20E 69 C8
Monterey U.S.A. 36°37N 121°55W 110 C2
Monteria Colombia 8°46N 75°53W 120 B2
Monterrey Mexico 25°40N 100°19W 114 B4
Montes Claros Brazil 16°30S 43°50W 122 C2
Montevideo Uruguay 34°50S 56°11W 121 F4
Montgomery U.K. 52°34N 3°8W 26 B7
Montgomery U.S.A. 32°23N 86°19W 111 D9
Monticello U.S.A. 40°45N 86°46W 112 E4
Montluçon France 46°22N 2°36E 66 C5
Montmagny Canada 46°58N 70°34W 113 B12
Montpelier Idaho, U.S.A. 42°19N 111°18W 110 B4
Montpelier Vt., U.S.A. 44°16N 72°35W 113 C11
Montpellier France 43°37N 3°52E 66 E5
Montréal Canada 45°30N 73°33W 113 C11
Montreux Switz. 46°26N 6°55E 64 E4
Montrose U.K. 56°44N 2°27W 19 J13
Montrose U.S.A. 38°29N 107°53W 110 C5
Montserrat ☑ W. Indies 16°40N 62°10W 115 D12
Monywa Burma 22°7N 95°11E 85 H19
Monza Italy 45°35N 9°16E 68 B3
Monze, C. Pakistan 24°47N 66°37E 84 G5
Moorfoot Hills U.K. 55°44N 3°8W 21 C9
Moorhead U.S.A. 46°53N 96°45W 111 A7
Moose Jaw Canada 50°24N 105°30W 108 D9
Moosehead L. U.S.A. 45°38N 69°40W 113 C13
Moosomin Canada 50°9N 101°40W 108 D9
Moosonee Canada 51°17N 80°39W 109 D11
Mopti Mali 14°30N 4°0W 94 F5
Mora Sweden 61°2N 14°38E 63 E6
Moradabad India 28°50N 78°50E 84 E11
Morant Bay Jamaica 17°53N 76°25W 114 a
Morant Pt. Jamaica 17°55N 76°12W 114 a
Morar, L. U.K. 56°57N 5°40W 18 J6
Moratuwa Sri Lanka 6°45N 79°55E 84 R11
Morava → Serbia 44°36N 21°4E 69 B9
Morava → Slovak Rep. 48°10N 16°59E 65 D9
Moravian Hts. Czech Rep. 49°30N 15°40E 56 F9
Moray □ U.K. 57°31N 3°18W 19 G11
Moray Firth U.K. 57°40N 3°52W 19 G10
Morden Canada 49°15N 98°10W 108 E10
Mordvinia □ Russia 54°20N 44°30E 70 D7
Moreau → U.S.A. 45°18N 100°43W 110 A6
Morebattle U.K. 55°31N 2°22W 21 C11
Morecambe U.K. 54°5N 2°52W 22 D3
Morecambe B. U.K. 54°7N 3°0W 22 D3
Moree Australia 29°28S 149°54E 98 F9
Morehead U.S.A. 38°11N 83°26W 112 F6
Morelia Mexico 19°42N 101°7W 114 D4
Morena, Sierra Spain 38°20N 4°0W 67 C3
Moresby I. Canada 52°30N 131°40W 108 D6
Moreton-in-Marsh U.K. 51°59N 1°41W 24 C5
Moretonhampstead U.K. 50°39N 3°46W 27 F6
Morgan City U.S.A. 29°42N 91°12W 111 E8
Morgantown U.S.A. 39°38N 79°57W 112 F8
Morioka Japan 39°45N 141°8E 81 D7
Morlaix France 48°36N 3°52W 66 B2
Morley U.K. 53°45N 1°36W 23 E5
Morocco ■ N. Afr. 32°0N 5°50W 94 B4
Morogoro Tanzania 6°50S 37°40E 96 F7
Morón Cuba 22°8N 78°39W 115 C9
Mörön Mongolia 49°38N 100°9E 78 B9
Morondava Madag. 20°17S 44°17E 97 J8
Moroni Comoros Is. 11°40S 43°16E 91 H8
Morotai Indonesia 2°10N 128°30E 83 D7
Morpeth U.K. 55°10N 1°41W 22 B5
Morphou Cyprus 35°12N 32°56E 86 C3
Morrinhos Brazil 17°45S 49°10W 122 C1
Morris Jesup, Kap Greenland 83°40N 34°0W 104 A16
Morte Bay U.K. 51°9N 4°14W 27 E5
Morte Pt. U.K. 51°11N 4°14W 27 E5
Mortehoe U.K. 51°11N 4°12W 27 E5
Mortimer's Cross U.K. 52°16N 2°50W 24 B3
Morton Fen U.K. 52°49N 0°20W 23 G8
Morvan France 47°5N 4°3E 66 C6
Morwenstow U.K. 50°54N 4°33W 27 F4
Moscos Is. Burma 14°0N 97°30E 85 N20
Moscow Russia 55°45N 37°37E 70 C6
Moscow U.S.A. 46°44N 117°0W 110 A3
Mosel → Europe 50°22N 7°36E 64 C4
Moses Lake U.S.A. 47°8N 119°17W 110 A3
Moshi Tanzania 3°22S 37°18E 96 E7
Mosjøen Norway 65°51N 13°12E 63 D6
Mossbaai S. Africa 34°11S 22°8E 97 L4
Mossley U.K. 53°33N 2°1W 23 E4
Mossoró Brazil 5°10S 37°15W 120 C6
Most Czech Rep. 50°31N 13°38E 64 C7
Mostaganem Algeria 35°54N 0°5E 94 A6
Mostar Bos.-H. 43°22N 17°50E 69 C7
Mosul Iraq 36°15N 43°5E 86 B5
Motherwell U.K. 55°47N 3°58W 21 C8
Motihari India 26°30N 84°55E 85 F14
Motril Spain 36°31N 3°37W 67 D4
Mottisfont U.K. 51°2N 1°32W 24 D5
Mouila Gabon 1°50S 11°0E 96 E2
Moule à Chique, C. St. Lucia 13°43N 60°57W 115 f
Moulins France 46°35N 3°19E 66 C5
Moulmein Burma 16°30N 97°40E 85 L20
Moulouya, O. → Morocco 35°5N 2°25W 94 B5
Moulton U.K. 52°17N 0°52W 25 B7
Moundou Chad 8°40N 16°10E 95 G9
Moundsville U.S.A. 39°55N 80°44W 112 F7
Mount Barker Australia 35°5S 138°52E 98 H6
Mount Desert I. U.S.A. 44°21N 68°20W 113 C13
Mount Gambier Australia 37°50S 140°46E 98 H7
Mount Hagen Papua N. G. 5°52S 144°16E 98 B7
Mount Isa Australia 20°42S 139°26E 98 E6
Mount Magnet Australia 28°2S 117°47E 98 F2
Mount Pleasant U.S.A. 43°36N 84°46W 112 D5
Mount Sterling U.S.A. 38°4N 83°56W 112 F6
Mount Vernon Ind., U.S.A. 37°56N 87°54W 112 F3
Mount Vernon Ohio, U.S.A. 40°23N 82°29W 112 E6
Mountain Ash U.K. 51°40N 3°23W 26 D7
Mountain Home U.S.A. 43°8N 115°41W 110 B3
Mountain View U.S.A. 19°33N 155°7W 110 J17
Mountmellick Ireland 53°7N 7°20W 31 B8

Mountrath Ireland 53°0N 7°28W 31 C8
Mount's Bay U.K. 50°5N 5°31W 27 G2
Mountsorrel U.K. 52°44N 1°8W 23 G6
Mourne → U.K. 54°52N 7°26W 28 B7
Mourne Mts. U.K. 54°10N 6°0W 29 C9
Moville Ireland 55°11N 7°3W 29 A7
Moy → Ireland 54°8N 9°8W 28 C3
Moyen Atlas Morocco 33°0N 5°0W 94 B4
Mozambique ■ Africa 19°0S 35°0E 97 H7
Mozambique Chan. Africa 17°30S 42°30E 90 H8
Mozdok Russia 43°45N 44°48E 71 F7
Mpanda Tanzania 6°23S 31°1E 96 F6
Mpumalanga S. Africa 29°50S 30°33E 97 K6
Msaken Tunisia 35°49N 10°33E 95 A8
Mthatha S. Africa 31°36S 28°49E 97 L5
Mtwara-Mikindani Tanzania 10°20S 40°20E 96 G8
Muar Malaysia 2°3N 102°34E 82 D2
Mubi Nigeria 10°18N 13°16E 95 F8
Much Dewchurch U.K. 51°58N 2°45W 24 C3
Much Marcle U.K. 51°59N 2°29W 24 C4
Much Wenlock U.K. 52°35N 2°33W 23 G3
Muchinga Mts. Zambia 11°30S 31°30E 97 G6
Muck U.K. 56°50N 6°15W 18 J4
Muckle Flugga U.K. 60°51N 0°54W 18 A16
Muckle Roe U.K. 60°23N 1°27W 18 B15
Mucuri Brazil 18°0S 39°36W 122 C3
Mudanjiang China 44°38N 129°30E 79 C14
Mufulira Zambia 12°32S 28°15E 97 G5
Muğla Turkey 37°15N 28°22E 71 G4
Muine Bheag Ireland 52°42N 6°58W 31 C9
Muir of Ord U.K. 57°32N 4°28W 19 G9
Muktsar India 30°30N 74°30E 84 D9
Mulanje, Mt. Malawi 16°2S 35°33E 97 H7
Mulde → Germany 51°53N 12°15E 64 C7
Mulhacén Spain 37°4N 3°20W 67 D4
Mulhouse France 47°40N 7°20E 66 C7
Mull U.K. 56°25N 5°56W 20 B4
Mull, Sound of U.K. 56°30N 5°50W 20 A4
Mullaghareirk Mts. Ireland 52°20N 9°10W 30 D4
Mullet Pen. Ireland 54°13N 10°2W 28 C1
Mullingar Ireland 53°31N 7°21W 28 D7
Mullion U.K. 50°1N 5°16W 27 G3
Mulroy B. Ireland 55°15N 7°46W 28 A6
Multan Pakistan 30°15N 71°36E 84 D7
Mumbai India 18°56N 72°50E 84 K8
Mumbles Hd. U.K. 51°34N 3°59W 27 D6
Muna Indonesia 5°0S 122°30E 83 F6
Muncie U.S.A. 40°12N 85°23W 112 E5
Mundesley U.K. 52°53N 1°25E 25 A11
Mundo Novo Brazil 11°50S 40°29W 122 B2
Munger India 25°23N 86°30E 85 G15
Munich Germany 48°8N 11°34E 64 D6
Munising U.S.A. 46°25N 86°40W 112 B4
Münster Germany 51°58N 7°37E 64 C4
Munster □ Ireland 52°18N 8°44W 30 D5
Murashi Russia 59°30N 49°0E 70 C8
Murat → Turkey 38°46N 40°0E 71 G7
Murchison → Australia 27°45S 114°0E 98 F1
Murcia Spain 38°5N 1°10W 67 D5
Murcia □ Spain 37°50N 1°30W 67 D5
Mureş → Romania 46°15N 20°13E 65 E11
Murfreesboro U.S.A. 35°51N 86°24W 111 C9
Muriaé Brazil 21°8S 42°23W 122 D2
Müritz Germany 53°25N 12°42E 64 B7
Murmansk Russia 68°57N 33°10E 70 A5
Murom Russia 55°35N 42°3E 70 C7
Muroran Japan 42°25N 141°0E 81 B7
Murray → U.S.A. 36°37N 88°19W 112 G3
Murray → Australia 35°20S 139°22E 98 H6
Murton U.K. 54°49N 1°22W 22 C6
Mururoa French Polynesia 21°52S 138°55W 103 K14
Murwara India 23°46N 80°28E 85 H12
Muş Turkey 38°45N 41°30E 71 G7
Mûsa, Gebel Egypt 28°33N 33°59E 86 D3
Muscat Oman 23°37N 58°36E 87 F9
Musgrave Ranges Australia 26°0S 132°0E 98 F5
Musina S. Africa 22°20S 30°5E 97 J6
Muskegon U.S.A. 43°14N 86°16W 112 D4
Muskegon → U.S.A. 43°14N 86°21W 112 D4
Muskogee U.S.A. 35°45N 95°22W 111 C7
Musselburgh U.K. 55°57N 3°2W 21 C9
Musselshell → U.S.A. 47°21N 107°57W 110 A5
Mutare Zimbabwe 18°58S 32°38E 97 H6
Mutton I. Ireland 52°49N 9°32W 30 C3
Muynak Uzbekistan 43°44N 59°10E 87 A9
Muz Tag China 36°25N 87°25E 78 D6
Muzaffarabad Pakistan 34°25N 73°30E 84 B8
Muzaffarnagar India 29°26N 77°40E 84 E10
Muztagh-Ata China 38°17N 75°7E 78 D4
Mwanza Tanzania 2°30S 32°58E 96 E6
Mweelrea Ireland 53°39N 9°49W 28 D2
Mwene-Ditu Dem. Rep. of the Congo 6°35S 22°27E 96 F4
Mweru, L. Zambia 9°0S 28°40E 96 F5
My Tho Vietnam 10°29N 106°23E 82 B3
Myanmar = Burma ■ Asia 21°0N 96°30E 85 J20
Mycenae Greece 37°43N 22°46E 69 F10
Myddle U.K. 52°49N 2°47W 23 G3
Myingyan Burma 21°30N 95°20E 85 J19
Mymensingh Bangla. 24°45N 90°24E 85 G17
Mynydd Du U.K. 51°52N 3°50W 26 D6
Mynydd Preseli U.K. 51°57N 4°48W 26 D4
Mysore India 12°17N 76°41E 84 N10
Mytishchi Russia 55°50N 37°50E 70 C6

N

Naab → Germany 49°1N 12°2E 64 D6
Naas Ireland 53°12N 6°40W 31 B9
Naberezhnyye Chelny Russia 55°42N 52°19E 70 C9
Nabeul Tunisia 36°30N 10°44E 95 A8
Nābulus West Bank 32°14N 35°15E 86 C3
Nacala Mozam. 14°32S 40°34E 97 G8
Nacogdoches U.S.A. 31°36N 94°39W 111 D8
Nacozari de García Mexico 30°25N 109°38W 114 A3
Nadiad India 22°41N 72°56E 84 H8
Nador Morocco 35°14N 2°58W 94 B5
Nafferton U.K. 54°1N 0°23W 23 D8
Nafud Desert Si. Arabia 28°15N 41°0E 86 D5

Naga Phil. 13°38N 123°15E 83 B6
Nagaland □ India 26°0N 94°30E 85 G19
Nagano Japan 36°40N 138°10E 81 E6
Nagaoka Japan 37°27N 138°51E 81 E6
Nagappattinam India 10°46N 79°51E 84 P11
Nagasaki Japan 32°47N 129°50E 81 G1
Nagaur India 27°15N 73°45E 84 F8
Nagercoil India 8°12N 77°26E 84 Q10
Nagles Mts. Ireland 52°8N 8°30W 30 D6
Nagorno-Karabakh □ Azerbaijan 39°55N 46°45E 71 F8
Nagoya Japan 35°10N 136°50E 81 F5
Nagpur India 21°8N 79°10E 84 J11
Nagqu China 31°29N 92°3E 78 E7
Naguabo Puerto Rico 18°13N 65°44W 115 d
Naha Japan 26°13N 127°42E 79 F14
Nailsea U.K. 51°26N 2°44W 24 D3
Nailsworth U.K. 51°41N 2°14W 24 C4
Nain Canada 56°34N 61°40W 109 D13
Nairn U.K. 57°35N 3°53W 19 G10
Nairobi Kenya 1°17S 36°48E 96 E7
Naivasha Kenya 0°40S 36°30E 96 E7
Najafābād Iran 32°40N 51°15E 87 C7
Najd Si. Arabia 26°30N 42°0E 86 E5
Najibabad India 29°40N 78°20E 84 E11
Najrān Si. Arabia 17°34N 44°18E 89 D3
Nakhodka Russia 42°53N 132°54E 79 C15
Nakhon Ratchasima Thailand 14°59N 102°12E 82 B2
Nakhon Sawan Thailand 15°35N 100°10E 82 A2
Nakhon Si Thammarat Thailand 8°29N 100°0E 82 C2
Nakina Canada 50°10N 86°40W 109 D11
Nakuru Kenya 0°15S 36°4E 96 E7
Nalchik Russia 43°30N 43°33E 71 F7
Nallamalai Hills India 15°30N 78°50E 84 M11
Nam Co China 30°30N 90°45E 78 E7
Namak, Daryācheh-ye Iran 34°30N 52°0E 87 C8
Namaland Namibia 26°0S 17°0E 97 K3
Namangan Uzbekistan 41°0N 71°40E 87 A12
Namcha Barwa China 29°40N 95°10E 78 F8
Namib Desert Namibia 22°30S 15°0E 97 J3
Namibe Angola 15°7S 12°11E 97 H2
Namibia ■ Africa 22°0S 18°9E 97 J3
Nampa U.S.A. 43°34N 116°34W 110 B3
Namp'o N. Korea 38°52N 125°10E 79 D14
Nampula Mozam. 15°6S 39°15E 97 H7
Namumea Tuvalu 5°41S 176°9E 99 B14
Namur Belgium 50°27N 4°52E 64 C3
Nan-ch'ang China 28°42N 115°55E 79 F12
Nanaimo Canada 49°10N 124°0W 108 E7
Nanchong China 30°43N 106°2E 78 E10
Nancy France 48°42N 6°12E 66 B7
Nanda Devi India 30°23N 79°59E 84 D11
Nanded India 19°10N 77°20E 84 K10
Nandurbar India 21°20N 74°15E 84 J9
Nanga Parbat Pakistan 35°10N 74°35E 84 B9
Nangarhār □ Afghan. 34°20N 70°0E 87 C12
Nanjing China 32°2N 118°47E 79 E12
Nanning China 22°48N 108°20E 78 G10
Nanping China 26°38N 118°10E 79 F12
Nansen Sd. Canada 81°0N 91°0W 109 A10
Nantes France 47°12N 1°33W 66 C3
Nantong China 32°1N 120°52E 79 E13
Nantucket I. U.S.A. 41°16N 70°5W 113 E12
Nantwich U.K. 53°4N 2°31W 23 F3
Nanuque Brazil 17°50S 40°21W 122 C2
Nanyang China 33°11N 112°30E 79 E11
Nanyuki Kenya 0°2N 37°4E 96 D7
Napa U.S.A. 38°18N 122°17W 110 C2
Napier N.Z. 39°30S 176°56E 99 H14
Naples Italy 40°50N 14°15E 68 D6
Napo → Peru 3°20S 72°40W 120 C2
Nappa U.S.A. 53°58N 2°13W 23 E4
Narayanganj Bangla. 23°40N 90°33E 85 H17
Narberth U.K. 51°47N 4°44W 26 D4
Narbonne France 43°11N 3°0E 66 E5
Narborough U.K. 52°34N 1°13W 23 G6
Nares Str. Arctic 80°0N 70°0W 109 A13
Narmada → India 21°38N 72°36E 84 J8
Narodnaya Russia 65°5N 59°58E 70 A10
Narva Estonia 59°23N 28°12E 63 F9
Narvik Norway 68°28N 17°26E 63 D7
Naryan-Mar Russia 67°42N 53°12E 70 A9
Naryn Kyrgyzstan 41°26N 75°58E 78 C4
Naseby U.K. 52°24N 0°59W 25 B7
Nashua U.S.A. 42°45N 71°28W 113 D12
Nashville U.S.A. 36°10N 86°47W 111 C9
Nasik India 19°58N 73°50E 84 K8
Nasirabad India 26°15N 74°45E 84 F9
Nasiriyah Iraq 31°0N 46°15E 86 D6
Nassau Bahamas 25°5N 77°20W 115 B9
Nasser, L. Egypt 23°0N 32°30E 95 D12
Natal Brazil 5°47S 35°13W 120 C6
Natashquan Canada 50°14N 61°46W 109 D13
Natashquan → Canada 50°7N 61°50W 109 D13
Natchez U.S.A. 31°34N 91°24W 111 D8
Natchitoches U.S.A. 31°46N 93°5W 111 D8
Nathdwara India 24°55N 73°50E 84 G8
Natitingou Benin 10°20N 1°26E 94 F6
Natron, L. Tanzania 2°20S 36°0E 96 E7
Natuna Besar, Kepulauan Indonesia 4°0N 108°15E 82 D3
Nauru ■ Pac. Oc. 1°0S 166°0E 102 H8
Navarino, I. Chile 55°0S 67°40W 121 H3
Navarra □ Spain 42°40N 1°40W 67 A5
Navenby U.K. 53°6N 0°31W 23 F7
Naver → U.K. 58°32N 4°14W 19 E8
Navoiy Uzbekistan 40°9N 65°22E 76 E7
Navojoa Mexico 27°6N 109°26W 114 B3
Navsari India 20°57N 72°59E 84 J8
Nawabshah Pakistan 26°15N 68°25E 84 F6
Naxçıvan □ Azerbaijan 39°25N 45°26E 71 G8
Naxos Greece 37°8N 25°25E 69 F11
Naypyidaw Burma 19°44N 96°12E 85 K20
Nazaré Brazil 13°2S 39°0W 122 B3
Nazas → Mexico 25°12N 104°12W 114 B4
Nazca Peru 14°50S 74°57W 120 D2
Naze, The U.K. 51°53N 1°18E 25 C11

Nazret   **Orléans**

Name	Location	Coordinates	Ref
Nazret	Ethiopia	8°32N 39°22E	89 F2
Ndjamena	Chad	12°10N 15°0E	95 F8
Ndola	Zambia	13°0S 28°34E	97 G5
Neagh, Lough	U.K.	54°37N 6°25W	29 B9
Near Is.	U.S.A.	52°30N 174°0E	108 D1
Neath	U.K.	51°39N 3°48W	26 D6
Neblina, Pico da	Brazil	0°48N 66°2W	120 B3
Nebraska □	U.S.A.	41°30N 99°30W	110 B7
Nébrodi, Monti	Italy	37°54N 14°35E	68 F6
Neckar →	Germany	49°27N 8°29E	64 D5
Necochea	Argentina	38°30S 58°50W	121 F4
Needham Market	U.K.	52°9N 1°4E	25 B11
Needles, The	U.K.	50°39N 1°35W	24 E5
Neenah	U.S.A.	44°11N 88°28W	112 C3
Neepawa	Canada	50°15N 99°30W	108 D10
Neftekumsk	Russia	44°46N 44°50E	71 F7
Nefteyugansk	Russia	61°5N 72°42E	76 C8
Negaunee	U.S.A.	46°30N 87°36W	112 B4
Negele	Ethiopia	5°20N 39°36E	89 F2
Negombo	Sri Lanka	7°12N 79°50E	84 R11
Negra, Pta.	Peru	6°6S 81°10W	117 D2
Negril	Jamaica	18°22N 78°20W	114 a
Negro →	Argentina	41°2S 62°47W	121 G3
Negro →	Brazil	3°0S 60°0W	120 C3
Negros	Phil.	9°30N 122°40E	83 C6
Neijiang	China	29°35N 104°55E	78 F9
Neisse →	Europe	52°4N 14°46E	64 B8
Neiva	Colombia	2°56N 75°18W	120 C2
Nellore	India	14°27N 79°59E	84 M11
Nelson	Canada	49°30N 117°20W	108 E8
Nelson	N.Z.	41°18S 173°16E	99 J13
Nelson	U.K.	53°50N 2°13W	23 E4
Nelson →	Canada	54°33N 98°2W	108 D10
Neman →	Lithuania	55°25N 21°10E	63 F8
Nenagh	Ireland	52°52N 8°11W	30 C6
Nene →	U.K.	52°49N 0°11E	25 A9
Nenjiang	China	49°10N 125°10E	79 B14
Neosho →	U.S.A.	36°48N 95°18W	111 C7
Nepal ■	Asia	28°0N 84°30E	85 E14
Nephi	U.S.A.	39°43N 111°50W	110 C4
Nephin	Ireland	54°1N 9°22W	28 C3
Nephin Beg Range	Ireland	54°0N 9°40W	28 C2
Nerastro, Sarīr	Libya	24°20N 20°37E	95 D10
Neryungri	Russia	57°38N 124°28E	77 D13
Ness, L.	U.K.	57°15N 4°32W	19 H8
Neston	U.K.	53°17N 3°4W	23 F2
Netherbury	U.K.	50°46N 2°45W	24 E3
Netherlands ■	Europe	52°0N 5°30E	64 B3
Netherlands Antilles ☑	W. Indies	12°15N 69°0W	115 E11
Netley	U.K.	50°52N 1°20W	24 E5
Nettilling L.	Canada	66°30N 71°0W	109 C12
Nettlebed	U.K.	51°34N 0°59W	25 C7
Nettleham	U.K.	53°16N 0°29W	23 F8
Neuchâtel	Switz.	47°0N 6°55E	64 E4
Neuchâtel, Lac de	Switz.	46°53N 6°50E	64 E4
Neuquén	Argentina	38°55S 68°0W	121 F3
Neusiedler See	Austria	47°50N 16°47E	65 E9
Neva →	Russia	59°56N 30°20E	70 C5
Nevada □	U.S.A.	39°0N 117°0W	110 C3
Nevers	France	47°0N 3°9E	66 C5
Nevinnomyssk	Russia	44°40N 42°0E	71 F7
New Abbey	U.K.	54°59N 3°37W	21 E9
New Alresford	U.K.	51°5N 1°8W	24 D6
New Amsterdam	Guyana	6°15N 57°36W	120 B4
New Bedford	U.S.A.	41°38N 70°56W	113 E12
New Britain	Papua N. G.	5°50S 150°20E	98 B9
New Britain	U.S.A.	41°40N 72°47W	113 E11
New Brunswick	U.S.A.	40°30N 74°27W	113 E10
New Brunswick □	Canada	46°50N 66°30W	113 B14
New Caledonia ☑	Pac. Oc.	21°0S 165°0E	99 E12
New Castle Ind.,	U.S.A.	39°55N 85°22W	112 F5
New Castle Pa.,	U.S.A.	41°0N 80°21W	112 E7
New Delhi	India	28°36N 77°11E	84 E10
New England	U.S.A.	43°0N 71°0W	111 B12
New Forest △	U.K.	50°53N 1°34W	24 E5
New Galloway	U.K.	55°5N 4°9W	20 D7
New Georgia Is.	Solomon Is.	8°15S 157°30E	99 B10
New Glasgow	Canada	45°35N 62°36W	109 E13
New Guinea	Oceania	4°0S 136°0E	98 B7
New Hampshire □	U.S.A.	44°0N 71°30W	113 D12
New Haven	U.S.A.	41°18N 72°55W	113 E11
New Hebrides = Vanuatu ■	Pac. Oc.	15°0S 168°0E	99 D12
New Holland	U.K.	53°42N 0°21W	23 E8
New Iberia	U.S.A.	30°1N 91°49W	111 D8
New Ireland	Papua N. G.	3°20S 151°50E	98 A9
New Jersey □	U.S.A.	40°0N 74°30W	113 E10
New Lexington	U.S.A.	39°43N 82°13W	112 F6
New Liskeard	Canada	47°31N 79°41W	109 E12
New London	U.S.A.	41°22N 72°6W	113 E11
New Madrid	U.S.A.	36°36N 89°32W	112 G3
New Mexico □	U.S.A.	34°30N 106°0W	110 D5
New Mills	U.K.	53°23N 2°0W	23 F5
New Milton	U.K.	50°45N 1°40W	24 E5
New Orleans	U.S.A.	29°57N 90°4W	111 E8
New Philadelphia	U.S.A.	40°30N 81°27W	112 E7
New Plymouth	N.Z.	39°4S 174°5E	99 H13
New Providence	Bahamas	25°25N 78°35W	115 B9
New Quay	U.K.	52°13N 4°21W	26 C5
New Radnor	U.K.	52°15N 3°9W	26 C7
New Romney	U.K.	50°59N 0°57E	25 E10
New Ross	Ireland	52°23N 6°57W	31 D9
New Rossington	U.K.	53°29N 1°4W	23 F6
New Siberian Is.	Russia	75°0N 142°0E	77 B15
New South Wales □	Australia	33°0S 146°0E	98 G8
New York	U.S.A.	40°43N 74°0W	113 E11
New York □	U.S.A.	43°0N 75°0W	113 D9
New Zealand ☑	Oceania	40°0S 176°0E	99 J14
Newark Del.,	U.S.A.	39°41N 75°46W	113 F10
Newark N.J.,	U.S.A.	40°44N 74°10W	113 E10
Newark N.Y.,	U.S.A.	43°3N 77°6W	112 D9
Newark Ohio,	U.S.A.	40°3N 82°24W	112 E6
Newark-on-Trent	U.K.	53°5N 0°48W	23 F7
Newberry	U.S.A.	46°21N 85°30W	112 B5
Newbiggin-by-the-Sea	U.K.	55°11N 1°31W	22 B5
Newbigging	U.K.	55°42N 3°34W	21 C8
Newburgh	U.S.A.	41°30N 74°1W	113 E10
Newburn	U.K.	54°59N 1°43W	22 C5
Newbury	U.K.	51°24N 1°20W	24 D6
Newburyport	U.S.A.	42°49N 70°53W	113 D12
Newby Bridge	U.K.	54°17N 2°57W	22 D3
Newcastle	Australia	33°0S 151°46E	98 G9
Newcastle	Canada	47°1N 65°38W	113 B15
Newcastle	S. Africa	27°45S 29°58E	97 K5
Newcastle	U.K.	54°13N 5°54W	29 C10
Newcastle Emlyn	U.K.	52°2N 4°28W	26 C5
Newcastle-under-Lyme	U.K.	53°1N 2°14W	23 F4
Newcastle-upon-Tyne	U.K.	54°58N 1°36W	22 C5
Newcastle West	Ireland	52°27N 9°3W	30 D4
Newcastleton	U.K.	55°11N 2°49W	21 D10
Newent	U.K.	51°56N 2°24W	24 C4
Newfoundland	Canada	49°0N 55°0W	104 E14
Newfoundland & Labrador □	Canada	53°0N 58°0W	109 D14
Newham □	U.K.	51°31N 0°3E	25 C9
Newhaven	U.K.	50°47N 0°3E	25 E9
Newington Kent,	U.K.	51°6N 1°7E	25 D11
Newington Kent,	U.K.	51°21N 0°41E	25 D10
Newlyn	U.K.	50°6N 5°34W	27 G2
Newlyn East	U.K.	50°22N 5°5W	27 G3
Newman	Australia	23°18S 119°45E	98 E2
Newmarket	Ireland	52°13N 9°0W	30 D5
Newmarket	U.K.	52°15N 0°25E	25 B9
Newnham	U.K.	51°48N 2°27W	24 C4
Newport	Ireland	53°53N 9°33W	28 D2
Newport Essex,	U.K.	51°59N 0°14E	25 C9
Newport I. of W.,	U.K.	50°42N 1°17W	24 E6
Newport Pembs.,	U.K.	52°1N 4°51W	26 C4
Newport Telford & Wrekin,	U.K.	52°46N 2°22W	23 G4
Newport Ark.,	U.S.A.	35°37N 91°16W	111 C8
Newport Ky.,	U.S.A.	39°5N 84°29W	112 F5
Newport R.I.,	U.S.A.	41°29N 71°19W	113 E12
Newport Vt.,	U.S.A.	44°56N 72°13W	113 C11
Newport News	U.S.A.	36°58N 76°25W	111 C11
Newport Pagnell	U.K.	52°5N 0°43W	25 B7
Newquay	U.K.	50°25N 5°6W	27 G3
Newry	U.K.	54°11N 6°21W	29 C9
Newton Abbot	U.K.	50°32N 3°37W	27 F6
Newton Arlosh	U.K.	54°53N 3°14W	22 C2
Newton Aycliffe	U.K.	54°37N 1°34W	22 C5
Newton Ferrers	U.K.	50°19N 4°3W	27 G5
Newton le Willows	U.K.	53°28N 2°38W	23 F3
Newton St. Cyres	U.K.	50°46N 3°36W	27 F6
Newton Stewart	U.K.	54°57N 4°30W	20 E6
Newtonmore	U.K.	57°4N 4°8W	19 H9
Newtown	U.K.	52°31N 3°19W	26 B7
Newtown St. Boswells	U.K.	55°34N 2°39W	21 C10
Newtownabbey	U.K.	54°40N 5°56W	29 B10
Newtownards	U.K.	54°36N 5°42W	29 B10
Newtownstewart	U.K.	54°43N 7°23W	28 B7
Neyshābūr	Iran	36°10N 58°50E	87 B9
Nganglong Kangri	China	33°0N 81°0E	78 E5
Ngaoundéré	Cameroon	7°15N 13°35E	96 C2
Ngoring Hu	China	34°55N 97°5E	78 E8
Ngorongoro	Tanzania	3°11S 35°32E	96 E7
Nguru	Nigeria	12°56N 10°29E	95 F8
Nha Trang	Vietnam	12°16N 109°10E	82 B3
Nhamundá →	Brazil	2°12S 56°41W	120 C4
Niagara Falls	Canada	43°7N 79°5W	109 E12
Niagara Falls	U.S.A.	43°5N 79°4W	112 D8
Niamey	Niger	13°27N 2°6E	94 F6
Nias	Indonesia	1°0N 97°30E	82 D1
Nicaragua ■	Cent. Amer.	11°40N 85°30W	114 E7
Nicaragua, L. de	Nic.	12°0N 85°30W	114 E7
Nice	France	43°42N 7°14E	66 E7
Nicholasville	U.S.A.	37°53N 84°34W	112 G5
Nicobar Is.	Ind. Oc.	8°0N 93°30E	53 D14
Nicosia	Cyprus	35°10N 33°25E	86 C3
Nicoya, Pen. de	Costa Rica	9°45N 85°40W	114 F7
Nidd →	U.K.	53°59N 1°23W	23 E6
Nidderdale	U.K.	54°5N 1°46W	22 D5
Niedersachsen □	Germany	52°50N 9°0E	64 B5
Nieuw Nickerie	Suriname	6°0N 56°59W	120 B4
Niğde	Turkey	37°58N 34°40E	86 B3
Niger ■	W. Afr.	17°30N 10°0E	94 E7
Niger →	W. Afr.	5°33N 6°33E	94 G7
Nigeria ■	W. Afr.	8°30N 8°0E	94 G7
Niigata	Japan	37°58N 139°0E	81 E6
Ni'ihau	U.S.A.	21°54N 160°9W	110 H14
Nijmegen	Neths.	51°50N 5°52E	64 C3
Nikolayev	Ukraine	46°58N 32°0E	71 E5
Nikolayevsk-na-Amur	Russia	53°8N 140°44E	77 D15
Nikopol	Ukraine	47°35N 34°25E	71 E5
Nikšić	Montenegro	42°50N 18°57E	69 C8
Nile →	Africa	30°10N 31°6E	95 B12
Nimach	India	24°30N 74°56E	84 G9
Nîmes	France	43°50N 4°23E	66 E6
Nimrūz □	Afghan.	30°0N 62°0E	87 D10
Nineveh	Iraq	36°25N 43°10E	86 B5
Ningbo	China	29°51N 121°28E	79 F13
Ningjing Shan	China	30°0N 98°20E	78 F8
Ningxia Hui □	China	38°0N 106°0E	78 D10
Niobrara →	U.S.A.	42°46N 98°3W	110 B7
Niort	France	46°19N 0°29W	66 C3
Nipawin	Canada	53°20N 104°0W	108 D9
Nipigon	Canada	49°0N 88°17W	112 A3
Nipigon, L.	Canada	49°50N 88°30W	109 E11
Nipissing, L.	Canada	46°20N 80°0W	109 E12
Niquelândia	Brazil	14°33S 48°23W	122 D1
Niš	Serbia	43°19N 21°58E	69 C9
Niterói	Brazil	22°53S 43°0W	122 D2
Nith →	U.K.	55°14N 3°33W	21 D8
Nitra	Slovak Rep.	48°19N 18°4E	65 D10
Nitra →	Slovak Rep.	47°46N 18°10E	65 D10
Niuafo'ou	Tonga	15°30S 175°58W	99 D15
Niue	Pac. Oc.	19°2S 169°54W	99 D17
Nivernais	France	47°15N 3°30E	66 C5
Nizamabad	India	18°45N 78°7E	84 K11
Nizhnekamsk	Russia	55°38N 51°49E	70 C9
Nizhnevartovsk	Russia	60°56N 76°38E	76 C8
Nizhniy Novgorod	Russia	56°20N 44°0E	70 C7
Nizhniy Tagil	Russia	57°55N 59°57E	70 C10
Nizhyn	Ukraine	51°5N 31°55E	71 D5
Nizwá	Oman	22°56N 57°32E	89 C6
Nkawkaw	Ghana	6°36N 0°49W	94 G5
Nkongsamba	Cameroon	4°55N 9°55E	96 D1
Noakhali	Bangla.	22°48N 91°10E	85 H17
Nobeoka	Japan	32°36N 131°41E	81 G2
Noblesville	U.S.A.	40°3N 86°1W	112 E5
Nogales	Mexico	31°19N 110°56W	114 A2
Nogales	U.S.A.	31°21N 110°56W	110 D4
Noirmoutier, Î. de	France	46°58N 2°10W	66 C2
Nola	C.A.R.	3°35N 16°4E	96 D3
Nome	U.S.A.	64°30N 165°25W	108 C3
Nordelph	U.K.	52°35N 0°17E	25 A9
Norderstedt	Germany	53°42N 10°1E	64 B5
Nordfriesische Inseln	Germany	54°40N 8°20E	64 A5
Nordkapp	Norway	71°10N 25°50E	63 C9
Nordrhein-Westfalen □	Germany	51°45N 7°30E	64 C4
Nordvik	Russia	74°2N 111°32E	77 B12
Nore →	Ireland	52°25N 6°58W	31 D9
Norfolk Nebr.,	U.S.A.	42°2N 97°25W	111 B7
Norfolk Va.,	U.S.A.	36°50N 76°17W	111 C11
Norfolk □	U.K.	52°39N 0°54E	25 A10
Norfolk Broads △	U.K.	52°45N 1°30E	25 A11
Norfolk I.	Pac. Oc.	28°58S 168°3E	99 F12
Norham	U.K.	55°43N 2°9W	22 A4
Norilsk	Russia	69°20N 88°6E	77 C9
Norman	U.S.A.	35°13N 97°26W	110 C7
Norman Wells	Canada	65°17N 126°51W	108 C7
Normandie	France	48°45N 0°10E	66 B4
Normanton	Australia	17°40S 141°10E	98 D7
Normanton	U.K.	53°42N 1°24W	23 E6
Norristown	U.S.A.	40°7N 75°21W	113 E10
Norrköping	Sweden	58°37N 16°11E	63 F7
Norrland	Sweden	62°15N 15°45E	63 E7
Norseman	Australia	32°8S 121°43E	98 G3
Norte, Serra do	Brazil	11°20S 59°0W	120 D4
North, C.	Canada	47°2N 60°20W	113 B17
North America		40°0N 100°0W	104 F10
North Ayrshire □	U.K.	55°45N 4°44W	20 C6
North Battleford	Canada	52°50N 108°17W	108 D9
North Bay	Canada	46°20N 79°30W	109 E12
North Berwick	U.K.	56°4N 2°42W	21 B10
North C.	Canada	47°5N 64°0W	113 B15
North C.	N.Z.	34°23S 173°4E	99 G13
North Canadian →	U.S.A.	35°22N 95°37W	110 C7
North Carolina □	U.S.A.	35°30N 80°0W	111 C11
North Cerney	U.K.	51°45N 1°57W	24 C5
North Channel	Canada	46°0N 83°0W	112 B6
North Channel	U.K.	55°13N 5°52W	20 D4
North Dakota □	U.S.A.	47°30N 100°15W	110 A7
North Dorset Downs	U.K.	50°51N 2°30W	24 E4
North Downs	U.K.	51°19N 0°21E	25 D9
North Esk →	U.K.	56°46N 2°24W	19 J13
North European Plain	Europe	55°0N 25°0E	56 E10
North Foreland	U.K.	51°22N 1°28E	25 D11
North Harris	U.K.	58°0N 6°55W	18 F4
North Hill	U.K.	50°33N 4°27W	27 F5
North Hykeham	U.K.	53°11N 0°35W	23 F7
North I.	N.Z.	38°0S 175°0E	99 H14
North Korea ■	Asia	40°0N 127°0E	79 D14
North Magnetic Pole	Arctic	82°42N 114°24W	54 A2
North Minch	U.K.	58°5N 5°55W	18 F6
North Molton	U.K.	51°3N 3°49W	27 E6
North Ossetia □	Russia	43°30N 44°30E	71 F7
North Petherton	U.K.	51°5N 3°1W	24 D2
North Platte	U.S.A.	41°8N 100°46W	110 B6
North Platte →	U.S.A.	41°7N 100°42W	110 B6
North Pole	Arctic	90°0N 0°0	54 A
North Pt.	Barbados	13°20N 59°37W	114 b
North Ronaldsay	U.K.	59°22N 2°26W	19 D13
North Saskatchewan →	Canada	53°15N 105°5W	108 D9
North Sea	Europe	56°0N 4°0E	56 D6
North Sea Canal = Nord-Ostsee-Kanal	Germany	54°12N 9°32E	64 A5
North Somercotes	U.K.	53°27N 0°8E	23 F9
North Sunderland	U.K.	55°34N 1°40W	22 A5
North Tawton	U.K.	50°48N 3°54W	27 F6
North Thompson →	Canada	50°40N 120°20W	108 D7
North Thoresby	U.K.	53°28N 0°4W	23 F8
North Tidworth	U.K.	51°15N 1°40W	24 D5
North Tyne →	U.K.	55°0N 2°8W	22 C4
North Uist	U.K.	57°40N 7°15W	18 G3
North Vernon	U.S.A.	39°0N 96°43W	114 D5
North Walsham	U.K.	52°50N 1°22E	25 A11
North West C.	Australia	21°45S 114°9E	98 E1
North West Frontier □	Pakistan	34°0N 72°0E	84 B8
North West Highlands	U.K.	57°33N 4°58W	19 G8
North West River	Canada	53°30N 60°10W	109 D13
North York Moors △	U.K.	54°23N 0°53W	22 D7
North Yorkshire △	U.K.	54°27N 0°51W	22 D7
North Yorkshire □	U.K.	54°15N 1°25W	22 D6
Northallerton	U.K.	54°20N 1°26W	22 D6
Northam	Australia	31°35S 116°42E	98 G2
Northam	U.K.	51°2N 4°13W	27 E5
Northampton	Australia	28°27S 114°33E	98 F1
Northampton	U.K.	52°15N 0°53W	25 B7
Northamptonshire □	U.K.	52°16N 0°55W	25 B7
Northern Areas □	Pakistan	36°30N 73°0E	84 B9
Northern Circars	India	17°30N 82°30E	85 L13
Northern Ireland □	U.K.	54°45N 7°0W	29 B8
Northern Marianas ☑	Pac. Oc.	17°0N 145°0E	102 F6
Northern Sporades	Greece	39°15N 23°30E	69 E10
Northern Territory □	Australia	20°0S 133°0E	98 E5
Northfleet	U.K.	51°26N 0°20E	25 D9
Northiam	U.K.	50°59N 0°36E	25 E9
Northleach	U.K.	51°49N 1°50W	24 C5
Northrepps	U.K.	52°54N 1°21E	25 A11
Northumberland □	U.K.	55°12N 2°0W	22 B4
Northumberland △	Northumberland, U.K.	55°15N 2°20W	22 B4
Northumberland Str.	Canada	46°20N 64°0W	109 E13
Northwest Territories □	Canada	63°0N 118°0W	108 C8
Northwich	U.K.	53°15N 2°31W	23 F3
Northwold	U.K.	52°33N 0°36E	25 A10
Norton N. Yorks.,	U.K.	54°8N 0°47W	22 D7
Norton Suffolk,	U.K.	52°16N 0°52E	25 B10
Norton Fitzwarren	U.K.	51°1N 3°8W	24 D2
Norton Sd.	U.S.A.	63°50N 164°0W	108 C3
Norwalk	U.S.A.	41°15N 82°37W	112 E6
Norway ■	Europe	63°0N 11°0E	63 E6
Norway House	Canada	53°59N 97°50W	108 D10
Norwegian B.	Canada	77°30N 90°0W	109 B11
Norwegian Sea	Atl. Oc.	66°0N 1°0E	56 B6
Norwich	U.K.	52°38N 1°18E	25 A11
Norwich	U.S.A.	42°32N 75°32W	113 D10
Noss Hd.	U.K.	58°28N 3°3W	19 F11
Nossa Senhora do Socorro	Brazil	10°52S 37°7W	122 B3
Nossob →	S. Africa	26°55S 20°45E	97 K4
Notre Dame B.	Canada	49°45N 55°30W	109 E14
Nottaway →	Canada	51°22N 78°55W	109 D12
Nottingham	U.K.	52°58N 1°10W	23 G6
Nottingham □	U.K.	63°20N 77°55W	109 C12
Nottinghamshire □	U.K.	53°10N 1°3W	23 F6
Nouâdhibou	Mauritania	20°54N 17°0W	94 D2
Nouâdhibou, Râs	Mauritania	20°50N 17°0W	94 D2
Nouakchott	Mauritania	18°9N 15°58W	94 E2
Nouméa	N. Cal.	22°17S 166°30E	99 E12
Nova Friburgo	Brazil	22°16S 42°30W	122 D2
Nova Iguaçu	Brazil	22°45S 43°28W	122 D2
Nova Scotia □	Canada	45°10N 63°0W	113 C16
Nova Venécia	Brazil	18°45S 40°24W	122 C2
Novara	Italy	45°28N 8°38E	68 B3
Novaya Zemlya	Russia	75°0N 56°0E	76 B6
Novgorod	Russia	58°30N 31°25E	70 C5
Novi Pazar	Serbia	43°12N 20°28E	69 C9
Novi Sad	Serbia	45°18N 19°52E	69 B8
Novocherkassk	Russia	47°27N 40°15E	71 E7
Novokuybyshevsk	Russia	53°7N 49°58E	70 D8
Novokuznetsk	Russia	53°45N 87°10E	76 D9
Novomoskovsk	Russia	54°5N 38°15E	70 D6
Novorossiysk	Russia	44°43N 37°46E	71 F6
Novoshakhtinsk	Russia	47°46N 39°58E	71 E6
Novosibirsk	Russia	55°0N 83°5E	76 D9
Novotroitsk	Russia	51°10N 58°15E	70 D10
Novyy Urengoy	Russia	65°48N 76°52E	76 C8
Nowy Sącz	Poland	49°40N 20°41E	65 D11
Noyabrsk	Russia	64°34N 76°21E	76 C8
Nubia	Africa	21°0N 32°0E	90 D7
Nubian Desert	Sudan	21°30N 33°30E	95 D12
Nueces →	U.S.A.	27°51N 97°30W	110 E7
Nueltin L.	Canada	60°30N 99°30W	108 C10
Nueva Rosita	Mexico	27°57N 101°13W	114 B4
Nuevitas	Cuba	21°30N 77°20W	115 C9
Nuevo Laredo	Mexico	27°30N 99°31W	114 B5
Nuku'alofa	Tonga	21°10S 175°12W	99 E16
Nukulaelae	Tuvalu	9°23S 179°52E	99 B14
Nukus	Uzbekistan	42°27N 59°41E	87 A9
Nullarbor Plain	Australia	31°10S 129°0E	98 G4
Numan	Nigeria	9°29N 12°3E	95 G8
Numazu	Japan	35°7N 138°51E	81 F6
Nunavut □	Canada	66°0N 85°0W	109 C11
Nuneaton	U.K.	52°32N 1°27W	23 G6
Nunivak I.	U.S.A.	60°10N 166°30W	108 C3
Nunney	U.K.	51°12N 2°22W	24 D4
Núoro	Italy	40°20N 9°20E	68 D3
Nuremberg	Germany	49°27N 11°3E	64 D6
Nusaybin	Turkey	37°3N 41°10E	71 G7
Nuuk	Greenland	64°10N 51°35W	54 C5
Nuweveldberge	S. Africa	32°10S 21°45E	97 L4
Nyagan	Russia	62°30N 65°38E	76 C7
Nyahururu	Kenya	0°2N 36°27E	96 D7
Nyaingêntanglha Shan	China	30°0N 90°0E	78 E7
Nyâlâ	Sudan	12°2N 24°58E	95 F10
Nyasa, L.	Africa	12°30S 34°30E	97 G6
Nyíregyháza	Hungary	47°58N 21°47E	65 E11
Nysa	Poland	50°30N 17°22E	65 C9
Nzérékoré	Guinea	7°49N 8°48W	94 G4

O

Name	Location	Coordinates	Ref
Oa, Mull of	U.K.	55°35N 6°20W	20 C3
Oadby	U.K.	52°36N 1°5W	23 G6
Oahe, L.	U.S.A.	44°27N 100°24W	110 A6
O'ahu	U.S.A.	21°28N 157°58W	110 H16
Oak Hill	U.S.A.	37°59N 81°9W	112 G7
Oak Ridge	U.S.A.	36°1N 84°16W	111 C10
Oakengates	U.K.	52°41N 2°26W	23 G4
Oakham	U.K.	52°40N 0°43W	23 G7
Oakland	U.S.A.	37°48N 122°18W	110 C2
Oates Land	Antarctica	69°0S 160°0E	55 C11
Oaxaca	Mexico	17°3N 96°43W	114 D5
Ob →	Russia	66°45N 69°30E	76 C7
Ob, G. of	Russia	69°0N 73°0E	76 C8
Oba	Canada	49°4N 84°7W	109 E11
Oban	U.K.	56°25N 5°29W	20 B5
Oberhausen	Germany	51°28N 6°51E	64 C4
Obi, Kepulauan	Indonesia	1°23S 127°45E	83 E7
Óbidos	Brazil	1°50S 55°30W	120 C4
Obihiro	Japan	42°56N 143°12E	81 B8
Obozerskiy	Russia	63°34N 40°21E	70 B7
Obshchi Syrt	Russia	52°0N 53°0E	56 E16
Ocala	U.S.A.	29°11N 82°8W	111 E10
Occidental, Cordillera	Colombia	5°0N 76°0W	117 C3
Occidental, Grand Erg	Algeria	30°20N 1°0E	94 B6
Ocean City	U.S.A.	39°17N 74°35W	113 F10
Oceanside	U.S.A.	33°12N 117°23W	110 D3
Ochil Hills	U.K.	56°14N 3°40W	21 B9
Ocho Rios	Jamaica	18°24N 77°6W	114 a
Oconto	U.S.A.	44°53N 87°52W	112 C4
Odawara	Japan	35°20N 139°6E	81 F6
Odense	Denmark	55°22N 10°23E	63 F6
Oder →	Europe	53°33N 14°38E	64 B8
Odessa	Ukraine	46°30N 30°45E	71 E5
Odessa	U.S.A.	31°52N 102°23W	110 D6
Odiham	U.K.	51°15N 0°55W	25 D7
Odintsovo	Russia	55°40N 37°16E	70 C6
Odzi	Zimbabwe	19°0S 32°20E	97 H6
Offa	Nigeria	8°13N 4°42E	94 G6
Offaly □	Ireland	53°15N 7°30W	31 B8
Offenbach	Germany	50°6N 8°44E	64 C5
Ogaden	Ethiopia	7°30N 45°30E	89 F3
Ōgaki	Japan	35°21N 136°37E	81 F5
Ogasawara Gunto	Pac. Oc.	27°0N 142°0E	102 E6
Ogbomosho	Nigeria	8°1N 4°11E	94 G6
Ogden	U.S.A.	41°13N 111°58W	110 B4
Ogdensburg	U.S.A.	44°42N 75°30W	113 C10
Ogooué →	Gabon	1°0S 9°0E	96 E1
Ohio □	U.S.A.	40°15N 82°45W	112 E5
Ohio →	U.S.A.	36°59N 89°8W	111 C9
Ohře →	Czech Rep.	50°30N 14°10E	64 C8
Ohrid, L.	Macedonia	41°8N 20°52E	69 D9
Oise →	France	49°0N 2°4E	66 B5
Oistins	Barbados	13°4N 59°33W	115 g
Oistins B.	Barbados	13°4N 59°33W	115 g
Ōita	Japan	33°14N 131°36E	81 G2
Ojos del Salado, Cerro	Argentina	27°0S 68°40W	121 E3
Oka →	Russia	56°20N 43°59E	70 C7
Okara	Pakistan	30°50N 73°31E	84 D8
Okavango Delta	Botswana	18°45S 22°45E	97 H4
Okayama	Japan	34°40N 133°54E	81 F3
Okazaki	Japan	34°57N 137°10E	81 F5
Okeechobee, L.	U.S.A.	27°0N 80°50W	111 E10
Okehampton	U.K.	50°44N 4°0W	27 F5
Okhotsk	Russia	59°20N 143°10E	77 D15
Okhotsk, Sea of	Asia	55°0N 145°0E	77 D15
Oki-Shotō	Japan	36°5N 133°15E	81 E3
Okinawa-Jima	Japan	26°32N 128°0E	79 F14
Oklahoma □	U.S.A.	35°20N 97°30W	110 C7
Oklahoma City	U.S.A.	35°30N 97°30W	110 C7
Oktyabrskiy	Russia	54°28N 53°28E	70 D9
Öland	Sweden	56°45N 16°38E	63 F7
Olavarría	Argentina	36°55S 60°20W	121 F3
Ólbia	Italy	40°55N 9°31E	68 D3
Old Basing	U.K.	51°16N 1°3W	24 D6
Old Crow	Canada	67°30N 139°55W	108 C6
Old Fletton	U.K.	52°33N 0°14W	25 A8
Old Leake	U.K.	53°2N 0°5E	23 F9
Old Town	U.S.A.	44°56N 68°39W	113 C13
Oldbury	U.K.	51°38N 2°33W	24 C3
Oldcastle	Ireland	53°46N 7°10W	29 D7
Oldenburg	Germany	53°9N 8°13E	64 B5
Oldham	U.K.	53°33N 2°7W	23 E4
Oldmeldrum	U.K.	57°20N 2°19W	19 H13
Olean	U.S.A.	42°5N 78°26W	112 D8
Olekminsk	Russia	60°25N 120°30E	77 C13
Olenek →	Russia	73°0N 120°10E	77 B13
Oléron, Î. d'	France	45°55N 1°15W	66 D3
Ólgiy	Mongolia	48°56N 89°57E	78 B6
Olímpia	Brazil	20°44S 48°54W	122 D1
Oliveira	Brazil	20°39S 44°50W	122 D2
Ollagüe	Chile	21°15S 68°10W	120 E3
Ollerton	U.K.	53°12N 1°1W	23 F6
Olmaliq	Uzbekistan	40°50N 69°35E	76 E7
Olney	U.K.	52°10N 0°41W	25 B7
Olney	U.S.A.	38°44N 88°5W	112 F3
Olomouc	Czech Rep.	49°38N 17°12E	65 D9
Olsztyn	Poland	53°48N 20°29E	65 B11
Olt →	Romania	43°43N 24°51E	65 G13
Olympia	Greece	37°39N 21°39E	69 F9
Olympia	U.S.A.	47°3N 122°53W	110 A2
Olympus, Mt.	Greece	40°6N 22°23E	69 D10
Olympus, Mt.	U.S.A.	47°48N 123°43W	110 A2
Omagh	U.K.	54°36N 7°19W	28 B7
Omaha	U.S.A.	41°17N 95°58W	111 B7
Oman ■	Asia	23°0N 58°0E	89 C6
Oman, G. of	Asia	24°30N 58°30E	87 E9
Ombersley	U.K.	52°16N 2°13W	24 B4
Omdurmân	Sudan	15°40N 32°28E	95 E12
Ometepec	Mexico	16°41N 98°25W	114 D5
Omsk	Russia	55°0N 73°12E	76 D8
Ōmuta	Japan	33°5N 130°26E	81 G2
Ondangwa	Namibia	17°57S 16°4E	97 H3
Öndörhaan	Mongolia	47°19N 110°39E	79 B11
Onega →	Russia	63°58N 38°2E	70 B6
Onega, L.	Russia	61°44N 35°22E	70 B6
Onega B.	Russia	64°24N 36°38E	70 B6
Oneida	U.S.A.	43°6N 75°39W	113 D10
O'Neill	U.S.A.	42°27N 98°39W	110 B7
Oneonta	U.S.A.	42°27N 75°4W	113 D10
Onitsha	Nigeria	6°6N 6°42E	94 G7
Onny →	U.K.	52°24N 2°47W	23 H3
Onslow B.	U.S.A.	34°20N 77°15W	111 D11
Ontario	U.S.A.	44°2N 116°58W	110 B3
Ontario □	Canada	48°0N 83°0W	109 E11
Ontario, L.	N. Amer.	43°20N 78°0W	112 D8
Ontonagon	U.S.A.	46°52N 89°19W	112 B3
Oostende	Belgium	51°15N 2°54E	64 C2
Opava	Czech Rep.	49°57N 17°58E	65 D9
Opole	Poland	50°42N 17°58E	65 C9
Oradea	Romania	47°2N 21°58E	65 E11
Öræfajökull	Iceland	64°2N 16°39W	63 B2
Oral	Kazakhstan	51°20N 51°20E	71 D9
Oran	Algeria	35°45N 0°39W	94 A5
Orange	Australia	33°15S 149°7E	98 G8
Orange	France	44°8N 4°47E	66 D6
Orange	U.S.A.	38°15N 78°7W	112 F8
Orange →	S. Africa	28°41S 16°28E	97 K3
Orange, C.	Brazil	4°20N 51°30W	120 B4
Orangeburg	U.S.A.	33°30N 80°52W	111 D10
Orangeville	Canada	43°55N 80°5W	112 D7
Ordos Desert	China	39°0N 109°0E	79 D10
Ordu	Turkey	40°55N 37°53E	71 F6
Örebro	Sweden	59°20N 15°18E	63 F7
Oregon □	U.S.A.	44°0N 121°0W	110 B2
Orekhovo-Zuyevo	Russia	55°50N 38°55E	70 C6
Orel	Russia	52°57N 36°3E	70 D6
Orem	U.S.A.	40°19N 111°42W	110 B4
Orenburg	Russia	51°45N 55°6E	70 D10
Orford	U.K.	52°6N 1°33E	25 B12
Orford Ness	U.K.	52°5N 1°35E	25 B12
Orhon Gol →	Mongolia	50°21N 106°0E	78 A10
Oriental, Cordillera	Colombia	6°0N 73°0W	117 C3
Oriental, Grand Erg	Algeria	30°0N 6°30E	94 B7
Orihuela	Spain	38°7N 0°55W	67 C5
Orinoco →	Venezuela	9°15N 61°30W	120 B3
Orissa □	India	20°0N 84°0E	85 K14
Oristano	Italy	39°54N 8°36E	68 E3
Orizaba	Mexico	18°51N 97°6W	114 D5
Orizaba, Pico de	Mexico	18°58N 97°15W	114 D5
Orkney □	U.K.	59°2N 3°13W	19 D11
Orkney Is.	U.K.	59°0N 3°0W	19 E12
Orlando	U.S.A.	28°32N 81°22W	111 E10
Orléanais	France	48°0N 2°0E	66 C5
Orléans	France	47°54N 1°52E	66 C4

Orléans, Î. d' Canada 46°54N 70°58W 113 B12
Ormara Pakistan 25°16N 64°33E 84 G4
Ormesby St. Margaret U.K. 52°41N 1°41E 25 A12
Ormoc Phil. 11°0N 124°37E 83 B6
Ormskirk U.K. 53°35N 2°54W 23 E3
Örnsköldsvik Sweden 63°17N 18°40E 63 E7
Oronsay U.K. 56°1N 6°15W 20 B3
Orsha Belarus 54°30N 30°25E 70 D5
Ortegal, C. Spain 43°43N 7°52W 67 A2
Oruro Bolivia 18°0S 67°9W 120 D3
Oruzgan □ Afghan. 33°0N 66°0E 87 C11
Orwell → U.K. 51°59N 1°18E 25 C11
Ōsaka Japan 34°42N 135°30E 81 F4
Osh Kyrgyzstan 40°37N 72°49E 76 E8
Oshakati Namibia 17°45S 15°40E 97 H3
Oshawa Canada 43°50N 78°50W 109 E12
Oshkosh U.S.A. 44°1N 88°33W 112 C3
Oshogbo Nigeria 7°48N 4°37E 94 G6
Osijek Croatia 45°34N 18°41E 69 B8
Osizweni S. Africa 27°49S 30°7E 97 K6
Oskaloosa U.S.A. 41°18N 92°39W 111 B81
Oskarshamn Sweden 57°15N 16°27E 63 F7
Öskemen Kazakhstan 50°0N 82°36E 76 E9
Oslo Norway 59°54N 10°43E 63 F6
Oslofjorden Norway 59°20N 10°35E 63 F6
Osmaniye Turkey 37°5N 36°10E 71 G6
Osmotherley U.K. 54°22N 1°18W 22 D6
Osnabrück Germany 52°17N 8°3E 64 B5
Osorno Chile 40°25S 73°0W 121 G2
Ossa, Mt. Australia 41°52S 146°3E 98 J8
Ossett U.K. 53°41N 1°34W 23 E5
Ostend = Oostende Belgium 51°15N 2°54E 64 C2
Österdalälven → Sweden 60°30N 15°7E 63 E6
Östersund Sweden 63°10N 14°38E 63 E6
Ostfriesische Inseln Germany 53°42N 7°0E 64 B4
Ostrava Czech Rep. 49°51N 18°18E 65 D10
Ostrołęka Poland 53°4N 21°32E 65 B11
Ostrów Wielkopolski Poland 51°36N 17°44E 65 C9
Ostrowiec-Świętokrzyski
  Poland 50°55N 21°22E 65 C11
Oswaldtwistle U.K. 53°43N 2°26W 23 E4
Oswego U.S.A. 43°27N 76°31W 112 D9
Oswestry U.K. 52°52N 3°3W 23 G2
Oturu Japan 43°10N 141°0E 81 B7
Otjiwarongo Namibia 20°30S 16°33E 97 J3
Otley U.K. 53°54N 1°41W 23 E5
Otranto Italy 40°9N 18°28E 69 D8
Otranto, Str. of Italy 40°15N 18°40E 69 D8
Ōtsu Japan 35°0N 135°50E 81 F4
Ottawa Canada 45°26N 75°42W 113 C10
Ottawa U.S.A. 41°21N 88°51W 112 E3
Ottawa Is. Canada 59°35N 80°10W 109 D11
Otter → U.K. 50°38N 3°19W 27 F7
Otterburn U.K. 55°14N 2°11W 22 B4
Ottery St. Mary U.K. 50°44N 3°17W 27 F7
Ottumwa U.S.A. 41°1N 92°25W 111 B81
Ouachita → U.S.A. 31°38N 91°49W 111 D8
Ouachita Mts. U.S.A. 34°30N 94°30W 111 D8
Ouagadougou Burkina Faso 12°25N 1°30W 94 F5
Oubangi →
  Dem. Rep. of the Congo 0°30S 17°50E 96 E3
Oudtshoorn S. Africa 33°35S 22°14E 97 L4
Ouezzane Morocco 34°51N 5°35W 94 B4
Oughterard Ireland 53°26N 9°18W 30 D4
Oujda Morocco 34°41N 1°55W 94 B5
Oulton U.K. 52°30N 1°43E 25 B12
Oulton Broad U.K. 52°28N 1°42E 25 B12
Oulu Finland 65°1N 25°29E 63 D9
Oulujärvi Finland 64°25N 27°15E 63 E9
Oulujoki → Finland 65°1N 25°30E 63 D9
Oundle U.K. 52°29N 0°28W 25 B8
Ourense Spain 42°19N 7°55W 67 A2
Ouro Fino Brazil 22°16S 46°25W 122 D1
Ouro Prêto Brazil 20°20S 43°30W 122 D2
Ouse → E. Sussex, U.K. 50°47N 0°4E 25 E9
Ouse → N. Yorks., U.K. 53°44N 0°55W 23 E7
Outaouais → Canada 45°27N 74°8W 109 E12
Outer Hebrides U.K. 57°30N 7°40W 18 H2
Outjo Namibia 20°5S 16°7E 97 J3
Outwell U.K. 52°37N 0°14E 25 A9
Ovalle Chile 30°33S 71°18W 121 F2
Ovamboland Namibia 18°30S 16°0E 97 H3
Over Wallop U.K. 51°9N 1°36W 24 D5
Overton U.K. 51°15N 1°15W 24 D6
Oviedo Spain 43°25N 5°50W 67 A3
Owatonna U.S.A. 44°5N 93°14W 111 B8
Owen Sound Canada 44°35N 80°55W 109 E11
Owen Stanley Ra. Papua N. G. 8°30S 147°0E 98 B8
Owens L. U.S.A. 36°26N 117°57W 110 C3
Owensboro U.S.A. 37°46N 87°7W 112 G4
Owo Nigeria 7°10N 5°39E 94 G7
Owosso U.S.A. 43°0N 84°10W 112 D5
Owston Ferry U.K. 53°29N 0°47W 23 F7
Owyhee → U.S.A. 43°49N 117°2W 110 B3
Oxford U.K. 51°46N 1°15W 24 C6
Oxfordshire □ U.K. 51°48N 1°16W 24 C6
Oxnard U.S.A. 34°12N 119°11W 110 D3
Oyama Japan 36°18N 139°48E 81 E6
Oyem Gabon 1°34N 11°31E 96 D2
Oykel → U.K. 57°56N 4°26W 19 G9
Oyo Nigeria 7°46N 3°56E 94 G6
Ozark Plateau U.S.A. 37°20N 91°40W 111 C81
Ozarks, L. of the U.S.A. 38°12N 92°38W 111 C81

P

Paarl S. Africa 33°45S 18°56E 97 L3
Pab Hills Pakistan 26°30N 66°45E 84 F5
Pabbay U.K. 57°46N 7°14W 18 G3
Pabna Bangla. 24°1N 89°18E 85 G16
Pacaraima, Sa. S. Amer. 4°0N 62°30W 120 B3
Pacasmayo Peru 7°20S 79°35W 120 C2
Pachuca Mexico 20°7N 98°44W 114 C5
Pacific Ocean 10°0N 140°0W 103 G14
Padang Indonesia 1°0S 100°20E 82 E2
Padangsidempuan Indonesia 1°30N 99°15E 82 D1
Paddock Wood U.K. 51°11N 0°24E 25 D9
Paderborn Germany 51°42N 8°45E 64 C5
Padiham U.K. 53°48N 2°18W 23 E4
Padre I. U.S.A. 27°10N 97°25W 111 E7

Padstow U.K. 50°33N 4°58W 27 F4
Padstow B. U.K. 50°34N 4°57W 27 F4
Padua Italy 45°25N 11°53E 68 B4
Paducah U.S.A. 37°5N 88°37W 112 G3
Pag Croatia 44°25N 15°3E 68 B6
Pagadian Phil. 7°55N 123°30E 83 C6
Page U.S.A. 36°57N 111°27W 110 C4
Pāhala U.S.A. 19°12N 155°29W 110 J17
Paignton U.K. 50°26N 3°35W 27 G6
Paine Grande, Cerro Chile 50°59S 73°4W 121 H2
Painesville U.S.A. 41°43N 81°15W 112 E7
Painswick U.K. 51°47N 2°10W 24 C4
Painted Desert U.S.A. 36°0N 111°0W 110 C4
Paintsville U.S.A. 37°49N 82°48W 112 G6
País Vasco □ Spain 42°50N 2°45W 67 A4
Paisley U.K. 55°50N 4°25W 20 C7
Paita Peru 5°11S 81°9W 120 C1
Pakistan ■ Asia 30°0N 70°0E 84 E7
Paktiā □ Afghan. 33°0N 69°15E 87 C12
Pakxe Laos 15°5N 105°52E 82 A3
Palagruža Croatia 42°24N 16°15E 68 C7
Palani Hills India 10°14N 77°33E 84 P10
Palanpur India 24°10N 72°25E 84 G8
Palapye Botswana 22°30S 27°7E 97 J5
Palau ■ Palau 7°30N 134°30E 102 G5
Palawan Phil. 9°30N 118°30E 82 C5
Palembang Indonesia 3°0S 104°50E 82 E2
Palencia Spain 42°1N 4°34W 67 A3
Palermo Italy 38°7N 13°22E 68 E5
Palestine U.S.A. 31°46N 95°38W 111 D7
Palghat India 10°46N 76°42E 84 P10
Palgrave U.K. 52°22N 1°6E 25 B11
Pali India 25°50N 73°20E 84 G8
Palikir Micronesia 6°55N 158°9E 102 G7
Palk Strait Asia 10°0N 79°45E 84 Q11
Palm Springs U.S.A. 33°50N 116°33W 110 D3
Palma de Mallorca Spain 39°35N 2°39E 67 C7
Palmares Brazil 8°41S 35°28W 122 A3
Palmas Brazil 10°12S 48°21W 122 B1
Palmas, C. Liberia 4°27N 7°46W 94 H4
Palmeira dos Índios Brazil 9°25S 36°37W 122 A3
Palmer U.S.A. 61°36N 149°7W 108 C5
Palmer Land Antarctica 73°0S 63°0W 55 D18
Palmerston North N.Z. 40°21S 175°39E 99 J14
Palmira Colombia 3°32N 76°16W 120 B2
Palmyra Syria 34°36N 38°15E 86 C4
Palmyra Is. Pac. Oc. 5°52N 162°5W 103 G11
Palopo Indonesia 3°0S 120°16E 83 E6
Palu Indonesia 1°0S 119°52E 83 E5
Palu Turkey 38°45N 40°0E 71 G7
Pamiers France 43°7N 1°39E 66 E4
Pamir Tajikistan 37°40N 73°0E 87 B13
Pamlico Sd. U.S.A. 35°20N 76°0W 111 C11
Pampa U.S.A. 35°32N 100°58W 110 C6
Pampas Argentina 35°0S 63°0W 121 F3
Pamplona-Iruña Spain 42°48N 1°38W 67 A5
Pana U.S.A. 39°23N 89°5W 112 F3
Panaji India 15°25N 73°50E 84 M8
Panamá Panama 9°0N 79°25W 115 F9
Panama ■ Cent. Amer. 8°48N 79°55W 115 F9
Panamá, G. de Panama 8°4N 79°20W 115 F9
Panama, Isthmus of Cent. Amer. 9°0N 79°0W 115 F9
Panama Canal Panama 9°10N 79°37W 115 F9
Panama City U.S.A. 30°10N 85°40W 111 D9
Panay Phil. 11°10N 122°30E 83 B6
Pančevo Serbia 44°52N 20°41E 69 B9
Panevėžys Lithuania 55°42N 24°25E 63 F9
Pangani Tanzania 5°25S 38°58E 96 F7
Pangbourne U.K. 51°29N 1°6W 24 D6
Pangkalpinang Indonesia 2°0S 106°0E 82 E3
Pangnirtung Canada 66°8N 65°43W 109 C13
Pantar Indonesia 8°28S 124°10E 83 F6
Pante Macassar E. Timor 9°30S 123°58E 83 F6
Panzhihua China 26°33N 101°44E 78 F9
Papa Stour U.K. 60°20N 1°42W 18 A14
Papa Westray U.K. 59°20N 2°55W 19 D12
Papantla Mexico 20°27N 97°19W 114 C5
Papeete Tahiti 17°32S 149°34W 103 J13
Paphos Cyprus 34°46N 32°25E 86 C3
Papua □ Indonesia 4°0S 137°0E 83 E9
Papua, G. of Papua N. G. 9°0S 144°50E 98 B7
Papua New Guinea ■ Oceania 8°0S 145°0E 98 B8
Pará □ Brazil 3°20S 52°0W 120 C4
Paracatu Brazil 17°10S 46°50W 122 C1
Paracel Is. S. China Sea 15°50N 112°0E 82 A4
Paragould U.S.A. 36°3N 90°29W 111 C81
Paraguaçu → Brazil 12°45S 38°54W 122 B3
Paraguaná, Pen. de Venezuela 12°0N 70°0W 120 A3
Paraguari Paraguay 25°36S 57°0W 121 E4
Paraguay ■ S. Amer. 23°0S 57°0W 121 E4
Paraguay → Paraguay 27°18S 58°38W 121 E4
Paraíba □ Brazil 7°0S 36°0W 120 C6
Parakou Benin 9°25N 2°40E 94 G6
Paramaribo Suriname 5°50N 55°10W 120 B4
Paraná Argentina 31°45S 60°30W 121 F3
Paraná □ Brazil 12°30S 47°48W 122 B1
Paraná □ Brazil 24°30S 51°0W 121 E4
Paraná → Argentina 33°43S 59°15W 121 F4
Paranaguá Brazil 25°30S 48°30W 122 E1
Paranaíba → Brazil 20°0S 51°4W 120 E4
Paranapanema → Brazil 22°40S 53°9W 121 E4
Parbhani India 19°8N 76°52E 84 K10
Pardo → Brazil 15°40S 39°0W 122 C3
Pardubice Czech Rep. 50°3N 15°45E 64 C8
Parecis, Serra dos Brazil 13°0S 60°0W 120 D4
Parepare Indonesia 4°0S 119°40E 83 E5
Parima, Serra Brazil 2°30N 64°0W 120 B3
Pariñas, Pta. Peru 4°30S 81°20W 117 D2
Parintins Brazil 2°40S 56°50W 120 C4
Pariparit Kyun Burma 14°52N 93°41E 85 M18
Paris France 48°53N 2°20E 66 B5
Paris U.S.A. 33°40N 95°33W 111 D7
Park Falls U.S.A. 45°56N 90°27W 112 C2
Parkersburg U.S.A. 39°16N 81°34W 112 F7
Parla Spain 40°14N 3°46W 67 B4
Parma Italy 44°48N 10°20E 68 B4
Parnaguá Brazil 10°10S 44°38W 122 B2
Parnaíba Brazil 2°54S 41°47W 120 C5
Parnaíba → Brazil 3°0S 41°50W 120 C5

Pärnu Estonia 58°28N 24°33E 63 F8
Paros Greece 37°5N 25°12E 69 F11
Parracombe U.K. 51°11N 3°56W 27 E6
Parrett → U.K. 51°12N 3°1W 24 D2
Parry Is. Canada 77°0N 110°0W 109 B9
Parry Sound Canada 45°20N 80°0W 109 E12
Parsons U.S.A. 37°20N 95°16W 111 C7
Partney U.K. 53°12N 0°7E 23 F9
Parton U.K. 54°35N 3°33W 22 C1
Partry Mts. Ireland 53°40N 9°28W 28 D3
Paru → Brazil 1°33S 52°38W 120 C4
Parvān □ Afghan. 35°0N 69°0E 87 C12
Pas, The Canada 53°45N 101°15W 108 D9
Pasadena Calif., U.S.A. 34°9N 118°8W 110 D3
Pasadena Tex., U.S.A. 29°43N 95°13W 111 E7
Pascua, I. de Chile 27°7S 109°23W 103 K17
Paso Robles U.S.A. 35°38N 120°41W 110 C2
Passage West Ireland 51°52N 8°21W 30 E6
Passau Germany 48°34N 13°28E 64 D7
Passo Fundo Brazil 28°10S 52°20W 121 E4
Passos Brazil 20°45S 46°29W 122 D1
Pastaza → Peru 4°50S 76°52W 120 C2
Pasto Colombia 1°13N 77°17W 120 B2
Patagonia Argentina 45°0S 69°0W 121 G3
Patan India 23°54N 72°14E 84 H8
Pateley Bridge U.K. 54°5N 1°44W 22 D5
Paterson U.S.A. 40°54N 74°9W 113 E10
Pathankot India 32°18N 75°45E 84 C9
Pathfinder Res. U.S.A. 42°28N 106°51W 110 B5
Patiala India 30°23N 76°26E 84 D9
Patkai Bum India 27°0N 95°30E 85 F19
Patmos Greece 37°21N 26°36E 69 F12
Patna India 25°35N 85°12E 85 G14
Patos Brazil 6°55S 37°16W 120 C6
Patos, L. dos Brazil 31°20S 51°0W 121 F4
Patos de Minas Brazil 18°35S 46°32W 122 C1
Patra Greece 38°14N 21°47E 69 E9
Patrington U.K. 53°41N 0°1W 23 E8
Patrocínio Brazil 18°57S 47°0W 122 C1
Patten U.S.A. 46°0N 68°38W 113 C13
Patterdale U.K. 54°32N 2°56W 22 C3
Patuakhali Bangla. 22°18N 90°41E 85 H17
Paulatuk Canada 69°25N 124°0W 108 C7
Paulistana Brazil 8°9S 41°9W 122 A2
Paull U.K. 53°44N 0°14W 23 E8
Paulo Afonso Brazil 9°21S 38°15W 122 A3
Pavia Italy 45°7N 9°8E 68 B3
Pavlodar Kazakhstan 52°33N 77°0E 76 D8
Pavlohrad Ukraine 48°30N 35°52E 71 E6
Pavlovo Russia 55°58N 43°5E 70 C7
Pawtucket U.S.A. 41°53N 71°23W 113 E12
Paxton U.S.A. 40°27N 88°6W 112 E3
Payakumbuh Indonesia 0°20S 100°35E 82 E2
Payette U.S.A. 44°5N 116°56W 110 B3
Payne L. Canada 59°30N 74°30W 109 D12
Paysandú Uruguay 32°19S 58°8W 121 F4
Payson U.S.A. 34°14N 111°20W 110 D4
Paz, B. de la Mexico 24°9N 110°25W 114 C2
Pazardzhik Bulgaria 42°12N 24°20E 69 C11
Peace → Canada 59°0N 111°25W 108 D8
Peace River Canada 56°15N 117°18W 108 D8
Peacehaven U.K. 50°48N 0°0 25 E8
Peak District △ U.K. 53°24N 1°46W 23 F5
Pearl City U.S.A. 21°24N 157°59W 110 H16
Pearl Harbor U.S.A. 21°21N 157°57W 110 H16
Peasenhall U.K. 52°16N 1°27E 25 B11
Peawanuck Canada 55°15N 85°12W 109 D11
Pechora Russia 65°10N 57°11E 70 A10
Pechora → Russia 68°13N 54°15E 70 A9
Pechora B. Russia 68°40N 54°0E 70 A9
Pecos U.S.A. 31°26N 103°30W 110 D6
Pecos → U.S.A. 29°42N 101°22W 110 E6
Pécs Hungary 46°5N 18°15E 65 E10
Pedra Azul Brazil 16°2S 41°17W 122 C2
Pedro Afonso Brazil 9°0S 48°10W 122 A1
Peebles U.K. 55°40N 3°11W 21 C9
Peel I. of Man 54°13N 4°40W 29 C12
Peel → Canada 67°0N 135°0W 108 C6
Peel Fell U.K. 55°18N 2°34W 22 B3
Peel Sd. Canada 73°0N 96°0W 108 B10
Pegswood U.K. 55°11N 1°39W 22 B5
Pegu Burma 17°20N 96°29E 85 L20
Pegu Yoma Burma 19°0N 96°0E 85 K20
Pegwell Bay U.K. 51°18N 1°24E 25 D11
Peixe Brazil 12°0S 48°40W 122 B1
Peje Kosovo 42°40N 20°17E 69 C9
Pekalongan Indonesia 6°53S 109°40E 82 F3
Pekanbaru Indonesia 0°30N 101°15E 82 D2
Pekin U.S.A. 40°35N 89°40W 112 E3
Peking = Beijing China 39°53N 116°21E 79 D12
Pelagie, Is. Italy 35°39N 12°33E 68 G5
Pelée, Mt. Martinique 14°48N 61°10W 114 c
Peleng Indonesia 1°20S 123°30E 83 E6
Peljesac Croatia 42°55N 17°25E 68 C7
Pelly → Canada 62°47N 137°19W 108 C6
Pelly Bay Canada 68°38N 89°50W 109 C11
Peloponnesos □ Greece 37°10N 22°0E 69 F10
Pelotas Brazil 31°42S 52°23W 121 F4
Pelvoux, Massif du France 44°52N 6°20E 66 D7
Pematangsiantar Indonesia 2°57N 99°5E 82 D1
Pemba Mozam. 12°58S 40°30E 97 G8
Pemba I. Tanzania 5°0S 39°45E 96 F7
Pembridge U.K. 52°13N 2°52W 24 B3
Pembroke Canada 45°50N 77°7W 109 E12
Pembroke U.K. 51°41N 4°55W 26 D4
Pembrokeshire □ U.K. 51°52N 4°56W 26 D3
Pembrokeshire Coast △ U.K. 51°50N 5°2W 26 D3
Pembury U.K. 51°8N 0°20E 25 D9
Pen-y-Ghent U.K. 54°10N 2°14W 22 D4
Penarth U.K. 51°26N 3°11W 27 F7
Peñas, G. de Chile 47°0S 75°0W 121 G2
Pend Oreille, L. U.S.A. 48°10N 116°21W 110 A3
Pendeen U.K. 50°9N 5°41W 27 G2
Pendle Hill U.K. 53°52N 2°19W 23 E4
Pendleton U.S.A. 45°40N 118°47W 110 A3
Penedo Brazil 10°15S 36°36W 122 B3
Penetanguishene Canada 44°50N 79°55W 112 C8
Penicuik U.K. 55°50N 3°13W 21 C9
Peninsular Malaysia □
  Malaysia 4°0N 102°0E 82 D2

Penistone U.K. 53°31N 1°37W 23 E5
Penkridge U.K. 52°44N 2°6W 23 G4
Penmarch, Pte. de France 47°48N 4°22W 66 C1
Penn Yan U.S.A. 42°40N 77°3W 112 D9
Pennines U.K. 54°45N 2°27W 22 C4
Pennsylvania □ U.S.A. 40°45N 77°30W 112 E8
Penong Australia 31°56S 133°1E 98 G5
Penrith Australia 33°43S 150°38E 98 G9
Penrith U.K. 54°40N 2°45W 22 C3
Penryn U.K. 50°9N 5°7W 27 G3
Pensacola U.S.A. 30°25N 87°13W 111 D9
Pensacola Mts. Antarctica 84°0S 40°0W 55 E1
Penshurst U.K. 51°10N 0°12E 25 D9
Penticton Canada 49°30N 119°38W 108 E8
Pentire Pt. U.K. 50°35N 4°56W 27 F4
Pentland Firth U.K. 58°43N 3°10W 19 E11
Pentland Hills U.K. 55°48N 3°25W 21 C9
Penwortham U.K. 53°45N 2°46W 23 E3
Penygroes U.K. 53°3N 4°17W 26 A5
Penza Russia 53°15N 45°5E 70 D8
Penzance U.K. 50°7N 5°33W 27 G2
Peoria U.S.A. 40°42N 89°36W 112 E3
Perabumulih Indonesia 3°27S 104°15E 82 E2
Perdido, Mte. Spain 42°40N 0°5E 67 A6
Pereira Colombia 4°49N 75°43W 120 B2
Pergamino Argentina 33°52S 60°30W 121 F3
Péribonka → Canada 48°45N 72°5W 109 E12
Périgueux France 45°10N 0°42E 66 D4
Perlas, Punta de Nic. 12°30N 83°30W 104 H11
Perm Russia 58°0N 56°10E 70 C10
Pernambuco □ Brazil 8°0S 37°0W 122 A3
Pernik Bulgaria 42°35N 23°2E 69 C10
Perpignan France 42°42N 2°53E 66 E5
Perranporth U.K. 50°20N 5°11W 27 G3
Perranzabuloe U.K. 50°19N 5°9W 27 G3
Perryton U.S.A. 36°24N 100°48W 110 C6
Perryville U.S.A. 37°43N 89°52W 112 G3
Persepolis Iran 29°55N 52°50E 87 D7
Pershore U.K. 52°7N 2°4W 24 B4
Persian Gulf Asia 27°0N 50°0E 87 E7
Perth Australia 31°57S 115°52E 98 G2
Perth Canada 44°55N 76°15W 112 C9
Perth U.K. 56°24N 3°26W 21 B9
Perth & Kinross □ U.K. 56°45N 3°55W 19 J9
Peru ■ S. Amer. 4°0S 75°0W 120 C2
Peru U.S.A. 40°45N 86°4W 112 E4
Peru-Chile Trench Pac. Oc. 20°0S 72°0W 103 K20
Perúgia Italy 43°7N 12°23E 68 C5
Pervomaysk Ukraine 48°10N 30°46E 71 E5
Pervouralsk Russia 56°59N 59°59E 70 C10
Pésaro Italy 43°54N 12°55E 68 C5
Pescara Italy 42°28N 14°13E 68 C6
Peshawar Pakistan 34°2N 71°37E 84 B7
Pesqueira Brazil 8°20S 36°42W 122 A3
Petah Tiqwa Israel 32°6N 34°53E 86 C3
Peter I. Br. Virgin Is. 18°22N 64°35W 115 e
Peterborough Canada 44°20N 78°20W 109 E12
Peterborough U.K. 52°35N 0°15W 25 A8
Peterchurch U.K. 52°2N 2°56W 24 B3
Peterculter U.K. 57°6N 2°16W 19 H13
Peterhead U.K. 57°31N 1°48W 19 G14
Peterlee U.K. 54°47N 1°20W 22 C6
Petersburg Alaska, U.S.A. 56°48N 132°58W 108 D6
Petersburg Va., U.S.A. 37°14N 77°24W 112 G9
Petersfield U.K. 51°1N 0°56W 25 D7
Petit-Canal Guadeloupe 16°25N 61°31W 114 b
Petit Piton St. Lucia 13°51N 61°5W 115 f
Petite Terre, Îles de la
  Guadeloupe 16°13N 61°9W 114 b
Petitot → Canada 60°14N 123°29W 108 C7
Petitsikapau L. Canada 54°37N 66°25W 109 D13
Peto Mexico 20°8N 88°55W 114 C7
Petoskey U.S.A. 45°22N 84°57W 112 C5
Petra Jordan 30°20N 35°22E 86 D3
Petrolândia Brazil 9°5S 38°20W 122 A3
Petrolina Brazil 9°24S 40°30W 122 A2
Petropavl Kazakhstan 54°53N 69°13E 76 D7
Petropavlovsk-Kamchatskiy
  Russia 53°3N 158°43E 77 D16
Petrópolis Brazil 22°33S 43°9W 122 D2
Petrozavodsk Russia 61°41N 34°20E 70 B5
Petworth U.K. 51°0N 0°36W 25 E7
Pevensey U.K. 50°49N 0°23E 25 E9
Pevensey Levels U.K. 50°50N 0°20E 25 E9
Pewsey U.K. 51°20N 1°45W 24 D5
Pewsey, Vale of U.K. 51°22N 1°40W 24 D5
Pforzheim Germany 48°52N 8°41E 64 D5
Phalodi India 27°12N 72°24E 84 F8
Phan Rang Vietnam 11°34N 109°0E 82 B3
Phan Thiet Vietnam 11°1N 108°9E 82 B3
Philadelphia U.S.A. 39°57N 75°9W 113 E10
Philippine Sea Pac. Oc. 18°0N 125°0E 72 G14
Philippine Trench Pac. Oc. 12°0N 126°6E 83 B7
Philippines ■ Asia 12°0N 123°0E 83 B6
Phillips U.S.A. 45°42N 90°24W 112 C2
Phitsanulok Thailand 16°50N 100°12E 82 A2
Phnom Penh Cambodia 11°33N 104°55E 82 B2
Phoenix U.S.A. 33°26N 112°4W 110 D4
Phoenix Is. Kiribati 3°30S 172°0W 99 A16
Phra Nakhon Si Ayutthaya
  Thailand 14°25N 100°30E 82 B2
Phuket Thailand 7°53N 98°24E 82 C1
Piacenza Italy 45°1N 9°40E 68 B3
Piatra Neamţ Romania 46°56N 26°21E 65 E14
Piauí □ Brazil 7°0S 43°0W 120 C5
Piauí → Brazil 6°38S 42°42W 120 C5
Piave → Italy 45°32N 12°44E 68 B5
Picardie □ France 49°50N 3°0E 66 B5
Pichilemu Chile 34°22S 72°0W 121 F2
Pickering U.K. 54°15N 0°46W 22 D7
Pickering, Vale of U.K. 54°14N 0°45W 22 D7
Picos Brazil 7°5S 41°28W 120 C5
Picton Canada 44°1N 77°9W 112 C9
Pidley U.K. 52°23N 0°2W 25 B8
Pidurutalagala Sri Lanka 7°10N 80°50E 84 R12
Piedmont U.S.A. 34°42N 82°28W 111 D10
Piedras Negras Mexico 28°42N 100°31W 114 B4
Piemonte □ Italy 45°0N 8°0E 68 B2
Pierre U.S.A. 44°22N 100°21W 110 B6
Pietermaritzburg S. Africa 29°35S 30°25E 97 K6
Pikes Peak U.S.A. 38°50N 105°3W 110 C5

Pikeville U.S.A. 37°29N 82°31W 112 G6
Pilar Paraguay 26°50S 58°20W 121 E4
Pilcomayo → Paraguay 25°21S 57°42W 121 E4
Pilibhit India 28°40N 79°50E 84 E11
Pilica → Poland 51°52N 21°17E 65 C11
Pilling U.K. 53°56N 2°54W 23 E3
Pilton U.K. 51°10N 2°36W 24 D3
Pimentel Peru 6°45S 79°55W 120 C2
Pinar del Río Cuba 22°26N 83°40W 115 C8
Pinatubo, Mt. Phil. 15°8N 120°21E 83 A6
Pinchbeck U.K. 52°50N 0°9W 23 G8
Pinckneyville U.S.A. 38°5N 89°23W 112 F3
Pindus Mts. Greece 40°0N 21°0E 69 E9
Pine Bluff U.S.A. 34°13N 92°1W 111 D8
Pine Point Canada 60°50N 114°28W 108 C8
Pinega → Russia 64°30N 44°19E 70 B8
Pingdingshan China 33°43N 113°27E 79 E11
Pingliang China 35°35N 106°31E 78 D10
P'ingtung Taiwan 22°38N 120°30E 79 G13
Pingxiang Guangxi Zhuangzu,
  China 22°6N 106°46E 78 G10
Pingxiang Jiangxi, China 27°43N 113°48E 79 F11
Pinheiro Brazil 2°31S 45°5W 120 C5
Pinhoe U.K. 50°44N 3°28W 27 F7
Pinsk Belarus 52°10N 26°1E 70 D4
Piombino Italy 42°55N 10°32E 68 C4
Piotrków Trybunalski
  Poland 51°23N 19°43E 65 C10
Pipmuacan, Rés. Canada 49°45N 70°30W 113 A12
Piracicaba Brazil 22°45S 47°40W 122 D1
Pirapora Brazil 17°20S 44°56W 122 C2
Pireas Greece 37°57N 23°42E 69 F10
Pirmasens Germany 49°12N 7°36E 64 D4
Pisa Italy 43°43N 10°23E 68 C4
Pisagua Chile 19°40S 70°15W 120 D2
Pishan China 37°30N 78°33E 78 D4
Pistóia Italy 43°55N 10°54E 68 C4
Pit → U.S.A. 40°47N 122°6W 110 B2
Pitcairn I. Pac. Oc. 25°5S 130°5W 103 K14
Piteå Sweden 65°20N 21°25E 63 D8
Piteşti Romania 44°52N 24°54E 65 F13
Pitlochry U.K. 56°42N 3°44W 19 J10
Pittsburg U.S.A. 37°25N 94°42W 111 C7
Pittsburgh U.S.A. 40°26N 79°58W 112 E8
Pittsfield U.S.A. 42°27N 73°15W 113 D11
Piura Peru 5°15S 80°38W 120 C1
Placentia Canada 47°20N 54°0W 109 E14
Placentia B. Canada 47°0N 54°40W 109 E14
Placetas Cuba 22°15N 79°44W 115 C9
Plainview U.S.A. 34°11N 101°43W 110 D6
Plata, Río de → S. Amer. 34°45S 57°30W 121 F4
Platte → Mo., U.S.A. 39°16N 94°50W 111 C8
Platte → Nebr., U.S.A. 41°4N 95°53W 104 E10
Plattsburgh U.S.A. 44°42N 73°28W 113 C11
Plauen Germany 50°30N 12°8E 64 C7
Plenty, B. of N.Z. 37°45S 177°0E 99 H14
Plessisville Canada 46°14N 71°47W 113 B12
Pleven Bulgaria 43°26N 24°37E 69 C11
Plock Poland 52°32N 19°40E 65 B10
Ploiești Romania 44°57N 26°5E 65 F14
Plovdiv Bulgaria 42°8N 24°44E 69 C11
Plymouth U.K. 50°22N 4°10W 27 G5
Plymouth Ind., U.S.A. 41°21N 86°19W 112 E4
Plymouth Wis., U.S.A. 43°45N 87°59W 112 D4
Plympton U.K. 50°23N 4°5W 27 G5
Plymstock U.K. 50°21N 4°7W 27 G5
Plzeň Czech Rep. 49°45N 13°22E 64 D7
Po → Italy 44°57N 12°4E 68 B5
Pobedy, Pik Kyrgyzstan 42°0N 79°58E 78 C4
Pocatello U.S.A. 42°52N 112°27W 110 B4
Pocklington U.K. 53°56N 0°46W 23 E7
Poços de Caldas Brazil 21°50S 46°33W 122 D1
Podgorica Montenegro 42°30N 19°19E 69 C8
Podolsk Russia 55°25N 37°30E 70 C6
Pohang S. Korea 36°1N 129°23E 79 D14
Pohnpei Micronesia 6°55N 158°10E 102 G7
Point Hope U.S.A. 68°21N 166°47W 108 C3
Point L. Canada 65°15N 113°4W 108 C8
Point Pleasant U.S.A. 38°51N 82°8W 112 F6
Pointe-à-Pitre Guadeloupe 16°10N 61°32W 114 b
Pointe-Noire Congo 4°48S 11°53E 96 E2
Pointe-Noire Guadeloupe 16°14N 61°47W 114 b
Poitiers France 46°35N 0°20E 66 C4
Poitou France 46°40N 0°10W 66 C3
Pokhara Nepal 28°14N 83°58E 85 E13
Poland ■ Europe 52°0N 20°0E 65 C10
Polatsk Belarus 55°30N 28°50E 70 C4
Polden Hills U.K. 51°7N 2°50W 24 D3
Polegate U.K. 50°49N 0°16E 25 E9
Polesworth U.K. 52°37N 1°36W 23 G5
Polevskoy Russia 56°26N 60°11E 70 C11
Polokwane S. Africa 23°54S 29°25E 97 J5
Polperro U.K. 50°20N 4°32W 27 G4
Polruan U.K. 50°19N 4°38W 27 G4
Poltava Ukraine 49°35N 34°35E 71 E5
Polynesia Pac. Oc. 10°0S 162°0W 103 F11
Pomeranian Lakes Poland 53°40N 16°37E 65 B9
Ponca City U.S.A. 36°42N 97°5W 111 C7
Ponce Puerto Rico 18°1N 66°37W 115 d
Pond Inlet Canada 72°40N 77°0W 109 B12
Ponferrada Spain 42°32N 6°35W 67 A2
Ponta Grossa Brazil 25°7S 50°10W 121 E4
Pontardawe U.K. 51°43N 3°51W 26 D6
Pontardulais U.K. 51°43N 4°3W 26 D5
Pontarlier France 46°54N 6°20E 66 C7
Pontchartrain, L. U.S.A. 30°5N 90°5W 111 D9
Ponte Nova Brazil 20°25S 42°54W 122 D2
Pontefract U.K. 53°42N 1°18W 23 E6
Ponteland U.K. 55°3N 1°45W 22 B5
Pontevedra Spain 42°26N 8°40W 67 A1
Pontiac Ill., U.S.A. 40°53N 88°38W 112 E3
Pontiac Mich., U.S.A. 42°38N 83°18W 112 D6
Pontianak Indonesia 0°3S 109°15E 82 E3
Pontine Mts. Turkey 41°0N 36°45E 71 F6
Pontivy France 48°5N 2°58W 66 B2
Pontrilas U.K. 51°56N 2°52W 24 C3
Pontypool U.K. 51°42N 3°2W 26 D7
Pontypridd U.K. 51°36N 3°20W 26 D7
Ponziane, Ísole Italy 40°55N 12°57E 68 D5
Poole U.K. 50°43N 1°59W 24 E5

Poole Harbour

Poole Harbour U.K. 50°41N 2°0W 24 E5
Pooley Bridge U.K. 54°37N 2°48W 22 C3
Poopó, L. de Bolivia 18°30S 67°35W 120 D3
Popayán Colombia 2°27N 76°36W 120 B2
Poplar Bluff U.S.A. 36°46N 90°24W 111 C81
Popocatépetl, Volcán Mexico 19°2N 98°38W 114 D5
Porbandar India 21°44N 69°43E 84 J6
Porcupine → U.S.A. 66°34N 145°19W 108 C5
Pori Finland 61°29N 21°48E 63 E8
Porlock U.K. 51°13N 3°35W 27 E6
Poronaysk Russia 49°13N 143°0E 79 B17
Port Alberni Canada 49°14N 124°50W 108 E7
Port Antonio Jamaica 18°10N 76°26W 114 a
Port Arthur U.S.A. 29°54N 93°56W 111 E8
Port-au-Prince Haiti 18°40N 72°20W 115 D10
Port Augusta Australia 32°30S 137°50E 98 G6
Port Carlisle U.K. 54°57N 3°11W 22 C2
Port-Cartier Canada 50°2N 66°50W 109 D13
Port-de-Paix Haiti 19°50N 72°50W 115 D10
Port Elgin Canada 44°25N 81°25W 112 C7
Port Elizabeth S. Africa 33°58S 25°40E 97 L5
Port Ellen U.K. 55°38N 6°11W 20 C3
Port Erin I. of Man 54°5N 4°45W 29 C12
Port-Gentil Gabon 0°40S 8°50E 96 E1
Port Glasgow U.K. 55°56N 4°41W 20 C6
Port Harcourt Nigeria 4°40N 7°10E 94 H7
Port Hawkesbury Canada 45°36N 61°22W 109 E13
Port Hedland Australia 20°25S 118°35E 98 E2
Port Hope Simpson Canada 52°33N 56°18W 109 D14
Port Huron U.S.A. 42°58N 82°26W 112 D6
Port Isaac U.K. 50°35N 4°50W 27 F4
Port Isaac B. U.K. 50°36N 4°50W 27 F4
Port Laoise Ireland 53°2N 7°18W 31 B8
Port Lincoln Australia 34°42S 135°52E 98 G6
Port-Louis Guadeloupe 16°28N 61°32W 114 b
Port Louis Mauritius 20°10S 57°30E 91 H9
Port McNeill Canada 50°35N 127°6W 108 D7
Port Macquarie Australia 31°25S 152°25E 98 G9
Port Maria Jamaica 18°22N 76°54W 114 a
Port Morant Jamaica 17°54N 76°19W 114 a
Port Moresby Papua N. G. 9°24S 147°8E 98 B8
Port Nolloth S. Africa 29°17S 16°52E 97 K3
Port of Spain Trin. & Tob. 10°40N 61°31W 120 A3
Port Pirie Australia 33°10S 138°1E 98 G6
Port Said Egypt 31°16N 32°18E 95 B12
Port St. Lucie U.S.A. 27°18N 80°21W 111 E10
Port St. Mary U.K. 54°5N 4°44W 29 C12
Port Shepstone S. Africa 30°44S 30°28E 97 L6
Port Sudan Sudan 19°32N 37°9E 95 E13
Port Talbot U.K. 51°35N 3°47W 27 D6
Port Vila Vanuatu 17°45S 168°18E 99 D12
Port Washington U.S.A. 43°23N 87°53W 112 D4
Port William U.K. 54°46N 4°35W 20 E6
Portadown U.K. 54°25N 6°27W 29 C9
Portaferry U.K. 54°23N 5°33W 29 C10
Portage U.S.A. 43°33N 89°28W 112 D3
Portage la Prairie Canada 49°58N 98°18W 108 E10
Portarlington Ireland 53°9N 7°14W 31 B8
Porthcawl U.K. 51°29N 3°42W 27 E6
Porthleven U.K. 50°4N 5°19W 27 G3
Porthmadog U.K. 52°55N 4°8W 26 B5
Portishead U.K. 51°29N 2°46W 24 D3
Portknockie U.K. 57°42N 2°51W 19 G12
Portland Maine, U.S.A. 43°39N 70°16W 113 D12
Portland Oreg., U.S.A. 45°32N 122°37W 110 A2
Portland, I. of U.K. 50°33N 2°26W 24 E4
Portland Bight Jamaica 17°52N 77°5W 114 a
Portland Bill U.K. 50°31N 2°28W 27 F9
Portland Pt. Jamaica 17°42N 77°11W 114 a
Portmarnock Ireland 53°26N 6°8W 31 B10
Portmore Jamaica 17°53N 76°53W 114 a
Porto Portugal 41°8N 8°40W 67 B1
Pôrto Alegre Brazil 30°5S 51°10W 121 F4
Porto Esperança Brazil 19°37S 57°29W 120 D4
Porto Nacional Brazil 10°40S 48°30W 122 B1
Porto-Novo Benin 6°23N 2°42E 94 G6
Porto Seguro Brazil 16°26S 39°5W 122 C3
Porto Tórres Italy 40°50N 8°24E 68 D3
Porto-Vecchio France 41°35N 9°16E 66 F8
Pôrto Velho Brazil 8°46S 63°54W 120 C3
Porton U.K. 51°8N 1°43W 24 D5
Portpatrick U.K. 54°51N 5°7W 20 E6
Portree U.K. 57°25N 6°12W 18 H5
Portrush U.K. 55°12N 6°40W 29 A8
Portslade U.K. 50°50N 0°12W 25 E8
Portsmouth U.K. 50°48N 1°6W 24 E6
Portsmouth N.H., U.S.A. 43°5N 70°45W 113 D12
Portsmouth Ohio, U.S.A. 38°44N 82°57W 112 F6
Portsmouth Va., U.S.A. 36°58N 76°23W 111 C11
Portsoy U.K. 57°41N 2°41W 19 G12
Portstewart U.K. 55°11N 6°43W 29 A8
Porttipahdan tekojärvi Finland 68°5N 26°40E 63 D9
Portugal ■ Europe 40°0N 8°0W 67 C1
Portumna Ireland 53°6N 8°14W 30 B6
Posadas Argentina 27°30S 55°50W 121 E4
Posse Brazil 14°4S 46°18W 122 B1
Postmasburg S. Africa 28°18S 23°5E 97 K4
Potchefstroom S. Africa 26°41S 27°7E 97 K5
Potenza Italy 40°38N 15°48E 68 D6
Poti Georgia 42°10N 41°38E 71 F7
Potiskum Nigeria 11°39N 11°2E 95 F8
Potomac → U.S.A. 38°0N 76°23W 112 F9
Potosí Bolivia 19°38S 65°50W 120 D3
Potsdam Germany 52°23N 13°3E 64 B7
Potsdam U.S.A. 44°40N 74°59W 113 D10
Potter Heigham U.K. 52°42N 1°34E 25 A12
Potterne U.K. 51°20N 2°0W 24 D4
Potters Bar U.K. 51°42N 0°11W 25 C8
Potterspury U.K. 52°5N 0°52W 25 B7
Pottstown U.S.A. 40°15N 75°39W 113 E10
Pottsville U.S.A. 40°41N 76°12W 113 E9
Pottuvil Sri Lanka 6°55N 81°50E 84 R12
Poughkeepsie U.S.A. 41°42N 73°56W 113 E11
Poulaphouca Res. Ireland 53°8N 6°33W 31 B9
Poulton-le-Fylde U.K. 53°51N 2°58W 23 E3
Poundstock U.K. 50°44N 4°34W 27 F3
Pouso Alegre Brazil 22°14S 45°57W 122 D1
Powder → U.S.A. 46°45N 105°26W 110 A5
Powell, L. U.S.A. 36°57N 111°29W 110 C4
Powell River Canada 49°50N 124°35W 108 E7

Powers U.S.A. 45°41N 87°32W 112 C4
Powick U.K. 52°10N 2°14W 24 B4
Powys □ U.K. 52°20N 3°20W 26 C7
Poyang Hu China 29°5N 116°20E 79 F12
Poza Rica Mexico 20°33N 97°27W 114 C5
Poznań Poland 52°25N 16°55E 65 B9
Pozzuoli Italy 40°49N 14°7E 68 D6
Prado Brazil 17°20S 39°13W 122 C3
Praia C. Verde Is. 15°2N 23°34W 91 E1
Praia Grande Brazil 24°0S 46°24W 122 D1
Prairie du Chien U.S.A. 43°3N 91°9W 112 D2
Prata Brazil 19°25S 48°54W 122 C1
Prato Italy 43°53N 11°6E 68 C4
Pratt U.S.A. 37°39N 98°44W 110 C7
Prawle Pt. U.K. 50°12N 3°44W 27 G6
Praya Indonesia 8°39S 116°17E 82 F5
Prees U.K. 52°54N 2°40W 23 G3
Preesall U.K. 53°55N 2°57W 23 E3
Prescott Canada 44°45N 75°30W 113 C10
Prescott U.S.A. 34°33N 112°28W 110 D4
Presidencia Roque Saenz Peña Argentina 26°45S 60°30W 121 E3
Presidente Prudente Brazil 22°5S 51°25W 120 E4
Presidio U.S.A. 29°34N 104°22W 110 E6
Prespa, L. Macedonia 40°55N 21°0E 69 D9
Presque Isle U.S.A. 46°41N 68°1W 113 B13
Prestatyn U.K. 53°20N 3°24W 26 A7
Prestbury U.K. 51°54N 2°2W 24 C4
Presteigne U.K. 52°17N 3°0W 26 C7
Preston Borders, U.K. 55°49N 2°19W 21 C11
Preston Dorset, U.K. 50°38N 2°26W 24 E4
Preston Lancs., U.K. 53°46N 2°42W 23 E3
Preston U.K. 42°6N 111°53W 110 B4
Prestonpans U.K. 55°58N 2°58W 21 C10
Prestwich U.K. 53°32N 2°17W 23 E4
Prestwick U.K. 55°29N 4°37W 20 D6
Pretoria S. Africa 25°44S 28°12E 97 K5
Pribilof Is. U.S.A. 57°0N 170°0W 108 D2
Price U.S.A. 39°36N 110°49W 110 C4
Prieska S. Africa 29°40S 22°42E 97 K4
Prilep Macedonia 41°21N 21°32E 69 D9
Prince Albert Canada 53°15N 105°50W 108 D9
Prince Albert Pen. Canada 72°30N 116°0W 108 B8
Prince Albert Sd. Canada 70°25N 115°0W 108 B8
Prince Alfred, C. Canada 74°20N 124°40W 109 B7
Prince Charles I. Canada 67°47N 76°12W 109 C12
Prince Charles Mts. Antarctica 72°0S 67°0E 55 D6
Prince Edward I. □ Canada 46°20N 63°20W 113 B16
Prince Edward Is. Ind. Oc. 46°35S 38°0E 53 G11
Prince George Canada 53°55N 122°50W 108 D7
Prince Gustaf Adolf Sea Canada 78°30N 107°0W 109 B9
Prince of Wales, C. U.S.A. 65°36N 168°5W 104 C3
Prince of Wales I. Canada 73°0N 99°0W 108 B10
Prince of Wales I. U.S.A. 55°47N 132°50W 108 D6
Prince Patrick I. Canada 77°0N 120°0W 109 B8
Prince Rupert Canada 54°20N 130°20W 108 D6
Princes Risborough U.K. 51°43N 0°49W 25 C7
Princeton Ill., U.S.A. 41°23N 89°28W 112 E3
Princeton Ind., U.S.A. 38°21N 87°34W 112 F4
Princeton Ky., U.S.A. 37°7N 87°53W 112 G4
Princeton W. Va., U.S.A. 37°22N 81°6W 112 G7
Príncipe São Tomé & Príncipe 1°37N 7°25E 90 F4
Pripet → Europe 51°20N 30°15E 65 C16
Pripet Marshes Europe 52°10N 27°10E 65 B15
Priština Kosovo 42°40N 21°13E 69 C9
Privas France 44°45N 4°37E 66 D6
Prizren Kosovo 42°13N 20°45E 69 C9
Probolinggo Indonesia 7°46S 113°13E 82 F4
Probus U.K. 50°17N 4°58W 27 G4
Progreso Mexico 21°20N 89°40W 114 C7
Prome Burma 18°49N 95°13E 85 K19
Propriá Brazil 10°13S 36°51W 122 B3
Provence France 43°40N 5°46E 66 E6
Providence U.S.A. 41°49N 71°24W 113 E12
Providencia, I. de Colombia 13°25N 81°26W 115 E8
Provins France 48°33N 3°15E 66 B5
Provo U.S.A. 40°14N 111°39W 110 B4
Prudhoe U.K. 54°57N 1°52W 22 C5
Prudhoe Bay U.S.A. 70°18N 148°22W 108 B5
Pruszków Poland 52°9N 20°49E 65 B11
Prut → Romania 45°28N 28°10E 65 F15
Pryluky Ukraine 50°30N 32°24E 71 D5
Przemyśl Poland 49°50N 22°45E 65 D12
Pskov Russia 57°50N 28°25E 70 C4
Puddletown U.K. 50°44N 2°20W 24 E4
Pudsey U.K. 53°47N 1°40W 23 E5
Puducherry India 11°59N 79°50E 84 P11
Puebla Mexico 19°3N 98°12W 114 D5
Pueblo U.S.A. 38°16N 104°37W 110 C6
Puerca, Pta. Puerto Rico 18°13N 65°36W 115 d
Puerto Aisén Chile 45°27S 73°0W 121 G2
Puerto Barrios Guatemala 15°40N 88°32W 114 D7
Puerto Cabello Venezuela 10°28N 68°1W 120 A3
Puerto Cabezas Nic. 14°0N 83°30W 115 E8
Puerto Carreño Colombia 6°12N 67°22W 120 B3
Puerto Cortés Honduras 15°51N 88°0W 114 D7
Puerto Deseado Argentina 47°55S 66°0W 121 G3
Puerto La Cruz Venezuela 10°13N 64°38W 120 A3
Puerto Madryn Argentina 42°48S 65°4W 121 G3
Puerto Maldonado Peru 12°30S 69°10W 120 D3
Puerto Montt Chile 41°28S 73°0W 121 G2
Puerto Plata Dom. Rep. 19°48N 70°45W 115 D10
Puerto Princesa Phil. 9°46N 118°45E 83 C5
Puerto Rico ☑ W. Indies 18°15N 66°45W 115 d
Puerto San Julián Argentina 49°18S 67°43W 121 G3
Puerto Suárez Bolivia 18°58S 57°52W 120 D4
Puerto Wilches Colombia 7°21N 73°54W 120 B2
Puertollano Spain 38°43N 4°7W 67 C3
Puffin I. Ireland 51°50N 10°24W 30 E2
Puget Sound U.S.A. 47°50N 122°30W 110 A2
Pukapuka Cook Is. 10°53S 165°49W 103 J11
Pukaskwa △ Canada 48°20N 86°0W 112 A4
Pula Croatia 44°54N 13°57E 68 B5
Pulacayo Bolivia 20°25S 66°41W 120 E3
Pulaski U.S.A. 37°3N 80°47W 111 C10
Pulborough U.K. 50°58N 0°30W 25 E8
Pulham Market U.K. 52°26N 1°13E 25 B11
Pulham St. Mary U.K. 52°26N 1°16E 25 B11

Pullman U.S.A. 46°44N 117°10W 110 A3
Pumlumon Fawr U.K. 52°28N 3°46W 26 C6
Pune India 18°29N 73°57E 84 K8
Punjab □ India 31°0N 76°0E 84 D10
Punjab □ Pakistan 32°0N 72°30E 84 E9
Puno Peru 15°55S 70°3W 120 D2
Punta, Cerro de Puerto Rico 18°10N 66°37W 115 d
Punta Arenas Chile 53°10S 71°0W 121 H2
Puntland Somali Rep. 8°0N 49°0E 89 F4
Punxsutawney U.S.A. 40°57N 78°59W 112 E8
Purbeck, Isle of U.K. 50°39N 1°59W 24 E5
Purfleet U.K. 51°29N 0°16E 25 D9
Puri India 19°50N 85°58E 85 K14
Purley on Thames U.K. 51°29N 1°3W 24 D6
Purnia India 25°45N 87°31E 85 G15
Puruliya India 23°17N 86°24E 85 H15
Purus → Brazil 3°42S 61°28W 120 C3
Putian China 25°23N 119°0E 79 F12
Putorana, Gory Russia 69°0N 95°0E 77 C10
Puttalam Sri Lanka 8°1N 79°55E 84 Q11
Putumayo → S. Amer. 3°7S 67°58W 120 C3
Puvirnituq Canada 60°2N 77°10W 109 C12
Puy-de-Dôme France 45°46N 2°57E 66 D5
Pwllheli U.K. 52°53N 4°25W 26 B5
Pyatigorsk Russia 44°2N 43°6E 71 F7
Pyinmana Burma 19°45N 96°12E 85 K20
P'yŏngyang N. Korea 39°0N 125°30E 79 D14
Pyramid L. U.S.A. 40°1N 119°35W 110 C3
Pyrénées Europe 42°45N 0°18E 66 E4

Q

Qaanaaq Greenland 77°30N 69°10W 54 B4
Qā'emshahr Iran 36°30N 52°53E 87 B8
Qaidam Basin China 37°0N 95°0E 78 D8
Qandyaghash Kazakhstan 49°28N 57°25E 71 E10
Qaqortoq Greenland 60°43N 46°0W 54 C5
Qarqan He → China 39°30N 88°30E 78 D6
Qarqaraly Kazakhstan 49°26N 75°30E 78 B4
Qarshi Uzbekistan 38°53N 65°48E 87 B11
Qatar ■ Asia 25°30N 51°15E 87 E7
Qattâra Depression Egypt 29°30N 27°30E 95 C11
Qazvin Iran 36°15N 50°0E 86 B7
Qena Egypt 26°10N 32°43E 95 C12
Qeqertarsuaq Greenland 69°15N 53°38W 54 C5
Qeshm Iran 26°55N 56°10E 87 E9
Qiemo China 38°8N 85°32E 78 D6
Qijiaojing China 43°28N 91°36E 78 C7
Qikiqtarjuaq Canada 67°33N 63°0W 109 C13
Qilian Shan China 38°30N 96°0E 78 D8
Qingdao China 36°5N 120°20E 79 D13
Qinghai □ China 36°0N 98°0E 78 D8
Qinghai Hu China 36°40N 100°10E 78 D9
Qinhuangdao China 39°56N 119°30E 79 D12
Qinzhou China 21°58N 108°38E 78 G10
Qiqihar China 47°26N 124°0E 79 B13
Qira China 37°0N 80°48E 78 D5
Qitai China 44°2N 89°35E 78 C6
Qitaihe China 45°48N 130°51E 79 B15
Qom Iran 34°40N 51°0E 87 C7
Qostanay Kazakhstan 53°10N 63°35E 76 D7
Quadring U.K. 52°54N 0°10W 23 G8
Quang Ngai Vietnam 15°13N 108°58E 82 A3
Quantock Hills U.K. 51°8N 3°10W 24 D2
Quanzhou China 24°55N 118°34E 79 G12
Quaqtaq Canada 60°55N 69°40W 109 C13
Quartu Sant'Élena Italy 39°15N 9°10E 68 E3
Québec Canada 46°52N 71°13W 113 B12
Québec □ Canada 48°0N 74°0W 109 D12
Queen Charlotte Is. Canada 53°20N 132°10W 108 D6
Queen Charlotte Sd. Canada 51°0N 128°0W 108 D7
Queen Elizabeth Is. Canada 76°0N 95°0W 104 B10
Queen Maud G. Canada 68°15N 102°30W 108 C9
Queenborough U.K. 51°25N 0°46E 25 D9
Queensbury U.K. 53°46N 1°50W 23 E5
Queensland □ Australia 22°0S 142°0E 98 E7
Queenstown N.Z. 45°1S 168°40E 99 K12
Queenstown S. Africa 31°52S 26°52E 97 L5
Queimadas Brazil 11°0S 39°38W 122 B3
Quelimane Mozam. 17°53S 36°58E 97 H7
Quendale, B. of U.K. 59°53N 1°20W 18 C15
Querétaro Mexico 20°36N 100°23W 114 C4
Quesnel Canada 53°0N 122°30W 108 D7
Quesnel L. Canada 52°30N 121°20W 108 D7
Quetta Pakistan 30°15N 66°55E 84 D5
Quezaltenango Guatemala 14°50N 91°30W 114 E6
Quezon City Phil. 14°37N 121°2E 83 B6
Qui Nhon Vietnam 13°40N 109°13E 82 B3
Quibdó Colombia 5°42N 76°40W 120 B2
Quilán, C. Chile 43°15S 74°30W 121 G2
Quilon India 8°50N 76°38E 84 Q10
Quilpie Australia 26°35S 144°11E 98 F7
Quimper France 48°0N 4°9W 66 B1
Quincy Ill., U.S.A. 39°56N 91°23W 111 C81
Quincy Mass., U.S.A. 42°14N 71°0W 113 D12
Quito Ecuador 0°15S 78°35W 120 C2
Qujing China 25°32N 103°41E 78 F9
Qulsary Kazakhstan 46°59N 54°1E 71 E9
Qŭnghirot Uzbekistan 43°2N 58°50E 87 A9
Quorndon U.K. 52°46N 1°10W 23 G6
Qŭqon Uzbekistan 40°31N 70°56E 87 A12
Quseir Egypt 26°7N 34°16E 95 C12
Quzhou China 28°57N 118°54E 79 F12

R

Raahe Finland 64°40N 24°28E 63 E8
Raasay U.K. 57°25N 6°4W 18 H5
Raasay, Sd. of U.K. 57°30N 6°8W 18 H5
Raba Indonesia 8°36S 118°55E 83 F5
Rabat Morocco 34°2N 6°48W 94 B4
Rabaul Papua N. G. 4°24S 152°18E 98 A9
Rābigh Si. Arabia 22°50N 39°5E 89 C2
Race, C. Canada 46°40N 53°5W 109 E14
Rach Gia Vietnam 10°5N 105°5E 82 B3
Racine U.S.A. 42°44N 87°47W 112 D4
Rackheath U.K. 52°45N 1°22E 25 A11
Radcliffe U.K. 53°34N 2°18W 23 E4
Radcliffe-on-Trent U.K. 52°57N 1°2W 23 G6

Radford U.S.A. 37°8N 80°34W 112 G7
Radley U.K. 51°41N 1°14W 24 C6
Radnor Forest U.K. 52°17N 3°10W 26 C7
Radom Poland 51°23N 21°12E 65 C11
Radstock U.K. 51°17N 2°26W 24 D4
Rae Canada 62°50N 116°3W 108 C8
Rae Bareli India 26°18N 81°20E 85 F12
Rae Isthmus Canada 66°40N 87°30W 109 C11
Rafaela Argentina 31°10S 61°30W 121 F3
Rafsanjān Iran 30°30N 56°5E 87 D9
Ragusa Italy 36°55N 14°44E 68 F6
Rahimyar Khan Pakistan 28°30N 70°25E 84 E7
Raichur India 16°10N 77°20E 84 L10
Raigarh India 21°56N 83°25E 85 J13
Rainbow Lake Canada 58°30N 119°23W 108 D8
Rainham U.K. 51°22N 0°37E 25 D10
Rainier, Mt. U.S.A. 46°52N 121°46W 110 A2
Rainworth U.K. 53°7N 1°7W 23 F6
Rainy L. Canada 48°42N 93°10W 108 E10
Raipur India 21°17N 81°45E 85 J12
Raj Nandgaon India 21°5N 81°5E 85 J12
Rajahmundry India 17°1N 81°48E 85 L12
Rajapalaiyam India 9°25N 77°35E 84 Q10
Rajasthan □ India 26°45N 73°30E 84 F8
Rajkot India 22°15N 70°56E 84 H7
Rajshahi Bangla. 24°22N 88°39E 85 G16
Rajshahi □ Bangla. 25°0N 89°0E 85 G16
Raleigh U.S.A. 35°47N 78°39W 111 C11
Rame Head U.K. 50°19N 4°13W 27 G5
Ramgarh India 23°40N 85°35E 85 H14
Ramna Stacks U.K. 60°35N 1°24W 18 A15
Rampside U.K. 54°6N 3°9W 22 D2
Rampur India 28°50N 79°5E 84 E11
Ramree I. Burma 19°0N 93°40E 85 K19
Ramsbottom U.K. 53°38N 2°19W 23 E4
Ramsbury U.K. 51°26N 1°36W 24 D5
Ramsey I. of Man 54°20N 4°22W 29 C13
Ramsey Cambs., U.K. 52°27N 0°7W 25 B8
Ramsey Essex, U.K. 51°55N 1°13E 25 C11
Ramsgate U.K. 51°20N 1°25E 25 D11
Rancagua Chile 34°10S 70°50W 121 F2
Ranchi India 23°19N 85°27E 85 H14
Randalstown U.K. 54°45N 6°19W 29 B9
Randers Denmark 56°29N 10°1E 63 F6
Rangoon Burma 16°45N 96°20E 85 L20
Rangpur Bangla. 25°42N 89°22E 85 G16
Rankin Inlet Canada 62°30N 93°0W 108 C10
Rannoch U.K. 56°41N 4°20W 19 J9
Rannoch, L. U.K. 56°41N 4°20W 19 J9
Rannoch Moor U.K. 56°38N 4°48W 19 J8
Rantoul U.S.A. 40°19N 88°9W 112 E3
Rapa French Polynesia 27°35S 144°20W 103 K13
Rapallo Italy 44°21N 9°14E 68 B3
Raper, C. Canada 69°44N 67°6W 109 C13
Rapid City U.S.A. 44°5N 103°14W 110 B6
Rarotonga Cook Is. 21°30S 160°0W 103 K12
Ra's al Khaymah U.A.E. 25°50N 55°59E 87 E9
Rasht Iran 37°20N 49°40E 86 B7
Rat Islands U.S.A. 52°0N 178°0E 108 D1
Ratangarh India 28°5N 74°35E 84 E9
Rath Luirc Ireland 52°21N 8°40W 30 D5
Rathcoole Ireland 53°17N 6°29W 31 B10
Rathdrum Ireland 52°56N 6°14W 31 C10
Rathkeale Ireland 52°32N 8°56W 30 C5
Rathlin I. U.K. 55°18N 6°14W 29 A9
Rathmelton Ireland 55°2N 7°38W 28 A6
Ratlam India 23°20N 75°0E 84 H9
Ratnagiri India 16°57N 73°18E 84 L8
Raton U.S.A. 36°54N 104°24W 110 C6
Rattray Hd. U.K. 57°38N 1°50W 19 G14
Rauma Finland 61°10N 21°30E 63 E8
Raunds U.K. 52°21N 0°32W 25 B7
Raurkela India 22°14N 84°50E 85 H14
Ravenglass U.K. 54°22N 3°24W 22 D2
Ravenna Italy 44°25N 12°12E 68 B5
Ravenstonedale U.K. 54°26N 2°25W 22 D4
Ravi → Pakistan 30°35N 71°49E 84 D7
Rawalpindi Pakistan 33°38N 73°8E 84 C8
Rawlins U.S.A. 41°47N 107°14W 110 B5
Rawmarsh U.K. 53°27N 1°21W 23 F6
Rawson Argentina 43°15S 65°5W 121 G3
Rawtenstall U.K. 53°42N 2°17W 23 E4
Ray, C. Canada 47°33N 59°15W 109 E14
Rayleigh U.K. 51°36N 0°37E 25 C10
Rayong Thailand 12°40N 101°20E 82 B2
Raz, Pte. du France 48°2N 4°47W 66 C1
Ré, Î. de France 46°12N 1°30W 66 C3
Reading U.K. 51°27N 0°58W 25 D7
Reading U.S.A. 40°20N 75°56W 113 E10
Reay Forest U.K. 58°22N 4°55W 19 F8
Rebiana Desert Libya 24°30N 21°0E 95 D10
Recife Brazil 8°0S 35°0W 122 A3
Reconquista Argentina 29°10S 59°45W 121 E4
Red → U.S.A. 31°1N 91°45W 111 D8
Red Bluff U.S.A. 40°11N 122°15W 110 B2
Red Deer Canada 52°20N 113°50W 108 D8
Red Dial U.K. 54°49N 3°10W 22 C2
Red L. Canada 51°3N 93°49W 104 D10
Red L. U.S.A. 48°8N 94°45W 111 A8
Red Lake Canada 51°3N 93°49W 108 D10
Red Oak U.S.A. 41°1N 95°14W 111 B7
Red River of the North → N. Amer. 49°0N 97°15W 108 D10
Red Sea Asia 25°0N 36°0E 89 C2
Red Wing U.S.A. 44°34N 92°31W 111 B81
Redbridge □ U.K. 51°35N 0°7E 25 C9
Redcar U.K. 54°37N 1°4W 22 C6
Redding U.S.A. 40°35N 122°24W 110 B2
Redditch U.K. 52°18N 1°55W 24 B5
Rede → U.K. 55°9N 2°13W 22 B4
Redesmouth U.K. 55°8N 2°13W 22 B4
Redhill U.K. 51°14N 0°9W 25 D8
Redlynch U.K. 50°59N 1°41W 24 E5
Redmile U.K. 52°55N 0°48W 23 G7
Redmire U.K. 54°19N 1°55W 22 D5
Redon France 47°40N 2°6W 66 C2
Redruth U.K. 50°14N 5°14W 27 G3
Ree, L. Ireland 53°35N 8°0W 28 D6
Reedham U.K. 52°34N 1°34E 25 A12

Reepham U.K. 52°46N 1°9E 25 A11
Reese → U.S.A. 40°48N 117°4W 110 B3
Reeth U.K. 54°23N 1°56W 22 D5
Regensburg Germany 49°1N 12°6E 64 D7
Réggio di Calábria Italy 38°6N 15°39E 68 E6
Réggio nell'Emília Italy 44°43N 10°36E 68 B4
Regina Canada 50°27N 104°35W 108 D9
Reichenbach Germany 50°37N 12°17E 64 C7
Reigate U.K. 51°14N 0°12W 25 D8
Reims France 49°15N 4°1E 66 B6
Reina Adelaida, Arch. Chile 52°20S 74°0W 121 H2
Reindeer L. Canada 57°15N 102°15W 108 D9
Remanso Brazil 9°41S 42°4W 122 A2
Renfrew Canada 45°30N 76°40W 112 C9
Renfrew U.K. 55°52N 4°24W 20 C7
Rennell Solomon Is. 11°40S 160°10E 99 C11
Rennes France 48°7N 1°41W 66 B3
Reno U.S.A. 39°31N 119°48W 110 C3
Repton U.K. 52°50N 1°33W 23 G5
Republican → U.S.A. 39°4N 96°48W 111 C7
Repulse Bay Canada 66°30N 86°30W 109 C11
Resistencia Argentina 27°30S 59°0W 121 E4
Resolute Canada 74°42N 94°54W 109 B10
Resolution I. Canada 61°30N 65°0W 109 C13
Reston U.K. 55°51N 2°10W 21 C11
Retford U.K. 53°19N 0°56W 23 F7
Rethimno Greece 35°18N 24°30E 69 G11
Réunion ☑ Ind. Oc. 21°0S 56°0E 91 J9
Reus Spain 41°10N 1°5E 67 B6
Reutlingen Germany 48°29N 9°12E 64 D5
Revda Russia 56°48N 59°57E 70 C10
Revelstoke Canada 51°0N 118°10W 108 D8
Revillagigedo, Is. de Pac. Oc. 18°40N 112°0W 114 D2
Rewa India 24°33N 81°25E 85 G12
Rexburg U.S.A. 43°49N 111°47W 110 B4
Rey Malabo Eq. Guin. 3°45N 8°50E 96 D1
Reykjavík Iceland 64°10N 21°57W 63 B1
Reynosa Mexico 26°7N 98°18W 114 B5
Rēzekne Latvia 56°30N 27°17E 63 F9
Rhayader U.K. 52°18N 3°29W 26 C7
Rheidol → U.K. 52°25N 4°5W 26 C5
Rheine Germany 52°17N 7°26E 64 B4
Rheinland-Pfalz □ Germany 50°0N 7°0E 64 C4
Rhine → Europe 51°52N 6°2E 64 C4
Rhinelander U.S.A. 45°38N 89°25W 112 C3
Rhinns Pt. U.K. 55°40N 6°29W 20 C3
Rhins, The U.K. 54°52N 5°3W 20 E5
Rhode Island □ U.S.A. 41°40N 71°30W 113 E12
Rhodes Greece 36°15N 28°10E 69 F13
Rhodope Mts. Bulgaria 41°40N 24°20E 69 D11
Rhondda U.K. 51°39N 3°31W 26 D6
Rhône → France 43°28N 4°42E 66 E6
Rhosllanerchrugog U.K. 53°1N 3°3W 26 A7
Rhossili U.K. 51°34N 4°17W 27 D5
Rhossili B. U.K. 51°32N 4°14W 27 D5
Rhum U.K. 57°0N 6°20W 18 J5
Rhum, Sound of U.K. 56°55N 6°14W 18 J5
Rhyl U.K. 53°20N 3°29W 26 A7
Rhymney U.K. 51°46N 3°17W 26 D7
Riau, Kepulauan Indonesia 0°30N 104°20E 82 D2
Ribble → U.K. 53°52N 2°25W 23 E4
Ribeirão Prêto Brazil 21°10S 47°50W 122 D1
Riberalta Bolivia 11°0S 66°0W 120 D3
Riccall U.K. 53°50N 1°3W 23 E6
Rice Lake U.S.A. 45°30N 91°44W 112 C2
Richards Bay S. Africa 28°48S 32°6E 97 K6
Richfield U.S.A. 38°46N 112°5W 110 C4
Richland U.S.A. 46°17N 119°18W 110 A3
Richland Center U.S.A. 43°21N 90°23W 112 D2
Richlands U.S.A. 37°6N 81°48W 112 G7
Richmond U.K. 54°25N 1°43W 22 D5
Richmond Ind., U.S.A. 39°50N 84°53W 112 F5
Richmond Ky., U.S.A. 37°45N 84°18W 112 G5
Richmond Va., U.S.A. 37°33N 77°27W 112 G9
Richmond-upon-Thames □ U.K. 51°27N 0°17W 25 D8
Rickmansworth U.K. 51°38N 0°29W 25 C8
Ridgecrest U.S.A. 35°38N 117°40W 110 C3
Ridgway U.S.A. 41°25N 78°44W 112 E8
Ridsdale U.K. 55°9N 2°9W 22 B4
Rievaulx U.K. 54°16N 1°7W 22 D6
Rift Valley Africa 7°0N 30°0E 90 G7
Rīga Latvia 56°53N 24°8E 63 F8
Riga, G. of Latvia 57°40N 23°45E 63 F8
Rīgestān Afghan. 30°15N 65°0E 87 D11
Rigolet Canada 54°10N 58°23W 109 D14
Rijeka Croatia 45°20N 14°21E 68 B6
Rillington U.K. 54°9N 0°42W 22 D7
Rímini Italy 44°3N 12°33E 68 B5
Rimouski Canada 48°27N 68°30W 109 E13
Ringmer U.K. 50°53N 0°5E 25 E9
Ringwood U.K. 50°50N 1°47W 24 E5
Rio Branco Brazil 9°58S 67°49W 120 C3
Rio Claro Brazil 22°19S 47°35W 122 D1
Rio Cuarto Argentina 33°10S 64°25W 121 F3
Rio de Janeiro Brazil 22°54S 43°12W 122 D2
Rio de Janeiro □ Brazil 22°50S 43°0W 122 D2
Rio Gallegos Argentina 51°35S 69°15W 121 H3
Rio Grande Brazil 32°0S 52°20W 121 F4
Rio Grande Puerto Rico 18°23N 65°50W 115 d
Rio Grande → N. Amer. 25°58N 97°9W 111 E7
Rio Grande de Santiago → Mexico 21°36N 105°26W 114 C3
Rio Grande do Norte □ Brazil 5°40S 36°0W 120 C6
Rio Grande do Sul □ Brazil 30°0S 53°0W 121 E4
Rio Largo Brazil 9°28S 35°50W 122 A3
Rio Muni □ Eq. Guin. 1°30N 10°0E 96 D2
Riohacha Colombia 11°33N 72°55W 120 A2
Ripley Derby, U.K. 53°3N 1°24W 23 F6
Ripley N. Yorks., U.K. 54°3N 1°34W 22 D5
Ripon U.K. 54°9N 1°31W 22 D5
Ripon U.S.A. 43°51N 88°50W 112 D3
Risca U.K. 51°37N 3°5W 27 D7
Rishton U.K. 53°46N 2°26W 23 E4
Rivera Uruguay 31°0S 55°50W 121 F4
Riverhead U.S.A. 40°55N 72°40W 113 E12
Riverside U.S.A. 33°59N 117°22W 110 D3
Riverton U.S.A. 43°2N 108°23W 110 B5
Rivière-du-Loup Canada 47°50N 69°30W 109 E13
Rivière-Pilote Martinique 14°26N 60°53W 114 c

Rivière-Salée · Santa Rosa

Rivière-Salée Martinique 14°31N 61°0W 114 c
Rivne Ukraine 50°40N 26°10E 65 C14
Riyadh Si. Arabia 24°41N 46°42E 88 E6
Rize Turkey 41°0N 40°30E 71 F7
Rizhao China 35°25N 119°30E 79 D12
Road Town Br. Virgin Is. 18°27N 64°37W 115 e
Roade U.K. 52°9N 0°53W 25 B7
Roanne France 46°3N 4°4E 66 C6
Roanoke U.S.A. 37°16N 79°56W 112 G8
Roanoke → U.S.A. 35°57N 76°42W 111 C11
Roberton U.K. 55°25N 2°54W 21 D10
Roberval Canada 48°32N 72°15W 109 E12
Robin Hood's Bay U.K. 54°27N 0°32W 22 D7
Robson, Mt. Canada 53°10N 119°10W 108 D8
Roca, C. da Portugal 38°40N 9°31W 67 C1
Rocester U.K. 52°57N 1°50W 23 G5
Rocha Uruguay 34°30S 54°25W 121 F4
Rochdale U.K. 53°38N 2°9W 23 E4
Roche U.K. 50°24N 4°50W 27 G4
Rochefort France 45°56N 0°57W 66 D3
Rochester Medway, U.K. 51°23N 0°31E 25 D10
Rochester Northumberland, U.K. 55°17N 2°17W 22 B4
Rochester Ind., U.S.A. 41°4N 86°13W 112 E4
Rochester Minn., U.S.A. 44°1N 92°28W 111 B81
Rochester N.H., U.S.A. 43°18N 70°59W 113 D12
Rochester N.Y., U.S.A. 43°10N 77°37W 112 D9
Rochford U.K. 51°34N 0°43E 25 C10
Rock Hill U.S.A. 34°56N 81°1W 111 D10
Rock Island U.S.A. 41°30N 90°34W 112 E2
Rock Springs U.S.A. 41°35N 109°14W 110 B5
Rockall Atl. Oc. 57°37N 13°42W 56 D3
Rockcliffe U.K. 54°57N 3°0W 22 C3
Rockford U.S.A. 42°16N 89°6W 112 D3
Rockhampton Australia 23°22S 150°32E 98 E9
Rockingham U.S.A. 52°31N 0°43W 25 A7
Rockingham Forest U.K. 52°29N 0°42W 25 B7
Rockland U.S.A. 44°6N 69°7W 113 C13
Rocky Mount U.S.A. 35°57N 77°48W 111 C11
Rocky Mts. N. Amer. 49°0N 115°0W 108 D7
Rodez France 44°21N 2°33E 66 D5
Roding → U.K. 51°31N 0°0C 25 C9
Rodrigues Ind. Oc. 19°45S 63°20E 53 E13
Roe → U.K. 55°6N 6°59W 29 A8
Roes Welcome Sd. Canada 65°0N 87°0W 109 C11
Rogans Seat U.K. 54°26N 2°7W 22 C4
Rogate U.K. 51°0N 0°50W 25 D7
Rogers City U.S.A. 45°25N 83°49W 112 C6
Rohri Pakistan 27°45N 68°51E 84 F6
Rojo, C. Mexico 21°33N 97°20W 114 C5
Rolla U.S.A. 37°57N 91°46W 111 C8
Roma Australia 26°32S 148°49E 98 F8
Romaine → Canada 50°18N 63°47W 109 D13
Romania ■ Europe 46°0N 25°0E 65 F12
Romans-sur-Isère France 45°3N 5°3E 66 D6
Rome Italy 41°54N 12°28E 68 D5
Rome Ga., U.S.A. 34°15N 85°10W 111 D9
Rome N.Y., U.S.A. 43°13N 75°27W 113 D10
Romney U.S.A. 39°21N 78°45W 112 F8
Romney Marsh U.K. 51°2N 0°54E 25 D10
Romorantin-Lanthenay France 47°21N 1°45E 66 C4
Romsey U.K. 51°0N 1°29W 24 E6
Rona U.K. 57°34N 5°59N 18 G6
Roncador, Serra do Brazil 12°30S 52°30W 120 D4
Rondônia □ Brazil 11°0S 63°0W 120 D3
Rondonópolis Brazil 16°28S 54°38W 120 D4
Ronge, L. la Canada 55°6N 105°17W 108 D9
Ronne Ice Shelf Antarctica 77°30S 60°0W 55 D18
Roosevelt → Brazil 7°35S 60°20W 120 C3
Roosevelt I. Antarctica 79°30S 162°0W 55 D12
Ropsley U.K. 52°54N 0°30W 23 G8
Roquetas de Mar Spain 36°46N 2°36W 67 D4
Roraima □ Brazil 2°0N 61°30W 120 B3
Roraima, Mt. Venezuela 5°10N 60°40W 120 B3
Rosario Argentina 33°0S 60°40W 121 F3
Rosario Mexico 22°58N 105°53W 114 C3
Rosario de la Frontera Argentina 25°50S 65°0W 121 E3
Roscommon Ireland 53°38N 8°11W 28 D5
Roscommon □ Ireland 53°49N 8°23W 28 D5
Roscrea Ireland 52°57N 7°49W 30 C7
Roseau Dominica 15°17N 61°24W 115 D12
Roseburg U.S.A. 43°13N 123°20W 110 B2
Rosedale Abbey U.K. 54°21N 0°52W 22 D7
Rosehearty U.K. 57°42N 2°7N 19 G13
Rosenheim Germany 47°51N 12°7E 64 E7
Rosetown Canada 51°35N 107°59W 108 D9
Roseville U.S.A. 38°45N 121°17W 110 C2
Roslavl Russia 53°57N 32°55E 70 D5
Ross Ice Shelf Antarctica 80°0S 180°0E 55 E12
Ross-on-Wye U.K. 51°54N 2°34W 24 C3
Ross River Canada 62°30N 131°30W 108 C6
Ross Sea Antarctica 74°0S 178°0E 55 D11
Rossall Pt. U.K. 53°55N 3°3W 23 E2
Rossan Pt. Ireland 54°42N 8°47W 28 B4
Rosses, The Ireland 55°2N 8°20W 28 A5
Rossignol L. Canada 44°12N 65°10W 113 C15
Rosslare Ireland 52°17N 6°24W 31 D10
Rosslare Harbour Ireland 52°15N 6°20W 31 D10
Rossosh Russia 50°15N 39°28E 71 D6
Rostock Germany 54°5N 12°8E 64 A7
Rostov Russia 47°15N 39°45E 71 E6
Roswell Ga., U.S.A. 34°2N 84°22W 111 D10
Roswell N. Mex., U.S.A. 33°24N 104°32W 110 D6
Rothbury U.K. 55°19N 1°58W 22 B5
Rothbury Forest U.K. 55°19N 1°50W 22 B5
Rother → U.K. 50°59N 0°45E 25 E10
Rotherham U.K. 53°26N 1°20W 23 F6
Rothes U.K. 57°32N 3°13W 19 G11
Rothesay U.K. 55°50N 5°3W 20 C5
Rothwell Northants., U.K. 52°25N 0°48W 25 B7
Rothwell W. Yorks., U.K. 53°45N 1°28W 23 E6
Roti Indonesia 10°50S 123°0E 83 F6
Rotorua N.Z. 38°9S 176°16E 99 H14
Rotterdam Neths. 51°55N 4°30E 64 C3
Rottingdean U.K. 50°48N 0°4W 25 E8
Rotuma Fiji 12°25S 177°5E 99 C14
Roubaix France 50°40N 3°10E 66 A5
Rouen France 49°27N 1°4E 66 B4
Round Mt. Australia 30°26S 152°16E 98 G9

Rousay U.K. 59°10N 3°2W 19 D11
Roussillon France 42°30N 2°35E 66 E5
Rouyn-Noranda Canada 48°20N 79°0W 109 E12
Rovaniemi Finland 66°29N 25°41E 63 D9
Rovigo Italy 45°4N 11°47E 68 B4
Rowanburn U.K. 55°5N 2°55W 21 D10
Roxas Phil. 11°36N 122°49E 83 B6
Roxburgh U.K. 55°35N 2°28W 21 D10
Roxby U.K. 53°38N 0°38W 23 E7
Royal Canal Ireland 53°30N 7°13W 31 B8
Royal Leamington Spa U.K. 52°18N 1°31W 24 B5
Royal Tunbridge Wells U.K. 51°7N 0°16E 25 D9
Royale, Isle U.S.A. 48°0N 88°54W 112 B3
Royan France 45°37N 1°2W 66 D3
Royston U.K. 52°3N 0°0 25 B8
Royton U.K. 53°34N 2°8W 23 E4
Rub' al Khālī Si. Arabia 19°0N 48°0E 89 D4
Rubery U.K. 52°24N 2°1W 24 B4
Rubh a' Mhail U.K. 55°56N 6°8W 20 C3
Rubha Hunish U.K. 57°42N 6°20W 18 G5
Rubtsovsk Russia 51°30N 81°10E 78 A5
Ruby L. U.S.A. 40°10N 115°28W 110 B3
Rudnyy Kazakhstan 52°57N 63°7E 76 D7
Rudston U.K. 54°6N 0°20W 22 D8
Ruffling Pt. Br. Virgin Is. 18°44N 64°27W 115 e
Rufford U.K. 53°38N 2°50W 23 E3
Rufiji → Tanzania 7°50S 39°15E 96 F7
Rugby U.K. 52°23N 1°16W 24 B6
Rugeley U.K. 52°46N 1°55W 23 G5
Rügen Germany 54°22N 13°24E 64 A7
Ruhr → Germany 51°27N 6°43E 64 C4
Ruki → Dem. Rep. of the Congo 0°5N 18°17E 96 E3
Rukwa, L. Tanzania 8°0S 32°20E 96 F6
Rumania = Romania ■ Europe 46°0N 25°0E 65 F12
Rumford U.S.A. 44°33N 70°33W 113 C12
Runaway Bay Jamaica 18°27N 77°20W 114 a
Runcorn U.K. 53°21N 2°44W 23 F3
Rundu Namibia 17°52S 19°43E 97 H3
Rungwe Tanzania 9°11S 33°32E 96 F6
Ruoqiang China 38°55N 88°10E 78 D6
Rupert U.S.A. 42°37N 113°41W 110 B4
Rupert → Canada 51°29N 78°45W 109 D12
Ruse Bulgaria 43°48N 25°59E 69 C12
Rush Ireland 53°31N 6°6W 31 A10
Rushden U.K. 52°18N 0°35W 25 B7
Rushville Ill., U.S.A. 40°7N 90°34W 112 E2
Rushville Ind., U.S.A. 39°37N 85°27W 112 F5
Ruskington U.K. 53°3N 0°22W 23 F8
Russellville U.S.A. 35°17N 93°8W 111 C8
Russia ■ Eurasia 62°0N 105°0E 77 C11
Rustavi Georgia 41°30N 45°0E 71 F8
Rustenburg S. Africa 25°41S 27°14E 97 K5
Rutherglen U.K. 55°49N 4°13W 20 C7
Ruthin U.K. 53°6N 3°19W 26 A7
Ruthwell U.K. 55°0N 3°25W 21 E9
Rutog China 33°27N 79°42E 78 E4
Ruvuma → Tanzania 10°29S 40°28E 96 G8
Ruwenzori Africa 0°30N 29°55E 96 D5
Rwanda ■ Africa 2°0S 30°0E 96 E5
Ryan, L. U.K. 55°0N 5°2W 20 E5
Ryazan Russia 54°40N 39°40E 70 D6
Rybachi Pen. Russia 69°43N 32°0E 70 A5
Rybinsk Russia 58°5N 38°50E 70 C6
Rybinsk Res. Russia 58°30N 38°25E 70 C6
Rydal U.K. 54°27N 2°59W 22 D3
Ryde U.K. 50°43N 1°9W 24 E6
Rye U.K. 50°57N 0°45E 25 E10
Rye → U.K. 54°11N 0°44W 22 D7
Rye Bay U.K. 50°52N 0°49E 25 E10
Ryhope U.K. 54°53N 1°21W 22 C6
Ryton U.K. 52°22N 1°25W 24 B6
Ryukyu Is. Japan 26°0N 126°0E 79 F14
Rzeszów Poland 50°5N 21°58E 65 C11
Rzhev Russia 56°20N 34°20E 70 C5

S

Saale → Germany 51°56N 11°54E 64 C6
Saar → Europe 49°41N 6°32E 64 D4
Saarbrücken Germany 49°14N 6°59E 64 D4
Saaremaa Estonia 58°30N 22°30E 63 F8
Sabadell Spain 41°28N 2°7E 67 B7
Sabah □ Malaysia 6°0N 117°0E 82 C5
Sabhā Libya 27°9N 14°29E 95 C8
Sabinas Mexico 27°51N 101°7W 114 B4
Sabinas Hidalgo Mexico 26°30N 100°10W 114 B4
Sabine → U.S.A. 29°59N 93°47W 111 E8
Sable, C. Canada 43°29N 65°38W 113 D15
Sable, C. U.S.A. 25°9N 81°8W 111 E10
Sable I. Canada 44°0N 60°0W 109 E14
Sachsen □ Germany 50°55N 13°10E 64 C7
Sachsen-Anhalt □ Germany 52°0N 12°0E 64 C7
Saco U.S.A. 43°30N 70°27W 113 D12
Sacramento U.S.A. 38°35N 121°29W 110 C2
Sacramento → U.S.A. 38°3N 121°56W 110 C2
Sacramento Mts. U.S.A. 32°30N 105°30W 110 D5
Sado Japan 38°0N 138°25E 81 D6
Safford U.S.A. 32°50N 109°43W 110 D5
Saffron Walden U.K. 52°1N 0°16E 25 B9
Safi Morocco 32°18N 9°20W 94 B4
Saga Japan 33°15N 130°16E 81 G2
Sagaing Burma 21°52N 95°59E 85 J19
Sagar India 23°50N 78°44E 84 H11
Saginaw U.S.A. 43°26N 83°56W 112 D6
Saginaw B. U.S.A. 43°50N 83°40W 112 D6
Sagua la Grande Cuba 22°50N 80°10W 115 C8
Saguenay → Canada 48°22N 71°0W 113 A12
Sagunt Spain 39°42N 0°18W 67 C5
Sahara Africa 23°0N 5°0E 94 D6
Saharanpur India 29°58N 77°33E 84 E10
Sahel Africa 16°0N 5°0E 94 E5
Sahiwal Pakistan 30°45N 73°8E 84 D8
Saidpur Bangla. 25°48N 89°0E 85 G16
St. Abb's Head U.K. 55°55N 2°8W 21 C11
St. Agnes Corn., U.K. 50°19N 5°13W 27 G3
St. Agnes Corn., U.K. 49°54N 6°21W 27 H1
St. Agnes Hd. U.K. 50°19N 5°15W 27 G3
St. Albans U.K. 51°45N 0°19W 25 C8
St. Albans Vt., U.S.A. 44°49N 73°5W 113 C11
St. Albans W. Va., U.S.A. 38°23N 81°50W 112 F7

St. Alban's Head U.K. 50°34N 2°4W 24 E4
St. Andrews U.K. 56°20N 2°47W 21 B10
St. Ann's U.K. 55°14N 3°28W 21 D9
St. Ann's Bay Jamaica 18°26N 77°12W 114 a
St. Anthony Canada 51°22N 55°35W 109 D14
St. Asaph U.K. 53°15N 3°27W 26 A7
St-Augustin Canada 51°13N 58°38W 109 D14
St. Augustine U.S.A. 29°54N 81°19W 111 E10
St. Austell U.K. 50°20N 4°47W 27 G4
St. Bees U.K. 54°30N 3°35W 22 C1
St. Bees Hd. U.K. 54°31N 3°38W 22 C1
St. Blazey U.K. 50°22N 4°43W 27 G4
St. Brides B. U.K. 51°49N 5°9W 26 D3
St-Brieuc France 48°30N 2°46W 66 B2
St. Buryan U.K. 50°4N 5°37W 27 G2
St. Catharines Canada 43°10N 79°15W 112 D8
St. Catherine's Pt. U.K. 50°34N 1°18W 24 E6
St. Charles U.S.A. 38°47N 90°29W 112 F2
St. Clair, L. N. Amer. 42°27N 82°39W 112 D6
St. Clears U.K. 51°49N 4°31W 26 D4
St. Cloud U.S.A. 45°34N 94°10W 111 A8
St. Columb Major U.K. 50°26N 4°58W 27 G4
St. Croix U.S. Virgin Is. 17°45N 64°45W 115 D12
St. David's U.K. 51°53N 5°16W 26 D3
St. David's Head U.K. 51°54N 5°19W 26 D3
St-Denis France 48°56N 2°20E 66 B5
St. Dennis U.K. 50°23N 4°53W 27 G4
St-Dizier France 48°38N 4°56E 66 B6
St. Dominick U.K. 50°29N 4°16W 27 G5
St. Elias, Mt. U.S.A. 60°18N 140°56W 108 C5
St. Elias Mts. N. Amer. 60°33N 139°28W 108 D6
St. Enoder U.K. 50°22N 4°59W 27 G3
St. Erth U.K. 50°9N 5°26W 27 G3
St-Étienne France 45°27N 4°22E 66 D6
St-Félicien Canada 48°40N 72°25W 113 A11
St-Flour France 45°2N 3°6E 66 D5
St. Gallen Switz. 47°26N 9°22E 64 E5
St. George U.S.A. 37°6N 113°35W 110 C4
St-Georges Canada 46°8N 70°40W 113 B12
St. George's Grenada 12°5N 61°43W 115 E12
St. George's Channel Europe 52°0N 6°0W 31 E11
St. Germans U.K. 50°23N 4°19W 27 G5
St. Helena Atl. Oc. 15°58S 5°42W 52 F9
St. Helens U.K. 53°27N 2°44W 23 F3
St. Helens, Mt. U.S.A. 46°12N 122°12W 110 A2
St. Helier U.K. 49°10N 2°7W 27 J9
St-Hyacinthe Canada 45°40N 72°58W 109 E12
St. Ignace U.S.A. 45°52N 84°44W 112 C5
St. Issey U.K. 50°30N 4°57W 27 G4
St. Ives Cambs., U.K. 52°20N 0°4W 25 B8
St. Ives Corn., U.K. 50°12N 5°30W 27 G3
St. Ives B. U.K. 50°13N 5°27W 27 G3
St-Jean, L. Canada 48°40N 72°0W 113 A11
St-Jérôme Canada 45°47N 74°0W 113 C11
St. John Canada 45°20N 66°8W 109 E13
St. John → N. Amer. 45°12N 66°5W 104 E13
St. John I. U.S. Virgin Is. 18°20N 64°42W 115 e
St. John's Antigua & B. 17°6N 61°51W 115 D12
St. John's Canada 47°35N 52°40W 109 E14
St. Johns U.S.A. 43°0N 84°33W 112 D5
St. Johns → U.S.A. 30°24N 81°24W 111 E10
St. Johns Chapel U.K. 54°44N 2°10W 22 C4
St. John's Pt. Ireland 54°34N 8°27W 28 B5
St. Johnsbury U.S.A. 44°25N 72°1W 113 C11
St-Joseph Martinique 14°39N 61°4W 114 c
St. Joseph Mich., U.S.A. 42°6N 86°29W 112 D4
St. Joseph Mo., U.S.A. 39°46N 94°50W 111 C8
St. Joseph, L. Canada 51°10N 90°35W 109 D10
St. Just U.K. 50°7N 5°42W 27 G2
St. Keverne U.K. 50°3N 5°6W 27 G3
St. Kilda U.K. 57°49N 8°34W 62 C2
St. Kitts & Nevis ■ W. Indies 17°20N 62°40W 115 D12
St. Lawrence → Canada 49°30N 66°0W 109 E13
St. Lawrence, Gulf of Canada 48°25N 62°0W 109 E13
St. Lawrence I. U.S.A. 63°30N 170°30W 108 C3
St. Levan U.K. 50°2N 5°41W 27 G2
St-Lô France 49°7N 1°5W 66 B3
St-Louis Guadeloupe 15°56N 61°19W 114 b
St. Louis Senegal 16°8N 16°27W 94 E2
St. Louis U.S.A. 38°37N 90°11W 112 F2
St. Lucia ■ W. Indies 14°0N 60°57W 115 f
St. Mabyn U.K. 50°30N 4°47W 27 F4
St. Magnus B. U.K. 60°25N 1°35W 18 B14
St-Malo France 48°39N 2°1W 66 B2
St-Marc Haiti 19°10N 72°41W 115 D10
St. Margaret's-at-Cliffe U.K. 51°9N 1°23E 25 D11
St-Martin ☑ W. Indies 18°0N 63°0W 115 D12
St-Martin, C. Martinique 14°52N 61°14W 114 c
St. Martins Barbados 13°5N 59°28W 115 g
St. Martin's U.K. 49°58N 6°17W 27 H1
St. Mary Bourne U.K. 51°15N 1°24W 24 D6
St. Mary's Corn., U.K. 49°55N 6°18W 27 H1
St. Mary's Orkney, U.K. 58°54N 2°54W 19 E12
St. Marys U.S.A. 41°26N 78°34W 112 E8
St. Mary's Sd. U.K. 49°54N 6°20W 27 H1
St. Matthew I. U.S.A. 60°24N 172°42W 108 C2
St. Mawes U.K. 50°10N 5°2W 27 G3
St. Merryn U.K. 50°32N 5°1W 27 F3
St. Michael's Mount U.K. 50°7N 5°29W 27 G3
St. Minver U.K. 50°33N 4°53W 27 F4
St. Moritz Switz. 46°30N 9°51E 64 E5
St-Nazaire France 47°17N 2°12W 66 C2
St. Neots U.K. 52°14N 0°15W 25 B8
St-Omer France 50°45N 2°15E 66 A5
St. Osyth U.K. 51°47N 1°5E 25 C11
St. Paul U.S.A. 44°56N 93°5W 111 B8
St. Paul, Î. Ind. Oc. 38°55S 77°34E 53 F13
St. Peter Port U.K. 49°26N 2°33W 27 J8
St. Petersburg Russia 59°55N 30°20E 70 C5
St. Petersburg U.S.A. 27°46N 82°40W 111 E10
St-Pierre Martinique 14°45N 61°10W 114 c
St-Pierre-et-Miquelon ☑ N. Amer. 46°55N 56°10W 109 E14
St-Quentin France 49°50N 3°16E 66 B5
St. Stephen Canada 45°16N 67°17W 113 C14
St. Teath U.K. 50°35N 4°45W 27 F4
St. Thomas Canada 42°45N 81°10W 112 D7

St. Thomas I. U.S. Virgin Is. 18°20N 64°55W 115 e
St-Tropez France 43°17N 6°38E 66 E7
St. Tudy U.K. 50°33N 4°45W 27 F4
St. Vincent, G. Australia 35°0S 138°0E 98 G6
Ste-Anne Guadeloupe 16°13N 61°24W 114 b
Ste. Genevieve U.S.A. 37°59N 90°2W 112 G2
Ste-Marie Canada 46°26N 71°0W 113 B12
Ste-Marie Martinique 14°48N 61°1W 114 c
Ste-Rose Guadeloupe 16°20N 61°45W 114 b
Saintes France 45°45N 0°37W 66 D3
Saintes, Îs. des Guadeloupe 15°50N 61°35W 114 b
Saintfield U.K. 54°28N 5°49W 29 C10
Saintonge France 45°40N 0°50W 66 D3
Saipan N. Marianas 15°12N 145°45E 102 F6
Saitama Japan 35°54N 139°38E 81 F7
Saitama □ Japan 35°54N 139°38E 81 F7
Sajama Bolivia 18°7S 69°0W 120 D3
Sakakawea, L. U.S.A. 47°30N 101°25W 110 A6
Sakarya Turkey 40°48N 30°25E 71 F5
Sakata Japan 38°55N 139°50E 81 D6
Sakhalin Russia 51°0N 143°0E 77 D15
Sakurajima Japan 31°35N 130°39E 81 H2
Sala Sweden 59°58N 16°35E 63 F7
Sala-y-Gómez Pac. Oc. 26°28S 105°28W 103 K17
Salado → La Pampa, Argentina 37°30S 67°0W 121 F3
Salado → Santa Fe, Argentina 31°40S 60°41W 121 F3
Salālah Oman 16°56N 53°59E 89 D5
Salamanca Spain 40°58N 5°39W 67 B3
Salamanca U.S.A. 42°10N 78°43W 112 D8
Salar de Uyuni Bolivia 20°30S 67°45W 120 E3
Salavat Russia 53°21N 55°55E 70 D10
Salaverry Peru 8°15S 79°0W 120 C2
Salayar Indonesia 6°7S 120°30E 83 F6
Salcombe U.K. 50°14N 3°47W 27 G6
Saldanha S. Africa 33°0S 17°58E 97 L3
Sale Australia 38°6S 147°6E 98 H8
Salé Morocco 34°3N 6°48W 94 B4
Sale U.K. 53°26N 2°19W 23 F4
Salekhard Russia 66°30N 66°35E 76 C7
Salem India 11°40N 78°11E 84 P11
Salem Ind., U.S.A. 38°36N 86°6W 112 F4
Salem Mass., U.S.A. 42°31N 70°53W 113 D12
Salem Ohio, U.S.A. 40°54N 80°52W 112 E7
Salem Oreg., U.S.A. 44°56N 123°2W 110 B2
Salem Va., U.S.A. 37°18N 80°3W 112 G7
Salerno Italy 40°41N 14°47E 68 D6
Salford U.K. 53°30N 2°18W 23 F4
Salford Priors U.K. 52°10N 1°53W 24 B5
Salida U.S.A. 38°32N 106°0W 110 C5
Salina U.S.A. 38°50N 97°37W 110 C7
Salina Cruz Mexico 16°10N 95°12W 114 D5
Salinas Ecuador 2°10S 80°58W 120 C1
Salinas U.S.A. 36°40N 121°39W 110 C2
Salinas → U.S.A. 36°45N 121°48W 110 C2
Salinas Grandes Argentina 30°0S 65°0W 121 E3
Salisbury U.K. 51°4N 1°47W 24 D5
Salisbury U.S.A. 38°22N 75°36W 113 F10
Salisbury I. Canada 63°30N 77°0W 109 C12
Salisbury Plain U.K. 51°14N 1°55W 24 D5
Salmon U.S.A. 45°11N 113°54W 110 A4
Salmon → U.S.A. 45°51N 116°47W 110 A3
Salmon Arm Canada 50°40N 119°15W 108 D8
Salmon River Mts. U.S.A. 44°50N 115°30W 110 B4
Salon-de-Provence France 43°39N 5°6E 66 E6
Salsk Russia 46°28N 41°30E 71 E7
Salt → U.S.A. 33°23N 112°19W 110 D4
Salt Lake City U.S.A. 40°45N 111°53W 110 B4
Salta Argentina 24°57S 65°25W 121 E3
Saltash U.K. 50°24N 4°14W 27 G5
Saltburn by the Sea U.K. 54°35N 0°58W 22 C7
Saltcoats U.K. 55°38N 4°47W 20 C6
Saltee Is. Ireland 52°7N 6°37W 31 D10
Saltfleet U.K. 53°25N 0°11E 23 F9
Saltfleetby U.K. 53°23N 0°10E 23 F9
Saltillo Mexico 25°25N 101°0W 114 B4
Salton Sea U.S.A. 33°15N 115°45W 110 D3
Saltwood U.K. 51°4N 1°2E 25 D11
Salvador Brazil 13°0S 38°30W 122 B3
Salvador, El ■ Cent. Amer. 13°50N 89°0W 114 E7
Salween → Burma 16°31N 97°37E 85 L20
Salyan Azerbaijan 39°33N 48°59E 71 G8
Salzburg Austria 47°48N 13°2E 64 E7
Salzgitter Germany 52°9N 10°19E 64 B6
Samangān □ Afghan. 36°15N 68°3E 87 B12
Samar Phil. 12°0N 125°0E 83 B7
Samara Russia 53°8N 50°6E 70 D9
Samarinda Indonesia 0°30S 117°9E 82 E5
Samarqand Uzbekistan 39°40N 66°55E 87 B11
Sambalpur India 21°28N 84°4E 85 J14
Sambhal India 28°35N 78°37E 84 E11
Sambhar India 26°52N 75°6E 84 F9
Samoa ■ Pac. Oc. 14°0S 172°0W 99 C16
Samos Greece 37°45N 26°50E 69 F12
Samothraki Greece 40°28N 25°28E 69 D11
Sampford Courtenay U.K. 50°47N 3°58E 74 F4
Samsun Turkey 41°15N 36°22E 71 F6
Samui, Ko Thailand 9°30N 100°0E 85 b
San → Poland 50°45N 21°51E 65 C11
San Ambrosio Pac. Oc. 26°28S 79°53W 117 F3
San Andrés, I. de Caribbean 12°42N 81°46W 115 E8
San Andres Mts. U.S.A. 33°0N 106°30W 110 D5
San Andrés Tuxtla Mexico 18°27N 95°13W 114 D5
San Angelo U.S.A. 31°28N 100°26W 110 D6
San Antonio Chile 33°40S 71°40W 121 F2
San Antonio U.S.A. 29°25N 98°29W 110 E7
San Antonio → U.S.A. 28°30N 96°54W 111 E7
San Antonio Oeste Argentina 40°40S 65°0W 121 G3
San Bernardino U.S.A. 34°7N 117°19W 110 D3
San Bernardino Str. Phil. 13°0N 125°0E 83 B6
San Bernardo Chile 33°40S 70°50W 121 F2
San Blas, C. U.S.A. 29°40N 85°21W 111 E9
San Carlos Phil. 10°29N 123°25E 83 B6
San Carlos de Bariloche Argentina 41°10S 71°25W 121 G2
San Carlos de Bolívar Argentina 36°15S 61°6W 121 F3
San Cristóbal Argentina 30°20S 61°10W 121 F3
San Cristóbal Solomon Is. 10°30S 161°0E 99 C11
San Cristóbal Venezuela 7°46N 72°14W 120 B2
San Cristóbal de las Casas Mexico 16°45N 92°38W 114 D6

San Diego U.S.A. 32°42N 117°9W 110 D3
San Felipe Venezuela 10°20N 68°44W 120 A3
San Félix Pac. Oc. 26°23S 80°0W 103 K20
San Fernando Chile 34°30S 71°0W 121 F2
San Fernando Spain 36°28N 6°17W 67 D2
San Fernando de Apure Venezuela 7°54N 67°15W 120 B3
San Francisco U.S.A. 37°46N 122°23W 110 C2
San Francisco, C. de Colombia 6°18N 77°29W 117 C3
San Francisco de Macorís Dom. Rep. 19°19N 70°15W 115 D10
San Germán Puerto Rico 18°4N 67°4W 115 d
San Gottardo, P. del Switz. 46°33N 8°33E 64 E5
San Ignacio Bolivia 16°20S 60°55W 120 D3
San Joaquín → U.S.A. 38°4N 121°51W 110 C2
San Jorge, G. Argentina 46°0S 66°0W 121 G3
San José Costa Rica 9°55N 84°2W 115 F8
San Jose Phil. 12°27N 121°4E 83 B6
San Jose → U.S.A. 34°25N 106°45W 110 D5
San José de Chiquitos Bolivia 17°53S 60°50W 120 D3
San José de Jáchal Argentina 30°15S 68°46W 121 F3
San José de Mayo Uruguay 34°27S 56°40W 121 F4
San Juan Argentina 31°30S 68°30W 121 F3
San Juan Dom. Rep. 18°49N 71°12W 115 D10
San Juan Puerto Rico 18°28N 66°7W 115 d
San Juan → Nic. 10°56N 83°42W 115 E8
San Juan de los Morros Venezuela 9°55N 67°21W 120 B3
San Juan Mts. U.S.A. 37°30N 107°0W 110 C5
San Lorenzo, Mte. Argentina 47°40S 72°20W 121 G2
San Lucas, C. Mexico 22°52N 109°53W 114 C3
San Luis Argentina 33°20S 66°20W 121 F3
San Luis Obispo U.S.A. 35°17N 120°40W 110 C2
San Luis Potosí Mexico 22°9N 100°59W 114 C4
San Marcos U.S.A. 29°53N 97°56W 110 E7
San Marino ■ Europe 43°56N 12°25E 68 C5
San Matías, G. Argentina 41°30S 64°0W 121 G3
San Miguel El Salv. 13°30N 88°12W 114 E7
San Miguel de Tucumán Argentina 26°50S 65°20W 121 E3
San Nicolás Argentina 33°25S 60°10W 121 F3
San Pedro Ivory C. 4°50N 6°33W 94 H4
San Pedro de las Colonias Mexico 25°45N 102°59W 114 B4
San Pedro de Macorís Dom. Rep. 18°30N 69°18W 115 D11
San Pedro Sula Honduras 15°30N 88°0W 114 D7
San Pietro Italy 39°8N 8°17E 68 E3
San Rafael Argentina 34°40S 68°21W 121 F3
San Remo Italy 43°49N 7°46E 68 C2
San Salvador El Salv. 13°40N 89°10W 114 E7
San Salvador de Jujuy Argentina 24°10S 64°48W 121 E3
San Salvador I. Bahamas 24°0N 74°40W 115 C10
San Sebastián Puerto Rico 18°20N 66°59W 115 d
San Severo Italy 41°41N 15°23E 68 D6
San Valentin, Mte. Chile 46°30S 73°30W 121 G2
Sana' Yemen 15°27N 44°12E 89 D3
Sanaga → Cameroon 3°35N 9°38E 96 D1
Sanandaj Iran 35°18N 47°1E 86 C6
Sancti Spíritus Cuba 21°52N 79°33W 115 C9
Sancy, Puy de France 45°32N 2°50E 66 D5
Sandakan Malaysia 5°53N 118°4E 82 C5
Sanday U.K. 59°16N 2°31W 19 D12
Sandbach U.K. 53°9N 2°21W 23 F4
Sandgate U.K. 51°4N 1°10E 25 D11
Sandhurst U.K. 51°21N 0°48W 25 D7
Sandown U.K. 50°40N 1°10W 24 E6
Sandpoint U.S.A. 48°17N 116°33W 110 A3
Sandray U.K. 56°53N 7°31W 18 J2
Sandringham U.K. 52°51N 0°31E 25 A9
Sandusky U.S.A. 41°27N 82°42W 112 E6
Sandwich U.K. 51°16N 1°21E 25 D11
Sandy U.K. 52°8N 0°17W 25 B8
Sandy U.S.A. 40°32N 111°50W 110 B4
Sandy L. Canada 53°2N 93°0W 108 D10
Sanford, Mt. U.S.A. 62°13N 144°8W 108 C5
Sangihe, Pulau Indonesia 3°35N 125°30E 83 D7
Sangli India 16°55N 74°33E 84 L9
Sangre de Cristo Mts. U.S.A. 37°30N 105°20W 110 C5
Sanikiluaq Canada 56°32N 79°14W 109 D12
Sankt Pölten Austria 48°12N 15°38E 64 D8
Sankuru → Dem. Rep. of the Congo 4°17S 20°25E 96 E4
Şanlıurfa Turkey 37°12N 38°50E 71 G6
Sanlúcar de Barrameda Spain 36°46N 6°21W 67 D2
Sanmenxia China 34°47N 111°12E 79 E11
Sanming China 26°15N 117°40E 79 F12
Sanquhar U.K. 55°22N 3°54W 21 D8
Sant Feliu de Guíxols Spain 41°45N 3°1E 67 B7
Santa Ana El Salv. 14°0N 89°31W 114 E7
Sant' Antíoco Italy 39°4N 8°27E 68 E3
Santa Barbara U.S.A. 34°25N 119°42W 110 D3
Santa Catarina □ Brazil 27°25S 48°30W 121 E5
Santa Clara Cuba 22°20N 80°0W 115 C9
Santa Clarita U.S.A. 34°24N 118°33W 110 D3
Santa Coloma de Gramenet Spain 41°27N 2°13E 67 B7
Santa Cruz Bolivia 17°43S 63°10W 120 D3
Santa Cruz U.S.A. 36°58N 122°1W 110 C2
Santa Cruz de Tenerife Canary Is. 28°28N 16°15W 94 C2
Santa Cruz Is. Solomon Is. 10°30S 166°0E 99 C12
Santa Cruz Mts. Jamaica 17°58N 77°43W 114 a
Santa Fé Argentina 31°35S 60°41W 121 F3
Santa Fe U.S.A. 35°41N 105°57W 110 C5
Santa Inés, I. Chile 54°0S 73°0W 121 H2
Santa Isabel Solomon Is. 8°0S 159°0E 99 B10
Santa Maria Brazil 29°40S 53°48W 121 E4
Santa María → Mexico 31°0N 107°14W 114 A3
Santa María Mexico 34°57N 120°26W 110 D2
Santa Marta, Sierra Nevada de Colombia 10°55N 73°50W 120 A2
Santa Rosa Argentina 36°40S 64°17W 121 F3
Santa Rosa U.S.A. 38°26N 122°43W 110 C2

Santai   Soldotna

Santai *China* 31°5N 104°58E **78 E9**
Santana do Livramento
  Brazil 30°55S 55°30W **121 F4**
Santander *Spain* 43°27N 3°51W **67 A4**
Santanilla, Is. *Honduras* 17°22N 83°57W **115 D8**
Santarém *Brazil* 2°25S 54°42W **120 C4**
Santarém *Portugal* 39°12N 8°42W **67 C1**
Santiago *Chile* 33°26S 70°40W **121 F2**
Santiago de Compostela *Spain* 42°52N 8°37W **67 A1**
Santiago de Cuba *Cuba* 20°0N 75°49W **115 D9**
Santiago de los Caballeros
  Dom. Rep. 19°30N 70°40W **115 D10**
Santiago del Estero
  Argentina 27°50S 64°15W **121 E3**
Santo Amaro *Brazil* 12°30S 38°43W **122 B3**
Santo André *Brazil* 23°39S 46°29W **122 D1**
Santo Antônio de Jesus
  Brazil 12°58S 39°16W **122 B3**
Santo Domingo *Dom. Rep.* 18°30N 69°59W **115 D11**
Santo Domingo de los Colorados
  Ecuador 0°15S 79°9W **120 C2**
Santorini *Greece* 36°23N 25°27E **69 F11**
Santos *Brazil* 24°0S 46°20W **122 D1**
Santos Dumont *Brazil* 22°55S 43°10W **122 D2**
Sanya *China* 18°14N 109°29E **79 H10**
São Bernardo do Campo
  Brazil 23°45S 46°34W **122 D1**
São Borja *Brazil* 28°39S 56°0W **121 E4**
São Caitano *Brazil* 8°21S 36°6W **122 A3**
São Carlos *Brazil* 22°0S 47°50W **122 D1**
São Francisco → *Brazil* 10°30S 36°24W **122 B3**
São Gonçalo *Brazil* 22°48S 43°5W **122 D2**
São João da Boa Vista *Brazil* 22°0S 46°52W **122 D1**
São João de Meriti *Brazil* 22°48S 43°22W **122 D2**
São João del Rei *Brazil* 21°8S 44°15W **122 D2**
São João do Piauí *Brazil* 8°21S 42°15W **122 A2**
São José do Rio Preto *Brazil* 20°50S 49°20W **122 D1**
São José dos Campos *Brazil* 23°7S 45°52W **122 D1**
São Lourenço *Brazil* 22°7S 45°3W **122 D2**
São Luís *Brazil* 2°39S 44°15W **120 C5**
São Marcos → *Brazil* 18°15S 47°37W **122 C1**
São Marcos, B. de *Brazil* 2°0S 44°0W **120 C5**
São Mateus *Brazil* 18°44S 39°50W **122 C3**
São Paulo *Brazil* 23°32S 46°38W **122 D1**
São Paulo □ *Brazil* 22°0S 49°0W **120 E5**
São Roque, C. de *Brazil* 5°30S 35°16W **120 C6**
São Sebastião do Paraíso
  Brazil 20°54S 46°59W **122 D1**
São Tomé *São Tomé & Príncipe* 0°10N 6°39E **91 f**
São Tomé & Príncipe ■ *Africa* 0°12N 6°39E **91 F4**
São Vicente *Brazil* 23°57S 46°23W **122 D1**
São Vicente, C. de *Portugal* 37°0N 9°0W **67 D1**
Saône → *France* 45°44N 4°50E **66 D6**
Sapele *Nigeria* 5°50N 5°40E **94 G7**
Sapporo *Japan* 43°0N 141°21E **81 B7**
Saqqez *Iran* 36°15N 46°20E **86 B6**
Sar-e Pol *Afghan.* 36°10N 66°0E **87 B11**
Saraburi *Thailand* 14°30N 100°55E **82 B2**
Sarajevo *Bos.-H.* 43°52N 18°26E **69 C8**
Saranac Lakes *U.S.A.* 44°20N 74°28W **113 C10**
Saransk *Russia* 54°10N 45°10E **70 D8**
Sarapul *Russia* 56°28N 53°48E **70 C9**
Sarasota *U.S.A.* 27°20N 82°32W **111 E10**
Saratoga Springs *U.S.A.* 43°5N 73°47W **113 D11**
Saratov *Russia* 51°30N 46°2E **71 D8**
Sarawak □ *Malaysia* 2°0N 113°0E **82 D4**
Sarda → *India* 27°21N 81°23E **85 F12**
Sardinia □ *Italy* 40°0N 9°0E **68 D3**
Sargasso Sea *Atl. Oc.* 27°0N 72°0W **104 G13**
Sargodha *Pakistan* 32°10N 72°40E **84 C8**
Sarh *Chad* 9°5N 18°23E **95 G9**
Sārī *Iran* 36°30N 53°4E **87 B8**
Sariwon *N. Korea* 38°31N 125°46E **79 D14**
Sark □ *U.K.* 49°25N 2°22W **27 J9**
Sarlat-la-Canéda *France* 44°54N 1°13E **66 D4**
Sarmiento *Argentina* 45°35S 69°5W **121 G3**
Sarnia *Canada* 42°58N 82°23W **109 E11**
Sarreguemines *France* 49°5N 7°4E **66 B7**
Sarthe → *France* 47°33N 0°31W **66 C3**
Sasebo *Japan* 33°10N 129°43E **81 G1**
Saskatchewan □ *Canada* 54°40N 106°0W **108 D9**
Saskatchewan → *Canada* 53°37N 100°40W **108 D9**
Saskatoon *Canada* 52°10N 106°38W **108 D9**
Sássari *Italy* 40°43N 8°34E **68 D3**
Sassnitz *Germany* 54°29N 13°39E **64 A7**
Satmala Hills *Andhra Pradesh,*
  India 19°45N 78°45E **84 K11**
Satmala Hills *Maharashtra,*
  India 20°15N 74°40E **84 J9**
Satna *India* 24°35N 80°50E **85 G12**
Satpura Ra. *India* 21°25N 76°10E **84 J10**
Satu Mare *Romania* 47°46N 22°55E **65 E12**
Saudi Arabia ■ *Asia* 26°0N 44°0E **89 B3**
Sault Ste. Marie *Canada* 46°30N 84°20W **112 B5**
Saumur *France* 47°15N 0°5W **66 C3**
Saundersfoot *U.K.* 51°43N 4°42W **26 D4**
Saurimo *Angola* 9°40S 20°12E **96 F4**
Sava → *Serbia* 44°50N 20°26E **69 B9**
Savai'i *Samoa* 13°28S 172°24W **99 C16**
Savanna-la-Mar *Jamaica* 18°10N 78°10W **114 a**
Savannah *U.S.A.* 32°5N 81°6W **111 D10**
Savannah → *U.S.A.* 32°2N 80°53W **111 D10**
Savannakhet *Laos* 16°30N 104°49E **82 A2**
Savoie □ *France* 45°26N 6°25E **66 D7**
Savona *Italy* 44°17N 8°30E **68 B3**
Sawatch Range *U.S.A.* 39°0N 106°30W **110 C5**
Sawbridgeworth *U.K.* 51°48N 0°9E **25 C9**
Sawel Mt. *U.K.* 54°50N 7°2W **29 B7**
Sawston *U.K.* 52°8N 0°10E **25 B9**
Sawtry *U.K.* 52°27N 0°17W **25 B8**
Sawu *Indonesia* 10°35S 121°50E **83 F6**
Sawu Sea *Indonesia* 9°30S 121°50E **83 F6**
Saxilby *U.K.* 53°16N 0°38W **23 F7**
Saxlingham Nethergate *U.K.* 52°32N 1°18E **25 A11**
Saxmundham *U.K.* 52°13N 1°30E **25 B12**
Sayan Mts. *Russia* 54°0N 96°0E **77 D10**
Saydā *Lebanon* 33°35N 35°25E **86 C3**
Sayre *U.S.A.* 41°59N 76°32W **112 E9**
Sázava → *Czech Rep.* 49°53N 14°24E **64 D8**
Scafell Pike *U.K.* 54°27N 3°14W **22 D2**

Scalby *U.K.* 54°18N 0°26W **22 D8**
Scalloway *U.K.* 60°9N 1°17W **18 B15**
Scalpay Highl., *U.K.* 57°18N 6°0W **18 H6**
Scalpay W. Isles, *U.K.* 57°52N 6°40W **18 G4**
Scamblesby *U.K.* 53°17N 0°5W **23 F8**
Scandicci *Italy* 43°45N 11°11E **68 C4**
Scandinavia *Europe* 64°0N 12°0E **56 C8**
Scapa Flow *U.K.* 58°53N 3°3W **19 E11**
Scarba *U.K.* 56°11N 5°43W **20 B4**
Scarborough *U.K.* 54°17N 0°24W **22 D8**
Scariff I. *Ireland* 51°44N 10°15W **30 E2**
Scarning *U.K.* 52°41N 0°54E **25 A10**
Scarp *U.K.* 58°1N 7°8W **18 F3**
Schaffhausen *Switz.* 47°42N 8°39E **64 E5**
Schelde → *Belgium* 51°15N 4°16E **64 C3**
Schenectady *U.S.A.* 42°49N 73°57W **113 D11**
Schiehallion *U.K.* 56°40N 4°6W **20 A7**
Schleswig *Germany* 54°31N 9°34E **64 A5**
Schleswig-Holstein □ *Germany* 54°30N 9°30E **64 A5**
Schœlcher *Martinique* 14°36N 61°7W **114 c**
Schreiber *Canada* 48°45N 87°20W **112 A4**
Schwäbische Alb *Germany* 48°20N 9°30E **64 D5**
Schwarzwald *Germany* 48°30N 8°20E **64 D5**
Schwerin *Germany* 53°36N 11°22E **64 B6**
Schwyz *Switz.* 47°2N 8°39E **64 E5**
Scilly Is. *U.K.* 49°56N 6°22W **27 H1**
Scioto → *U.S.A.* 38°44N 83°1W **112 F6**
Scole *U.K.* 52°22N 1°10E **25 B11**
Scone *U.K.* 56°25N 3°24W **21 B9**
Scopwick *U.K.* 53°8N 0°24W **23 F8**
Scotia Sea *Antarctica* 56°5S 56°0W **55 B18**
Scotland □ *U.K.* 57°0N 4°0W **62 C5**
Scott I. *Antarctica* 67°0S 179°0E **55 C11**
Scottish Borders □ *U.K.* 55°35N 2°50W **21 C10**
Scottsbluff *U.S.A.* 41°52N 103°40W **110 B6**
Scottsburg *U.S.A.* 38°41N 85°47W **112 F5**
Scrabster *U.K.* 58°36N 3°33W **19 E10**
Scranton *U.S.A.* 41°25N 75°40W **113 E10**
Scremerston *U.K.* 55°44N 2°0W **22 A5**
Scunthorpe *U.K.* 53°36N 0°39W **23 E7**
Scutari *Albania* 42°4N 19°32E **69 C8**
Scutari *Turkey* 41°1N 29°0E **86 A2**
Seaford *U.K.* 50°47N 0°7E **25 E9**
Seaford *U.S.A.* 38°39N 75°37W **113 F10**
Seaforth, L. *U.K.* 57°52N 6°36W **18 G4**
Seaham *U.K.* 54°50N 1°20W **22 C6**
Seahouses *U.K.* 55°34N 1°39W **22 A5**
Seal → *Canada* 59°4N 94°48W **108 D10**
Seamer *U.K.* 54°15N 0°26W **22 D8**
Seascale *U.K.* 54°24N 3°29W **22 D2**
Seaton Cumb., *U.K.* 54°40N 3°31W **22 C1**
Seaton Devon, *U.K.* 50°42N 3°5W **27 F7**
Seaton Delaval *U.K.* 55°5N 1°33W **22 A6**
Seattle *U.S.A.* 47°36N 122°19W **110 A2**
Sebastián Vizcaíno, B.
  Mexico 28°0N 114°30W **114 B2**
Şebinkarahisar *Turkey* 40°22N 38°28E **71 F6**
Sedalia *U.S.A.* 38°42N 93°14W **111 C8**
Sedan *France* 49°43N 4°57E **66 B6**
Sedbergh *U.K.* 54°20N 2°31W **22 D3**
Sedgefield *U.K.* 54°40N 1°26W **22 C6**
Seend *U.K.* 51°21N 2°4W **24 D4**
Segesta *Italy* 37°56N 12°50E **68 F5**
Ségou *Mali* 13°30N 6°16W **94 F4**
Segovia *Spain* 40°57N 4°10W **67 B3**
Séguéla *Ivory C.* 7°55N 6°40W **94 G4**
Sehore *India* 23°10N 77°5E **84 H10**
Seil *U.K.* 56°18N 5°38W **20 B4**
Seine → *France* 49°26N 0°26E **66 B4**
Sekondi-Takoradi *Ghana* 4°58N 1°45W **94 H5**
Selborne *U.K.* 51°6N 0°56W **25 D7**
Selby *U.K.* 53°47N 1°5W **23 E6**
Selebi-Phikwe *Botswana* 21°58S 27°48E **97 J5**
Selenge Mörön → *Asia* 52°16N 106°16E **78 A10**
Selkirk *Canada* 50°10N 96°55W **108 D10**
Selkirk *U.K.* 55°33N 2°50W **21 C10**
Selkirk Mts. *Canada* 51°15N 117°40W **108 D8**
Sellafield *U.K.* 54°25N 3°29W **22 D2**
Selma *U.S.A.* 32°25N 87°1W **111 D9**
Selsey *U.K.* 50°44N 0°47W **25 E7**
Selsey Bill *U.K.* 50°43N 0°47W **25 E7**
Selvas *Brazil* 6°30S 67°0W **120 C3**
Selwyn L. *Canada* 60°0N 104°30W **108 C9**
Selwyn Mts. *Canada* 63°0N 130°0W **108 C6**
Semarang *Indonesia* 7°0S 110°26E **82 F4**
Semey *Kazakhstan* 50°30N 80°10E **78 A5**
Semnān *Iran* 35°40N 53°23E **87 B8**
Sena Madureira *Brazil* 9°5S 68°45W **120 C3**
Sendai *Japan* 38°15N 140°53E **81 D7**
Seneca L. *U.S.A.* 42°40N 76°54W **112 D9**
Senegal ■ *W. Afr.* 14°30N 14°30W **94 F3**
Sénégal → *W. Afr.* 15°48N 16°32W **94 E2**
Senegambia *Africa* 12°45N 12°0W **90 E2**
Senhor-do-Bonfim *Brazil* 10°30S 40°10W **122 B2**
Senja *Norway* 69°25N 17°30E **63 D7**
Senkaku-Shoto *E. China Sea* 25°45N 123°30E **79 F13**
Senlis *France* 49°13N 2°35E **66 B5**
Sennen *U.K.* 50°4N 5°42W **27 G2**
Sens *France* 48°11N 3°15E **66 B5**
Seoul *S. Korea* 37°31N 126°58E **79 D14**
Seph → *U.K.* 54°17N 1°9W **22 D6**
Sept-Îles *Canada* 50°13N 66°22W **109 D13**
Seram *Indonesia* 3°10S 129°0E **83 E7**
Seram Sea *Indonesia* 2°30S 128°30E **83 E7**
Serang *Indonesia* 6°8S 106°10E **82 F3**
Serbia ■ *Europe* 43°20N 20°0E **69 B9**
Serdar *Turkmenistan* 39°4N 56°23E **87 B9**
Seremban *Malaysia* 2°43N 101°53E **82 D2**
Serengeti Plain *Tanzania* 2°40S 35°0E **96 E7**
Sergipe □ *Brazil* 10°30S 37°30W **122 B3**
Sergiyev Posad *Russia* 56°20N 38°10E **70 C6**
Serhetabat *Turkmenistan* 35°20N 62°18E **87 C10**
Serifos *Greece* 37°9N 24°30E **69 F11**
Serov *Russia* 59°29N 60°35E **70 C11**
Serowe *Botswana* 22°25S 26°43E **97 J5**
Serpukhov *Russia* 54°55N 37°28E **70 D6**
Serra *Brazil* 20°7S 40°18W **122 D2**
Serra de Mesa, Barragem de
  Brazil 14°30S 49°10W **122 B1**
Serrinha *Brazil* 11°39S 39°0W **122 B3**

Sète *France* 43°25N 3°42E **66 E5**
Sete Lagoas *Brazil* 19°27S 44°16W **122 C2**
Sétif *Algeria* 36°9N 5°26E **94 A7**
Settat *Morocco* 33°0N 7°40W **94 B4**
Settle *U.K.* 54°5N 2°16W **22 D4**
Settlement, The *Br. Virgin Is.* 18°43N 64°22W **115 e**
Setúbal *Portugal* 38°30N 8°58W **67 C1**
Setúbal, B. de *Portugal* 38°40N 8°56W **67 C1**
Seul, Lac *Canada* 50°20N 92°30W **108 D10**
Sevan, L. *Armenia* 40°30N 45°20E **71 F8**
Sevastopol *Ukraine* 44°35N 33°30E **71 F5**
Seven → *U.K.* 54°12N 0°52W **22 D7**
Sevenoaks *U.K.* 51°16N 0°11E **25 D9**
Severn → *Canada* 56°2N 87°36W **109 D11**
Severn → *U.K.* 51°35N 2°40W **24 C3**
Severn Beach *U.K.* 51°33N 2°39W **24 C3**
Severn Stoke *U.K.* 52°6N 2°12W **24 B4**
Severnaya Zemlya *Russia* 79°0N 100°0E **77 B10**
Severodvinsk *Russia* 64°27N 39°58E **70 B6**
Severomorsk *Russia* 69°5N 33°27E **70 A5**
Sevier → *U.S.A.* 39°4N 113°6W **110 C4**
Sevier L. *U.S.A.* 38°54N 113°9W **110 C4**
Seville *Spain* 37°23N 5°58W **67 D2**
Seward *U.S.A.* 60°7N 149°27W **108 C5**
Seward Peninsula *U.S.A.* 65°30N 166°0W **108 C3**
Seychelles ■ *Ind. Oc.* 5°0S 56°0E **91 G9**
Seyðisfjörður *Iceland* 65°16N 13°57W **63 A3**
Seydişehir *Turkey* 37°25N 31°51E **71 G5**
Seymour *U.S.A.* 38°58N 85°53W **112 F5**
Sfântu Gheorghe *Romania* 45°52N 25°48E **65 F13**
Sfax *Tunisia* 34°49N 10°48E **95 B8**
Shaanxi □ *China* 35°0N 109°0E **79 D10**
Shabeelle → *Somali Rep.* 2°0N 44°0E **89 G3**
Shache *China* 38°20N 77°10E **78 D4**
Shaftesbury *U.K.* 51°0N 2°11W **24 D4**
Shahjahanpur *India* 27°54N 79°57E **84 F11**
Shakhty *Russia* 47°40N 40°16E **71 E7**
Shaki *Nigeria* 8°41N 3°21E **94 G6**
Shaldon *U.K.* 50°32N 3°31W **27 F6**
Shaluli Shan *China* 30°40N 99°55E **78 E8**
Shamo, L. *Ethiopia* 5°45N 37°30E **89 F2**
Shan □ *Burma* 21°30N 98°30E **85 J21**
Shandong □ *China* 36°0N 118°0E **79 D12**
Shandong Pen. *China* 37°0N 121°0E **79 D13**
Shanghai *China* 31°15N 121°26E **79 E13**
Shangqiu *China* 34°26N 115°36E **79 E12**
Shangrao *China* 28°25N 117°59E **79 F12**
Shangshui *China* 33°42N 114°35E **79 E11**
Shanklin *U.K.* 50°38N 1°11W **24 E6**
Shannon → *Ireland* 52°35N 9°30W **30 C4**
Shannon ✈ (SNN) *Ireland* 52°42N 8°57W **30 C5**
Shannon, Mouth of the
  Ireland 52°30N 9°55W **30 D3**
Shantou *China* 23°18N 116°40E **79 G12**
Shanxi □ *China* 37°0N 112°0E **79 D11**
Shaoguan *China* 24°48N 113°35E **79 G11**
Shaoxing *China* 30°0N 120°35E **79 F13**
Shaoyang *China* 27°14N 111°25E **79 F11**
Shap *U.K.* 54°32N 2°40W **22 C3**
Shapinsay *U.K.* 59°3N 2°51W **19 D12**
Shaqra' *Si. Arabia* 25°15N 45°16E **86 E6**
Shaqrā' *Yemen* 13°22N 45°44E **89 E4**
Sharjah *U.A.E.* 25°23N 55°26E **87 E8**
Shark B. *Australia* 25°30S 113°32E **98 F1**
Sharm el Sheikh *Egypt* 27°53N 34°18E **95 C12**
Sharon *U.S.A.* 41°14N 80°31W **112 E7**
Sharpness *U.K.* 51°43N 2°28W **24 C4**
Sharya *Russia* 58°22N 45°20E **70 C8**
Shashi *China* 30°25N 112°14E **79 E11**
Shasta, Mt. *U.S.A.* 41°25N 122°12W **110 B2**
Shatt al Arab *Asia* 29°57N 48°34E **86 D7**
Shawano *U.S.A.* 44°47N 88°36W **112 C3**
Shawbury *U.K.* 52°48N 2°39W **23 G3**
Shawinigan *Canada* 46°35N 72°50W **109 E12**
Shawnee *U.S.A.* 35°20N 96°55W **111 C7**
Shebbear *U.K.* 50°51N 4°15W **27 F5**
Sheboygan *U.S.A.* 43°46N 87°45W **112 D4**
Sheelin, L. *Ireland* 53°48N 7°20W **28 D6**
Sheep Haven *Ireland* 55°11N 7°52W **28 A6**
Sheerness *U.K.* 51°26N 0°47E **25 D10**
Sheffield *U.K.* 53°23N 1°28W **23 F6**
Shefford *U.K.* 52°2N 0°20W **25 B8**
Shehy Mts. *Ireland* 51°47N 9°15W **30 E3**
Shelburne *Canada* 43°47N 65°20W **113 D15**
Shelby *U.S.A.* 48°30N 111°51W **110 A4**
Shelbyville Ill., *U.S.A.* 39°24N 88°48W **112 F3**
Shelbyville Ind., *U.S.A.* 39°31N 85°47W **112 F5**
Shelikhov G. *Russia* 59°30N 157°0E **77 D16**
Shenandoah *U.S.A.* 40°49N 76°12W **113 E9**
Shenandoah → *U.S.A.* 39°19N 77°44W **112 F9**
Shendî *Sudan* 16°46N 33°22E **95 E12**
Shenfield *U.K.* 51°38N 0°22E **25 C9**
Shenyang *China* 41°48N 123°27E **79 C13**
Shenzhen *China* 22°32N 114°5E **79 a**
Shepparton *Australia* 36°23S 145°26E **98 H8**
Sheppey, I. of *U.K.* 51°25N 0°48E **25 D10**
Shepshed *U.K.* 52°47N 1°18W **23 G6**
Shepton Mallet *U.K.* 51°11N 2°33W **24 D3**
Sherborne *U.K.* 50°57N 2°31W **24 E3**
Sherborne St. John *U.K.* 51°17N 1°7W **24 D6**
Sherbrooke *Canada* 45°28N 71°57W **113 C12**
Sherburn *N. Yorks., U.K.* 54°11N 0°32W **22 D7**
Sherburn *N. Yorks., U.K.* 53°48N 1°15W **23 E6**
Shere *U.K.* 51°13N 0°27W **25 D8**
Sherfield English *U.K.* 51°1N 1°34W **24 D5**
Sheridan *U.S.A.* 44°48N 106°58W **110 B5**
Sheriff Hutton *U.K.* 54°5N 1°0W **22 D7**
Sheringham *U.K.* 52°56N 1°13E **25 A11**
Sherkin I. *Ireland* 51°28N 9°26W **30 F4**
Sherman *U.S.A.* 33°38N 96°36W **111 D7**
Sherston *U.K.* 51°34N 2°14W **24 C4**
Sherwood Forest *U.K.* 53°6N 1°7W **23 F6**
Shetland □ *U.K.* 60°30N 1°30W **18 B15**
Shetland Is. *U.K.* 60°30N 1°30W **18 B15**
Sheyenne → *U.S.A.* 47°2N 96°50W **111 A7**
Shiant Is. *U.K.* 57°54N 6°22W **18 G4**
Shibām *Yemen* 15°59N 48°36E **89 D4**
Shiel, L. *U.K.* 56°48N 5°34W **18 J6**
Shifnal *U.K.* 52°39N 2°23W **23 G4**
Shihezi *China* 44°15N 86°2E **78 C6**

Shijiazhuang *China* 38°2N 114°28E **79 D11**
Shikarpur *Pakistan* 27°57N 68°39E **84 F6**
Shikoku □ *Japan* 33°30N 133°30E **81 G3**
Shilbottle *U.K.* 55°22N 1°40W **22 B5**
Shildon *U.K.* 54°38N 1°38W **22 C5**
Shiliguri *India* 26°45N 88°25E **85 F16**
Shillelagh *Ireland* 52°45N 6°32W **31 C9**
Shillingstone *U.K.* 50°53N 2°15W **24 E4**
Shillong *India* 25°35N 91°53E **85 G17**
Shimla *India* 31°2N 77°9E **84 D10**
Shimoga *India* 13°57N 75°32E **84 N9**
Shimonoseki *Japan* 33°58N 130°55E **81 G2**
Shin, L. *U.K.* 58°5N 4°30W **19 F8**
Shinyanga *Tanzania* 3°45S 33°27E **96 E6**
Shipdham *U.K.* 52°38N 0°54E **25 A10**
Shipley *U.K.* 53°50N 1°47W **23 E5**
Shipston-on-Stour *U.K.* 52°3N 1°37W **24 B5**
Shipton under Wychwood
  U.K. 51°51N 1°36W **24 C5**
Shīrāz *Iran* 29°42N 52°30E **87 D8**
Shire → *Africa* 17°42S 35°19E **97 H7**
Shirebrook *U.K.* 53°12N 1°13W **23 F6**
Shivpuri *India* 25°26N 77°42E **84 G10**
Shizuishan *China* 39°15N 106°50E **78 D10**
Shizuoka *Japan* 34°57N 138°24E **81 F6**
Shoeburyness *U.K.* 51°32N 0°49E **25 C10**
Shoreham by Sea *U.K.* 50°50N 0°16W **25 E8**
Shreveport *U.S.A.* 32°31N 93°45W **111 D8**
Shrewsbury *U.K.* 52°43N 2°45W **23 G3**
Shrewton *U.K.* 51°12N 1°54W **24 D5**
Shrirampur *India* 22°44N 88°21E **85 H16**
Shrivenham *U.K.* 51°36N 1°38W **24 C5**
Shropshire □ *U.K.* 52°36N 2°45W **23 G3**
Shuangliao *China* 43°29N 123°30E **79 C13**
Shuangyashan *China* 46°28N 131°5E **79 B15**
Shule *China* 39°25N 76°3E **78 D4**
Shumagin Is. *U.S.A.* 55°7N 160°30W **108 C4**
Shumen *Bulgaria* 43°18N 26°55E **69 C12**
Shwebo *Burma* 22°30N 95°45E **85 H19**
Shymkent *Kazakhstan* 42°18N 69°36E **87 A12**
Si Kiang = Xi Jiang → *China* 22°5N 113°20E **79 G11**
Siahan Range *Pakistan* 27°30N 64°40E **84 F4**
Sialkot *Pakistan* 32°32N 74°30E **84 C9**
Šiauliai *Lithuania* 55°56N 23°15E **63 F8**
Šibenik *Croatia* 43°48N 15°54E **68 C6**
Siberia *Russia* 60°0N 100°0E **72 B11**
Siberut *Indonesia* 1°30S 99°0E **82 E1**
Sibi *Pakistan* 29°30N 67°54E **84 E5**
Sibiu *Romania* 45°45N 24°9E **65 F13**
Sible Hedingham *U.K.* 51°59N 0°37E **25 C10**
Sibolga *Indonesia* 1°42N 98°45E **82 D1**
Sibsey *U.K.* 53°2N 0°1E **23 F9**
Sibu *Malaysia* 2°18N 111°49E **82 D4**
Sibuyan Sea *Phil.* 12°30N 122°20E **83 B6**
Sichuan □ *China* 30°30N 103°0E **78 E9**
Sicily □ *Italy* 37°30N 14°30E **68 F6**
Sicuani *Peru* 14°21S 71°10W **120 D2**
Sidi-bel-Abbès *Algeria* 35°13N 0°39W **94 A5**
Sidlaw Hills *U.K.* 56°32N 3°2W **21 A9**
Sidlesham *U.K.* 50°47N 0°47W **25 E7**
Sidmouth *U.K.* 50°40N 3°15W **27 F7**
Sidney *Nebr., U.S.A.* 41°8N 102°59W **110 B6**
Sidney *Ohio, U.S.A.* 40°17N 84°9W **112 E5**
Sidra, G. of *Libya* 31°40N 18°30E **95 B9**
Siedlce *Poland* 52°10N 22°20E **65 B12**
Siegen *Germany* 50°51N 8°0E **64 C5**
Siena *Italy* 43°19N 11°21E **68 C4**
Sierra Blanca Peak *U.S.A.* 33°23N 105°49W **110 D5**
Sierra Leone ■ *W. Afr.* 9°0N 12°0W **94 G3**
Sierra Madre *Mexico* 16°0N 93°0W **104 H10**
Sierra Madre Occidental
  Mexico 27°0N 107°0W **114 B3**
Sierra Madre Oriental *Mexico* 25°0N 100°0W **114 C4**
Sierra Nevada *Spain* 37°3N 3°15W **67 D4**
Sierra Nevada *U.S.A.* 39°0N 120°30W **110 C2**
Sierra Vista *U.S.A.* 31°33N 110°18W **110 D4**
Sifnos *Greece* 37°0N 24°45E **69 F11**
Sighty Crag *U.K.* 55°7N 2°38W **22 B3**
Sikar *India* 27°33N 75°10E **84 F9**
Sikasso *Mali* 11°18N 5°35W **94 F4**
Sikeston *U.S.A.* 36°53N 89°35W **112 G3**
Sikhote Alin Ra. *Russia* 45°0N 136°0E **79 B16**
Sikkim □ *India* 27°50N 88°30E **85 F16**
Silesia *Poland* 51°0N 16°30E **64 C9**
Silifke *Turkey* 36°22N 33°58E **71 G5**
Siling Co *China* 31°50N 89°20E **78 E6**
Silloth *U.K.* 54°52N 3°23W **22 C2**
Silsden *U.K.* 53°55N 1°55W **23 E5**
Silver City *U.S.A.* 32°46N 108°17W **110 D5**
Silvermine Mts. *Ireland* 52°47N 8°15W **30 C6**
Silverstone *U.K.* 52°5N 1°2W **24 B6**
Silverton *U.K.* 50°49N 3°29W **27 F7**
Simcoe, L. *Canada* 44°25N 79°20W **112 C8**
Simeulue *Indonesia* 2°45N 95°45E **82 D1**
Simferopol *Ukraine* 44°55N 34°3E **71 F5**
Simi *Greece* 36°35N 27°50E **69 F12**
Simonsbath *U.K.* 51°8N 3°46W **27 E6**
Simonside *U.K.* 55°17N 1°59W **22 B5**
Simplonpass *Switz.* 46°15N 8°3E **64 E5**
Simpson Desert *Australia* 25°0S 137°0E **98 F6**
Simpson Pen. *Canada* 68°34N 88°45W **109 C11**
Sinai *Egypt* 29°0N 34°0E **95 C12**
Sincelejo *Colombia* 9°18N 75°24W **120 B2**
Sinclair's B. *U.K.* 58°31N 3°5W **19 E11**
Sind Sagar Doab *Pakistan* 32°0N 71°30E **84 D7**
Sindh □ *Pakistan* 26°0N 69°0E **84 G6**
Sines *Portugal* 37°56N 8°51W **67 D1**
Singapore ■ *Asia* 1°17N 103°51E **82 D2**
Singaraja *Indonesia* 8°7S 115°6E **82 F5**
Singida *Tanzania* 4°49S 34°48E **96 E6**
Singkawang *Indonesia* 1°0N 108°57E **82 D3**
Singleton *U.K.* 50°55N 0°46W **25 E7**
Sinkiang □ *China* 42°0N 86°0E **78 C6**
Sinop *Turkey* 42°1N 35°11E **71 F6**
Sintra *Portugal* 38°47N 9°25W **67 C1**
Sion *Switz.* 46°14N 7°20E **64 E4**
Sion Mills *U.K.* 54°48N 7°29W **28 B7**
Sioux City *U.S.A.* 42°30N 96°24W **111 B7**
Sioux Falls *U.S.A.* 43°33N 96°44W **111 B7**

Sioux Lookout *Canada* 50°10N 91°50W **108 D10**
Siping *China* 43°8N 124°21E **79 C13**
Sir James MacBrien, Mt.
  Canada 62°7N 127°41W **108 C7**
Siracusa *Italy* 37°4N 15°17E **68 F6**
Sirajganj *Bangla.* 24°25N 89°47E **85 G16**
Sirsa *India* 29°33N 75°4E **84 E9**
Sīstān *Asia* 30°50N 61°0E **87 D10**
Sitapur *India* 27°38N 80°45E **85 F12**
Sitges *Spain* 41°17N 1°47E **67 B6**
Sitka *U.S.A.* 57°3N 135°20W **108 D6**
Sittingbourne *U.K.* 51°21N 0°45E **25 D10**
Sittwe *Burma* 20°18N 92°45E **85 J18**
Sivas *Turkey* 39°43N 36°58E **71 G6**
Sivrihisar *Turkey* 39°30N 31°35E **71 G5**
Siwa *Egypt* 29°11N 25°31E **95 C11**
Siwalik Range *Nepal* 28°0N 83°0E **85 F13**
Siwan *India* 26°13N 84°21E **85 F14**
Six Cross Roads *Barbados* 13°7N 59°28W **115 g**
Sixmilebridge *Ireland* 52°44N 8°46W **30 C5**
Sizewell *U.K.* 52°12N 1°37E **25 B12**
Sjælland *Denmark* 55°30N 11°30E **63 F6**
Skagerrak *Denmark* 57°30N 9°0E **63 F5**
Skagway *U.S.A.* 59°28N 135°19W **108 D6**
Skeena → *Canada* 54°9N 130°5W **108 D6**
Skegness *U.K.* 53°9N 0°20E **23 F9**
Skeleton Coast *Namibia* 20°0S 13°0E **97 J2**
Skellefteå *Sweden* 64°45N 20°50E **63 E8**
Skellefteälven → *Sweden* 64°45N 21°10E **63 E8**
Skellingthorpe *U.K.* 53°15N 0°37W **23 F7**
Skelmersdale *U.K.* 53°33N 2°48W **23 E3**
Skelmorlie *U.K.* 55°52N 4°53W **20 C6**
Skelton Cleve., *U.K.* 54°34N 0°58W **22 C7**
Skelton Cumb., *U.K.* 54°43N 2°51W **22 C3**
Skerries, The *U.K.* 53°25N 4°36W **26 A4**
Skiathos *Greece* 39°12N 23°30E **69 E10**
Skibbereen *Ireland* 51°33N 9°16W **30 E4**
Skiddaw *U.K.* 54°39N 3°9W **22 C2**
Skien *Norway* 59°12N 9°35E **63 F5**
Skikda *Algeria* 36°50N 6°58E **94 A7**
Skipsea *U.K.* 53°58N 0°13W **23 E8**
Skipton *U.K.* 53°58N 2°3W **23 E4**
Skopelos *Greece* 39°9N 23°47E **69 E10**
Skopje *Macedonia* 42°1N 21°26E **69 C9**
Skovorodino *Russia* 54°0N 124°0E **77 D13**
Skowhegan *U.S.A.* 44°46N 69°43W **113 C13**
Skull *Ireland* 51°32N 9°34W **30 E3**
Skye *U.K.* 57°15N 6°10W **18 H5**
Skyros *Greece* 38°55N 24°34E **69 E11**
Slaidburn *U.K.* 53°58N 2°26W **23 E4**
Slaney → *Ireland* 52°26N 6°33W **31 D9**
Slatina *Romania* 44°28N 24°22E **65 F13**
Slave → *Canada* 61°18N 113°39W **108 C8**
Slave Coast *W. Afr.* 6°0N 2°30E **94 G6**
Slave Lake *Canada* 55°17N 114°43W **108 D8**
Sleaford *U.K.* 53°0N 0°24W **23 F8**
Sleat, Sd. of *U.K.* 57°5N 5°47W **18 H6**
Sledmere *U.K.* 54°4N 0°35W **22 D7**
Sleeper Is. *Canada* 58°30N 81°0W **109 D11**
Sleights *U.K.* 54°27N 0°40W **22 D7**
Slieve Aughty *Ireland* 53°4N 8°30W **30 B5**
Slieve Bloom *Ireland* 53°4N 7°40W **31 B7**
Slieve Donard *U.K.* 54°11N 5°55W **29 C10**
Slieve Gamph *Ireland* 54°6N 9°0W **28 C4**
Slieve Gullion *U.K.* 54°7N 6°26W **29 C9**
Slieve League *Ireland* 54°40N 8°42W **28 B4**
Slieve Mish *Ireland* 52°12N 9°50W **30 D2**
Slievenamon *Ireland* 52°25N 7°34W **31 D7**
Sligo *Ireland* 54°16N 8°28W **28 C5**
Sligo □ *Ireland* 54°8N 8°42W **28 C4**
Sligo B. *Ireland* 54°18N 8°40W **28 C4**
Sliven *Bulgaria* 42°42N 26°19E **69 C12**
Slough *U.K.* 51°30N 0°36W **25 C7**
Slovak Rep. ■ *Europe* 48°30N 20°0E **65 D10**
Slovenia ■ *Europe* 45°58N 14°30E **64 F8**
Slovyansk *Ukraine* 48°55N 37°36E **71 E6**
Słupsk *Poland* 54°30N 17°3E **65 A9**
Slutsk *Belarus* 53°2N 27°31E **70 D4**
Slyne Hd. *Ireland* 53°25N 10°10W **28 E1**
Smallwood Res. *Canada* 54°5N 64°30W **109 D13**
Smederevo *Serbia* 44°40N 20°57E **69 B9**
Smerwick Harbour *Ireland* 52°12N 10°23W **30 D2**
Smethwick *U.K.* 52°30N 1°57W **23 G5**
Smiths Falls *Canada* 44°55N 76°0W **113 C9**
Smoky → *Canada* 56°10N 117°21W **108 D8**
Smoky Hill → *U.S.A.* 39°4N 96°48W **111 C7**
Smolensk *Russia* 54°45N 32°5E **70 D5**
Snaefell *I. of Man* 54°16N 4°27W **29 C13**
Snainton *U.K.* 54°14N 0°33W **22 D7**
Snaith *U.K.* 53°42N 1°1W **23 E6**
Snake → *U.S.A.* 46°12N 119°2W **110 A3**
Snape *U.K.* 52°10N 1°30E **25 B12**
Snettisham *U.K.* 52°53N 0°31E **25 A10**
Snizort, L. *U.K.* 57°33N 6°28E **18 G5**
Snøhetta *Norway* 62°19N 9°16E **63 E5**
Snow Hill *U.S.A.* 38°11N 75°24W **113 F10**
Snowdon *U.K.* 53°4N 4°5W **26 A3**
Snowdonia □ *U.K.* 53°7N 3°59W **26 A6**
Snowy Mts. *Australia* 36°30S 148°20E **98 H8**
Sobat, Nahr → *Sudan* 9°22N 31°33E **95 G12**
Sobradinho, Represa de *Brazil* 9°30S 42°0W **122 A2**
Sobral *Brazil* 3°50S 40°20W **120 C5**
Soc Trang *Vietnam* 9°37N 105°50E **82 C3**
Sochi *Russia* 43°35N 39°40E **71 F6**
Société, Îs. de la
  French Polynesia 17°0S 151°0W **103 J12**
Socorro *U.S.A.* 34°4N 106°54W **110 D5**
Socotra *Yemen* 12°30N 54°0E **89 E5**
Söderhamn *Sweden* 61°18N 17°10E **63 E7**
Sofia *Bulgaria* 42°45N 23°20E **69 C10**
Sognefjorden *Norway* 61°10N 5°50E **63 E5**
Sohâg *Egypt* 26°33N 31°43E **95 C12**
Soham *U.K.* 52°21N 0°21E **25 B9**
Sokhumi *Georgia* 43°0N 41°0E **71 F7**
Sokodé *Togo* 9°0N 1°11E **94 G6**
Sokoto *Nigeria* 13°2N 5°16E **94 F7**
Solapur *India* 17°43N 75°56E **84 L9**
Soldotna *U.S.A.* 60°29N 151°3W **108 C4**

Soledad   Taunus

Soledad *Colombia* 10°55N 74°46W **120** A2
Solent, The *U.K.* 50°45N 1°25W **24** E6
Solihull *U.K.* 52°26N 1°47W **23** H5
Solikamsk *Russia* 59°38N 56°50E **70** C10
Solingen *Germany* 51°10N 7°5E **64** C4
Sóller *Spain* 39°46N 2°43E **67** C7
Sologne *France* 47°40N 1°45E **66** C4
Solomon Is. ■ *Pac. Oc.* 6°0S 155°0E **99** B10
Solomon Sea *Papua N. G.* 7°0S 150°0E **98** B9
Solon *China* 46°32N 121°10E **79** B13
Solothurn *Switz.* 47°13N 7°32E **64** E4
Solway Firth *U.K.* 54°49N 3°35W **22** C1
Somali Pen. *Africa* 7°0N 46°0E **90** F8
Somali Rep. ■ *Africa* 7°0N 47°0E **89** F4
Somaliland □ *Somali Rep.* 9°0N 46°0E **89** F4
Sombrerete *Mexico* 23°38N 103°39W **114** C4
Somerby *U.K.* 52°42N 0°50W **23** G7
Somerset *U.S.A.* 37°5N 84°36W **112** G5
Somerset □ *U.K.* 51°9N 3°0W **24** D2
Somerset I. *Canada* 73°30N 93°0W **108** B10
Somersham *U.K.* 52°24N 0°1W **25** B8
Somerton *U.K.* 51°2N 2°43W **24** D3
Somme → *France* 50°11N 1°38E **66** A4
Songhua Hu *China* 43°35N 126°50E **79** C14
Songhua Jiang → *China* 47°45N 132°30E **79** B15
Songkhla *Thailand* 7°13N 100°37E **82** C2
Songpan *China* 32°40N 103°30E **78** E9
Sonid Youqi *China* 42°45N 112°48E **79** C11
Sonning *U.K.* 51°28N 0°54W **25** D7
Sonora → *Mexico* 29°5N 110°55W **114** B2
Sonoran Desert *U.S.A.* 33°40N 113°30W **110** D4
Sonoyta *Mexico* 31°51N 112°50W **114** A2
Sonsonate *El Salv.* 13°43N 89°44W **114** E7
Sopot *Poland* 54°27N 18°31E **65** A10
Sorel-Tracy *Canada* 46°0N 73°10W **113** C11
Soria *Spain* 41°43N 2°32W **67** B4
Sorocaba *Brazil* 23°31S 47°27W **122** D1
Søroya *Norway* 70°40N 22°30E **63** C8
Sosnowiec *Poland* 50°20N 19°10E **65** C10
Soufrière *Guadeloupe* 16°5N 61°40W **114** b
Soufrière *St. Lucia* 13°51N 61°3W **115** f
Soufrière Bay *St. Lucia* 13°51N 61°4W **115** f
Sound, The *U.K.* 50°20N 4°10W **27** G5
Souris → *N. Amer.* 49°40N 99°34W **108** D9
Sousse *Tunisia* 35°50N 10°38E **95** A8
South Africa ■ *Africa* 32°0S 23°0E **97** L4
South America 10°0S 60°0W **117** E5
South Australia □ *Australia* 32°0S 139°0E **98** G6
South Ayrshire □ *U.K.* 55°18N 4°41W **20** D6
South Bend *U.S.A.* 41°41N 86°15W **112** E4
South Benfleet *U.K.* 51°33N 0°36E **25** C10
South Brent *U.K.* 50°25N 3°51W **27** G6
South Carolina □ *U.S.A.* 34°0N 81°0W **111** D10
South Cave *U.K.* 53°47N 0°37W **23** E7
South Charleston *U.S.A.* 38°22N 81°44W **112** F7
South China Sea *Asia* 10°0N 113°0E **82** C4
South Dakota □ *U.S.A.* 44°15N 100°0W **110** B7
South Dorset Downs *U.K.* 50°40N 2°26W **24** E4
South Downs *U.K.* 50°52N 0°25W **25** E8
South East C. *Australia* 43°40S 146°50E **98** J8
South Elkington *U.K.* 53°23N 0°4W **23** F8
South Esk → *U.K.* 56°43N 2°31W **19** J12
South Foreland *U.K.* 51°8N 1°24E **25** D11
South Georgia *Antarctica* 54°30S 37°0W **55** B1
South Harris *U.K.* 57°50N 7°0W **18** G4
South Hayling *U.K.* 50°47N 0°56W **25** E7
South I. *N.Z.* 44°0S 170°0E **99** J13
South Korea ■ *Asia* 36°0N 128°0E **79** D14
South Lanarkshire □ *U.K.* 55°37N 3°53W **21** C8
South Magnetic Pole *Antarctica* 64°8S 138°8E **55** C9
South Molton *U.K.* 51°1N 3°51W **27** E6
South Nahanni → *Canada* 61°3N 123°21W **108** C7
South Negril Pt. *Jamaica* 18°16N 78°22W **114** a
South Orkney Is. *Antarctica* 63°0S 45°0W **55** C18
South Ossetia □ *Georgia* 42°21N 44°2E **71** F7
South Petherton *U.K.* 50°57N 2°46W **24** E3
South Petherwin *U.K.* 50°36N 4°24W **27** F5
South Platte → *U.S.A.* 41°7N 100°42W **110** B6
South Pole *Antarctica* 90°0S 0°0E **55** E
South Pt. *Barbados* 13°2N 59°32W **115** g
South Queensferry *U.K.* 55°59N 3°23W **21** C9
South Ronaldsay *U.K.* 58°48N 2°58W **19** E12
South Sandwich Is. *Antarctica* 57°0S 27°0W **55** B2
South Saskatchewan →
  Canada 53°15N 105°5W **108** D9
South Shetland Is. *Antarctica* 62°0S 59°0W **55** C18
South Shields *U.K.* 55°0N 1°25W **22** C6
South Tawton *U.K.* 50°44N 3°55W **27** F6
South Tyne → *U.K.* 54°59N 2°8W **22** C4
South Uist *U.K.* 57°20N 7°15W **18** H3
South Woodham Ferrers *U.K.* 51°39N 0°37E **25** C10
South Yorkshire □ *U.K.* 53°27N 1°36W **23** F5
Southam *U.K.* 52°18N 1°23W **24** B6
Southampton *U.K.* 50°54N 1°23W **24** E6
Southampton I. *Canada* 64°30N 84°0W **109** C11
Southborough *U.K.* 51°9N 0°16E **25** D9
Southend-on-Sea *U.K.* 51°32N 0°44E **25** C10
Southern Alps *N.Z.* 43°41S 170°11E **99** J13
Southern Indian L. *Canada* 57°10N 98°30W **108** D9
Southern Ocean *Antarctica* 62°0S 60°0E **53** H13
Southern Uplands *U.K.* 55°28N 3°52W **21** D8
Southery *U.K.* 52°31N 0°24E **25** A9
Southminster *U.K.* 51°40N 0°51E **25** C10
Southport *U.K.* 53°39N 3°0W **23** E2
Southwark □ *U.K.* 51°29N 0°6W **25** D8
Southwell *U.K.* 53°4N 0°57W **23** F7
Southwick *U.K.* 50°50N 0°13W **25** E8
Southwold *U.K.* 52°20N 1°41E **25** B12
Sovetsk *Russia* 55°6N 21°50E **63** F8
Sowerby *U.K.* 54°14N 1°21W **22** D6
Soweto *S. Africa* 26°14S 27°52E **97** K5
Spain ■ *Europe* 39°0N 4°0W **67** B4
Spalding *U.K.* 52°48N 0°9W **23** G8
Spanish *Canada* 46°12N 82°20W **112** B6
Spanish Town *Br. Virgin Is.* 18°27N 64°26W **115** e
Spanish Town *Jamaica* 18°0N 76°57W **114** a
Sparkford *U.K.* 51°2N 2°33W **24** D3
Sparks *U.S.A.* 39°32N 119°45W **110** C3
Sparta *Greece* 37°5N 22°25E **69** F10
Sparta *U.S.A.* 43°56N 90°49W **112** D2

Spartanburg *U.S.A.* 34°56N 81°57W **111** D10
Spartivento, C. *Italy* 37°55N 16°4E **68** F7
Speightstown *Barbados* 13°15N 59°39W **115** g
Speke *U.K.* 53°21N 2°52W **23** F3
Spencer *U.S.A.* 43°9N 95°9W **111** B7
Spencer G. *Australia* 34°0S 137°20E **98** G6
Spennymoor *U.K.* 54°42N 1°36W **22** C5
Sperrin Mts. *U.K.* 54°50N 7°0W **29** B7
Spey → *U.K.* 57°40N 3°6W **19** G11
Spilsby *U.K.* 53°10N 0°6E **23** F9
Spithead *U.K.* 50°45N 1°10W **24** E6
Split *Croatia* 43°31N 16°26E **68** C7
Spofforth *U.K.* 53°57N 1°27W **23** E6
Spokane *U.S.A.* 47°40N 117°24W **110** A3
Spooner *U.S.A.* 45°50N 91°53W **112** C2
Spratly Is. *S. China Sea* 8°20N 112°0E **82** C4
Spree → *Germany* 52°32N 13°12E **64** B7
Spring Hall *Barbados* 13°18N 59°36W **115** g
Springbok *S. Africa* 29°42S 17°54E **97** K3
Springfield *Ill., U.S.A.* 39°48N 89°39W **112** F3
Springfield *Mass., U.S.A.* 42°6N 72°35W **113** D11
Springfield *Mo., U.S.A.* 37°13N 93°17W **111** C8
Springfield *Ohio, U.S.A.* 39°55N 83°49W **112** F6
Springfield *Oreg., U.S.A.* 44°3N 123°1W **110** B2
Springhill *Canada* 45°40N 64°4W **113** C15
Springs *S. Africa* 26°13S 28°25E **97** K5
Sproatley *U.K.* 53°47N 0°11W **23** E8
Spurn Hd. *U.K.* 53°35N 0°8E **23** E9
Srebrenica *Bos.-H.* 44°6N 19°18E **69** B8
Sredinnyy Ra. *Russia* 57°0N 160°0E **77** D16
Sri Lanka ■ *Asia* 7°30N 80°50E **84** R12
Srikakulam *India* 18°14N 83°58E **85** K13
Srinagar *India* 34°5N 74°50E **84** B9
Stacks Mts. *Ireland* 52°20N 9°34W **30** D3
Staffa *U.K.* 56°27N 6°21W **20** B3
Stafford *U.K.* 52°49N 2°7W **23** G4
Staffordshire □ *U.K.* 52°53N 2°10W **23** G4
Staindrop *U.K.* 54°36N 1°47W **22** C5
Staines *U.K.* 51°26N 0°29W **25** D8
Stainforth *U.K.* 53°37N 1°0W **23** E7
Stainmore Forest *U.K.* 54°29N 2°5W **22** C4
Stainton *U.K.* 53°18N 0°24W **23** F8
Staithes *U.K.* 54°34N 0°46W **22** C7
Stakhanov *Ukraine* 48°35N 38°40E **71** E6
Stalbridge *U.K.* 50°57N 2°23W **24** E4
Stalham *U.K.* 52°47N 1°31E **25** A12
Stallingborough *U.K.* 53°35N 0°12W **23** E8
Stalybridge *U.K.* 53°28N 2°3W **23** F4
Stamford *U.K.* 52°39N 0°29W **23** G8
Stamford *U.S.A.* 41°3N 73°32W **113** E11
Stamford Bridge *U.K.* 54°0N 0°54W **23** E7
Stamfordham *U.K.* 55°3N 1°53W **22** B5
Standish *U.K.* 53°35N 2°41W **23** E3
Standish *U.S.A.* 43°59N 83°57W **112** D6
Stanford on Teme *U.K.* 52°18N 2°25W **24** B4
Stanhope *U.K.* 54°45N 2°1W **22** C4
Stanley *Falk. Is.* 51°40S 59°51W **121** H4
Stanley *U.K.* 54°53N 1°41W **22** C5
Stannington *U.K.* 55°7N 1°40W **22** B5
Stanovoy Ra. *Russia* 55°0N 130°0E **77** D13
Stansted, London ✈ (STN)
  U.K. 51°54N 0°14E **25** C9
Stansted Mountfitchet *U.K.* 51°54N 0°11E **25** C9
Stanwix *U.K.* 54°55N 2°56W **22** C3
Stapleford *U.K.* 52°57N 1°16W **23** G6
Staplehurst *U.K.* 51°9N 0°34E **25** D10
Stara Zagora *Bulgaria* 42°26N 25°39E **69** C11
Staraya Russa *Russia* 57°58N 31°23E **70** C5
Starbuck I. *Kiribati* 5°37S 155°55W **103** H12
Start B. *U.K.* 50°15N 3°39W **27** G6
Start Pt. *U.K.* 50°13N 3°39W **27** G6
Staryy Oskol *Russia* 51°19N 37°55E **71** D6
State College *U.S.A.* 40°48N 77°52W **112** E9
Staten, I. = Estados, I. de Los
  Argentina 54°40S 64°30W **121** H3
Staunton *U.K.* 51°57N 2°17W **24** B4
Staunton *U.S.A.* 38°9N 79°4W **112** F8
Stavanger *Norway* 58°57N 5°40E **63** F5
Staveley *Cumb., U.K.* 54°23N 2°48W **22** D3
Staveley *Derby, U.K.* 53°16N 1°21W **23** F6
Stavropol *Russia* 45°5N 42°0E **71** E7
Steiermark □ *Austria* 47°26N 15°0E **64** E8
Steinkjer *Norway* 64°1N 11°31E **63** E6
Stellarton *Canada* 45°32N 62°30W **113** C16
Stellenbosch *S. Africa* 33°58S 18°50E **97** L3
Stenhousemuir *U.K.* 56°2N 3°48W **21** B8
Stephenville *Canada* 48°31N 58°35W **109** E14
Steppe *Asia* 50°0N 50°0E **72** C7
Sudeten *Europe* 50°20N 16°45E **65** C9
Sterling *Colo., U.S.A.* 40°37N 103°13W **110** B6
Sterling *Ill., U.S.A.* 41°48N 89°42W **112** E3
Sterlitamak *Russia* 53°40N 56°0E **70** D10
Stettiner Haff *Germany* 53°47N 14°15E **64** B8
Stettler *Canada* 52°19N 112°40W **108** D8
Steubenville *U.S.A.* 40°22N 80°37W **112** E7
Stevenage *U.K.* 51°55N 0°13W **25** C8
Stevens Point *U.S.A.* 44°31N 89°34W **112** C3
Stevenston *U.K.* 55°39N 4°45W **20** D6
Stewart *Canada* 55°56N 129°57W **108** D6
Stewart → *Canada* 63°19N 139°26W **108** C6
Stewart I. *N.Z.* 46°58S 167°54E **99** K12
Stewarton *U.K.* 55°40N 4°32W **20** D6
Steyning *U.K.* 50°53N 0°18W **25** E8
Steyr *Austria* 48°3N 14°25E **64** D8
Stikine → *Canada* 56°40N 132°30W **108** D6
Stillington *U.K.* 54°6N 1°6W **22** D6
Stillwater *U.S.A.* 36°7N 97°4W **111** A8
Stiperstones *U.K.* 52°36N 2°55W **23** G3
Stirling *U.K.* 56°8N 3°57W **21** B8
Stirling □ *U.K.* 56°12N 4°18W **20** B7
Stockbridge *U.K.* 51°7N 1°29W **24** D6
Stockholm *Sweden* 59°19N 18°4E **63** F7
Stockport *U.K.* 53°25N 2°9W **23** F4
Stocksbridge *U.K.* 53°29N 1°35W **23** F5
Stockton *U.S.A.* 37°58N 121°17W **110** C2
Stockton-on-Tees *U.K.* 54°35N 1°19W **22** C6
Stoer, Pt. of *U.K.* 58°16N 5°23W **18** F7
Stoke *U.K.* 51°26N 0°41E **25** D10
Stoke Ferry *U.K.* 52°34N 0°31E **25** A10
Stoke Fleming *U.K.* 50°19N 3°37W **27** G6

Stoke Mandeville *U.K.* 51°47N 0°47W **25** C7
Stoke-on-Trent *U.K.* 53°1N 2°11W **23** F4
Stoke Prior *U.K.* 52°19N 2°4W **24** B4
Stokesley *U.K.* 54°28N 1°12W **22** D6
Stone *Bucks., U.K.* 51°48N 0°52W **25** C7
Stone *Staffs., U.K.* 52°55N 2°9W **23** G4
Stonehaven *U.K.* 56°59N 2°12W **19** J13
Stonehouse *U.K.* 51°45N 2°16W **24** C4
Stonham Aspal *U.K.* 52°12N 1°8E **25** B11
Stony Stratford *U.K.* 52°3N 0°50W **25** B7
Stony Tunguska → *Russia* 61°50N 90°13E **77** C10
Stora Lulevatten *Sweden* 67°10N 19°30E **63** D7
Storavan *Sweden* 65°45N 18°10E **63** D7
Store Bælt *Denmark* 55°20N 11°0E **63** F6
Stormberge *S. Africa* 31°16S 26°17E **97** L5
Stornoway *U.K.* 58°13N 6°23W **18** F5
Storsjön *Sweden* 63°9N 14°30E **63** E6
Stort → *U.K.* 51°46N 0°2E **25** C9
Storuman *Sweden* 65°5N 17°10E **63** D7
Stotfold *U.K.* 52°1N 0°13W **25** B8
Stour → *Dorset, U.K.* 50°43N 1°47W **24** E5
Stour → *Kent, U.K.* 51°18N 1°22E **25** D11
Stour → *Suffolk, U.K.* 51°57N 1°4E **25** C11
Stour → *Worcs., U.K.* 52°21N 2°17W **24** B4
Stourbridge *U.K.* 52°28N 2°8W **23** H4
Stourport-on-Severn *U.K.* 52°21N 2°17W **24** B4
Stow *U.K.* 55°42N 2°50W **21** C10
Stow Bardolph *U.K.* 52°38N 0°24E **25** A9
Stow-on-the-Wold *U.K.* 51°56N 1°42W **24** C5
Stowmarket *U.K.* 52°12N 1°0E **25** B10
Strabane *U.K.* 54°50N 7°27W **28** B7
Stradbroke *U.K.* 52°19N 1°16E **25** B11
Stralsund *Germany* 54°18N 13°4E **64** A7
Strangford L. *U.K.* 54°30N 5°37W **29** C10
Stranraer *U.K.* 54°54N 5°1W **20** E5
Strasbourg *France* 48°35N 7°42E **66** B7
Stratford *Canada* 43°23N 81°0W **112** D7
Stratford St. Mary *U.K.* 51°58N 1°0E **25** C10
Stratford-upon-Avon *U.K.* 52°12N 1°42W **24** B5
Strath Avon *U.K.* 57°18N 3°23W **19** H11
Strath Dearn *U.K.* 57°20N 4°0W **19** H9
Strath Glass *U.K.* 57°22N 4°42W **19** H8
Strath Halladale *U.K.* 58°30N 3°51W **19** F10
Strath Naver *U.K.* 58°24N 4°12W **19** F9
Strath of Kildonan *U.K.* 58°14N 3°56W **19** F10
Strath Spey *U.K.* 57°9N 3°49W **19** H10
Strath Tay *U.K.* 56°40N 3°48W **21** A8
Strathaven *U.K.* 55°40N 4°5W **20** D7
Strathbogie *U.K.* 57°25N 2°45W **19** H12
Strathmore *Angus, U.K.* 56°37N 3°7W **19** J11
Strathmore *Highl., U.K.* 58°22N 4°40W **19** F8
Strathpeffer *U.K.* 57°35N 4°32W **19** G8
Strathroy *Canada* 42°58N 81°38W **112** D7
Strathy Pt. *U.K.* 58°36N 4°1W **19** E9
Stratton *U.K.* 50°49N 4°32W **27** F4
Stratton St. Margaret *U.K.* 51°35N 1°44W **24** C6
Streatley *U.K.* 51°31N 1°8W **24** C6
Street *U.K.* 51°8N 2°44W **24** D3
Strensall *U.K.* 54°3N 1°4W **22** D6
Stretford *U.K.* 53°28N 2°17W **23** F4
Stroma *U.K.* 58°41N 3°7W **19** E11
Strómboli *Italy* 38°47N 15°13E **68** E6
Stromeferry *U.K.* 57°21N 5°33W **18** H6
Stromness *U.K.* 58°58N 3°17W **19** E11
Stronsay *U.K.* 59°7N 2°35W **19** D12
Stroud *U.K.* 51°45N 2°13W **24** C4
Stuart L. *Canada* 54°30N 124°30W **108** D7
Studland *U.K.* 50°39N 1°58W **24** E5
Studley *U.K.* 52°16N 1°54W **24** B5
Sturgeon Bay *U.S.A.* 44°50N 87°23W **112** C4
Sturgeon Falls *Canada* 46°25N 79°57W **112** B8
Sturminster Marshall *U.K.* 50°48N 2°5W **24** E4
Sturminster Newton *U.K.* 50°55N 2°18W **24** E4
Sturt Stony Desert *Australia* 28°30S 141°0E **98** F6
Sturton *U.K.* 53°19N 0°39W **23** F7
Stuttgart *Germany* 48°48N 9°11E **64** D5
Stuttgart *U.S.A.* 34°30N 91°33W **111** D8
Suakin *Sudan* 19°8N 37°20E **95** E13
Şuba' *Si. Arabia* 27°10N 35°40E **86** E3
Subotica *Serbia* 46°6N 19°39E **69** A8
Suceava *Romania* 47°38N 26°16E **65** E14
Suck → *Ireland* 53°17N 8°3W **30** B6
Sucre *Bolivia* 19°0S 65°15W **120** D3
Sudan ■ *Africa* 15°0N 30°0E **95** F11
Sudbury *Canada* 46°30N 81°0W **112** B7
Sudbury *Derby, U.K.* 52°54N 1°45W **23** G5
Sudbury *Suffolk, U.K.* 52°2N 0°45E **25** B10
Südd *Sudan* 8°20N 30°0E **95** G12
Sudeten *Europe* 50°20N 16°45E **65** C9
Suez *Egypt* 29°58N 32°31E **95** C12
Suez, G. of *Egypt* 28°40N 33°0E **95** C12
Suez Canal *Egypt* 31°0N 32°20E **95** B12
Suffolk □ *U.K.* 52°16N 1°0E **25** B11
Sugluk *Canada* 62°14N 75°38W **109** C12
Şuḥār *Oman* 24°20N 56°40E **87** E9
Suihua *China* 46°32N 126°55E **79** B14
Suining *China* 30°26N 105°35E **78** E10
Suir → *Ireland* 52°16N 7°9W **31** D8
Sukabumi *Indonesia* 6°56S 106°50E **82** F3
Sukhona → *Russia* 61°15N 46°39E **70** C6
Sukkur *Pakistan* 27°42N 68°54E **84** F6
Sulaiman Range *Pakistan* 30°30N 69°50E **84** D6
Sulawesi *Indonesia* 2°0S 120°0E **83** E6
Sullana *Peru* 4°52S 80°39W **120** C1
Sullom Voe *U.K.* 60°27N 1°20W **18** B15
Sulu Arch. *Phil.* 6°0N 121°0E **83** C6
Sulu Sea *E. Indies* 8°0N 120°0E **83** C6
Sumare *Brazil* 22°49S 47°16W **122** D1
Sumatra *Indonesia* 0°40N 100°20E **82** D2
Sumba *Indonesia* 9°45S 119°35E **83** F5
Sumbawa *Indonesia* 8°26S 117°30E **82** F5
Sumburgh Hd. *U.K.* 59°52N 1°17W **18** C15
Summer L. *U.S.A.* 42°50N 120°45W **110** B2
Summerside *Canada* 46°24N 63°47W **109** E13
Sumqayıt *Azerbaijan* 40°34N 49°38E **71** F8
Sumter *U.S.A.* 33°55N 80°21W **111** D10
Sumy *Ukraine* 50°57N 34°50E **71** D5
Sun Valley *U.S.A.* 43°42N 114°21W **110** B4
Sunart, L. *U.K.* 56°42N 5°43W **18** J6

Sunbury *U.S.A.* 40°52N 76°48W **112** E9
Sunda, Selat *Indonesia* 6°20S 105°30E **82** F3
Sunda Is. *Indonesia* 5°0S 105°0E **102** H2
Sundarbans *Asia* 22°0N 89°0E **85** J16
Sunderland *U.K.* 54°55N 1°23W **22** C6
Sundsvall *Sweden* 62°23N 17°17E **63** E7
Sungaipenuh *Indonesia* 2°1S 101°20E **82** E2
Sunk Island *U.K.* 53°39N 0°6W **23** E8
Sunninghill *U.K.* 51°24N 0°39W **25** D7
Sunshine Coast *Australia* 26°30S 153°0E **98** F9
Superior *U.S.A.* 46°44N 92°6W **112** B1
Superior, L. *N. Amer.* 47°0N 87°0W **112** B4
Sür *Lebanon* 33°19N 35°16E **86** C3
Sura → *Russia* 56°6N 46°0E **70** C8
Surabaya *Indonesia* 7°17S 112°45E **82** F4
Surakarta *Indonesia* 7°35S 110°48E **82** F4
Surat *India* 21°12N 72°55E **84** J8
Surgut *Russia* 61°14N 73°20E **76** C8
Surigao *Phil.* 9°47N 125°29E **83** C7
Suriname ■ *S. Amer.* 4°0N 56°0W **120** B4
Surrey □ *U.K.* 51°15N 0°31W **25** D7
Surt *Libya* 31°11N 16°39E **95** B9
Surtsey *Iceland* 63°20N 20°30W **63** B1
Susquehanna → *U.S.A.* 39°33N 76°5W **112** F9
Sussex *Canada* 45°45N 65°37W **113** C15
Sutherland *U.K.* 58°12N 4°50W **19** F8
Sutlej → *Pakistan* 29°23N 71°3E **84** E7
Sutterton *U.K.* 52°55N 0°9W **23** G8
Sutton □ *U.K.* 51°21N 0°11W **25** D8
Sutton Bridge *U.K.* 52°47N 0°11E **23** G9
Sutton Coldfield *U.K.* 52°35N 1°49W **23** G5
Sutton Courtenay *U.K.* 51°39N 1°16W **24** C6
Sutton in Ashfield *U.K.* 53°8N 1°16W **23** F6
Sutton-on-Sea *U.K.* 53°18N 0°16E **23** F9
Sutton Scotney *U.K.* 51°9N 1°20W **24** D6
Suva *Fiji* 18°6S 178°30E **99** D14
Suvorov Is. *Cook Is.* 13°15S 163°5W **103** J11
Suwałki *Poland* 54°8N 22°59E **65** A12
Suzhou *China* 31°19N 120°38E **79** E13
Svalbard *Arctic* 78°0N 17°0E **54** B8
Svealand *Sweden* 60°20N 15°0E **63** E7
Sverdrup Chan. *Canada* 79°56N 96°25W **109** B10
Sverdrup Is. *Canada* 79°0N 97°0W **109** B10
Svir → *Russia* 60°30N 32°48E **70** B5
Swadlincote *U.K.* 52°47N 1°33W **23** G5
Swaffham *U.K.* 52°39N 0°42E **25** A10
Swakopmund *Namibia* 22°37S 14°30E **97** J2
Swale → *U.K.* 54°5N 1°20W **22** D6
Swan Hill *Australia* 35°20S 143°33E **98** H7
Swan River *Canada* 52°10N 101°16W **108** D9
Swanage *U.K.* 50°36N 1°58W **24** E5
Swansea *U.K.* 51°37N 3°57W **27** D6
Swansea B. *U.K.* 51°32N 3°57W **27** D6
Swartberge *S. Africa* 33°20S 22°0E **90** K6
Swaziland ■ *Africa* 26°30S 31°30E **97** K6
Sweden ■ *Europe* 57°0N 15°0E **63** F7
Sweetwater *U.S.A.* 32°28N 100°25W **110** D6
Swellendam *S. Africa* 34°1S 20°26E **97** l4
Swift Current *Canada* 50°20N 107°45W **108** D9
Swilly, L. *Ireland* 55°12N 7°33W **28** A6
Swindon *U.K.* 51°34N 1°46W **24** C5
Swineshead *U.K.* 52°57N 0°10W **23** G8
Swinford *Ireland* 53°57N 8°58W **28** D4
Swinton *Borders, U.K.* 55°43N 2°15W **21** C11
Swinton *Gt. Man., U.K.* 53°31N 2°20W **23** E4
Swinton *S. Yorks., U.K.* 53°29N 1°20W **23** F6
Switzerland ■ *Europe* 46°30N 8°0E **64** E5
Swords *Ireland* 53°28N 6°13W **31** B9
Sydney *Australia* 33°52S 151°12E **98** G9
Sydney *Canada* 46°7N 60°7W **113** C17
Syktyvkar *Russia* 61°45N 50°40E **70** B9
Sylhet *Bangla.* 24°54N 91°52E **85** G17
Sylhet □ *Bangla.* 24°50N 91°50E **85** G17
Symington *U.K.* 55°36N 3°36W **21** C8
Symonds Yat *U.K.* 51°51N 2°38W **24** C3
Syracuse *U.S.A.* 43°3N 76°9W **113** D9
Syrdarya → *Kazakhstan* 46°3N 61°0E **76** E7
Syria ■ *Asia* 35°0N 38°0E **86** C4
Syrian Desert *Asia* 32°0N 40°0E **86** C4
Syston *U.K.* 52°42N 1°3W **23** G6
Syzran *Russia* 53°12N 48°30E **70** D8
Szczecin *Poland* 53°27N 14°27E **64** B8
Szczecinek = Sichuan □ *China* 30°30N 103°0E **78** E9
Szeged *Hungary* 46°16N 20°10E **65** E11
Székesfehérvár *Hungary* 47°15N 18°25E **65** E10
Szekszárd *Hungary* 46°22N 18°42E **65** E10
Szolnok *Hungary* 47°10N 20°15E **65** E11
Szombathely *Hungary* 47°14N 16°38E **65** E9

T'aitung *Taiwan* 22°43N 121°4E **79** G13
Taiwan ■ *Asia* 23°30N 121°0E **79** G13
Taiwan Str. *Asia* 24°40N 120°0E **79** G12
Taiyuan *China* 37°52N 112°33E **79** D11
Ta'izz *Yemen* 13°35N 44°2E **89** E3
Tak *Thailand* 16°52N 99°8E **82** A1
Takamatsu *Japan* 34°20N 134°5E **81** F4
Takaoka *Japan* 36°47N 137°0E **81** E5
Takasaki *Japan* 36°20N 139°0E **81** E6
Takeshima = Tokdo *Asia* 37°15N 131°52E **81** E2
Takhār □ *Afghan.* 36°40N 70°0E **87** B12
Taklamakan Desert *China* 38°0N 83°0E **78** D5
Talara *Peru* 4°38S 81°18W **120** C1
Talaud, Kepulauan *Indonesia* 4°30N 126°50E **83** D7
Talavera de la Reina *Spain* 39°55N 4°46W **67** C3
Talca *Chile* 35°28S 71°40W **121** F2
Talcahuano *Chile* 36°40S 73°10W **121** F2
Taldyqorghan *Kazakhstan* 45°10N 78°45E **76** E8
Talgarth *U.K.* 52°0N 3°14W **26** D7
Taliabu *Indonesia* 1°50S 125°0E **83** E6
Tallaght *Ireland* 53°17N 6°19W **31** B10
Tallahassee *U.S.A.* 30°27N 84°17W **111** D10
Tallinn *Estonia* 59°22N 24°48E **63** F8
Taloyoak *Canada* 69°32N 93°32W **108** C10
Taltal *Chile* 25°23S 70°33W **121** E2
Tamale *Ghana* 9°22N 0°50W **94** G5
Tamana *Kiribati* 2°30S 175°59E **99** A13
Tamanrasset *Algeria* 22°50N 5°30E **94** D7
Tamar → *U.K.* 50°27N 4°15W **27** G5
Tambov *Russia* 52°45N 41°28E **71** D7
Tame → *U.K.* 52°44N 1°43W **23** G5
Tamerton Foliot *U.K.* 50°25N 4°11W **27** G5
Tamil Nadu □ *India* 11°0N 77°0E **84** P10
Tampa *U.S.A.* 27°56N 82°27W **111** E10
Tampa B. *U.S.A.* 27°50N 82°30W **111** E10
Tampere *Finland* 61°30N 23°50E **63** E8
Tampico *Mexico* 22°13N 97°51W **114** C5
Tamworth *Australia* 31°7S 150°58E **98** G9
Tamworth *U.K.* 52°39N 1°41E **23** G5
Tana → *Kenya* 2°32S 40°31E **96** E8
Tana → *Norway* 70°30N 28°14E **63** C9
Tana, L. *Ethiopia* 13°5N 37°30E **89** E2
Tanami Desert *Australia* 18°50S 132°0E **98** D5
Tanana → *U.S.A.* 65°10N 151°58W **108** C4
Tandil *Argentina* 37°15S 59°6W **121** F4
Tandragee *U.K.* 54°21N 6°24W **29** C9
Tanezrouft *Algeria* 23°9N 0°11E **94** D6
Tanga *Tanzania* 5°5S 39°2E **96** F7
Tanganyika, L. *Africa* 6°40S 30°0E **96** F6
Tanggula Shan *China* 32°40N 92°10E **78** E7
Tanggula Shankou *China* 32°42N 92°27E **78** E7
Tangier *Morocco* 35°50N 5°49W **94** A4
Tangshan *China* 39°38N 118°10E **79** D12
Tanimbar, Kepulauan
  Indonesia 7°30S 131°30E **83** F8
Tanjungbalai *Indonesia* 2°55N 99°44E **82** D1
Tanjungpandan *Indonesia* 2°43S 107°38E **82** E3
Tanjungredeb *Indonesia* 2°9N 117°29E **82** D5
Tanna *Vanuatu* 19°30S 169°20E **99** D12
Tannu Ola *Asia* 51°0N 94°0E **77** D10
Tanta *Egypt* 30°45N 30°57E **95** B12
Tanworth *U.K.* 52°20N 1°50W **24** B5
Tanzania ■ *Africa* 6°0S 34°0E **96** F6
Taolanaro *Madag.* 25°2S 47°0E **97** K9
Taos *U.S.A.* 36°24N 105°35W **110** C5
Tapachula *Mexico* 14°54N 92°17W **114** E6
Tapajós → *Brazil* 2°24S 54°41W **120** C4
Tapti → *India* 21°8N 72°41E **84** J8
Taquaritinga *Brazil* 21°24S 48°30W **122** D1
Tarakan *Indonesia* 3°20N 117°35E **82** D5
Taransay *U.K.* 57°54N 7°0W **18** G3
Táranto *Italy* 40°28N 17°14E **68** D7
Táranto, G. di *Italy* 40°8N 17°20E **68** D7
Tarawa *Kiribati* 1°30N 173°0E **102** G9
Taraz *Kazakhstan* 42°54N 71°22E **87** A12
Tarbagatay, Khrebet *Kazakhstan* 48°0N 83°0E **76** E9
Tarbat Ness *U.K.* 57°52N 3°47W **19** G10
Tarbela Dam *Pakistan* 34°8N 72°52E **84** B8
Tarbert *Argyll & Bute, U.K.* 55°52N 5°25W **20** C5
Tarbert *W. Isles, U.K.* 57°54N 6°49W **18** G4
Tarbes *France* 43°15N 0°3E **66** E4
Tarcoola *Australia* 30°44S 134°36E **98** G5
Taree *Australia* 31°50S 152°30E **98** G9
Tarfaya *Morocco* 27°55N 12°55W **94** C3
Târgovişte *Romania* 44°55N 25°27E **65** F13
Târgu Jiu *Romania* 45°5N 23°19E **65** F12
Târgu Mureş *Romania* 46°31N 24°38E **65** E13
Tarija *Bolivia* 21°30S 64°40W **120** E3
Tarim Basin *China* 40°0N 84°0E **78** D5
Tarim He → *China* 39°30N 88°30E **78** D6
Tarleton *U.K.* 53°41N 2°50W **23** E3
Tarn □ *France* 44°5N 1°6E **66** E4
Tarnów *Poland* 50°3N 21°0E **65** C11
Taroudannt *Morocco* 30°30N 8°52W **94** B4
Tarporley *U.K.* 53°10N 2°40W **23** F3
Tarragona *Spain* 41°5N 1°17E **67** B6
Tarsus *Turkey* 36°58N 34°55E **71** G5
Tartu *Estonia* 58°20N 26°44E **63** F9
Tarțūs *Syria* 34°55N 35°55E **86** C3
Tashkent *Uzbekistan* 41°20N 69°10E **87** A12
Tasiilaq *Greenland* 65°40N 37°20W **54** C6
Tasikmalaya *Indonesia* 7°18S 108°12E **82** F3
Tasman Sea *Pac. Oc.* 36°0S 160°0E **99** H10
Tasmania □ *Australia* 42°0S 146°30E **98** J8
Tassili n'Ajjer *Algeria* 25°47N 8°1E **94** C7
Tatar Str. *Russia* 50°0N 141°0E **77** E14
Tatarstan □ *Russia* 55°30N 51°30E **70** C9
Tatnam, C. *Canada* 57°16N 91°0W **109** D10
Tatra *Slovak Rep.* 49°20N 20°0E **65** D11
Tatta *Pakistan* 24°42N 67°55E **84** G5
Tattenhall *U.K.* 53°7N 2°46W **23** F3
Tatuí *Brazil* 23°25S 47°53W **122** D1
Tatvan *Turkey* 38°31N 42°15E **71** G7
Taubaté *Brazil* 23°0S 45°36W **122** D1
Tauern *Austria* 47°15N 12°40E **64** E7
Taunggyi *Burma* 20°50N 97°0E **85** J20
Taunton *U.K.* 51°1N 3°5W **24** D2
Taunton *U.S.A.* 41°54N 71°6W **113** E12
Taunus *Germany* 50°13N 8°34E **64** C5

Taurus Mts.   Umnak I.

Taurus Mts. *Turkey* 37°0N 32°30E **71 G5**
Tavan Bogd Uul *Mongolia* 49°10N 87°49E **78 B6**
Tavistock *U.K.* 50°33N 4°9W **27 F5**
Taw → *U.K.* 51°4N 4°4W **27 E5**
Tawas City *U.S.A.* 44°16N 83°31W **112 C6**
Tawau *Malaysia* 4°20N 117°55E **82 D5**
Taxkorgan Tajik Zizhixian *China* 37°49N 75°14E **78 D4**
Tay → *U.K.* 56°37N 3°38W **21 A8**
Tay, Firth of *U.K.* 56°25N 3°8W **21 B9**
Tay, L. *U.K.* 56°32N 4°8W **20 A7**
Taylor, Mt. *U.S.A.* 35°14N 107°37W **110 C5**
Taylorville *U.S.A.* 39°33N 89°18W **112 F3**
Tayport *U.K.* 56°27N 2°52W **21 B10**
Taz → *Russia* 67°32N 78°40E **76 C8**
Taza *Morocco* 34°16N 4°6W **94 B5**
Tbilisi *Georgia* 41°43N 44°50E **71 F7**
Tebay *U.K.* 54°26N 2°35W **22 D3**
Tébessa *Algeria* 35°22N 8°8E **94 A7**
Tees → *U.K.* 54°37N 1°10W **22 C6**
Teesdale *U.K.* 54°37N 2°10W **22 C4**
Teesside *U.K.* 54°36N 1°15W **22 C6**
Tegal *Indonesia* 6°52S 109°8E **82 F3**
Tegucigalpa *Honduras* 14°5N 87°14W **114 E7**
Tehrān *Iran* 35°41N 51°25E **87 C7**
Tehuantepec *Mexico* 16°21N 95°13W **114 D5**
Tehuantepec, G. de *Mexico* 15°50N 95°12W **114 D5**
Tehuantepec, Istmo de *Mexico* 17°15N 94°30W **114 D6**
Teifi → *U.K.* 52°5N 4°41W **26 C4**
Teign → *U.K.* 50°32N 3°32W **27 F6**
Teignmouth *U.K.* 50°33N 3°31W **27 F6**
Tejen *Turkmenistan* 37°23N 60°31E **87 B10**
Tekirdağ *Turkey* 40°58N 27°30E **71 F4**
Tel Aviv-Jaffa *Israel* 32°4N 34°48E **86 C3**
Tela *Honduras* 15°40N 87°28W **114 D7**
Telegraph Creek *Canada* 58°0N 131°10W **108 D6**
Teles Pires → *Brazil* 7°21S 58°3W **120 C4**
Telford *U.K.* 52°40N 2°27W **23 G4**
Tell City *U.S.A.* 37°57N 86°46W **112 G4**
Tellicherry *India* 11°45N 75°30E **84 P9**
Telpos Iz *Russia* 63°16N 59°13E **70 B10**
Teluk Intan *Malaysia* 4°3N 101°0E **82 D2**
Tema *Ghana* 5°41N 0°0 **94 G5**
Teme → *U.K.* 52°11N 2°13W **24 B4**
Temirtau *Kazakhstan* 50°5N 72°56E **76 D8**
Témiscaming *Canada* 46°44N 79°5W **112 B8**
Temple *U.S.A.* 31°6N 97°21W **111 D7**
Temple Combe *U.K.* 51°0N 2°24W **24 D4**
Temple Ewell *U.K.* 51°8N 1°17E **25 D11**
Temple Sowerby *U.K.* 54°38N 2°36W **22 C3**
Templemore *Ireland* 52°47N 7°51W **30 C7**
Temuco *Chile* 38°45S 72°40W **121 F2**
Tenali *India* 16°15N 80°35E **85 L12**
Tenbury Wells *U.K.* 52°19N 2°35W **24 B3**
Tenby *U.K.* 51°40N 4°42W **26 D4**
Tenerife *Canary Is.* 28°15N 16°35W **94 C2**
Tengchong *China* 25°0N 98°28E **78 D8**
Tengger Desert *China* 38°0N 104°0E **78 D9**
Tennant Creek *Australia* 19°30S 134°15E **98 E5**
Tennessee □ *U.S.A.* 36°0N 86°30W **111 C9**
Tennessee → *U.S.A.* 37°4N 88°34W **111 C9**
Tenterden *U.K.* 51°4N 0°42E **25 D10**
Teófilo Otoni *Brazil* 17°50S 41°30W **122 C2**
Tepic *Mexico* 21°30N 104°54W **114 C4**
Teraina *Kiribati* 4°43N 160°25W **103 G12**
Téramo *Italy* 42°39N 13°42E **68 C5**
Teresina *Brazil* 5°9S 42°45W **120 C5**
Termiz *Uzbekistan* 37°15N 67°15E **87 B11**
Ternate *Indonesia* 0°45N 127°25E **83 D7**
Terni *Italy* 42°34N 12°37E **68 C5**
Ternopil *Ukraine* 49°30N 25°40E **65 D13**
Terrace *Canada* 54°30N 128°35W **108 D7**
Terrassa *Spain* 41°34N 2°1E **67 B7**
Terre Haute *U.S.A.* 39°28N 87°25W **112 F4**
Terschelling *Neths.* 53°25N 5°20E **64 B3**
Teruel *Spain* 40°22N 1°8W **67 B5**
Tesiyn Gol → *Mongolia* 50°40N 93°20E **78 A7**
Teslin *Canada* 60°10N 132°43W **108 C6**
Teslin → *Canada* 61°34N 134°35W **104 C6**
Test → *U.K.* 50°56N 1°29W **24 E6**
Tetbury *U.K.* 51°38N 2°10W **24 C4**
Tete *Mozam.* 16°13S 33°33E **97 H6**
Tetney *U.K.* 53°29N 0°1W **23 F8**
Tétouan *Morocco* 35°35N 5°21W **94 A4**
Tetovo *Macedonia* 42°1N 20°59E **69 C9**
Teuco → *Argentina* 25°35S 60°11W **121 E3**
Teutoburger Wald *Germany* 52°5N 8°22E **64 B5**
Teviot → *U.K.* 55°29N 2°38W **21 D10**
Teviotdale *U.K.* 55°25N 2°50W **21 D10**
Teviothead *U.K.* 55°20N 2°56W **21 D10**
Tewkesbury *U.K.* 51°59N 2°9W **24 C4**
Texarkana *U.S.A.* 33°26N 94°3W **111 D8**
Texas □ *U.S.A.* 31°40N 98°30W **110 D7**
Texel *Neths.* 53°5N 4°50E **64 B3**
Teynham *U.K.* 51°20N 0°50E **25 D10**
Tezpur *India* 26°40N 92°45E **85 F18**
Thabana Ntlenyana *Lesotho* 29°30S 29°16E **97 K5**
Thabazimbi *S. Africa* 24°40S 27°21E **97 J5**
Thailand ■ *Asia* 16°0N 102°0E **82 A2**
Thailand, G. of *Asia* 11°30N 101°0E **82 B2**
Thal Desert *Pakistan* 31°10N 71°30E **84 D7**
Thame *U.K.* 51°45N 0°58W **25 C7**
Thame → *U.K.* 51°39N 1°9W **24 C6**
Thames → *Canada* 42°20N 82°25W **112 D6**
Thames → *U.K.* 51°29N 0°34E **25 D10**
Thane *India* 19°12N 72°59E **84 K8**
Thanet, I. of *U.K.* 51°21N 1°20E **25 D11**
Thanjavur *India* 10°48N 79°12E **84 P11**
Thar Desert *Pakistan* 28°0N 72°0E **84 F8**
Thargomindah *Australia* 27°58S 143°46E **98 F7**
Thasos *Greece* 40°40N 24°40E **69 D11**
Thatcham *U.K.* 51°24N 1°15W **24 D6**
Thaxted *U.K.* 51°57N 0°22E **25 C10**
The Everglades *U.S.A.* 25°50N 81°0W **111 E10**
The Pas *Canada* 53°45N 101°15W **108 D9**
The Wash *U.K.* 52°58N 0°20E **25 A9**
The Weald *U.K.* 51°4N 0°20E **25 D9**
Theale *U.K.* 51°26N 1°5W **24 D6**
Thebes *Egypt* 25°40N 32°35E **95 C12**

Thelon → *Canada* 64°16N 96°4W **108 C9**
Thermopolis *U.S.A.* 43°39N 108°13W **110 B5**
Thermopylæ *Greece* 38°48N 22°35E **69 E10**
Thessalon *Canada* 46°20N 83°30W **112 B6**
Thessaloniki *Greece* 40°38N 22°58E **69 D10**
Thetford *U.K.* 52°25N 0°45E **25 B10**
Thetford Mines *Canada* 46°8N 71°18W **109 E12**
Thiers *France* 45°52N 3°33E **66 D5**
Thiès *Senegal* 14°50N 16°51W **94 F2**
Thika *Kenya* 1°1S 37°5E **96 E7**
Thimphu *Bhutan* 27°31N 89°45E **85 F16**
Thionville *France* 49°20N 6°10E **66 B7**
Thira = Santorini *Greece* 36°23N 25°27E **69 F11**
Thirlmere *U.K.* 54°32N 3°4W **22 C2**
Thirsk *U.K.* 54°14N 1°19W **22 D6**
Thlewiaza → *Canada* 60°29N 94°40W **108 C10**
Thomasville *U.S.A.* 30°50N 83°59W **111 D10**
Thompson *Canada* 55°45N 97°52W **108 D10**
Thornaby on Tees *U.K.* 54°33N 1°18W **22 C6**
Thornbury *U.K.* 51°36N 2°31W **24 C3**
Thorndon *U.K.* 52°17N 1°9E **25 B11**
Thorne *U.K.* 53°37N 0°57W **23 E7**
Thorney *U.K.* 52°37N 0°6W **25 A8**
Thornham *U.K.* 52°58N 0°35E **25 A10**
Thornhill *U.K.* 54°37N 3°13W **22 C2**
Thornton *U.K.* 53°52N 2°59W **23 E3**
Thornton Dale *U.K.* 54°15N 0°42W **22 D7**
Thorpe *U.K.* 52°38N 1°22E **25 A11**
Thorpe le Soken *U.K.* 51°51N 1°11E **25 C11**
Thrace *Turkey* 41°0N 27°0E **69 D12**
Thrace, Sea of *Greece* 40°30N 25°0E **69 D11**
Thrapston *U.K.* 52°24N 0°32W **25 B7**
Three Gorges Dam *China* 30°45N 111°15E **79 E11**
Threlkeld *U.K.* 54°37N 3°3W **22 C2**
Threshfield *U.K.* 54°4N 2°1W **22 D4**
Thunder B. *U.S.A.* 45°0N 83°20W **112 C6**
Thunder Bay *Canada* 48°20N 89°15W **112 A3**
Thüringer Wald *Germany* 50°35N 11°0E **64 C6**
Thurlby *U.K.* 52°45N 0°22W **23 G8**
Thurles *Ireland* 52°41N 7°49W **30 C7**
Thurmaston *U.K.* 52°40N 1°5W **23 G6**
Thurso *U.K.* 54°51N 3°2W **22 C2**
Thurso → *U.K.* 58°36N 3°32W **19 E10**
Thurso *U.K.* 58°36N 3°32W **19 E10**
Thurston I. *Antarctica* 72°0S 100°0W **55 D16**
Tian Shan *Asia* 40°30N 76°0E **78 C4**
Tianjin *China* 39°7N 117°12E **79 D12**
Tianmen *China* 30°39N 113°9E **79 E11**
Tianshui *China* 34°32N 105°40E **78 E10**
Tiaret *Algeria* 35°20N 1°21E **94 A6**
Tibastī, Sarīr *Libya* 22°50N 18°30E **95 D9**
Tiber → *Italy* 41°44N 12°14E **68 D5**
Tiberias, L. = Galilee, Sea of *Israel* 32°45N 35°35E **86 C3**
Tibesti *Chad* 21°0N 17°30E **95 D9**
Tibet = Xizang Zizhiqu □ *China* 32°0N 88°0E **78 E6**
Tibet, Plateau of *Asia* 32°0N 86°0E **72 E10**
Tiburón, I. *Mexico* 29°0N 112°25W **114 B2**
Ticehurst *U.K.* 51°3N 0°25E **25 D9**
Ticino → *Italy* 45°9N 9°14E **68 B3**
Tickhill *U.K.* 53°26N 1°6W **23 F6**
Ticonderoga *U.S.A.* 43°51N 73°26W **113 D11**
Tideswell *U.K.* 53°17N 1°47W **23 F5**
Tieling *China* 42°20N 123°55E **79 C13**
Tierra de Campos *Spain* 42°10N 4°50W **67 A3**
Tierra del Fuego, I. Grande de *Argentina* 54°0S 69°0W **121 H3**
Tiffin *U.S.A.* 41°7N 83°11W **112 E6**
Tighina *Moldova* 46°50N 29°30E **65 E15**
Tignish *Canada* 46°58N 64°2W **113 B15**
Tigris → *Asia* 31°0N 47°25E **86 D6**
Tijuana *Mexico* 32°32N 117°1W **114 A1**
Tikhoretsk *Russia* 45°56N 40°5E **71 E7**
Tikhvin *Russia* 59°35N 33°30E **70 C5**
Tikrīt *Iraq* 34°35N 43°37E **86 C5**
Tiksi *Russia* 71°40N 128°45E **77 B13**
Tilburg *Neths.* 51°31N 5°6E **64 C3**
Tilbury *U.K.* 51°27N 0°22E **25 D9**
Till → *U.K.* 55°41N 2°13W **22 A4**
Tillicoultry *U.K.* 56°9N 3°45W **21 B8**
Tilmanstone *U.K.* 51°12N 1°18E **25 D11**
Tilt → *U.K.* 56°46N 3°51W **19 J10**
Timaru *N.Z.* 44°23S 171°14E **99 J13**
Timișoara *Romania* 45°43N 21°15E **65 F11**
Timmins *Canada* 48°28N 81°25W **109 E11**
Timor *Asia* 9°0S 125°0E **83 F7**
Timor Leste = East Timor ■ *Asia* 8°50S 126°0E **83 F7**
Timor Sea *Ind. Oc.* 12°0S 127°0E **72 K14**
Tingewick *U.K.* 51°59N 1°2W **24 C6**
Tinogasta *Argentina* 28°5S 67°32W **121 E3**
Tinos *Greece* 37°33N 25°8E **69 F11**
Tintagel *U.K.* 50°39N 4°46W **27 F4**
Tintagel Hd. *U.K.* 50°40N 4°47W **27 F4**
Tipperary *Ireland* 52°28N 8°10W **30 D6**
Tipperary □ *Ireland* 52°37N 7°55W **30 C7**
Tipton *U.K.* 52°32N 2°4W **23 G4**
Tipton *U.S.A.* 41°46N 91°8W **112 E2**
Tiptree *U.K.* 51°48N 0°46E **25 C10**
Tiranë *Albania* 41°18N 19°49E **69 D8**
Tiraspol *Moldova* 46°55N 29°35E **65 E15**
Tirebolu *Turkey* 40°58N 38°45E **71 F6**
Tiree *U.K.* 56°31N 6°55W **20 B2**
Tiree, Passage of *U.K.* 56°30N 6°30W **20 B2**
Tirich Mir *Pakistan* 36°15N 71°55E **84 A7**
Tirol □ *Austria* 47°3N 10°43E **64 E6**
Tiruchchirappalli *India* 10°45N 78°45E **84 P11**
Tirunelveli *India* 8°45N 77°45E **84 Q10**
Tiruppur *India* 11°5N 77°22E **84 P10**
Tisa → *Serbia* 45°15N 20°17E **69 B9**
Tisbury *U.K.* 51°4N 2°5W **24 D4**
Tisdale *Canada* 52°50N 104°0W **108 D9**
Titchfield *U.K.* 50°50N 1°15W **24 E6**
Titicaca, L. *S. Amer.* 15°30S 69°30W **120 D3**
Titusville *U.S.A.* 41°38N 79°41W **112 E8**
Tiverton *U.K.* 50°54N 3°29W **27 F7**
Tivoli *Italy* 41°58N 12°45E **68 D5**
Tizi-Ouzou *Algeria* 36°42N 4°3E **94 A6**
Tlaxiaco *Mexico* 17°25N 97°35W **114 D5**
Tlemcen *Algeria* 34°52N 1°21W **94 B5**

Toamasina *Madag.* 18°10S 49°25E **97 H9**
Toba, Danau *Indonesia* 2°30N 97°30E **82 D1**
Toba Kakar *Pakistan* 31°30N 69°0E **84 D6**
Tobago *Trin. & Tob.* 11°10N 60°30W **120 A3**
Tobermory *Canada* 45°12N 81°40W **112 C7**
Tobermory *U.K.* 56°38N 6°5W **20 A3**
Tobol → *Russia* 58°10N 68°12E **76 D7**
Tobolsk *Russia* 58°15N 68°10E **76 D7**
Tocantins → *Brazil* 1°45S 49°10W **120 C5**
Toddington *U.K.* 51°57N 0°32W **25 C7**
Todmorden *U.K.* 53°43N 2°6W **23 E4**
Todos os Santos, B. de *Brazil* 12°48S 38°38W **122 B3**
Toe Hd. *U.K.* 57°50N 7°8W **18 G3**
Togliatti *Russia* 53°32N 49°24E **70 D8**
Togo ■ *W. Afr.* 8°30N 1°35E **94 G6**
Tok *U.S.A.* 63°20N 142°59W **108 C5**
Tokachi-Dake *Japan* 43°17N 142°5E **81 B8**
Tokat *Turkey* 40°22N 36°35E **71 F6**
Tokdo *Asia* 37°15N 131°52E **81 E2**
Tokelau Is. *Pac. Oc.* 9°0S 171°45W **99 B16**
Tokushima *Japan* 34°4N 134°34E **81 F4**
Tokuyama *Japan* 34°3N 131°50E **81 F2**
Tōkyō *Japan* 35°43N 139°45E **81 F6**
Toledo *Spain* 39°50N 4°2W **67 C3**
Toledo *U.S.A.* 41°39N 83°33W **112 E6**
Toledo, Montes de *Spain* 39°33N 4°20W **67 C3**
Toliara *Madag.* 23°21S 43°40E **97 J8**
Tolima *Colombia* 4°40N 75°19W **120 B2**
Tollesbury *U.K.* 51°45N 0°51E **25 C10**
Toluca *Mexico* 19°17N 99°40W **114 D5**
Tomah *U.S.A.* 43°59N 90°30W **112 D2**
Tomakomai *Japan* 42°38N 141°36E **81 B7**
Tomaszów Mazowiecki *Poland* 51°30N 20°2E **65 C10**
Tombador, Serra do *Brazil* 12°0S 58°0W **120 D4**
Tombigbee → *U.S.A.* 31°8N 87°57W **111 D9**
Tombouctou *Mali* 16°50N 3°0W **94 E5**
Tomini, Teluk *Indonesia* 0°10S 121°0E **83 E6**
Tomintoul *U.K.* 57°15N 3°23W **19 H11**
Tomsk *Russia* 56°30N 85°5E **76 D9**
Tonbridge *U.K.* 51°11N 0°17E **25 D9**
Tone → *U.K.* 50°58N 3°20W **27 F7**
Tong *U.K.* 52°40N 2°17W **23 G4**
Tonga ■ *Pac. Oc.* 19°50S 174°30W **99 D16**
Tonga Trench *Pac. Oc.* 18°0S 173°0W **99 D16**
Tongareva *Cook Is.* 9°0S 158°0W **103 H12**
Tongatapu Group *Tonga* 21°0S 175°0W **99 E16**
Tongchuan *China* 35°6N 109°3E **79 D10**
Tonghua *China* 41°42N 125°58E **79 C13**
Tongliao *China* 43°38N 122°18E **79 C13**
Tongling *China* 30°55N 117°48E **79 E12**
Tongue *U.K.* 58°29N 4°25W **19 F9**
Tongue → *U.S.A.* 46°25N 105°52W **110 A5**
Tonk *India* 26°6N 75°54E **84 F9**
Tonkin, G. of *Asia* 20°0N 108°0E **78 H10**
Tonle Sap *Cambodia* 13°0N 104°0E **82 B2**
Tonopah *U.S.A.* 38°4N 117°14W **110 C3**
Toowoomba *Australia* 27°32S 151°56E **98 F9**
Topeka *U.S.A.* 39°3N 95°40W **111 C7**
Topolobampo *Mexico* 25°36N 109°3W **114 B3**
Topsham *U.K.* 50°41N 3°28W **27 F7**
Tor B. *U.K.* 50°25N 3°33W **27 G6**
Torbay *U.K.* 50°26N 3°31W **27 G6**
Torne älv → *Europe* 65°50N 24°12E **63 D8**
Torneträsk *Sweden* 68°24N 19°15E **63 D7**
Tornio *Finland* 65°50N 24°12E **63 D8**
Toro, Cerro del *Chile* 29°10S 69°50W **121 E3**
Toronto *Canada* 43°39N 79°20W **112 D8**
Torpoint *U.K.* 50°23N 4°13W **27 G5**
Torquay *U.K.* 50°27N 3°32W **27 G6**
Torre del Greco *Italy* 40°47N 14°22E **68 D6**
Torrejón de Ardoz *Spain* 40°27N 3°29W **67 B4**
Torrelavega *Spain* 43°20N 4°5W **67 A3**
Torremolinos *Spain* 36°38N 4°30W **67 D3**
Torrens, L. *Australia* 31°0S 137°50E **98 G6**
Torrent *Spain* 39°27N 0°28W **67 C5**
Torreón *Mexico* 25°33N 103°26W **114 B4**
Torres Strait *Australia* 9°50S 142°20E **98 C7**
Torridge → *U.K.* 51°0N 4°13W **27 E5**
Torridon, L. *U.K.* 57°35N 5°50W **18 G6**
Torthorwald *U.K.* 55°6N 3°32W **21 D8**
Tortola *Br. Virgin Is.* 18°19N 64°45W **115 e**
Tortosa *Spain* 40°49N 0°31E **67 B6**
Toruń *Poland* 53°2N 18°39E **65 B10**
Torver *U.K.* 54°20N 3°6W **22 D2**
Tory I. *Ireland* 55°16N 8°14W **28 A5**
Toscana □ *Italy* 43°25N 11°0E **68 C4**
Toshka Lakes *Egypt* 22°50N 31°0E **95 D12**
Tsugaru Str. *Japan* 41°35N 141°0E **81 C7**
Totland *U.K.* 50°41N 1°32W **24 E5**
Totley *U.K.* 53°20N 1°32W **23 F5**
Totnes *U.K.* 50°26N 3°42W **27 G6**
Totton *U.K.* 50°55N 1°29W **24 E6**
Tottori *Japan* 35°30N 134°15E **81 F4**
Toubkal, Djebel *Morocco* 31°0N 8°0W **94 B4**
Touggourt *Algeria* 33°6N 6°4E **94 B7**
Toul *France* 48°40N 5°53E **66 B6**
Toulon *France* 43°10N 5°55E **66 E6**
Toulouse *France* 43°37N 1°27E **66 E4**
Touraine *France* 47°20N 0°30E **66 C4**
Tournai *Belgium* 50°35N 3°25E **64 C2**
Tournon-sur-Rhône *France* 45°4N 4°50E **66 D6**
Tours *France* 47°22N 0°40E **66 C4**
Towanda *U.S.A.* 41°46N 76°27W **112 E9**
Towcester *U.K.* 52°8N 0°59W **25 B7**
Town Yetholm *U.K.* 55°33N 2°17W **21 C11**
Townsville *Australia* 19°15S 146°45E **98 D8**
Towraghondi *Afghan.* 35°13N 62°16E **84 B3**
Towson *U.S.A.* 39°24N 76°36W **112 F9**
Toyama *Japan* 36°40N 137°15E **81 E5**
Toyohashi *Japan* 34°45N 137°37E **81 F5**
Toyota *Japan* 35°3N 137°7E **81 F5**
Trabzon *Turkey* 41°0N 39°45E **71 F6**
Trafalgar, C. *Spain* 36°10N 6°2W **67 D2**
Trail *Canada* 49°5N 117°40W **108 E8**
Tralee *Ireland* 52°16N 9°42W **30 D3**
Tralee B. *Ireland* 52°17N 9°55W **30 D3**
Tramore *Ireland* 52°10N 7°10W **31 D8**
Tramore B. *Ireland* 52°9N 7°10W **31 D8**
Tranent *U.K.* 55°57N 2°57W **21 C10**
Trang *Thailand* 7°33N 99°38E **82 C1**

Transantarctic Mts. *Antarctica* 85°0S 170°0W **55 E12**
Transylvania *Romania* 46°30N 24°0E **65 E12**
Transylvanian Alps *Romania* 45°30N 25°0E **65 F13**
Trápani *Italy* 38°1N 12°29E **68 E5**
Trasimeno, L. *Italy* 43°8N 12°6E **68 C5**
Traverse City *U.S.A.* 44°46N 85°38W **112 C5**
Trawbreaga B. *Ireland* 55°20N 7°25W **28 A7**
Trawsfynydd *U.K.* 52°54N 3°55W **26 B6**
Tredegar *U.K.* 51°47N 3°14W **26 D7**
Tregaron *U.K.* 52°14N 3°56W **26 C6**
Treinta y Tres *Uruguay* 33°16S 54°17W **121 F4**
Trelew *Argentina* 43°10S 65°20W **121 G3**
Trent → *U.K.* 53°41N 0°42W **23 E7**
Trentham *U.K.* 52°58N 2°11W **23 G4**
Trento *Italy* 46°4N 11°8E **68 A4**
Trenton *Canada* 44°10N 77°34W **112 C9**
Trenton *U.S.A.* 40°14N 74°46W **113 E10**
Tres Arroyos *Argentina* 38°26S 60°20W **121 F3**
Três Corações *Brazil* 21°44S 45°15W **122 D1**
Três Lagoas *Brazil* 20°50S 51°43W **120 E4**
Três Pontas *Brazil* 21°23S 45°29W **122 D1**
Tres Puntas, C. *Argentina* 47°0S 66°0W **121 G3**
Três Rios *Brazil* 22°6S 43°15W **122 D2**
Tresco *U.K.* 49°57N 6°20W **27 H1**
Treviso *Italy* 45°40N 12°15E **68 B5**
Trevose Hd. *U.K.* 50°32N 5°3W **27 F3**
Tribal Areas □ *Pakistan* 33°0N 70°0E **84 C7**
Trichur *India* 10°30N 76°18E **84 P10**
Trier *Germany* 49°45N 6°38E **64 D4**
Trieste *Italy* 45°40N 13°46E **68 B5**
Trim *Ireland* 53°33N 6°48W **29 D8**
Trimdon *U.K.* 54°42N 1°24W **22 C6**
Trimley *U.K.* 51°59N 1°20E **25 C11**
Trincomalee *Sri Lanka* 8°38N 81°15E **84 Q12**
Trindade *Atl. Oc.* 20°20S 29°50W **52 F8**
Trinidad *Bolivia* 14°46S 64°50W **120 D3**
Trinidad *Cuba* 21°48N 80°0W **115 C9**
Trinidad *U.S.A.* 37°10N 104°31W **110 C6**
Trinidad & Tobago ■ *W. Indies* 10°30N 61°20W **115 E12**
Trinity → *U.S.A.* 29°45N 94°43W **111 E8**
Trinity B. *Canada* 48°20N 53°10W **109 E14**
Trinity Is. *U.S.A.* 56°33N 154°25W **108 D4**
Tripoli *Lebanon* 34°31N 35°50E **86 C3**
Tripoli *Libya* 32°49N 13°7E **95 B8**
Tripolitania *N. Afr.* 31°0N 13°0E **95 B8**
Tripura □ *India* 24°0N 92°0E **85 H18**
Tristan da Cunha *Atl. Oc.* 37°6S 12°20W **52 F9**
Trivandrum *India* 8°41N 77°0E **84 Q10**
Trnava *Slovak Rep.* 48°23N 17°35E **65 D9**
Trois-Rivières *Canada* 46°25N 72°34W **109 E12**
Trois-Rivières *Guadeloupe* 15°57N 61°40W **114 b**
Trollhättan *Sweden* 58°17N 12°20E **63 F6**
Trombetas → *Brazil* 1°55S 55°35W **120 C4**
Tromsø *Norway* 69°40N 18°56E **63 D7**
Tronador *Argentina* 41°10S 71°50W **121 G2**
Trondheim *Norway* 63°36N 10°25E **63 E6**
Trondheimsfjorden *Norway* 63°35N 10°30E **63 E6**
Troon *U.K.* 55°33N 4°39W **20 C6**
Trossachs, The *U.K.* 56°14N 4°24W **20 B7**
Trostan *U.K.* 55°3N 6°10W **29 A9**
Trotternish *U.K.* 57°32N 6°15W **18 G5**
Trou Gras Pt. *St. Lucia* 13°51N 60°53W **115 f**
Trout L. *N.W.T., Canada* 60°40N 121°14W **108 C7**
Trout L. *Ont., Canada* 51°20N 93°15W **108 D10**
Trowbridge *U.K.* 51°18N 2°12W **24 D4**
Troy *Turkey* 39°57N 26°12E **71 G4**
Troy *Ala., U.S.A.* 31°48N 85°58W **111 D9**
Troy *N.Y., U.S.A.* 42°44N 73°41W **113 D11**
Troy *Ohio, U.S.A.* 40°2N 84°12W **112 E5**
Troyes *France* 48°19N 4°3E **66 B6**
Trujillo *Honduras* 16°0N 86°0W **114 D7**
Trujillo *Peru* 8°6S 79°0W **120 C2**
Trujillo *Venezuela* 9°22N 70°38W **120 B2**
Truk *Micronesia* 7°25N 151°46E **102 G7**
Trull *U.K.* 51°0N 3°6W **24 E2**
Trumpington *U.K.* 52°10N 0°7E **25 B9**
Truro *Canada* 45°21N 63°14W **109 E13**
Truro *U.K.* 50°16N 5°4W **27 G3**
Tsavo *Kenya* 2°59S 38°28E **96 E7**
Tsetserleg *Mongolia* 47°36N 101°32E **78 B9**
Tshikapa *Dem. Rep. of the Congo* 6°28S 20°48E **96 F4**
Tsiigehtchic *Canada* 67°15N 134°0W **108 C6**
Tsimlyansk Res. *Russia* 48°0N 43°0E **71 E7**
Tskhinvali *Georgia* 42°14N 44°1E **71 F7**
Tsuchiura *Japan* 36°5N 140°15E **81 E7**
Tsugaru Str. *Japan* 41°35N 141°0E **81 C7**
Tsumeb *Namibia* 19°9S 17°44E **97 H3**
Tsuruoka *Japan* 38°44N 139°50E **81 D6**
Tsushima *Japan* 34°20N 129°20E **81 F1**
Tuam *Ireland* 53°31N 8°51W **28 D4**
Tuamotu, Îs. *French Polynesia* 17°0S 144°0W **103 J13**
Tuapse *Russia* 44°5N 39°10E **71 F6**
Tubarão *Brazil* 28°30S 49°0W **121 E5**
Tübingen *Germany* 48°31N 9°4E **64 D5**
Tubruq *Libya* 32°7N 23°55E **95 B10**
Tubuaï, Îs. *French Polynesia* 25°0S 150°0W **103 K13**
Tucson *U.S.A.* 32°13N 110°58W **110 D4**
Tucumcari *U.S.A.* 35°10N 103°44W **110 C6**
Tucupita *Venezuela* 9°2N 62°3W **120 B3**
Tucuruí *Brazil* 3°42S 49°44W **120 C5**
Tucuruí, Represa de *Brazil* 4°0S 49°30W **120 C5**
Tuguegarao *Phil.* 17°35N 121°42E **83 A6**
Tuktoyaktuk *Canada* 69°27N 133°2W **108 C6**
Tula *Russia* 54°13N 37°38E **70 D6**
Tulancingo *Mexico* 20°5N 98°22W **114 C5**
Tulare *U.S.A.* 36°13N 119°21W **110 C3**
Tulcán *Ecuador* 0°48N 77°43W **120 B2**
Tulcea *Romania* 45°13N 28°46E **65 F15**
Tulita *Canada* 64°57N 125°30W **108 C7**
Tulla *Ireland* 52°53N 8°46W **30 C5**
Tullamore *Ireland* 53°16N 7°31W **31 B7**
Tulle *France* 45°16N 1°46E **66 D4**
Tullow *Ireland* 52°49N 6°45W **31 C8**
Tulsa *U.S.A.* 36°10N 95°55W **111 C7**
Tumaco *Colombia* 1°50N 78°45W **120 B2**
Tumbes *Peru* 3°37S 80°27W **120 C1**

Tumucumaque, Serra *Brazil* 2°0N 55°0W **120 B4**
Tunis *Tunisia* 36°50N 10°11E **95 A8**
Tunisia ■ *Africa* 33°30N 9°10E **95 A7**
Tunja *Colombia* 5°33N 73°25W **120 B2**
Tunstall *U.K.* 52°9N 1°27E **25 B11**
Tupaciguara *Brazil* 18°35S 48°42W **122 C1**
Tupelo *U.S.A.* 34°16N 88°43W **111 D9**
Tupiza *Bolivia* 21°30S 65°40W **120 E3**
Turfan Basin *China* 42°40N 89°25E **78 C6**
Turgutlu *Turkey* 38°30N 27°43E **71 G4**
Turin *Italy* 45°3N 7°40E **68 B2**
Turkana, L. *Africa* 3°30N 36°5E **96 D7**
Turkey ■ *Eurasia* 39°0N 36°0E **71 G6**
Türkmenabat *Turkmenistan* 39°6N 63°34E **87 B10**
Türkmenbashi *Turkmenistan* 40°5N 53°5E **87 A8**
Turkmenistan ■ *Asia* 39°0N 59°0E **87 B9**
Turks & Caicos Is. ☑ *W. Indies* 21°20N 71°20W **115 C10**
Turku *Finland* 60°30N 22°19E **63 E8**
Turnberry *U.K.* 55°18N 4°49W **20 D6**
Turneffe Is. *Belize* 17°20N 87°50W **114 D7**
Turpan *China* 43°58N 89°10E **78 C6**
Turriff *U.K.* 57°32N 2°27W **19 G13**
Tuscaloosa *U.S.A.* 33°12N 87°34W **111 D9**
Tuscany = Toscana □ *Italy* 43°25N 11°0E **68 C4**
Tutbury *U.K.* 52°51N 1°41W **23 G5**
Tuticorin *India* 8°50N 78°12E **84 Q11**
Tutuila *Amer. Samoa* 14°19S 170°50W **99 C16**
Tutume *Botswana* 20°30S 27°5E **97 J5**
Tuva □ *Russia* 51°30N 95°0E **77 D10**
Tuvalu ■ *Pac. Oc.* 8°0S 178°0E **99 B14**
Tuxford *U.K.* 53°14N 0°54W **23 F7**
Tuxpan *Mexico* 20°57N 97°24W **114 C5**
Tuxtla Gutiérrez *Mexico* 16°45N 93°7W **114 D6**
Tuz Gölü *Turkey* 38°42N 33°18E **71 G5**
Tuzla *Bos.-H.* 44°34N 18°41E **69 B8**
Tver *Russia* 56°55N 35°59E **70 C6**
Tweed → *U.K.* 55°45N 2°0W **21 C11**
Tweedmouth *U.K.* 55°45N 2°0W **22 A5**
Tweedshaws *U.K.* 55°27N 3°29W **21 D9**
Twenty *U.K.* 52°47N 0°17W **23 G8**
Twin Falls *U.S.A.* 42°34N 114°28W **110 B4**
Two Harbors *U.S.A.* 47°2N 91°40W **112 B2**
Two Rivers *U.S.A.* 44°9N 87°34W **112 C4**
Twyford *Hants., U.K.* 51°1N 1°19W **24 D6**
Twyford *Wokingham, U.K.* 51°28N 0°51W **25 D7**
Tychy *Poland* 50°9N 18°59E **65 C10**
Tydd St. Mary *U.K.* 52°45N 0°7E **23 G9**
Tyler *U.S.A.* 32°21N 95°18W **111 D7**
Tyndrum *U.K.* 56°26N 4°42W **20 B6**
Tyne → *U.K.* 54°59N 1°32W **22 C5**
Tyne & Wear □ *U.K.* 55°6N 1°17W **22 B6**
Tynemouth *U.K.* 55°1N 1°26W **22 B6**
Tyrol = Tirol □ *Austria* 47°3N 10°43E **64 E6**
Tyrone □ *U.K.* 54°38N 7°11W **29 B7**
Tyrrhenian Sea *Medit. S.* 40°0N 12°30E **68 E5**
Tyumen *Russia* 57°11N 65°29E **76 D7**
Tywardreath *U.K.* 50°21N 4°42W **27 G4**
Tywi → *U.K.* 51°48N 4°21W **26 D5**
Tywyn *U.K.* 52°35N 4°5W **26 B5**
Tzaneen *S. Africa* 23°47S 30°9E **97 J6**

U

U.S.A. = United States of America ■
  N. Amer. 37°0N 96°0W **110 C7**
U.S. Virgin Is. ☑ *W. Indies* 18°20N 65°0W **115 e**
Uaupés → *Brazil* 0°2N 67°16W **120 B3**
Ubá *Brazil* 21°8S 43°0W **122 D2**
Ubaitaba *Brazil* 14°18S 39°20W **122 B3**
Ube *Japan* 33°56N 131°15E **81 G2**
Uberaba *Brazil* 19°50S 47°55W **122 C1**
Uberlândia *Brazil* 19°0S 48°20W **122 C1**
Ubon Ratchathani *Thailand* 15°15N 104°50E **82 A2**
Ucayali → *Peru* 4°30S 73°30W **120 C2**
Uckfield *U.K.* 50°58N 0°7E **25 E9**
Udagamandalam *India* 11°30N 76°44E **84 P10**
Udaipur *India* 24°36N 73°44E **84 G8**
Uddingston *U.K.* 55°49N 4°5W **20 C7**
Udine *Italy* 46°3N 13°14E **68 A5**
Udmurtia □ *Russia* 57°30N 52°30E **70 C9**
Udon Thani *Thailand* 17°29N 102°46E **82 A2**
Udupi *India* 13°25N 74°42E **84 N9**
Uele → *Dem. Rep. of the Congo* 3°45N 24°45E **96 D4**
Ufa *Russia* 54°45N 55°55E **70 D10**
Uffculme *U.K.* 50°54N 3°20W **27 F7**
Ufford *U.K.* 52°8N 1°23E **25 B11**
Uganda ■ *Africa* 2°0N 32°0E **96 D6**
Ugborough *U.K.* 50°22N 3°53W **27 G6**
Uig *U.K.* 57°35N 6°21W **18 G5**
Uinta Mts. *U.S.A.* 40°45N 110°30W **110 B4**
Uitenhage *S. Africa* 33°40S 25°28E **97 L5**
Ujjain *India* 23°9N 75°43E **84 H9**
Ujung Pandang *Indonesia* 5°10S 119°20E **83 F5**
Ukhta *Russia* 63°34N 53°41E **70 B9**
Ukiah *U.S.A.* 39°9N 123°13W **110 C2**
Ukraine ■ *Europe* 49°0N 32°0E **71 E5**
Ulaangom *Mongolia* 50°5N 92°10E **78 A7**
Ulaanjirem *Mongolia* 45°5N 105°30E **78 B10**
Ulan Bator *Mongolia* 47°55N 106°53E **78 B10**
Ulan Ude *Russia* 51°45N 107°40E **79 A10**
Ulceby Cross *U.K.* 53°15N 0°7E **23 F9**
Ulhasnagar *India* 19°15N 73°10E **84 K8**
Uliastay *Mongolia* 47°56N 97°28E **78 B8**
Ullapool *U.K.* 57°54N 5°9W **18 G7**
Ulleungdo *S. Korea* 37°30N 130°30E **81 E2**
Ullswater *U.K.* 54°34N 2°52W **22 C3**
Ulm *Germany* 48°23N 9°58E **64 D5**
Ulster □ *U.K.* 54°35N 6°30W **29 B9**
Ulungur He → *China* 47°1N 87°24E **78 B6**
Uluru *Australia* 25°23S 131°5E **98 F5**
Ulva *U.K.* 56°29N 6°13W **20 B3**
Ulverston *U.K.* 54°13N 3°5W **22 D2**
Ulyanovsk *Russia* 54°20N 48°25E **70 D8**
Uman *Ukraine* 48°40N 30°12E **71 E5**
Umeå *Sweden* 63°45N 20°20E **63 E8**
Umeälven → *Sweden* 63°45N 20°20E **63 E8**
Umlazi *S. Africa* 29°59S 30°54E **97 L6**
Umm al Qaywayn *U.A.E.* 25°30N 55°35E **87 E8**
Umnak I. *U.S.A.* 53°15N 168°20W **108 D3**

Umuarama | Wheatley Hill

Umuarama Brazil 23°45S 53°20W 121 E4
Unalakleet U.S.A. 63°52N 160°47W 108 C3
Unalaska U.S.A. 53°53N 166°32W 108 D3
Unalaska I. U.S.A. 53°35N 166°50W 108 D3
'Unayzah Si. Arabia 26°6N 43°58E 86 E5
Uncía Bolivia 18°25S 66°40W 120 D3
Ungava, Pén. d' Canada 60°0N 74°0W 109 D12
Ungava B. Canada 59°30N 67°30W 109 D13
União dos Palmares Brazil 9°10S 36°2W 122 A3
Unimak I. U.S.A. 54°45N 164°0W 108 D3
Union City U.S.A. 36°26N 89°3W 112 G3
Uniontown U.S.A. 39°54N 79°44W 112 F8
United Arab Emirates ■ Asia 23°50N 54°0E 87 F8
United Kingdom ■ Europe 53°0N 2°0W 62 E6
United States of America ■ N. Amer. 37°0N 96°0W 110 C7
Unst U.K. 60°44N 0°53W 18 A16
Unzen-Dake Japan 32°45N 130°17E 81 G2
Upavon U.K. 51°18N 1°48W 24 D5
Upington S. Africa 28°25S 21°15E 97 K4
'Upolu Samoa 13°58S 172°0W 99 C16
Upper Heyford U.K. 51°56N 1°15W 24 C6
Upper Klamath L. U.S.A. 42°25N 121°55W 110 B2
Uppingham U.K. 52°36N 0°43W 23 G7
Uppsala Sweden 59°53N 17°38E 63 F7
Upton U.K. 53°13N 2°53W 23 F3
Upton-upon-Severn U.K. 52°2N 2°12W 24 B4
Upwey U.K. 50°39N 2°29W 24 E4
Ur Iraq 30°55N 46°25E 86 D6
Ural → Kazakhstan 47°0N 51°48E 71 E9
Ural Mts. Eurasia 60°0N 59°0E 70 C10
Uranium City Canada 59°34N 108°37W 108 D9
Uraricoera → Brazil 3°2N 60°30W 120 B3
Urbana Ill., U.S.A. 40°7N 88°12W 112 E3
Urbana Ohio, U.S.A. 40°7N 83°45W 112 E6
Ure → U.K. 54°5N 1°20W 22 D5
Urganch Uzbekistan 41°40N 60°41E 87 A10
Urmia Iran 37°40N 45°0E 86 B6
Urmia, L. Iran 37°50N 45°30E 86 B6
Urmston U.K. 53°27N 2°21W 23 F4
Uroyan, Mts. de Puerto Rico 18°12N 67°0W 115 d
Uruaçu Brazil 14°30S 49°10W 122 B1
Uruapan Mexico 19°24N 102°3W 114 D4
Urubamba → Peru 10°43S 73°48W 120 D2
Uruguai → Brazil 26°0S 53°30W 121 E4
Uruguaiana Brazil 29°50S 57°0W 121 E4
Uruguay ■ S. Amer. 32°30S 56°30W 121 F4
Uruguay → S. Amer. 34°12S 58°18W 117 G5
Ürümqi China 43°45N 87°45E 78 C6
Usa → Russia 66°16N 59°49E 70 A10
Uşak Turkey 38°43N 29°28E 71 G4
Usakos Namibia 21°54S 15°31E 97 J3
Usedom Germany 53°55N 14°2E 64 B8
Ushant France 48°28N 5°6W 66 B1
Ushuaia Argentina 54°50S 68°23W 121 H3
Usk → U.K. 51°33N 2°58W 27 D8
Usolye Sibirskoye Russia 52°48N 103°40E 77 D11
Uspallata, P. de Argentina 32°37S 69°22W 121 F3
Usselby U.K. 53°26N 0°21W 23 F8
Ussuriysk Russia 43°48N 131°59E 81 B2
Ust-Ilimsk Russia 58°3N 102°39E 77 D11
Ust-Kut Russia 56°50N 105°42E 77 D11
Ústí nad Labem Czech Rep. 50°41N 14°3E 64 C8
Ustica Italy 38°42N 13°11E 68 E5
Usu China 44°27N 84°40E 78 C5
Usumacinta → Mexico 18°24N 92°38W 114 D6
Utah □ U.S.A. 39°20N 111°30W 110 C4
Utah L. U.S.A. 40°12N 111°48W 110 B4
Utica U.S.A. 43°6N 75°14W 113 D10
Utrecht Neths. 52°5N 5°8E 64 B3
Utsunomiya Japan 36°30N 139°50E 81 E6
Uttar Pradesh □ India 27°0N 80°0E 84 F12
Uttaradit Thailand 17°36N 100°5E 82 A2
Uttarakhand □ India 30°0N 79°30E 84 D11
Uttoxeter U.K. 52°54N 1°52W 23 G5
Utuado Puerto Rico 18°16N 66°42W 115 d
Uusikaupunki Finland 60°47N 21°25E 63 E8
Uvalde U.S.A. 29°13N 99°47W 110 E7
Uvira Dem. Rep. of the Congo 3°22S 29°3E 96 E5
Uvs Nuur Mongolia 50°20N 92°30E 78 A7
Uyuni Bolivia 20°28S 66°47W 120 E3
Uzbekistan ■ Asia 41°30N 65°0E 87 A10
Uzhhorod Ukraine 48°36N 22°18E 65 D12

V
Vaal → S. Africa 29°4S 23°38E 97 K4
Vaasa Finland 63°6N 21°38E 63 E8
Vadodara India 22°20N 73°10E 84 H8
Vadsø Norway 70°3N 29°50E 63 C9
Vaduz Liech. 47°8N 9°31E 64 E5
Váh → Slovak Rep. 47°43N 18°7E 65 D9
Vail U.S.A. 39°40N 106°20W 110 C5
Vaila U.K. 60°12N 1°36W 18 B14
Val-d'Or Canada 48°7N 77°47W 109 E12
Valdai Hills Russia 57°0N 33°30E 70 C5
Valdés, Pen. Argentina 42°30S 63°45W 121 G3
Valdez U.S.A. 61°7N 146°16W 108 C5
Valdivia Chile 39°50S 73°14W 121 F2
Valdosta U.S.A. 30°50N 83°17W 111 D10
Vale of Glamorgan □ U.K. 51°28N 3°25W 27 F7
Valença Brazil 13°20S 39°5W 122 B3
Valence France 44°57N 4°54E 66 D6
Valencia Spain 39°27N 0°23W 67 C5
Valencia Venezuela 10°11N 68°0W 120 A3
Valencia □ Spain 39°20N 0°40W 67 C5
Valencia, G. de Spain 39°30N 0°20E 67 C6
Valencia I. Ireland 51°54N 10°22W 30 E2
Valenciennes France 50°20N 3°34E 66 A5
Valera Venezuela 9°19N 70°37W 120 B2
Valladolid Mexico 20°41N 88°12W 114 C7
Valladolid Spain 41°38N 4°43W 67 B3
Valledupar Colombia 10°29N 73°15W 120 A2
Vallejo U.S.A. 38°7N 122°14W 110 C2
Vallenar Chile 28°30S 70°50W 121 E2
Valletta Malta 35°54N 14°31E 68 d
Valley U.K. 53°16N 4°34W 26 A4
Valley City U.S.A. 46°55N 98°0W 110 A7
Valparaíso Chile 33°2S 71°40W 121 F2
Van Turkey 38°30N 43°20E 71 G7

Van, L. Turkey 38°30N 43°0E 71 G7
Van Buren U.S.A. 47°10N 67°58W 113 B13
Van Wert U.S.A. 40°52N 84°35W 112 E5
Vanadzor Armenia 40°48N 44°30E 71 F7
Vancouver Canada 49°15N 123°7W 108 E7
Vancouver U.S.A. 45°38N 122°40W 110 A2
Vancouver I. Canada 49°50N 126°0W 108 E7
Vandalia U.S.A. 38°58N 89°6W 112 F3
Vanderhoof Canada 54°0N 124°0W 108 D7
Vänern Sweden 58°47N 13°30E 63 F6
Vännäs Sweden 63°58N 19°48E 63 E7
Vannes France 47°40N 2°47W 66 C2
Vanrhynsdorp S. Africa 31°36S 18°44E 97 L3
Vantaa Finland 60°18N 24°56E 63 E8
Vanua Levu Fiji 16°33S 179°15E 99 D14
Vanuatu ■ Pac. Oc. 15°0S 168°0E 99 D12
Varanasi India 25°22N 83°0E 85 G13
Varangerfjorden Norway 70°3N 29°25E 63 C9
Varberg Sweden 57°6N 12°20E 63 F6
Vardak □ Afghan. 34°0N 68°0E 87 C12
Vardø Norway 70°23N 31°5E 63 C10
Varese Italy 45°48N 8°50E 68 B3
Varginha Brazil 21°33S 45°25W 122 D1
Varna Bulgaria 43°13N 27°56E 69 C12
Vasa Barris → Brazil 11°10S 37°10W 122 B3
Vasterås Sweden 59°37N 16°38E 63 F7
Västervik Sweden 57°43N 16°33E 63 F7
Vaté Vanuatu 17°40S 168°25E 99 D12
Vatersay U.K. 56°55N 7°32W 18 J2
Vatican City ■ Europe 41°54N 12°27E 68 D5
Vatnajökull Iceland 64°30N 16°48W 63 B2
Vättern Sweden 58°25N 14°30E 63 F6
Vaughn U.S.A. 34°36N 105°13W 110 D5
Vava'u Group Tonga 18°40S 174°0W 99 D16
Vega Norway 65°40N 11°55E 63 D6
Vega Baja Puerto Rico 18°27N 66°23W 115 d
Vegreville Canada 53°30N 112°5W 108 D8
Vélez-Málaga Spain 36°48N 4°5W 67 D3
Velhas → Brazil 17°13S 44°49W 122 C2
Velikiye Luki Russia 56°25N 30°32E 70 C5
Veliko Tŭrnovo Bulgaria 43°5N 25°41E 69 C11
Velikonda Range India 14°45N 79°10E 84 M11
Vellore India 12°57N 79°10E 84 N11
Velsk Russia 61°10N 42°5E 70 B7
Vendée □ France 46°50N 1°35W 66 C3
Vendôme France 47°47N 1°3E 66 C4
Venézia, G. di Italy 45°15N 13°0E 68 B5
Venezuela ■ S. Amer. 8°0N 66°0W 120 B3
Venezuela, G. de Venezuela 11°30N 71°0W 120 A2
Vengurla India 15°53N 73°45E 84 M8
Venice Italy 45°27N 12°21E 68 B5
Ventnor U.K. 50°36N 1°12W 24 E6
Ventoux, Mt. France 44°10N 5°17E 66 D6
Ventspils Latvia 57°25N 21°32E 63 F8
Veracruz Mexico 19°11N 96°8W 114 D5
Veraval India 20°53N 70°27E 84 J7
Vercelli Italy 45°19N 8°25E 68 B3
Verde → U.S.A. 33°33N 111°40W 110 D4
Verdun France 49°9N 5°24E 66 B6
Vereeniging S. Africa 26°38S 27°57E 97 K5
Verkhoyansk Russia 67°35N 133°25E 77 C14
Verkhoyansk Ra. Russia 66°0N 129°0E 77 C13
Vermont □ U.S.A. 44°0N 73°0W 113 D11
vernal U.S.A. 40°27N 109°32W 110 B5
Vernon Canada 50°20N 119°15W 108 D8
Vernon U.S.A. 34°9N 99°17W 110 D7
Verona Italy 45°27N 10°59E 68 B4
Versailles France 48°48N 2°7E 66 B5
Vert, C. Senegal 14°45N 17°30W 94 F2
Verwood U.K. 50°52N 1°52W 24 E5
Verviers Belgium 50°37N 5°52E 64 C3
Veryan U.K. 50°13N 4°56W 27 G4
Veryan B. U.K. 50°13N 4°51W 27 G4
Vesoul France 47°40N 6°11E 66 C7
Vesterålen Norway 68°45N 15°0E 63 D7
Vestfjorden Norway 67°55N 14°0E 63 D6
Vesuvio Italy 40°49N 14°26E 68 D6
Veszprém Hungary 47°8N 17°57E 65 E9
Vianópolis Brazil 16°40S 48°35W 122 C1
Viaréggio Italy 43°52N 10°14E 68 C4
Vicenza Italy 45°33N 11°33E 68 B4
Vichada → Colombia 4°55N 67°50W 120 B3
Vichy France 46°9N 3°26E 66 C5
Vickerstown U.K. 54°6N 3°15W 22 D2
Vicksburg U.S.A. 32°21N 90°53W 111 D8
Victoria Canada 48°30N 123°25W 108 E7
Victoria China 22°17N 114°9E 79 a
Victoria U.S.A. 28°48N 97°0W 111 E7
Victoria □ Australia 37°0S 144°0E 98 H7
Victoria Falls Zimbabwe 17°58S 25°52E 97 H5
Victoria I. Canada 71°0N 111°0W 108 B8
Victoria Ld. Antarctica 75°0S 160°0E 55 D11
Victoria Str. Canada 69°31N 100°30W 108 C9
Victoriaville Canada 46°4N 71°56W 113 B12
Vidin Bulgaria 43°59N 22°50E 69 C10
Viedma, L. Argentina 49°30S 72°30W 121 G2
Vienna Austria 48°12N 16°22E 64 D9
Vienne France 45°31N 4°53E 66 D6
Vienne → France 47°13N 0°5E 66 C4
Vientiane Laos 17°58N 102°36E 82 A2
Vieques Puerto Rico 18°8N 65°25W 115 d
Vierge Pt. St. Lucia 13°49N 60°53W 115 f
Vierzon France 47°13N 2°5E 66 C5
Vietnam ■ Asia 19°0N 106°0E 82 A3
Vieux Fort St. Lucia 13°46N 60°58W 115 f
Vigévano Italy 45°19N 8°51E 68 B3
Vigo Spain 42°12N 8°41W 67 A1
Vijayawada India 16°31N 80°39E 85 L12
Vikna Norway 64°55N 10°58E 63 D6
Vila Nova de Gaia Portugal 41°4N 8°40W 67 B1
Vila Velha Brazil 20°20S 40°17W 122 D2
Vilaine → France 47°30N 2°27W 66 C2
Vilhelmina Sweden 64°35N 16°39E 63 E7
Vilhena Brazil 12°40S 60°5W 120 D3
Vilkitski Str. Russia 78°0N 103°0E 77 B11
Villa Bella Bolivia 10°25S 65°22W 120 D3
Villa Maria Argentina 32°20S 63°10W 121 F3
Villach Austria 46°37N 13°51E 64 E7
Villahermosa Mexico 17°59N 92°55W 114 D6
Villajoyosa Spain 38°30N 0°12W 67 C5

Villarrica Paraguay 25°40S 56°30W 121 E4
Villavicencio Colombia 4°9N 73°37W 120 B2
Ville-Marie Canada 47°20N 79°30W 112 B8
Villeneuve-sur-Lot France 44°24N 0°42E 66 D4
Vilnius Lithuania 54°38N 25°19E 63 G9
Vilyuy → Russia 64°24N 126°26E 77 C13
Vilyuysk Russia 63°40N 121°35E 77 C13
Viña del Mar Chile 33°0S 71°30W 121 F2
Vincennes U.S.A. 38°41N 87°32W 112 F4
Vindhya Ra. India 22°50N 77°0E 84 H10
Vineland U.S.A. 39°29N 75°2W 113 F10
Vinnytsya Ukraine 49°15N 28°30E 65 D15
Virden Canada 49°50N 100°56W 108 E9
Virgin → U.S.A. 36°28N 114°21W 110 C4
Virgin Gorda Br. Virgin Is. 18°30N 64°26W 115 e
Virgin Is. (British) ☑ W. Indies 18°30N 64°30W 115 e
Virgin Is. (U.S.) ☑ W. Indies 18°20N 65°0W 115 e
Virginia S. Africa 28°8S 26°55E 97 K5
Virginia U.S.A. 47°31N 92°32W 111 A8
Virginia □ U.S.A. 37°30N 78°45W 112 G8
Virginia Beach U.S.A. 36°49N 76°9W 111 C11
Viroqua U.S.A. 43°34N 90°53W 112 D2
Vis Croatia 43°4N 16°10E 68 C7
Visalia U.S.A. 36°20N 119°18W 110 C3
Visby Sweden 57°37N 18°18E 63 F7
Viscount Melville Sd. Canada 74°10N 108°0W 109 B9
Vishakhapatnam India 17°45N 83°20E 85 L13
Vistula → Poland 54°22N 18°55E 65 A10
Vitebsk Belarus 55°10N 30°15E 70 C5
Viterbo Italy 42°25N 12°6E 68 C5
Viti Levu Fiji 17°30S 177°30E 99 D14
Vitim → Russia 59°26N 112°34E 77 D12
Vitória Brazil 20°20S 40°22W 122 D2
Vitória da Conquista Brazil 14°51S 40°51W 122 B2
Vitoria-Gasteiz Spain 42°50N 2°41W 67 A4
Vittória Italy 36°57N 14°32E 68 F6
Vizianagaram India 18°6N 83°30E 85 K13
Vladikavkaz Russia 43°0N 44°35E 71 F7
Vladimir Russia 56°15N 40°30E 70 C7
Vladivostok Russia 43°10N 131°53E 77 E14
Vlissingen Neths. 51°26N 3°34E 64 C2
Vlorë Albania 40°32N 19°28E 69 D8
Vltava → Czech Rep. 50°21N 14°30E 64 D8
Voe U.K. 60°21N 1°16W 18 B15
Vogelsberg Germany 50°31N 9°12E 64 C5
Vohimena, Tanjon' i Madag. 25°36S 45°8E 97 K9
Voi Kenya 3°25S 38°32E 96 E7
Vojvodina □ Serbia 45°20N 20°0E 69 B9
Volga → Russia 46°0N 48°30E 71 E8
Volga Hts. Russia 51°0N 46°0E 71 D8
Volgodonsk Russia 47°33N 42°5E 71 E7
Volgograd Russia 48°40N 44°25E 71 E7
Volgograd Res. Russia 50°0N 45°20E 71 D8
Vologda Russia 59°10N 39°45E 70 C6
Volos Greece 39°24N 22°59E 69 E10
Volsk Russia 52°5N 47°22E 70 D8
Volta → Ghana 5°46N 0°41E 94 G6
Volta, L. Ghana 7°30N 0°0 94 G6
Volta Redonda Brazil 22°31S 44°5W 122 D2
Volzhskiy Russia 48°56N 44°46E 71 E7
Vorkuta Russia 67°48N 64°20E 70 A11
Voronezh Russia 51°40N 39°10E 71 D6
Vosges France 48°20N 7°10E 66 B7
Vostok I. Kiribati 10°5S 152°23W 103 J12
Votkinsk Russia 57°0N 53°55E 70 C9
Vratsa Bulgaria 43°15N 23°30E 69 C10
Vryburg S. Africa 26°55S 24°45E 97 K4
Vryheid S. Africa 27°45S 30°47E 97 K6
Vulcano Italy 38°24N 14°58E 68 E6
Vung Tau Vietnam 10°21N 107°4E 82 B3
Vyazma Russia 55°10N 34°15E 70 C5
Vyborg Russia 60°43N 28°47E 70 B4
Vychegda → Russia 61°18N 46°36E 70 B8
Vyrnwy, L. U.K. 52°48N 3°31W 26 B6
Vyshniy Volochek Russia 57°30N 34°30E 70 C5

W
Waal → Neths. 51°37N 5°0E 64 C3
Wabasca → Canada 58°22N 115°20W 108 D8
Wabash U.S.A. 40°48N 85°49W 112 E5
Wabash → U.S.A. 37°48N 88°2W 112 G3
Waco U.S.A. 31°33N 97°9W 111 D7
Wad Medani Sudan 14°28N 33°30E 95 F12
Waddesdon U.K. 51°51N 0°55W 25 C7
Waddingham U.K. 53°27N 0°32W 23 F7
Waddington U.K. 53°10N 0°32W 23 F7
Waddington, Mt. Canada 51°23N 125°15W 108 D7
Wadebridge U.K. 50°31N 4°51W 27 F4
Wadhurst U.K. 51°3N 0°20E 25 D9
Wadi Halfa Sudan 21°53N 31°19E 95 D12
Wager B. Canada 65°26N 88°40W 109 C11
Wagga Wagga Australia 35°7S 147°24E 98 H8
Wah Pakistan 33°45N 72°40E 84 C8
Wahiawā U.S.A. 21°30N 158°2W 110 H15
Waigeu Indonesia 0°20S 130°40E 83 E8
Wailuku U.S.A. 20°53N 156°30W 110 H16
Wainfleet All Saints U.K. 53°7N 0°15E 23 F9
Wakayama Japan 34°15N 135°15E 81 F4
Wake I. Pac. Oc. 19°18N 166°36E 102 F8
Wakefield Jamaica 18°26N 77°42W 114 a
Wakefield U.K. 53°41N 1°29W 23 E6
Wakkanai Japan 45°28N 141°35E 81 A7
Walberswick U.K. 52°19N 1°40E 25 B12
Walbrzych Poland 50°45N 16°18E 64 C9
Walbury Hill U.K. 51°21N 1°28W 24 D6
Waldron U.K. 50°56N 0°13E 25 D9
Wales □ U.K. 52°19N 4°43W 26 C4
Walgett Australia 30°0S 148°5E 98 G8
Walker L. U.S.A. 38°42N 118°43W 110 C3
Walla Walla U.S.A. 46°4N 118°20W 110 A3
Wallaceburg Canada 42°34N 82°23W 112 D6
Wallachia Romania 44°35N 25°0E 65 F13
Wallasey U.K. 53°25N 3°2W 23 F2
Wallingford U.K. 51°35N 1°8W 24 C6
Wallis & Futuna, Is. Pac. Oc. 13°18S 176°10W 99 C15

Walls U.K. 60°14N 1°33W 18 B14
Wallsend U.K. 54°59N 1°31W 22 C5
Walmer U.K. 51°11N 1°25E 25 D11
Walney, I. of U.K. 54°6N 3°15W 22 D2
Walpole U.K. 52°45N 0°13E 25 A9
Walsall U.K. 52°35N 1°58W 23 G5
Walsenburg U.S.A. 37°38N 104°47W 110 C6
Walsoken U.K. 52°41N 0°11E 25 A9
Waltham U.K. 53°31N 0°7W 23 E8
Waltham Abbey U.K. 51°41N 0°1E 25 C9
Waltham Forest □ U.K. 51°35N 0°0 25 C9
Waltham on the Wolds U.K. 52°50N 0°48W 23 G7
Walton-on-the-Naze U.K. 51°51N 1°17E 25 C11
Walvis Bay Namibia 23°0S 14°28E 97 J2
Wamba Dem. Rep. of the Congo 2°10N 27°57E 96 D5
Wanborough U.K. 51°33N 1°42W 24 C5
Wandsworth □ U.K. 51°27N 0°11W 25 D8
Wanganui N.Z. 39°56S 175°3E 99 H14
Wanleweyne Somali Rep. 2°37N 44°54E 89 G3
Wansbeck → U.K. 55°10N 1°32W 22 B5
Wantage U.K. 51°35N 1°25W 24 C6
Wanxian China 30°42N 108°20E 78 E10
Wapakoneta U.S.A. 40°34N 84°12W 112 E5
Warangal India 17°58N 79°35E 84 L11
Warboys U.K. 52°24N 0°4W 25 B8
Ward Ireland 53°26N 6°20W 31 B10
Wardha India 20°45N 78°39E 84 J11
Wardington U.K. 52°7N 1°17W 24 B6
Wardle U.K. 53°7N 2°35W 23 F3
Ward's Stone U.K. 54°1N 2°36W 23 D3
Ware U.K. 51°49N 0°2E 25 C8
Wareham U.K. 50°42N 2°7W 24 E4
Wark U.K. 55°6N 2°14W 22 B4
Warkworth U.K. 55°21N 1°37W 22 B5
Warley U.K. 52°30N 1°59W 23 H5
Warminster U.K. 51°12N 2°10W 24 D4
Warrego → Australia 30°24S 145°21E 98 G8
Warren Mich., U.S.A. 42°28N 83°1W 112 D6
Warren Ohio, U.S.A. 41°14N 80°49W 112 E7
Warren Pa., U.S.A. 41°51N 79°9W 112 E8
Warrenpoint U.K. 54°6N 6°15W 29 C9
Warri Nigeria 5°30N 5°41E 94 G7
Warrington U.K. 53°24N 2°35W 23 F3
Warrnambool Australia 38°25S 142°30E 98 H7
Warsaw Poland 52°14N 21°0E 65 B11
Warsaw U.S.A. 41°14N 85°51W 112 E5
Warsop U.K. 53°12N 1°9W 23 F6
Warta → Poland 52°35N 14°39E 64 B8
Warwick U.K. 52°18N 1°35W 24 B5
Warwick U.S.A. 41°42N 71°28W 113 E12
Warwickshire □ U.K. 52°14N 1°38W 24 B5
Wasatch Ra. U.S.A. 40°0N 111°30W 110 B4
Wash, The U.K. 52°58N 0°20E 23 E9
Washburn U.S.A. 46°40N 90°54W 112 B2
Washford U.K. 51°9N 3°21W 24 D2
Washington U.K. 54°55N 1°30W 22 C6
Washington D.C., U.S.A. 38°53N 77°2W 112 F9
Washington Ind., U.S.A. 38°40N 87°10W 112 F4
Washington Pa., U.S.A. 40°10N 80°15W 112 E7
Washington □ U.S.A. 47°30N 120°30W 110 A2
Washington, Mt. U.S.A. 44°16N 71°18W 113 C12
Washington I. U.S.A. 45°23N 86°54W 112 C4
Wasilla U.S.A. 61°35N 149°26W 108 C5
Waskaganish Canada 51°30N 78°40W 109 D12
Wast Water U.K. 54°26N 3°18W 22 D2
Watampone Indonesia 4°29S 120°25E 83 E6
Watchet U.K. 51°10N 3°19W 24 D2
Waterbeach U.K. 52°16N 0°12E 25 B9
Waterbury U.S.A. 41°33N 73°3W 113 E11
Waterford Ireland 52°15N 7°8W 31 D8
Waterford □ Ireland 52°10N 7°40W 31 D7
Waterford Harbour Ireland 52°8N 6°58W 31 D9
Watergate B. U.K. 50°26N 5°4W 27 G3
Waterloo Canada 43°30N 80°32W 112 D7
Waterloo Ill., U.S.A. 38°20N 90°9W 112 F2
Waterloo Iowa, U.S.A. 42°30N 92°21W 111 B8
Watermeet U.S.A. 46°16N 89°11W 112 B3
Watertown N.Y., U.S.A. 43°59N 75°55W 113 D10
Watertown S. Dak., U.S.A. 44°54N 97°7W 111 B7
Watertown Wis., U.S.A. 43°12N 88°43W 112 D3
Waterville U.S.A. 44°33N 69°38W 113 C13
Watford U.K. 51°40N 0°24W 25 C8
Watlington Norfolk, U.K. 52°40N 0°24E 25 A9
Watlington Oxon., U.K. 51°38N 1°0W 24 C6
Watrous Canada 51°40N 105°25W 108 D9
Watsa Dem. Rep. of the Congo 3°4N 29°30E 96 D5
Watseka U.S.A. 40°47N 87°44W 112 E4
Watson Lake Canada 60°6N 128°49W 108 C7
Watton U.K. 52°34N 0°51E 25 A10
Waukegan U.S.A. 42°22N 87°50W 112 D4
Waukesha U.S.A. 43°1N 88°14W 112 D3
Waupaca U.S.A. 44°21N 89°5W 112 C3
Waupun U.S.A. 43°38N 88°44W 112 D3
Wausau U.S.A. 44°58N 89°38W 112 C3
Wautoma U.S.A. 44°4N 89°18W 112 C3
Wauwatosa U.S.A. 43°2N 88°0W 112 D4
Waveney → U.K. 52°35N 1°39E 25 A12
Waver → U.K. 54°50N 3°15W 22 C2
Wâw Sudan 7°45N 28°1E 95 G11
Waycross U.S.A. 31°13N 82°21W 111 D10
Wayne U.S.A. 38°13N 82°27W 112 F6
Waynesboro U.S.A. 38°4N 78°53W 112 F8
Waynesburg U.S.A. 39°54N 80°11W 112 F7
Wazirabad Pakistan 32°30N 74°8E 84 C9
Weald, The U.K. 51°4N 0°20E 25 D9
Wear → U.K. 54°55N 1°23W 22 C6
Weardale U.K. 54°44N 2°5W 22 C4
Wearhead U.K. 54°45N 2°13W 22 C4
Weaver → U.K. 53°17N 2°35W 23 F3
Weaverham U.K. 53°16N 2°35W 23 F3
Webster Springs U.S.A. 38°29N 80°25W 112 F7
Weddell Sea Antarctica 72°30S 40°0W 55 D1
Wedmore U.K. 51°13N 2°44W 24 D3
Wednesbury U.K. 52°34N 2°1W 23 G4
Wednesfield U.K. 52°37N 2°2W 23 G4
Weedon Bec U.K. 52°15N 1°5W 24 B6
Weifang China 36°44N 119°7E 79 D12
Weihai China 37°30N 122°6E 79 D13
Weipa Australia 12°40S 141°50E 98 C7

Welch U.S.A. 37°26N 81°35W 112 G7
Weldon U.K. 55°17N 1°45W 22 B5
Welford Northants., U.K. 52°25N 1°3W 24 B6
Welford W. Berkshire, U.K. 51°27N 1°24W 24 D6
Welkom S. Africa 28°0S 26°46E 97 K5
Welland Canada 43°0N 79°15W 112 D8
Welland → U.K. 52°51N 0°5W 23 G8
Wellesley Is. Australia 16°42S 139°30E 98 D6
Wellingborough U.K. 52°19N 0°41W 25 B7
Wellington N.Z. 41°19S 174°46E 99 J13
Wellington Somst., U.K. 50°58N 3°13W 24 E2
Wellington Telford & Wrekin, U.K. 52°42N 2°30W 23 G3
Wellington, I. Chile 49°30S 75°0W 121 G2
Wellington Chan. Canada 75°0N 93°0W 109 B10
Wells U.K. 51°13N 2°39W 24 D3
Wells-next-the-Sea U.K. 52°57N 0°51E 25 A10
Wellsboro U.S.A. 41°45N 77°18W 112 E9
Wellsville U.S.A. 42°7N 77°57W 112 D9
Welney U.K. 52°31N 0°15E 25 A9
Wels Austria 48°9N 14°1E 64 D8
Welshpool U.K. 52°39N 3°8W 26 B7
Welton U.K. 53°18N 0°29W 23 F8
Welwyn Garden City U.K. 51°48N 0°12W 25 C8
Wem U.K. 52°52N 2°44W 23 G3
Wembury U.K. 50°19N 4°6W 27 G5
Wemindji Canada 53°0N 78°49W 109 D12
Wemyss Bay U.K. 55°53N 4°53W 20 C6
Wenatchee U.S.A. 47°25N 120°19W 110 A2
Wendover U.K. 51°45N 0°44W 25 C7
Wenlock Edge U.K. 52°30N 2°43W 23 H3
Wensleydale U.K. 54°17N 2°0W 22 D4
Wensu China 41°15N 80°10E 78 C5
Wensum → U.K. 52°40N 1°15E 25 A11
Wenzhou China 28°0N 120°38E 79 F13
Weobley U.K. 52°11N 2°50W 24 B3
Werrington U.K. 50°39N 4°23W 27 F5
Weser → Germany 53°36N 8°28E 64 B5
West Antarctica Antarctica 80°0S 90°0W 55 D15
West Auckland U.K. 54°38N 1°43W 22 C5
West Bank ■ Asia 32°6N 35°13E 86 C3
West Bend U.S.A. 43°25N 88°11W 112 D3
West Bengal □ India 23°0N 88°0E 85 H16
West Berkshire □ U.K. 51°25N 1°17W 24 D6
West Beskids Europe 49°30N 19°0E 65 D10
West Bridgford U.K. 52°55N 1°8W 23 G6
West Bromwich U.K. 52°32N 1°59W 23 G5
West Burra U.K. 60°5N 1°21W 18 B15
West Calder U.K. 55°51N 3°33W 21 C8
West Coker U.K. 50°55N 2°40W 24 E3
West Falkland Falk. Is. 51°40S 60°0W 121 H3
West Fen U.K. 53°5N 0°5W 23 F8
West Frankfort U.S.A. 37°54N 88°55W 111 C9
West Grinstead U.K. 50°58N 0°19W 25 E8
West Haddon U.K. 52°20N 1°3W 24 B6
West Kirby U.K. 53°23N 3°11W 23 F2
West Linton U.K. 55°46N 3°21W 21 C9
West Lulworth U.K. 50°37N 2°14W 24 E4
West Malling U.K. 51°17N 0°26E 25 D9
West Meon U.K. 51°1N 1°5W 24 D6
West Mersea U.K. 51°46N 0°56E 25 C10
West Midlands □ U.K. 52°26N 2°0W 23 H5
West Moors U.K. 50°49N 1°53W 24 E5
West Palm Beach U.S.A. 26°43N 80°3W 111 E10
West Point U.S.A. 37°32N 76°48W 112 G9
West Rasen U.K. 53°23N 0°24W 23 F8
West Seneca U.S.A. 42°51N 78°48W 112 D8
West Siberian Plain Russia 62°0N 75°0E 72 B9
West Sussex □ U.K. 50°55N 0°30W 25 E8
West Virginia □ U.S.A. 38°45N 80°30W 112 F7
West Yorkshire □ U.K. 53°45N 1°40W 23 E5
Westbourne U.K. 50°52N 0°55W 25 E7
Westbrook U.S.A. 43°41N 70°22W 113 D12
Westbury Shrops., U.K. 52°41N 2°55W 23 G3
Westbury Wilts., U.K. 51°15N 2°11W 24 D4
Westbury-on-Severn U.K. 51°50N 2°25W 24 C4
Wester Ross U.K. 57°37N 4°51W 18 G6
Westerham U.K. 51°16N 0°5E 25 D9
Western Australia □ Australia 25°0S 118°0E 98 F2
Western Ghats India 14°0N 75°0E 84 N9
Western Isles □ U.K. 57°30N 7°10W 18 D1
Western Sahara ■ Africa 25°0N 13°0W 94 D3
Westerwald Germany 50°38N 7°56E 64 C4
Westfield U.K. 50°55N 0°35E 25 E10
Westhill U.K. 57°9N 2°19W 19 H13
Westhoughton U.K. 53°33N 2°31W 23 E3
Westmeath □ Ireland 53°33N 7°34W 28 D6
Westminster U.S.A. 39°34N 76°59W 112 F9
Weston U.K. 52°51N 2°1W 23 G4
Weston U.S.A. 39°2N 80°28W 112 F7
Weston-super-Mare U.K. 51°21N 2°58W 24 D3
Westport Ireland 53°48N 9°31W 28 D2
Westray U.K. 59°18N 3°0W 19 D11
Westruther U.K. 55°45N 2°35W 21 C10
Westward Ho! U.K. 51°2N 4°15W 27 E5
Wetar Indonesia 7°48S 126°30E 83 F7
Wetaskiwin Canada 52°55N 113°24W 108 D8
Wetherby U.K. 53°56N 1°23W 23 E6
Wetwang U.K. 54°1N 0°35W 23 D7
Wewak Papua N. G. 3°38S 143°41E 98 A7
Wexford Ireland 52°20N 6°25W 31 D10
Wexford □ Ireland 52°20N 6°25W 31 D10
Wexford Harbour Ireland 52°20N 6°25W 31 D10
Wey → U.K. 51°22N 0°27W 25 D8
Weybourne U.K. 52°57N 1°9E 25 A11
Weybridge U.K. 51°22N 0°27W 25 D8
Weyburn Canada 49°40N 103°50W 108 E9
Weymouth U.K. 50°37N 2°28W 24 E4
Wha Ti Canada 63°8N 117°16W 108 C8
Whale Cove Canada 62°10N 92°34W 108 C10
Whales, B. of Antarctica 78°0S 160°0W 55 D12
Whalley U.K. 53°49N 2°24W 23 E4
Whalsay U.K. 60°22N 0°59W 18 B16
Whalton U.K. 55°8N 1°46W 22 B5
Whangarei N.Z. 35°43S 174°21E 99 H13
Whaplode U.K. 52°42N 0°3W 23 G8
Wharfe → U.K. 53°51N 1°9W 23 E6
Wharfedale U.K. 54°6N 2°1W 22 D4
Wheatley Hill U.K. 54°45N 1°23W 22 C6

Wheeler Pk. U.S.A. 38°57N 114°15W 110 C4
Wheeling U.S.A. 40°4N 80°43W 112 E7
Whernside U.K. 54°14N 2°24W 22 D4
Whicham U.K. 54°15N 3°21W 22 D2
Whimple U.K. 50°46N 3°20W 27 F7
Whipsnade U.K. 51°51N 0°32W 25 C7
Whissendine U.K. 52°43N 0°46W 23 G7
Whitburn U.K. 55°52N 3°40W 21 C8
Whitby U.K. 54°29N 0°37W 22 D7
Whitchurch Devon, U.K. 50°32N 4°9W 27 F5
Whitchurch Hants., U.K. 51°14N 1°20W 24 D6
Whitchurch Hereford, U.K. 51°51N 2°39W 24 C3
Whitchurch Shrops., U.K. 52°59N 2°40W 23 G3
White → Ark., U.S.A. 33°57N 91°5W 111 D8
White → Ind., U.S.A. 38°25N 87°45W 112 F4
White → Utah, U.S.A. 40°4N 109°41W 110 B5
White Esk → U.K. 55°13N 3°11W 21 D9
White Horse, Vale of U.K. 51°37N 1°30W 24 C5
White Horse Hill U.K. 51°34N 1°33W 24 C5
White Mts. Calif., U.S.A. 37°30N 118°15W 110 C3
White Mts. N.H., U.S.A. 44°15N 71°15W 111 B12
White Nile → Sudan 15°38N 32°31E 95 E12
White Sea Russia 66°30N 38°0E 70 A6
Whiteadder Water → U.K. 55°51N 2°25W 21 C11
Whitecourt Canada 54°10N 115°45W 108 D8
Whitefish Pt. U.S.A. 46°45N 84°59W 112 B5
Whitehall U.S.A. 44°22N 91°19W 112 C2
Whitehaven U.K. 54°33N 3°35W 22 C1
Whitehorse Canada 60°43N 135°3W 108 C6
Whitesand B. U.K. 50°21N 4°18W 27 G5
Whitewater U.S.A. 42°50N 88°44W 112 D3
Whithorn U.K. 54°44N 4°26W 20 E7
Whitley Bay U.K. 55°3N 1°27W 22 B6
Whitney, Mt. U.S.A. 36°35N 118°18W 110 C3
Whitstable U.K. 51°21N 1°3E 25 D11
Whittington Derby, U.K. 53°16N 1°26W 23 F6
Whittington Shrops., U.K. 52°52N 3°0W 23 G3
Whittlesey U.K. 52°33N 0°8W 25 A8
Whittlesford U.K. 52°7N 0°9E 25 B9
Whitwell Derby, U.K. 53°17N 1°12W 23 F6
Whitwell I. of W., U.K. 50°36N 1°15W 24 E6
Whitwick U.K. 52°45N 1°22W 23 G6
Whitworth U.K. 53°39N 2°11W 23 E4
Wholdaia L. Canada 60°43N 104°20W 108 C9
Whyalla Australia 33°2S 137°30E 98 G6
Wiarton Canada 44°40N 81°10W 112 C7
Wiay U.K. 57°24N 7°13W 18 H3
Wichita U.S.A. 37°42N 97°20W 111 C7
Wichita Falls U.S.A. 33°54N 98°30W 110 D7
Wick U.K. 58°26N 3°5W 19 F11
Wickford U.K. 51°36N 0°33E 25 C9
Wickham U.K. 50°54N 1°11W 24 E6
Wickham Market U.K. 52°9N 1°23E 25 B11
Wicklow Ireland 52°59N 6°3W 31 C10
Wicklow □ Ireland 52°57N 6°25W 31 C10
Wicklow Hd. Ireland 52°58N 6°0W 31 C11
Wicklow Mts. Ireland 52°58N 6°26W 31 C10
Wicklow Mts. △ Ireland 53°6N 6°21W 31 B11
Wickwar U.K. 51°36N 2°23W 24 C4
Widdrington U.K. 55°15N 1°35W 22 B5
Widecombe U.K. 50°34N 3°49W 27 F6
Widemouth U.K. 50°47N 4°34W 27 F4
Widnes U.K. 53°23N 2°45W 23 F3
Wiener Neustadt Austria 47°49N 16°16E 64 E9
Wiesbaden Germany 50°4N 8°14E 64 C5
Wigan U.K. 53°33N 2°38W 23 E3
Wight, I. of U.K. 50°41N 1°17W 24 E6
Wight, Isle of □ U.K. 50°41N 1°17W 24 E6
Wigmore U.K. 52°19N 2°51W 24 B3
Wigston U.K. 52°35N 1°6W 23 G6
Wigton U.K. 54°50N 3°10W 22 C2
Wigtown U.K. 54°53N 4°27W 20 E7
Wigtown B. U.K. 54°46N 4°15W 20 E7
Wilhelm, Mt. Papua N. G. 5°50S 145°1E 98 B8
Wilhelmshaven Germany 53°31N 8°7E 64 B5
Wilkes-Barre U.S.A. 41°15N 75°53W 113 E10
Wilkes Land Antarctica 69°0S 120°0E 55 D9
Wilkins Ice Shelf Antarctica 70°30S 72°0W 55 D17
Willemstad Neth. Ant. 12°5N 68°55W 115 E11
Willenhall U.K. 52°36N 2°2W 23 G4
Willesborough U.K. 51°8N 0°56E 25 D10
Williams Lake Canada 52°10N 122°10W 108 D7
Williamsburg U.S.A. 37°16N 76°43W 112 G9
Williamson U.S.A. 37°41N 82°17W 112 G6
Williamsport U.S.A. 41°15N 77°1W 112 E9
Willingdon U.K. 50°47N 0°17E 25 E9
Williston U.S.A. 48°9N 103°37W 110 A6
Williston L. Canada 56°0N 124°0W 108 D7
Williton U.K. 51°9N 3°19W 24 D3
Willmar U.S.A. 45°7N 95°3W 111 A7
Willoughby U.K. 53°13N 0°12E 23 F9
Wilmington U.K. 50°47N 3°7W 27 F7
Wilmington Del., U.S.A. 39°45N 75°33W 113 F10
Wilmington N.C., U.S.A. 34°14N 77°55W 111 D11
Wilmslow U.K. 53°19N 2°13W 23 F4
Wilnecote U.K. 52°36N 1°39W 23 G5
Wilton U.K. 51°5N 1°51W 24 D5
Wiltshire □ U.K. 51°18N 1°53W 24 D5
Wimblington U.K. 52°31N 0°4E 25 A9
Wimborne Minster U.K. 50°48N 1°59W 24 E5

Wincanton U.K. 51°3N 2°24W 24 D4
Winchelsea U.K. 50°55N 0°43E 25 E10
Winchester U.K. 51°4N 1°18W 24 D6
Winchester Ky., U.S.A. 37°59N 84°11W 112 G6
Winchester Va., U.S.A. 39°11N 78°10W 112 F8
Wind → U.S.A. 43°12N 108°12W 110 B5
Wind River Range U.S.A. 43°0N 109°30W 110 B5
Windermere U.K. 54°23N 2°55W 22 D3
Windhoek Namibia 22°35S 17°4E 97 J3
Windrush → U.K. 51°43N 1°24W 24 C6
Windsor Canada 42°18N 83°0W 109 E11
Windsor U.K. 51°29N 0°36W 25 D7
Windward Is. W. Indies 13°0N 61°0W 115 E12
Windward Passage Caribbean 20°0N 74°0W 115 D10
Wing U.K. 51°53N 0°43W 25 C7
Wingham U.K. 51°16N 1°13E 25 D11
Winisk → Canada 55°17N 85°5W 109 D11
Winkleigh U.K. 50°50N 3°58W 27 F6
Winkler Canada 49°10N 97°56W 108 E10
Winneba Ghana 5°25N 0°36W 94 G5
Winnebago, L. U.S.A. 44°0N 88°26W 112 D3
Winnemucca U.S.A. 40°58N 117°44W 110 B3
Winnipeg Canada 49°54N 97°9W 108 E10
Winnipeg, L. Canada 52°0N 97°0W 108 D10
Winnipegosis L. Canada 52°30N 100°0W 108 C9
Winona U.S.A. 44°3N 91°39W 111 B8
Winooski U.S.A. 44°29N 73°11W 113 C11
Winsford U.K. 53°12N 2°31W 23 F3
Winslow U.K. 51°57N 0°52W 25 C7
Winslow U.S.A. 35°2N 110°42W 110 C4
Winster U.K. 53°9N 1°39W 23 F5
Winston-Salem U.S.A. 36°6N 80°15W 111 C10
Winterborne Abbas U.K. 50°42N 2°33W 24 E3
Winterthur Switz. 47°30N 8°44E 64 E5
Winterton N. Lincs., U.K. 53°39N 0°37W 23 E7
Winterton Norfolk, U.K. 52°43N 1°41E 25 A12
Winton Australia 22°24S 143°3E 98 E7
Wirksworth U.K. 53°6N 1°35W 23 F5
Wirral U.K. 53°25N 3°0W 23 F2
Wisbech U.K. 52°41N 0°9E 25 A9
Wisborough Green U.K. 51°2N 0°30W 25 D7
Wisconsin □ U.S.A. 44°45N 89°30W 111 B9
Wisconsin Rapids U.S.A. 44°23N 89°49W 112 C3
Wishaw U.K. 55°46N 3°54W 21 C8
Wiske → U.K. 54°19N 1°27W 22 D6
Witham U.K. 51°48N 0°40E 25 C10
Witham → U.K. 52°59N 0°2W 23 G8
Withern U.K. 53°18N 0°8E 23 F9
Withernsea U.K. 53°44N 0°1E 23 E9
Witley U.K. 51°9N 0°39W 25 D7
Witney U.K. 51°48N 1°28W 24 C6
Wittersham U.K. 51°0N 0°43E 25 D10
Wiveliscombe U.K. 51°2N 3°19W 24 D2
Wivenhoe U.K. 51°51N 0°59E 25 C10
Wkra → Poland 52°27N 20°44E 65 B11
Włocławek Poland 52°40N 19°3E 65 B10
Woburn U.K. 51°59N 0°36W 25 C7
Woburn Sands U.K. 52°1N 0°39W 25 B7
Wodonga Australia 36°5S 146°50E 98 H8
Woking U.K. 51°19N 0°34W 25 D7
Wokingham U.K. 51°24N 0°49W 25 D7
Wolf Rock U.K. 49°57N 5°49W 27 H2
Wolfsburg Germany 52°25N 10°48E 64 B6
Wolin Poland 53°50N 14°37E 64 B8
Wollaston L. Canada 58°7N 103°10W 108 D9
Wollaston Pen. Canada 69°30N 115°0W 108 C8
Wollongong Australia 34°25S 150°54E 98 G9
Wolsingham U.K. 54°44N 1°52W 22 C5
Wolstenholme, C. Canada 62°35N 77°30W 104 C12
Wolverhampton U.K. 52°35N 2°7W 23 G4
Wolverton U.K. 52°3N 0°47W 25 B7
Wolviston U.K. 54°38N 1°18W 22 C6
Wombwell U.K. 53°32N 1°25W 23 E6
Wŏnsan N. Korea 39°11N 127°27E 79 D14
Wonston U.K. 51°8N 1°18W 24 D6
Woodbridge U.K. 52°6N 1°20E 25 B11
Woodbury U.K. 50°41N 3°24W 27 F7
Woodhall Spa U.K. 53°10N 0°12W 23 F8
Woodhouse U.K. 53°22N 1°21W 23 F6
Woodley U.K. 51°27N 0°53W 25 D7
Woodroffe, Mt. Australia 26°20S 131°45E 98 F5
Woods, L. of the N. Amer. 49°15N 94°45W 108 E10
Woodstock N.B., Canada 46°11N 67°37W 109 E13
Woodstock Ont., Canada 43°10N 80°45W 112 D7
Woodstock U.K. 51°51N 1°20W 24 C6
Woodstock U.S.A. 42°19N 88°27W 112 D3
Wookey U.K. 51°13N 2°41W 24 D3
Wookey Hole U.K. 51°14N 2°40W 24 D3
Wool U.K. 50°40N 2°12W 24 E4
Woolacombe U.K. 51°10N 4°13W 27 E5
Wooler U.K. 55°33N 2°1W 22 A4
Woonsocket U.S.A. 42°0N 71°31W 113 E11
Wootton Bassett U.K. 51°32N 1°54W 24 C5
Wootton Wawen U.K. 52°16N 1°47W 24 B5
Worcester S. Africa 33°39S 19°27E 97 L3
Worcester U.K. 52°11N 2°12W 24 B4
Worcester U.S.A. 42°16N 71°48W 113 D12
Worcestershire □ U.K. 52°13N 2°10W 24 B4
Worfield U.K. 52°34N 2°21W 23 G4
Workington U.K. 54°39N 3°33W 22 C1

Worksop U.K. 53°18N 1°7W 23 F6
Worms Germany 49°37N 8°21E 64 D5
Wortham U.K. 52°21N 1°3E 25 B11
Worthing Barbados 13°5N 59°35W 115 g
Worthing U.K. 50°49N 0°21W 25 E8
Worthington U.S.A. 43°37N 95°36W 111 B7
Wotton under Edge U.K. 51°37N 2°20W 24 C4
Wragby U.K. 53°18N 0°17W 23 F8
Wrangel I. Russia 71°0N 180°0E 77 B19
Wrangell U.S.A. 56°28N 132°23W 108 D6
Wrangell Mts. U.S.A. 61°30N 142°0W 108 C5
Wrangle U.K. 53°3N 0°7E 23 F9
Wrath, C. U.K. 58°38N 5°1W 18 E7
Wrekin, The U.K. 52°41N 2°32W 23 G3
Wrentham U.K. 52°23N 1°40E 25 B12
Wrexham U.K. 53°3N 3°0W 26 A8
Wrexham □ U.K. 53°1N 2°58W 26 D3
Wrigley Canada 63°16N 123°37W 108 C7
Writtle U.K. 51°44N 0°27E 25 C9
Wrocław Poland 51°5N 17°5E 65 C9
Wroughton U.K. 51°31N 1°47W 24 C5
Wroxham U.K. 52°42N 1°24E 25 A11
Wu Jiang → China 29°40N 107°20E 78 F10
Wuhai China 39°47N 106°52E 78 D10
Wuhan China 30°31N 114°18E 79 E11
Wuhu China 31°22N 118°21E 79 E12
Wuppertal Germany 51°16N 7°12E 64 C4
Würzburg Germany 49°46N 9°55E 64 D5
Wushi China 41°9N 79°13E 78 C4
Wutongqiao China 29°22N 103°50E 78 F9
Wuwei China 37°57N 102°34E 78 D9
Wuxi China 31°33N 120°18E 79 E13
Wuyi Shan China 27°0N 117°0E 79 F12
Wuzhong China 38°2N 106°12E 78 D10
Wuzhou China 23°30N 111°18E 79 G11
Wye → U.K. 51°10N 0°57E 25 D10
Wye → U.K. 51°38N 2°40W 24 C3
Wylye → U.K. 51°5N 1°51W 24 D5
Wymondham Leics., U.K. 52°45N 0°43W 23 G7
Wymondham Norfolk, U.K. 52°35N 1°7E 25 A11
Wyndham Australia 15°33S 128°3E 98 D4
Wyoming □ U.S.A. 43°0N 107°30W 110 B5
Wyre → U.K. 53°52N 2°57W 23 E3
Wyre Forest U.K. 52°24N 2°24W 23 H4

X

Xaçmaz Azerbaijan 41°31N 48°42E 71 F8
Xainza China 30°58N 88°35E 78 E6
Xalapa Mexico 19°32N 96°55W 114 D5
Xankändi Azerbaijan 39°52N 46°49E 71 G8
Xenia U.S.A. 39°41N 83°56W 112 F6
Xi Jiang → China 22°5N 113°20E 79 G11
Xiaguan China 25°32N 100°16E 78 F9
Xiamen China 24°25N 118°4E 79 G12
Xi'an China 34°15N 109°0E 79 E10
Xiang Jiang → China 28°55N 112°50E 79 F11
Xiangfan China 32°2N 112°8E 79 E11
Xianggang = Hong Kong □ China 22°11N 114°14E 79 a
Xiangtan China 27°51N 112°54E 79 F11
Xianyang China 34°20N 108°40E 79 E10
Xichang China 27°51N 102°19E 78 F9
Xigazê China 29°5N 88°45E 78 F6
Xilinhot China 43°52N 116°2E 79 C12
Xing'an China 25°38N 110°40E 79 F11
Xinghua China 32°58N 119°48E 79 E12
Xingu → Brazil 1°30S 51°53W 120 C4
Xining China 36°34N 101°40E 78 D9
Xinxiang China 35°18N 113°50E 79 D11
Xinyang China 32°6N 114°3E 79 E11
Xique-Xique Brazil 10°50S 42°40W 122 B2
Xizang Zizhiqu □ China 32°0N 88°0E 78 E6
Xuanhua China 40°40N 115°2E 79 C12
Xuanwei China 26°15N 103°59E 78 F9
Xuzhou China 34°18N 117°10E 79 E12

Y

Ya'an China 29°58N 103°5E 78 E9
Yablonovyy Ra. Russia 53°0N 114°0E 77 D12
Yabucoa Puerto Rico 18°3N 65°53W 115 d
Yacuiba Bolivia 22°0S 63°43W 120 E3
Yakeshi China 49°17N 120°43E 79 B13
Yakima U.S.A. 46°36N 120°31W 110 A2
Yakutat U.S.A. 59°33N 139°44W 108 D6
Yakutia □ Russia 66°0N 130°0E 77 C13
Yakutsk Russia 62°5N 129°50E 77 C13
Yala Thailand 6°33N 101°18E 82 C2
Yalong Jiang → China 26°40N 101°55E 78 F9
Yalta Ukraine 44°30N 34°10E 71 F5
Yalu Jiang → China 39°55N 124°19E 79 D13
Yamagata Japan 38°15N 140°15E 81 D7
Yamaguchi Japan 34°10N 131°32E 81 F2
Yamal Pen. Russia 71°0N 70°0E 76 B7
Yambol Bulgaria 42°30N 26°30E 69 C12
Yamethin Burma 20°29N 96°18E 85 J20
Yamoussoukro Ivory C. 6°49N 5°17W 94 G4

Yampa → U.S.A. 40°32N 108°59W 110 B5
Yamuna → India 25°30N 81°53E 85 G12
Yamzho Yumco China 28°48N 90°35E 78 F7
Yan'an China 36°35N 109°26E 79 D10
Yanbu 'al Baḥr Si. Arabia 24°0N 38°5E 86 E4
Yancheng China 33°23N 120°8E 79 E13
Yangambi Dem. Rep. of the Congo 0°47N 24°24E 96 D4
Yangjiang China 21°50N 111°59E 79 G11
Yangquan China 37°58N 113°31E 79 D11
Yangtse → China 31°48N 121°10E 79 E13
Yangzhou China 32°21N 119°26E 79 E12
Yanji China 42°59N 129°30E 79 C14
Yankton U.S.A. 42°53N 97°23W 111 B7
Yanqi China 42°5N 86°35E 78 C6
Yantai China 37°34N 121°22E 79 D13
Yaoundé Cameroon 3°50N 11°35E 96 D2
Yap Pac. Oc. 9°30N 138°10E 102 G5
Yapen Indonesia 1°50S 136°0E 83 E9
Yaqui → Mexico 27°37N 110°39W 114 B2
Yaraka Australia 24°53S 144°3E 98 E7
Yarcombe U.K. 50°51N 3°5W 27 F7
Yare → U.K. 52°35N 1°38E 25 A12
Yarkant He → China 40°26N 80°59E 78 C5
Yarkhun → Pakistan 36°17N 72°30E 84 A8
Yarm U.K. 54°31N 1°21W 22 C6
Yarmouth Canada 43°50N 66°7W 109 E13
Yarmouth U.K. 50°42N 1°29W 24 E6
Yaroslavl Russia 57°35N 39°55E 70 C6
Yarrow U.K. 55°33N 3°1W 21 C9
Yarumal Colombia 6°58N 75°24W 120 B2
Yate U.K. 51°32N 2°25W 24 C4
Yathkyed L. Canada 62°40N 98°0W 108 C10
Yatsushiro Japan 32°30N 130°40E 81 G2
Yatton U.K. 51°23N 2°49W 24 D3
Yauco Puerto Rico 18°2N 66°51W 115 d
Yavari → Peru 4°21S 70°2W 120 C2
Yaxley U.K. 52°31N 0°16W 25 A8
Yazd Iran 31°55N 54°27E 87 D8
Yazoo → U.S.A. 32°22N 90°54W 111 D8
Yazoo City U.S.A. 32°51N 90°25W 111 D8
Yealmpton U.K. 50°21N 4°1W 27 G5
Yecheng China 37°54N 77°26E 78 D4
Yelets Russia 52°40N 38°30E 70 D6
Yell U.K. 60°35N 1°5W 18 A15
Yell Sd. U.K. 60°33N 1°15W 18 A15
Yellow = Huang He → China 37°55N 118°50E 79 D12
Yellow Sea China 35°0N 123°0E 79 D13
Yellowhead Pass Canada 52°53N 118°25W 108 D8
Yellowknife Canada 62°27N 114°29W 108 C8
Yellowstone → U.S.A. 47°59N 103°59W 110 A6
Yellowstone Nat. Park △ U.S.A. 44°40N 110°30W 110 B5
Yemen ■ Asia 15°0N 44°0E 89 E3
Yenisey → Russia 71°50N 82°40E 76 B9
Yeo → U.K. 51°24N 2°54W 24 D3
Yeola India 20°2N 74°30E 84 J9
Yeovil U.K. 50°57N 2°38W 24 E3
Yerevan Armenia 40°10N 44°31E 71 F7
Yes Tor U.K. 50°41N 4°0W 27 F5
Yeu, Î. d' France 46°42N 2°20W 66 C2
Yevpatoriya Ukraine 45°15N 33°20E 71 E5
Yeysk Russia 46°40N 38°12E 71 E6
Yibin China 28°45N 104°32E 78 F9
Yichang China 30°40N 111°20E 79 E11
Yichun China 47°44N 128°52E 79 B14
Yinchuan China 38°30N 106°15E 78 D10
Yingkou China 40°37N 122°18E 79 C13
Yining China 43°58N 81°10E 78 C5
Yishan China 24°28N 108°38E 78 G10
Yixing China 31°21N 119°48E 79 E12
Yiyang China 28°35N 112°18E 79 F11
Yogyakarta Indonesia 7°49S 110°22E 82 F4
Yokkaichi Japan 34°55N 136°38E 81 F5
Yokohama Japan 35°27N 139°28E 81 F6
Yokosuka Japan 35°20N 139°40E 81 F6
Yonago Japan 35°25N 133°19E 81 F3
Yong'an China 25°59N 117°25E 79 F12
Yongzhou China 26°17N 111°37E 79 F11
Yonkers U.S.A. 40°56N 73°52W 113 E11
Yonne → France 48°23N 2°58E 66 B5
York U.K. 53°58N 1°6W 23 E6
York U.S.A. 39°58N 76°44W 112 F9
York, C. Australia 10°42S 142°31E 98 C7
York, Vale of U.K. 54°15N 1°25W 22 D6
Yorkshire Dales △ U.K. 54°12N 2°10W 22 D5
Yorkshire Wolds U.K. 54°8N 0°31W 22 D7
Yorkton Canada 51°11N 102°28W 108 D9
Yosemite Nat. Park △ U.S.A. 37°45N 119°40W 110 C3
Yoshkar Ola Russia 56°38N 47°55E 70 C8
Youghal Ireland 51°56N 7°52W 30 E7
Youghal B. Ireland 51°55N 7°49W 30 E7
Youlgreave U.K. 53°11N 1°40W 23 F5
Youngstown U.S.A. 41°6N 80°39W 112 E7
Yoxall U.K. 52°46N 1°47W 23 G5
Yoxford U.K. 52°16N 1°31E 25 B12
Yozgat Turkey 39°51N 34°47E 71 G5
Yreka U.S.A. 41°44N 122°38W 110 B2

Ystalyfera U.K. 51°46N 3°48W 26 D6
Ythan → U.K. 57°19N 1°59W 19 H14
Yu Jiang → China 23°22N 110°3E 79 G11
Yuan Jiang → China 28°55N 111°50E 79 F11
Yuba City U.S.A. 39°8N 121°37W 110 C2
Yucatán Mexico 19°30N 89°0W 114 D7
Yucatan Basin Cent. Amer. 19°0N 86°0W 104 H11
Yucatan Channel Caribbean 22°0N 86°30W 114 C7
Yueyang China 29°21N 113°5E 79 F11
Yukon → U.S.A. 62°32N 163°54W 108 C3
Yukon Territory □ Canada 63°0N 135°0W 108 C6
Yulin China 38°20N 109°30E 79 D10
Yuma U.S.A. 32°43N 114°37W 110 D4
Yumen China 39°50N 97°30E 78 D8
Yungas Bolivia 17°0S 66°0W 120 D3
Yunnan □ China 25°0N 102°0E 78 G9
Yurimaguas Peru 5°55S 76°7W 120 C2
Yushu China 33°5N 96°55E 78 E8
Yutian China 36°52N 81°42E 78 D5
Yuzhno-Sakhalinsk Russia 46°58N 142°45E 79 B17
Yuzhou China 34°10N 113°28E 79 E11
Yvetot France 49°37N 0°44E 66 B4

Z

Zāb al Kabīr → Iraq 36°1N 43°24E 86 B5
Zābol □ Afghan. 32°0N 67°0E 87 D11
Zabrze Poland 50°18N 18°50E 65 C10
Zacatecas Mexico 22°47N 102°35W 114 C4
Zadar Croatia 44°8N 15°14E 68 B6
Zagaoua Chad 15°30N 22°24E 95 E10
Zagazig Egypt 30°40N 31°30E 95 B12
Zagreb Croatia 45°50N 15°58E 68 B7
Zagros Mts. Iran 33°45N 48°5E 86 C7
Zāhedān Iran 29°30N 60°50E 87 D10
Zahlah Lebanon 33°52N 35°50E 86 C3
Zakynthos Greece 37°47N 20°54E 69 F9
Zalantun China 48°0N 122°43E 79 B13
Zambezi → Africa 18°35S 36°20E 97 H7
Zambia ■ Africa 15°0S 28°0E 97 G5
Zamboanga Phil. 6°59N 122°3E 83 C6
Zamora Mexico 19°59N 102°16W 114 D4
Zamora Spain 41°30N 5°45W 67 B3
Zamość Poland 50°43N 23°15E 65 C12
Zanesville U.S.A. 39°56N 82°1W 112 F6
Zanjan Iran 36°40N 48°35E 86 B7
Zanzibar Tanzania 6°12S 39°12E 96 F7
Zaouiet Reggâne Algeria 26°32N 0°3E 94 C6
Zaoyang China 32°10N 112°45E 79 E11
Zaozhuang China 34°50N 117°35E 79 E12
Zapala Argentina 39°0S 70°5W 121 F2
Zaporozhye Ukraine 47°50N 35°10E 71 E6
Zaragoza Spain 41°39N 0°53W 67 B5
Zaranj Afghan. 30°55N 61°55E 87 D10
Zárate Argentina 34°7S 59°0W 121 F4
Zaria Nigeria 11°0N 7°40E 94 F7
Zarzis Tunisia 33°31N 11°2E 95 B8
Zaskar Mts. India 33°15N 77°30E 84 C10
Zaysan, L. Kazakhstan 48°0N 83°0E 76 E9
Zeebrugge Belgium 51°19N 3°12E 64 C2
Zeil, Mt. Australia 23°30S 132°23E 98 E5
Zelenograd Russia 56°1N 37°12E 70 C6
Zenica Bos.-H. 44°10N 17°57E 69 B7
Zhangjiakou China 40°48N 114°55E 79 C11
Zhangye China 38°50N 100°23E 78 D9
Zhangzhou China 24°30N 117°35E 79 G12
Zhanjiang China 21°15N 110°20E 79 G11
Zhaoqing China 23°0N 112°20E 79 G11
Zhaotong China 27°20N 103°44E 78 F9
Zhejiang □ China 29°0N 120°0E 79 F13
Zhengzhou China 34°45N 113°34E 79 E11
Zhezqazghan Kazakhstan 47°44N 67°40E 76 E7
Zhigansk Russia 66°48N 123°27E 77 C13
Zhlobin Belarus 52°55N 30°0E 70 D5
Zhob Pakistan 31°20N 69°31E 84 D6
Zhongdian China 27°48N 99°42E 78 F8
Zhuhai China 22°17N 113°34E 79 a
Zhumadian China 32°59N 114°2E 79 E11
Zhytomyr Ukraine 50°20N 28°40E 65 C15
Zibo China 36°47N 118°3E 79 D12
Zielona Góra Poland 51°57N 15°31E 64 C8
Zigong China 29°15N 104°48E 78 F9
Ziguinchor Senegal 12°35N 16°20W 94 F2
Žilina Slovak Rep. 49°12N 18°42E 65 D10
Zimbabwe ■ Africa 19°0S 30°0E 97 H5
Zinder Niger 13°48N 9°0E 94 F7
Ziway, L. Ethiopia 8°0N 38°50E 89 F2
Zlatoust Russia 55°10N 59°40E 70 C10
Zlín Czech Rep. 49°14N 17°40E 65 D9
Zonguldak Turkey 41°28N 31°50E 71 F5
Zrenjanin Serbia 45°22N 20°23E 69 B9
Zug Switz. 47°10N 8°31E 64 E5
Zunyi China 27°42N 106°53E 78 F10
Zürich Switz. 47°22N 8°32E 64 E5
Zuwārah Libya 32°58N 12°1E 95 B8
Zvishavane Zimbabwe 20°17S 30°2E 97 J6
Zwelitsha S. Africa 32°55N 27°22E 97 L5
Zwickau Germany 50°44N 12°30E 64 C7
Zwolle Neths. 52°31N 6°6E 64 B4

Published in Great Britain in 2009 by Philip's, a division of Octopus Publishing Group Ltd, www.octopusbooks.com 2–4 Heron Quays, London E14 4JP

An Hachette UK Company www.hachette.co.uk

www.philips-maps.co.uk

Ninety-sixth edition

Copyright © 2009 Philip's

ISBN 978-1-84907-013-3 (PAPERBACK EDITION)

ISBN 978-1-84907-012-6 (HARDBACK EDITION)

Philip's World Atlases are published in association with The Royal Geographical Society (with The Institute of British Geographers).

The Society was founded in 1830 and given a Royal Charter in 1859 for 'the advancement of geographical science'. Today it is a leading world centre for geographical learning – supporting education, teaching, research and expeditions, and promoting public understanding of the subject.

Further information about the Society and how to join may be found on its website at: www.rgs.org

PHOTOGRAPHIC ACKNOWLEDGEMENTS

Satellite images in the atlas are courtesy of the following: EROS pp. 8, 9, 12tl, 12tr, 14bl, 14br; China RSGS p. 14tl; ESA 10b, 15b; Fugro-NPA (www.satmaps.com) pp. 10t, 11t, 14tr, 15t, 17, 49, 88, 123. 130; GeoEye p. 16b; NASA pp. 11bl, 12b; Precision Terrain Surveys Ltd p. 16t.

SATELLITE IMAGE OF THE SEVERN ESTUARY

This Landsat false-colour composite image was captured in October. The cities of Bristol and Cardiff are clearly visible, as are the Black Mountains and the Brecon Beacons in Wales. Images such as this are used for recording and monitoring land use. *(EROS)*